HIDDEN®

Carolinas

Including Asheville, Great Smoky Mountains, Outer Banks and Charleston

Catherine O'Neal

SIXTH EDITION

Ulysses Press®
BERKELEY, CALIFORNIA

Published by: ULYSSES PRESS
P.O. Box 3440
Berkeley, CA 94703
www.ulyssespress.com

ISSN 1523-9201
ISBN 1-56975-484-5

Printed in Canada by Transcontinental Printing

20 19 18 17 16 15 14 13 12 11 10 9

MANAGING EDITOR: Claire Chun
COPY EDITORS: Lee Micheaux, Lily Chou
EDITORIAL ASSOCIATES: Leona Benten, Amy Hough, Joyce Liao
TYPESETTER: Lisa Kester
CARTOGRAPHY: Stellar Cartography
COVER DESIGN: Sarah Levin, Leslie Henriques
INDEXER: Sayre Van Young
COVER PHOTOGRAPHY: © Thinkstock/gettyimages.com
   (boardwalk to Bodie Island Light in North Carolina's
   Outer Banks)
ILLUSTRATOR: Hanako Wakiyama
CONTRIBUTOR: Marin Van Young

Distributed in the United States by Publishers
Group West and in Canada by Raincoast Books

For Cheryl MacNeal,
who lightens life

and for Joanna Pearlman,
always a positive force

What's Hidden?

At different points throughout this book, you'll find special listings marked with this symbol:

◄ HIDDEN

This means that you have come upon a place off the beaten tourist track, a spot that will carry you a step closer to the local people and natural environment of the Carolinas.

The goal of this guide is to lead you beyond the realm of everyday tourist facilities. While we include traditional sightseeing listings and popular attractions, we also offer alternative sights and adventure activities. Instead of filling this guide with reviews of standard hotels and chain restaurants, we concentrate on one-of-a-kind places and locally owned establishments.

Our authors seek out locales that are popular with residents but usually overlooked by visitors. Some are more hidden than others (and are marked accordingly), but all the listings in this book are intended to help you discover the true nature of the Carolinas and put you on the path of adventure.

Write to us!

If in your travels you discover a spot that captures the spirit of the Carolinas, or if you live in the region and have a favorite place to share, or if you just feel like expressing your views, write to us and we'll pass your note along to the author.

We can't guarantee that the author will add your personal find to the next edition, but if the writer does use the suggestion, we'll acknowledge you in the credits and send you a free copy of the new edition.

ULYSSES PRESS
3286 Adeline Street, Suite 1
Berkeley, CA 94703
E-mail: readermail@ulyssespress.com

Contents

Maps

OUTDOOR ADVENTURE SYMBOLS

The following symbols accompany national, state and regional park listings, as well as beach descriptions throughout the text.

▲	Camping			Waterskiing
	Hiking			Windsurfing
	Biking			Canoeing or Kayaking
	Horseback Riding			Boating
	Swimming			Boat Ramps
	Surfing			Fishing

ONE

Carolinas Wandering

On one end of the Carolinas there is the ocean, a great vault of fabulous blue heaving against wispy islands and shores of monstrous dunes. On the other end are mountains, broad and green and towering, acutely silent, eternally cool, wrapped in mist and a halo of clouds.

In between the water and peaks are foothills and farmlands, corn and tobacco fields running into crisp sky, sprinklings of whitewashed, clapboard, no-name roads roughed with clay, and far-reaching forests of palmetto and slash pine where white-tailed deer and bald eagles reside.

The land is not only eclectic but vast. Together, North and South Carolina cover some 82,811 square miles—considerably more than all the New England states combined. To cross the Carolinas by car is to pass through many dimensions, to enter many eras and to observe many ways. The scenery is forever changing, from wild and watery swamps to subtle, sunlit plantations, from cultured cosmopolitan cities to wooded mountain hollows where folks carve their own dulcimers. Not far from bustling Charlotte, North Carolina, there's a quiet western town where no cars—only horses—are allowed on Main Street. The surf-and-beer scene of North Carolina's Outer Banks is but a few country miles from the cotton towns where LeAnn Rimes rules the radio and Baptist preachers reign on Sunday mornings.

New South ideas prevail in larger cities, but elsewhere the Old South thrives. Sweet tea is sipped on front porches. Blue crabs are caught in the tidal marshes. Cotton and apples are picked in the fall. Pecan trees make music during afternoon storms, their nuts clacking in the wind. White magnolia blossoms perfume the roadsides and gardens. And in true Southern fashion, everyone asks how you're doing.

There is much history in the Carolinas. Wilbur and Orville Wright took their first flight from a monstrous sand dune on the Outer Banks. The country's first

English child was born a few miles away. The first hunk of North American gold was found in a North Carolina creek, though the finder chose to use it as a doorstop.

Beautiful Charleston, South Carolina, is one of the United States' oldest cities, founded in 1670 and saturated with early Americana; some 4000 historic buildings fill its downtown, many dating to the 1700s. Horse-drawn carriages convey visitors along ancient cobbled streets, and Gullah women, African-American descendants of plantation slaves, weave sweetgrass baskets on the sidewalks. Lofty antebellum plantations, with their lavish gardens, dot the coastal plain of South Carolina.

It is for these reasons—compelling history, scenery and the Southern state of mind—that so many travelers keep finding the Carolinas. Every year, more than nine million visitors find Great Smoky Mountains National Park in North Carolina—twice as many as those who go to the Grand Canyon, making it the nation's most-visited national park. Nearly 14 million visitors make an annual trip to Myrtle Beach to soak up sun and swim in the sea. Some 21 million travelers take North Carolina's Blue Ridge Parkway, and why not? The road is a glorious ride amid bluish mountain peaks, with not a single stop sign or traffic light along the way.

Hidden Carolinas is designed to help you explore these two great states. It will lead you to countless popular spots, offering advice on how best to enjoy them, then take you to off-the-beaten-path locales, places usually known only to locals. The book will tell the story of the region's history, its flora and fauna. Each chapter will suggest places to stay and eat, to sightsee and shop, and to enjoy the outdoors and the nightlife, covering a range of tastes and budgets.

The book sets out in Asheville, North Carolina, taking visitors in Chapter Two through this lovely Blue Ridge city and gateway to North Carolina's mountains. Chapter Three wanders along the state's Southern Mountains sprinkled with small towns and filled with waterfalls. From there, Chapter Four picks up the Great Smoky Mountains of North Carolina, including the tourist towns of Maggie Valley and Cherokee, and the Cherokee reservation. Chapter Five presents a driving tour along the North Carolina portion of the Blue Ridge Parkway, one of the nation's most appealing roads.

Chapter Six heads up into the High Country, the mountainous northwestern corner of North Carolina with both popular resort areas and far-flung hamlets. Chapter Seven wanders east through North Carolina's Piedmont, home to several big cities and over three million people. Chapter Eight runs down the North Carolina coast, with its rich maritime mood and dramatic barrier isles known as the Outer Banks. Chapter Nine moves southward along South Carolina's coast, through the sands and golf courses of Myrtle Beach to old-world Charleston and the megaresort called Hilton Head. Finally, Chapter Ten wanders across inland South Carolina, with its fields of cotton and deep pine woods, and foothills culminating in westerly mountains and lakes.

What you choose to see and do is up to you. Whether you prefer to park your towel in the sand or picnic on a plantation, wander through stately sculpture gardens or stroll glittering city streets, swing a golf club or wade in a mountain creek, you will find your place in the Carolinas.

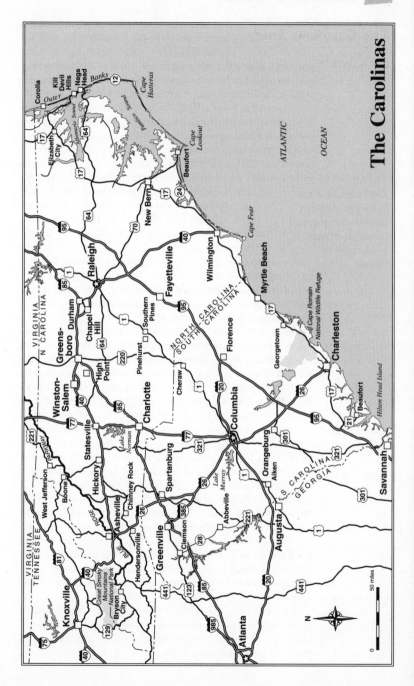

The Carolinas

▼▼▼▼▼▼▼▼▼▼▼▼▼▼
The Carolinas Story

GEOLOGY

The Southern Appalachians are old mountains, much older than the Himalayas or even the Swiss Alps. They were created half a billion years ago, during the Paleozoic period, when two enormous land masses collided to form the supercontinent of Pangea. Where they crashed, the land exploded in a torrent of high, ragged mountains that resembled today's Himalayas. When Pangea later broke apart, the mountains formed a dramatic, easterly wrinkle down the side of a land mass—the future North America.

Over the eons, erosion wore away and rounded the mountains' sharp peaks, and a luxuriant blanket of vegetation spread across their shoulders and valleys. Today's Southern Appalachians are foremost green and flourishing, with double and triple canopies of forest carpeted with ferns and pillow-soft layers of leaves and filled with flowers nearly all year. In winter, though, the mountains become rocky skeletons, revealing their ancient beginnings of granite, gneiss and schist. Wandering through these mountains, which run along the western sides of North and South Carolina, it is easy to believe their age, for the rocky outcroppings and gorges look primeval and the summits honed by interminable time.

The Piedmont is even older than the Appalachians, having existed before the collision of continents into Pangea.

What were originally pools of water between the Appalachian ridges have now become wind gaps, and there is many a summit where you can sit high above the world and hear the winds sing. Wind and water constantly shape and reshape the mountains, sometimes carving bizarre and haunting profiles. Chimney Rock in North Carolina is a great pedestal of granite, 225 feet high and poking into blue sky, its summit offering views of wind-etched ravines all around. North Carolina's Grandfather Mountain, another freak of wind and erosion, most resembles a patriarch lying on his back, bushy brows and goatee aimed toward heaven.

The crystalline nature of Appalachian rocks has made many a Carolinian rich. In the late 1800s, rubies were discovered in the mountains of North Carolina, including pigeon-blood rubies, the rarest rubies in the world. Commercial mines thrived for a while and then closed. Today's visitors, however, can still pan for rubies and sapphires, garnets, kyanite, moonstone and other stones and minerals, though few strike it big. Almost half the country's supply of feldspar, a chalky rock used in everything from dinner plates to house paint, comes from the small Appalachian town of Spruce Pine, North Carolina.

East of Appalachia lies an immense expanse of foothills known as the Piedmont. In geologic terms it is called the Fall Line, named for the line of waterfalls, rapids and rivers that course through on their way from mountains to sea. Carolinas' towns grew around these agitated waters, harnessing their energy for the water wheels of industry.

The Coastal Plain, which lies east of the Appalachians along the Carolinas' seaboard, was once covered by the Atlantic Ocean, and today the earth bears traces of sea sediment. Not until over 15,000 years ago did the coast and its barrier islands begin to take their current shape. Near the end of the Ice Age when the sea level subsided, wicked ocean winds drove sandbars up into lofty dunes. When the sea rose at the end of the Wisconsin Advance, the waves pushed the dunes close to shore.

There they remain today, a strand of barrier islands running the length of the Carolinas, forever windwhipped and at the mercy of currents and tides. The wildest isles are the Outer Banks of North Carolina, where dunes reach 150 feet high and look like something from the Mojave Desert, and where Mother Nature is constantly moving islands around, without the slightest concern for human development. Here, you can hang glide off a giant pillar of sand more than 15,000 years old.

FLORA

Nowhere is Carolinas' flora more abundant than in the mountains. Across the Blue Ridge and Great Smoky Mountains of North Carolina are fantastic forests of maples, hickories, sourwoods, poplar and elms, sycamores, sweet gums and Carolina silverbells. Caverns of hemlock conceal creeks and streams and run for thousands of feet down mountains. Pines and oaks protrude from windier slopes and outcroppings. Fraser fir and red spruce, rarely found south of Maine, grow on the highest points. There is so much green, and so little development, that the very air takes on a moist, Edenic tint.

Flowers fill the mountain scenery with flamboyant color, starting on the lowest slopes in March and ending on the loftiest peaks with a September finale. Take a spring ride along North Carolina's Blue Ridge Parkway and you will witness trilliums, lady's slippers, jack-in-the-pulpits and showy orchids. Millions of mountain laurel shrubs release their pinkish blossoms, fountains of flowers gushing from cliffsides. Dogwood trees, which are native to the forests and also planted profusely around Carolinas' gardens, put out their pearlwhite blossoms in spring.

Solomon's seal comes along in May, though nothing is so splendid as the opening of the Catawba rhododendrons around mid-June. The mountain shrubs with their purple-pink blooms grow so thick they look like shimmering rose-hued seas. Mountain laurel and flame azaleas, their blooms a blazing orange, crowd in with the rhododendron for extra extravagance.

The lower forests of South Carolina's Upcountry, where elevations average about 2000 feet, are dominated by poplar, oak and pine trees, and there are sprinklings of fraser magnolias, also called umbrella trees for their thick leaf canopies that protect from rain. Their supple white blossoms emerge in April and May, and breathe sweetness into the forest air. Here also are rare Oconee bells, found only around the Carolinas and Georgia, each with five bell-shaped petals shaded sunny yellow inside.

Scruffy forests of pine and oak and sandhills run across the Carolinas' Piedmont and coastal plain. The longleaf pine is North Carolina's state tree, though its name is too enchanting for its look: tall, skinny and ruddy-colored, with bristly limbs and shingly bark, and sprays of dark green needles. South Carolina's state tree, the palmetto, is no more beautiful, being similarly dull in color and design.

Turtles enjoy official status in the Carolinas: South Carolina's state reptile is the loggerhead turtle, while North Carolina prefers the Eastern box turtle.

All across the Carolinas, kudzu overtakes whole trees and cars and hills. Kudzu is pretty but treacherous: the vine and its heart-shaped leaves grow rapidly, as much as a foot a day, swallowing everything in its path, including native foliage that animals need to survive. Kudzu came from Asia to the South in the 1870s, when farmers planted it to enrich their soil and the federal government used it to control riverbank erosion. By the time everyone learned of its destructive nature, it was too late. Now kudzu is called "The Scourge of the South."

Only the hardiest flora survive along the shifting, sun-beaten dunes of North Carolina's Outer Banks. Arrowleaf morning glory, with its leathery leaves and funnel-shaped flowers, is a vine that climbs the dunes. Virginia creeper will grow almost anywhere but has a dull green flower—not exciting. Sea purslane and blanket flowers also survive along the salt-washed beaches.

North Carolina's coastal plain is completely different. Lonesome pine woods stretch for miles, and there are vast wetlands whose rich, mucky soils harbor dazzling wildflowers, seas of saw grass, woods of pine and oak, and rare carnivorous plants. There is a chunk of woods, Croatan National Forest, with five insect-eating plants, including the Venus flytrap, the pitcher plant, and the butterwort, which washes its victims in anesthesia.

The myrtle trees of Myrtle Beach, South Carolina, are wax myrtles. The area's first settlers found the shrubby, wind-tolerant plants growing along the shores. Today, there are also many crepe myrtles, much prettier than wax myrtles, with buttery-smooth, chalk-white trunks and spidery limbs tasseled with white and lavender blossoms in summer. Fat, fluffy hydrangeas, whose pink and blue blooms look like powder puffs, decorate local gardens, as do velvety white gardenias.

South of Myrtle Beach across the watery Lowcountry, bald cypress trees cling to the sides of swamps and black rivers, and reedy

tidal grass spills across horizons. The limbs of the live oak, so ma-
gisterial and primal, draped in ethereal moss, stretch across the
Lowcountry sky. They cover roadways, sometimes for miles, a cool,
dark tunnel of filigreed greenery. Within Lowcountry gardens and
plantations, particularly around Charleston, grow vigorous plantings of jasmine and honeysuckle, Carolina jessamine and tea olive,
daphne and sweet bay. There are walls of pittosporum and wisteria, gardens of roses and stands of magnolias. Walk among
Charleston's gardens and you will breathe the sweet scent of the
Carolinas.

Once there were bison, cougars and elk in the Carolinas mountains, but white settlers hunted them to extinction. There are still
black bears, wild turkeys, foxes, bobcats, mink and white-tailed
deer in the mountains, particularly in North Carolina's Great
Smoky and Blue Ridge mountains.

The bears are big, up to 300 pounds, and there are about 400
who live in Great Smoky Mountains National Park. During the
winter, they snooze in their dens. When they awake in spring,
they are naturally quite ravenous and go foraging for nuts, berries,
insects and small animals. Unfortunately, despite warnings to the
contrary, park visitors sometimes feed the bears, which causes the
burly creatures to become aggressive. A pushy, hungry bear is not
something you want to encounter on a hiking trail.

Even worse, the bears become easier prey for poachers—increasingly a problem, as bear body parts, from the paws to the
teeth, bring big bucks on the black market. In Asian markets, the
gallbladder of a black bear is worth up to US$2000, and rangers
in Great Smoky Mountains National Park have found massive
bear carcasses, intact except for the tiny gallbladder.

The Smokies are also plagued by non-native, exotic wild hogs
whose ancestors escaped from a nearby hunting preserve in 1912
and invaded the mountain forests. They compete with bears and
other animals for food, breed huge litters and have virtually no
enemies. About 2000 hogs live in the Smokies, though you will
rarely see them, since they are nocturnal.

You probably will see a woodchuck, possibly two, as the
furry groundhogs love to burrow in the mown green roadsides
of the Great Smoky Mountains National Park. Ruffed grouse,
brownish birds the size of chickens, are also common in the park.
Beavers, once gone from the Smokies, have reappeared but are
still scarce.

Even if you don't make it to the mountains, you may see a
white-tailed deer, wild turkey or a fox, especially a red fox, which
all thrive in forests across the Piedmont and coastal plains.

Trout, particularly rainbow and brown trout, fill the rivers,
creeks and streams that flow seaward across the Carolinas. In the

lakes you will find bass, catfish, sunfish, croaker and bream. And the sea holds such good-to-eat fish as flounder, whiting, Spanish mackerel, gray sea trout, small bluefish, sheepshead and cobia.

Tundra swans winter in lakes along the Carolina coast; some 45,000 gather at North Carolina's Lake Mattamuskeet National Wildlife Refuge. Otters live in the rivers. Muskrat and bobcat roam coastal forests. Alligators prowl the lakes, marshes and streams.

There are thousands of shorebirds, snow geese and hooded mergansers, wood ducks, sandpipers and herons, common brown pelicans and egrets. There are raptors, too, such as bald eagles and osprey, also called fish hawks, who pluck fish from the water. There is nothing quite like watching an osprey glide by with a plump, silvery fish fluttering in its razor-sharp talons.

HISTORY   **NATIVE PEOPLE**   Most Carolina histories recount only the last 400 years, when white men conquered these coasts and mountains. Far more fascinating are the 10,000 years before, when the first Carolinians arrived. Near the end of the Ice Age, they made their way from Asia across a ribbon of land today covered by the Bering Strait. They arrived in what is now North America and spread across the continent in a sea of humanity.

Some walked thousands of miles over several years, following the wild game animals and the warmth that beckoned from the south. They were of many tribes and languages, dress, religion and government. In the Carolinas, the Hatteras and Yammassee tribes settled along the coast; the Catawba, Chowanoc, Waxhaw and Tuscarora found homes in the Piedmont sandhills and forest; and the Cherokee took to the mountains.

The Cherokee became the mightiest and most populous tribe. They were taller, more rugged than the people of other tribes, and they were brilliant hunters and marksmen. The women gathered nuts, berries and vegetables—potatoes and mushrooms, chestnuts and hickory nuts, huckleberries and mulberries—using them for food and medicine. At least 2000 years ago, the Cherokees were growing gardens of corn, beans, pumpkins and squash.

Most native tribes were not nomadic, but lived in permanent homes of log, split canes and twigs that were covered with grass and clay (despite the pervasive tepees advertised around the Carolinas today). Every family had a hothouse where they holed up on the coldest winter days; partly underground and encased in thick earthworks, it had a fire inside that burned all the time. Their villages were clustered alongside streams and at the mouths of rivers rich with trout, redhorse and catfish. The men hunted deer, bear, wild turkey and bison.

There were wars between tribes, but for the most part the earliest Carolinians lived a peaceful existence. The Cherokee had a national government with a board of nine men, as well as seven women, whose specific duties included deciding the fate of war prisoners. There were seven clans with names such as Wild Potato, Bird and Long Hair. Women could fight and vote.

Despite all this, the Europeans considered them savage. When the first white men and women arrived in the mid-1500s, there were about 35,000 native people living in the Carolinas. Three hundred years later, there were fewer than 2000.

EUROPEAN SETTLEMENT   The Spanish first found the Carolinas in Francisco Cordillo's 1521 expedition along the coast. Five years later, a Spanish judge named Vasquez de Ayllón brought 500 men, women and children from Santo Domingo Island to what is now Georgetown, South Carolina, and tried to establish a colony. The judge died, disease and starvation set in and the weather was unusually nasty; 150 survivors fled back to Santo Domingo.

It was the European hunting methods that brought the local bison population to extinction.

Not until 1584 was there another Carolina colony, when Sir Walter Raleigh dispatched two English ships carrying 107 men to the shores of North Carolina. Upon arriving on today's Outer Banks, Captain Arthur Barlowe wrote of a land overflowing with grapes and with the "beating and surge of the sea," and "woods full of deer, conies, hares and fowl . . . in incredible abundance." He also wrote of a native man, perhaps of the Hatteras or Yamasee tribe, who came aboard a ship, was given clothing and food, then returned with a bounty of fish for the colonists.

But winter soon set in and the men ran low on food and supplies. Before a year was over, they returned to England. A second colony came in 1587, this time with women, and within a few months the first English child was born in North America. Her name was Virginia Dare, and though it is a common name today, appearing on everything from roads to inns, no one knows the fate of the girl. This second colony also ran low on food and supplies and dispatched a ship to England, but the ship got caught up in the war with Spain and could not return for three years. By then, the settlers were gone. They became known as the lost colony.

The white settlers who first made permanent homes in the Carolinas came down from Virginia in the 1650s. Most were planters with hopes of owning huge hunks of land, which they found and secured along North Carolina's fertile coastal plain. Crude farming and fishing outposts sprang up alongside rivers and sounds.

South Carolina's first lasting colony came in 1670, when the English built a coastal settlement and called it Albemarle Point. Ten years later they moved to a nearby peninsula and named it Charles Town, today's Charleston. French, English and Irish immigrants came to town and got rich trading deerskins, sugar and rum, and the trading port quickly became the center of the Carolina Colonial universe—a cultural, artistic, affluent mecca with grand homes and formal gardens.

As European settlers spread out, they pushed aside the native Carolinians. Entire tribes were eliminated by disease, while others were driven westward to the rugged Carolina mountains. Still others, such as the Yamasee, fought bloodily but unsuccessfully for their land, eventually fleeing to Florida in 1718, where they were later obliterated.

Pirates also waged war with colonists, terrorizing the coastal cities in the early eighteenth century. Blackbeard, Stede Bonnet and many other buccaneers, including several women, found the hidden coves and blackwater swamps of the Carolinas perfect lairs. Blackbeard was killed in 1718 at Cape Fear, North Carolina, by a British Navy lieutenant; Bonnet was captured at the same time, shipped to Charleston, and hung.

The early 1700s also brought the beginning of Southern plantation life. South Carolina's fertile, watery fringe made it perfect for rice growing, and by the mid-1700s, plantations covered much of the coast. Most planters grew indigo and cotton, as well, though all these crops were labor-intensive.

And so some of history's bleaker moments were played out in the Carolinas as thousands of Africans were shipped here and enslaved on plantations. Charleston boasted the busiest slave markets around, and South Carolina's economy was built on rice and slavery. By 1775, black slaves outnumbered white South Carolinians by 30,000, though they were unable to overthrow their oppressors. Reminders of those times are evident today in the grim former slave quarters and the nameless tombstones of slave cemeteries.

There are many reminders, too, of the Revolutionary War, particularly in South Carolina, where several battles and skirmishes were fought. British troops failed to capture Charleston in 1776, but succeeded in 1780. Shortly thereafter, the British were defeated

TAR HEELS

It was around the time of the Revolutionary War that North Carolinians were named Tar Heels. One story says that a British general remarked after intense fighting that "those Carolina boys stick in there like they've got tar on their heels." Another version is that General Cornwallis' troops crossed the Tar River (where turpentine mills dumped their waste) and emerged with the black stuff on their feet. Cornwallis is said to have observed that "anyone who wades in a Carolina stream would get tar heels."

by Continental forces at Kings Mountain and then at Cowpens, both in northwestern South Carolina.

CIVIL WAR AND RECONSTRUCTION   No event so shaped the Carolinas as did the Civil War, simply called "The War" around both states today. The shooting started in Charleston on April 12, 1861, a most appropriate place for the war's beginning, as the city coquettishly called itself the "Cradle of Secession." Union General William Tecumseh Sherman called South Carolina the "hell-hole of Secession" and vowed to crush the state, the first to secede the Union and the premier champion of slavery.

North Carolina was the last state to secede, having opposed secession until May 1861, when it was asked to send troops to the Union Army. Instead, North Carolina sent 125,000 men to fight with the Confederacy—about a quarter of the entire Confederate Army—and lost more soldiers by war's end than any other Southern state.

Sherman kept his promise about South Carolina. In 1865, during the war's final months, he and 61,000 troops swept across the state, demolishing railroad lines, burning fields and plantations, blackening the sky with columns of smoke. Sherman set fire to Columbia, the state capital, and wiped out 84 city blocks. His troops then spent three days getting drunk, plundering and raping.

The troops never reached Charleston, having been held back by the Lowcountry's mucky labyrinth of swamp, creeks and rivers, but the city fell anyway. A Union siege begun in 1863 left the city in shambles by February 1865, when the Confederate flag was permanently lowered over Charleston.

Post-war, the Carolinas were mostly a wasteland. Plantations, abandoned or reduced to cinders, covered the Piedmont and coastal plain. Cities lay in ruins. Slaves were technically free but enjoyed few economic or social rights. The Ku Klux Klan reared up, horribly, from the Civil War wreckage to begin its secretive tyranny. Federal law guaranteed African Americans the right to vote, go to school and own land, but the Klan believed otherwise. Many Carolinian blacks died at the bad end of a hanging rope, in the sweaty darkness of a Southern night.

North Carolina planters divvied up their land and rented portions to sharecroppers, many of whom were former slaves. Three decades after the war, cotton and tobacco dominated the land, and mills populated the towns and cities. Forests were logged and the wood turned into tables, chairs and desks, and soon North Carolina became a hub of furniture making. Textile mills spilled over into South Carolina, where hydroelectricity was the new source of energy and where destitute farmers were desperate for work. By 1900, thousands had left the fields for the mills.

MODERN TIMES Twenty-first-century North Carolina is still dominated by furniture and tobacco manufacturing, though the latter—a perilous, controversial business—continues to trouble the state. In the 1950s, North Carolina focused on technology and engineering, opening the Research Triangle Park between Raleigh and Durham to attract industry. Today, the 6800-acre park is a high-tech haven whose tenants include IBM, Burroughs-Wellcome and Northern Telecom.

Greensboro, North Carolina, was the seat of social reform in 1960, when four black students staged a sit-in at an F. W. Woolworth lunch counter. It sparked lunch-counter sit-inns across the nation, and helped bring about the Civil Rights Act of 1964.

The drug AZT was created in North Carolina, and several local researchers have received the Nobel Prize for their findings.

The Carolinas' most progressive city, Charlotte, North Carolina, is today a sparkling New South hub with a burgeoning banking and insurance industry and a sleek downtown. It is often compared to Atlanta—and unfairly, since Charlotte lacks the crime, congestion and urban chaos of the big Georgia city to the south.

South Carolina's hub of business and technology can be found at Greenville and Spartanburg, in the state's hilly Upcountry. In the 1990s, nearby Greer was chosen over dozens of other cities worldwide as the site of BMW's newest auto manufacturing plant.

As for Charleston, that grand antebellum dame by the sea has emerged as one of the top tourist cities in the nation, its downtown saturated with marvelous Old South architecture and New South cafés and boutiques. National magazines have named Charleston among the top ten destinations in the United States, and its historic inns among the country's most desirable.

Indeed, since the turn of the century, tourism has defined the Carolinas. Mountain resort towns have long drawn thousands of summer visitors to their fabulously forested, cool environs, and today they draw millions. Beaches attract sun-and-sand seekers and, lately, anyone who wants to swing a golf club. More than 120 golf courses are along the South Carolina coast, with the majority, about 100, in Myrtle Beach. Winter retreats such as Aiken, South Carolina, attracted Northerners after the Civil War—"Yankee" aristocrats built grand mansions and called them cottages, and called themselves "The Winter Colony."

Perhaps the greatest statement about modern Carolinas tourism is that Carolinians themselves do much of the wandering, preferring the beauty and familiarity of their own states to any others. City people head for the mountains in summer; mountain folk drive over to the beaches, seeking out the secluded isles and hidden coves of the Lowcountry in South Carolina and the Outer

Banks in North Carolina. Just about everyone makes a pilgrimage to Charleston, usually in spring or fall, to walk among the ancient cobbled streets and redolent gardens.

Choosing the Carolinas as a vacation destination is easy; deciding where to go is another matter. The two states are so vast and varied that it would take many visits to experience all they have to offer. To help you decide, here are brief descriptions of the regions presented in this book, but they are only teasers. To get the big picture, read the more detailed introductions to each chapter, then delve into the material on the particular regions that appeal to you most.

Where to Go

Asheville, North Carolina, is ringed with Blue Ridge mountains and filled with beautiful old architecture, moneyed neighborhoods and a young, hip population. Roughly 69,000 people live in this city where, in the 1880s, George Vanderbilt built his exquisite Biltmore Estate, today the country's largest private home and a major Carolinas attraction. Asheville is the gateway to North Carolina's mountains; the Blue Ridge Parkway runs alongside the city, and the Great Smoky Mountains are barely 30 miles to the west.

North Carolina's **Southern Mountains** start just south of Asheville and run west more than a hundred miles. Two-lane Route 64 is the main thread through this deeply wooded region where heights average 2000 to 3000 feet. Waterfalls, apple orchards and national forests fill the scenery, and there are a few small resort towns, some with chichi shops and golf courses, others with down-home appeal.

The western edge of North Carolina explodes with the lush, green, misty peaks of the **Great Smoky Mountains**. Most lie within Great Smoky Mountains National Park. Split between North Carolina and Tennessee, it's the country's most popular national park, with more than nine million annual visitors. Old homesteads and grist mills and farms, extraordinary vistas of valleys and mountain ranges, and rich, dazzling plant and animal life await in this cool and luxuriant place. Old-time resort towns just outside the park offer venerable lodging and dining, plenty of outdoor pursuits and Southern hospitality.

A scenic road across mountain peaks, the **Blue Ridge Parkway** runs from the Smokies northeast all the way into Virginia. There are 252 miles of this national parkway in North Carolina, all offering postcard views, whether they be of a century-old log cabin framed in split-rail fence, a mountain lake enveloped in evergreens, cold-running streams filled with trout, or apple orchards cascading into valleys. No stop signs, no traffic lights and barely any development—just dozens of historic and scenic stops.

You can exit the parkway right into the resort towns of the **High Country**. North Carolina's highest mountains are here, with 6684-foot Mount Mitchell, tallest mountain east of the Mississippi, ruling the scenery. Little Switzerland, Linville and Blowing Rock are some of the scenic, elite hamlets sprinkled across the High Country, and there is the slightly larger city of Boone, named for the frontiersman who once blazed the buffalo trails through these parts. The High Country is North Carolina's hub of snow skiing, and summer headquarters for golf and tennis, hiking and fishing, fine dining and just plain living well.

Prior to becoming the Palmetto State, South Carolina had a less appealing nickname—the Iodine State (due to the high levels of the mineral found in its vegetation).

The Piedmont makes up that great swath of central North Carolina, painted with clay, covered with foothills and tobacco fields, and studded with the Carolinas' major population centers. More than three million people call the Piedmont home, most living in Winston-Salem, Charlotte, Raleigh, Durham or Chapel Hill. Picturesque college campuses, burgeoning banking, insurance and high-tech industries, furniture and tobacco factories, and lovely old Southern homes dominate the region, though rambling countryside and Old South ways are easy to find.

Stretching nearly 300 miles between Virginia and South Carolina, the **North Carolina Coast** is a wonderful tapestry of rivers and sounds and scrub pine forest, pretty old fishing villages and a necklace of barrier isles called the Outer Banks. The Banks boast long, lonesome beaches and popular ones, too, and constant winds that whip the sand into the East Coast's highest dunes. Ferry boats deliver visitors and their cars to various islands.

The **South Carolina Coast** encompasses 200 miles of rivers and swamps, silver sand beaches and long-lasting forests, towns dating to the 1600s and Civil War plantations. Myrtle Beach, on the north end, has the prettiest beaches, the kitschiest ambiance and more than 100 golf courses. South of here is the Lowcountry, a watery world of tidal creeks and savannahs where rice and indigo plantations once thrived, and where today shrimp and crab are abundant. Charleston—old, elegant and supremely Southern —is the heart of the Lowcountry, and then there is the pretty town of Beaufort and the exclusive resort island of Hilton Head, where golfing reigns supreme.

Inland South Carolina starts with the appealing capital, Columbia, then spreads out to handsome, moneyed Aiken and its thoroughbred horse culture. It also takes in the northwestern corner of the state, called the Upcountry, with low, green mountains, lakes cupped in evergreen spires, and dozens of hidden places to discover.

The Carolinas stay comfortable most of the time, rarely getting extremely cold or hot—temperatures hover in the 80s during summer and the 60s during spring and fall. In winter, the mercury drops down in the 30s and 40s, lower in the mountains and higher on the coast, and rain is frequent.

Spring and fall bring some of the most pleasant days and nights in all but the highest regions of the Carolinas. The weather is typically dry and sunny, the flowers blooming in spring and leaves blazing orange, purple and red in fall, creating a crisp, colorful experience. This is high season for the mountains, when the most visitors take to the winding roads. It's also peak time in certain coastal cities, such as New Bern, North Carolina, and Charleston, South Carolina, when the gardens put on a spectacular show.

The mountains are glorious in summer, with their light-sweater nights, T-shirt days and endless shades of green. Summer rain comes suddenly and frequently in the mountains, particularly the Great Smoky Mountains, but it rarely lasts long—usually just minutes—and the sun is back in all its warmth and glory. When visiting the East's highest peak, Mount Mitchell, North Carolina, dress warmly. This wind-lashed summit has seen snow year-round. Temperatures can drop 10° in an hour, 20° in three hours.

People in the Piedmont region of North Carolina and across inland South Carolina head for the mountains on summer weekends to escape the still, humid heat of the cities, where temperatures can creep up into the 90s. On winter weekends, the same folks go to the mountains to ski. The downhill and cross-country action typically starts in December and runs until mid- or late March, with December and March bringing the warmest ski weather.

Beaches along the Carolinas' coast are generally packed from Memorial Day to Labor Day, when temperatures average in the mid- to high 80s but the beaches are cooled by constant wind. On North Carolina's Outer Banks, the breeze is so dependable that many beachfront cottages don't bother with air conditioning. Water temperatures are another story—usually reaching the mid- to upper 70s, but rarely 80°.

Hurricanes, though they can be devastating, need not keep one away from the coast. Usually developing in September, hurricanes have also been known to occur earlier or much later. Unlike many other weather phenomena, they come with plenty of warning, allowing visitors to either batten down or depart for inland locations and higher ground. Besides, September can be a wonderful time on a Carolinas' beach. The kids are back in school, the rates have dropped considerably but the temperature only a little, and the sands are much more secluded.

CALENDAR OF EVENTS

Ever been to a grits festival, an opossum creep, a parade of pigs, or a mountain sweet talk play? Now's your chance. Annual events in the Carolinas are folksy, friendly fests where you'll get to know the local people and instantly feel at home.

Check with local chambers of commerce (listed in regional chapters of this book) to see what will be going on when you are in the area. Below is a sampling of some of the bigger events, and some home-style ones, too.

JANUARY

High Country The Hickory Ridge Olde Christmas, a traditional eighteenth-century holiday celebration re-enacted in Boone, North Carolina, features the "lighting of the cabins," hearth-baked puddings, and music.

Piedmont Pinehurst, North Carolina's Jazz Fest in January is a two-day musical gala at the grand old Pinehurst Resort.

FEBRUARY

High Country Bring your appetite to the Maggie Valley Chili Challenge, where chili chefs square off amid live concerts and craft booths.

North Carolina Coast A Revolutionary War skirmish is replayed at the anniversary Celebration of the Battle of Moores Creek Bridge, located northwest of Wilmington.

South Carolina Coast Get your steamed oysters by the bucket at Charleston's Lowcountry Oyster Festival, held on the lawns of Boone Hall Plantation.

Inland South Carolina Africa Alive uses art, music and dance to tell the story of early African culture. The event is held at the Museum of York County in Rock Hill.

MARCH

South Carolina Coast One of Charleston's biggest events, the Festival of Houses and Gardens, includes tours of five gardens, twelve neighborhoods and three plantations. Afternoon teas, oyster roasts, garden galas and walking tours are among the many events, which last from mid-March to mid-April.

Inland South Carolina One of South Carolina's biggest events, the Aiken Triple Crown, takes place on three consecutive March weekends. The venue is Aiken, the heart of thoroughbred racing country.

APRIL

Asheville From early April to early May, the Biltmore Estate's Festival of Flowers is a dazzling, colorful affair, with spring blooms filling the formal gardens and interior of Asheville's famed chateau.

Southern Mountains What more compelling place than Chimney Rock Park to celebrate Easter? The Chimney Rock Park Easter Sunrise Service, held at the spine-tingling top of the rock, is non-denominational.

Great Smoky Mountains   Go wild at the **Wildflower Pilgrimage** inside Great Smoky Mountains National Park. Nearly 100 hikes, walks, talks and auto tours get you close to the blooms.

Piedmont   In Southern Pines, North Carolina, the **Springfest/ Tour De Moore** features 30- and 100-mile bike races, crafts, food and entertainment.

North Carolina Coast   Wilmington goes all out for azaleas, with a parade, home and garden tours, and live entertainment during the **North Carolina Azalea Festival**.

Inland South Carolina   Lovely Edisto Memorial Gardens in Orangeburg explodes with roses in spring, offering festivities such as canoe racing, an arts-and-crafts fair and food during its three-day **South Carolina Festival of Roses**. **The World Grits Festival** in St. George has lots of gritty trappings, including grits grinding, a grits-eating contest and corn-shelling contest.

Asheville   Northeast of Asheville, the **Black Mountain Folk Festival** centers around crafts, dance and food.

MAY

High Country   Arts and crafts are the highlight of **Art in the Park** at Blowing Rock, North Carolina, held monthly through October.

Piedmont   Tanglewood Park, located south of Winston-Salem in Clemmons, North Carolina, hosts its ever-popular **Steeplechase at Tanglewood**. Over at the Charlotte Motor Speedway in Concord, North Carolina, there's big excitement generated during the **Coca-Cola 600** race.

North Carolina Coast   All the action's up high at the **Hang Gliding Spectacular** competitions and show in Nags Head.

South Carolina Coast   Little River has its **Blue Crab Festival,** one of the coast's biggest events, with more than 150 booths and exhibits and plenty of fresh, flaky blue crab. Charleston's most acclaimed annual gala, **Spoleto Festival**, is a two-week musical extravaganza focusing on opera but also featuring jazz, ballet, chamber music, theater, late-night cabaret—and lots and lots of parties. The Lowcountry's rich Gullah heritage is celebrated during the three-day-long **Gullah Festival** in Beaufort. Storytelling, basket-making, fine art, dance and music are just some of the activities.

Inland South Carolina   Ever heard of a custom-built lobster racetrack? You have now. The one in the town of Aiken is the site of the **Lobster Race**, where you can watch the crustaceans crawl down a track, listen to big band music, peruse arts and crafts, and savor fresh-cooked seafood (read lobster).

Great Smoky Mountains   Pretty downtown Dillsboro, North Carolina, is lined with art, craft and food vendors as well as sidewalk entertainers during the **Dillsboro Heritage Festival**.

JUNE

High Country   When the world's largest wild rhododendron gardens bloom on Roan Mountain, Bakersville folks hold the **North**

Carolina Rhododendron Festival, with a 10K race, golf tournament and carnival rides. Nature lovers and photographers won't want to miss the **Grandfather Mountain Nature Photography Weekend**, with lectures and contests on the mountain in Linville, North Carolina.

Piedmont   Make yourself heard at the **National Hollerin' Contest** in Spivey's Corner, which "focuses on hollerin' as a traditional form of entertainment" and features crafts and music as well.

North Carolina Coast   Nags Head celebrates June with the **Rogallo Kite Festival,** featuring kite-flying workshops and competitions. Beaufort's **Annual Old Home Tours** are a wonderful way to see inside some of North Carolina's most beautiful historic houses.

South Carolina Coast   Myrtle Beach's **Sun Fun Festival** is a week-long parade of events: sporting contests, beauty pageants, sand-castle-building contests, outdoor concerts and fireworks. **Harborwalk** at Georgetown is a riverside party with live music, artwork and Lowcountry fare.

JULY   Many communities celebrate the **Fourth of July** with parades, fireworks and other festivities.

Great Smoky Mountains   Waynesville, North Carolina, hosts its popular **Folkmoot, U.S.A.**, highlighted by international music and dance. The town also has a July **Street Dance** accompanied by mountain and bluegrass music and Southern cooking.

High Country   Grandfather Mountain's famous **Highland Games & Gathering of Scottish Clans** draws thousands of people to the scenic mountainside in Linville, North Carolina. Highland dancing, athletic competitions, Scottish fiddling and harps, piping and drumming, Celtic jam, and Scottish folk music fill four days of celebration.

North Carolina Coast   The **Wright Kite Festival** in Kill Devil Hills is held on the spot where Wilbur and Orville Wright took their first flight. The Outer Banks beaches of Ocracoke Island are the site of the **Ocracoke Sand Sculpture Contest** every Fourth of July. Gospel singing and croakers team up at the **Pamlico County Croaker Festival** in tiny seaside Oriental. Arts and crafts, fireworks and a parade are also on the agenda. (A croaker is a small, white-fleshed fish that, well, *croaks* when you catch him.) In Wilmington there are three days of blues concerts and boat cruises during the annual **Cape Fear Blues Festival**.

Inland South Carolina   Gaffney pays homage to the peach during the **South Carolina Peach Festival**, with concerts by nationally known musicians, truck and tractor pulls, and lots of peachy eats. Watermelons more your style? Pageland hosts the **Watermelon Festival**, where events range from melon-eating and seed-spitting contests to rodeos.

Southern Mountains   Hendersonville's **North Carolina Apple Festival** features four days of celebration. There's a jazz concert, a gem and mineral show, food and art booths, and a King Apple Parade.

North Carolina Coast   Fresh, summery seafare will water your mouth at the **Corolla Seafood Festival** on the northern Outer Banks. Down on the Cape Fear Coast, Snead's Ferry dishes up pearly pink shellfish at the **Annual Shrimp Festival**, which includes a parade, arts-and-crafts booths and entertainment.

AUGUST

Blue Ridge Parkway   The **World Gee Haw Whimmy Diddle Contest** at the Folk Art Center in Oteen is all about whimmy diddles, an Appalachian folk toy that's a stick with notches along one side and a propeller on the end. Take another stick, rub it along the notches, and the propeller turns, making a "gee haw" sound. Besides the contest—who can make the most gees and haws in twelve seconds—there are crafts, food and music.

Piedmont   Kernersville, North Carolina, holds the **Honeybee Festival**, with art, food and music honoring the state insect. **Mayberry Days** in Mount Airy, North Carolina—the setting fictionalized in "The Andy Griffith Show"—offers down-home fun: pie-eating contests, pig-pickin' cookouts and Opie's Playground, where kids can go worm-digging and play hopscotch. Durham, North Carolina, home of Carolina blues, hosts the **Bull Durham Blues Festival** with two days of bluesy music and plenty to eat.

South Carolina Coast   Charleston hosts the **Scottish Games and Highland Gathering**, complete with medieval competitions, bagpipe playing and Scottish dancing. The **Candlelight Tour of Houses and Gardens** in Charleston covers the private homes and gardens seen in the Festival of Houses and Gardens in March.

Inland South Carolina   During **Aiken's Makin'**, historic Aiken fills with arts, crafts, musicians and local celebrities who compete in foot races.

SEPTEMBER

Octoberfests are in full gear around the Carolinas, with most offering German food and beer and oompah-pah music.

High Country   Banner Elk, North Carolina, holds the **Wooly Worm Festival**, where locals turn out to race caterpillars on strings, after which there is plenty of food and drink and music.

Piedmont   The biggest barbecue bash around is Lexington, North Carolina's **Barbecue Festival**, where dozens of Carolina cooks take to the streets with their pigs and smokers. There's a barbecue cook-off, arts and crafts, and a parade of pigs.

North Carolina Coast   Thousands of mum lovers stream to the town of Wilmington for the **Chrysanthemum Festival** at Tryon Palace.

South Carolina Coast   Seafood chefs dish up their Low Country best at the **Beaufort Shrimp Festival**. Owners of beautiful old

OCTOBER

Beaufort homes open their doors to visitors for the **Fall Festival of Houses and History**. You can continue your tour down on Edisto Island during **Edisto's Golden Age**, which offers visits to churches and plantations dating to the early 1700s.

Inland South Carolina Columbia's "Lantern Tour Through Time" is a walk in the woods with stops at several "camps"—Colonial, Civil War, African-American story-telling. The event kicks off the city's **Archaeology Festival**. **Fall for Greenville** welcomes the fall season with a lineup of musical and performing-arts events, downtown art fests and a finale of fireworks in an alcohol-free environment. Fountain Inn, in South Carolina's Upcountry, sponsors the **Aunt Het Festival**, where nineteenth century–style fun includes weaving and pottery demonstrations and street dances.

NOVEMBER **Asheville** The much-celebrated **Christmas at Biltmore Estate**, where the beautiful Asheville chateau is elaborately decorated in Victorian holiday style, begins in early November and runs to early January.

Piedmont Seagrove, North Carolina, holds its **Seagrove Pottery Festival**, where artistically inclined browsers can choose from dozens of styles and artists.

DECEMBER Candlelight and historic home tours, parades and Santa festivals prevail across North and South Carolina communities throughout December, culminating in New Year's Eve galas.

Asheville **New Year's Eve Celebration** at the Grove Park Inn starts on December 30 and continues for three days, with highlights including a mountain theme party and nonstop dining and entertainment.

Piedmont Winston-Salem's **Old Salem Christmas** features Moravian customs from past centuries—visitors can observe Christmas candles being made and attend "lovefeasts," which (before you get too excited) are meals of sweetened buns and coffee.

North Carolina Coast The **First Flight Anniversary Celebration** in Kill Devil Hills commemorates Wilbur and Orville Wright's history-making flight. New Bern's Tryon Palace is lavished with Colonial holiday decor most of the month for the **Tryon Palace Candlelight Tours**, featuring home and garden tours and cider and cookies.

▼▼▼▼▼▼▼▼▼▼
Before You Go

VISITORS CENTERS

For information on North Carolina, contact the **North Carolina Division of Travel & Tourism**. ~ 301 North Wilmington Street, Raleigh, NC 27601; 919-733-4171, 800-847-4862, fax 919-733-8582; www.visitnc.com. For a free copy of the *North Carolina Scenic Byways* booklet, which describes hidden roads and off-the-beaten-path trails all around the state, contact the **North Carolina Department of Transportation**. ~ 1557 Mail Service Center, Raleigh, NC 27699-1557; 919-733-2920.

In South Carolina, the **South Carolina Division of Parks, Recreation & Tourism** is the place for general information. ~ 1205 Pendleton Street, Columbia, SC 29201; 803-734-0122, 888-727-6453, fax 803-734-0138; www.discoversouthcarolina.com. Most Carolinas cities and small towns have visitor information centers or chambers of commerce; many of them are listed in *Hidden Carolinas* under the appropriate regions.

PACKING

Packing for the Carolinas depends a lot on when and where you visit. In summer, you can get by in most areas with light, casual clothing, some shorts and cool slacks, T-shirts and cotton blouses, a bathing suit (two, if you're beach bound), sandals and sturdy, comfortable walking shoes, and something a little dressy for night. If you're headed for the mountains, definitely pack a sweater or lightweight jacket for those cool summer nights.

For big-city forays, you can take along fancier clothes for ultra-deluxe dining, but very few places require coat and tie. Dress is more conservative in small towns, particularly those with laws prohibiting the sale of alcohol and where Sunday churchgoing is de rigueur. Short-shorts and micro-skirts are not.

Spring and fall call for more substantial wear: jeans and a sweatshirt, sweatpants and a warm jacket. Bring your warmest clothes in winter: thick sweaters and socks, hats and gloves, down jackets and ski clothes, especially if you're headed for the mountain slopes. Heavy-soled hiking boots come in handy even in the cities, where winter rains are dependable.

With their glorious assortment of flora, it's no surprise that rain is a constant factor in the Carolinas. Take along an umbrella and raincoat, any time or place you visit.

Though the Carolinas are not the Caribbean, you can get just as impressive a sunburn here. Bring a good sunscreen, especially to the beach, where sand and water reflect the sun's rays more intensely. If you'll be on the Outer Banks, pack protective sunglasses to shield your eyes from constant winds and occasional airborne sand.

Mosquito repellent is essential in summer, particularly in the coastal forests and swamps. If you plan to do any hiking in the wetlands or crabbing in the tidal marshes, wear canvas shoes that you don't mind wading in. If you plan on doing a lot of fishing; pack polarized glasses, which help you see beneath the water's surface.

Bring along a camera; mountain sunsets and seaside sunrises are sensational. Binoculars enhance both birdwatching and beachwatching. Good street and road maps are a must. Many roads in the Carolinas are winding and poorly marked (or unmarked), but these offer some of the most scenic, worthwhile wandering. Anyway, if you get lost, Carolinians will gladly point you in the right direction.

LODGING   Lodging in the Carolinas ranges from log cabins hidden in the woods to grand old mountainside inns, from funky seaside cottages to lavish beachfront hotels with fantasy gardens and swimming pools. Charleston, South Carolina, is a haven of exquisite lodges and inns, many more than 100 years old, including the John Rutledge House, which Rutledge built in 1763 for his bride.

Bed and breakfasts abound throughout both states. Some are in historic farmhouses or port town mansions with rambling quarters and plenty of space and privacy for guests. Other places are small homes with a spare room or two, with plenty of space for the host family but little seclusion or privacy for guests. Be sure to ask whether a bed and breakfast is a real inn or not. All of the bed and breakfasts listed in this book offer generous, private quarters for guests.

Chain motels line most main thoroughfares and mom-and-pop enterprises still successfully vie for lodgers in every region. Large hotels with names you'd know anywhere appear in most cities of any size. All along the Carolinas' coast, you'll find old-fashioned beach houses, many on stilts, where the salt-laden wind blows in off the water and the seagulls screech along the surf. Many are available by the week-only in summer but offer rates in the budget to moderate range.

State park cabins and villas, usually in the woods or along the shore, offer some of the least expensive lodging in the Carolinas. Naturally, it is some of the hardest to procure. You may have to book a year in advance—and then settle for your second or third choice of dates. Weekly stays are usually required in high season.

Whatever your preference and budget, you can probably find something to suit your taste with the help of the regional chapters in this book. Remember, rooms are often scarce and rates steepest in the high season—spring through fall in the mountains and on the beaches, spring and fall (but not summer) in Charleston. Ski season is also peak time in North Carolina's High Country. Across the North Carolina Piedmont and inland South Carolina, most cities offer constant year-round rates.

Off-season rates are often drastically reduced in many places (ultra-deluxe summer rooms on Myrtle Beach, for instance, are budget-priced in winter), allowing for a week's, or even a month's, stay to be a real bargain. Then, of course, there may be nasty weather. Whatever you do, plan ahead and make reservations, especially in the prime tourist seasons.

Accommodations in this book are organized by region and classified according to price range. Rates referred to are high-season rates, so if you are looking for low-season bargains, it's good to inquire. *Budget* lodgings generally are less than $70 per night for two people and are satisfactory—clean but modest. *Moderate*-priced lodgings run from $70 to $110; what they have to offer in the way of luxury will depend on where they are located, but they tend to have larger rooms and more attractive surroundings. For a *deluxe* accommodation, you can expect to spend between $110 and $180 for a double; you'll generally find spacious rooms, a fashionable lobby, a restaurant or two, and perhaps some boutiques. *Ultra-deluxe* facilities, priced above $180, are a region's finest, offering all the amenities of a deluxe hotel plus plenty of resort extras such as a health club and spa, 24-hour room service and gourmet dining.

If you crave a room facing the mountainside or the sea, be sure to ask specifically. Be warned that "waterfront" can mean sound or inlet or even a creek in some cases. If you are trying to save money, lodgings a block or so from the beach, or in town instead of on the mountain, usually have lower rates. The savings are often worth the short stroll to the beach or scenic ride up the mountain.

DINING

Southern fare, from New South nouveau and Old South country cooking to Lowcountry cuisine, stars at Carolinas restaurants everywhere. In big cities and college towns, you won't have trouble finding just about any kind of eatery, from ethnic to European to vegetarian.

Within a particular chapter of *Hidden Carolinas*, restaurants are categorized geographically, with each entry describing the establishment according to price. Restaurants serve lunch and dinner unless otherwise noted. Dinner entrées at *budget* restaurants usually cost $9 or less per person. The ambiance is less formal, service usually speedy and the crowd is often a local one. *Moderate*-priced restaurants range between $9 and $16 at dinner; surroundings are casual but pleasant, the menu offers more variety and the pace is usually slower than at budget eateries. *Deluxe* establishments tab their entrées from $16 to $25; cuisines may be simple or sophisticated, depending on the location, but the decor is plusher and the service more personalized. *Ultra-deluxe* dining rooms, where entrées begin at $25, are often the gourmet places; here cooking has become a fine art and the service should be impeccable.

In most major urban areas of the Carolinas, you can order alcohol by the glass any day of the week—though you must order it after 1 p.m. on Sunday.

Some restaurants change hands often and are occasionally closed in low season. Efforts have been made in this book to include places with established reputations for good eating. When possible, restaurants with seasonal schedules have been noted. Breakfast and lunch menus vary less in price from restaurant to restaurant than evening dinners.

LIQUOR

Now, about alcohol: Carolinas' laws on liquor consumption vary from town to town and county to county. Particularly in "dry" rural areas along the Bible Belt, alcohol sales are limited in some form or even altogether. Some places permit wine and beer sales but no hard liquor; others limit all liquor sales to package stores but no restaurants—and forget nightclubs. Sunday liquor sales are banned in many rural areas. Often, restaurants will permit you to bring your own alcohol, though sometimes only wine and beer. If a drink with dinner is important to you, call before dining out.

TRAVELING WITH CHILDREN

The Carolinas are a wonderful place to bring children. The prevailing Southern culture focuses not just on hospitality but on the family, and most activities, lodging and restaurants accommodate children. Two major North Carolina ski resorts are geared toward families, and what child wouldn't love a city (Myrtle Beach) with 50 mini golf courses? Then there are miles of beaches, dozens of lakes and hundreds of parks perfect for family travelers.

Some Carolinas' inns, guesthouses and bed and breakfasts don't accept children, so be sure of the policy when you make reservations. If you need a crib or cot, arrange for it with your hotel ahead of time.

If you are traveling by air, try to reserve bulkhead seats where there is plenty of room. Take along extras you may need, such as diapers, changes of clothing, snacks and toys, or small games. When traveling by car, be sure to take along the extras, too. Make sure you have plenty of water and juices to drink; dehydration can be a subtle problem.

A first-aid kit is a must for any trip. Along with adhesive bandages, antiseptic cream and something to stop itching, include any medicines your child's pediatrician might recommend to treat allergies (particularly if you visit in spring), colds, diarrhea or any chronic problems your child may have.

At the beach, take extra care with children's skin the first few days. Tender young skin can suffer severe sunburn before you know it. Hats for the kids are a good idea, along with liberal applications of a good sunscreen. Never take your eyes off children at the shore.

All-night stores are scarce in rural areas, and stores in small towns often close early. You may go a long distance between stores that can supply you with essentials, so be sure to be well-stocked with diapers, baby food and other necessities when on the go.

Many towns, parks and attractions offer special activities designed just for children. Consult local newspapers and/or call the numbers in this book to see what's happening where you're going.

WOMEN TRAVELING ALONE

Traveling solo grants an independence and freedom different from that of traveling with a partner, but single travelers are more vulnerable to crime and must take additional precautions.

It's unwise to hitchhike and probably best to avoid inexpensive accommodations on the outskirts of town; the money saved does not outweigh the risk. Bed and breakfasts, youth hostels and YWCAs are generally your safest bet for lodging, and they also foster an environment ideal for bonding with fellow travelers.

Keep all valuables well-hidden and clutch cameras and purses tightly. Avoid late-night treks or strolls through undesirable parts of town, but if you find yourself in this situation, continue walking with a confident air until you reach a safe haven. A fierce scowl never hurts.

These hints should by no means deter you from seeking out adventure. Wherever you go, stay alert, use your common sense and trust your instincts. If you are hassled or threatened in some way, never be afraid to scream for assistance. It's a good idea to carry change for a phone call and to know the number to call in case of emergency. For more hints, get a copy of *Safety and Security For Women Who Travel* (Travelers Tales).

GAY & LESBIAN TRAVELERS

The Carolinas are not known for their broadmindedness (this *is* the South) and there are, undoubtedly, deeply rural places where gay and lesbian travelers will not feel comfortable. However, in many areas they will not only feel comfortable but especially welcome. And several regions are fast emerging as gay and lesbian hot spots.

It is within these regions that *Hidden Carolinas* will steer you to gay-friendly and gay-specific lodging, dining, shopping and nightlife. In Chapter Two, you'll find gay-friendly lodging, bookstores and night spots in the dynamic city of Asheville. The big cities of Piedmont, covered in Chapter Seven, offer lots of danceclubs and other popular night spots for gay and lesbian travelers.

Gay headquarters on North Carolina's coast is Wilmington; check Chapter Eight for gay-friendly lodging, nightlife and beaches in this progressive coastal town. Across the line in South Carolina, Charleston has a thriving community of gay artists, writers and affluent nine-to-fivers. Their favorite lodges, night spots and beaches are outlined in Chapter Nine.

EXTRA! EXTRA!

For gay and lesbian happenings around the Carolinas, pick up a copy of the *Front Page*, a free bi-weekly available in bookstores, cafes and gay nightclubs. ~ 919-829-0181; www.frontpagenews.com. For the latest in nightlife, check out www.gaybarsonline.com.

SENIOR TRAVELERS   The Carolinas are an ideal place for older vacationers; countless museums, historic sights and even restaurants and lodges offer senior discounts that cut a substantial chunk off vacation costs. And many older travelers from hotter climes flock to the Carolina mountains for its cool summers.

The AARP offers membership to anyone 50 or over. Benefits of AARP membership include travel discounts with a number of firms. ~ 601 E Street Northwest, Washington, DC 20049; 888-687-2277; www.aarp.org.

Elderhostel offers reasonably priced, all-inclusive educational programs at a variety of Carolinas' locations throughout the year. ~ 11 Avenue de Lafayette, Boston, MA 02111; 877-426-8056, fax 617-426-0701; www.elderhostel.org.

Be extra careful about health matters. In addition to the medications you ordinarily use, it's a good idea to bring along the prescriptions for obtaining more. Consider carrying a copy of your medical record with you—including your medical history and current medical status as well as your doctor's name, telephone number and address. Make sure that your insurance covers you while you're away from home.

DISABLED TRAVELERS   Many travel destinations throughout the Carolinas are fully accessible to travelers with disabilities. Every state park campground in South Carolina has two wheelchair-accessible sites that can be reserved in advance. The city of Myrtle Beach provides beachgoing wheelchairs. Many museums, botanical gardens and even mountain parks are designed with wheelchair visitors in mind.

Plenty of wheelchair visitors have ridden the half-mile concrete ramp up to the top of Clingmans Dome, which is the highest spot in Great Smoky Mountains National Park.

Helpful information on traveling with disabilities is available from several national groups, including the Society for Accessible Travel & Hospitality. ~ 347 5th Avenue, Suite 610, New York, NY 10016; 212-447-7284, fax 212-725-8253; www.sath.org. Travelin' Talk, a network of people and organizations, also provides assistance. ~ P.O. Box 1796, Wheatridge, CO 80034; 303-232-2979; www.travelintalk.net.

The travel guide *Traveling Like Everybody Else: A Practical Guide for Disabled Travelers*, by Jacqueline Freedman and Susan Gersten, lists tour operators and provides information on many other resources.

FOREIGN TRAVELERS   **Passports and Visas**   Most foreign visitors need a passport and tourist visa to enter the United States. Contact your nearest U.S. Embassy or Consulate well in advance to obtain a visa and to check on any other entry requirements.

Customs Requirements   Foreign travelers are allowed to carry in the following: 200 cigarettes (1 carton), 50 cigars or 2 kilograms (4.4 pounds) of smoking tobacco; one liter of alcohol for personal use only (you must be 21 years of age to bring in alcohol); and US$100 worth of duty-free gifts that may include an additional 100 cigars. You may bring in any amount of currency, but must fill out a form if you bring in over US$10,000. Carry any prescription drugs in clearly marked containers. (You may have to produce a written prescription or doctor's statement for the customs officers.) Meat or meat products, seeds, plants, fruits, and narcotics may not be brought into the United States. Contact the **U.S. Customs Service** for further information. ~ 1300 Pennsylvania Avenue NW, Washington, DC 20229; 202-354-1000; www.cbp.gov.

Driving   If you plan to rent a car, an international driver's license should be obtained before arriving in the United States. Some car rental agencies require both a foreign license and an international driver's license. Many also require a lessee to be at least 25 years of age; all require a major credit card. Seat belts are mandatory for the driver and all passengers. Children under the age of six or under 60 pounds should be in the back seat in approved child-safety restraints.

Currency   United States money is based on the dollar. Bills come in denominations of $1, $5, $10, $20, $50 and $100. Every dollar is divided into 100 cents. Coins are the penny (1 cent), nickel (5 cents), dime (10 cents) and quarter (25 cents). Half-dollar and dollar coins are rarely used. You may not use foreign currency to purchase goods and services in the United States. Consider buying traveler's checks in dollar amounts. You may also use credit cards affiliated with an American company such as Interbank, Barclay Card and American Express.

Electricity and Electronics   Electric outlets use currents of 110 volts, 60 cycles. For appliances made for other electrical systems, you need a transformer or other adapter. Travelers who use laptop computers for telecommunication should be aware that modem configurations for U.S. telephone systems may be different from their European counterparts. Similarly, the U.S. format for videotapes is different from that in Europe; U.S. Park Service visitors centers and other stores that sell souvenir videos often have them available in European format.

Weights and Measures   The United States uses the English system of weights and measures. American units and their metric equivalents are: 1 inch = 2.5 centimeters; 1 foot (12 inches) = 0.3 meter; 1 yard (3 feet) = 0.9 meter; 1 mile (5280 feet) = 1.6 kilometers; 1 ounce = 28 grams; 1 pound (16 ounces) = 0.45 kilograms; 1 quart (liquid) = 0.9 liter.

▼▼▼▼▼▼▼▼▼▼▼▼▼▼

Outdoor Adventures

CAMPING

The Carolinas offer a wide variety of camping opportunities, from primitive camping in wilderness areas to recreational vehicle parks that resemble fashionable resorts. For a listing of North Carolina state parks and recreation areas, contact **North Carolina State Parks and Recreation Division**. ~ 512 North Salisbury Street, Raleigh, NC 27604; 919-733-4181; e-mail parkinfo@ncmail.net. In South Carolina, write or call **South Carolina State Parks**. ~ 1205 Pendleton Street, Columbia, SC 29202; 803-734-1700.

Information on camping in national forests in North Carolina is available from the **U.S. Forest Service**. ~ P.O. Box 2750, Asheville, NC 28802; 828-257-4200. If you're visiting the Smokies, contact the **Great Smoky Mountains National Park**. ~ 107 Park Headquarters Road, Gatlinburg, TN 37738; 865-436-1226. For South Carolina national forests, contact the **U.S. Forest Service**. ~ 4931 Broad River Road, Columbia, SC 29212-3530; 803-561-4000.

An accommodations directory published by the **North Carolina Division of Travel & Tourism** lists public campgrounds and cabins across the state. ~ 301 North Wilmington Street, Raleigh, NC 27601; 919-733-4171, 800-847-4862, fax 919-733-8582; www.visitnc.com. The **Carolinas Association of RV Parks and Campgrounds** publishes a guide to numerous privately owned campgrounds. ~ 605 Poole Drive, Garner, NC 27529; 919-779-5709; www.campingcarolinas.com.

PERMITS   Primitive campsites are provided in certain state parks and recreation areas. You need a permit for wilderness camping away from designated sites in national forests and in certain wilderness areas of state parks and seashores. To obtain permits and information, contact individual sites, as found in the "Beaches & Parks" sections of the regional chapters of this book.

◆◆

SNOW HEELS

As winter blankets the mountains of North Carolina, ski season heats up. Ski enthusiasts head for the High Country, where Sugar Mountain, Beech Mountain, Hawksnest and Appalachian Mountain offer the best downhill action. Much of the snow is machine-made and can sometimes get icy, though daily grooming helps keep the runs smooth and navigable. Specifics on individual resorts are listed in Chapter Six. For additional information on ski events and services, contact High Country Host. ~ 1700 Blowing Rock Road, Boone, NC 28607; 828-264-1299, 800-438-7500; www.mountainsofnc.com.

Boating is one of the more popular activities in the Carolinas. You can bring your own boat and travel the Intracoastal Waterway or laze away the day on a quiet lake with a fishing pole. And if you have no boat, you can rent or charter a craft of just about any size or speed. Various chapters in this book offers suggestions on how to go about finding the vessel of your choice. Most marinas and other rental agencies will arm you with maps in advance.

BOATING

A *Coastal Boating Guide* to North Carolina is available from the **North Carolina Department of Transportation Map Section**. ~ 1503 Mail Service Center, Raleigh, NC 27699; 919-733-7600, 877-368-4968; www.ncdot.org. For information on boating regulations in South Carolina, contact the **South Carolina Department of Natural Resources and Law Enforcement**. ~ P.O. Box 167, Columbia, SC 29202; 803-734-4002; www.dnr. state.sc.us.

Or, if you're planning a trip along the Intracoastal Waterway, consider buying the *Mid-Atlantic Waterway Guide* (Communication Channels, Inc.), which details sounds, bridges, bays and connecting rivers through Virginia, North and South Carolina, and Georgia.

Even in winter, you'll find diehard surfers and windsurfers riding the waves in their wetsuits. Swimming, waterskiing, jetboating and floating on inflatable rafts are popular activities in the summer.

WATER SAFETY

People have drowned in Carolinas waters, but drownings are easily avoided when you respect the power of the water, heed appropriate warnings and use good sense.

Wherever you swim, never do it alone. Always swim in designated areas, preferably where there are lifeguards. On the ocean, always face the incoming waves. They can bring unpleasant surprises even to the initiated. If you go surfing, learn the proper techniques and how to spot dangers from an expert before you start out. Respect signs warning of dangerous currents and undertows. North Carolina's Outer Banks are particularly prone to rough seas and strong currents, so be aware when swimming there. If you get caught in a rip current or any tow that makes you feel out of control, don't try to swim against it. Head across it, paralleling the shore. Exercise caution in the use of floats, inner tubes or rafts; unexpected currents can quickly carry you out to sea.

There are some jellyfish that inflict a mild sting, but that is easily treated with an over-the-counter antiseptic. If you go oystering or crabbing, swim in or wade in murky waters where shellfish dwell, wear canvas or rubber boots to protect your feet.

If you're going canoeing or whitewater rafting, always scout the river from land before the first trip, and check available literature. Rivers may have danger areas such as falls, boulders, rapids and dams.

FISHING &
CRABBING

Sitting near dead center on the Atlantic coast and sharing two big migratory basins—the Mid-Atlantic Bight and the South Atlantic Bight—the Carolinas offer some of the East Coast's best fishing. As well, the network of sounds, basins and estuaries provide breeding and feeding grounds for dozens of fish and shellfish.

Unfortunately, like most areas along the Atlantic, commercial overfishing and rising consumer demand has in recent years taken its toll, reducing the populations of several types of fish. Gray trout, red drum, black sea bass and summer flounder are being caught faster than they can replace themselves. Recent regulations banning certain commercial fishing (but not recreational sport-fishing) are intended to replenish the waters.

Still, nearly 1.7 million sport anglers take to the Carolinas' coastal waters every year, and with considerable success, catching more than 26 million fish. King mackerel, Southern flounder, Spanish mackerel and croakers are still abundant, as are blue crabs.

Crabbing is a major pastime, particularly in South Carolina's Lowcountry. It's an easy and inexpensive endeavor, requiring some string, a weight, some chicken parts and a dip net. Tie the weight and chicken onto the string, throw it out in the creek or tidal flats, wait for a blue crab to mosey along, and scoop him out with the net.

Inland, lakes and streams offer excellent angling. You can fly-fish for trout, or use a rod 'n' reel baited with anything from corn kernels and crickets to nightcrawlers. You can also try for catfish, bream, bass and sunfish—all part of many Carolinians' diet.

If you'd like to try a kind of fishing that's new to you, you will find guided services available just about everywhere boats are rented and bait sold. Charter fishing is the costliest way to go out to sea; party boats (also called head boats) take a crowd but are less expensive and usually great fun. On rivers, lakes and tiny hidden streams, guides can show you the best place to throw a hook or skim a fly.

In North Carolina, you don't need a license to fish in saltwater (though state officials have long proposed the idea), but you do need one for freshwater fishing. Occasionally, special stamps, such as trout stamps, are required as well. Fishing licenses and stamps are available from local bait-and-tackle stores and from the Licensing Section of the **North Carolina Wildlife Resources Commission.** ~ 322 Chapanoke Road, Raleigh, NC 27603; 919-662-4370.

No matter where you fish in South Carolina—saltwater or freshwater—you'll need a license, available from many bait-and-tackle shops and marinas. Or, contact the **Licensing Division of the South Carolina Department of Natural Resources.** ~ P.O. Box 11710, Columbia, SC 29211; 803-734-3838.

TWO

Asheville

George Vanderbilt called Asheville "the most beautiful land in the world." The year was 1888, and it was no shallow praise from a savvy tycoon who had traveled to Europe more than a dozen times. But then, Vanderbilt was certainly not the first to be charmed by this North Carolina place, set in a bowl of Blue Ridge Mountains, painted with persistent clear skies, emblazoned in summer with lavender bursts of rhododendron and in autumn with the fire-red of maples.

"Eden Land" is what the area's first permanent settlers called Asheville. Arriving in 1785 from northern Ireland, they were mainly Scottish-Irish immigrants who couldn't make a living after the British slapped steep tariffs on wool. No longer in the sheep business, they turned hardy mountaineers who built crude wood shacks, hunted the depths of surrounding forests and farmed small garden patches. One local frontierswoman, Elizabeth Patton, caught the eye of an itinerant frontiersman named Davy Crockett. The couple was wed in the town of Asheville, incorporated in 1797 and named after North Carolina Governor Samuel Ashe.

Asheville's fate as a thriving crossroads and summer escape was set in the 1820s when pioneers carved the Buncombe Turnpike toll trail from the Eastern Seaboard to western South Carolina. It ran right through the middle of town and brought hundreds of wagons and stagecoaches, and drovers herding cattle and flocks of turkeys headed for southern markets. The passers-through left, telling of a "Land of Sky," where mountains lapped at the clouds and the air was cooler and kinder than most.

The Civil War plunged Asheville into decline, putting its resort destiny on brief hold, but by the 1880s the town was turning into a summer social mecca. In 1883 the local newspaper pronounced Asheville the "Paris of the South," raving about its art studios and extravagant parties, 1000-volume library above the drugstore, hunting forays and railroad excursions.

A train brought George Vanderbilt from New York to Asheville in the late 1880s, and with Vanderbilt money he bought several mountains and began building what would come to be recognized as one of the world's most beautiful estates. Designed after the grand French chateaux he had come to love during his travels, today Vanderbilt's fabulous Biltmore Estate is one of the Carolinas' most-visited attractions. Vanderbilt eventually bought 125,000 acres and founded the country's first forestry school; much of the land is now Pisgah National Forest, a vast tract of woods running west of Asheville.

Like Vanderbilt, Edwin Wiley Grove was so smitten with Asheville that he put his fortune there. The St. Louis inventor of Grove's Tasteless Chill Tonic created the Grove Park Inn as a monument to himself, opening the great granite resort in 1913 before a throng of dignitaries. It was—and still is—an extraordinary place, earthy and elegant, roosting atop Sunset Mountain, its rock-studded facade glinting mightily in the mountain sun.

Many of the architects, masons and other minds behind the Grove Park Inn and Biltmore Estate also turned their talents on downtown Asheville. The result is obvious today: a tremendous blend of styles, from Byzantine and Florentine to Romanesque and Art Deco. Though many buildings fell into near-ruin after the Depression, they have been (and are still being) vigorously revived, so that downtown Asheville today has a fresh-scrubbed, vibrant look.

And while the nineteenth-century bluebloods polished Asheville with money and affluence, the young sophisticates and outdoor adventurers of the twenty-first century have bestowed a markedly hip edge. Pretty and gritty coffeehouses, trendy bistros, "smoke free" nightclubs and retro boutiques crowd this ever-growing stronghold of American counterculture. Dozens of galleries showcase Appalachian art and music, from mountain pottery to hand-carved dulcimers. Everything in Asheville is on a small scale—the population is only 68,900—and rarely crowded. A number of national magazines have lately listed Asheville as one of the top ten U.S. cities to live in. Some have suggested that a large measure of Asheville's appeal is derived from what the city *doesn't* have. Exulted one transplanted Atlanta artist: "I like Asheville because there's no traffic, pollution, serious crime. For the first time in my life, I don't lock my doors at night."

Asheville is also a perfect place to start the Carolinas' experience, not only because it's good-looking and hip, but because it's the gateway to the mountains. North Carolina's southern mountains and South Carolina's Upcountry spread out beneath the city like a rippled apron. The Blue Ridge Parkway, that slow, wonderful glide past hundreds of awe-inspiring peaks, cuts along the eastern side of Asheville and squiggles its way west to Great Smoky Mountains National Park. Mt. Mitchell, eastern America's highest peak at 6684 feet, is only 30 miles from Asheville, right off the parkway.

Many people bent on seeing those mountains, however, inevitably get side-tracked in Asheville, spending days instead of hours, finding there's more to do than they had imagined. At day's end, they will hopefully find themselves on the terrace of the Grove Park Inn, where they can watch the sun put down behind the soft peaks of the Blue Ridge, leaving a purple afterglow across this most beautiful land.

Route 240, the main approach to downtown Asheville, is also known as the Billy Graham Freeway in honor of the world-famous evangelist who is an Asheville native. It delivers visitors to a place of neatly tended blocks with broad, tidy streets, the most stylish of buildings, and a palpable air of business. Great church domes glimmer beneath the glass silhouettes of slender midrises, and sensuous Art Deco facades ramble beneath oaks and dogwoods. Entire blocks look like 21st-century beat scenes, with youths garbed in tie-dye and army-issue boots, their hands warming little cups of double espresso. Gallery windows tempt with clever artwork, and bakeries and coffeehouses send good smells into the street.

Downtown Asheville

Downtown Asheville is entirely enjoyable. It's easy to walk and offers plenty for the eye, palate and shopping list. You won't even have trouble finding a parking space—without a meter, if you're

SIGHTS

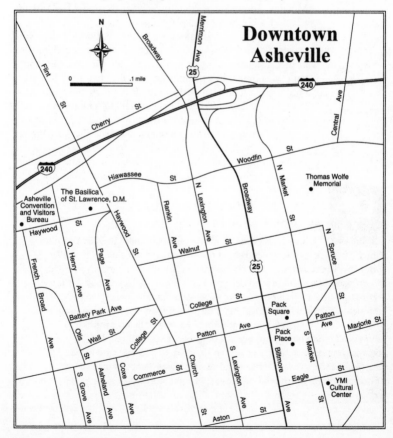

Downtown Asheville

lucky. Park near **Pack Square**, known simply as "The Square" in the 1820s when the Buncombe Turnpike (a loose term for a wagon trail) ran through town and brought in all sorts of business. Back then The Square was often filled with livestock on its way to the market; today it is a public park punctuated by a granite obelisk monument to Zebulon Baird Vance, whose law practice once stood on the spot. ~ Corner of Patton Avenue and Broadway.

The park came to the city compliments of George Willis Pack, a Cleveland lumberman who brought his sick wife to Asheville in 1883, hoping the cool, dry air would make her feel better. He took a liking to the town, buying up land and erecting buildings he would later donate to the people. One of these was the 1926 library, now **Pack Place**, Asheville's showpiece center for art, science and culture. There are two performing arts spaces, as well as four museums easily seen in a day. Buy a ticket for just one museum, or save money with a combination ticket. All museums are closed Monday. Admission. ~ 2 South Pack Square; 828-257-4500, fax 828-251-5652; www.packplace.org.

A slow, soulful stroll along the 1.7-mile **Asheville Urban Trail** provides a most pleasant introduction to the city's architecture, history and culture. Over two dozen sculptures dot the looped path, including a boy on stilts and a giant "flat iron" like those once used at the Asheville Laundry. Pick up an audiocassette at Pack Place (2 South Pack Square; 828-257-4500) for a self-guided tour. Or join the guided treks by calling 828-258-0710.

Least impressive of the museums, the **Asheville Art Museum** has several small galleries that are home to a small permanent collection, mostly twentieth-century pieces, including bronze sculpture, serigraphs, lithographs and screen-printing. ~ 828-253-3227.

sights

AUTHOR FAVORITE

"In winter, the wind blew howling blasts under the skirts of [the house]: its back end was built high off the ground on wet columns of rotting brick." So wrote Wolfe in *Look Homeward, Angel*, his first and most acclaimed autobiographical novel. In it he depicted a sad and strange childhood in the boardinghouse in which he grew up, watching the traveling salesmen pass through, enduring the social and racial turmoil of a city not fully recovered from the Civil War. Wolfe's internal turmoil was fueled by his parents' endless bickering; his mother was a workaholic miser who ran the boardinghouse, while his father was an alcoholic stonecutter who hated the house and its flow of transients. The house now stands as the **Thomas Wolfe Memorial**. See page 36 for more information.

Adults will be more taken with the **Colburn Earth Science Museum**, where walls glitter with exhibits of thousands of precious stones, manuscripts tell of the state's stone age and interactive displays explore the geologic forces that shape the Earth. In the 1800s, more than 100 mines were open in the Piedmont area; today, the world's largest granite quarry—a mile long and 1800 feet wide—is still in operation near Mt. Airy, in the northern Piedmont. The museum is named for Burnham Standish Colburn, the local man who had the world's largest collection of hiddenite. ~ 828-254-7162.

Not in the same building but actually part of the Pack Place museum family, the **YMI Cultural Center** houses a small but accomplished exhibit of African-American art within its historic brick walls. The handsome Tudor building dates to 1892, when George Vanderbilt decided the "Negro" craftsmen who worked on his Biltmore Estate should have a community center. The craftsmen built this Young Men's Institute, then they bought it from Vanderbilt in 1905. Over the years it went from western North Carolina's hub for black art and culture to abandonment back to flourishing cultural center. Today, the permanent artifacts include tribal masks and sculptures; traveling exhibits tend to be of stellar quality. Closed Sunday and Monday. Admission. ~ Market and Eagle streets; 828-252-4614, fax 828-257-4539; www.ymicc.org, e-mail ymicc@aol.com.

Stop by the **Asheville Convention and Visitors Bureau** for walking-tour maps and detailed information on the city. ~ 151 Haywood Street; 828-258-6101, 888-247-9811; www.explore asheville.com.

In the early 1900s, Asheville's architectural aura was being helped along by places like the **First Baptist Church**. Its gigantic rust-colored dome lends a European air to the city skyline; its steps and portico of Italian pink marble excite up close. The church was designed after the great domed cathedrals of Florence, and its well-known architect, Douglas Ellington, clearly understood Florentine design. If you go inside you can see the stained glass all around the sanctuary, and the pipe organs and chandeliers that are overwhelming in size. ~ 5 Oak Street; 828-252-4781; www.fbca.net.

The city's other big and beautiful church is **The Basilica of St. Lawrence, D.M.**, built early in the twentieth century in the style of the Spanish Renaissance. Listed on the National Register of Historic Places, the immense terra cotta church was constructed without the use of wood or steel. The interior features an incredible free-standing elliptical dome of tile and concrete, stained glass, intricate seventeenth-century woodcarvings and frescoes. The noted Spanish architect Rafael Gustavino worked on the Biltmore

House before designing the church. Gustavino's work in the ancient method of building domes and vaults with tile and mortar can also be seen at Grand Central Station and Carnegie Hall in New York City. ~ 97 Haywood Street; 828-252-6042.

A few blocks east, huddling in the shadows of Asheville's more statuesque buildings, the **Thomas Wolfe Memorial** is the dim and drafty boardinghouse that forged the life of author Thomas Wolfe. Only Tom lived with his mother in the boardinghouse, taking his meals alone in a cubbyhole to maximize space for boarders, sleeping in whatever bedroom was available at day's end. His father lived across the street with seven of the children. The 1883 Queen Anne house was, tragically, a victim of arson in the summer of 1998, though the main structure and some of the original furnishings were saved. Restoration on the State Historic Site is complete and the adjacent Visitor Center is open and offers visitors a look at various Wolfe artifacts, including his writing desk and the Remington typewriter retrieved by his siblings from his New York apartment. He did most of his writing after moving to New York, and he also died there at age 38 of a rare tuberculosis of the brain. Before his death he returned to Asheville and found good feelings, writing of "the cool sweet magic of starred mountain night, the huge attentiveness of dark, the slope, the trees, the living silence of the houses waiting. . . ." Closed Monday. Admission. ~ 52 North Market Street; 828-253-8304, fax 828-252-8171; www.wolfememorial.com.

LODGING   Downtown's most chic lodging is at **Haywood Park Hotel**. Elegant in a minimalist way, its style is crisp and airy with lots of open space. The lobby soars with white pillars, brass rails, and staircases that curve up to 33 suites with elegant crown moulding and baths of Spanish marble. Continental breakfast is delivered to your room with the daily paper. ~ 1 Battery Park Avenue; 828-252-2522, 800-228-2522, fax 828-253-0481; www.haywood park.com. ULTRA-DELUXE.

Next door to the Thomas Wolfe Memorial, the **Renaissance Hotel Asheville** is tall, sleek and corporate-looking. Nearly all of the 281 rooms and four suites have a sweeping view of the city with a backdrop of the Blue Ridge Mountains. There's an indoor pool and an outdoor pool for warm-weather swimming as well as one restaurant serving breakfast, lunch and dinner. ~ 1 Thomas Wolfe Plaza; 828-252-8211, 800-468-3571, fax 828-236-9616; www.renaissancehotels.com. DELUXE.

HIDDEN ►   On the northern fringe of downtown and impossible to miss, **Beaufort House Victorian Inn** is daubed with deep salmon, white and burgundy, decorated with bay and arched windows and a big gazebo with wraparound porch. The Queen Anne confection, designed in 1894 by famed local architect A. L. Melton, is for-

Inn

Organics

In the northeast corner of downtown Asheville lie luxuriant wooded neighborhoods where, if you listen closely, you can hear the servants polishing the silver. If you follow Macon Avenue north you will come upon the place where perhaps more silver has been polished over time than anywhere else—the **Grove Park Inn Resort & Spa**, Asheville's legendary haunt of the wealthy and well-known. ~ 290 Macon Avenue; 828-252-2711, 800-438-5800, fax 828-252-6040; www.groveparkinn.com.

Newspaper editor Fred Seely first had the idea for an earthy but luxurious inn crafted of natural material to match nature. In 1912 he took his idea for "organic architecture" to his father-in-law, E.W. Grove, who had made millions by inventing Grove's Tasteless Chill Tonic and Grove's Bromo-Quinine (potions whose benefits remain questionable today). Grove had as much ego as money, so he commissioned the inn as a monument to himself. Italian stonemasons and tons of Appalachian granite were brought in, and artists and craftspeople created natural-style furnishings. Within a year the 150-room resort opened to a slew of celebrities. Soon everyone who was anyone wanted to come to the Grove Park Inn.

Things aren't quite that momentous today, thank goodness. (Really, who wants to put on pantyhose just to walk through the lobby?) While country clubbers filter in throughout the year, the average guest is just as likely to be an all-American family vacationer. You'll find them out on the tennis courts and golf course that descend Sunset Mountain, and in the indoor and outdoor pools. Naturally the inn is much bigger today—510 rooms, thanks to the addition of two wings in the 1980s—though its "organic" mood remains largely intact. The famous roof of red clay still droops over the granite lodge like folds of dough, and original hammered-copper lights decorate some of the historic rooms.

Plan your tour late in the day so you can be on the Sunset Terrace when the ruby ball vanishes behind Mt. Pisgah. Find a chair, order a drink, and look down on Asheville and across the Pisgah Mountains—the view is amazing. Then retreat to the lobby and find a spot near one of the famous stone fireplaces, famous because they look big enough to drive a car through.

$140

Chestnut Inn   176 E. Chestnut   828-285-0705
Lion & Rose   800-546-6988 $135
Corner Oak Manor - Near Biltmore $125-135   828-253-3525

mal inside; its polished wood walls gleam and its eight luxuriant bedrooms and three cottages are rich with antiques, lace and carved woods. Each is completely different, from the two-bedroom suite that takes up the top floor to the carriage house with an 18-foot cathedral ceiling. Enjoy the mountain views while soaking in the jacuzzi. Considering its Hollywood pedigree (actor Charlton Heston was once owner), it's no surprise this is Asheville's most glamourous retreat. ~ 61 North Liberty Street; 828-254-8334, 800-261-2221, fax 828-251-2082; www.beauforthouse.com, e-mail info@beauforthouse.com. DELUXE TO ULTRA-DELUXE.

DINING   Joining the bistro mania that's clutching the country, **Café on the Square** is a warm and casual spot with vibrant art and a glass wall overlooking Pack Square. It's always thronged with locals who come to eat bistro bites like Cajun fried eggplant with shrimp andouille sausage and crawfish *beurre blanc* and pecan-crusted chicken. Start with seared tuna with wasabi vinaigrette—it's wonderful. No lunch on Sunday from May through October. ~ 1 Biltmore Avenue; 828-251-5565, fax 828-251-0846. www.cafeonthesquare.com. DELUXE.

The **New French Bar** is Asheville's answer to a Paris-style sidewalk café, with a few regional favorites thrown in for local flavor. Croissants and brioches for weekend brunch, then crab cake po' boys, salad nicoise and asiago-crusted chicken breast on weekdays, make this a popular gathering place. ~ 12 Biltmore Avenue; 828-254-5070, fax 828-254-5076. MODERATE.

Across the way, **Beanstreets** coffeehouse is where the suit-and-tie crowd readies itself for the early-morning shock of business. The espresso and café mochas do the trick, accompanied by a bowl of fruit, scone or wrap. Even better are the omelettes and the simple, home-cooked lunches—thick stews and soups, and sandwiches made with just-baked bagels, croissants and baguettes.

AUTHOR FAVORITE

With a prepossessing name like **Savoy Cucina Italiana**, it's tough to imagine the restaurant was once a gas station. Not that anyone cares, since the Savoy—now transformed with warm bronze walls, wrought-iron railings, and linen tablecloths—is easily the city's hottest dining spot. Order from the copious martini and wine list, then fill up on fresh seafood with an Italian flair. The fennel-dusted ahi over basil gnocchi in gorgonzola cream is, like everything else, exceptional. ~ 641 Merrimon Avenue; 828-253-1077; www.savoycucina.com. ULTRA-DELUXE.

The atmosphere is bright and gallerylike, with walls showcasing local art. ~ 3 Broadway; 828-255-8180. BUDGET.

Salsa's, just half a block below Pack Square, blends Mexican and Caribbean cuisine in the deft hands of its Puerto Rican owner-chef, Hector Diaz. You've never had enchiladas and burritos like these before: smoked salmon? roasted pumpkin? The scrumptious dishes incorporate local organic ingredients whenever possible. ~ 6 Patton Avenue; 828-252-9805. MODERATE.

Sooner or later, somebody was going to slip soy sauce in the collard greens. Sure enough, the collards at **Tupelo Honey Café** are spiced with soy and toasted garlic, and the cornbread is spiked with candied ginger. The Asian spin on Southern cooking is obviously just what Asheville folks want since Tupelo is packed for breakfast and lunch. Southerners who prefer the real Old South deal won't go away hungry: shrimp and grits, buttermilk biscuits and banana pudding are among the standouts in this sweet space with plank floors and hanging plants. Closed Monday. ~ 12 College Street; 828-255-4863; www.tupelohoney cafe.com. MODERATE TO DELUXE.

Talk about fusion cuisine. The **Flying Frog Café** mixes German, "urban Indian" and Continental tastes for delicious results. Try the *samosa tikki*, which are spicy fried potato cutlets with green peas, ginger and tamarind chutney. Stay exotic with the lamb *korma zaffrani* (in a creamy, saffron-spiked tomato curry with cilantro), or play it safe with the Cajun filet (mignon, that is). Either way, you'll be salivating all the way around this global café. Upstairs the wine bar offers deli- style dishes and over 50 vintages. Reservations recommended. Closed Tuesday. ~ Haywood Park Hotel, 1 Battery Park Avenue; 828-254-9411; www. flyingfrogcafe.com. ULTRA-DELUXE.

Laughing Seed Café is a vegetarian haunt, ridiculously popular and overcrowded at lunch and sometimes dinner, so go early or late. The food, imaginative, colorful and super fresh, is worth any inconvenience. Try the curried eggplant napoleon or East–West quesadillas with avocado and pineapple. Wash it down with a fruit smoothie or an organic beer or wine. Closed Tuesday. ~ 40 Wall Street; 828-252-3445; www.laughingseed.com. MODERATE.

SHOPPING

Downtown has it all—antique stores by the dozen, vintage boutiques, import shops, great bookstores with basement coffeehouses, and galleries showcasing Appalachian art and crafts.

American Folk showcases the pottery, paintings, sculptures and textiles of more than 60 talented regional artists. Among the whimsical creations are bottle-cap jewelry, hooked rugs, miniature tiled altars and whittled animal carvings. Closed Sunday in winter. ~ 64 Biltmore Avenue; 828-281-2134; www.amerifolk.com.

The Chocolate Fetish is known for its ragingly good truffles, though the indulgences also include caramels and barks, and hand-dipped chocolate turtles. Closed Sunday. ~ 36 Haywood Street; 828-258-2353; www.chocolatefetish.com.

The L.O.F.T. is located in an attic where "Lost Objects, Found Treasures" and other distinctive gifts may be discovered. Original folk art, handmade goods and unique furniture are some of the eclectic items for sale. ~ 53 Broadway Avenue; 828-259-9303.

Wonderfully worn and inviting, **Malaprop's Bookstore and Cafe** is Asheville's counterculture central. Shelves sag with the weight of books on everything from African dance to modern goddesses. A great source for gay and lesbian literature and regional travel maps, Malaprop's has a cozy café where all the cool people go. ~ 55 Haywood Street; 828-254-6734, fax 828-252-2369; www.malaprops.com.

If you're an antique hound, head for Broadway and Lexington avenues, just south of College Street. Within dozens of stores, relics run the gamut from Renaissance busts and miniatures and life-size carousels to American Indian baskets, bassinets and sleds. The quality ranges from heirloom to cast-off.

A bit touristy, but fun nevertheless, **T. S. Morrison & Company** is the oldest retail store in Asheville. This is the place to go for old-fashioned candy, gourmet country foods, nostalgic Raggedy Ann dolls, Hadley pottery, designer stationery and more. Closed Sunday from January through May. ~ 39 North Lexington; 828-258-1891, 828-253-2348; www.tsmorrison.com.

Downtown Books & News carries the kind of alternative publications you won't see in any of the chain stores. Underground magazines and newspapers, experimental sex books, pot-growing manuals and even free coffee while you browse. ~ 67 North Lexington Avenue; 828-253-8654.

AUTHOR FAVORITE

My favorite indoor shopping space in the Carolinas is the **Grove Arcade Public Market**. Built in 1929 and spectacularly ornate (you can't miss the gargoyles and entwined hearts in and outside the building), the Gothic Revival emporium was restored in late 2002. Besides the usual market suspects—fresh produce, cheeses, pies and coffees—the Grove carries both homespun and high-style works by local and international ~~artists~~. Peruse the stalls for everything from fine porcelain to ~~~~ carvings. ~ 1 Page Avenue; 828-252-7799; www.

The **Wall Street Shops** (between Battery Park Avenue and Otis Street) comprise a lively pedestrian mall. Ashevilleans are drawn to the cafés (see the Laughing Seed, above), galleries and crafts shops, and stunning climbing-wall plaza outside **Climb-max**, a great place to learn mountaineering techniques. Closed Monday. ~ 43 Wall Street; 828-252-9996. At **Fired Up!** you can fire and paint your own ceramic pottery. Closed Monday. ~ 26 Wall Street; 828-253-8181.

There are big night moves in downtown Asheville, lots of live music, wildly varied, with young but sophisticated crowds. For a rundown on clubs and bands, pick up a free copy of *Mountain Express* magazine from one of the local shops or restaurants. **NIGHTLIFE**

A leading venue for live music is **Stella Blue**, within whose dark walls you'll hear anything from alternative rock to blues, jazz, reggae and folk music. Tuesday is local band night. Cover. ~ 31 Patton Avenue; 828-236-2424; www.stellabluelive.com.

At **Beanstreets** coffeehouse, you can sink into a sofa and listen to the open mic on Thursday night, or enjoy some rhythm-and-blues or acoustic music on Friday nights. ~ 3 Broadway; 828-255-8180.

Vincenzos Ristorante & Bistro caps off every evening with live jazz or blues. ~ 10 North Market Street; 828-254-4698.

Hidden in a courtyard, its entrance obscured by chatty, smoking youths in retro garb, is the extremely hip **Vincent's Ear**. Impromptu ensembles, acoustic or avant-garde jazz—virtually anything goes at this bizarre bi-level beer and coffeehouse. In warm weather, most of the action's outside on the patio bar. Cover for live music. ~ 68-B North Lexington Avenue; 828-259-9119. ◀ HIDDEN

The **Jack of the Wood Pub and Brewery**, downstairs from the Laughing Seed Café, is an authentic British-style pub with handsome wood furnishings within its brick walls. There's live old time bluegrass or Celtic music Wednesday through Sunday. Weekend cover. ~ 95 Patton Avenue; 828-252-5445.

A wide variety of performance arts can be found at the intimate **Diana Wortham Theatre** located in Pack Place. Performances might include jazz concerts, Celtic music shows, poetry readings, modern dance or Appalachian flatfooters. ~ 2 South Pack Square; 828-257-4530.

GAY SCENE **O'Henry's** is a neighborhood bar on the edge of downtown Asheville. This afternoon and evening meetingspot for gay professionals is leather- and Levis-friendly. ~ 237 Haywood Street; 828-254-1891.

Asheville's gay nightlife central is **Club Hairspray**, with vintage '60s decor. The stage is hot on weekend nights when drag shows are the draw. The rest of the week a deejay spins deep house and the crowd cruises between the two bars and lets loose on the wooden dancefloor. Occasional cover. ~ 38 North French Broad Avenue; 828-258-2027; www.clubhairspray.com.

Scandals likewise draws young gay men and women to its enormous tri-level disco and showbars. There are extravagant drag shows on Fridays, Saturdays and "Scandalous Sundays." Cover. ~ 11 Grove Street; 828-252-2838; www.scandals-club.com.

A mixed clientele frequents **Tressa's** for the varied line-up of local bands playing flamenco-fusion, jazz, salsa and R&B. Upstairs there's a mellow smoke-free dance space with a fireplace. Closed Sunday. ~ 28 Broadway; 828-254-7072; www.tressas downtownjazzandblues.com.

Asheville Area

▼▼▼▼▼▼▼▼▼▼▼▼

Just outside downtown lie Asheville's better homes and gardens, gorgeous old inns and well-tended house museums, curling streets and their canopies of ancient oaks.

SIGHTS

HIDDEN ►

Near Asheville's most famous inn, the Grove Park, you'll discover the **Estes-Winn Automobile Museum**, where antique cars are queued up and polished to a high sheen, and date back to the inn's opening in 1913. There's a horse-drawn carriage from 1890, and a 1927 La France fire engine that was used to put out Asheville fires. Closed January through March. ~ At the Homespun Shops, 111 Grovewood Road, Asheville; 828-253-7651.

The **Botanical Gardens at Asheville** are like a secret hideout, with dark caverns of forest, tiny footbridges arching beneath enormous trees, streams trickling through beds of soft leaves, and cool air given over to birdsong. Covering ten acres, it's a great introduction to Appalachian greenery: giant sycamores, rock cap ferns, paper birches, largeleaf magnolias and many other species are labeled within the area. ~ 151 W. T. Weaver Boulevard, Asheville; 828-252-5190; www.ashevillebotanicalgardens.org, e-mail bgardens@bellsouth.net.

HIDDEN ►

The **Smith-McDowell House Museum** is said to be "Asheville's oldest brick home," built around 1840, though certainly not on a grand scale. It is, however, most definitely a warm and inviting home, with good-size rooms for entertaining and just sitting by the fire—indeed a place one would liked to have lived in back then. You'll learn how the home was restored by Asheville-Buncombe Technical College students, as you wander through rooms with rich period wallpapers and furnishings, and pretty vintage clothes draped here and there. Closed Monday. Admission. ~ 283 Victoria Road, on the Asheville-Buncombe Technical College campus, Asheville; 828-253-9231, fax 828-253-5518.

The **Biltmore Estate** is the reason hundreds of thousands of people come to Asheville every year. America's largest privately owned home—complete with winery, tremendous gardens, fine restaurants and shops, and history to match—it is one of the most-visited attractions in the Carolinas. The Biltmore House itself, a sensational French-style chateau, is, of course, the point of it all. When first seen from the long, poplar-lined drive, its architecture is so exquisite it's hard to believe the place is real. Indeed, from the first encounter with the elaborate facade to the last hour spent in the rose garden where sweet buds tower above, the eye is enchanted time and time again. Which is precisely how George Vanderbilt planned it.

Vanderbilt was 26 when he commissioned the Biltmore Estate in 1888. Despite his youth, he had traveled the world many times over, enjoying the bounty of Vanderbilt money. In the French wine country he found the architecture he loved most—sixteenth-century chateaux—and he brought it to Asheville. He hired famed architect Richard Morris Hunt, educated at Paris' De École des Beaux-Arts, to build his masterpiece. Then he hired one Frederick Law

Asheville Area

Olmsted, mastermind of landscape, to create the formal and informal gardens.

It took six years to build the 250-room mansion, and, when it opened in 1895, it was the largest private home in all the United States—a designation it still enjoys today. Vanderbilt filled his home with handsome furnishings and masterworks he had acquired during his travels, and made it comfortable for guests. Central heat, electric lights and indoor bathrooms—unheard of at the time—were installed, and so was an indoor swimming pool, bowling alley and gymnasium. From the limestone terraces, misty mountain views went on forever.

Upon returning home from a visit to the house, author Paul Leicester Ford recalled that ". . . as I read the proofs of this book I have found more than once that the pages have faded out of sight and in their stead I have seen Mt. Pisgah and the French Broad River, or the ramp and the terrace of the Biltmore House. . . ."

The panoramas endure, as does the grandeur of the house. Yet despite the colossal magnitude and elaborate design, the chateau is neither cold nor aseptic but full of warmth and light and air. As you step through the great Entrance Hall and into the Winter Garden, sunshine streams through a glass-paned rotunda, and greenery spills from pots. In the stupendous Banquet Hall, the acoustics are so perfect that two people seated at opposite ends of the long table can speak normally and hear each other.

Every room has something of intrigue. Walls of Spanish leather in the Breakfast Room. Bizarre murals, painted by former guests, in the underground Halloween Room. The two-lane Bowling Alley of hard maple and pine, possibly the oldest lanes in the world. The bright red Renaissance decor of Vanderbilt's bedroom; the yellow and purple designs of his wife, Edith's, room.

The tour of the house is self-guided, though there are docents everywhere (only a few of the 550 full-time employees are running the place) hoping someone will ask them a question. For an additional fee, you can hear a narrated tour over headphones, or you can pay even more and take a guided behind-the-scenes tour. The latter is best done on a second visit to Biltmore Estate. There's just too much to see the first time.

After the house there are The Gardens, formal and Italian, marbled with pebbled paths, decorated with reed-filled ponds and statuary, and dotted with shaded benches for contemplating the surroundings. Then there's The Winery, an enjoyable five-mile drive from the house (it's three miles from the main gate to the house), where you'll get a tour of the fermenting, aging and bottling rooms, and taste some Biltmore Estate vintages.

Some general advice for visiting: Wear comfortable shoes, take frequent breaks (the courtyard at the Stable Cafe is a good place) and plan to spend most of the day. Most of the estate is wheelchair accessible, including The Gardens. Three on-site restaurants offer lunch: **The Stable Cafe** (828-225-6370) has good moderate-priced entrées such as rotisserie chicken sandwiches, salads and great Southern desserts; **Deerpark Restaurant** (828-225-6260), open March through December, offers a seasonal buffet at a moderate to deluxe price. **The Bistro** at The Winery (828-225-6230) features gourmet pizzas, homemade pastas, breads and salads—all at a moderate to deluxe price.

If at all possible, visit Monday through Thursday; Fridays, weekends and holidays are more crowded. Most crowded is the whole month of December, when the house is elaborately decorated for the holidays, and the popular candlelight tours take place. Least congested is January through March, though The Gardens aren't much to look at then. Admission. ~ Route 25, off Route 40, south of downtown Asheville; 828-255-1333, 800-624-1575, fax 828-225-1296; www.biltmore.com, e-mail happenings@biltmore.com.

If you have a drop of stamina left, take a stroll around **Historic Biltmore Village**. The pretty cottages of red brick and stucco are the work of Vanderbilt, who bought the town of Best in 1889 and fashioned it as the attendant village of his Biltmore Estate. Many of his 80 employees lived here in the early 1900s; there was once a school, post office, church, train depot and even a hospital. The buildings have been given over to shops and restaurants, making it a prime place to visit. ~ Just west of Biltmore Estate and bounded roughly by Biltmore Avenue, Brook Street and All Souls Crescent, Asheville.

Due east of Asheville is the friendly Southern town of **Black Mountain**. Besides being a hub of front porches and antiques, Black Mountain is also home to numerous traditional and alternative religious camps. It started back in the early 1900s, when Presbyterians settled into nearby Montreat. Seeing the far-flung mountains as a good place to renew one's spiritual sense, others

sights

AUTHOR FAVORITE

Being a Francophile, I can't help but love the **Biltmore Estate**. The spectacular chateau rivals any in the Loire, and the exquisite French furnishings—from gilded Baroque clocks to Louis XVI fainting couches—send me straight to the 1700s. But it's the winery, redolent with varietals from Chablis and Alsace, where I feel most at home. See page 42 for more information.

Black Mountain: On the Porch Front

From Asheville, take Route 70 east until suburban scenes evaporate and the Swannanoa Valley opens like a bowl of deep green. After about 20 miles you'll come to Black Mountain, a pretty place that calls itself "The Front Porch of Western North Carolina." The reason: it sits on the cusp of the Blue Ridge and the Smokies, a small town welcome mat for all those mountains. In addition, Black Mountain has a lot of front porches, where friendly folks sit and let the Southern days slip away.

MONTE VISTA HOTEL   If you leave Asheville in the late morning, you'll arrive in Black Mountain just in time for lunch. On Sunday, you can't go wrong at Monte Vista Hotel, where you can fill up on fried chicken and mashed potatoes, fresh vegetables and pecan pie. The dining room of the 1919 hotel is a simple Southern affair, and the lobby is decorated with antiques and Appalachian art. Dinner only Thursday through Saturday. ~ 308 West State Street; 828-669-2119, 888-804-8438, fax 828-669-6226; www.montevistahotel.com. BUDGET TO MODERATE.

SHOPPING GALORE   Work off all (or at least part of) that filling fare with an around-town shopping stroll. Among the many galleries and antique stores, **Seven Sisters Gallery** has fine pottery, glass and fiber art, metal and wood crafts, and jewelry by hundreds of regional and national artists. ~ 117 Cherry Street; 828-669-5107; www.sevensistersgallery. com. In the same block, **Black Mountain Books** stocks great old reads, including some out-of-print books by Southern authors. ~ 103

soon followed: first the Baptists and then the YMCA, later the Disciples of Christ, the African Methodist Episcopalians, Freewill Baptists and lots of others. Thousands of people come to Black Mountain every summer for retreats—there are now upwards of fifteen of them, more than any other small town in America.

Also east of Asheville is tiny **Oteen**, known for the annual World Gee Haw Whimmy Diddle Contest. There's not much doing around Oteen, save for the third weekend of September when everyone brings out their whimmy diddles and starts geeing and hawing. A whimmy diddle is an Appalachian folk toy that's basically a stick with notches cut along the top and a propeller on the end. Rub the notches up and down with another stick and the propeller turns. The gee and haw come in when you rub along the right or left of the notches (gee is right; haw is left),

Cherry Street; 828-669-8149. More musically inclined? Check out **Song of the Wood**, which has an excellent collection of dulcimers. Closed Sunday. ~ 203 West State Street; 828-669-7675; www.songofthewood. com. Over on Broadway, **Treasure & Trivia** offers estate jewelry, crystal and porcelain, lamps and furniture fashioned in Victorian, English and Early American styles. ~ 106 Broadway; 828-669-5190. Take an easy downhill stroll on Broadway to **Black Mountain Iron Works**, where husband-and-wife blacksmiths customize everything from chandeliers and fireplace screens to balustrade railings. They also have a gallery with stained glass, pottery and other glass works, as well as metal provided by other blacksmiths. ~ 120 Broadway; 828-669-1001; www.blackmoun tainiron.com. From Broadway turn west on Sutton Street and follow the railroad tracks to **Ivy Corner Antique Mall**, where 14 antique dealers ply their goods. ~ 1 Cherry Lane; 828-669-2177. A little farther down Sutton is the **Old Depot Association & Gallery**, home to future antiques. Dozens of western North Carolina artists and craftspeople display their handmade wares here. ~ 207 Sutton Avenue; 828-669-6583; www.olddepot.org.

RED ROCKER INN   Of all the porches in this front porch capital, one of the most popular is at the Red Rocker Inn. Make a "supper" reservation and let innkeepers Margie and Craig Lindberg lavish you with their bountiful country victuals—roast pork with cornbread stuffing, mountain trout with buttered almonds and squash casserole. If you're too full to drive back to Asheville, spend the night in one of their elegant Old South rooms with names like Dogwood, Azalea and Savannah. Closed January. ~ 136 North Dougherty Street; phone/fax 828-669-5991, 888-669-5991; www.redrockerinn.com. MODERATE TO DELUXE.

making sounds a lot like a donkey might make. The contest, held on the parkway at the Folk Art Center, is to see who can make the most gees and haws in twelve seconds. For information on the next contest, call 828-298-7928.

Mountainside elegance, perhaps the ultimate to be found in the Carolinas, is why people have been finding the **Grove Park Inn Resort & Spa** for most of last century. Built of native granite and rich in local lore, it is high on amenities, low on snobbery. Things were not always this way at the Grove Park. When it opened in 1913, children were forbidden upstairs near the bedrooms and adults were forbidden to wear shoes after 10 p.m., for fear they would disturb a sleeping guest. Kids are not only welcome today, they have their own activities program (kids under 16 stay free).

LODGING

For adults, there's a championship golf course and tennis and racquetball courts, and several excellent restaurants and lounges. The most serene space, though, is the European-style spa with an indoor pool surrounded by fireplaces, waterfalls and high rock walls. Schedule a "Carolina Mud Pie Wrap" and you'll be bundled up with shea butter and warm mountain mud and stones.

The rooms number 510, including 142 in the original inn, with decor ranging from simple, earthy and comfortable to quite lavish. Many have mountain views that are stunning. The Great Hall, furnished with some of the famous original Roycrofters pieces, has stone fireplaces so enormous you can fit a whole tree. The staff can't seem to do enough for you. It's all the things you expect from a luxurious inn, but don't always find. ~ 290 Macon Avenue, Asheville; 828-252-2711, 800-438-5800, fax 828-252-6102; www.groveparkinn.com. ULTRA-DELUXE.

HIDDEN ► In Asheville's lovely and historic Montford neighborhood, the **AppleWood Manor Inn** is set among two acres of rolling lawn and gardens. A favorite of straight and gay professional couples, the 1910 Colonial Revival home has four guest rooms furnished in tasteful, homestyle decor, plus a cottage with kitchen. Three of the bedrooms have balconies and wood-burning fireplaces. Innkeepers Johan and Coby Verhey go all out for breakfast, serving delicious fare such as orange nutmeg french toast. ~ 62 Cumberland Circle, Asheville; 828-254-2244, 800-442-2197, fax 828-254-0899; www.applewoodmanor.com, e-mail innkeeper@apple woodmanor.com. DELUXE.

Richmond Hill Inn looks theatrical sitting high atop a hill, with dark silhouettes of mountains hovering behind and the lights of downtown Asheville glittering below. A beautiful, 12-room Queen Anne building presides over the grounds, complete with a rippling mountain brook, waterfalls and pretty parterre gardens. Fifteen rooms rest among the gardens, and nine cottages are up the hill. Every room is desirable, offering plenty of space, plush furnishings and modern amenities such as cable TV and telephones. Dine at the inn's casual garden pavilion for breakfast or enjoy dinner at the elegant Gabrielle's. There's also complimentary afternoon tea. Closed in January. ~ 87 Richmond Hill Drive, off Route 1923, three miles north of downtown Asheville; 828-252-7313, 888-742-7313, fax 828-252-8726; www.rich mondhillinn.com. ULTRA-DELUXE.

George Vanderbilt once toyed with the idea of building a hotel on his estate. He got as far as a cost estimate—$17,500. A hundred years and nearly $31 million later, **Inn on Biltmore Estate** was finally realized. The 213-room stucco hotel with slate and Indiana limestone flourishes is set on a hill above the estate winery, offering the best views around. Vanderbilt-era touches include a

formal library and carriage rides. ~ 1 Antler Hill Road, Asheville;
800-858-4130, 828-225-1600; www.biltmore.com. ULTRA-
DELUXE.

Less than a mile from the Biltmore Estate, the **Cedar Crest
Victorian Inn** enjoys a splendid location on a hill amid four acres
of gardens and forest. The interior of the 1891
Queen Anne home is a feast for the eyes, with   North Carolina was the
gorgeous stained glass, polished antiques, rich rugs   country's top producer
and elaborate woodworking, some of which was   of gold until Califor-
carved by Biltmore artisans. There are ten bedrooms   nia's rush in 1849.
and a 1915 bungalow—all are completely different but
beautifully decorated, from the canopied ceilings to the
deep clawfoot tubs. Stay overnight in the luxury suite and
enjoy the private veranda, king-sized bed, fireplace and
jacuzzi. Silver breakfast service and afternoon tea, lemonade,
warm beverage and dessert are included in the rates. ~ 674
Biltmore Avenue, Asheville; 828-252-1389, 800-252-0310, fax
828-253-7667; www.cedarcrestinn.com, e-mail stay@cedarcrest
inn.com. ULTRA-DELUXE.

For years, families have been finding **Pisgah View Ranch** a   ◀ HIDDEN
wonderful way to experience the mountains. It's way out in the
woods, surrounded by 2000 acres of tall trees and wending creeks
and stellar views of Mt. Pisgah. Accommodations are in cabins;
meals, famously large, are served family style. After supper
there's live entertainment June through October. During the day,
kids can chase butterflies, swim in the pool, ride horses and go
hiking. Rates include three daily meals and most activities.
Closed December through April. ~ Off Route 151, Candler;
828-667-9100, fax 828-665-2216. BUDGET TO MODERATE.

Chops at the Grove Park Inn Resort & Spa is the place to be when   **DINING**
the sun goes down. The breezy veranda opens to a view of the
mountainous countryside and offers hearty cuisine to match.
Prime rib and rainbow trout are among the fine choices. ~ 290
Macon Avenue, Asheville; 828-252-2711. DELUXE TO ULTRA-
DELUXE. Similarly spectacular views, except behind glass, can be
had at the hotel's formal **Horizons**. The fare is chichi Continental
and men are asked to wear jackets. Call for hours. ~ 290 Macon
Avenue; 828-252-2711, 800-438-5800. ULTRA-DELUXE.

Grovewood Cafe resides in a storybook cottage with vines
creeping up its stucco walls and flower-lined paths decorating the
lawn. Mozart streams through the tiny dining room with white
tablecloths and black lacquer chairs, and fare that is predomi-
nantly Continental. The menu is seasonal but favorites include
the Stilton and pear salad, the stuffed salmon and the pasta with
wild mushrooms. All soups, bread and desserts are homemade. ~

111 Grovewood Road, next to the Grove Park Inn, Asheville; 828-258-8956; www.grovewoodcafe.com. DELUXE.

In Historic Biltmore Village, **Rezaz Mediterranean Cuisine** furthers Asheville's fondness for international fare. Owner and chef Reza Setayesh puts a Turkish twist on meats with his appetizer of lamb and currant sausage with roasted grape and port wine sauce, then sets his sights on Morocco with a spiced lump crab cake with cinnamon tomato jam. You'll also find flavors from Greece and Israel in this sleek dining room with hardwood floors left over from the building's days as a hardware store. Closed Sunday. ~ 28 Hendersonville Road; 828-277-1510; www. rezaz.com. DELUXE.

Late-night dining takes on an international flavor at the **Usual Suspects**, where you can order latkes, Thai mussels and a delicious Cuban sandwich (house-braised pork, applewood smoked bacon and swiss cheese, all toasted on a hoagie). Eat under arched ceilings and exposed ducts, or, in summer, on the outdoor patio. Early birds will be rubbing elbows with neighborhood families, but as the evening progresses, the singles crowd rolls in. Open to 2 a.m. nightly (the kitchen serves until 1:30 a.m.). ~ 791 Merrimon Avenue; 828-350-8181. MODERATE.

Locals fill the cherrywood tables at **Asian Grill**, where Thai, Japanese and Chinese classics are joined by East-meets-West dishes. For the traditionalist there's assorted sushi, pad thai or kung pao chicken. The more adventurous can choose grilled scallops with a black bean scallion mustard cream sauce, salmon crusted with Japanese *furikake* and served with lime-ginger sauce, or beef medallions with snow peas and water chestnuts. Efficient service and a tranquil atmosphere keep people coming back for more. ~ 1851 Hendersonville Road, 828-277-1556. BUDGET TO DELUXE.

HIDDEN ►

Inside the Richmond Hill Inn, the handsome, cherry-paneled **Gabrielle's** is perfect for such Southern culinary formalities as mountain apple and Vidalia onion soup; and grilled black angus fillet with barbecue sauce, Dixie potatoes and smoked corn fritters. Menus change seasonally. There are modified winter hours in January and February. Highly recommended. Reservations required. ~ 87 Richmond Hill Drive, off Route 1923, three miles north of downtown Asheville; 828-252-7313, fax 828-252-8726; www.richmondhillinn.com. ULTRA-DELUXE.

SHOPPING   For a look at the kind of stellar art and crafts produced by Appalachian artists, go to **Grovewood Gallery**, in business since 1917. Furniture, blown glass, pottery, jewelry, and wood and garden arts reflect myriad styles and eras, with many prices in the moderate range. Step next door, and you'll see some of the artists at work. Closed Sunday from January through March. ~ 111 Grovewood

Biltmore
Browsing

Rarely do big attractions have such inviting shops as you'll find at the Biltmore Estate. A few to explore while you're here:

Bookbinders has big, glossy and expensive coffee-table books, as well as guides on Victorian etiquette and gold embossed bookmarks.

The Confectionery stocks gourmet chocolates and candies, herbal teas, and hard-to-find cooking items like petit-four cups.

Elaborate wreaths, miniature towns and cities, and ornaments galore— what else would you expect from a place called **A Christmas Past**?

Toymaker's is mainly for someone who collects frilly dolls, model trains, miniatures and other pricey specialty toys (in other words, keep the kids out unless you plan to detach yourself from a bit of cash).

Just east of Biltmore Estate (and outside the admission gate), **Historic Biltmore Village** (bounded by Biltmore Avenue, Brook Street and All Souls Crescent) is a neighborhood filled with shops. Among the terrific places to scour for art is **New Morning Gallery**, a spacious loft showcasing thousands of works by local as well as national artisans. Handblown glass, delicate pottery, jewelry, vases, tables and furniture are among the many offerings here. ~ 7 Boston Way; 828-274-2831.

Downstairs it's tough to miss **Bellagio**, whose windows reveal the sassiest apparel and jewelry. Take a look at the outrageous furniture upstairs in the New Morning Gallery. ~ 5 Biltmore Plaza; 828-277-8100.

Focusing on the out-of-doors, **The Compleat Naturalist** supplies stargazer books and guides on wildflowers, science kits for kids and the wildlife prints of artists such as Robert Batemen. ~ 2 Biltmore Plaza; 828-274-5430, 800-678-5430.

If you need a break from shopping, stop for tea at **Chelsea's Cafe and Tea Room**, then peruse the fancy French and English gifts and the food hall filled with all things culinary. ~ 6 Boston Way; 828-274-4400.

Road, across from the Grove Park Inn; 828-253-7651; www. grovewood.com.

Located southwest of downtown, **Western North Carolina Farmer's Market** is considered one of the best produce places in the Carolinas. Allow a few hours to check out the 125-plus stands heaped with the season's freshest, from sweet corn and sourwood honey to apples and butter beans. There are also local-made crafts, jams and jellies, and a good lunch spot called Moose's Cafe. ~ 570 Brevard Road; 828-253-1691; www.wnc farmersmarket.org.

The **Mast Store** is a historical emporium featuring such old-fashioned mercantile goods as cast-iron cookware, clothing, retro candies and toys from yesteryear. ~ 15 Biltmore Avenue; 828-232-1883; www.maststore.com.

Don't leave Asheville without visiting the **Folk Art Center**. It's the Carolinas' premier place for folk art, not the country kitsch too frequently encountered at roadside craft marts, but the earthy, ethereal works that reflect generations of working with natural elements. Save your money for this place; there seems no end to the terrific pottery, wood sculpture, quilts, baskets, jewelry and objets d'art. ~ Milepost 382, Blue Ridge Parkway; 828-298-7928.

NIGHTLIFE Video games, pool, $2 second-run movies and award-winning pizza draw families to the **Asheville Pizza & Brewing Company**. The big-screen TV features sports or cartoons, depending on the time of day. ~ 675 Merrimon Avenue; 828-254-1281; www. ashevillepizza.com.

For a neighborhood experience, **Fred's Speak Easy** is a small basement bar that features karaoke during the week and local jazz or rock bands on weekends. ~ 122 College Street; 828-281-0920.

PARKS Though no major parks exist within Asheville, great forests begin just beyond its borders. Pisgah National Forest and the Blue Ridge Parkway afford many possibilities for picnicking, camping, hiking, fishing and superior exploring. For details, see Chapter Three and Chapter Five.

▼▼▼▼▼▼▼▼▼▼▼▼▼
Outdoor Adventures

GOLF

Asheville's most picturesque course is the 18-hole Donald Rossdesign at the **Grove Park Inn Resort & Spa**. Try to schedule a late afternoon game so you'll catch the mountain sunset. ~ 290 Macon Avenue; 828-252-2711, 800-438-5800. The **Great Smokies Holiday Inn Sunspree Resort** has 18 holes. ~ 1 Holiday Inn Drive, off Route 240, Asheville; 828-254-3211. Also try the Donald Ross–designed **Buncombe County Golf Course**. ~ 222 Fairway Drive, Asheville; 828-298-1867. In Weaverville try **Reems Creek Golf**

Club. ~ Pink Fox Cove Road, Weaverville; 828-645-4393. If you play the 17th hole at the **Black Mountain Golf Club,** you'll have played the world's third-longest hole (distance: 747 yards; par: 6). ~ 15 Ross Street, Black Mountain; 828-669-2710.

At the city-owned **Ashton Park Tennis Center,** you'll find twelve clay courts. ~ 336 Hilliard Avenue between French Broad Avenue and Klingman Street, Asheville; 828-255-5193. The beautiful **Grove Park Inn Resort & Spa** has outdoor and indoor courts. ~ 290 Macon Avenue; 828-252-2711.

TENNIS

Mountain biking is most popular around Asheville, which means heading away from downtown. For excellent bike-trail maps, contact the North Carolina Department of Transportation's Bicycle Program. ~ 1552 Mail Service Center, Raleigh, NC 27699-1552; 919-733-2804. You may also contact the **Blue Ridge Bicycle Club** for a schedule of riding events including the annual Hilly Hellacious Hundred. ~ P.O. Box 309, Asheville, NC 28802; www.blueridgebicycleclub.org.

BIKING

If you get on the **Blue Ridge Parkway** around Milepost 382 five miles east of Asheville, you can ride southwest through Pisgah National Forest toward Mt. Pisgah, 27 miles away. Or, you can head northeast to Mt. Mitchell, about 30 miles away. The parkway's gently sloping curves and mountain vistas are a bicyclist's dream, though you should avoid the peak spring and fall seasons, when the road is jammed with cars. Also, be sure to stay on the paved road; bicycles are prohibited from parkway trails.

Pisgah National Forest, which sprawls west of Asheville, also offers biking possibilities. For information on where to ride, contact the Ranger Station Visitor Center. ~ 1001 Pisgah Highway, Pisgah Forest; 828-877-3265.

North of Asheville, **Route 251** follows the French Broad River and affords wonderful cycling. From the town of Woodfin north to Marshall, it's about a 26-mile round-trip ride.

Bike Rentals You can rent mountain bikes from **Hearn's Cycling & Fitness.** ~ 34 Broadway; 828-253-4800; www.hearns-cycling.com. Mountain bikes are also available from **Ski Country Sports.** ~ 1000 Merrimon Avenue; 828-254-2771; www.ski countrysports.com. Or you can try **Liberty Bikes.** ~ 1378 Hendersonville Highway, Asheville; 828-274-2453; www.liberty bikes.com.

In Black Mountain, rentals are available at **Epic Bicycle.** Are you up for trying their tandem mountain bike? ~ 102 Sutton Avenue; 828-669-5969.

All distances listed for hiking trails are one way unless otherwise noted.

HIKING

One of the most enjoyable trails in Asheville is the one at the **Botanical Gardens of Asheville** (.6 mile), an easy stroll along gravel trails and others strewn with pine needles.

Five miles east of Asheville at the Blue Ridge Parkway's Folk Art Center, you can get on the **Mountains-to-Sea Trail** (380 miles), being built by volunteers across the state. It follows the parkway northeast for a moderately difficult trek. In spring, the views of wildflowers are spectacular.

Adventure sports are limited within Asheville proper, but they abound in the nearby mountains. For information on whitewater rafting, skiing, canoeing and fishing, see Chapters Three, Four, Five and Six.

Transportation

CAR

Perched along the eastern rim of the Blue Ridge, Asheville is the gateway to North Carolina's mountains. It's at the junction of **Route 26**, which runs northwest from Columbia, South Carolina, and **Route 40**, which cuts west from Wilmington on the North Carolina seacoast, arching through Raleigh, Durham and Winston-Salem. Route 40 continues west and north from Asheville into Knoxville, Tennessee. The **Route 240** connector loops through downtown Asheville.

The **Blue Ridge Parkway** skirts the eastern side of Asheville and heads south to Cherokee, situated at the entrance to the Great Smoky Mountains National Park.

AIR

Asheville Regional Airport, off Route 26 about 15 miles south of downtown Asheville, is served by ComAir, Continental Express, Delta Connection, Northwest Airlines, US Airways and US Airways Express. Clean and well run, the attractive little airport is flanked by thick forest. ~ www.flyavl.com.

BUS

Greyhound Bus Lines offers bus service to Asheville from various points around the South. ~ Two Tunnel Road; 828-253-8451, 800-231-2222; www.greyhound.com.

CAR RENTALS

Avis Rent A Car (800-331-1212) and **Hertz Rent A Car** (800-654-3131) have locations at Asheville Regional Airport. **Enterprise Rent A Car** (800-325-8007) has a shuttle to the airport.

PUBLIC TRANSIT

The **Asheville Transit Authority** provides bus service throughout the city. ~ 828-253-5691.

TAXIS

Asheville taxi companies include **Beaver Lake Cab Company** (828-252-1913), **Your Cab** (828-259-9904), **New Blue Bird Taxi Company** (828-258-8331) and **Yellow Cab** (828-253-3311).

THREE

The Southern Mountains

Along the southern rim of the Blue Ridge, a thread of asphalt un-inspiringly dubbed Route 64 meanders through mountains and forests of remarkable beauty and mood. Wind swishes through giant boughs of trees, waterfalls thunder from a far cliff, slick white granite plummets into deep gorges. The lush scenery is broken only by towns, some small and simple with their old-time soda fountains and folks on front porches, others large and showy with their posh shops, plush golf courses and scads of nouveaux riches.

These are North Carolina's Southern Mountains, linked by Route 64 and stretching south of Asheville, from compelling Chimney Rock Park on the east to the unadorned gem-mining town of Franklin on the west. Angling off from Route 64 are numerous back roads with endless hidden possibilities, from the lonesome silhouette of a tobacco barn to the sawdust-floored country store where the proprietor gives you free apples. "Sweetest in the Appalachians," she says.

Long before the apples and country stores, the Southern Appalachians belonged to the Cherokees. Their homes of bark and twigs and clay mud were clustered at the mouths of mountain streams, where the American Indians fished for trout, catfish and redhorse. In the Edenic forest around them, they hunted deer, wild turkey, rabbit, groundhog and other game, and picked mushrooms, blackberries and chestnuts. Their tranquil existence was interrupted only occasionally by skirmishes with the Creeks and other tribes. Until the white man came.

Around 1540, Spanish explorer Hernando de Soto journeyed to the mountains looking for gold. He made his way along the Cullasaja River (bastardized from the Cherokee Kulsetsiyi, meaning "honey locust place"), stopping at what are now the towns of Highlands and Franklin. In Franklin he encountered the Cherokee village of Nikwasi but, finding no gold, he continued west to the Mississippi. Too bad de Soto wasn't looking for rubies or sapphires, since the rocky earth around Nikwasi was littered with them. More than 300 years later, state geologists did discover the gems and numerous others, and miners overran the area looking for their own motherlode. Today, there are few big gems left in Franklin but many mines where visitors can try their luck. As for Nikwasi, it is an abandoned hump of roadside ground, lost in the oblivion of town traffic.

In the centuries following de Soto, white settlers continued to trickle in to the Southern Mountains. In 1819, a treaty was forced on the Cherokees that pushed them west to the Nantahala Ridge, just outside the Southern Mountains. With American Indians out of the way, hardy farmers and other gutsy pioneers could settle in the rugged mountains. They cleared small valley patches and built log cabins with fieldstone chimneys. They planted corn and sorghum, raised hogs and chickens, and wove baskets.

Wealthy planters and businessmen arrived, too, many from Charleston and New Orleans, and established vast plantations and summer estates in Hendersonville and Flat Rock, just south of Asheville. One of the most famous estates is Connemara, built in 1838 by Charlestonian Christopher Memminger, who later became Treasury Secretary for the Confederacy. More than a hundred years later, Carl Sandburg bought the simple frame farmhouse in Flat Rock, surrounded by 240 acres of sloping lawns and mountain vistas. The author, poet, political activist and social reformist spent the last 22 years of his life there, inspired and captivated by the southern Blue Ridge. His dark, cramped writing room is part of the tour at his farm, now registered as a National Historic Site.

With the 1860s came the Civil War, but its effect on the Southern Mountains was more psychological than physical. Young soldiers left for distant battlefields and never returned. Union sympathies were strong, and families and communities fought bitter philosophical wars. News of the war's end in 1865 took awhile to reach remote mountain towns, and the final surrender of Confederate forces in North Carolina supposedly took place deep in the Southern Mountains, in Macon County.

Reconstruction brought prosperity and, more specifically, the railroad, which provided release from rural life. Hotels were built to accommodate new summer visitors arriving by train, while cabins were constructed for immigrants coming to work the ore and mineral mines. Loggers found the railroad easy transport for their wood and, by the early 1900s, the mountains had been transformed into one big lumber camp. The forests were stripped with abandon until 1916, when the federal government began buying chunks for national forests.

Today, there's little evidence of logging scars, though some lumber companies stayed in business until the 1950s. Indeed, the Southern Mountains are for the most part a place of nature, with dense, far-reaching forests and horizons dotted with green summits. The most fantastic summit, magnificent Chimney Rock, is the starting point for the Southern Mountains tour in the east. From the windy, mood-heightening plateau of Chimney Rock you can look down upon beautiful Lake Lure framed in verdant forest.

Farther west, apple orchards decorate the valleys and hills of Henderson County, home to 70 percent of North Carolina's apple crop.

In the autumn months, pumpkins grow in vast patches between the orchards, and you can stop alongside the road and select your own big orange ball.

The county seat of Hendersonville has a commercial veneer but a historic downtown with rows of pretty old homes and antique shops and galleries. Next

Text continued on page 60.

Southern Mountains

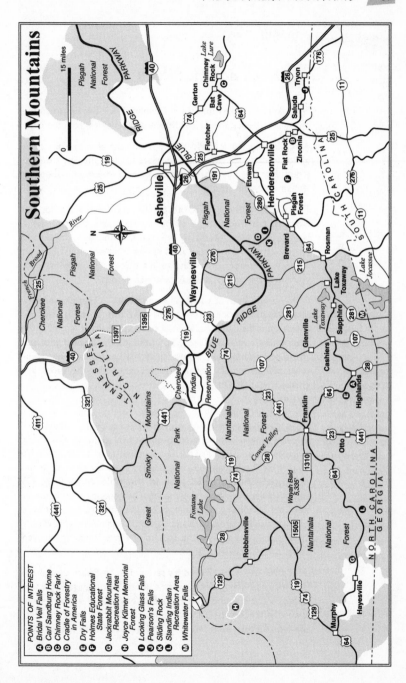

0   15 miles

N

POINTS OF INTEREST
Ⓐ Bridal Veil Falls
Ⓑ Carl Sandburg Home
Ⓒ Chimney Rock Park
Ⓓ Cradle of Forestry in America
Ⓔ Dry Falls
Ⓕ Holmes Educational State Forest
Ⓖ Jackrabbit Mountain Recreation Area
Ⓗ Joyce Kilmer Memorial Forest
Ⓘ Looking Glass Falls
Ⓙ Pearson's Falls
Ⓚ Sliding Rock
Ⓛ Standing Indian Recreation Area
Ⓜ Whitewater Falls

Two-day Weekend

Chimney Rock and Flat Rock

Day 1
- From Asheville, take Route 74 to Chimney Rock. The tiny town and monster-size rock are 23 low-lying mountain miles from the city.

- At **Chimney Rock Park** (page 60) ride the elevator 26 stories up for fabulous Carolinas scenery. Have lunch at the **Sky Lounge snack bar** (page 64), then head back down to town for shopping and an ice cream stop.

- Five miles southeast on Route 64-74A, you'll see a sign for the **Bottomless Pools** (page 62), a granite gneiss that's always a favorite with kids. Alternately, you can take the **Bat Cave tour** (page 62) with the Nature Conservancy, but you must have an advance reservation. You won't go in a cave or see many bats, but you'll love this walk in deep Appalachian woods.

- From here you can coast 20 miles southwest to **Hendersonville** (page 65) and check in to **Highland Lake Inn** (page 70). Have the concierge make dinner reservations at **Expressions** (page 71) for after you've rested up. Take a dip in the inn's swimming pool and amble down to the lake. Before dinner, have a stroll around downtown Hendersonville (bring a generous wallet—the shops are great!).

Day 2
- Sleep late and have a big country breakfast at the inn. Check out, and take a hidden sidetrip from downtown to **Jump Off Rock** (page 66). Then slowly make your way three miles south on Route 25 to **Flat Rock** (page 66), stopping for a moody moment at the **Episcopal Church of St. John in the Wilderness** (page 67) and the adjacent historical cemetery. Then spend a few hours at the **Carl Sandburg Home** (page 67). After the guided tour, have a look around the goat barn and buy some homemade goat cheese for a picnic overlooking the mountain views Sandburg enjoyed every day when he wrote.

- Hop over to Route 176 and it's seven miles to **Saluda** (page 68) for antiquing. It's only another eight miles to **Tryon** (page 69) but be forewarned: the road curls like a serpent's tale. On the other side of town is South Carolina, but in town, you can do some more antiquing and have an easy, early dinner at **Sidestreet Pizza** (page 72).

• If you're returning to Asheville, Route 26 is your fastest way back. From Tryon, take Route 108 northeast four miles and you'll hit the interstate. If you're heading west through the Southern Mountains, exit on Route 64 near Hendersonville.

door, tiny, old-moneyed Flat Rock is immensely appealing with its antebellum manses tucked into forest clearings. Westward awaits one of the most scenic drives in the Carolinas: Route 64's slow, twisting glide through misty, sun-streaked woods loaded with waterfalls and wildlife, much of it protected within the 500,000-acre Pisgah National Forest. There are only a few intermissions, like the busy little town of Brevard and the affluent nests of Cashiers and Highlands.

Brevard is tiny and unassuming, home to only 7000 people, but surrounded by forests filled with hundreds of waterfalls. "Land of Waterfalls" is how Brevardians advertise their town. Downtown, whitewashed clapboard and red-brick homes help create a soothing Southern scene.

Around Cashiers and Highlands are developments of recent invention, which seem overrun by Floridians determined to escape their sweltering summers, and which look suspiciously like Florida's own country club communities with their Disneyesque flower beds and faceless condominiums and townhouses. Fairways and greens are etched into the mountainsides, and tennis courts are parked in the valleys.

The "planned" look lessens a bit west in Franklin, a just-being-discovered Southern town with a long reputation for gem mining. Just north of Franklin in the Cowee Valley, rock hounds can pan for gems in real and imitation mines.

In between the better-known Southern Mountain towns are quirky places with quirky names like Bat Cave, whose blackened hollows harbor more salamanders than bats, and Zirconia and Sapphire, hamlets that recall the days before only tourists panned for gems.

Whether you search for the offbeat or the ordinary, the gem mine or the hidden sightseeing gem, the challenge of a golf fairway or a steep mountain trail, you will likely find it in these Southern Mountains.

▼▼▼▼▼▼▼▼▼▼▼▼▼▼
Chimney Rock Area

"I could stay all day and look across here," exalted one visitor upon reaching the top of Chimney Rock. It is a common sentiment, given the scale of this great granite pedestal with a sea of forest at its feet. The view from the rock's wind-polished, 225-foot-high summit is of sculpted peaks in every direction—on clear days the vistas stretch more than 75 miles—and the deeply etched ravines of Hickory Nut Gap and glassy blues of Lake Lure.

SIGHTS   The top of Chimney Rock offers much more than a view. Indeed, the moment you step off the narrow catwalk (don't look down on the way up) and onto the rock's plateau, the feeling hits: a vertiginous, leg-weakening, wind-against-body feeling that you won't forget, at least not anytime soon.

This was how Lucius Morse felt when he first climbed the chimney-shaped rock in the early 1900s, so he bought it. The doctor from St. Louis bought some of Chimney Rock Mountain, a total of 64 acres, and set about turning it into a park. Today, **Chimney Rock Park** covers 1000 acres of spectacular scenery. The habitats contained in the park range from rivers to cliffs, attracting a variety of birds year-round and ensuring prime birdwatching. Though the rock is its centerpiece, the park offers miles of trails to various vistas that become more amazing as you hike. Trails are usually iced over in winter, and the park's waterfalls are at least partly frozen into sheets of ice. Admission. ~ Route 64-74A, in the town of Chimney Rock; 828-625-9611, 800-277-9611.

The park entrance is in the little town of Chimney Rock; from the entrance, three miles of narrow pavement corkscrew through forest so thick it's dark on the brightest of days. On the way is a small **nature center** with displays on park geology, flora and fauna, and several picnic areas and playgrounds.

Scenes from the movie *The Last of the Mohicans*, starring Daniel Day-Lewis and Madeleine Stowe, were shot at Chimney Rock.

At the top of the road you come to an elevator shaft and a sign explaining that it took eight tons of dynamite and 18 months to blast the 258-foot-high hoistway for the shaft, which tunnels right through the middle of a solid rock mountain. The elevator rockets up through 26 stories of rock in 30 seconds before depositing visitors in a gift shop. You can buy a T-shirt, actual photos of the actual filming of *The Last of the Mohicans* (imagine!) and even a colorful brochure describing where various scenes were filmed—all items attesting that you were where the movie was made.

Here also is a snack bar where a glass wall lined with barstools looks across mood-altering mountain scenery. Outside the eatery are trailheads to Chimney Rock and to the **Opera Box**, a granite overhang whose graffiti-covered railing is all that separates you from a big plunge into a rocky abyss. A few steps up, **Devil's Head** perch lets you gaze across to the brooding profile of what looks like a Buddha's head balanced on a cliff.

Wheelchair travelers can go as far as the observation deck just below Chimney Rock, but, unfortunately, cannot reach the top of the rock, nor explore any trails. The views from the deck, however, are worth the price of admission.

After exploring the park, drive back down the mountain for a walk around the town of **Chimney Rock**. It won't take long, considering it's only a block long. Main Street attractions include Bubba's General Store and Rock River Ice Cream and Fudge, where locals enjoy homemade treats and watch passersby. ~ Route 64-74A.

From here it's about five miles southeast on Route 64-74A to lovely **Lake Lure**, which, like Chimney Rock Park, exists because of Dr. Lucius Morse. In 1926, Morse built a dam across the Rocky Broad River, corralling its waters into 1500 acres beneath the brow of Rumbling Bald Mountain. The instant lake meant instant lakefront property, and the area developed into a resort community. Now, pretty summer cabins rest beneath spires of evergreens along more than 25 miles of shoreline, and there's the small but much-esteemed **Lodge on Lake Lure.** ~ Charlotte Drive, off Route 64-74A; 828-625-2789, 800-733-2785.

Near the lodge are the **Bottomless Pools,** looking like liquid tornadoes captured inside deep craters. The phenomenon is caused by fractures in the ancient granite gneiss, which trap water on its way down the mountain to Lake Lure. Drop a twig into one of the three pools and it will stay there a very long time, swirling round so fast you can barely see it. Since Dr. Morse opened the pools in 1916, and *Ripley's Believe It or Not!* reported on them in the 1930s, the oddities have been attracting curious tourists. After seeing the pools and their respective waterfalls, there's really little to do other than enjoy the wooded trails. There are picnic facilities, and a wedding chapel for those who want to seal their love in the Southern Mountains. Closed December to mid-March. Admission. ~ Route 64-74A, Lake Lure; 828-625-8324.

Back northwest on Route 64-74A just past Chimney Rock, in a wooded hamlet along the Rocky Broad River, you may or HIDDEN ▶ may not see signs for the town of **Bat Cave.** That's because fans of the Caped Crusader have taken to pilfering the signs, perhaps carting them off to their own secret bat cave, never to be seen again. As quickly as the town can replace them, they disappear. Even worse, many visitors who do manage to find the town come to see bats in a cave, which is not possible. ~ Intersection of Route 64-74A and Route 9.

There is, in fact, a real Bat Cave (which the town of 457 residents is named for) located on the north slope of Hickory Nut Gorge. The property is protected and partly owned by The North Carolina Nature Conservancy. The Conservancy offers field trips HIDDEN ▶ to the 180-acre **Bat Cave Preserve,** designated a National Natural Landmark, from June to early August. However, these days visitors are only allowed as far as the mouth of the cave so they rarely see any bats. Years ago many bats inhabited the cave but now there are only a few, thanks to pesky human explorers. Bats disturbed during hibernation often die, since they store only a limited amount of food. The critically endangered Indiana myotis bat, once a resident here, did not survive the years of human visits.

Don't let the absence of bats dissuade you from taking this field trip: The two-hour hike is a wonderful walk in the woods, with opportunities to see waist-high wildflowers and 60-foot canopies of gnarled oak; many species of birds, including threatened warblers; and strange spiders and salamanders. The rare, red-and-white crevice salamander loves the rocks around Bat Cave and is frequently spotted on the tour. The cave itself, the guide will tell you, is actually part of an elaborate network of granite fissure caves whose passageways run for more than a mile—making it one of the world's longest caves of the type. There is a fee for the tour. ~ 4705 University Drive, Suite 290,

Durham, NC 27707; 919-403-8558, 828-749-1700; www.na
ture.org/northcarolina.

From Bat Cave you can head north to Asheville (see Chapter
Two) on Route 74, a pleasant country drive with views across
ravines carpeted with ferns and whitewashed homes with clothes
strung on backyard lines. Or, you can stay in the Southern Mountains and drive southwest on Route 64 through apple country.
This is **Henderson County**, North Carolina's number-one apple
producer, where orchards of Rome Beauties and Golden Delicious, Gingergolds and Jonagolds, and many other popular varieties and hybrids ripple across a horizon of hills. In the spring,
apple blossoms sweeten the air; in the fall, scarlet globes decorate the trees like Christmas ornaments. This is when signs invite
you to pick your own fruit; tote a basket home and your car will
smell of apples for many days. In the pint-size community of
Apple Valley, about four miles west of Bat Cave, you can also select a pumpkin from one of the roadside patches. ~ Route 64.

Small and pleasant, **Evening Shade River Lodging** consists of several clapboard buildings parked above the boulder-studded
Broad River, with green lawn cascading down to the water's
edge. Rooms have paneled walls, small TVs and air conditioning—all in all quite rustic, but impeccable—and there are balconies peeking down to the river. All rooms face the river with a
beautiful view of the mountains. A few rooms have kitchenettes.
~ Route 64-74A, Chimney Rock; 828-625-4774; www.evening
shade.net, e-mail relax@eveningshade.net. MODERATE.

LODGING

If a place with a lake *and* mountain view sounds appealing,
check into **The Lodge on Lake Lure**. Secluded and entirely comfortable, the venerable lodge built in the 1930s shortly after
Dr. Lucius Morse put a dam across the Rocky Broad River and
created 1500-acre Lake Lure. The sixteen rooms with private
bath are all attractively decorated, and include complimentary
breakfast. The dining room has sweeping views of the lake—and
those peaks. A paddleboat and canoes are provided for guests,
who are treated to an evening lake cruise and hors d'ouevre hour.

AUTHOR FAVORITE

Cuisine or a scene? It's an age-old restaurant dilemma, and in this
case I'm going for the view. Because at Chimney Rock Park's **Sky Lounge
snack bar**, it's a big one: drop-off gorges swirling with rivers and razor-
sharp granite pulling at savagely blue sky. Then again, the chili's homemade and not half bad. See page 64 for more information.

Reservations required for dinner Thursday through Saturday. ~ Charlotte Drive, off Route 64-74A, Lake Lure; 828-625-2789, 800-733-2785, fax 828-625-2421; www.lodgeonlakelure.com. DELUXE TO ULTRA-DELUXE.

HIDDEN ►

For serious mountain seclusion, wind a mile up a remote peak near Bat Cave to **Hickory Nut Gap Inn**. The stone and milled-wood hideaway was built during the 1940s as a weekend retreat by the founder of Trailways Bus Company. Now a B&B secured on 75 acres of wilderness, it has a giant screened porch with beautiful Blue Ridge views. Each of the six guest rooms is finished with different wood from surrounding forests, from black walnut and hickory to wormy chestnut. In winter, warm up by the living room fireplace, or downstairs in the sauna. There's also a game room with pool, Ping-Pong and even a regulation-size Brunswick bowling lane. ~ For reservations and directions, call 828-625-9108; www.hickorynutgapinn.com, e-mail hnginn@aol.com. DELUXE.

DINING

HIDDEN ►

Inside Chimney Rock Park is **Sky Lounge snack bar**, with the best view of any restaurant around. Grab a tray and order from the menu of filling, tasty deli sandwiches, chili and soups, and hot chocolate. Then grab a stool at the bar—glass walls face into the rock-etched Blue Ridge Mountains and Hickory Nut Gorge below. If you're planning to hike in the park, the eatery will prepare a picnic. ~ Route 64-74A; 828-625-4764; www.chimney rockpark.com. BUDGET.

You can have your fish and beef with a water view at **Lakeview Restaurant**, the fanciest of the three restaurants at Lake Lure Golf and Beach Resort (not jackets-for-men fancy, but more a smart Eddie Bauer look). Settle into a curved-back wood chair at a table draped in white linen, and savor grilled New York strip or trout almondine. Come at sunset, when the lake shimmers hot pink through big picture windows. ~ 112 Mountains Boulevard, Lake Lure; 828-625-3045; www.lakeluregolf.com. DELUXE.

SHOPPING

Right in "downtown" Chimney Rock, **Bubba O'Leary's General Store** is a big and bright emporium flooded with bluegrass music and stocked with everything from weathervanes and kitchenware to Pointer Brand overalls. ~ Route 64-74A, 384 Main Street, Chimney Rock; 828-625-2479.

HIDDEN ►

Just a few steps down the street, **Featherheads** carries works by American Indian and North Carolina artists. Mandalas and medicine wheels, jewelry, handmade bows and arrows and twig pens are among the unusual works sold here. ~ 398 Main Street, Chimney Rock; 828-625-1175; www.chimney-rock.com.

If your tastes lean toward country-style gifts, you literally could spend a day at **A Day in the Country**. Afghans, jams and jellies,

Christmas decor, baskets, antiques, dolls, pottery and more crowd into this 10,000-square-foot mecca. ~ Sugar Loaf Road, south of Route 64, Bat Cave; 828-692-7914; www.aditc.com.

NIGHTLIFE

There isn't any. The closest nightlife (and it's limited) is in Flat Rock and Hendersonville, about 20 minutes away. Another 20 minutes north in Asheville (see Chapter Two), you'll find plenty to satisfy night owls.

▼▼▼▼▼▼▼▼▼▼▼▼
Hendersonville & Flat Rock Area

An enviable location in the Blue Ridge foothills, an elevation (2200 feet) that guarantees chamber-of-commerce weather year-round, valleys that explode with apple orchards—these are the reasons people have been coming to Hendersonville and Flat Rock for over 150 years. The wealthy in particular have always liked the area; their grandiose antebellum and modern homes grace the neighborhoods. There are certainly plenty of creative ways to spend your money here, whether on fine dining or exclusive shopping. There are eight public golf courses and nearly a dozen performing-arts groups in this area of only 90,000 people.

SIGHTS

You can start your spree in **Hendersonville**. The city of 10,000 actually has two very different sides: the chaotic sprawl of strip malls and fast-food chains that creeps ever closer to Asheville; and the tranquil, affluent-feeling downtown where brick streets are edged with a panorama of flowers, and antique shops and galleries are sequestered beneath pretty awnings. The latter can be found just south of Route 64 in the historic district near **Main Street**, where more than 40 shops and eateries line ten square blocks.

Presiding over the area is the historic **Henderson County Courthouse** with its massive Corinthian columns, striking gold dome and lawn edged with tulips. It's currently closed to the public. ~ Corner of Main Street and 1st Avenue, Hendersonville. (The new working courthouse is at 200 North Grove Street.)

Information on all area sightseeing is available on the south end of historic Main Street at the **Henderson County Visitors Information Center**. ~ 201 South Main Street, Hendersonville;

HOW DO YOU LIKE THEM APPLES?

The most exciting time in downtown Hendersonville is the four days around Labor Day weekend (Friday through Monday), when the streets are transformed into a sea of fragrant scarlet for the **North Carolina Apple Festival**. There's mountain folk dancing, apple art and apple cuisine, and the wild and wacky King Apple Parade.

828-693-9708, 800-828-4244, fax 828-697-4996; www.historic hendersonville.org, e-mail tourism@historichendersonville.org.

From downtown Hendersonville, take Laurel Park Highway west, winding through manicured neighborhoods with grand homes, until you ascend **Jump Off Mountain**. At the top is a lookout point called **Jump Off Rock**, so named because a young Cherokee woman took the big leap after her lover, a Cherokee chieftain, was killed in tribal wars—or at least that's the story. Today, you'll want to stay firmly on the big flat rock and well behind the guardrail, and enjoy the bluish peaks that seem to race across the horizon.

A few minutes south of Hendersonville on Route 25 is **Flat Rock**, a town lying within a huge granite outcropping—hence the name. Little of the rock is visible, having been blasted out by developers or covered with thick woods. In fact, the town feels like a neighborhood in a forest. Within its four square miles of dense greenery are gracious nineteenth-century English country and antebellum homes, their lawns lined with boxwood hedges, their winding stone driveways laid by slaves.

The luxurious summer homes began to take shape in the early 1800s when the first aristocrats arrived from Charleston. In 1825, Charlestonians Susan and Charles Baring bought several hundred acres, fashioned it as an English country estate, and called it "Mountain Lodge." The wealthy rice planters set aside some land for a deer hunting club and invited their friends to come for the summer. In 1833 they built a chapel and rectory, but attendance was by invitation only. Authors Kenneth and Blanche Marsh, in their book *Historic Flat Rock*, tell how Susan "would allow no one to enter the church before the Barings' bright yellow carriage arrived. . . . The carriage door was opened by a footman, and Susan descended on her husband's arm. She then was preceded into the church by her maid carrying Susan's prayer book and a large turkey fan on a velvet cushion. . . . As soon as the Barings were seated, the bell would ring and the service could begin."

sights

AUTHOR FAVORITE

I can't imagine a more perfect setting for putting ideas onto paper than the **Carl Sandburg Home**. The view of lakes and Blue Ridge Mountains is serene, and the big, book-filled farmhouse speaks to material simplicity and mental complexity. You can catch a cheese-making demonstration at the main goat barn here and purchase cheese that's been marinated in herbs and olive oil and aged a month. If you're a fan of goat cheese, you'll love these wedges. See page 67 for more information.

The Barings are buried in a vault beneath the church, which is now the **Episcopal Church of St. John in the Wilderness**. Don't miss this exquisite old building, enveloped in tall trees that throw long shadows on its tawny tower and fluted eaves. According to the Barings' specifications, Charleston architect Edward Jones designed the church as an English rural chapel, with a tremendous ceiling of beamed pine arches and glittering windows of stained glass. On the pews, brass plates bear the names of many nineteenth-century parishioners.

From the church, terraces of hemlock run down to a **little cemetery** where monuments are etched with the names of Flat Rock's earliest rich and famous, including Christopher Gustavus Memminger, the first Treasury Secretary of the Confederacy. ~ Route 25, Flat Rock; 828-693-9783.

Less than a mile south of the church, Memminger built a summer house that was eventually purchased by Carl Sandburg. The **Carl Sandburg Home** is a big white farmhouse, simple and weathered, set on a hill above a lake, with forest and then Blue Ridge Mountains and puffs of clouds in the distance. It is a marvelous place to record deep thought, which, of course, is what Sandburg did here the last 22 years of his life.

An eighth-grade graduate who traveled as a hobo, then fought in the Spanish-American War, Sandburg became a poet, novelist, social commentator and political activist, among other things, although perhaps his most famous works are his Pulitzer Prize–winning biographies of Abraham Lincoln. In 1945, Sandburg had already won the Pulitzer when he and his wife, Paula, bought the 240-acre farm for $40,000. With it came 30 structures, including several barns and a pair of mountains and lakes. They called it Connemara, after the Connemara Mountains of Ireland. Sandburg was actually Swedish; his high, chiseled cheekbones and folksy, blond countenance are found in photos throughout the house.

Connemara is now a National Historic Site, a very popular one in fact. Guided, 30-minute tours of the house are given at various times throughout the day, but they fill up fast. Call before you go, then show up early. Wheelchair travelers have access to most sights, though some of the wooded trails are too narrow and bumpy to be navigated.

Visitors are often surprised to find the house is not fancy, but plain, even austere. Unlike most other Flat Rock residents, the Sandburgs eschewed the perks of wealth and fame, preferring to live modestly. Most impressive in the house is the books, more than 10,000 volumes spanning floor to ceiling in various rooms, that the Sandburgs spent much time reading and discussing. During the late evening and early morning hours, however, Sandburg wrote in a dim, cluttered attic chamber. He penned his only novel, *Remembrance Rock*, here. His green visor, left over from his days as a writer for the *Chicago Daily News*, rests on his desk, as does one of his cigars.

The entire house is virtually unchanged since the Sandburg days. *Newsweek* and *National Geographic* magazines, dating to the 1940s, are stacked everywhere (Sandburg refused to discard any reading material). In the dining room is the old Zenith television that Sandburg called the "thief of time," and watched only for news.

Paula and the Sandburg's daughters, Helga, Margaret and Janet, spent long days at the barn raising champion goats. Paula's well-bred herd, which numbered up to 200 and included famous Chikaming goats, earned her a worldwide reputation among goat traders and earned the couple a good living. Despite her business success, however, Carl Sandburg still traveled the lecture circuit, earning thousands of dollars for his appearances. He hated traveling, and while on the road wrote yearningly to Paula, to "speak to me of the drag on your heart, the iron drag of the long days."

From the house it's a short stroll through towering mountain ash and pines to the tin-roofed **main goat barn**, where you'll find descendants of Paula's original herds. Surrounding yards are filled with more animal life: swallows swoop in and out, a lavender-eyed cat goes on the prowl, chickens scratch around the dirt. Children especially enjoy the barn area, where they can pet the plump, bleating goats and sometimes watch them being milked. The goats' milk is used for cheese-making demonstrations.

There is much more to see at the Sandburg property, including a greenhouse and a silo (which the Sandburgs never used), a gazebo and a barn garage. Take a look at the copper-colored 1962 Willy's Jeep in the garage; Sandburg received it as a gift from the makers of *The Greatest Story Ever Told* after he helped write the movie script. Here also is Paula's set of farm wheels: a 1951 Ford tractor.

Carl Sandburg died in his bedroom at Connemara of a stroke in 1967. He was 90. In 1969, Paula deeded the property to the federal government as a historic site. She died nine years later. Margaret passed away in 1997. Admission. ~ Little River Road, just off Route 25, Flat Rock; 828-693-4178.

HIDDEN ►

Route 176 south of Flat Rock offers a peaceful, bucolic side trip through mountains marbled in forest and streams. After 12 miles you unexpectedly come upon **Saluda**, a tiny, two-block town of the quaintest order, sitting right against the railroad tracks. Its Main Street is decorated with two little general stores, a bakery, antique stores, and a renovated train depot where local artists sell unusual and traditional works. A crossroads between South Carolina and Georgia, Saluda was known among railroaders as having the steepest standard gauge tracks in the country. The tracks climb 600 feet up Saluda Mountain in just three miles. A **historical marker** right next to the tracks notes this trivia.

South of Saluda, Route 176 is a switchback trail that launches into a web of thick forest. Soon you'll see a sign announcing **Tryon**, "The Friendliest Town in the South." Folks here do seem friendly, though one suspects they'd also be a little off kilter, considering the whole town is lopsided, its brick buildings actually tilting against a mountain.   ◀ *HIDDEN*

Grab a paper, stroll down the steeply angled Main Street, browse the gift shops and have lunch at one of the eateries. If you explore much south of town, you'll run into South Carolina, only a half-mile from Tryon.

Continuing the westward tour of the South Mountains, head back north to Hendersonville and then west on Route 64 toward Brevard. Immediately west of town, the **Oakdale Cemetery** contains   ◀ *HIDDEN* a piece of literary intrigue. The **marble angel** atop the grave of Margaret Johnson, wife of a local preacher, closely resembles the one in Thomas Wolfe's book *Look Homeward, Angel*. Wolfe's fictional angel was carved by Gant, a character based on Wolfe's own father, who was a mason. The Asheville author chose the angel because his father, frustrated that he could not sculpt one, was forced to import European angel monuments for his clients. No one's sure exactly which angel inspired Wolfe, though Mrs. Johnson's compelling monument—her wings spread high and finger pointed toward heaven—is hauntingly similar to the one in the book. You can see the angel from Route 64; follow the cemetery roads back to where she stands, enclosed by a wrought-iron fence.

The Waverly Inn has been hosting guests since it opened in 1878.   **LODGING** The inviting three-story frame house, renovated in 2002, offers thirteen guest rooms and one suite, all with private baths, phones and TVs. Several gleam with pretty four-poster canopy beds,

AUTHOR FAVORITE

Charles Kuralt once stayed at **The Claddagh Inn** while researching local Americana. It was perfect for such research, since the turn-of-the-twentieth-century, sunshine-yellow house radiates solace and warmth. Old wooden rockers invite from a rambling porch shaded with trees. The fourteen bedrooms and two suites, all with private baths, are decorated with fine antiques and soothing colors. And the breakfasts, included in the rates, are like those you'd have on a farm: eggs, bacon and sausage, apple cinnamon pancakes and almond french toast, muffins and peach crisp. ~ 755 North Main Street, Hendersonville; 828-697-7778, 800-225-4700, fax 828-697-8664; www.claddaghinn.com, e-mail innkeepers@claddagh inn.com. MODERATE TO DELUXE.

clawfoot tubs and pedestal sinks. One room has a sun porch. Guests enjoy getting acquainted with one another during the early-evening social hour. All-you-can-eat breakfasts are cooked to order. ~ 783 North Main Street, Hendersonville; 828-693-9193, 800-537-8195, fax 828-692-1010; www.thewaverlyinn. com, e-mail info@waverlyinn.com. DELUXE TO ULTRA-DELUXE.

Built in 1902 and supremely restored a century later, the **Elizabeth Leigh Inn** has four sumptuous suites with all the intimate essentials—fireplace, king-size beds, plush foot stools for the wing-back chairs. The decor is a blend of English cottage and French country, apropos for the setting among grand old oaks and elms. ~ 908 5th Avenue West, Hendersonville; 828-698-9707, fax 503-907-8911; www.elizabethleighinn.com, e-mail elinn@bellsouth.net. ULTRA-DELUXE.

HIDDEN ▶ Outside of town, at the crest of a mountain surrounded by skyline views, **Echo Mountain Inn** offers an escape to the woods. There are four buildings, including a frame-and-stone main house built in 1896, with 34 rooms and suites, decorated in simple French-country style, with balloon valances. Many rooms have working fireplaces and wonderful mountain views, and all have air conditioners. There's a swimming pool. ~ 2849 Laurel Park Highway, Hendersonville; 828-693-9626, 888-324-6466; www.echoinn.com, e-mail info@echoinn.com. MODERATE TO DELUXE.

Tryon gets its news from *The Tryon Daily Bulletin*, whose masthead reads "The World's Smallest Daily Newspaper"—it's been printed on 8½" by 11" paper since 1928. Circulation is 5200.

Occasionally there is a place so pleasing in mood and design you really hate to leave. **Flat Rock Inn** is that place, no doubt because owners Sandi and Dennis Page spent much of their lives staying in guesthouses and seeing things from a guest's point of view. Their three-story, 1888 house is beautifully decorated and inviting, with four large, lovely, high-ceiling bedrooms and big baths, and much attention to detail, from the perfumed potions set beside the clawfoot tubs to the downy quilts and linens that envelop you at night. Every room has an air conditioner and a ceiling fan. Sandi's bountiful breakfasts and afternoon snacks, included in the rate, look like they might grace the cover of *Gourmet* magazine. Closed January. ~ 2810 Greenville Highway, Flat Rock; 828-696-3273, 800-266-3996; www.bbhost.com/flatrockinn, e-mail fribb@bellsouth.net. MODERATE TO DELUXE.

Secluded, wooded and on a 30-acre lake, **Highland Lake Inn** is where burned-out professionals come to unwind. Families and couples also find the slow pace relaxing. There are canoes down by the lake, a swimming pool for cooling off in summer, and an organic garden of vegetables, berries and herbs, most of which end up in the inspired dishes served by the inn's restaurant. Accommodations are in various simple, generous-size cabins and cottages amid the trees, plus a modern main lodge and inn. A nine-hole golf course is across the street. ~ Highland Lake Road, between Routes 25 and 176, Flat Rock; 828-693-6812, 800-635-0979, fax 828-696-8951; www.hlinn.com, e-mail front desk@hlinn.com. DELUXE.

Built in the early 1900s by the Southern Railway as a summer retreat for its clerks' union, the **Orchard Inn** now hosts travelers in search of seclusion. Hidden atop a mountain, the pale yellow farmhouse presides over sweeping green lawns swirled with wild-flowers, with the peaks of the Warrior Mountain Range unfolding in the distance. The thirteen guest rooms are informal with their wood floors and throw rugs or carpeting, simple antiques, and works by local artisans. Four spacious cottages, with private decks and fireplaces, overlook the woods or the mountains. ~ Route 176, one mile east of Saluda; 828-749-5471, 800-581-3800, fax 828-749-9805; www.orchardinn.com. DELUXE.

◄ HIDDEN

In the tiny, little-known town of Tryon, a half-mile north of the South Carolina line, **Pine Crest Inn** seems purposefully hidden from civilization. That's likely what drew guests F. Scott Fitzgerald and Ernest Hemingway to this classy former hunt club in the woods. Cottages of forest green crouch beneath spidery trees, and French doors open onto shaded verandas. A main lodge gleams with polished wood and stylish country motif, while a woodcutter cottage, swayback cabin and stone cottage offer unusual places to sleep. Most rooms have fireplaces; all have cable TV, phones and private baths. ~ 85 Pine Crest Lane, Tryon; 828-859-9135, 800-633-3001, fax 828-859-1936; www.pinecrestinn.com. ULTRA-DELUXE.

◄ HIDDEN

If you want to enjoy an exceptional meal in Hendersonville, you will inevitably be introduced to the name Tom Young. The culinary instructor, chef and owner of **Expressions** is famed for his fine productions of seasonal specialties served in an elegant bistro in historic downtown Hendersonville. Offerings change nightly but might include appetizers such as spicy fried calamari with lemon caper aioli or smoked trout with horseradish cream, and entrées like grilled tuna with mango sauce or roasted Manchester Farms quail with goat cheese, sun-dried tomatoes and hickory-smoked bacon. Sunday brunch. ~ 114 North Main Street, Hendersonville; 828-693-8516. DELUXE.

DINING

For light eats and a choice of over 125 beers, duck into **Hannah Flanagan's Pub & Eatery**. A classy place of brass and brick and well-polished wood floors, it serves good sandwiches, homemade soups and salads from late morning 'til late night. ~ 300

North Main Street, Hendersonville; 828-696-1665, fax 828-698-8002. MODERATE.

HIDDEN ▶   Built in 1881, **Poplar Lodge** is a popular place of immense proportions, with massive walls of poplar wood and soaring fieldstone fireplaces, and a dimly lit, hearthside atmosphere for dining. No longer a lodge, the restaurant offers big and tender pricey steaks, grilled chicken, pan-seared mountain trout, filet mignon, lobster tail, and a salad bar whose items extend well beyond lettuce and veggies (sardines, pepperoni, black-eyed peas, Vienna sausage, to name a few). Reservations recommended. Closed Monday. ~ 2550 Hebron Road, Hendersonville; 828-693-8400. DELUXE.

HIDDEN ▶   In a pretty dining room and glass-walled porch in the woods, **Highland Lake Inn** serves breakfast, lunch and dinner—some of the freshest, most innovative cooking around. The chefs need only look as far as the inn's organic farm for herbs, fruits and vegetables to grace the plates. The food is always different, depending on what's in season, but here's a sampling of dinner: mountain trout, grilled vegetable polenta cake, jumbo shrimp and beef kabobs. Don't miss it. ~ Highland Lake Road, between Routes 25 and 176, Flat Rock; 828-696-9094; www.hlinn.com. DELUXE.

HIDDEN ▶   Sitting near the railroad tracks, **Sidestreet Pizza** emits enticing Italian food smells from the front door. The thick- and thin-crust pizzas and toasted subs do live up to their smells; the "white pizza" with olive oil, garlic and cheese is unusually tasty. You can order out or eat on a wooden table with views of a jukebox and mirrored beer plaques. Closed Tuesday and Wednesday. ~ 201 South Trade Street, Tryon; 828-859-5325. BUDGET.

A meal at the **Pine Crest Inn** is one befitting a former hunt club: robust and meaty, steeped in sauces and arranged imaginatively on the plate. There's filet mignon served with chive mashed potatoes; roast breast of duck with a port wine and fig sauce; salmon topped with fresh herbs and braised leeks. The dining room, with its heavily beamed ceiling and big stone hearth, feels transported from the English countryside. ~ 85 Pine Crest Lane, Tryon; 828-859-9135. DELUXE.

SHOPPING   The best shopping is in downtown Hendersonville, home to more than three dozen shops and galleries. Concentrate first on Main Street.

If you're even slightly interested in cooking, check out the wonderful kitchenry, specialty foods, and underground wine cellar at **Purple Sage**. It's owned by Tom Young, chef and restaurateur of the highly regarded Expressions, just down the street. Closed Sunday. ~ 416 North Main Street, Hendersonville; 828-693-9555.

Much of Henderson County's apple crop is turned into jams, jellies, relishes and pies, which you can sample at the old-time **Curb Market**. Established in 1924 with only eight farmers selling from beneath umbrellas, the market today has 100 vendors offering all sorts of fruits, vegetables and home-style goods, from aprons and afghans to wreaths and walking sticks. Open Tuesday, Thursday and Saturday from April through December; open Tuesday and Saturday from January through March. ~ 221 North Church Street, Hendersonville; 828-692-8012; www. curbmarket.com.

The local night scene is limited to a beer and light tunes or the performing arts, the latter of which happen to be some of the best in the Carolinas. Actually, some say **Flat Rock Playhouse** is the best—certainly at least when it comes to summer stock theater. Opened in 1952 and made North Carolina's State Theater in 1961, it hosts the ever-popular Vagabond Players, who started in New York in 1937. Musicals, comedies and occasional drama from Broadway and London play here. The season runs from late April to mid-December. ~ Route 25, Flat Rock; 828-693-0731.

NIGHTLIFE

> The Curb Market's Ol' Timey Days (the first Saturday in June and the last Saturday in September) offers a plethora of food, live music, vintage cars and crafts.

The **Hendersonville Symphony Orchestra** presents several concerts a year, often featuring local and national guest artists. Location varies, so call for information. ~ 828-697-5884; e-mail hso@brinet.com.

One of the most popular nightspots in Hendersonville, **Hannah Flanagan's Pub & Eatery** hosts weekend (Thursday through Saturday) acoustic bands from bluegrass to rock and jazz. Naturally, you'll want to order a beer—there were over 125 brands at last count. ~ 300 North Main Street, Hendersonville; 828-696-1665.

The bar at **Poplar Lodge**, comfortably cluttered with antiques and oddities, is a fun place for a drink. ~ 2350 Hebron Road, Hendersonville; 828-693-8400.

◀ *HIDDEN*

HOLMES EDUCATIONAL STATE FOREST   A marvelous introduction to the Carolinas' mountain flora, the 235-acre forest has "talking trees" that tell about their origins and uses, and how they interact with animals and other plants. Simply push the button on an oak, hickory, tulip poplar or other hardwood, and a recording will give you the lowdown on the tree. The "Talking Tree Trail" is an easy half-mile, and there's a longer, three-mile "Forest Management Demonstration Trail" (which should be called something less stiff, like "Getting to Know Your Forest") where you can see exactly how big an acre is and learn other woodsy details. The forest also has a wetland and a pond. Closed

PARKS

◀ *HIDDEN*

Monday; closed late November to mid-March. Facilities include picnic tables and a covered shelter, restrooms (only picnic areas, restrooms, and the half-mile Crab Creek Trail are wheelchair accessible) and three amphitheaters. ~ From downtown Hendersonville, take Kanuga Road (which becomes Crab Creek Road) southwest for nine miles, a scenic drive through rolling hills and valleys; 828-692-0100.

▲ There are 10 semi-primitive tent sites for groups of 20 or more, with cold-water showers; no fee. The campground is just a short stroll from the parking area.

▼▼▼▼▼▼▼▼▼▼
Brevard Area

As Route 64 west leaves the suburban sprawl of Hendersonville behind, there is a welcome coolness in the air—and then forest, moist, quiet and dappled with sun filtering through 40-foot canopies of red oak and yellow and white pine, and rhododendron and flame azaleas coloring the roadsides. You know you are out of the city and in the country when you see signs for "Hunters' Dog Boxes" (the kind that goes on the back of a pickup truck to hold the hunting dogs). You'll also know when you see the signs for Pisgah National Forest.

SIGHTS

Pisgah National Forest is protected today because of George Vanderbilt, who in the late 1800s purchased several forests, totaling 125,000 acres, extending west from his famous Biltmore House in Asheville. Vanderbilt hired a friend named Gifford Pinchot, who had studied forestry in France, to manage and protect the area—and thus laid the groundwork for the first national forest. Not long after Vanderbilt died in 1914, the federal government acquired most of the forest and turned it into a game preserve, eventually more than tripling its size.

Brevard once held a festival called Transylvania Mania, complete with a Dracula look-alike contest. The event is now called Halloweenfest.

Pinchot was succeeded by Dr. Carl Schenck, a German forestry pioneer who created the Biltmore Forestry School. From the turn of the century until 1914, his students ran a trout hatchery, studied selective logging, and lived in rundown, deserted logging camps, giving them names such as Hell Hole and Rest for the Wicked.

Today, the school has been re-created as the **Cradle of Forestry in America**, a National Historic Site spanning 6500 acres of the Pisgah National Forest. Most areas here are wheelchair accessible, including the one-mile Biltmore Campus Trail and the remnants of Hell Hole. You'll find woodcarvers, basketmakers, weavers, quilters and blacksmiths demonstrating their skills. Also here is the Black Forest Lodge, one of several buildings designed by Carl Schenck to resemble Germany's Black Forest cottages. Schenck's hired rangers lived in these cottages while fending off illegal loggers and trappers.

You can learn all about Schenck, Pinchot and Vanderbilt and their progressive forestry ideas in a film shown in the 15,000-square-foot **Visitors Center**. Kids will love the hands-on and high-tech exhibits including touch-screen videos and a helicopter with a "virtual reality" screen that allows them to put out a forest fire. Another outstanding exhibit teaches kids about trees as they explore the trunk, branches and root system in a life-size replica. The site also uses scavenger hunts to teach youngsters. Visit the historic site between mid-April and October, since it's closed the rest of the year. Admission. ~ Route 276, north of Route 64 near Brevard; 828-877-3130.

Heading south back on Route 276, take the turnoff for **Pisgah Center for Wildlife Education**. This is a highly interesting and strange place, especially if you've never seen thousands of multi-size trout swimming furiously in tanks called "raceways." Kids love feeding the fish, which attack the food (a mixture of fish meal and vitamins), piranha-like. About 425,000 trout are raised at the hatchery every year and released into surrounding streams, which sounds like a lot, until you consider only 20 percent of North Carolina's streams are "non-native," meaning they're eligible for farm-raised fish. In other words, if you do catch a local trout, chances are it was born in a stream, not here in a tank. ~ Route 475; 828-877-4423.

Returning to Route 64, continue westward through Pisgah Forest to **Brevard**, which calls itself "Land of Waterfalls" and "Home of the White Squirrel," for the white squirrels, rare in this part of the world, that live in city parks. Brevard is also the seat of Transylvania County, a name supposedly unrelated to vampires or any place in Europe, but derived from "trans," meaning across, and "sylvania," meaning the woods. The *Transylvania Times* is the local newspaper.

There are no waterfalls in Brevard proper, but there is a busy little town center and a main street whose western end dramatically frames a mountain. As you come into town, take a look at the lovely **Brevard College**, where distinguished Federal-style buildings of red brick and white columns assemble on rambling green lawns planted with brilliant flowers. ~ North Broad Street, Brevard; 828-883-8292.

Home to 7000 people, the town gets its name from Ephraim Brevard, a surgeon and Revolutionary War colonel who died of battle wounds in 1781 at the age of 37. The colonel never actually set foot in Brevard, but he was well known here and throughout the South. It's not known whether he loved music, but one hopes he did, since his town is best known for the Brevard Music Festival, which for seven weeks every summer draws national and international performers and thousands of spectators from surrounding counties and states. It's held at the **Brevard Music Center**, which was founded in 1936 and moved to its present locale ten years later. ~ West Probart Street, Brevard; 828-884-2011.

More local history, as well as suggestions on things to see and do, are available from the **Brevard Chamber of Commerce**. (The director was born and raised in Brevard.) Closed Sunday. ~ 35 West Main Street; 828-883-3700, 800-648-4523; www.brevard ncchamber.org.

LODGING

HIDDEN ►

Key Falls Inn is a fine old Victorian farmhouse, built in 1860 and splendidly restored, with a stream and waterfall cascading through the property. Owners Janet Fogleman and her parents, Clark and Patricia Grosvenor, have put antiques nearly everywhere in the house, including in the four tastefully decorated bedrooms and one suite, all with private baths. There are porches for watching the mountains, and 35 acres of luxuriant grounds, including thick boxwood and azalea gardens and a tunnel of rhododendron leading to a bridge over the waterfall. The rates include full farm-style breakfasts and afternoon tea. A cabin that accommodates four people is available. Closed Thanksgiving weekend and the week between Christmas and New Year. ~ Everett Road, off Old Route 64; 828-884-7559, fax 828-885-8342; www.keyfallsinn. com, e-mail keyfallsinn@brinet.com. BUDGET TO DELUXE.

The **Inn at Brevard** stands out along Main Street with its crisp white exterior. Inside the 1885 mansion displays a cozy atmosphere, with oriental rugs adorning the hardwood floors and six entirely different bedrooms, all with private baths. Room rates include a full country breakfast. An adjacent two-story building has ten more rooms. ~ 410 East Main Street, Brevard; 828-884-2105, fax 828-885-7996; www.innatbrevard.8m.com, e-mail brevardinn@citicom.net. DELUXE.

DINING

Jordan Street Café is small (reservations are a must in summer) and wood-floored, with glass tables lit by pyramid-shaped lamps. When the weather's warm, you can eat out on the patio with a view of the mountains—the perfect backdrop for bacon-wrapped beef tenderloin topped with bleu cheese, or pecan-crusted salmon with blackberry sauce. The menu changes constantly. ~ 13 West Jordan Street, Brevard; 828-883-2558; www. jordanstreetcafe.com. DELUXE TO ULTRA-DELUXE.

At **The Bistro** you can dine beneath molded tin ceilings and look across to the beautiful old county courthouse. The dinner menu (served Thursday through Saturday) tends toward mountain-standard fare—trout, salmon, ribs—but lunchtime brings black-bean and veggie burgers, turkey chili, tortilla wraps and other food with flair. ~ Corner of Main and Broad streets, Brevard; 828-862-4746. MODERATE.

Three doors down, **Falls Landing** goes more upscale with crisp linens and custom-carved mahogany tables trimmed in cypress. In summer there's Maine lobster and Carolinas-caught mahimahi; steak, mountain trout and pasta are served year-round. Go during lunch for seafood burritos, crabcake sandwiches or Jamaican jerk chicken. Closed Sunday. ~ 23 East Main Street, Brevard; 828-884-2835. DELUXE.

On weekends, there's live music at several Brevard restaurants, ranging from country to easy listening to folk.

For Brevard's most imaginative cuisine, head to **Hobnob Restaurant**. Chef-owners Marc and Shellie Dambax bring their bent for bistro cuisine from Charleston, where they owned the excellent Market Street East. At Hobnob, the starters include grilled portobello mushroom in a parmesan basket with blue cheese sauce; the entrées may feature roasted duck with leek and asparagus risotto. The venue is warm and restful—pumpkin- and saffron-colored walls, burgundy tablecloths—and the Sunday brunch (try the shrimp and grits provençale) literally a local event. ~ 226 West Main Street, Brevard; 828-966-4662; www.hobnobrestaurant.com. MODERATE.

SHOPPING

Browsers should concentrate on the area around Main Street in downtown Brevard, a district sprinkled with some fine antique shops, boutiques and craft stores.

Across from Brevard College, join the students who frequent **Highland Books**, which specializes in regional titles, children's books and nature guides. The store's friendly staff can help you find what you're looking for. Closed Sunday. ~ 480 North Broad Street, Brevard; 828-884-2424.

The **White Squirrel Shoppe** is a curio shop with unusual gifts and antiques. ~ 2 West Main Street, Brevard; 828-877-3530. **The Carolina Connection** is country-themed, with primitive furniture, birdhouses and woven throws. Closed Sunday. ~ 6 South Broad Street, Brevard; 828-884-9786.

O. P. Taylor's is full of specialty toys like Brio trains, Breyer models and Corgi cars. ~ 2 South Broad Street, Brevard; 828-883-2309, 800-500-8697.

NIGHTLIFE

If you brought your disco duds, put them away. Bring out the blue jeans and cowboy boots (you *did* pack them, right?).

The upscale bar area at **Jordan Street Café** attracts a young and active crowd that shows up Monday, Wednesday and Friday for live jazz, funk or bluegrass music. ~ 30 West Jordan Street, Brevard; 828-883-2558.

If it's Thursday night, go to **Silvermont** for a real mountain hoedown, with old-time bluegrass and sometimes, if the local

Text continued on page 80.

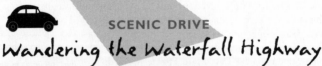

Wandering the Waterfall Highway

They range from curtains of quiet water to fast-flowing flumes to liquid thunder. You can drive under or behind them, slide down them, or lodge your body beneath them and have the best shower massage of your life. Most people, however, are content to simply stare at waterfalls, those indescribable tricks of nature: water freefalling its way to some darkened gorge or bright stream, crashing and fizzing before continuing on its way. Only the icy breath of winter can stop a waterfall, and it often does, suspending it in midair in a frozen sheet of silver fringed with icicles. There are hundreds, possibly thousands, of waterfalls in the Southern Mountains, their names—Umbrella Falls, Bridal Veil Falls, Sliding Rock, Slippery Witch—suggesting a distinct form, beauty or treachery. Some are located right alongside the road; others are a short and scenic hike from the pavement. But most all are reached from Route 64, also known as the Waterfall Highway.

HICKORY NUT FALLS   Start wandering the highway on the east end of the Southern Mountains in Chimney Rock Park. The park's number-one attention-getter is a stupendous chimney-shaped rock; number two is Hickory Nut Falls, one of the highest falls in the eastern United States with a straight-down drop of 404 feet, twice as long as Niagara, though significantly narrower. The easiest way to the bottom of the falls is via the Hickory Nut Falls Trail, a moderate, one-hour round-trip walk from the area just below the top parking lot. The two-hour Skyline Trail, which starts near Chimney Rock and whose views and steep steps will leave you breathless, leads to the top of the falls. Centuries-old chestnut oaks and hemlocks preside over this summit. This is a great spot for a picnic, and the folks down at the park's snack shop are happy to pack one—so ask before you go. Admission. ~ Route 64-74A in the town of Chimney Rock; 828-625-9611.

PEARSON'S FALLS   Westward on Route 64, then south on Route 176, between the tiny towns of Saluda and Tryon, look for the small sign for Pearson's Falls. A quarter-mile trail wends through carpets of ferns and trees dripping with bromeliads and orchids, delivering you to the granite terraces of the falls, where water tumbles 90 feet from step to step to step. These falls are out of the way and not so well known, so you will likely have them all to yourself. Enjoy. ~ 828-749-3031 for hours.

LOOKING GLASS FALLS   If a painter were to portray a perfect waterfall, it would be Looking Glass Falls. A broad, curving mantle of pure unbroken water, framed in granite ledges and speckled leaves of forest, flows 60 feet into a clear pool. This is a popular waterfall, close to the road, so you will likely share the moment with people snapping photos. ~ Route 276 north of Route 64, in Pisgah National Forest.

SLIDING ROCK   A spot that's even more crowded, but absolutely worth experiencing, lies two miles farther north on Route 276. Like it sounds, Sliding Rock is where water slides down rock—and you can, too. Put on a pair of sturdy shorts and shoes and take a fast ride down the 60-foot natural slide, landing in a seven-foot-deep pool as clear as air. People have been doing it for decades, and so have animals; Lassie supposedly took the big slide for a scene in her TV show. Kids will slide down relentlessly all day, even if the water averages 55° *in summer*. There are bathhouses and lifeguards on duty Memorial Day through Labor Day. In winter, the place is near empty. Admission.

WHITEWATER FALLS   Farther west on Route 64, near the community of Sapphire, head south on Route 281. Just before the South Carolina line, stop at Whitewater Falls. A most unusual cascade, it falls partly in North Carolina and partly in South Carolina. The North Carolina falls, or the upper falls, surge 411 feet down a stepped rock wall, making them the highest waterfalls east of the Rockies. Poets and writers have long attempted to capture the power and grandeur of this spot.

BRIDAL VEIL FALLS   Just past Highlands on Route 64 are a pair of outstanding falls. You can see Bridal Veil Falls from the highway, a cascade of whitewater as thin and glisteny as shredded lace. The water falls in millions of little droplets upon the rocks; in winter, the droplets freeze and look like rhinestones.

DRY FALLS   Barely a mile west of here is the turnoff for Dry Falls. You can hear the thunderous torrent from the parking area, but you'll have to walk a few minutes down to where it plummets, freeform, 75 feet into the Cullasaja River. Walk around behind the mammoth falls, into the dim, damp rock grotto, and you can watch the world *through* the falls—while staying completely dry. In winter, beware of icy conditions.

INFORMATION   There are many more falls along the highway, enough, in fact, to fill up weeks of wandering. For tips on where to find them, contact **Pisgah National Forest Ranger Station**. ~ Route 276; 828-877-3265. Also try **Brevard Chamber of Commerce**. ~ 35 West Main Street, Brevard; 828-883-3700, 800-648-4523. You can also contact the **Cashiers Area Chamber of Commerce**, which publishes a Waterfall Treasure Map. ~ 202 Route 64 West; 828-743-5191.

ladies are in the mood, clogging. As one resident puts it, the long-time event is "a bunch of local musicians who get together and just noodle away." ~ East Main Street, Brevard; 828-884-3156.

PARKS

PISGAH NATIONAL FOREST 🏃 🛶 A 504,180-acre forest that extends far north into North Carolina's High Country and Piedmont regions, Pisgah is a wilderness of waterfalls, rocky outcroppings, thick caverns of ferns and spiraling trees, and several mountain ranges, including the Black Mountains, with a ceiling reaching more than 6000 feet. There's a vast array of wildlife, from black bears, red squirrels, ravens and hawks to ruffed grouse, white-tailed deer and the rare and tiny saw-whet owl, which lives only in spruce and fir forests higher than 5000 feet.

Within the national forest, which reaches down into the Southern Mountains to the South Carolina line, there are many places for sightseeing, innertubing, camping out, swimming, fishing, rock climbing, waterfall watching and sliding. To simply drive through endlessly beautiful forest, take the **Forest Heritage National Scenic Byway**, a 77-mile loop along Routes 276, 64, 215 and 475.

Facilities include picnic sites, and hot showers at various locations. Good swimming is available at Lake Powhatan. The Davidson River is well-known for its abundance of rainbow trout. Other great spots: North and South Mills rivers, for trout and bream; and Lake Powhatan, for largemouth and smallmouth bass, bream, catfish and trout. A fishing license is required. A few areas have up to a $3 day-use fee. ~ Major access points are along Routes 64, 276, 191 and 215, and the Blue Ridge Parkway; 828-877-3265.

> Gorges State Park is home to a high concentration of rare plants, including tropical strains whose origins at the site are a puzzle to scientists.

🏕 There are nearly 300 tent and RV sites throughout the forest, plus several group camping areas. Those at Davidson River don't have hookups. Most campgrounds close November through March. Fees range from $7 to $18 per night, depending on the campground.

GORGES STATE PARK 🏃 🚵 🐎 🛶 ⛵ With steep elevations (in some places a rise of 2000 feet in only four miles), waterfalls and lots of rain, this park straddling the Carolinas border has much of the same dramatic scenery as the Pisgah National Forest. Wildlife here includes black bears, wild turkeys, foxes, coyotes, wild boar, deer and squirrels, as well as the largest known population of green salamanders in the state. There are no garbage facilities, so visitors must carry out whatever they bring in. Fishing is good for smallmouth bass and rainbow and brown trout (license required). Amenities include hiking, biking and horseback riding trails, boating (access from Devil's Fork

State Park in South Carolina), restrooms and picnic tables. ~ Route 64, west of Brevard in Sapphire; 828-966-9099.

▲ The Ray Fisher Place campground has 6 primitive sites ($9 per night), while the Lake Jocassee campground has 6 primitive sites (free).

West from Brevard to Cashiers, Route 64 is a virtual joy ride through sun-dappled mountain forest, with dips and dives and hairpin turns, and the occasional sign announcing "Boiled Peanuts" or "Trout Fishing Bait." Near Lake Toxaway, there's another sign letting you know when you cross the Eastern Continental Divide.

Cashiers & Highlands Area

The rural drama transforms into contemporary scenes at **Sapphire**, a community made up mainly of a 6000-acre planned resort called **Fairfield Sapphire Valley**. Sign after sign, tucked into the woods, announces this sprawling place of townhouses and lakes, golf courses and tennis courts. ~ 4000 Route 64 West; 828-743-3441.

SIGHTS

Just past here you'll find aesthetic **Cashiers**, pronounced CASH-ers, a town of a few blocks with quaint shops sitting 3486 comfortable feet up in the mountains. Floridians love this cool summer spot and seem to have taken over the town. As soon as you arrive, you notice something is missing: the Carolinas' mountain accent. These flatlanders haven't quite learned how to say "y'all."

For information on this part of the Southern Mountains, stop by the **Cashiers Area Chamber of Commerce**. Closed weekends. ~ Route 64 West; 828-743-5191; www.cashiers-nc.com, e-mail email@cashiers-nc.com.

Keep going westward on Route 64 for a thrilling trip into the **Nantahala National Forest**. The slender road corkscrews around cliffs of exposed rocks where streams dribble down and tunnel through great cathedrals of greenery. Random openings in the forest let you see far across horizons dotted with bluish peaks and silvery balds glinting with sun. A fortunate few people have hung homes on the mountainsides off Route 64 and given them names—Sky Watch, Sun Ledge—that hint at their extraordinary views. Very old, boldly painted pickup trucks, their mufflers in desperate need of repair, frequent this stretch of road, so don't be surprised when you meet one coming around a narrow bend.

Near the Macon County line, take the turnoff for Whiteside Mountain Road. After a mile of nothing but forest you'll arrive at **Whiteside Mountain Area Vista Point**. Take an hour or two and hike the two-mile switchback loop to the mountaintop, where you are met by sheer cliffs of white metamorphic rock climbing from 400 to 750 feet, hovering above a dark valley below and looking into the headwaters of the Chattooga River. The cliffs are formed of whiteside granite, where peregrine falcons perch.

West on Route 64, just a few minutes from where the falcons go, are places less natural and more contrived: miles of planned developments, retirement communities and golf resorts whose orderly townhomes and gardens look out of place among these wild mountains and streams. Strangely, the heart of this modern design is a town that was planned back around 1875.

Highlands was created by land developers Samuel T. Kelsey and Clinton C. Hutchinson, who bought 839 acres on this mountain plateau and published a brochure to entice investors. "No better climate in the world for health, comfort and enjoyment," it said, repeating the same words used for dozens of eastern mountain developments (folks today do admit there's a bit of pollen in the air). But the words worked, and by 1883 Highlands boasted 300 residents. Today, there are only about 3000, though you'd never know it, for up to 20,000 visitors crowd the tiny town in summer, staying in inns and manses with well-tended gardens and resorts where tee times (and tea times) are posted in the lobbies.

There is money in Highlands. You can see it in the shops of exclusive designs and hushed price tags, in the tony eateries where champagne is poured at lunch, and in the real-estate pages advertising prices you are certain must be misprints. Which is to say that Highlands is an enormously attractive town, with lush gardens and rows of perfect buildings and sidewalks overhung with colorful canopies. It is also a superior place to shop; dozens of stores, advertising highly imaginative items, crowd the downtown. And, despite the money, Highlands is far from stuffy—indeed, it is quite friendly. Even if you don't stay overnight—and you should—spend a day wandering around town.

Before you start exploring, stop by the **Highlands Chamber of Commerce** for brochures on local sights, restaurants, lodges and activities. Closed Saturday and Sunday from late October through June; closed Sunday the rest of the year. ~ 396 Oak Street, Highlands; 828-526-2112; www.highlandschamber.org.

LODGING   Spread across 6000 acres of mountains and valleys and woods, offering every imaginable amenity, from golf, tennis and canoeing to hiking trails and cross-country ski trails, **Fairfield Sapphire Valley Resort** is a virtual city. An excellent family retreat, it has extensive programs for children, and spacious modern condominiums and townhomes, most of them with kitchens and many with fireplaces and washers and dryers. There are two swimming pools, including an indoor Olympic pool with a huge vaulted tongue-in-groove ceiling, as well as a health club and recreation center with jacuzzi, sauna, weight room and game room. My favorite spot, though, is **The Library** (828-743-5512), a private restaurant and bar (open to guests and club members) built around a late-1800s farmhouse. You can read a book and have a cocktail (county laws prohibit liquor except in private clubs), a sandwich or one of the well-prepared nightly specials. ~ Route 64 West, Sapphire; 828-743-3441, 800-533-8268; www.fair fieldsapphirevalley.com. DELUXE TO ULTRA-DELUXE.

Woodlands Inn of Sapphire is a simple roadside place, unassuming and eclectic, set on the slope of a hill. Three two-story octagonal buildings feature spacious rooms and suites decorated in various motifs such as sunflower and ivy and flanked by windows that look into forest. Rooms have refrigerators and coffeepots. A full breakfast is served in the gathering room. Add to that a swimming pool, a staff that's exceedingly helpful, and reasonable rates, and you have a very good value. ~ 1305 Route 64 West, Sapphire; 828-966-4709, fax 828-884-6233; www.wood-landsinn.net, e-mail woodlandsinn@citicom.net. MODERATE.

Its name suggests a grand and formal lodge, but **High Hampton Inn and Country Club** is actually the opposite: warm, woody and rustic, like a huge mountain cabin. In fact, the only thing grand about the place is the trees. Two—a fraser fir and a bottlebrush buckeye near the golf course's 18th hole—are among the largest of their kind in America (both have certificates from the National Forestry Association). The lodge itself is built almost entirely out of wood, including a lot of wormy chestnut that succumbed to the blight of the 1920s (you can see the worm tunnels). A massive, four-sided stone fireplace graces the lobby. There are 117 wood-paneled rooms and 19 cottages, including a

AUTHOR FAVORITE

A place of great charm and solitude and style, **Millstone Inn** is situated in a 1930s former home trimmed in wood shakes and perched on a lush knoll of pine and rhododendron and mountain laurel. Birds sing from high in the treetops, and mountains and valleys are etched in the distance like a watercolor picture. In the main sitting room, an oriental rug reposes in front of a stone fireplace. The ambiance is elegant in the seven bedrooms, four suites and newly added cottage, with period and antique furnishings, exposed-beam ceilings and pine paneling. All have private baths, refrigerators and TVs. The highlight, though, is the wonderful deck off the main house with a spectacular vista of both Whiteside Mountain and Devil's Courthouse. Rates include breakfast. Closed January and February. ~ Off Route 64 West, Cashiers; 828-743-2737, 888-645-5786, fax 828-743-0208; www.millstoneinn.com. ULTRA-DELUXE.

lakeside grist mill honeymoon cottage. (Rooms are sans phones and TVs.) Mountain views are everywhere. A favorite of families and company retreats, the inn features a golf course, tennis courts, a lake, summer kids' program and restaurant (coat and tie required at night). Rates include three buffet meals a day. Closed late November through March. ~ Route 107, south of Cashiers; 828-743-2411, 800-334-2551, fax 828-743-5991; www.highhamptoninn.com. ULTRA-DELUXE.

Highlands Inn has seen town comings and goings since 1880, though ongoing restorations have given the place a light and airy feel. Plank cherry floors and comfortably worn sofas enhance the lobby. Three floors of rooms are decorated in country-manor style, with antique furnishings and wallpaper stenciling by noted local artist Donna Feltman. A gazebo room in the courtyard is surrounded by apple trees. Country-style breakfast is served. ~ Main Street at the corner of Fourth Street, Highlands; 828-526-9380, 800-964-6955; www.highlandsinn-nc.com. DELUXE.

Just across the street, **The Old Edwards Inn** is a prim, red-brick building with a lobby of leaded glass and forest-green carpets. There are nineteen rooms, some with canopy beds and balconies overlooking town, and some formally adorned with antique dressers and embroidered sofas. Feltman's fanciful stenciling is also prominent here. There are also two three-bedroom cabins available. Rates include a Continental breakfast. ~ Main Street at the corner of Fourth Street, Highlands; 828-526-9319, 888-526-9319; www.oldedwardsinn.com. MODERATE TO DELUXE.

Near the quieter west end of town, the corporate-style **Highlands Suite Hotel** is for those who prefer newer accommodations with less historical character. Rooms are spacious and modern, with amenities such as mini-refrigerators and microwaves and gas fireplaces. ~ 200 Main Street, Highlands; 828-526-4502, 877-553-3761, fax 828-526-4840; www.highlandssuitehotel. com. MODERATE TO ULTRA-DELUXE.

HIDDEN ► Slipped into a secluded Highlands neighborhood, **4½ Street Inn** feels closer to the country yet is still walking distance to town. Innkeepers Rick and Helene Siegel, who fled big-city Atlanta for the mountain quiet of this three-story, 1910 Victorian clapboard home, created a one-acre oasis of hemlock and blossoming rhododendron. Their raised herb, flower and vegetable gardens inspire the breakfast menus (try the ginger scones and corn-apple pancakes), and their attention to comfort shows in the ten guest rooms with handmade quilts, down comforters and plush linens and robes. Don't miss the afternoon wine hour on the back deck. ~ 55 4½ Street, Highlands; 828-526-4464, 888-799-4464; www. 4andahalfstinn.com, e-mail relax@4andahalfstinn.com. DELUXE.

HIDDEN ► Sophistication meets mighty mountain scenery at **Fire Mountain Inn**. A few miles from Highlands and hidden (there are no signs) atop Fire Mountain, the stylish retreat offers airy rooms and cabins with champagne-colored walls, sailcloth draperies, and pencil-post, honey-pine beds. The cabins come with two-person hot tubs and porches with heavenly valley views. For ultimate privacy, I stay in one of the treehouses, located down a little path from the inn and shrouded in a sea of solomon trees. Call ahead for directions. ~ 828-526-4446, 800-775-4446, fax 828-526-5518; www.firemt.com, e-mail reservations@firemt.com. ULTRA-DELUXE

DINING

At the wildly popular **Market Basket**, you eat in a smoke-free dining room with a cheery sunflower-and-vegetable motif. The menu, printed on a paper bag, is loaded with fresh veggies (each meal comes with eight to ten) such as stir fry in soy ginger sauce. You may also find baked garlic with feta cheese spread and sun-dried tomatoes; and a variety of fish, seafood, chicken and meats. If you order the "Hot Rock" menu, you'll cook your own meat (if you're a vegetarian, substitute tofu) on a tabletop slab of North Carolina granite. Dinner comes with live music—this spot is big fun. Closed Tuesday and Wednesday. ~ Route 107 South, Cashiers; 828-743-2216. DELUXE.

Creative bistro fare is the order of the day at the warm and intimate **Wild Thyme Gourmet**. Regulars favor sesame chicken salad on mixed greens with hot ginger dressing, baked crabcakes with dill mustard sauce, and salmon with a Vidalia onion crust. Ask for a table on the glassed-in porch, where you'll dine surrounded by rhododendrons. ~ 490 Carolina Way, Highlands; 828-526-4035. DELUXE.

If you need a break from elaborate food, try a local soda fountain. In Highlands, **Highland Hill Deli** has an ample selection   ◄ *HIDDEN* of lunch items. Well-prepared sandwiches, meaty chili and extra thick malts and shakes are a few of the offerings. ~ Corner of Highland and Fourth streets, Highlands; 828-526-9632. BUDGET.

Highland's Back Room Deli serves similar fare and is another   ◄ *HIDDEN* good place for overhearing locals converse about golf and the stock market. Closed Saturday and Sunday. Breakfast and lunch only. ~ West Main Street, in the Highlands Pharmacy Building, Highlands; 828-526-2048. BUDGET.

SMOKY SOUTHERN GOODNESS

The place for barbecue and bluegrass is **Carolina Smokehouse**, which pit cooks its chicken, ribs, pork and beef out back. The ambiance is predictably casual, with wood floors, chairs and tables, and license plates tacked to the wall. ~ Route 64, Cashiers; 828-743-3200. BUDGET TO MODERATE.

A venerable eatery in a beige-and-green cottage framed in tall trees and green lawn, **Wolfgang's on Main** was built as a house in 1880 by town pioneer, post master and mayor Jay Smith. These days, it's a restaurant with an eclectic menu. Steaks are the standout—order the filet mignon topped with crabmeat, leeks and gorgonzola cheese—or consider something Cajun like crawfish étouffée. The chef even tips his toque to Bavaria with schnitzels and *rostbraten*, a pan-fried sirloin topped with "tumble wood" onions and served on a cabernet reduction. Reservations recommended. Dinner only. Closed on Tuesday in the winter. ~ 474 Main Street, Highlands; 828-526-3807, fax 828-526-5754; www.wolfgangs.net, e-mail wom1@gte.net. DELUXE TO ULTRA-DELUXE.

HIDDEN ► **On the Verandah**, just west of Highlands, occupies a quiet spot along the Cullasaja River, barely two miles outside of Highlands. This is where premier seasonal and regional cuisine is served in a classy dining room with big windows on the woods. There are many desirable appetizers, salads and entrées—start with three-cheese-and-wild-mushroom napoleon, or Thai spring rolls with spicy pineapple dipping sauce. Entrées might include hazelnut-crusted halibut over garlic wilted spinach, Thai coconut ginger shrimp, or grilled black Angus rib eye with gorgonzola butter. The wine bar has garnered the *Wine Spectator*'s "Award of Excellence" for the last sixteen years. Closed after New Year's until mid-March. ~ 1536 Franklin Road, off Route 64; 828-526-2338; www.ontheverandah.com. ULTRA-DELUXE.

SHOPPING Cashiers has a handful of shops, but Highlands has dozens. People shop here long and leisurely, easily dropping thousands (and I mean dollars) in a few hours. Browsing, of course, is nearly as much fun.

Get your smoked trout, caviar spreads and bottled gourmet sauces at **Highlands Wine & Cheese Co.** There's also a selection of fine, affordable wines. Closed Sunday from Labor Day through Memorial Day. ~ 561 East Main Street, Highlands; 828-526-5210.

For upscale gifts visit **Lindy's Gifts and Collectibles**, where a display of Swarouski crystal greets you at the door. You can peruse Lladro or Armani figurines, items made by Faberge and Waterford, and fine linens to your heart's delight. Closed on Sunday in winter. ~ 349 Main Street, Highlands; 828-526-9637.

From June through November, **Scudder's Galleries** hosts *the* local event of the night in Highlands: an auction. Drop by during the day to peruse the offerings, everything from English and American antique furniture and art to centuries-old silver and crystal. ~ 352 Main Street, Highlands; 828-526-4111.

The Dry Sink, open more than two decades, is stocked with every imaginable kitchen item, along with brass door knockers and fine china. ~ 450 Main Street, Highlands; 828-526-5226.

The local favorite entertainer is guitarist and vocalist Cy Timmons, who has opened for such big names as Joan Rivers and Al Jarreau. These days he plays at **The Market Basket**. There's also bluegrass and piano music on some nights. Call for seasonal hours. ~ Route 107 South, Cashiers; 828-743-2216.

NIGHTLIFE

On weekends in the summertime, you can hear bluegrass on the front lawn of the **Carolina Smokehouse**. ~ Route 64, Cashiers; 828-743-3200.

For nightlife in Highlands, folks go to **Scudder's** (see "Shopping" above) for the nightly auction, sans alcohol. Or, they drive 12 miles south across the Georgia line to the **Sky Valley Resort**. ~ Off Route 106 in Georgia; 706-746-5302.

NANTAHALA NATIONAL FOREST 🏃 🦫 🛶 More than half a million acres of western North Carolina, stretching north to the Great Smoky Mountains and west to the Tennessee line, Nantahala (pronounced Nan-ta-HALE-a) National Forest is a picture of drama: sheer cliffs of white granite with sharp gorges at their feet, waterfalls booming into boulder-studded rivers, slick rock outcroppings slithering with salamanders, and one area where low bogs and marshes rear up into lofty peaks and ridges. Plant and animal life is vast and varied. Among the types of trees you'll find within this national forest are Canadian and Carolina hemlock, dry pine and oak, dwarf northern red oak and beech. Among the animals are deer, bear, red-tailed and broad-winged hawks, grouse, turkey vultures, owls, wild boar and even ravens and peregrine falcons.

PARKS

To hear live music in Cashiers, you'll have to brown bag your liquor and also order dinner.

Near Cashiers and Highlands are several opportunities for hiking, fishing, swimming, waterfall and wildlife watching, and camping within the national forest. While no boats are allowed at **Cliffside Lake Recreation Area**, there is excellent fishing and swimming, in addition to a day-use-only picnic area. The 15,000-acre **Ellicott Rock Wilderness** provides miles upon miles of hiking trails. Because it's a wilderness area there are no facilities, but restaurants and groceries are nearby in Highlands and Cashiers. Swimming is excellent and fishing is good for trout and bass at Cliffside Lake Recreation Area. You'll also find good trout fishing in Whitewater River, Cullasaja River and Chattooga River. ~ Route 64 serves as the access point to various forest facilities near Cashiers and Highlands, including Whiteside Mountain Area Vista Point, on Whiteside Mountain Road off Route 64, about

◄ HIDDEN

six miles east of Highlands; and Cliffside Lake Recreation Area, off Route 64 about four and a half miles west of Highlands. To get to Ellicott Rock Wilderness, take Horse Cove Road southeast of Highlands and veer right at the fork, which is Bull Pen Road. You'll see the signs for Ellicott Rock; 828-526-3765.

▲ There are 20 sites at Van Hook Glade, off Route 64 four and half miles west of Highlands, that will accommodate tents or small pull-through and pop-up trailer; $10 per night. Various other primitive sites are also located in the area. ~ 877-444-6777; www.reserveusa.com.

▼▼▼▼▼▼▼▼▼▼
Franklin Area

The drive on Route 64 from Highlands to Franklin is a zigzagging, hairpinning odyssey that skirts walls of sheer rock and presents vistas of heath-covered balds. The rock, and the intermittent waterfalls, belong to Cullasaja Gorge. If you feel a little queasy looking down and driving up and down, take a deep breath, turn up the bluegrass on the radio, and go for it!

SIGHTS

Eventually Route 64 irons out at **Franklin**, a budding mountain town built on gem mining. Franklin came to gem fame back in the late 1800s when a farmer discovered a large ruby on his land in the Cowee Valley, a lovely pastoral area about five miles north of Franklin. State geologists were sent to investigate, and when they confirmed there were indeed rubies and sapphires in these hills, Tiffany & Co. came to town. The New York gem giant bought hundreds of Cowee Valley acres and dug deep mines, but after four years never struck it big, unable to find the source of the gems. They did find some pigeon-blood rubies, rarest of all rubies, known only to exist in one other place in the world, the Mogock Valley of Burma.

Commercial mining lasted only about 30 years in the Cowee Valley, but rock hounds, ever hopeful of finding "the big one," have been coming to Franklin ever since. Of course, a big find is rare these days, though travelers can find small attractive stones and gem flakes. Besides rubies and sapphires, you may come across garnet,

◆◆

ROCK HOUND HINTS

Here's how to look for gems: Pick a mine, pay about five bucks (two bucks for kids) for several buckets of soil and rock, take your station at a long wooden trough lined with people and flowing with water, pour your soil and rock into the water, and sift through it. You're looking for small gem and mineral pieces, which look nothing like they do at the jewelry store, but rather are dull and crusty. The folks at the mine can provide tips on what to look for.

kyanite, rhodolite, moonstone and rutile, other fairly common gemstones and minerals. Even without exciting discoveries, most people (especially kids) find it fun sifting through the gravelly mud for several hours at a time.

Basically, two kinds of mines are found here. "Native" mines are located on actual mines and give you soil only from that mine. "Enriched" or "salted" mines are rarely situated in actual mines; they're just roadside operations that say they are mines but bring in soil from other parts of North Carolina or the United States. You have a much better chance of finding something, *anything*, at the enriched mines (here's where to take the kids). However, you've a better chance of finding something more valuable and exciting at a native mine. Most mines are closed during winter.

More gem tips are available from the friendly rockophiles who run the **Franklin Gem and Mineral Museum**—stop here before you start mining. A funky, musty, glittery place inside a mid-1800s jailhouse, the museum has two floors of "theme" rooms: a North Carolina Room with garnets, sapphires and rubies (you can't miss the 2¼-pound ruby) found around Franklin; a Fluorescent Room that showcases gems under a black light; and an Indian Room with arrowheads, peace pipes, spearpoints and obsidian. Here you can get a free guide to local gem mines and shops, most just a few miles north in the Cowee Valley. The museum staff can point out the "native" and "enriched" mines to you. Closed Sunday, and from November through April. ~ 25 Phillips Street, Franklin; 828-369-7831.

Mine maps are also available from the **Franklin Chamber of Commerce**, which has information on area attractions. Closed Saturday from November through April; closed Sunday year-round. ~ 425 Porter Street, Franklin; 828-524-3161, 866-372-5546, 800-336-7829; www.franklin-chamber.com.

If you go mining and think you've found something, you can take it to **Cowee Valley Lapidary**, an independent company that will analyze, appraise and set your gem, if you desire. ~ 1408 Ruby Mine Road, east of Route 28, in the Cowee Valley; 828-524-2321.

If mining's not on your mind, consider a cruise through the **Scottish Tartans Museum**. America's only official "center for tartan inquiries and Scottish heritage," the museum displays over 500 tartans and related regalia such as a replica of a seventh-century weaver's cottage. It's a spacious, merry place of beautiful woolen fabrics and near-encyclopedic history of Scottish culture and history. If you're moved to try a tartan, the gift shop not only sells kilts but—for gents too sheepish to own a skirt—will rent you one for the evening. Closed Sunday. ~ 86 East Main Street, Franklin; 828-524-7472; www.scottishtartans.org, e-mail tartans@scottishtartans.org.

HIDDEN ▸ Out in the rolling green Cowee Valley, one of the best gem finds is not at a mine but at **Perry's Water Gardens**. This private water-lily farm and mail-order business welcomes visitors to its ponds riotously decorated with empress lotuses, froebelises, white rushes, water lettuce, Venezuela poppies and hundreds more blooms and water plants. Check out the Hindu lotus, a colossal lily whose big pink blossom resembles a showerhead. Try to come between mid-July and mid-August, when most all the lilies are blooming. Spring is the second-best time to come. Don't even bother coming in the fall or winter. ~ 136 Gibson Aquatic Farm Road, north of Ruby Mine Road; 828-524-3264; www.tcfb.com/perwatg, e-mail perrywat@dnet.net.

HIDDEN ▸ One hour west of Franklin is one of the most mysterious and compelling sights in the area: **Wayah Bald** (pronounced Why-ya-bald), a 5335-foot-high rock summit that in spring blazes with azalea, dogwood and other brilliant blooms. The Cherokee supposedly named it Wayah, meaning wolf, for the wolves that patrolled the mountaintop. ~ Route 64 west to Route 1310, then head north.

LODGING   Right in town, **The Franklin Terrace** has long local roots—it was first an 1887 schoolhouse then a 1915 inn. Today's inn was redecorated in 2002 with softly lit amber walls, period antiques, and white wicker rockers lining the screened verandah. All nine rooms come with TVs and air conditioning (needed only in August and sometimes September). Breakfasts are fresh and colorful—lemon and pumpkin breads, muffins topped with sausage, cheese and poached eggs—and served in a window-lined room overlooking butterfly gardens. ~ 159 Harrison Avenue, Franklin; 828-524-7907, 800-633-2431; www.franklinterrace.com, e-mail stay@franklinterrace.com. MODERATE.

Mountain views and rustic charm are the hallmarks of the **Buttonwood Inn**, a two-story red battenboard structure originally built in the 1920s. Four cozy rooms are prettily decorated with homemade quilts, antiques and collectibles. Morning brings a hearty breakfast of soufflés, sausage or french toast stuffed with nuts or fruit. The inn's porch comes complete with a rocking chair to while away those lazy afternoons, especially lovely when the dogwood are in bloom. ~ 50 Admiral Drive, Franklin; 828-369-8985, 888-368-8985; www.buttonwoodbb.com, e-mail innkeeperbwbb@myexcel.com. MODERATE TO DELUXE.

Fourteen miles north of Franklin, **The Snow Hill Inn Bed & Breakfast** resides on fourteen acres with gardens, green lawns and views of eleven mountains. In fact, all eight rooms offer mountain sightings from picture windows trimmed in lace. The decor and amenities differ slightly, from the garden tub with complimentary sparkling wine in The Retreat room to the goose-down comforter in the Rose Garden room. Outside, there's are croquet and badminton lawns. ~ 531 Snow Hill Road, Franklin; 828-369-2100, 800-598-8136; www.bbonline.com/nc/snowhill, e-mail sheilaanddave@msn.com. MODERATE.

Otherwise, there's **Summit Inn**, homey and rustic and scattered with multifarious antiques. As the name suggests, the 1900 house of yellow poplar wood resides on a hill and enjoys views of the surrounding mountains. Fourteen bedrooms, most with private baths, are nicely decorated with pastel walls and four-poster beds. The low prices amazingly include a continental breakfast, and there's a popular restaurant serving some of the best food around. ~ 210 East Rogers Street, Franklin; 828-524-2006; www.summitinn.net. BUDGET.

DINING

Other than fast food, there's not a whole lot in the way of Franklin dining, and there's no place on Sunday nights—so plan ahead. **Seasons at the Summit** does casual mountain dining Thursday through Monday. Entrées may include chicken piccata, veal Provençal or herb-encrusted trout. Reservations recommended. ~ 210 East Rogers Street, Franklin; 828-524-2006. MODERATE.

The Italian kitchen at **Patriccio's** can be counted on for pasta, chicken (piccatas, parmigiano), seafood and steaks. Nothing terribly imaginative, but tasty. Closed Sunday. ~ 201 Highlands Road, Franklin; 828-524-9229. MODERATE.

Frog and Owl Mountain Bistro and Wine Bar does simple and straightforward fare like fried or poached trout, New York strips and filets, Mediterranean chicken, pasta, soups and salads. You eat on little café tables overlooking Main Street, sometimes flush with tourists just back from gem mining, sometimes dead calm, especially in winter. Brunch only on Sunday. Closed Monday. ~ 46 East Main Street, Franklin; 828-349-4112. MODERATE.

Franklin celebrates warm summer nights under the stars with "Pickin' on the Square," live entertainment provided by locals every Saturday at 6:30 p.m. from May through October. ~ Corner of East Main and Iowa streets; 866-372-5546.

Mama's serves a mean breakfast—homemade biscuits and gravy, stone-milled grits, cheese- and meat-packed omelettes. Lunch and dinner are also hearty and country-styled, from the fried chicken and barbecue pork to the hamburger steak with mushroom gravy. Closed Sunday. ~ 21 Heritage Hollow Road, Franklin; 828-369-8185; www.mamasrestaurant.com, e-mail info@mamasrestaurant.com. BUDGET.

SHOPPING

Gem shops, one after another, with their tedious, tacky facades, call to you from the highways. Most are reputable, though some have been known to falsify their merchandise. A list of gem shops is available from the **Franklin Chamber of Commerce**. ~ 425 Porter Street, Franklin; 828-524-3161, 800-336-7829.

NIGHTLIFE   The options for sophisticated play are limited in this area, but for families there's nothing like **The Fun Factory**. This is the place for playing laser tag and miniature golf, getting your swing on in the batting cages, making a customized teddy bear and racing go-karts. There is often karaoke on Friday nights, and occasional live Christian and country music on Saturday. ~ 1024 Georgia Road, Franklin; 828-349-8888, 866-482-2386.

PARKS   **NANTAHALA NATIONAL FOREST** The westernmost— and remotest—portion of this 527,000-acre forest runs from Franklin to the Tennessee and Georgia state lines. Most recreation areas and sights are west of Franklin, an hour or even three by car. But the drives are incredibly scenic and the forest deep and mysterious.

JOYCE KILMER MEMORIAL FOREST Far west in Nantahala, just before the Tennessee line, lies one of the few remaining stands of virgin southern Appalachian forest. Within Nantahala National Forest is Joyce Kilmer Memorial Forest, named for the poet and World War I soldier killed in battle. Here live big old hardwoods and Canadian hemlock, wild boar and bear, deer and salamanders. Kilmer's most famous poem was "Trees." ~ From the town of Robbinsville, head west on Route 143, then turn right onto Route 1127 until you see signs for the forest; 828-479-6431.

▲ There are tent sites nearby. Rattler Ford, a group site, accepts reservations and has hot-water showers (no hookups); $50 per night. Horse Cove is first-come, first-serve (no hookups); $10 per night.

HIDDEN ▶   **JACKRABBIT MOUNTAIN RECREATION AREA** The 7000-acre Jackrabbit Mountain Recreation Area offers good swimming at its beach and a picnic area. Boating is available on Lake Chatuge in Clay County, where you might also fish for bass. Trout live in surrounding mountain streams. Closed in winter. ~ Off Route 175 about seven miles east of the town of Hayesville; 828-837-5152.

▲ There are 103 tent and RV sites; $15 per night.

HIDDEN ▶   **STANDING INDIAN RECREATION AREA** Standing Indian Recreation Area offers a picnic area and several hiking trails. Anglers try to hook some trout in Nantahala River and Kimsey Creek, which is shallow enough for swimming. Facilities include restrooms and bathhouses at various access sites. Closed in winter. ~ Take Route 64 west of Franklin for 12 miles, go south on Old Route two miles, then continue south on Forest Road 67 for two miles. ~ 828-524-6441.

▲ There are 84 tent and RV sites, as well as hot-water showers, plus various primitive group sites throughout the forest; $14 per night.

HENDERSONVILLE & FLAT ROCK AREA In the Hendersonville area, there's **Crooked Creek Golf Club**. ~ Kanuga Road, Hendersonville; 828-692-2011. In Fletcher, try the **Broadmoor Golf Links**. ~ 101 French Broad Lane, Fletcher; 828-687-1500. **Orchard Trace Golf Club** has a par-3, 18-hole course. ~ 942 Sugarloaf Road, Hendersonville; 828-685-1006. **Cummings Cove Golf & Country Club** is also open to the public. ~ 3000 Cummings Road, Hendersonville; 828-891-9412. In Flat Rock, there's **Highland Lake Golf Course**, with a 9-hole, ~ 111 Highland Lake Road; 828-692-0143.

BREVARD AREA In the Brevard area, try **Sherwood Forest**. ~ Route 276 South, Brevard; 828-884-7825. The **Sapphire Mountain Golf Club** at Fairfield Sapphire Valley Resort has a waterfall hole. ~ Route 64, Sapphire; 828-743-1174.

FRANKLIN AREA In Franklin, play at **Mill Creek Country Club**. ~ 341 Country Club Drive, off Route 64 West; 828-524-6458. **Parker Meadows Golf Course** has a 9-hole course with seven par-3s and two par-4s. ~ Maxwell Home Road; 828-369-8008. Also try **Franklin Golf Course**. ~ 255 First Fairway Drive; 828-524-2288.

Outdoor Adventures

GOLF

Grab a racquet and head for the courts at **Silvermont**. ~ East Main Street, Brevard; 828-884-3156. Also try **Brevard Tennis & Athletic Club**. ~ Country Club Road, Brevard; 828-883-3005. **Fairfield Sapphire Valley Resort** is a private club with 16 courts. Fee. ~ Route 64, Sapphire; 828-743-1171. Work on your serve at **Cashiers Community Center**. ~ Route 64, Cashiers. **Highlands Recreation Park** has four courts available. ~ Cashiers Road, Highlands; 828-526-3556. There are also courts at **Franklin Parks and Recreation**. ~ Route 441 South, Franklin.

TENNIS

Hundreds of trails within Pisgah National Forest and Nantahala National Forest are open to equestrians. You can rent horses and guides at **Pisgah Forest Stables** from April through October. ~ Route 276 North, Pisgah Forest; 828-883-8258.

RIDING STABLES

AUTHOR FAVORITE

Whether you live for golf or rarely tee off, I guarantee you'll love the course at **High Hampton Inn & Country Club**. The scenery—mist-shrouded green forest and mountain-edged lakes—looks lifted from Scotland, and the course has bent-grass greens. The par-71, George C. Cobb–designed course welcomes the public in the afternoon when there's room. ~ Route 107 South; 828-743-2411 ext. 114.

The **Nantahala Village Riding Stable** offers hour-long to all-day guided excursions into the Nantahala National Forest. Reservations are suggested. No rides during winter. ~ 9400 Route 19 West, Bryson City; 828-488-9649, 828-488-2903.

BIKING

Southern Mountains cycling is for those who want a workout—the terrain here is anything but flat. Many roads, however, are gently sloped and marvelously remote, offering silent pedaling through deep woods. For excellent bike trail maps, contact the North Carolina Department of Transportation's Bicycle Program. ~ 1552 Mail Service Center, Raleigh, NC 27699-1552; 919-733-2804; www.dot.state.nc.us/transit/bicycle.

Backcountry Outdoors, located a few miles outside of Brevard, is another choice for bike rentals. ~ 18 Pisgah Highway, Pisgah Forest; 828-884-4262; www.backcountryoutdoors.com.

The first 15 miles of **Connemara Trail** offer a stomach-tingling plunge down Blue Ridge Mountains—a drop of more than 2400 feet. There are moderate hills and a few steep uphills on the 46-mile run, the first segment of the Southern Highlands Trail. Connemara commences at Wagon Road Gap on the Blue Ridge Parkway, then heads south to Route 276 east, picking up Route 176 in Brevard and winding eastward through Little River, Flat Rock, Saluda and Tryon.

Highlands Spur links the towns of Highlands and Franklin, taking scenic, little-traveled back roads for 19 miles. Start in Highlands on Route 28 west, then head north on Route 1546 to Route l545, jogging over to Route 1538, which eventually hooks up with Route 64. Here you will want to get on Route 1678, then Route 1672, and then Route 1564, following it into Franklin.

North of Franklin, the eight-mile **Cowee Valley Loop** takes you on a fairly leisurely easy tour of the area's gem mines, with pastoral views along the way. From Route 28 near West's Mill, pick up Route 1340 to Route 1341, then 1343 and 1345, winding your way back to Route 28.

Bike Rentals   Bring your bike to the Southern Mountains—bike rentals are tough to find. **Bike Ways** in Hendersonville does have a few mountain bikes for rent. Closed Sunday. ~ 607 Greenville Highway, Hendersonville; 828-692-0613.

HIKING

All distances listed for hiking trails are one way unless otherwise noted.

From leisurely walks by waterfalls to demanding day-long treks into and out of gorges, the Southern Mountains are a hiker's paradise. Many trails are part of the Appalachian Trail stretching from Maine to Georgia. Trail maps and information are available from local chambers of commerce. **Pisgah National Forest** also has some trail information. ~ 828-877-3265. If you visit **Nantahala Na-**

Trout
Tales

Have no doubt about it—this here's trout country. More than 1500 miles of streams are swimming with trout in the Southern Mountains, where despite the abundance of hatcheries, most trout aren't farm-raised. The best time to try for a trout is March through May; the second-best time is September and October. Summer isn't bad, it's just hotter, so the fish only bite in early morning and early evening.

You can flyfish for trout, or use a rod 'n' reel baited with anything from corn kernels and crickets to nightcrawlers. You can also pond fish at one of the private trout farms in the Southern Mountains, which you should know are often way out in the country, sometimes down a series of dirt roads, so call ahead for directions. (Call ahead anyway to make sure the fish are biting.) If you fish at a private pond, you don't need a fishing license but will simply pay a per-fish fee. If you fish anywhere else, pick up a license at a local bait-and-tackle store. Other than trout, you'll find catfish, bass and bream in the Southern Mountain streams and lakes.

Most lodges will arrange a fishing trip. If you'd rather make plans on your own, these outfits sell bait and tackle and licenses, and can provide guides. **Brookings** will take you flyfishing for trout in the Nantahala National Forest. ~ 3 Chestnut Square, Cashiers; 828-743-3768.

Private trout-fishing farms and ponds include **Morgan Mill Trout**. Closed on weekends in winter. ~ Route 64 West, Brevard; 828-883-3886.

tional Forest, trail maps are available. ~ 828-526-3765, 828-524-6441. You can purchase trail guides and books on hiking from The **Highland Hiker**. ~ 601 Main Street, Highlands; 828-526-5298.

CHIMNEY ROCK AREA   On the eastern end of the Southern Mountains, **Chimney Rock Park** offers three popular trails, ranging from the fairly easy **Forest Stroll** (.75 mile) to the bottom of Hickory Nut Falls to the steeper **Cliff Trail** (.75 mile) continuing onto the **Skyline Trail** (.75 mile). The latter two hikes take you on a geologic journey along ledges of gneiss rock, into a granite formation called Opera Box, and atop the fabulous Hickory Nut Falls. You'll see twisted-hair spikemoss, prickly pines, false indigo, witch hazel, false goat's beard, hairy alumroot, mountain magnolia, and many other shrubs and wildflowers. Get a trail guide at the park's visitors center. ~ 828-625-9281.

HENDERSONVILLE & FLAT ROCK AREA   In Hendersonville on Fourth Avenue East, the **Jackson Park Nature Trail** (1.5 miles) is a good way to exercise and learn about local plants and animals. The marked trail notes everything from Carolina chickadee birds and roundleaf yellow violet flowers to blackberries and wild roses.

HIDDEN ►

If you take the **Talking Tree Trail** (.45 mile) at Holmes Educational State Forest, you can hear each tree "tell" you all about itself. Each one is actually outfitted with a recorder; push a button on the tree and the recording starts playing. The forest also has a more challenging hike along the **Wildcat Rock Trail** (1 mile). It makes a loop through hardwoods and white pine, and on the way skirts a pond and delivers you to a scenic viewpoint. The walk in the **Soil and Water Study Area** (1.5 miles) takes you on a 200-foot-long boardwalk through a wetland studded with trillium and other forest flowers. To get to the forest from downtown Hendersonville, take Kanuga Road (which eventually becomes Crab Creek Road) southwest for nine miles.

HIDDEN ►

BREVARD AREA   Numerous moderate to difficult trails start just north of Brevard in the Pisgah National Forest. **Farlow Gap Trail** (3.1 miles), a moderately tough hike, follows the river, studded with rocks you can slide on, and passes a former fish hatchery. The strenuous **Looking Glass Rock Trail** (6.2 miles round-trip) rewards with spectacular mountain forest views, seen from a granite dome. Much of the terrain is rocky and steep, and the trail narrows along some stomach-loosening corners. **Butter Gap Trail** (2.7 miles) runs along an old railroad grade and affords views of a waterfall and the headwaters of a creek. The hike is moderately difficult. ~ Route 276, north of Route 64.

CASHIERS & HIGHLANDS AREA   Much of the **Whitewater Falls Trail** (1 mile round-trip) is paved, making it an easy hike. The trail, which begins off Route 281, off Route 107, 13 miles south of

Cashiers, wends past wading pools and picnic areas and culminates at the spectacular falls.

Short, steep and fantastically scenic, the **Glen Falls Trail** (.8 mile) plunges down past cascades and sweeping views into Blue Valley. The hike back up is tough but worth it. Good picnicking. To reach the trailhead, take Route 106 south from Highlands for a little less than two miles. When you see Glen Falls Scenic Area, go north on Route 1618 for a mile. There's a parking lot at the trailhead.

One of the more challenging day hikes, **Yellow Mountain Trail**   ◄ HIDDEN
(4.8 miles) takes you up and down three peaks, including the 5127-foot Yellow Mountain, the area's highest. An old wood-and-stone fire tower presides over the summit, a popular place to camp (no facilities). To get to the trailhead from Highlands, take Route 64 three miles east to Buck Creek Road (Shortoff Baptist Church is on the corner). Turn left and go 2.3 miles on Buck Creek Road, until you see a parking area on the left and trailhead on the right.

Even more hidden, and offering a slice of the past, **Hurrah**   ◄ HIDDEN
Ridge (.6 mile) is on part of the historical trail used by Blue Valley ranchers to drive their cattle to "The Flats" pastures of Scaly Mountain. The trail is short but steep and the terrain is rugged, following the rocky shoulder of Hurrah Ridge. To get there from Highlands, take Route 28 south 6 miles to Clear Creek Missionary Baptist Church. Turn right at the church and go six miles until the road ends at a broken culvert in the West Fork of Overflow Creek. Cross the creek and begin looking for the trailhead on the right.

The **Chinquapin Mountain Trail** (1.6 miles) climbs to the 4160-foot summit, affording vistas across the Blue Valley along the way. The marked trailhead is located off Route 106, two miles southwest of Highlands.

FRANKLIN AREA A 35-mile section of the **Bartram Trail** (81 miles), a National Recreation Trail, lies within the Nantahala National Forest. It's a moderate to strenuous hike and is a wonder-

WALK ON THE WHITESIDE

If you only take one hike in the Southern Mountains, choose **Whiteside Mountain** (2 miles), a switchback trail that climbs through dense forests of hemlock and dwarf northern red oak, with lookout points on the way up and possibilities for seeing broad-winged hawks, ravens and even a peregrine falcon. The climax—walls of sheer rock and mind-clearing views across the Chattooga River and endless summits. The trailhead is on Whiteside Mountain Road off Route 64 between Cashiers and Highlands.

ful escape in the woods, with vistas of cascading streams and strolls through cool, deep hardwood forest and fields of wildflowers. Directions to the trailhead are available from the national forest's Wayah District Office, off Route 64 just west of Franklin and Sloan Road. The trail begins past the office on Presley Road.

Much shorter and easier, the **Joyce Kilmer Memorial Loop** (2 miles) takes you close to the flora that Kilmer loved and wrote about. A spectacular grove of yellow poplar is here, and there are also many trillium, hemlock and crested dwarf iris. Wooden benches for resting and a footbridge for crossing a creek make this a most enjoyable hike. The trailhead starts in the parking lot of the Joyce Kilmer Memorial Forest (within Nantahala National Forest) off Route 416 west of Route 129.

Transportation

CAR

The major artery of the Southern Mountains is **Route 64**, which runs east–west through the main towns. Routes 64 and 85 link the Southern Mountains with eastern North Carolina. From South Carolina, **Route 26** runs north and joins Route 64 near Hendersonville. From Tennessee on the west, **Route 64-74A** connects with Route 64 near Murphy. From Georgia to the southwest, **Route 441** travels north to Franklin.

AIR

Asheville Regional Airport, about 12 miles north of downtown Hendersonville, is the closest commercial airport to the Southern Mountains. It is served by Continental Express, ComAir, Delta Connection, Northwest Airlines, US Airways and US Airways Express. ~ www.flyavl.com.

BUS

Greyhound Lines Inc. provides bus service to Hendersonville from major points across the nation. ~ 337 East 7th Avenue, Hendersonville; 828-693-1201, 800-231-2222; www.greyhound.com.

TRAIN

Amtrak will take you as far as Greenville, South Carolina, or Spartanburg, South Carolina, about 48 miles from Hendersonville, North Carolina. ~ 800-872-7245; www.amtrak.com.

CAR RENTALS

At the Asheville airport, there's **Avis Rent A Car** (800-331-1212) and **Hertz Rent A Car** (800-654-3131). **Enterprise Rent A Car** (800-325-8007) is also in Asheville though not at the airport. **U-Save Auto Rental** (828-696-2200) has an office in Hendersonville.

TAXIS

Carolina Taxi (Hendersonville; 828-693-3221) and **City Taxi** (Franklin; 828-369-5042) service their respective towns.

FOUR

The Great Smoky Mountains

The Great Smoky Mountains aren't smoky. They're damp and cool and unbelievably green. The white mantle that prompts their name is made up of fog and clouds, those swirling, shifting ghosts of high places, forever cloaking the peaks but rarely reaching down into the valleys. The ankles of the Smokies are, in fact, crisp, clear and colorful. Flowers bloom low on the mountains as late as December, when the summits are blanketed by snow.

It rains more in the Smokies than anywhere else in the southeastern United States; nearly 90 inches of rain fall in the highest forests every year. Perpetual moisture breeds life—rich, complex, inordinate plant and animal life. The virgin cove forests of the Smokies are primeval, grounded in rich soil and thronged with more variety and size of trees than any other forest in the Northern Hemisphere. Spruce fir forests rarely found south of Maine are here, too, and countless ferns and shrubs, grasses and wildflowers. Their names—witch hobble, scarlet painted cup, jack-in-the-pulpit—sound exotic to the ear.

Yet the Smokies aren't really exotic. They are soothing and sumptuous, full of warmth and mood and heights that don't soar but rise gently to five and six thousand feet. Wandering through their darkened depths feels like a mental massage, for everywhere there is subtlety: the faint trickling of streams and rain, the smooth roundness of creek stones and mountaintops, the simplicity of log cabins. White-tail deer, red squirrels, and black bear fill the forests, and trout crowd the streams. Only cars interrupt the quietude, but then that *is* the main way to see the Smokies.

Around nine million people see Great Smoky Mountains National Park every year, making it the nation's most visited national park (only half that many visit the Grand Canyon). The park's 520,000 acres are shared almost equally by North Carolina and Tennessee, though the scenery does not recognize state boundaries. The Smokies experience, unlike the Grand Canyon, does not involve seeing just one single wonder but reveling in many. Extraordinary views await visitors at every turn, and in between are old homesteads to be explored, streams to be fished, awesome summits to be scaled, trails to be taken. Visitors centers are museums focusing on mountain life, with lots of fascinating cultural and historical details on the Smokies' early Scotch-Irish settlers.

Despite all the tepees now used to promote Cherokee attractions, these early Americans were not nomadic but actually lived in homes of wood and clay. The men hunted bear, buffalo, wild turkey and other game, and fished the creeks for trout. The women grew squash, corn and beans, and gathered wild mushrooms, berries and nuts. They wrapped themselves in deerskin in summer, and buffalo and bear skins in winter. The Cherokee had seven clans, a written language and a national government, and women could vote and fight.

The Cherokee must have found it odd, then, that the Europeans considered them savage. White men began stealing Cherokee land in the 1790s and never stopped. The Smokies instantly changed—for while the Cherokee were content to live in the forest, the Europeans insisted on cutting down trees to make way for pastures, farmland and more settlers.

An acute logging push came in the early 1900s, when nearly 85 percent of current park land was owned by timber companies. Loggers, nicknamed "woodhicks" and looking precisely the part, traveled in packs and left destruction in their wake. The loggers earned a dollar for a 12-hour workday and were fed by cooks they referred to as "gut robbers." The cooks hunted during the day, though by this time elk, bison and beaver had disappeared, and deer, bear and turkey were getting more and more difficult to find.

When Congress authorized creation of Great Smoky Mountains National Park in 1926, 60 percent of the forests were gone. Patches of virgin forest remained and can be found today primarily in North Carolina.

In the past seven decades most of the cleared lands in the Great Smoky Mountains have been renewed, though it will take a hundred years, maybe more, for some varieties of trees to return. The elk and bison will never return without human assistance.

As for the Cherokee, they were nearly wiped out by smallpox and their vast lands reduced to a 56,573-acre reservation called Qualla Boundary. Today, the reservation juts into the national park like a puzzle piece and forms the park's North Carolina gateway. About 5000 Cherokees live on the reservation, some in secluded forest coves but many in the touristy town of Cherokee, which has a good museum, outdoor drama and re-created village that offer visitors an explanation of the old and new American Indian cultures.

Southwest of Cherokee, Bryson City is situated near the headwaters of the Nantahala River and hence the headquarters for whitewater rafting. In the opposite direction through the Soco Gap, the town of Maggie Valley is nearly as contrived as Cherokee, but in an old-fashioned way. Waynesville, southeast of Maggie Valley, is a genuine place with a handsome little downtown and an Old South flavor.

Except for this handful of small hamlets, and the emergence of soft mountains hovering in haze, there is nothing to suggest you are approaching the country's most popular national park.

Text continued on page 104.

Great Smoky Mountains

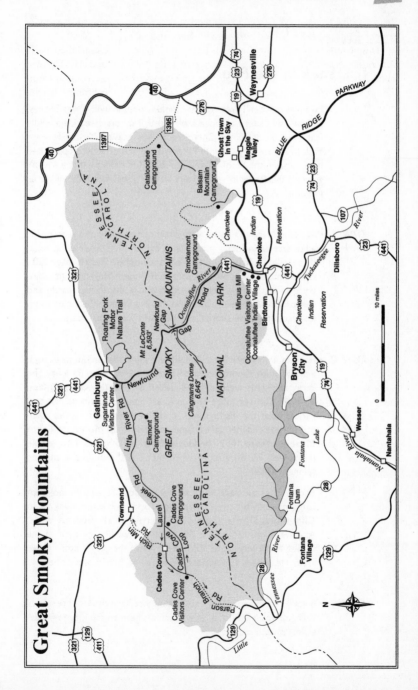

A Week in the Peaks

I was seven when I first saw the Smokies, slept in funky Maggie Valley, and had my picture snapped atop a real, live horse wearing a wildly feathered headpiece in Cherokee. It was heaven. My family went back nearly every year until I got too old and ornery to appreciate how amazing the Smokies are, especially for children. If you haven't gone on this family foray yet, start making plans! Your kids will never forget it.

DAY 1 • Arrive at Maggie Valley by early afternoon and stop at a grocery for a few staples, including picnic lunch fixings. Then take Fie Top Road three miles up from town to the **Cataloochee Ranch** (page 120). Check into a cabin, put the cold stuff in your fridge and get a fire going in the hearth. Let the kids explore the former cattle and sheep farm while you relax before heading over to the dining room for a country-style supper, included with your cabin rate.

DAY 2 • Have an early breakfast at Cataloochee (included in the rate), pack a picnic lunch, then take Route 19 to the Blue Ridge Parkway. The Parkway wends west and will deliver you to the **Oconaluftee Visitors Center** (page 104) in Great Smoky Mountains National Park. Peruse the displays, pick up some park maps and an auto-touring booklet, then take a family stroll down to **Mountain Farm Museum** (page 105). The kids will get a kick out of how simple (primitive?) life used to be when they see the outhouse and the spinning wheel.

• Back in the car, make your way to Signpost 16 and the poignant **Logging Exhibit** (page 108). Then corkscrew seven miles up to **Clingmans Dome** (page 108) for cold, windy, fabulous views. Afterward you can have a late lunch and wildflower stroll at the **Quiet Walkway** (page 105) or at any of the park's other picnic areas. Head back to Cataloochee for some R 'n' R and dinner.

DAY 3 • Enjoy a morning outdoors at Cataloochee. Take the kids horseback riding or trout fishing. If it's wintertime, head to the lodge's family-style, downhill ski area.

- Have lunch at the lodge, or down in Maggie Valley at **Saratoga's** (page 122).

DAY 4
- Rise early, have breakfast and check out of Cataloochee. Take Route 19 to **Cherokee** (page 112) and check into a generic motel (one night is fun!).

- Head back into the national park for a day at **Cades Cove** (page 106). If the weather's nice, consider renting bikes for a family ride around the cove.

DAY 5
- Have breakfast early and spend the morning in Cherokee. Older kids will enjoy the **Museum of the Cherokee Indian** (page 112), but all kids love the **Oconaluftee Indian Village** (page 112). Make sure you also stop at **Qualla Arts and Crafts** (page 117).

- Take Route 19 west of Bryson City to **Nantahala Village Mountain Resort & Meeting Center** (page 116) and check into a cabin. Swim in the pool, then have dinner at the excellent restaurant.

DAY 6
- Go whitewater rafting. Right at the village, **Nantahala Outdoor Center** (page 125) will help design the best family trip. If you have toddlers, make arrangements for them to spend the day at the center's day care. Older kids may want to join a one-day rafting course offered at this premier school. Spend your last night at Nantahala. And if you'd rather it not be your last, head over to **Fontana Village Resort** (page 116) for more family fun in the Smokies.

▼▼▼▼▼▼▼▼▼▼▼▼▼▼▼▼▼

Great Smoky Mountains National Park

Plenty of roads, including paved, gravel and bumpy dirt roads, penetrate Great Smoky Mountains National Park. But only one, the paved, two-lane New-found Gap Road, actually crosses the mountains. It's the most traveled route, cutting right through the middle of the national park, and connecting the Oconaluftee Visitor Center in North Carolina with the Sugarlands Visitor Center in Tennessee. The distance is 32 miles, but pretend it's at least 60, for the road dips and dives, backtracks and gets sidetracked along the way.

SIGHTS

Newfound Gap Road is so squiggly that, on a map, it looks like it was drawn by a two-year-old. Commercial vehicles are banned from the road, but RVs and buses aren't, so traffic frequently crawls along. Which is just fine, since the point is not to stay on the road but to get off it. Dozens of overlooks, side roads and stopovers provide access to park sights—and the only way to hidden spots. Many of these stops are numbered on little wooden signposts. As you travel toward Tennessee, the numbers get lower.

Maps and information are available at the **Oconaluftee Visitors Center** near Cherokee, at the park's main North Carolina entrance. The stone building, a former town courtroom, blends nicely into the woods and offers superb displays on early moun-taineer life as well as an excellent bookstore. Dozens of pamphlets, on subjects ranging from park wildflowers and wildlife to moun-tain people and waterfalls, are available free or sold for a mini-mal fee. Especially helpful are the brochures called *Auto Touring* and *Walks and Hikes*. ~ Newfound Gap Road, Signpost 21.

None of the visitors centers have public phone numbers, but there is a **main park number**: 865-436-1200. Unfortunately, it's one of those touch-tone, choose-the-right-category numbers that tries desperately to keep you from talking with a live person. Plan to be on hold awhile, especially during peak seasons. For instant park information, go online: www.nps.gov/grsm.

◆◆

sights

AUTHOR FAVORITE

I knew I was headed someplace special when my shins caught fire. Well, not literally, but they felt that way on the last straight-up stretch to **Clingmans Dome**. Then all of a sudden, I was standing in the clouds. The wind kept shifting and the air went from cool to warm and back to cool as I watched the valleys and forests roll in green tidal waves. See page 108 for more information.

From the Oconaluftee center, a trail wide enough for wheelchair visitors wends alongside a racing river down to the **Mountain Farm Museum**. You can peek inside a number of primitive wood buildings, including an old springhouse, outhouse, blacksmith shop, meat house, sorghum mill, apple house and bee gum stand. You can look through the door of the main house and see an old sewing machine and piano, and a loom and spinning wheel. The idea is that you'll understand how rough (and uncomplicated) life was here 200 years ago. In the summer, the garden is planted with lettuce, corn and tomatoes, and surrounding fields smell of sorghum or fresh-cut hay. Always there is the rush of the river, just out of sight.

By now you may be wondering when and if you'll have to stop and pay admission to Great Smoky Mountains National Park. You won't. And you can visit almost anytime. The park is open all day and night every day of the year, except when snow shuts down the roads. Newfound Gap Road rarely closes (some folks use it to commute to work, lucky souls) but many of the side roads are blocked in winter.

The main roads are also sometimes blocked—by too much traffic—on summer weekends and during spring blooming and fall foliage seasons. Everything's more crowded—trails, picnic areas, fishing spots. Campgrounds are booked months in advance. If you don't care to share your scenic overlook with a mob, plan to visit any time *other* than these high seasons. May and September are usually wonderful months, both weatherwise and crowdwise.

After the Oconaluftee Visitors Center, the next stop north along Newfound Gap Road is **Mingus Mill**. From the parking area it's a cool walk through yellow poplar forest streaked with sunlight to the vintage 1876 cast-iron turbine mill. (The trail, unfortunately, is not paved and so there is no access for wheelchairs.) For 50 years the mill turned corn into meal and wheat into flour for the nearby hamlet of Mingus Creek. The grinding was actually done by great stones carved from the mountains and smoothed and scored by stonecutters' tools—hence the name "stoneground" meal. The mill is cranked up occasionally from April through October, but the cornmeal is stoneground at a commercial mill in Tennessee. ~ At Signpost 20.

Heading toward Tennessee, the Newfound Gap Road tunnels through enormous forest, with trees towering over ten stories high and sunlight flashing from above. In summer there seems to be a thousand shades of green and a thousand angles and silhouettes passing from low to high, set against the ink-blue sky. On a more human level, a **Quiet Walkway** curls through shoulder-high wildflowers filled with the songs of crickets. Take a seat on the smooth

Text continued on page 108.

The Tennessee Side of the Smokies

The Smokies don't stop where Tennessee starts (half the national park, in fact, is across the state line), so get on Newfound Gap Road, cross into Tennessee, and watch the mountain balds glisten all around. Above the road, sheer, cinnamon-colored cliffs are glossy and veiled with water. Tunnels, their openings draped in luscious ferns, present themselves around turns, and you'll need your headlights to see inside their darkened lengths. As you keep driving, you'll feel the day pass in measured shades of sunlit color, like a slow technicolor dream.

CADES COVE   The early 1800s settlers of Cades Cove were no doubt taken by the same scenery that's so stunning today. Making their way slowly on horses and wagons, they bought land from speculators, who had bought it from the state of Tennessee, which had taken it from the Cherokees. The settlers cleared forests, planted orchards, corn, wheat and rye, and built the most fundamental, inviting homes of hewn logs and simple wood frames. By 1850, 685 people lived in the Cove, though in ten years' time more than half had gone west in search of gold and more fertile pastures. The Cove became nearly a ghost town after that. What you see today is not too different from Cades Cove back then. Seven simple log homes are sprinkled along the 11-mile, one-way **Cades Cove Loop**, and there are churches, barns, a blacksmith shop, mills, a smokehouse and a corncrib. All are accessible by wheelchair, and tell a poignant story of long, productive days spent growing and gathering food, chopping wood, milking cows, grinding corn and wheat, smoking meat, "putting up" the vegetables, helping build a house when someone needed it, helping bury someone when they needed that, too. Callused hands these people had, twenty-first-century ulcers they did not. About halfway around the loop, the **Cades Cove Visitors Center** has information on the area, including a worthwhile auto-tour booklet. The center is closed from November to mid-April, though the loop stays open except for the nastiest of winter days. ~ To get to Cades Cove, take Cades Cove Loop 23 miles from Newfound Gap Road.

RICH MOUNTAIN ROAD   From Cades Cove Loop you can drive the lovely, reclusive Rich Mountain Road. Make sure it's between spring and fall, though, because the road shuts down in winter, buried for months in snow and slush. The road heads north from the loop for seven miles and following a path first cut by the Cherokee. It's a single-lane gravel trail, though a wide one, that fishtails up Rich Mountain and then descends into the rich woods and pastures of Tuckaleechee Cove, eventually joining Route 321 into Townsend, Tennessee.

PARSON BRANCH ROAD   Parson Branch offers an entirely different drive; the road is flanked by luscious foliage, dense, wet and green, riddled with streams and waterfalls and boulders covered in furry green algae. There are some patches of pavement along the road, but most of the eight-mile stretch is gravelly and skinny, heading southwest from Cades Cove through Tennessee to Route 129. Thankfully, RVs and trailers are banned from both Parson Branch and Rich Mountain roads.

SUGARLANDS VISITORS CENTER   Back on Newfound Gap Road, the Sugarlands Visitors Center is the last place before the Tennessee boundary of Great Smoky Mountains National Park. Exhibits here are more elaborate than at Oconaluftee Visitor Center; taxidermied animals are everywhere, and so are photographs of large and small Smokies critters, with lengthy details about their lives and times. The ubiquitous woodchuck, one learns, loves to graze on wildflowers along the roadways and is nicknamed "whistle pig." If you haven't already seen one, keep an eye out. They're easy to spot. ~ Signpost 1.

GATLINBURG   Right after Sugarlands and all the solitude and silence of the Smokies is Gatlinburg, Tennessee. It's a rude encounter, a town with more gimmickry and gaucherie than any in western North Carolina (come to think of it, in all of North Carolina). Depending on your taste in towns, of course, you may find Gatlinburg big fun. Like a caricature of a Swiss village, it is overrun with chalets whose occupants—souvenir shops, burger joints, pinball palaces, mom-and-pop motels—cater to tourists in a not-so-subtle way. Good luck finding a parking space.

ROARING FORK MOTOR NATURE TRAIL   One reason to go to Gatlinburg is to get to Roaring Fork Motor Nature Trail. The paved, one-way loop lasts only five and a half miles but forges through exhilarating, eclectic scenery—first a parade of hills, then solid green walls of woods, then light and airy poplar forest where cornfields once stood. Numbered signposts invite travelers to stop, see, feel and smell the surroundings: an old wagon trail, an 1865 dog-trot cabin, a waterfall called "The Place of a Thousand Drips." Closed in winter. ~ Off Route 441, about four miles south of Gatlinburg.

CATALOOCHEE   Many more back-road trips await in the national park. Most are difficult to reach, some are rough and rugged and closed in winter, but all offer a wonderful way to see the Smokies—in solitude. The isolated **Cataloochee Road**, on the park's southeastern side in North Carolina, is a six-mile trek through vast valleys decorated with pastures to **Cataloochee Historic District**, the remains of an 1800s hamlet. ~ Off Route 40.

boulder and watch the bees suck nectar from purple flowers and the orange and black butterflies duck in and out of clearings. Amid the intense aroma of fraser fir, you can look at spiderwebs so elaborate they seem to have no end, and caterpillars packaged neatly in their cocoons. ~ At the Collins Creek Picnic Area, Signpost 18.

Such subtleties are what the Smokies are all about. Along Newfound Gap Road, myriad paths invite discovery of nature—and self-discovery. Quiet walkways abound, their signs beckoning with trails that have "no particular destination, so walk as far as you like and then return."

Occasionally, the silence is interrupted by angry screams and the violent rustling of leaves. Don't worry; it's just the tiny red squirrel, the "mountain boomer," foraging for food. Much less noisy but a whole lot bigger, the black bear occasionally shows up along trails and roadsides, usually searching for food to maintain its 200- to 400-pound bulk. Don't give him any. Bears who get food become bolder and are easy prey for poachers. How else to act? "Theories abound about how to act if you should confront a bear," says the *Great Smoky Mountains National Park Handbook*. "All such theories assume . . . that bear behavior is predictable. It is not." *Note*: Most park rangers recommend just quietly going about your business.

You don't have to leave Newfound Gap Road to see the Oconaluftee River, which presents itself again and again, sometimes as a fizzing stream and at other times as a dead-calm mirror of water. You can park at the **Oconaluftee River** stop and walk by water as clear as air and inlaid with silken smooth rocks.

The Oconaluftee River is nicknamed "The Lufty," though its real name is *Ekwanulti*, or "place-by-the-river" in Cherokee, a word white settlers butchered into Oconaluftee.

The displays at the **Logging Exhibit** are comical. A caption for a black-and-white photo of early loggers reads: "Definitely not soup-eating people." These bulky, craggy, rheumy-eyed henchmen for the lumber companies hacked and drank their way through the Smokies, and had a life expectancy of about 40 years. Between 1900 and 1920, they wiped out over three-quarters of the Smokies. Had the decimation not been so sudden and so deft, perhaps there would be no national park. ~ Just south of Newfound Gap.

Admittedly, it is difficult to imagine the Smokies almost gone, considering their splendor today. As you drive northward, valleys are rippled and so soft looking you want to reach out to feel their greenness. Some overlooks are tightly plaited with sharp summits, others are smooth and rambling and awash in purple haze. The highest point in the park, spectacular 6643-foot **Clingmans Dome**, is up a seven-mile road that snakes across rocky precipices, which is followed by a steep half-mile hike up the mountain. The turnoff for the road comes just before the Tennessee line (you'll recognize it as the place where everyone else is turning), though it is closed in winter.

The drive to the dome is eerie. Fog and frigid air roll down the mountainsides and wash over your car, and giant trees dangle from black boulders overhead. Storms come often to this corner of the Smokies, even when the sun stays firmly over Newfound Gap. The forests change quickly, and by the time you reach the top you can see red spruce and fraser firs growing side by side—unusual outside of Central Canada.

Sadly, most of the mature fraser firs are dead, having been felled by the wee balsam woolly adelgid, an insect that invaded from Europe earlier this century. More than a hundred variety of trees do surround the dome, including the mountain ash with its flaming red bunches of berries, and nearly 1500 types of flowering plants—all lovers of the constant moisture available way up here.

A half-mile trail of concrete spirals to the top of the dome (a mile round-trip) and is steep enough to make your shins ache. Still, millions of visitors have walked or taken their wheelchairs up into the clouds to be on the Clingmans Dome platform, in hopes of catching a glimpse of the thickly woven forest and creased hills and valleys that run into sheer blue sky.

It makes perfect sense that the only lodge in Great Smoky Mountains National Park is thoroughly hidden. To get to **LeConte Lodge,** you have to hike five and a half miles up the third-highest Appalachian mountain, 6593 feet to be exact, and that's *after* making a reservation a year in advance. The signs at the trailheads for the lodge say: "None of the five trails should be considered a stroll. You may encounter ice and snow as late as May and as early as October." You may also encounter bears, who have figured out just what goes on at the lodge (lots of home cooking). Do not feed or approach them, but continue calmly (as possible) on the trail.

The lodge's seven hand-hewn cabins and three group buildings with individual bedrooms sit atop Mount LeConte and are extremely primitive—no showers or electricity (put that television right out of your mind). There are flush toilets that freeze up in the coldest weather, and fresh water you carry to a metal washbasin (bring a washcloth and hand towel) for freshening up. The views are fabulous, the two meals a day fresh and filling, the mood soul-cleansing. Most people stay one night, a few stay two. Room rates include breakfast and dinner. Most important: The lodge starts taking reservations for the *following season* on October 1 of each year, and usually books up by October 31. The season runs from late March to late November. ~ 865-429-5704;

LODGING

www.lecontelodge.com, e-mail reservations@lecontelodge.com.
ULTRA-DELUXE.

Otherwise, there's camping. Ten developed campgrounds are sprinkled throughout the park and accommodate tents and some RVs and trailers, though there are no hookups. There are picnic tables, fireplaces, restrooms and fresh water at each campground. One of the most popular campgrounds in the Smokies is **Smokemont** in North Carolina. ~ Newfound Gap Road, Signpost 19. Also try **Elkmont** campgrounds. ~ Little River Road, Signpost 3, on the way to Cades Cove. In Tennessee there is **Cades Cove**. ~ Cades Cove Loop, about 23 miles from Newfound Gap Road. These campgrounds are open year-round, but reservations are accepted only for the high season—May 15 through October 31 —by contacting **Biospherics**. ~ 800-365-2267. You may also want to contact **Great Smoky Mountains National Park Services**. ~ 865-436-1200, fax 865-436-1220. You can call up to five months in advance, which is a good idea for weekends in summertime and fall foliage in October. The fee is $14 to $20 per night.

HIDDEN ▶   For less crowded camping, try **Cataloochee** in North Carolina. ~ Cataloochee Road, off Route 40, on the park's southeastern

HIDDEN ▶   side. Or try **Balsam Mountain** campgrounds, also in North Carolina. ~ Balsam Mountain Road, off Route 19, south of Cataloochee. These and the park's other five campgrounds are open April through October, but you can't make reservations. Fees range from $12 to $17 per night.

Backcountry campsites, including 16 hike-in shelters, are also scattered throughout the park. A backcountry permit is required, though there is no fee. Pick up a permit at any of the visitors centers and ranger stations. Campers can also get a permit by contacting the park's Backcountry Office, which accepts reservations for specific backcountry sites for up to 30 days in advance. The office is open Monday through Friday from 8 a.m. to 4:30 p.m. ~ 865-436-1231.

DINING   There aren't any dining establishments in these parts, so be sure to pack a picnic and find a table. Dozens of picnic tables are set

---

DAM FOG

Near Bryson City, North Carolina, on the Great Smoky Mountains National Park's southern end, **Lakeview Drive** goes for six scenic miles, then dead ends. The lake is **Fontana Lake**, framed in deep green hills and corralled by a dam 25 miles downstream, whose waters come from the Tuckasegee River. Take a dawn drive and see fog curl off the glassy water like steam rising from a vat, a haunting morning mountain portrait. ~ Off Route 19.

among the thick green woods, beside the thunder of waterfalls and faint swish of slow-going streams, and atop mountains that look across to more mountains. Better views and atmosphere can't be had anywhere.

Try the stellar bookstore at the **Oconaluftee Visitors Center**. ~ Newfound Gap Road, near the North Carolina park entrance. Also check out the **Cades Cove Visitors Center**. ~ Cades Cove Loop. There is also a good selection of materials at **Sugarlands Visitors Center**. ~ Newfound Gap Road, near the Tennessee park entrance. All of these bookstores have volumes on everything relating to the Smokies. Pioneer life, the Cherokees, photo essays, birdwatching and wildflower guides, audio tapes on Smokies' sights, children's coloring books, jigsaw puzzles—good things to fill the mind while wandering the mountains.

SHOPPING

A mountaintop drenched in full moonlight, the flash of a white-tail deer vanishing into blackness, the ferocious rustling of a red squirrel, the angry grunts of wild boar—these are the night scenes of Great Smoky Mountains National Park. Spend a night in the woods and you may find it more thrilling than any nightclub.

NIGHTLIFE

To better understand what goes on after dusk and also during the day, rangers lead nighttime walks and host fireside chats and slide shows on the Smokies. For example in fall they might describe how animals, particularly the black bear, hibernate. In the spring, you'll hear what happens when they wake up with a big appetite. Programs are held throughout the park. For a schedule, call 865-436-1291.

Cherokee & Bryson City

At the threshold of Great Smoky Mountains National Park and the heart of the 56,573-acre Cherokee Indian Reservation, Cherokee, North Carolina, is both tourist haven and cultural and business center. Route 441 North runs the brief length of town, strung with chain motels, putt-putt golf, sidewalk vendors, gem-mining troughs, a skylift across from the Fort Tomahawk Mall, and tribal casinos whose cacophonous, neon interior flickers with video poker, video craps and video blackjack machines (but no tables). Tour buses regularly pull up and disgorge their contents into the casino, which stays open 24 hours a day. Then there are seemingly countless roadside stands selling "Indian" souvenirs. The miniature tepees and wigwams and long feather headdresses aren't authentic; the Cherokee lived in permanent wood and clay mud homes and wore headbands with a few feathers. There's also a matter of human decency—or lack of it. The Redskin Motel and Wigwam Motel surely could be better named.

SIGHTS

There is still good reason to stop in **Cherokee**. Start with the **Museum of the Cherokee Indian**, which sets things straight about these peaceful, highly intelligent people. The video and audio displays and exhibits of artifacts tell how the Cherokee lived in the Smokies for thousands of years and let the land be. How they assembled villages along the rivers, hunted only animals they could eat or use for clothing and how, like the ancient Maya, they turned to the forest for medicine, employing more than 400 plants for healing. They were artists and craftspeople, passionate dancers and worshipers of one god called *YOWA*. They had seven clans (two were named Wild Potato and Long Hair) and a leader named Sequoyah who, in 1821, created the Cherokee written language. Shortly thereafter, in a holocaust called "The Trail of Tears," the Cherokees were driven from their homes and herded like cattle to Oklahoma. More than 4000 died. Admission. ~ Route 441 North, Cherokee; 828-497-3481; www.cherokeemuseum.org.

Oconaluftee Indian Village re-creates a 1750 Cherokee town. Take the one-hour tour (which is offered every ten minutes) and walk through cool, fragrant forest on spongy paths of peat moss, wide and firm enough for wheelchairs. You can pause at various huts and homes to watch the craftspeople and hear them tell about their works. Women make beaded necklaces using thread from hemp and needles made of deer hooves, and weave baskets of river cane and white oak, dying them with roots and bark. Men carve blowguns from river cane and demonstrate their aim, and make bear traps of logs, fish traps of hickory bark and buckskin, and teeny bird traps with teeny trap doors on top. Each exhibit is only as good as its narrators, and some are more enthusiastic than others. At the end, everyone gathers in a seven-sided council chamber (a side for each clan) to hear what they haven't heard yet about the modern Cherokees: few know the language Sequoyah created in the nineteenth century, most are Baptist and speak with a Southern accent, and their land is held in a federal trust. Open mid-May to late October. Admission. ~ Route 441 North, Cherokee; 828-497-2315; www.ocanalufteevillage.com.

Sequoyah, leader of the Cherokees, is thought to be the only person ever to design and perfect an entire alphabet.

For more information on the Cherokee area, stop by the **Cherokee Visitors Center**. ~ Route 441 North, Cherokee; 828-497-9195, 800-438-1601; www.cherokee-nc.com.

It's 15 squiggly miles on Route 19 west from Cherokee to Bryson City. Part of the way is through the thickly wooded Cherokee Indian Reservation and its speck-sized Birdtown. The road rises and falls and S-curves all over the place, and your ears pop as you careen around green caverns and mountains.

Bryson City is a country outpost, a thin wedge of town between the Nantahala River and the mountains. A handsome city hall with a four-sided clock tower presides over the downtown of red brick, and there's Clampitt Hardware, ancient-looking Nabers Drive-In, and The Best Little Hair House in Town.

Here also is a depot for the **Great Smoky Mountains Railroad,** a big attraction offering big fun around these parts. The reconditioned steam and diesel-electric locomotives, brightly painted primary colors, follow routes laid in the 1890s. Numerous trips are offered, the most popular being a four-and-a-half-hour excursion down into the deep, densely wooded Nantahala Gorge, stopping for lunch at a restaurant in the gorge. Adventurers should opt for the seven-hour gorge trip that includes whitewater rafting on the Nantahala River. Trips are offered on varying days and times, from early July to early October. ~ Everett Street, Bryson City; 828-586-8811, 800-872-4681; www.gsmr.com.

The railway's other popular excursion is a four-hour round-trip to the Tuckasegee River from **Dillsboro,** offered year-round. And on summer Saturdays, there's a dinner ride in an old-fashioned dining car (on the menu: cornish game hen with wild rice and pecans, filet mignon and grilled seasonal vegetables with brandy creme or zinfandel demi-glace). It's recommended that reservations for all excursions be made several weeks ahead. ~ Depot: Front Street, Bryson City; 828-586-8811, 800-872-4681.

LODGING

In Cherokee there are dozens of motor court–style motels, some looking more worn than others, crowded along Route 441 and just off it. Otherwise, there are about 30 private campgrounds. The **Cherokee Visitors Center** can provide a list of accommodations. ~ Route 441 North, Cherokee; 828-497-9195, 800-438-1601; www.cherokee-nc.com.

Better, though, is a stay in one of the engaging inns or bed and breakfasts around Bryson City.

◄ *HIDDEN*

A more comfortable place than **Fryemont Inn** cannot be imagined. The fetching, 1923 bark-covered building sits on a hill, with a fountain-filled pond and a vast porch overlooking the Smoky Mountains. An enormous stone fireplace and long table set with board games make the lobby extra inviting. Rich woods are rampant throughout; 37 rooms are paneled with chestnut and have private baths, ceiling fans, and pocket windows that draw in the cool mountain air. Rates include breakfast and dinner. Closed December to mid-April. For plusher accommodations, take one of the eight air-conditioned suites in the inn's ultra-deluxe-priced cottages, open year-round. ~ Fryemont Street, off Veterans Boulevard, Bryson City; 828-488-2159, 800-845-4879; www.frye montinn.com, e-mail fryemont@dnet.net. DELUXE TO ULTRA-DELUXE.

Text continued on page 116.

Best Country Cookin'
in the Smokies

If mountains of mashed potatoes dripping with fresh-churned butter, peppery crusted fried chicken that crumbles to the touch, fat slabs of the sweetest ham, soup bowls bubbling with butter beans, and the fluffiest hot biscuits drizzled with honey sound like a good way to eat, then go to **The Jarrett House**.

You won't be alone. Every year tens of thousands of people eat at this venerable old house in the captivating little town of Dillsboro, along Route 441 about 13 miles south of Cherokee. Many patrons are on their way to catch a train, or are getting off a train. The popular **Great Smoky Mountains Railroad** has its main depot in Dillsboro and operates four-hour sightseeing tours to Bryson City along the Tuckasegee River. ~ Front Street; 828-586-8811, 800-872-4681; www.gsmr.com.

Most days from morning till night, you can see folks in the front-porch rockers at The Jarrett House, waiting for their turn at one of the wood tables in the dining room. The mood here is pure Southern hospitality: courteous waitresses in pinafores, lacy wreaths on the doors, baskets of fresh flowers on every table, the shine of white china, the clang of dishes, the air redolent with country-cooked food.

Things move quickly; minutes after you're seated and the sweet iced tea is poured into glasses, the waitress returns with bowls and platters burdened with so many meats and vegetables, potatoes and breads, you are certain she is heading for another table. She isn't.

The bowls and platters are left on the table, and you help yourself to all the food. If a dish starts looking empty, it's quickly refilled. Everything is good, right down to the legendary vinegar pie, which is made with vinegar but tastes nothing like vinegar—more like a candy custard tucked between two crumbly crusts. Alcoholic beverages are not served, but you can bring a bottle of wine. Most people don't. ~ 100 Haywood Street, Dillsboro; phone/fax 828-586-0265, 800-972-5623; www.jarretthouse.com. MODERATE.

Part of The Jarrett House appeal is its past as the Mount Beulah Hotel, built in 1884 by William Allen Dills after the Western North Carolina

Railway starting passing through the area. In 1886, the hotel became famous after two women visited from the North Carolina coast—and smoked.

The other reason the place is so appealing are its current owners, the Hartbarger family, famous for their gracious, sincere hospitality and ability to keep things running smoothly. The Jarrett House is also their inn, with 16 guest rooms in the main, three-story building decorated with handsome antiques like clawfoot tubs, poster beds, pitchers and bowls. Seven plush, modern rooms in an annex have decks that overlook the town and mountains. All rooms have air conditioning. Closed December through March. ~ MODERATE.

From The Jarrett House you can walk around **Dillsboro** and enjoy its charm. Peaked roofs and church steeples angle against blue mountain sky, and bakeries and coffee and tea houses open their doors to the sunshine of spring and summer. Colorful clapboard stores framed in white picket gather along two blocks of **Haywood Street** and **Front Street** and the lanes in between, and you can shop for hours.

The Cheddar Box easily satisfies a cheese fetish. The cookbooks, fudge and gourmet teas and coffees here make great gifts. ~ Front Street; 828-586-4442.

Bradley's General Store is just what you hope for from an old-time emporium: two rambling floors filled with bins of dime candy, homemade jams and jellies crowned with checkered cloth, rag rugs, antique bikes, oxen yokes and stuffed animals for the kids. Plus, there's a soda fountain. ~ 52 Front Street; 828-586-3891.

There are two outstanding galleries. The first is **The Golden Carp**, whose original watercolors, vases, baskets and other gifts draw from eclectic styles. ~ Webster Street; 828-586-5477. The other is **Dogwood Crafters**, a nonprofit cooperative where about 100 artists contribute everything from stained glass and wood sculpture to linens, baskets, quilts and pottery. ~ 90 Webster Street; 828-586-2248.

For barbecue, go to **Dillsboro Smokehouse** and have hickory-smoked beef, pork, baby back ribs or turkey attended by barbecue beans, hush-puppies, yam patties and onion rings. Low-fat, heart-healthy items are also on the menu. ~ Haywood Street; 828-586-9556. BUDGET TO MODERATE.

HIDDEN ▶   Two miles east of Bryson City, a mile up a mountain road through hemlock and spruce forest, is the aptly named **Hemlock Inn**. The low-slung, pewter-colored building resembles a mountain motel, and there are several cabins tucked in the woods. The 22 rooms are plain but modern, with carpet, wood paneling and poster beds. It's awfully quiet up here, except during big family-style breakfasts and dinners which are included in the rates. The inn is closed early November to mid-April. ~ Route 19, Bryson City; 828-488-2885, fax 828-488-8985; www.hemlockinn.com, e-mail hemlock@dnet.net. DELUXE TO ULTRA-DELUXE.

Right in whitewater country, the popular **Nantahala Village Mountain Resort & Meeting Center** is surrounded by 200 acres of lush mountain forest. Choose from 11 rooms in the 1948 stone lodge along the road or drive up the hill and stay in one of 50 cabins, many outfitted with porches that look into trees. The decor is simple and woodsy. There's a swimming pool and a restaurant (offering fine dining), a recreation hall and riding stables. Closed January and February. ~ Route 19, about nine miles west of Bryson City; 828-488-2826, 800-438-1507, fax 828-488-9634; www.nvnc.com, e-mail nvinfo@nvnc.com. DELUXE.

HIDDEN ▶   Stuck way out in the western corner of the Smokies, **Fontana Village Resort** is where one goes to really get away. Families in particular have been finding this place since it opened in back in 1947, right after the Tennessee Valley Authority built Fontana Dam and created 31-mile-long Fontana Lake. As you might expect, there are plenty of water activities—including fishing, canoeing, boating, scenic cruising and houseboat rentals—as well as mountain biking, horseback riding, miniature golf, nightly dances and bonfires, arts-and-crafts workshops, tennis courts, shuffle-board courts and three swimming pools (translation: The kids will be out of your hair). In season, guests have a choice of dining at one of two casual eateries, or picking up some groceries at the general store. Accommodations vary from older, moderately priced rooms in rustic cottages and the inn to more contemporary, amenity-packed cottages with ultra-deluxe price tags. Call for hours from Labor Day to Memorial Day. ~ Off Route 28, about 36 miles west of Bryson City; 828-498-2211, 800-849-2258, fax 828-498-2345; www.fontanavillage.com. MODERATE.

DINING

HIDDEN ▶   In a big dining room warmed by a big fireplace, the **Fryemont Inn** serves time-honored Southern dishes with great success. There's plenty of trout on the menu, as well as braised lamb shank, baked Virginia ham with raisin sauce and roast breast of turkey with pecan dressing; specials and side dishes tend to change with the season. Despite the polished surroundings—gleaming wood floors, white and plum linens—dress is mountain casual. Big breakfasts are also served, but there's no lunch. Cocktails available.

Closed December to late April. ~ Fryemont Street, off Veterans Boulevard, Bryson City; 828-488-2159. MODERATE.

Next door to Fryemont, dining is more homey at the **Randolph House,** though reservations are a must. Owners Bill and Ruth Randolph Adams serve on the terrace of their whitewashed 1895 home or inside in the little dining room. Entrées vary nightly, but might include veal Marsala, stuffed trout, shrimp scampi or prime rib. Best are the homemade desserts: apple pie, rich fruit cobblers, peanut butter supremes. There's wine, beer and mixed beverages. Closed November to mid-April. ~ 223 Fryemont Road, off Spring Street, Bryson City; 828-488-3472. MODERATE.

◄ *HIDDEN*

The folks at **Hemlock Inn** go real casual. They bring out dishes of down-home cookin'—green beans, broccoli casserole, spaghetti, country ham, carrot cake, homemade biscuits—and set them on lazy Susans in the middle of big wood tables. Then everyone helps themselves. You'll need a reservation if you're not staying at the inn. Closed November to mid-April. ~ Off Route 19, Bryson City; 828-488-2885; www.innbook.com/hemlock. html. MODERATE.

◄ *HIDDEN*

Nothing seems more enjoyable after whitewater rafting on the Nantahala River than sitting on the sun porch of **Nantahala Village Grill,** nursing a cup of hot herbal tea, and looking out across the forest and hills. If it's lunchtime, order the homemade soup and the Great Smoky Sandwich, with smoked turkey, monterey jack cheese, bacon and chive mayonnaise. There's lots of chicken and pasta on the dinner menu, plus vegetarian specials and the perennial country ham and mountain trout. The main dining room is atmospheric with its worn wood floors and granddaddy fireplace. Brown bagging. Closed December to mid-March. ~ Route 19-74, about nine miles west of Bryson City; 828-488-9616; www.nvnc.com. MODERATE TO DELUXE.

Bypass all those souvenir shops in Cherokee selling bogus "Indian" items and instead go to **Qualla Arts and Crafts.** The delicate and detailed pieces at this artists' cooperative include soapstone carvings, white oak baskets, soft sculpture dolls and low-fired

SHOPPING

AUTHOR FAVORITE

A sure sign a Southern cook knows her stuff is the size of her fried chicken: petite pieces fry faster, are crispier and sweeter, and hence fly out of the kitchen. They do that at **The Jarrett House.** I can't help but eat too much—though I do save room for the marvelous vinegar pie. See page 114 for more information.

pottery so fragile it cannot hold water. ~ Route 441 North, Cherokee; 828-497-3103.

NIGHTLIFE The story of the Cherokee, from their ancestors' crossing of the Bering Straight 10,000 years ago to their being nearly decimated by white men, is replayed on summer nights in the outdoor pageant **Unto These Hills**. The production is both popular and well-done. During its mid-June-through-August run each year, nearly 100,000 people crowd the amphitheater, built after World War II by Cherokee stonemasons and American GIs. Call ahead for tickets or purchase them at the door. Closed September to mid-June. ~ Route 441 North, Cherokee; 828-497-2111, 866-554-4557; www.untothesehills.com, e-mail chevatt@dnet.net.

Cherokee is a dry area (no liquor sold in establishments), so you'll have to go to Bryson City for a drink and some music.

HIDDEN ▶ Most relaxing is the **Fryemont Inn**, an inn/restaurant with a cozy lounge. ~ Fryemont Road, off Spring Street, Bryson City; 828-488-2159.

The lounge at **Smokey Ridge Restaurant** is a fine place for a drink. Closed Sunday through Wednesday. ~ 385 Arlington Avenue, Bryson City; 828-488-2300.

▼ ▼ ▼ ▼ ▼ ▼ ▼ ▼ ▼ ▼ ▼ ▼
Maggie Valley & Waynesville Area

Constantly linked by promotional ads and separated geographically by only 12 hilly miles, Maggie Valley and Waynesville aren't at all alike. Maggie Valley came to life around 1900 as a resort town and exists today for tourists; its main drag, Route 19, is edged with country novelty shops and motels whose neon signs give a simple "Yes" or "No." Waynesville is a real live working town with a hardware store and pharmacy and an actual downtown with a Main Street. There are places to shop and stay here, but they don't shout their presence. Rather, they are stowed under painted awnings or along side streets.

SIGHTS Situated seventeen miles east of Maggie Valley, the **Old Pressley** is one of the oldest operating mines in North Carolina and the source of the 1445-carat Star of the Carolinas sapphire (found in the late 1980s and now housed in Asheville, in the Colburn Gem and Mineral Museum). You might be able to find your own huge sapphire or moonstone, but even if you don't, you can picnic with mountain views and learn more about mineral deposits in the gift shop at this ancient volcanic site. ~ 240 Pressley Mine Road, Canton; 828-648-6320; www.oldpressleymine.com, e-mail cjohnboy2@aol.com.

Soco Gardens Zoo is a compact but pretty place with animals in small pens. Wheelchair-accessible paths wend through the gardens, with views of a bear, wallabies, a snow leopard, jaguars, emus and other creatures. Most popular with kids are the two snake shows, one venomous and one nonvenomous, and the petting area. Closed November through April. Admission. ~ 3578 Soco Road, off Route 19, Maggie Valley; 828-926-1746; www. socogardenszoo.com.

Go the opposite direction on Route 19 to Route 276 North, then head about two miles to **Hemphill Road** for a drive through the country. You're actually climbing the mountain (switch to low gear when the car starts groaning), with panoramas of whitewashed fences and cranberry-red barns, angus cattle grazing on knolls and apple trees burdened with fruit, narrow little churches propped up on hills and homes perched across creeks, and tobacco drying in old sheds.

◄ HIDDEN

For more information on Maggie Valley or Waynesville, stop by Gateways to the Smokies. ~ 1233 North Main Street, Waynesville; 800-334-9036.

To get to **Waynesville**, though, you'll have to go back to Route 19 and take Route 276 South. You'll pass through a commercial area with fast-food chains before arriving in the handsome downtown of red-brick buildings, with low peaks off in the distance. Take awhile to walk around, browse the handful of shops and visit the **Museum of North Carolina Handicrafts**. Among the 2000-plus pieces of talent: rivercane baskets trimmed in honeysuckle vine, handmade flutes, fiddles and dulcimers, and fiber art colored with walnut hulls and pokeberry. Closed November through April. Admission. ~ 49 Shelton Street; 828-452-1551.

If you love golf, stay at **Maggie Valley Resort & Country Club**. The front nine holes of the picturesque, par-72 championship course lie on the valley floor, the back nine climb the mountain. The two-bedroom, two-bath luxury condominiums overlook the greens and fairways, and so do many of the rooms in the main lodge. The rates range from moderate to ultra-deluxe. In winter, you pay budget rates and play unlimited golf—but then there is the snow. A good restaurant, exercise room and pool are among the other amenities. ~ 1819 Country Club Drive, off Route 19, Maggie Valley; 828-926-1616, 800-438-3861, fax 828-926-2906; www.maggievalleyresort.com, e-mail golf@maggievalley resort.com. DELUXE.

LODGING

The rustic little houses at **Twinbrook Resort Cottages**, stashed in the woods, have kitchens, fireplaces and porches stacked with firewood. Carl and Viola Henry started the place in 1947 and their extensive family provides exuberant hospitality. Cottages have pine-paneled walls and old-time decor, televisions and microwaves, all in all clean and homey. You can pitch horseshoes, swim in the indoor pool or take the kids to the playground. ~ Off Route 19, Maggie Valley; 828-926-1388, 800-305-8946, fax 828-926-2943; www.twinbrookresort.com. DELUXE TO ULTRA-DELUXE.

The **Cataloochee Ranch** is a comfy compound high on a mountain, formerly a sheep and cattle farm but now a place to ski, hike, trout fish and ride horseback. Wildflower meadows cascade down this 1000-acre property and peaks ripple across the horizon. There's a historic ranch house, a newer lodge and several cabins with decor ranging from rustic to modern. Braided rugs, patterned quilts and wood walls give a home-style ambiance. Families usually go for the cabins, which have refrigerators, fireplaces and coffeemakers. The Cataloochee ski area, open at night, is a mile away. Other activities include clogging, square dancing and lawn games. The regular season is April to November, when breakfast and dinner are included in the rates; open select weekends for skiing during the winter. ~ Fie Top Road, three miles off Route 19, Maggie Valley; 828-926-1401, 800-868-1401, fax 828-926-9249; www.cataloochee-ranch.com. ULTRA-DELUXE.

About 30 minutes northwest of Waynesville, **WindDancers** has stylish rooms in log buildings set among llama pastures in a Smoky Mountain cove. The llamas will tote your gourmet lunch should you choose a guided hike across the 270-acre ranch. Or you can stick close to your room, which features a gas log fireplace, high-beamed ceilings and tub for two. Every room comes with a deck and mountain view. There are nine rooms, including two two-bedroom suites with kitchens. Rates include breakfast. ~ 1966 Martins Creek Road, Clyde; 828-627-6986, 877-627-3330, fax 828-627-0754; www.winddancersnc.com, e-mail info@winddancersnc.com. DELUXE TO ULTRA-DELUXE.

HIDDEN ►

The **Yellow House** is indeed yellow, a handsome two-story home decorated with columns and chimneys and set along a knoll riotously planted with flowers, shrubs and soft green lawn. The three rooms and seven suites are luxurious and beautifully adorned. All have private baths and working fireplaces, and most have a private balcony or patio; suites boast a two-person whirlpool tub. You can take breakfast in your room, the dining room or the veranda; hors d'oeuvres are served in the evening— civilized living. ~ 89 Oak View Drive at Plott Creek Road, off Route 23-74, one mile west of Waynesville; 828-452-0991, 800-563-1236, fax 828-452-1140; www.theyellowhouse.com. DELUXE TO ULTRA-DELUXE.

HIDDEN ►

If one wanted to completely disappear into the woods, but in a luxurious way, there could not be a better place than **The Swag**. Guest rooms and private cabins are stylish and woodsy, variously adorned with stone fireplaces, secluded balconies and porches, plush quilts and Appalachian art. Great Smoky Mountains National Park starts out back, and you can hike for miles and be swallowed by deep green, dark woods. On cool nights, slip into the warmth of a big hot tub beneath an inky mountain sky. Room rates include all meals—fresh, imaginative regional fare. BYOB. Closed mid-November to late April. ~ Hemphill Road, six and a half miles off Route 276 North, Waynesville; 828-926-0430, 800-789-7672, fax 828-926-2036; www.theswag.com, e-mail letters@theswag.com. ULTRA-DELUXE.

Not quite as reclusive but still offering mountain privacy, the **Old Stone Inn** consists of seven stone and poplar buildings ◄ HIDDEN tucked among several acres of woods. Rooms and suites are simply furnished, and many are paneled in wood. A guest lounge offers opportunities for gazing into the fireplace, quiet conversation and sipping a glass of wine. Rates include breakfast, and Continental dishes from local ingredients are available at dinnertime. Closed January to Good Friday. ~ 109 Dolan Road, off Route 276 South, Waynesville; 828-456-3333, 800-432-8499; www.oldstoneinn.com. MODERATE TO DELUXE.

Balsam Mountain Inn is a big place among big mountains, a ◄ HIDDEN Colonial Revival manse with high-ceilinged rooms, book-filled libraries and long windows looking at the tips of 6000-foot Balsams. Yet the mood here is intimate, as befitting a turn-of-the-twentieth-century, weatherboard hotel that once drew travelers seeking restoration in area mineral springs. All 50 rooms have private baths and are warmly, simply decorated with wicker, oak and willow furnishings, antique iron beds and beadboard walls. The closest town, Balsam, is but a pindot in the woods, but Waynesville is only about ten miles away and the Blue Ridge Parkway is a half-mile. Hearty and healthy breakfasts (go for the french toast with sour cream and mountain blueberries) are included in the rate. ~ Off Route 74-23, a half-mile south of the

AUTHOR FAVORITE

The first time I drove to **The Swag** I feared I would fall off the earth: the dirt road simply doesn't want to stop—which makes the exquisitely designed inn at the end all that much more desirable, knowing you have the views, the artwork, the whole luxurious mountaintop (nearly) all to yourself. Parked on a mountaintop 5000 feet high, with gorgeous green lawn and fantastic views in every direction, this extraordinary place was put together with hand-hewn logs from numerous historic mountain buildings, including an 1800s church. See page 120 for more information.

Blue Ridge Parkway, Balsam; 828-456-9498, 800-224-9498, fax 503-212-9855; www.balsammountaininn.com, e-mail relax@ balsammountaininn.com. MODERATE TO DELUXE.

DINING

Maggie Valley is not known as a culinary haven, and Waynesville is only a notch better. "For a special night out," one valley chef says, "you'll have to drive to Asheville—we all do." You can, however, find filling down-home fare that satisfies on a cool mountain day.

Funky and favored by locals, **Saratoga's** serves homogenous American fare like chili, prime rib and fried onion rings, patty melts, chopped sirloin and soup from a can. The booths are mismatched, and there are paintings planted strangely in the rafters. ~ 2723 Soco Road, Maggie Valley; 828-926-1448. BUDGET TO MODERATE.

HIDDEN ►

For some of the best barbecue in the area, and the most unusual name, try another local hangout, **Butts on the Creek**, where you can, in fact, sit on a deck that butts onto Jonathan Creek. The hand-hewn wood interior is a rustic backdrop for housemade desserts (like Key lime pie and blackberry cobbler), hickory-smoked meats and fried corn on the cob. Side dishes vary from sweet potato casserole to creamed spinach, or you can go with the barbecue standards of cole slaw or beans. Closed Monday and from November through April. ~ 1580 Soco Road, Maggie Valley; 828-926-7885. BUDGET TO MODERATE.

Family-style **Snappy's** has reliable low-priced Italian food. The extensive menu lists lasagnas, calzones, chicken or eggplant parmesan, spaghetti, stromboli, and baked ziti, flounder, ham steak, pizzas and hot dogs. The decor is pleasant enough, with marble tabletops and silk ferns dangling from the ceiling. ~ Route 19, in the Eagle Shopping Plaza, Maggie Valley; 828-926-6126. BUDGET.

HIDDEN ►

With a reservation you can dine finely at **The Swag** for dinner. The chef at this remote mountaintop inn selects the freshest ingredients—trout from the farm down the mountain, just-picked apples and cranberries, herbs and vegetables from the backyard

---

A RESERVATION IN THE WOODS

Even if you don't stay at **Balsam Mountain Inn**, consider driving out for dinner. It's about ten miles from Waynesville, stashed way in the woods with 6000-foot peaks floating all around, the air crisp and reviving. You'll need a reservation to enjoy savory, well-prepared fare such as pecan-encrusted catfish, shrimp with garlic cheddar grits, grilled free-range chicken, blackened tuna and sunburst trout. ~ Off Route 74-23, just south of the Blue Ridge Parkway, Balsam; 828-456-9498; www.balsammountaininn.com. DELUXE.

garden—and turns them into luscious dishes. Tomato basil soup, grilled rainbow trout, cumin-crusted pork with red-currant wine sauce, and a variety of sorbets are examples of the everchanging menu. The dining room is an enormous wood space with a lofty ceiling. BYOB. Closed mid-November to late April. ~ Hemphill Road, six and a half miles off Route 276, Waynesville; 828-926-0430; www.theswag.com. ULTRA-DELUXE.

In a spacious house, **Bogart's** gives an open feeling with its soaring ceiling, stained-glass windows and loft dining room. The atmosphere is lively but tame enough for kids. The menu reads pub food: burgers, chili, French onion soup, broiled or fried trout, and colossal stuffed baked potatoes. Beer and wine served. Closed Sunday. ~ 303 South Main Street, Waynesville; 828-452-1313. BUDGET.

Route 19 through Maggie Valley is country craft central. The stores are, for the most part, pleasant places to pour through potpourri, pottery, antiques and lovely souvenirs for the folks back home (how about a bird mobile or cake-in-a-jar?).   **SHOPPING**

A stream bubbles behind **Maggie Mountaineer Crafts**, while the inside is perfumed by potpourri. Ceramics, butter churns, silk flowers, homemade fudge and mountain apples in season are available at this agreeable place. ~ Route 19, Maggie Valley; 828-926-3129; www.maggiemountaineercrafts.com.

In the market for Harley Davidson boots, wallets, belts and buckles or the like? Stop in at **Jack's Leather Shack**. ~ Route 19, Maggie Valley; 828-926-1055.

How about accessories for church? **Aunt Bee's Blessing Shop** stocks Bibles, hymnals and various other religious-themed items. Closed Sunday. ~ Route 19, Market Square, Maggie Valley; 828-926-3031.

Do your Christmas shopping anytime at **Cabbage Rose**, where the ornaments, imported from around the world, number in the thousands. Victorian gifts, collectibles and floral arrangements are also available. ~ Route 19, Maggie Valley; 828-926-3079.

Just west of Maggie Valley on Route 19 at **Soco Gap**, a number of craft shops are hinged along the mountainside, their excessive signs all announcing the "most photographed Smoky Mountains view." Some charge to look, but others just hope you'll be persuaded to step in and buy something. The view of the valley is admittedly soul-stirring: neatly plaited fields, crisp white farmhouses, soft mountains floating all around.

It's a little out of the way, but the gift shop at **The Swag** stocks   ◄ HIDDEN
some lovely local crafts, including birdhouses, jewelry, quilts and handpainted umbrellas. ~ Hemphill Road, six and a half miles off Route 276 North, Waynesville; 828-926-0430; theswag.com.

GateKeepers has collectibles, home accessories and pottery. Closed Sunday. ~ 4 North Main Street, Waynesville; 828-456-8820.

The colored-pencil scenes at T. Pennington Art Gallery are of western North Carolina landmarks and scenery, and are all done by owner Teresa Pennington. Closed Sunday. ~ 15 North Main Street, Waynesville; 828-452-9284.

Main Street in Waynesville is the perfect place to find high-quality artistry. Earthworks has a stellar selection of American Indian art and jewelry, as well as bronze sculpture, serigraphs and environmental T-shirts. ~ 21 North Main Street, Waynesville; 828-452-9500.

Mast General Store is a cousin of the first and famous Mast store in Valle Crucis. Spend an hour or two scanning great stuff—outdoor gear, cookware, jewelry, boots and tennis shoes, gourmet coffees, etc. ~ 63 North Main Street, Waynesville; 828-452-2101.

NIGHTLIFE Wednesday is jazz night at Saratoga's Cafe, while weekends bring entertainment by solo artists. The simplified soup-and-sandwich joint and local meeting spot serves beer and wine. ~ Route 19, Maggie Valley; 828-926-1448.

Put your clogging shoes on and head for Stompin' Ground. The big barn hosts a number of regional and national clogging teams, clomping to country, bluegrass and gospel Friday and Saturday nights from May through October. ~ Route 19, Maggie Valley; 828-926-1288.

If you happen to be a clog dancer, you'll find a warm welcome at the Stompin' Ground in Maggie Valley.

Maggie Valley Opry House is a wildly popular pickin' parlor. Live bluegrass and mountain music and dancing featured nightly May to mid-November. Cover. ~ Route 19, Maggie Valley; 828-926-9336.

Eagle Nest Entertainment is an 800-seat theater that hosts occasional events, sometimes big names. Cover. ~ Route 19, Maggie Valley; 828-926-9658.

Have a beer in the bar at Bogart's, a casual, crowded tavern serving good food and wine. ~ 303 South Main Street, Waynesville; 828-452-1313.

Outdoor Adventures

RIVER RUNNING

This is whitewater country. The Nantahala River, which runs southwest of Bryson City, is *the* place for rafting, kayaking, canoeing and innertubing. I like rafting the best. You can feel the smoothness of the riverbed stones under the raft's thin rubbery bottom. Anyone who has never tried whitewater rafting because of that deep-in-the-gut fear should try it here: The river is kind most of the time, the rapids are easy to exciting, and the surroundings sublime. The banks of the Nantahala are smothered in Edenic forest, and the air is fragrant and brisk. Every now and then the Great Smoky Mountains Railway chugs by overhead and people wave from the colorful train cars. Otherwise, there's only the sound of water running downriver.

The premier whitewater outfitter is **Nantahala Outdoor Center**. Reputed to be one of the nation's best whitewater schools, it offers one- to seven-day courses on everything from rafting, kayaking and canoeing to "frugal floating" downriver and mountain cycling. You can also join a half-day, all-day, or overnight trip involving any of the above. Students can stay in dorm-style bunkhouses, basic motel rooms or rental homes. There are three restaurants here, too. ~ 13077 Route 19 West, about 13 miles west of Bryson City; 828-488-2175, 800-232-7238; www.noc.com.

Among the other whitewater companies, **Endless River Adventures** has guided kayak and rafting excursions. ~ Bryson City; 828-488-6199, 800-224-7238; www.endlessriveradventures.com. **Tuckasegee Outfitters** does rafting and innertube trips down the tamer Tuckasegee River. ~ Route 74, near the junction of Route 441 South; 828-586-5050, 800-539-5683.

Also contact **Wildwater, LTD Rafting**, near Nantahala Village, for guided raft trips. ~ 10345 Route 19 West, Bryson City; 828-488-9130, 800-451-9972; www.wildwaterrafting.com.

FISHING

The Great Smoky Mountains need no introduction to trout fishers. More than 700 miles of streams and creeks offer fishing for rainbow and brown trout, smallmouth bass and rock bass. There are also brook trout, though it is illegal to catch them. There are limits on rainbow and brown trout as well. Only single-hook artificial lures may be used at all within the park (in other words, no live bait!), and a fishing license, available at bait-and-tackle shops outside the park, is required for anyone thirteen and older. If you plan to do some serious angling, pick up a copy of *Smoky Mountains Trout Fishing Guide* by Don Kirk.

Within the Cherokee Reservation are 30 miles of streams, three ponds—and plenty of trout and bass. Call the **Fish & Game Management of the Eastern Band of Cherokee Indians** for information on fishing on the reservation. ~ 828-497-5201.

In Bryson City, **Endless River Adventures** offers guided floatfishing cruises in dories as well as lake touring. You can flyfish or use a spinning rod to catch smallmouth bass, walleye and trout. ~ 828-488-6199.

You don't need a license to fish at a trout farm, but you will pay a per-fish fee. Some of these places are out in the boonies, down no-name country roads, so call ahead for directions. In Cherokee, contact **Morgan Mills Trout Farm**. ~ Big Cove Road, Cherokee; 828-497-9227. Or try **Fontana Village Trout Pond**. ~ Route 28, Fontana Dam; 828-498-2211. Also try **Holland's**

Trout Pond. ~ Holland Road, off Route 19, Maggie Valley. Fishing is open to the public at **Soco Gap Trout Farm.** ~ Route 19 West, Maggie Valley; 828-926-3635. You may also fish at **Ferguson's Trout Pond.** ~ Route 209, off Route 19, Maggie Valley; 828-627-6404.

SKIING

It's not Aspen, but there are ten runs at **Cataloochee Ski Area,** with a vertical drop of 740 feet and three chairlifts. Open for night skiing, it's a good place for first-timers. ~ Off Route 19, Maggie Valley; 828-926-0285.

GOLF

What could be better than teeing up on a crisp mountain morning, while watching the fog roll off the greens? You'll find a beautiful course at **Maggie Valley Resort.** ~ 1819 Country Club Drive, Maggie Valley; 828-926-1616, 800-438-3861. Check out the green at **Waynesville Country Club Inn.** ~ Country Club Drive, Waynesville; 828-452-4617, 800-627-6250. Tee off at **Springdale Country Club.** ~ Route 276, 11 miles south of Waynesville; 828-235-8451, 800-553-3027.

TENNIS

HIDDEN ▶

The crisp, cool mountain air is ideal for tennis. Practice your serve at the **Waynesville Country Club Inn.** ~ Country Club Drive, Waynesville; 828-425-2258, 800-627-6250. Also try **Fontana Village.** ~ Off Route 28, about 36 miles west of Bryson City; 828-498-2211, 800-849-2258.

The town of Canton (20 minutes east of Maggie Valley) has four courts open to the public year-round.

RIDING STABLES

Five stables within Great Smoky Mountains National Park offer guided trail rides from spring through fall. You can ride by the hour, half-day or full-day, or even take an overnight trip. All require reservations. Stables are located at **Smokemont Campground.** ~ North of Cherokee; 828-497-2373. In Tennessee, try

AUTHOR FAVORITE

One of the key reasons people come to this part of North Carolina is the river. The **Nantahala** is a great whitewater river, with Class II and III rapids (Class V being the most advanced and terrifying) that are perfect for novices and families with young children. You can raft, kayak or canoe down the immensely scenic river bordered with trees. Numerous whitewater outfitters line Route 19-74 about nine to 14 miles west of Bryson City, but by far the best is Nantahala Outdoor Center. ~ 13077 Route 19 West, about 13 miles west of Bryson City; 828-488-2175, 800-232-7238, fax 828-488-0301. For more on whitewater pursuits, see page 124.

Cades Cove. ~ 865-448-6286. You may also ride at **McCarter Stables.** ~ 865-436-5354. Or try **Smoky Mountain Stables.** ~ 865-436-5634.

Outside the park, you can saddle up at **Fontana Village.** ~ Route 28, about 36 miles west of Bryson City; 828-498-2211, 800-849-2258. Also try **Cataloochee Ranch.** ~ Fie Top Road, three miles from Route 19, Maggie Valley; 828-926-1401, 800-868-1401. If you're in Waynesville try riding at **Utah Mountain Riding Stables.** ~ Off Route 276, Waynesville; 828-926-1143. Also try **Queen's Farm Stables.** ~ 2607 Dellwood Road, off Route 19, Waynesville; 828-926-0718.

◄ HIDDEN

For excellent bike-trail maps, contact the North Carolina Department of Transportation's Bicycle Program. ~ 1552 Mail Service Center, Raleigh, NC 27699-1552; 919-733-2804.

BIKING

The steep, curvy, often unpaved roads of Great Smoky Mountains National Park make bicycling tough. One place that's great to bike is the **Cades Cove Loop** (11 miles one way) in Tennessee, a trek on gentle pavement, with spectacular scenery and historic stopovers to match.

Outside the park, **Route 28** (26 miles) from Route 19-74 west to Fontana Village is a little-traveled road through fairly easy to steep mountain terrain. At **Fontana Village** are numerous short and easy bike trails.

Bike Rentals   A concession at **Cades Cove Campground** within Great Smoky Mountains National Park rents bikes. You can also rent a mountain bike from **Euchella Mountain & Lake Cabins.** ~ Route 74, about 12 miles west of Bryson City; 828-488-8835. **Nantahala Outdoor Center** has mountain bikes and great trail maps, too. ~ 13077 Route 19 West, Bryson City; 828-488-2175, 888-662-1662 ext. 158. A bike-rental concession at **Fontana Village** is open year-round. ~ Route 28; 828-498-2211.

All distances listed for hiking trails are one way unless otherwise noted.

HIKING

GREAT SMOKY MOUNTAINS NATIONAL PARK   More than 800 miles of trails plunge into the deepest, most peaceful parts of Great Smoky Mountains National Park. Pick up a copy of the park's *Day Hikes* fold-out map and brochure, which lists more than 25 trails. It's only $1, and is available at the park's visitors centers. The Great Smoky Mountains Natural History Association sells books that thoroughly detail all the trails, including the excellent 575-page *Hiking Trails of the Smokies*, available for $16.95. ~ 416 Cherry Street, Gatlinburg, TN 37738; 865-436-0120.

Near the Deep Creek picnic shelter, take the moderately difficult **Juney Whank Falls Trail** (.3 mile) for a look at some beautiful

◄ HIDDEN

cascades. Also here are two easy trails, **Indian Creek Falls Trail** (3.9 miles) and **Toms Branch Falls** (.5 mile), with more water views.

From the Smokemont Campground, two lengthy, moderate-to-rugged trails lead into the deep woods. **Chasteen Creek Trail** (4 miles) passes a 15-foot waterfall on its switchback course up Hughes Ridge. **Smokemont Loop** (3.8 miles) is a cool walk through oak and cove hardwood forest.

In early summer, the **Forney Ridge Trail** (5.7 miles) is ablaze with azaleas. A moderate trek down 600 feet to the mountain clearing, it starts at the Clingmans Dome parking area.

The sign at **Chimney Tops Trail** (2 miles) says, "The view is worth the climb." Naturally, it's a popular hike, despite the vigorous, can't-catch-your-breath trek (including some rock scrambling) up 1335 feet to the twin summits the Cherokee called *Duniskwalguni*, or "forked antlers." Early mountaineers called them chimneys, and indeed you can peer down what appears to be a flue. The big view from up here is across Sugarland Valley, looking fabulous with its peaks marbled in moss and mountain laurel and rhododendron. The trail, which starts at Signpost 6 on Newfound Gap Road in Tennessee, is along a path first worn by the Cherokee.

Hike the first mile and a half of **Alum Cave Bluffs Trail** and you've taken the easy route, a fairly carefree walk along Alum Creek through hardwood and hemlock forest to Arch Rock, a natural tunnel. Go the last, strenuous three and a half miles to the bluffs and you'll be surrounded by mysterious rocky scenery, some masked in ferns, herbs and lichens. The trailhead is at Signpost 8 on Newfound Gap Road in Tennessee.

HIDDEN ▶   The pace of **Upper Little River Trail** (5.1 miles) is leisurely and the scenery includes spectacularly clear water rushing around boulders. Pick up the trail at the locked gate just above Elkmont Campground.

You can walk behind a waterfall if you take **Grotto Falls Trail** (3 miles), an easy stroll through dense, lush hardwood forest. You'll find the trailhead near Milepost 5 on the Roaring Fork Motor Nature Trail in Tennessee.

CHEROKEE AND BRYSON CITY   South of Bryson City near Wesser, the tough **Wesser Creek Trail** (3.5 miles) gives both a good workout and good views of the Nantahala range. Parts of the trail are narrow and straight up. You'll find the beginning along Route 1107, about one and a half miles off Route 19.

▼ ▼ ▼ ▼ ▼ ▼ ▼ ▼ ▼ ▼   The Great Smoky Mountains begin about 40 miles west
Transportation   of Asheville, North Carolina. **Route 40** heads west from
Asheville, then runs north along the eastern edge of
CAR   Great Smoky Mountains National Park. **Route 23** angles off Route
40 toward Waynesville. **Route 19** doglegs from Route 23 to

Maggie Valley and Cherokee, North Carolina's main entrance to the national park.

Newfound Gap Road, also called **Route 441**, slices through the middle of Great Smoky Mountains National Park for 32 miles, until Gatlinburg, Tennessee. The park is almost equally divided, crosswise, between North Carolina and Tennessee.

Asheville Regional Airport in Asheville, North Carolina, is about 40 miles from the Great Smoky Mountains. For information on airlines, airport shuttle service and car rentals, see the "Transportation" section of Chapter Two.

AIR

FIVE

The Blue Ridge Parkway

This is about a journey, not a place. It is a long, pure journey: 252 miles of mountains rippling blue against bold bright sky, water tumbling down granite walls in luscious torrents, white clouds shifting across deep green valleys. There are no stop signs or traffic lights, no neon or billboards to sully the scenery, so high above the rest of the world.

The Blue Ridge Parkway, that soul-cleansing journey across mountain peaks, is in fact called a "highway in the sky," though highway is too harsh a name. The trip along this two-lane road is slow and soothing, full of forests and flowers and curves, and many tunnels blasted through the middle of mountains. There is also the constant rush of air, whether one is nearing a rocky summit or snaking along famous Linn Cove Viaduct, an elevated S-curve around a mountain that gives the sensation of flying.

Actually, the Blue Ridge Parkway is 469 miles long, though only 252 of those miles are in North Carolina. The rest are in Virginia, the genesis of the parkway, a super-scenic star in the National Park system. Milepost zero is a mountain pass called Rockfish Gap in Virginia's Shenandoah National Park. From here, the parkway bends southwest, crossing the North Carolina line 217 miles later at Cumberland Knob, an outpost west of Mount Airy. The road keeps heading southwest, first through gently rolling farmland, then along the humpback mountains of North Carolina's High Country and its resort areas of Blowing Rock, Boone and Linville. The parkway passes by Asheville before finishing at Great Smoky Mountains National Park. A more perfect finale cannot be imagined.

More than 21 million people take the Blue Ridge Parkway every year. Despite its popularity and closeness to resort areas, the parkway seems far from civilization, as both the road and the strips of land on either side are a national park. Unfortunately, the strips are too narrow and development has crept in on portions of the parkway, mainly in Virginia. In North Carolina, you can drive a hundred miles and see a home or two, but you will never see a fast-food chain.

Neither will you notice a gypsy moth, balsam woolly adelgid or dogwood anthracnose, though you can occasionally see their destruction. The moth eats at oaks and maples and other low-elevation trees until they are ragged. The adelgid strikes higher on the mountains, injecting fraser firs with a liquid that deprives them of water and nutrients. The fir holocaust is apparent on the highest ridges, where the beautiful giants lay slain, entombed in a white, woolly material.

The lovely dogwood tree is also under attack. The dogwood anthracnose has been around for decades, but only in the last few years has it gotten serious. Like so many human diseases, it has no cure, at least not yet. Neither have park officials found a way to fight the gypsy moth or woolly aphid, though they are constantly trying.

Despite human and natural predators, the parkway remains a splendorous backwoods journey, which is just how its creators intended it. In the mid-1930s, Virginia Senator Harry F. Byrd proposed a road linking the Shenandoah National Park with Great Smoky Mountains National Park. It would trace the rim of the Blue Ridge and several other mountain ranges for nearly 500 miles and it would be paved—not a simple job considering the harsh, vertical terrain. Mountain folk, accustomed to riding on bumpy dirt roads that shut down in winter, scoffed at the idea of a "hard road" through the mountains.

But President Franklin Delano Roosevelt liked the idea, having just driven on Shenandoah's Skyline Drive, where he enjoyed the scenery immensely. More importantly, it would give hundreds of post-Depression workers a job and hopefully bring some tourism to the area. He helped sell the idea to Congress, and Virginia and North Carolina purchased the land for the road. The parkway was placed under the control of the National Park Service.

It would be several years before short spans were built and the Parkway opened—but fifty years before the journey was complete. In 1987, long after FDR had died, the Blue Ridge Parkway was finally made whole with the Linn Cove Viaduct, the section around Grandfather Mountain.

Today, you can get on the parkway and not have the drive interrupted even once. But of course that's not what the Blue Ridge Parkway is all about, for sprinkled along its squiggly length are dozens of stopovers, places to catch a dazzling view or picnic by a stream, to explore century-old log cabins or sit at a coffee shop and hear farmers talk about putting up hay. Here, at constantly cool altitudes that reach 6000 feet, are galleries where you can buy exquisite mountain art and crafts, and sprawling parks where you can fish, hike or pitch a tent and sleep close to the stars, emboldened by mountain darkness.

Along the Blue Ridge journey the scenery is forever changing, from dark to light and then dark again, from brilliantly clear to hauntingly hazy, from remote stretches of pastureland to deep woods to crowded portions peopled by sightseers in RVs.

Blossoms decorate the parkway nearly all year. Dandelions open as early as February and mask the roadsides until June. Dwarf iris, buttercups and mayapples come along in March, and then there are Indian paintbrushes and golden groundsels. The blooming of the dogwoods and mountain laurel in April and May and the rhododendrons in June is nearly celestial, as entire mountains shimmer in pink and white and yellow.

The parkway is wonderful right before and after a rain. When a storm nears, there is cool, blunt stillness, and blue darkness painting the sky. Afterward mist rises from the road, sun glints off wet leaves, animals emerge from the forest—the musky smell of renewal. During a storm, however, it is best to pull off the parkway, lest one miscalculate the sharp angle of a mountain curve.

On the coldest days, when the rain turns to snow and ice, much of the Parkway closes. On the sections that stay open, the Blue Ridge journey is both eerie and invigorating. You can drive next to waterfalls suspended by the icy breath of winter, and revel in the skeletal silhouettes of trees.

SIGHTS   Winter does shut down some parts of the road, so it's best to call ahead before setting out. Most parkway facilities are closed from November through April. For information, contact the **Blue Ridge Parkway**. ~ 199 Hemphill Knob Road, Asheville, NC 28803; 828-298-0398, emergencies 800-727-5928; www.nps.gov/blri.

You can also get information at any of the visitors centers, including the one at **Cumberland Knob**, the parkway's first stopover after you cross from Virginia into North Carolina. Distances on the parkway are measured by mileposts, those little concrete markers with black numbers on the side of the road. Heading into North Carolina, the numbers get bigger. ~ Milepost 217.5.

Cumberland Knob is also the historical beginning of the Blue Ridge Parkway, the first section built back in the 1930s, 12.7 miles of lonesome road with a big view. The picnic area and hiking trails here are compliments of the Civilian Conservation Corps. The visitor center can supply all sorts of literature on the park, including excellent maps, blooming schedules and hiking trail guides. There's also a bookstore where you can pick up a copy of the *Blue Ridge Parkway Guide* by former park ranger and naturalist, William G. Lord. The thorough, two-volume guide lists every stop on the 469-mile-long parkway, delving deep into the history, flora and fauna of the mountains.

After Cumberland Knob the parkway wends southwest through North Carolina quiet country, north of the High Country and west of the Piedmont, a nowheresville where valleys run deep and long, and cows graze in pastures framed in split-log fences, crooked and weathered. It doesn't take long to get used to the parkway; who wouldn't enjoy driving through a seemingly endless Eden, pausing only to gaze at something extraordinarily beautiful, even historic?

There are motorists who, strangely, pull off at overlooks and historical markers and never roll down their car windows, preferring to take their views and history from the air conditioned, music-flooded comfort of their car. The Blue Ridge is not something to be experienced with the radio playing, nor should it be done hurriedly. The speed limit is 45 miles per hour, less on hairpin curves, though a slower pace allows better vistas. Commercial vehicles are banned from the parkway but tour buses and RVs aren't, so if you find your view blocked by one, pull over at the

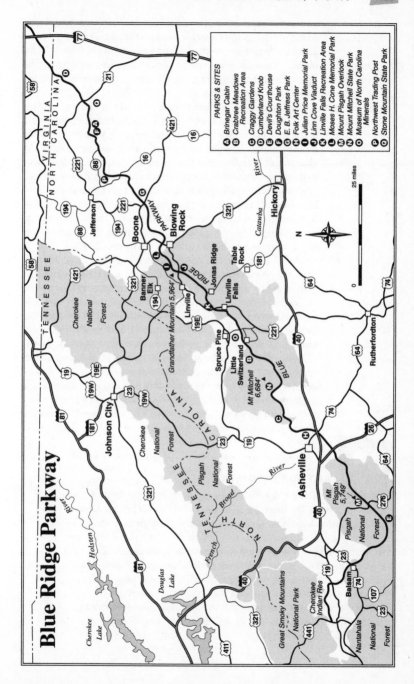

Blue Ridge Parkway

PARKS & SITES
- Ⓐ Brinegar Cabin
- Ⓑ Crabtree Meadows Recreation Area
- Ⓒ Craggy Gardens
- Ⓓ Cumberland Knob
- Ⓔ Devil's Courthouse
- Ⓕ Doughton Park
- Ⓖ E. B. Jeffress Park
- Ⓗ Folk Art Center
- Ⓘ Julian Price Memorial Park
- Ⓙ Linn Cove Viaduct
- Ⓚ Linville Falls Recreation Area
- Ⓛ Moses H. Cone Memorial Park
- Ⓜ Mount Pisgah Overlook
- Ⓝ Mount Mitchell State Park
- Ⓞ Museum of North Carolina Minerals
- Ⓟ Northwest Trading Post
- Ⓠ Stone Mountain State Park

next scenic stop—there's one around nearly every corner. Many scenic overlooks offer a single picnic table where you can dine in peace while listening to the rush of a stream or the buzz of bumblebees. The stopovers I describe below are just a sampling of the sights you'll encounter traveling northeast to southwest along the parkway in North Carolina.

Brinegar Cabin is where mountaineer Martin Brinegar and his wife, Caroline, lived in the late 1800s. Martin built the crude wood house with twin stone chimneys and the teeny springhouse down by the stream. Caroline wove on a loom, raised pole beans and gourds and kept the place free of snakes, using rocks and sticks to subdue the rattlers and copperheads that slithered onto her turf. The cabin is normally locked, but you can peek in and see Caroline's loom. On some summer weekends there are weaving demonstrations and other pioneer happenings at the cabin. On a nearby marker is a picture of the somber-looking Brinegars, who now rest in a cemetery just off the parkway. ~ Milepost 238.5.

Pull over at Milepost 264.4 for a look at **The Lump**. Actually there are two lumps, a big one and a little one right next to it, a pair of nubby hills poking up from carpets of crisp forest. The sky seems bluer and the forest greener up here, which is why people have been finding this spot for hundreds of years—first the Cherokee, then farmers and fox hunters, and finally millions of visitors, all drinking in a big Blue Ridge view. ~ Milepost 264.4.

Keep driving southwest through sparse farm country, with sun-blistered split-rail fence trailing along the road and rhododendrons gushing from the roadside like fountains of color. There are lots of places to stop and catch your breath, then have it taken away again by some fantastic view. The mileposts keep getting higher and so does the ear-popping terrain, until you near Mile-

sights

AUTHOR FAVORITE

The Blue Ridge Parkway certainly offers an indulgent abundance of delectable views, but there are a few that render me breathless. Definitely don't miss **Stone Mountain Overlook**, where you can gaze across a valley to the granite Piedmont mountain, only 500 to 600 feet high, which in summer looks like it has a serious bald spot. In winter when the trees go naked, the baldness is rampant. A lonely picnic table, engraved with years of graffiti, invites solitary dining. ~ Milepost 232.5. Three miles later, **Devil's Garden** is another distant view to a rocky crevice between two Piedmont hills. Best that you are not at the garden itself, as rattlesnakes and copperheads make their homes among the arid granite ledges. ~ Milepost 235.7.

post 300 and the parkway changes. There are more cars and RVs, more exits, more homes and backyards littered with toys and swingsets within plain view of the parkway.

This is the heart of the High Country and its longtime mountain resort towns of Blowing Rock, Boone and Linville. Here, too, is famous Grandfather Mountain, a mountain with an old-man profile and a mile-high swinging bridge that dangles in the cool, treacherous mountain air. Over the next few miles, exits will direct you into these pretty, popular areas with their exclusive country clubs, old-time mountain attractions and ski resorts. You can spend a few hours or a few weeks around here, taking the parkway in measured doses while enjoying local sights.

One parkway sight that's nearly always thronged with people is **Moses H. Cone Memorial Park**. The focus is **Flat Top Manor**, a handsome whitewashed house whose rocker-lined porch faces pleated valleys and meadows and shimmering, maple-lined Bass Lake. Both the manor and compelling mountain scenes belonged to Moses H. Cone, who, in the late 1800s came from Baltimore and, with his brother, Ceasar, started making blue jeans. North Carolina was a perfect place for manufacturing denim, having miles of cotton fields and railroad lines, and plenty of cheap labor as well. They built mills in Greensboro and Moses Cone became known as "The Denim King." He soon trained his sights on the nearby Blue Ridge, bought 3600 acres of land, and began customizing his estate. He built two lakes and stocked them with trout and bass. He planted more than 75 varieties of apples. He carved 25 miles of carriage trails, and he created the 20-room Flat Top Manor. Then he died in 1908, leaving his wife, Bertha, to manage and enjoy his Eden for the next 39 years. Today, the manor sells a stellar selection of Appalachian art and crafts, as well as books on this bold, brawny mountain country. After browsing, most folks find a chair on the porch and take in the lovely panoramic views. ~ Mileposts 292 to 295.

The setting at **Price Lake** is equally as powerful, though different. Instead of far-reaching hills and valleys, there is the hypnotic blueness of the lake, silhouettes of elms and rhododendron reflecting along its edges, vibrantly colored mallard ducks skimming its surface. From the surrounding forest comes intense birdsong, and butterflies floating against dusky sky. ~ Milepost 296.7.

Within a few miles comes the most famous curve on the parkway, the S-shaped **Linn Cove Viaduct** around Grandfather Mountain, a driving experience often compared to riding on air. Look up after the viaduct at the cliffs of exposed granite, with great evergreens sprouting like twigs, and you will feel absolutely elfish in proportion. ~ Milepost 304.4.

Pull over at Milepost 306.6 and you'll know why Grandfather Mountain was given this name. From the **Grandfather Mountain**

Alone at the Last Great Overlooks

The last 60 miles of Blue Ridge Parkway supply some of its quietest, least-crowded moments—time to enjoy being the only car on the road (often, anyway). Don't hesitate to stop and stretch your legs at the overlooks. You may just find yourself alone with these views.

CHERRY COVE OVERLOOK   Pull over at Cherry Cove and look 1000 feet down onto black cherry groves. In early summer they fill the cove with white blossoms; by July, their dark fruit pops out and birds descend in droves. ~ Milepost 415.7.

DEVIL'S COURTHOUSE   Walk up the barren granite bluff, taking care to stay on the trail, as many rare and exotic flora lie just off it. Spruce and balsam forests climb up to the "courthouse," but there is little life at the top, for the wind is too wicked to allow it. ~ Milepost 422.4.

HAYWOOD-JACKSON OVERLOOK   Pull over at Haywood-Jackson and look across the Great Balsam Range—or what's left of it. The balsam woolly adelgid, a wingless insect with a ravenous appetite for the sap of

Overlook his gnarly profile stands out; you can see the old man lying on his back, bushy eyebrows and goatee in full view. In winter, when the leaves fall away from the ridgeline trees, his features are sharper, his eyes more sunken and deeper in slumber. ~ Milepost 306.6.

The same folks you saw at Grandfather Mountain will stop at **Linville Falls**, one of the most popular and spectacular sights along the parkway. More like an angry torrent than a breezy cascade, the falls rush through Linville Gorge, its granite walls wet and worn by water and topped by vigorously growing trees. It takes some effort to get there, though. Three trails go to the falls: a 1-mile round-trip to the Upper Falls, where there's a short set of cascades down a 12-foot drop; a 1.5-mile round-trip to the Lower Falls, a forceful 60-foot gush down granite; and a 2-mile round-trip trek to Erwin's View, where you can see all the falls. In other words, the farther you hike, the better the view. ~ Milepost 316.3.

HIDDEN ►

The easiest, shortest walk to the falls is, appropriately, from the town of **Linville Falls**. ~ Exit the parkway at Milepost 317.5 and follow Route 221 south about a mile. Ask around town; most anyone can direct you to the trail.

fraser firs, or she-balsams, has felled many of the great firs of Great Balsam Range. Acid rain, which weakens the firs, only hastens their demise. The trees lie, defeated, in abject heaps. You can see them also atop Mount Mitchell, and in other high spruce-fir forests along the parkway. As the voracious woolly adelgid, an invader from Europe, is fed, so the native spruce-fir moss spider slowly starves, having fewer and fewer spruces and firs to feed on. ~ Milepost 431.

THE FINAL STRETCH   Farther down the parkway, **Locust Gap** is named for black locust trees. ~ Milepost 433.3. **Licklog Gap** is named for the cows that used to gather here to lick the salt logs. ~ Milepost 435.7. There are **apple orchards** across Richland Creek. ~ Milepost 444.6. The **cross** on Mount Lynn Lowery lights up at night. This 60-foot cross serves as a memorial to Lynn Lowery, who died in 1962 of leukemia at the age of 15. ~ Milepost 445.2. More overlooks, more tunnels, more gaps—including **Big Witch Gap** and its witchy story—await along the parkway. ~ Milepost 461.6. Then there is the end, **Oconaluftee River Bridge**. ~ Milepost 469. There is, however, no remorse at this journey's end, for if you cross the bridge you will be in the cool, sheltered depths of Great Smoky Mountains National Park.

By the time you reach Milepost 325 or so, you can see apple orchards cascading down the mountainsides. If it's May, there will be pinkish-white blossoms coloring the trees and perfuming the air. Pull over at **Heffner Gap** and look down at the plaited orchards filling the landscape. ~ Milepost 326.

You can still see some orchards at the **Table Rock Overlook**, but in the far South Carolina distance there's the sharp flatness of Table Rock Mountain, its granite crown glinting above a sea of verdant forest. ~ Milepost 329.7.

The **Museum of North Carolina Minerals** is a pleasant enough place, offering an overview of the state's mining industry and gem finds, including exhibits on minerals and mountain geology. But if you're really into rocks, go to the extensive Colburn Gem and Mineral Museum in Asheville, a short drive from the parkway (see Chapter Two). ~ Milepost 331.

Farther along the parkway, a spur road veers off the parkway and right into **Little Switzerland**, a pin-size town of the quaintest order, with A-frame chalets etched into the mountain and open to hillsides and valleys in every direction. For more on visiting this lovely place, see Chapter Six. ~ Milepost 334.

By now you are deep in the Black Mountain range, presided over by Mount Mitchell, loftiest peak east of the Mississippi, its crown measuring in at 6684 feet. From 4821 feet at **Mount Mitchell Overlook**, you can look up at the forested rise. ~ Milepost 349.9.

Farther down the parkway, if you exit at Route 128 into **Mount Mitchell State Park**, you can drive up the mountain. ~ Milepost 355.4.

"Miracle on the Mountain" is how a sign describes the blossoming of the Catawba rhododendrons at **Craggy Gardens**. Until you come face to face with an entire mountain clothed in pinkish purple, it is indeed impossible to imagine. The "miracle" happens between mid-June and early July, preceded by another show—spring wildflowers and fruit bearers opening in unison, mayapples, blackberries and violets, toothworts, mountain ash and wild crabapples, creating a technicolor display among the rocky summits. There is a visitors center here, a large picnic area and trails among the gardens. ~ Milepost 363.4 to 369.6.

Keep going south on the parkway and you will arrive at what George Vanderbilt called "the most beautiful land in the world." The turn-of-the-twentieth-century tycoon didn't make empty exclamations; he spent millions of dollars buying and protecting the land, eventually acquiring 125,000 acres that included Mount Pisgah. At **Mount Pisgah Overlook** you'll see the massive mountain, 5749 feet high and named after the smaller peak on Jordan's Dead Sea. ~ Milepost 407.4. But it's the surrounding scenery—far-reaching forests, cloud-tipped summits, the closeness of the sky—that makes people not want to leave. If you're struck by the same feeling, consider staying at **Pisgah Inn**. ~ Milepost 408.6. Or try the **Mount Pisgah Campground**. ~ Milepost 408.8. You will not be disappointed.

LODGING   There are slim pickings for accommodations on the parkway: Only two lodges provide accommodations on the parkway in North Carolina and, not surprisingly, you often have to book months ahead to get a room. However, just off the parkway, dozens of hotels, motels and inns, many open year-round, can be found in picturesque cities and towns such as Asheville, Little Switzerland, Blowing Rock and Boone. For more on these, see Chapters Two, Four and Six.

The 24 rooms of **Bluffs Lodge** are basic and clean, but the views from 3700 feet are incredible. The location at Doughton Park means there are lots of activities: hiking, fishing and campfire programs. The coffee shop here serves good food. Closed November through April. ~ Doughton Park, Milepost 240; 336-372-4499. MODERATE.

Larger and higher up, **Pisgah Inn** has 50 rooms and a fireplace suite, all with sensational, 5000-foot-high panoramas. All rooms

Curve
Ahead

The Linn Cove Viaduct is 1243 feet long, 35 feet wide and shaped like an S. From underneath it looks like a giant conveyer belt that's not moving. On top, its smooth concrete surface is open to the skies, and driving the viaduct feels a little like flying. The squeamish do best to keep their eyes on the road, instead of the nothingness all around.

On one side of the road there is Grandfather Mountain, the reason for Linn Cove Viaduct. When road engineers are confronted by a mountain, they typically dynamite through it, erasing forests and ancient trees, nests of animals, even entire ecosystems. When Blue Ridge Parkway creators arrived at Grandfather Mountain, they went around him.

Linn Cove Viaduct conforms to Grandfather Mountain, obeying his every curve, dip and rise. Seven vertical piers support the roadbed, which weighs 7650 tons and is held together by wire cables and epoxy glue. The roadbed has 153 sections, no two alike, that were cast a mile away and assembled on site like a puzzle.

There is nothing like Linn Cove Viaduct anywhere else in the world, and thus some have suggested its engineering genius is of da Vincian proportions. On a wall of the **Linn Cove Visitor Center** hang many awards for the road's design, including a 1984 Presidential Award. ~ Milepost 304.4. The viaduct was completed in 1987, nearly 50 years after the Blue Ridge Parkway was begun, and was part of the final link of the 469-mile scenic road. A ceremony was held beneath the bushy brows and slumbering eyes of Grandfather Mountain.

At the visitors center you can browse among the construction exhibits and a bookstore, then take a paved trail (open to wheelchair visitors) that runs beneath the viaduct. If the road's magnitude and the surrounding blue mist of the woods inspire you, head off on one of the longer, unpaved trails up Grandfather Mountain.

have televisions, and VCR and video rentals are available; some are wheelchair accessible. Closed early November to early April. ~ Mount Pisgah recreation area, Milepost 408.6; 828-235-8228, fax 828-648-9719; www.pisgahinn.com. MODERATE TO DELUXE.

DINING   There are three places serving good, hot, home cooking along the Blue Ridge Parkway in North Carolina. Incredibly, some of the waitresses have been on the job for more than 50 years.

At **Bluffs Lodge Coffee Shop** you get BLTs, barbecue and lots of Southern talk. Closed November through April. ~ Doughton Park, Milepost 240; 336-372-4744. BUDGET.

The **Crabtree Meadows Coffee Shop** is a snack bar with hot dogs and such. Closed November through April. ~ Crabtree Meadows, Milepost 339.5. BUDGET.

The **Pisgah Inn** dining room serves full-course fare like rainbow trout, steak and fried chicken. There are daily specials, too. Closed mid-November to early April. ~ Mount Pisgah recreation area, Milepost 408.6; 828-235-8228, fax 828-648-9719. MODERATE.

SHOPPING   Few people equate great shopping with national parks, but the arts and crafts at the **Parkway Craft Center** (Moses H. Cone Memorial Park, Milepost 294; 828-295-7938) and **Folk Art Center** (Milepost 382, near Asheville; 828-298-7928) are some of the finest in the Carolinas. More than 700 artists from the southern Appalachians contribute singular, beautiful works, with price tags ranging from cheap to steep—though most people spend more than they planned. Wavy clocks, delicate stone and painted jewelry, shiny goblets and platters, zany light-switch covers, white oak baskets, luxurious rugs and throws—everything is high quality and unusual.

The Parkway Craft Center is in a gracious, whitewashed, turn-of-the-twentieth-century manor built by textile magnate Moses H. Cone. Entirely different but just as engaging, the Folk Art Center is a bi-level building looking like something Frank Lloyd Wright might have designed, with a deeply overhung roof and lots of glass letting in views of the forest. On many days you can watch artisans working just outside the building.

AUTHOR FAVORITE

Hours vanished as I walked through the doors of the **Folk Art Center** and the **Parkway Craft Center**. The hundreds of intriguing and beautiful art pieces, crafted by Appalachian artisans, are a wonderful telescope to mountain life. See above for more information.

Elsewhere on the parkway, the **Northwest Trading Post** has jams and jellies (including some excellent elderberry jelly) made by local ladies, as well as bird feeders carved from mountain woods, quilts, cookbooks, cornbread and hushpuppy mixes, and homemade breads and pastries. ~ Milepost 285.6, south of Doughton Park.

Books on the parkway, wildlife, wildflowers, the history of western North Carolina and other mountain-related topics are on sale at several stopovers, including **Cumberland Knob** (Milepost 217.5), **Doughton Park** (Milepost 241.1), the **Linn Cove Viaduct** (Milepost 304.4), **Museum of North Carolina Minerals** (Milepost 331), **Craggy Gardens** (Milepost 364.6) and **Mount Pisgah** (Milepost 408.6).

NIGHTLIFE

There are, of course, no nightclubs along the Blue Ridge Parkway, but there is usually a nighttime show. As the sun settles down behind the mountains, the blue ridges turn ripe plum and the granite outcroppings are softened by shadows. Blackness eases into the woods, like a bear slipping into his winter slumber. This is a good time to stroll beside a stream or sit upon a summit and watch for foxes, raccoons, bobcats, skunks and other nocturnal creatures emerging from their daytime slumber.

If you'd rather not be alone, join one of the evening walks, campfire talks or slide shows led by parkway rangers. They're usually held on weekends from June through October. ~ 828-298-0398.

The biggest summer weekend bash is on Saturday nights at the **Blue Ridge Music Center**. Here, from an amphitheater ringed with mountaintops, musicians let loose with their banjos, fiddles and harmonicas. The talent is a mix of regional and national (Rick Skaggs, Doc Watson), but the music stays true to the old-time bluegrass of the Blue Ridge. Cover for national performers. ~ Milepost 213, part of the Cumberland Knob stopover.

PARKS

Odd as it may seem, there are several parks within Blue Ridge Parkway, all run by the National Park Service, as is the Parkway itself. Reached by spur roads off the parkway, they range from several hundred acres to several thousand and offer exceptional hiking, fishing, picnicking and camping.

Parkway campgrounds are open May through October on a first-come, first-served basis. Fees for all sites are $14. If you dislike crowds, stay away in October and on summer and holiday weekends. September and summer weekdays are wonderful.

DOUGHTON PARK 🏃 🛶 A 6000-acre chunk of Blue Ridge forest, coves, meadows and creeks, Doughton (pronounced DOW-ton) is the largest park on the parkway. It was once called The Bluffs, out of respect for big Bluff Mountain that splits the park nearly down the middle, though now it is named for the late Robert Lee "Muley Bob" Doughton, a North Carolina congressman and advocate for the parkway (the lodge and restaurant here are still called The Bluffs). If you go to Wildcat Rocks and take the well-worn path past the bronze marker honoring Congressman Doughton, you'll come to a bluff overlooking Basin Cove. The Cove is where folks used to go hog huntin'. It's also where Martin Caudill built his cabin, 1500 feet below the bluff, in 1895. Look straight down and you'll see it. For fishing try for rainbow trout in Basin Cove and Cove Creek. Facilities include restrooms, a coffee shop, gas pumps, a lodge, a picnic area, a camp store and a souvenir shop. ~ Located between Mileposts 238.5 and 244.7; 336-372-8568.

▲ There are 110 tent sites and 25 trailer sites (no hookups), each with fireplace and picnic table. Restrooms and drinking water provided; no showers; $14 per night. ~ 336-372-8877.

E. B. JEFFRESS PARK 🏃 These 600 acres are a monument to a man who helped found the parkway. E. B. Jeffress was chairman of North Carolina's state highway commission in the 1930s when he worked to secure land throughout the area. His namesake park is low on facilities but long on lush forest. Walk the half-mile Cascades Nature Trail beneath spidery limbs of magnolia, birch and rhododendron, to where Falls Creek rushes down a rocky chute, and you will know why Jeffress liked it here. Facilities include picnic tables, restrooms (closed in winter) and a self-guided nature trail. ~ Milepost 271.9; 828-295-7591.

Moses H. Cone Memorial Park's Bass Lake and Trout Lake, which Moses Cone built and stocked, still yield plenty of catches for parkway fishers.

MOSES H. CONE MEMORIAL PARK 🏃 🐎 ⛴ Some of the prettiest Blue Ridge country sprawls across this former turn-of-the-twentieth-century estate of textile magnate Moses H. Cone. Virgin forest of hemlock and yellow poplar, great stands of fraser fir, ridgeline meadows, valleys punctuated with the liquid blue of lakes, brilliant rhododendron and mountain laurel, and two mountains fill these 3500 acres of luscious landscape. Cone and his wife, Bertha, are buried on the side of Flat Top Mountain, not far from their 20-room manor that's now the Parkway Craft Center. Their 25 miles of carriage trails still carry horseback riders in summer, but are enjoyed even more by hikers. In summer, there are ranger-led programs and demonstrations at the craft center. Facilities include restrooms, nature and hiking trails and horseback-riding trails. ~ Located from Milepost 292 to 295; 828-295-7591.

JULIAN PRICE MEMORIAL PARK 🏃 ⛴ 🚣 ⛴ Julian Price liked his employees, so he bought them several thousand acres of prime mountain country. The land was actually meant as a company vacation retreat, though after buying up numerous parcels in the 1930s and early 1940s, Price subsequently died, and the employees of Jefferson Standard Life Insurance Company never got to enjoy their mountain nirvana. Today, anyone can enjoy these beautiful wilds, 4200 acres etched with poplar and chestnut and maple forest, and secret streams snaking through darkened hollows; some mountain headwaters have been corralled to create 47-acre Price Lake, cushioned in dense forest with many butterflies and birds. Rent a rowboat or canoe and paddle onto the lake; the trout fishing is great. Facilities include picnic grounds, restrooms, numerous nature and hiking trails, and rowboat and canoe rentals. ~ Located between Mileposts 295.1 and 298; 828-295-7591.

▲ There are 129 tent sites and 68 trailer sites (no hookups), all with fireplaces and picnic tables; $14 per night. ~ 828-963-5911.

LINVILLE FALLS RECREATION AREA 🏃 🛶 More than 60 picnic tables edge Linville River as you enter this 440-acre park and, incredibly, most are usually filled. People like it here; the woods are moist and mind-clearing, and there is water everywhere. Linville Falls plunge through Linville Gorge, gushing and rushing through primeval forest and walls of granite. Several trails lead to various stages of the falls. The park comes compliments of John D. Rockefeller, Jr., though it is named for William Linville and his son, who were killed in their sleep by Cherokees as they camped beside the river. It was 1766, and the pair never got to the falls or gorge that now bear their name. Brook trout, brown trout and rainbow trout are common in state hatchery-supported Linville River. You can also try for trout in Camp Creek. Facilities include a visitors center with a bookstore, a picnic area, restrooms and hiking trails. ~ Milepost 316.3; 828-765-1045.

▲ Fifty tent sites and 20 trailer sites come with fireplaces and picnic tables but no hookups; $14 per night. Ask for tent site number 15, so secluded that park rangers call it the "honeymoon suite." ~ 828-765-7818; www.reserveusa.com.

CRABTREE MEADOWS RECREATION AREA 🏃 A peaceful, rambling lawn of wildflowers runs into forest, and then there are mountains in the distance. If you come in May, you will see lady's slippers, columbines and crested dwarf iris garbed in glory. A month later, mountain laurel, rhododendrons, beard tongues and goatsbeards explode with color. In summer, there are naturalist shows at the amphitheater. As parkway parks go, Crabtree is not big, only 253 acres, but it is nearly always beautiful. Facilities include a coffee shop, a souvenir shop, restrooms, picnic areas and hiking and nature trails. ~ Milepost 339.5; 828-765-6082.

▲ There are 71 tent sites and 22 trailer sites (no hookups) with fireplaces and picnic tables; $14 per night. ~ 828-675-5444.

MOUNT MITCHELL STATE PARK 🏃 Six Black Mountain peaks over 6000 feet high reside within the park, though one gets all the attention. Mount Mitchell is the highest mountain in the range and also in the eastern United States, rising 6684 feet above sea level. The main parking lot of the 1677-acre park is near Mount Mitchell's summit, and an observation tower is smack on top of the summit. Down on the Blue Ridge Parkway you may be comfortable in short sleeves, but up here it's sweater weather year-round. The clouds insert themselves into the parking lots and picnic areas, and the wind blows in brisk sheets. The park stays open year-round, but winters can be brutal and snow can close the entrance road. Average snowfall is over 100 inches. In the summer, the sunshine is brilliant. Go at dusk and watch the surrounding mountains turn purple and orange as the sun bleeds down between the peaks. A more spectacular show cannot be had in these mountains. Facilities include observation tower, museum, picnic tables, grills and shelters, hiking trails and a restaurant and concession that are open May through October. ~ Exit the Blue Ridge Parkway at Milepost 355.4 and take Route 128 up Mount Mitchell. It's about a five-mile drive to the parking lot; 828-675-4611.

> Mount Mitchell State Park is home to the highest peak in the eastern United States. Dress warmly—snow flurries have been reported here even in the summer.

▲ Nine primitive tent sites on a first-come, first-served basis; $15 per site.

MOUNT PISGAH 🏃 Twice as high as its Biblical namesake near the Dead Sea in Jordan, North Carolina's Mount Pisgah soars 5721 feet above a resplendent sea of velvety green valleys and foothills. The parkway runs right by the mount, with places to stay and dine among forested wilds. Facilities include a picnic area, restrooms, a camp store, an amphitheater and hiking trails. ~ Facilities are located between Milepost 407.8 and 408.8.

▲ There are 70 sites for tents and 67 for trailers, all with fireplaces and picnic tables (no hookups); $14 per night. ~ 828-271-4779.

Outdoor Adventures

If it's golf or tennis you seek, you'll find them in the resort towns just a few miles off the parkway. See Chapters Two and Six for places to play.

SPORT-FISHING   The streams and lakes of the Blue Ridge Parkway are prime trout waters. You must have a North Carolina or Virginia fishing license to fish on the parkway, and must abide by various state and federal rules on bait, lures and flies. Different waters have different rules, so before you cast your line in, pick up a copy of the Blue Ridge Parkway's *Fishing Regulations and Opportunities* brochure from any visitors center.

There are many places to try your luck. For brook trout, try **Chestnut Creek**. ~ Milepost 215.2 to 217. If you're looking for brook and rainbow trout there a a couple of choices. One of these is at **Big Pine Creek**. ~ Milepost 221.5 to 225.5. Head down to **Little Glade Mill Pond**, near the site of an old turbine mill, for rainbow trout and bluegill. ~ Milepost 230. The other spot is **Meadow Fork Creek**. ~ Milepost 246 to 248.5. **Bass Lake** is the place for (what else?) smallmouth bass. ~ Milepost 293. For brown trout, try **Simms Creek**. ~ Milepost 296. Three types of trout—brown, brook and rainbow—can be found at **Price Lake**. ~ Milepost 297. You'll find more of the same at **Linville River**. ~ Milepost 317.

CANOEING

You can rent a canoe or rowboat at **Julian Price Memorial Park** and paddle out onto lovely Price Lake. ~ Milepost 295 to 299; 828-963-5911.

BIKING

For excellent bike-trail maps, contact the North Carolina Department of Transportation's Bicycle Program. ~ 1552 Mail Service Center, Raleigh, NC 27699-1552; 919-733-2804.

Unfortunately, the Blue Ridge Parkway was not built with bicyclists in mind, as there is no bike lane. Still, it is ever-popular with cyclists, who wear helmets and kneepads and ride single file along the edge of the two-lane road. Reflectors or white lights are required—and necessary since there are 26 pitch-black tunnels to be taken, as well as frequent fog. A headlight is the safest bet.

Cycling is most enjoyable when there aren't a lot of automobiles, usually Monday through Thursday. Avoid holidays and all of July and October, when traffic is heaviest. Stay on paved roads or in parking areas; biking is prohibited on trails and boardwalks.

Several stretches of the parkway are steeper than they seem, and you may find yourself struggling to scale 1000 feet in just three miles. The parkway's helpful *Bicycling* brochure lists the "major uphills" and can be procured at any of the visitors centers.

Portions of the parkway lie within the 700-mile-long Mountains-to-Sea bike route from Murphy in the western North Carolina mountains to Manteo on the Outer Banks. The strenuous **Sliding Rock** segment begins near the Great Smoky Mountains and lasts for 55 miles. It starts with a tough 12-mile climb to Richland Balsam, then slopes down and back up to Devil's Courthouse and its circle view into four states. Shining Rock Wilderness and Mount Pisgah are among the other scenic stops. There are numerous tunnels along this stretch, so use care when riding through their darkened lengths. ~ Where Route 23-74 intersects the parkway.

The 53-mile **Craggy Pinnacle** segment of the Mountains-to-Sea route picks up the parkway just south of Asheville. For 30 miles you climb up and across the Black Mountains, then descend into Buck Creek Gap, passing through several tunnels on the way. You can rest at Craggy Gardens, Mount Mitchell State Park or Crabtree Meadows. ~ Milepost 364.1.

Farther north and a favorite of bikers, the 52-mile **Brown Mountain Lights** segment has plenty of places to stop, including the Museum of North Carolina Minerals, Linville Falls and the Linville Gorge Wilderness Area. Most of the ride, which starts near Little Switzerland, is downhill.

Bike Rentals There are no bike rentals on the Blue Ridge Parkway, but there are a few in surrounding towns. For a list of places, see Chapters Two, Four and Six.

HIKING

Hikers can choose from more than 100 trails along the Blue Ridge Parkway. Some disappear into cool, dim Edenic forest, others rear up rocky ledges into wind and sun, and still stay near the water, wending along a lake, river or creek edge. A list of parkway trails and fliers on individual trails are available from any visitors center, or by calling 828-298-0398. All distances listed for hiking trails are one way unless otherwise noted.

Park brochures describe **Cumberland Knob Trail** (.5 mile) as an ideal lazy-day walk, great for little ones who need to burn some energy. The mostly paved path starts at the Cumberland Knob Visitors Center. ~ Milepost 217.5.

Several longer trails in Doughton Park are easy enough for flatlanders. **Bluff Mountain Trail** (7.5 miles) stays near the parkway on its trek from Brinegar Cabin to Basin Cove Overlook. **Fodder Stack Trail** (1.5 miles) tunnels through pine and hardwood forest, with wildflowers at your feet in spring and early summer. ~ Milepost 241.

Cinnamonbush, oaks and sourwood trees crowd the popular **Jumpin' Off Rocks Trail** (1 mile). The climax, of course, is a potentially perilous bluff thrust against a vault of blue sky. ~ Starts at Milepost 260.3.

The 25 miles of turn-of-the-twentieth-century carriage trails at Moses H. Cone Memorial Park are perfect for hiking. One of the most enjoyable, **Bass Lake Trail** (1.7 miles) circles the picturesque lake.

A short walk to a big view, **Beacon Heights Trail** (.44 mile) delivers hikers to a granite point with a view of the Blue Ridge foothills and streams down below. ~ The trailhead is at Milepost 305.2.

The long and winding **Tanawha Trail** (13.5 miles) curves around Grandfather Mountain, following the parkway for several miles. Among the highlights: shady glens of birch and beech trees, tunnels of mountain laurel and rhododendron, footbridges across racing creeks, and far-reaching views across the Piedmont. Most of the trek is quite easy. ~ Begins at Milepost 305.5 below Linn Cove Viaduct.

Within Mount Mitchell State Park, **Mount Mitchell Trail** (13 miles) is the one hard-core hikers use to climb the East's highest peak. The strenuous trek connects the tops of Black Mountain and Mount Mitchell. Make it a two-day venture: one to go down Black Mountain, a strenuous 3600 feet, and another for the arduous climb up Mount Mitchell. Spend the night at the base of Black Mountain at Black Mountain Campground, operated by Pisgah National Forest. (Fee is $13 per individual site, $50 for group campsites.) ~ 828-675-5616.

More in the mood for a mountain stroll? Head down easy **Balsam Trail** (.75 mile), a self-guided nature trail on Mount Mitchell. The trailhead is at the lower summit parking lot in Mount Mitchell State Park. ~ Exit at Route 128, Milepost 355.4.

If you take the **Richland Balsam Trail** (1.5 miles), you'll walk across the highest peak on the parkway, 6053 feet high, though the mountain actually goes up to 6410 feet. The easy-to-moderate, self-guided loop navigates the lush forest of fraser firs and red spruce across Richland Balsam. ~ Pick up the trailhead at Milepost 431.

Transportation

CAR

The Blue Ridge Parkway runs for 252 miles through western North Carolina, connecting Cumberland Knob in the north with the Great Smoky Mountains in the south. **Route 40** comes over from Raleigh in the east, running through Winston-Salem before intersecting the parkway near Asheville. **Route 26** veers up from South Carolina and joins Route 40 in Asheville.

AIR

Asheville Regional Airport is about five miles from the Blue Ridge Parkway. Exit at Milepost 388.1 and get on Route 25 south. For information on airlines, airport shuttles and car rentals, see "Transportation" in Chapter Two.

SIX

The High Country

If you want to get high, go to northwest North Carolina. The land swells more boldly here than anywhere else in the South, with big, broad mountains reaching up past 6000 feet, their peaks dressed in firs. The air is cooler, the nights blacker, the mornings coated with clouds.

Millions of people go to the High Country every year, to ski down a mountain or hike up it, to fish or canoe rock-bound rivers, to attend various folksy-themed attractions or pick apples on a hillside. Others simply come for mental and spiritual renewal, to be among "the masters," as Thomas Wolfe called these mountains, "rimmed in life . . . absolute unity in the midst of eternal change."

Hundreds of Blue Ridge and Black mountains are packed into this tiny, extreme northwest corner of North Carolina, heart of the Southern Highlands. Their sides glint with granite and quartzite, their summits merge with sky. Ancient rivers twist along their feet, liquid highways wending across several states. The New River commences in Blowing Rock and flows northward into West Virginia. Actually, it is not new at all but extremely old, the oldest river on the continent.

The Toe River cuts through the high ragged peaks of the southern High Country—from Roan Mountain and Winter Star to Grassy Ridge and 6684-foot Mount Mitchell, the tallest mountain east of the Mississippi. At Mount Mitchell, the Toe forms the headwaters of the Nolichucky River, which tumbles down through deep Nolichucky River Gorge. Whitewater rafters take Nolichucky for a serious ride on rapids.

Some of the mountains are etched into haunting shapes. The High Country's most famous shape, the old man of Grandfather Mountain, lies sleeping on his back, his bushy brows and goatee in full view. For centuries his profile has perplexed those who look upon the 5964-foot mountain, highest in the Blue Ridge. Today it is possible to see him up close, as the entire mountain has become a tourist attraction.

Long before the old man was hosting tourists, he was home to the Cherokee. Along with smaller, sometimes unfriendly tribes such as the Yeatkins, Catawbas and Sauras, the Cherokees lived low on the mountains and across the valleys. They were skilled at fishing and hunting and enduring the raw winters of this high region.

When white pioneers began pushing up into the mountains around 1670, they deftly subdued the tribes, first with disease and whiskey, eventually by murder. A hundred years later, American Indians were gone from the High Country, having retreated westward into the Great Smoky Mountains. In the 1830s they would be driven even farther west, all the way to Oklahoma, herded like cattle in a holocaust called the "Trail of Tears."

With the Cherokee out of the way, though, white men didn't rush to the mountains. Mainly rugged hunters and trappers set up camps in the 1700s, collecting pelts for trade and trading stories with flatlanders about the brutal, mysterious mountains. Daniel Boone came to the High Country in 1760 and stayed for nine years, but he spread word of "high, far-seeing places." He helped bring German, Scotch-Irish and English settlers to the area along an old buffalo trail.

By the early 1800s, settlers were growing corn and other crops, raising chickens and cows, hunting and fishing, and spinning their own clothes on wooden wheels. They dug deep into the Appalachian earth and created a folksy culture rich in music and living well off the land. They carved and strung their own dulcimers and banjos, put up their own jams, jellies and apple butter, hunted hogs, turkey and deer, and aged their moonshine in the cool confines of fern grottoes.

In a few decades the mountaineer families had grown into communities with roads firm enough for wagons and stagecoaches. By the late 1800s, mining companies invaded the area looking for minerals and ore. Then came loggers, who skinned the mountains of their fabulous firs, chestnuts, pines and other virgin forests. The federal government more or less came to the rescue, and national forests put an end to the frenzied lumbering, though some forests are still aggressively logged today.

Tourism has lately taken hold of the region (the name High Country was invented by promoters, though it is admittedly a fine name), but the mountaineers' culture survives and there are still hidden destinations to discover. Not far from the modern and moneyed country clubs and new log home developments are weathered old farmsteads with their springhouses guarding the creek, and crude cabins with apple butter for sale, stacked high on washtubs. People in the High Country still till the land, pick their banjos on the front porch, and wake well before daylight to go hunting.

The High Country tour begins and ends with the old ways. In the south, the Toe River Valley is mountain wilderness except for a few hamlets like Little Switzerland, an alpine-style village that's minuscule in size but big on mountain views. In mineral-rich Spruce Pine, massive feldspar mines feed a commercial market, while visitors can forage for gemstones. At the head of the Toe River Valley, 6285-foot Roan Mountain explodes with Catawba rhododendrons each year in late June.

North of here is the heart of the High Country, with the resort towns of Linville, Banner Elk, Blowing Rock and Boone, and four ski resorts, including the highest ski slopes in the eastern United States. Dozens of fine restaurants, grand old inns, country club communities, exclusive boutiques and golf courses appeal to year-round visitors. This is also some of the hottest real estate in the Carolinas. Flat-l anders have been buying property at such a furious pace that the average price of a mountain acre has quadrupled in five years.

Northward, the High Country relaxes again. The mountains relent into foothills and folded pasture, the meticulous country clubs melt into rambling farms and scattered rural towns. Three remote state parks offer outstanding backwoods hiking, canoeing and scenery. Up here is also the North Carolina start of the Blue Ridge Parkway (see Chapter Five).

Whether you seek the backwoods experience or one on a golf green, you can have it in the High Country. You can stay at a plush resort or check into an 1800s farmhouse. Ride the folksy Tweetsie Railroad, or join a week-long canoe trek into wooded mountain depths. Have a croissant and cappuccino at a '90s coffeehouse, or grits and gravy at a '50s coffee shop.

If it's local color you want, go for the grits.

▼▼▼▼▼▼▼▼▼▼▼▼
Toe River Valley

The Toe River does not wind lazily. It flows urgently through the southern High Country, frothing beneath lofty mountains, their sides blanketed with hardwood forest and ankles covered in wildflower meadows. Where the Toe reaches 6684-foot Mount Mitchell, it forms the Nolichucky River, tumbling down through rock-lined Nolichucky River Gorge, one of the deepest gorges east of the Grand Canyon. Whitewater rafters like the Nolichucky; the rapids are Class III and IV (Class V is highest) and there are plenty of boulders that get in the way.

Botanists like the Toe River Valley for its inordinately rich flora. Over the centuries, Europeans have come looking for exotic Appalachian species to decorate the formal gardens of France and England. Artisans, too, have found inspiration in the scenery, and today you will find their tiny glass-blowing, weaving and pottery studios tucked down side roads.

SIGHTS

Some of their creations end up in **Little Switzerland** (Route 226A), a pin-size resort village propped atop a mountain and backing up to the Blue Ridge Parkway. The views here are mind-cleansing. The mountains cascade in waves down from the village, and the air is scented with fir and spruce. A few dozen A-frame chalets have deep wood exteriors and fanciful eaves and doors, and are charmingly arranged along sloping roads. Vast green lawns run downhill, and there are signs welcoming you to someone's "haus." Right "in town" are a handful of shops all in a row.

In the winter, Little Switzerland shuts down, and only about two dozen people live there. Spring through fall, it's a wonderful stopover, with pretty, woodsy places to stay and eat.

About 16 miles northeast from here on the Blue Ridge Parkway, take the exit for Route 221 south. Follow it about a mile to

HIDDEN ▶ the town of **Linville Falls** named for the formidable cascade

Way Up in the High Country

- The calm, farflung Northern High Country is a great day away from busy Boone and Blowing Rock. Get going by 9 a.m. and make your way north on Route 194 and then Route 221. It's about 33 miles to **West Jefferson** (page 175), but the roads bend and curve, offering striking scenery, so allow an hour for the trip.

- Stop by for a look at the **frescoes of St. Mary's Church** (page 175). It's a poignant place you won't want to rush through, and the outside of the church will make you reach for your camera. Allow at least 30 minutes.

- Check out the cheese-making at **Ashe County Cheese Company** (page 175). Then you'll want to sample and perhaps purchase a wheel of this high-quality stuff.

- Leave West Jefferson on Route 221 north, then get on Route 16 north to Crumpler. The drive to **Shatley Springs Inn** (page 176) will take about 20 minutes and get you there just in time for lunch. If it's a weekend be prepared to wait up to 30 minutes—entirely worth it for the stellar Southern cooking.

- Head back south on Route 16 to Route 221 and follow it 24 miles as it arches north and southeast and becomes Route 21. Total driving time is about 50 minutes. Near where 21 connects with the Blue Ridge Parkway, take the turnoff for Route 1002 and **Stone Mountain State Park** (page 177). These 13,450 acres of tall, luscious woods are some of the most spectacular and solitary in all the Carolinas, which is why you will feel you're truly "way up" in the High Country. If it's summer, get on the John P. Franklin Parkway ("parkway" being a bit deceiving, since it's dirt and gravel), keep a lookout for turtles and snakes, and stop for a stroll through a stream.

- Leave the park at least one and a half hours before dark. The drive back to Boone and Blowing Rock on the Blue Ridge Parkway is 65 miles of fabulous sunset watching.

through nearby Linville Gorge (for more on getting to the falls, see Chapter Five). The town is but an eyeblink, with a gas station that is either deserted or deluged with people heading to a low-key, old-time attraction called **Linville Caverns**. The temperature inside is always a cool 52° so bring along a jacket. Open year-round, but closed weekdays from December through February. Admission. ~ Route 221, about three miles south of Linville Falls; 828-756-4171, 800-419-0540; www.linvillecaverns.com.

The caverns were found over a hundred years ago by two fishermen who followed a trout-gorged stream inside a mountain. They purportedly described the caverns as looking like "the arch of some grand old cathedral," though today some will think themselves in the belly of the *Alien* monster. Cavern walls are brown and gooey, with stalactites and stalagmites resembling a ribcage. The floors are sopping and slick, the passageways comfortable to skinny. The guide will tell you to take care as the group files along behind him for the 30-minute tour. Trout-filled streams still run through, though they are now stocked due to past overfishing. The trout are blind because they live in the dark. The caverns are lit for human visitors, though musky blackness hovers just beyond the spotlights.

After you've seen the caverns, backtrack on Route 221 to the Blue Ridge Parkway. Head 14 miles southwest on the parkway, until you reach the **Museum of North Carolina Minerals**. This museum contains the **Mitchell County Chamber of Commerce**, which can supply maps and information on the region. Take Route 226 north from the museum and plunge into backcountry, where there are no tourist attractions. ~ Milepost 331; 828-765-9483, 800-227-3912; www.mitchell-county.com.

One of the first settlements you'll come to is **Spruce Pine**, a mountain hamlet of 2500 that produces half the nation's supply of feldspar. For those not up on their feldspar, it's a chalklike rock that's blasted out of the ground and ground into a powder. The powder goes into everything from house paint and dinner plates to false teeth and toilet bowls. ~ Route 226, just north of Route 19E.

Besides feldspar, Spruce Pine is also mined commercially for quartz and mica, though dozens of gems—including aquamarine, emeralds, garnets and sapphires—have been found here. On Topaz Street in downtown Spruce Pine, the **Gunter Building** is charcoal-colored and rock-studded, fashioned in the 1930s from biotite mica. The world's only biotite mica belt is, naturally, in the area. ~ Corner of Topaz Street and Upper Oak Avenue.

Keep on Route 226 north about three miles to Penland Road and turn left. Go about a mile on Penland Road and take a right at the sign for **Penland School of Crafts**. The road squiggles up a hill to several wood buildings in the woods, which house the school started in 1929 by "Miss Lucy" Morgan. Miss Lucy, new

HIDDEN ►

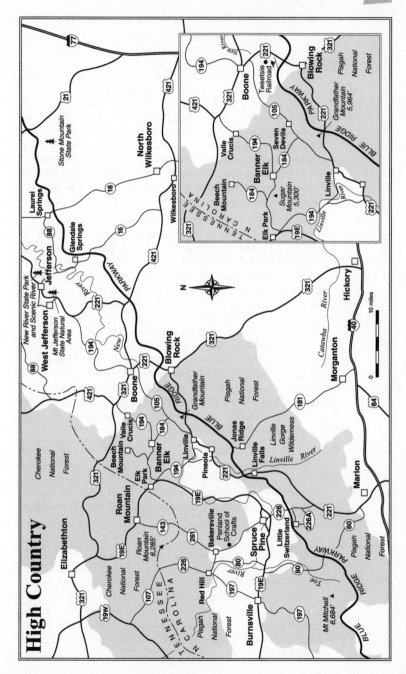

High Country

Inset map labels:

New River
194
221
221
Blowing Rock
Pisgah National Forest
Boone
421
321
321
Tweetsie Railroad
PARKWAY
Grandfather Mountain 5,964'
105
BLUE RIDGE
Valle Crucis
194
Seven Devils
184
221
Banner Elk
Beech Mountain
184
Sugar Mountain 5,300'
Linville
Linville River
221
TENNESSEE
NORTH CAROLINA
321
Elk Park
194
19E

Main map labels:

77
21
Stone Mountain State Park
North Wilkesboro
421
18
16
Wilkesboro
421
Laurel Springs
88
Glendale Springs
Jefferson
New River State Park and Scenic River
221
PARKWAY
West Jefferson
Mt Jefferson State Natural Area
88
194
New River
N
321
Hickory
Catawba River
40
321
10 miles
0
Blowing Rock
321
Boone
321
105
Grandfather Mountain
Pisgah National Forest
181
64
Beech Mountain
194
Valle Crucis
184
BLUE RIDGE
Banner Elk
Elk Park
194
Linville
Pineola
221
Jonas Ridge
Linville Gorge Wilderness
Linville Falls
Linville River
Morganton
Cherokee National Forest
321
Roan Mountain
19E
143
261
Bakersville
Penland School of Crafts
226
Spruce Pine
Little Switzerland
226A
221
Marion
80
Pisgah National Forest
Elizabethton
Roan Mountain 6,285'
19E
226
107
Red Hill
197
Toe River
80
19E
80
PARKWAY
19W
321
Cherokee National Forest
TENNESSEE
NORTH CAROLINA
Pisgah National Forest
Burnsville
197
Mt Mitchell 6,684'
BLUE RIDGE

Roan Mountain Country

LOAFERS GLORY   From Bakersville, you can get on Route 226 and drive straight up to Roan Mountain, but it's vastly more interesting to go the long way, passing through teeny country towns and upland meadows ensconced in wildflowers. Then there is the rushing Toe River bundled in boulders and forest. Three miles west of Bakersville, Loafers Glory is best known for its name, compliments of local womenfolk who thought their husbands lazed around the general store too much—at least that's the story.

KONA   No doubt the area's most disgruntled wife was Frankie Silver. You can see her former house about seven miles south of Route 80 in mite-size Kona, where she hacked her husband, Richard, to death with an ax as he snoozed near the fireplace (maybe he, too, was a loafer?). It was 1831, and only a few days before Christmas. She cut the body into pieces and tossed them in the roaring fire, but they didn't burn too well. Her in-laws found what was left of Richard in the hearth. Frankie went to prison, escaped, was caught and finally hung from a scaffold in 1833. Her last words, according to local lore, were a 60-line poem to Richard: *"....There shall I meet that mournful face, Whose blood I spilled upon this place: With flaming eyes to me he'll say: 'Why did you take my life away?'"* You can't go inside the **Silver Homestead** to have a look at where the dirty deed occurred, but you can gaze at the outside of the two-story, poplar- and oak-log cabin, built around the turn of the eighteenth century. Therein lived seven generations of Silvers. ~ Route 80, just south of the Kona Baptist Church.

RELIEF AND POPLAR   Back north on Route 80, you can pass through more hillside hamlets if you head west on Route 197. There's Red Hill and Tipton Hill and then Relief, named for Hart's Relief, a medicinal potion sold here in the 1870s, and a hot seller it was, not in the least because it was mostly grain alcohol. A few miles past Relief is Poplar, a pop-

in town, thought the local ladies needed a way to earn money. She lured in Edward Worst, a nationally famous weaver, and within a few years Worst's classes had students from as far away as California and Maine. Soon other artistic skills were added, including pewter "beating" and leather tooling, and the Penland School secured a national reputation. Today, it's one of the top glass-art centers in the country. ~ 828-765-2359, fax 828-765-7389; www.penland.org, e-mail office@penland.org.

ular place for launching canoes and rafts into the Toe River for a down-stream run.

ROAN MOUNTAIN   At Red Hill, you can work your way north on Route 226, then northwest on Route 261 to the Toe River Valley's most compelling sight. Roan Mountain ripples down in waves, spreading half its deep green mass in North Carolina and half in Tennessee. The mountain is most famous for its splendorous gardens of Catawba rhododendron. Around late June they explode with color, and Roan's 6285-foot summit is cloaked with purple, pink and scarlet. The gardens are vast, some 600 acres, the largest wild rhododendron patch in the world. Fraser firs cascade down from the gardens, and then there are rambling meadows. To walk among the rhododendron, park at the Rhododendron Gardens area along Route 261, just before the North Carolina–Tennessee line. Across the state line in the town of Roan Mountain, Tennessee, is the entrance to Roan Mountain State Park. The gardens are not in the park, though many people assume they are.

PINEOLA   Back down Roan, follow Route 19E south to Route 194 south, then wind lazily through foothills and tall summits all the way to Pineola. Pronounced "Pine-O-la," it's a mountain patch that has barely changed over the years, unlike touristy Linville, Boone and Blowing Rock just down the road. Pineola has nurseries that sell mountain exotics and also do a big Christmas tree business. It has a scattering of log homes that blend into the woods, a countrified coffee shop, and the **Pineola Inn and Country Store**. ~ Route 221 at Route 181; 828-733-4979. You can spend the night at the inn or stop in the store for a few minutes and browse the **Indian Artifacts Museum** tucked in back. Thousands of relics dating back thousands of years line the glass cases. Most of the pipes, ax heads, spearheads and beautiful arrowheads are from the collection of Tom Dellinger, who spent several decades with his eye to the ground. There's also a display of Confederate currency at the museum. But perhaps most intriguing is the seven-foot-long diamondback rattlesnake skin, 26 rattles and double fangs intact. You can buy it (unless someone else has by now) for several hundred dollars.

Back on Route 226, it's another nine miles or so to the town of **Bakersville**, county seat of Mitchell County. This pleasant little place at the foot of Roan Mountain is presided over by the **Mitchell County Courthouse**, built in 1907 in neoclassical Revival style. ~ Corner North Mitchell Avenue and Crimson Laurel Way.

Accommodations are scarce in this secluded mountain region. The place of choice is absolutely the **Switzerland Inn**, whose chalet-

LODGING

style lodge nestles in the crest of a mountain, with long green lawns dotted with perfect triangles of fir and spruce trees. A warm, homey place, it has a wood-paneled lobby with a fireplace and vast windows looking across the valleys. Guest rooms in the main lodge are simple but spacious, with boxy balconies facing into the woods or offering sensational mountain panoramas. Several cottages offer more space and privacy. There's a good restaurant as well as a swimming pool, tennis courts and shuffleboard. Rates include full breakfast. Closed early November to mid-April. ~ Route 226A, at Blue Ridge Parkway Milepost 334, Little Switzerland; 828-765-2153, 800-654-4026, fax 828-765-0049; www.switzerlandinn.com, e-mail swissinn@wnclink.com. DELUXE TO ULTRA-DELUXE.

A minute from Little Switzerland, **Big Lynn Lodge** overlooks the Catawba River Valley from its 3100-foot-high, mountainside perch. Hike or ride horseback through the Blue Ridge Mountains, then return to your suite with private balcony and river views. There are also older, motel-style rooms with Berber carpets and plain white walls, and rustic cabins (knotty pine walls and ceilings but no TV or air conditioning) that offer wonderful scenes of the valley and mountains. A dining room (order the sweet potato casserole) adds to the amenities. ~ Route 226A, Little Switzerland; 828-765-4257, 800-654-5232, fax 828-765-0301; www.biglynnlodge.com, e-mail info@biglynnlodge.com. MODERATE TO DELUXE.

Four miles north of the Blue Ridge Parkway, **Richmond Inn** is in Spruce Pine but offers the ambiance of the countryside. From the rambling flagstone terrace of this gabled house you can look down upon the North Toe River valley ringed with mountains. Eight guest rooms, all with private baths, are done in antiques and cozy accoutrements, and some have poster beds. Rates include a large country breakfast. ~ 51 Pine Avenue, Spruce Pine; 828-765-6993, 877-765-6993, fax 828-766-7224; www.richmond-inn.com, e-mail richmondinn@msn.com. MODERATE.

The Nu Wray Inn, established in 1833, is western North Carolina's oldest continuously operating inn. Guests love the two-tiered porch, where rocking chairs await after a day of exploring surrounding Blue Ridge Mountains. Twenty-six guest rooms and suites reflect the inn's history with 19th-century antiques; most have the original pine flooring. Full country breakfasts (sausage and biscuits) are served fireside in winter. ~ 102 Town Square, Burnsville; 828-682-2339, 800-368-9729; www.nuwrayinn.com, e-mail nuwrayinn@aol.com. MODERATE.

The basic, motel-style accommodations of **Pineola Inn** appeal mainly to cross-country skiers, fishers and anyone else looking for the low-key life. Rooms are modern, with cable TV, phones,

The Mystery of the Brown Mountain Lights

The lights are blue and red, or purple and green. They quiver, halo-like above the mountain, or shine clear and steady like a planet's beacon. They are the ghosts of American Indians, or UFO invaders.

No two tales of the Brown Mountain Lights are the same. In fact, many people who go to Jonas Ridge and search the sky above Brown Mountain see nothing but silvery stars embedded in black night. The boulders and guardrails at Jonas Ridge, near Pineola, have been etched by disbelievers: "These lights are a fake. Go home." And: "Been here ten times. Never saw nothing."

The federal government believed enough to send weather and geological researchers to investigate. *National Geographic* magazine dispatched photographers in search of the lights. So far, nothing conclusive.

But talk to some locals and they will tell you the lights really do exist. Spring and fall nights, when the sky is crisp clear, are best, they say. Hikers, cross-country skiers and coon hunters all claim to have seen the lights. Sometimes they move across the mountaintops; other times they hover in bands of color like a rainbow.

Some old-timers say they've never witnessed the enigma after hundreds of looks at the mountain. They blame reported sightings on too much moonshine and other mind-warping substances, and human hunger for a good story. At the Mountain Top Restaurant, a few miles north of Jonas Ridge, the lights are a frequent topic at the Liar's Table, where locals come to shoot the breeze and tell questionable stories.

If you can't resist a look yourself, go to **Jonas Ridge Overlook** in Pisgah National Forest, along Route 181 about five miles south of Route 221. Arrive at sunset with a bottle of wine and watch the orange globe slink down around the mountaintops. When it's good and dark, gaze across to horseshoe-shaped Brown Mountain, 2600 feet high. Even if you don't see the lights, at least you got a great sunset.

air conditioning and heating, and several have kitchenettes. There's a cross-country ski shop here, and trails that start right outside the door. ~ Route 221 at Route 181, Pineola; 828-733-4979; www.pineolainn.com. BUDGET.

DINING

The mountaintop **Chalet Restaurant** at Switzerland Inn is a big, wood-paneled dining room with picture windows that drink in miles of mountain views. The fare is hearty, as befitting a woodsy mountain setting, with blackened prime rib, roast duck, citrus chicken, jerk chicken, twin lobster tails, chicken pot pie and mountain trout at dinner. Sandwiches, soups and salads are offered as well for lunch, and there's a full-course breakfast. Friday nights are host to a seafood and prime rib buffet. Full bar. ~ Route 226A, Little Switzerland; 828-765-2153. MODERATE TO DELUXE.

Around the corner in "downtown" Little Switzerland, the **Switzerland Cafe and General Store** has nearly two dozen tables and a dozen wonderful desserts, from fudgy, peanut-buttery tortes and cakes to dazzling fruit pies. Herbal teas, good soups and sandwiches are also served at this cheery place. ~ Route 226A, Little Switzerland; 828-765-5289. BUDGET TO MODERATE.

Carolina BBQ is a down-home restaurant with slow-cooked pork, chicken and ribs, all served with a choice of three sauces (vinegar, mild and spicy Mad Dog). Side dishes include chili cheese fries, cole slaw, hush puppies, and jalapeño poppers. Red-and-white-checked tablecloths, banquettes and friendly service encourage you to take your time. No dinner on Sunday. ~ 500 Pineola Street, Newland; 828-737-0700, fax 828-737-0708. BUDGET.

SHOPPING

Beautiful Appalachian crafts, impeccably coaxed or carved into shape by local artisans, can be found throughout the valley. One of the most famous glass-art schools, the Penland School of Crafts,

STUDIO DELIGHTS

Some Penland crafters and other area artisans welcome visitors to their studios, usually by appointment. These places are often wonderfully hidden down dirt roads or sequestered in woods, and make for an enjoyable afternoon drive. A list of studios is available from the **Mitchell County Chamber of Commerce**. ~ In the Museum of North Carolina Minerals, Blue Ridge Parkway Milepost 331; 828-765-9483, 800-227-3912. You can also call the **Toe River Arts Council**. ~ 828-682-7215 or 828-765-0520.

is here, and there are many little-known studios where you can
buy directly from artisans.

The most formal shopping is in Little Switzerland, a teeny village with a handful of shops, most closed from November to early
April.

Two galleries carry exclusive items as well as homespun gifts.
The Trillim Gallery has delicate glass works, gemstone jewelry
and pottery. ~ Route 226A; 828-765-0024. **Hearthside Hand-
mades** is for those with country leanings. ~ Route 226A; 828-
765-7982.

Little Switzerland also possesses the best bookstore in the High
Country. The volumes at **Grassy Mountain Book Shop** are ancient to new, and they're stacked floor-to-ceiling, musty and dusty
but easy to browse. You can pick up original works by Carl Sandburg, Thomas Wolfe and other North Carolina authors, many
well priced. And if you don't find what you want, the owners
will search far and wide to get it. Closed November to early
April. ~ Route 226A; 828-765-9070.

Next door, **Switzerland General Store** also has great browsing. Baskets, pottery, local-made jams and jellies, and gourmet
coffee are among the merchandise. ~ Route 226A; 828-765-5289.

In downtown Spruce Pine, **Twisted Laurel Gallery** showcases
the works of more than 140 area artists. There is, of course,
plenty of blown glass, stained glass and pottery, but you'll also
find fiber art, clocks, paintings and sculpture. Closed Sunday and
Monday from April through December; closed Sunday through
Thursday from January through March. ~ 221 Locust Avenue,
Spruce Pine; 828-765-1562.

For five generations, the Woody Family has been making
chairs in the woods along Grassy Creek. Author Muriel Earley
Sheppard, in her 1935 book *Cabins in the Laurel*, wrote that they
"turn chairs on a lathe run by a water wheel when they are not
grinding meal. . . ." Today, the chairs at **Woody's Chair Shop** are
still made without nails or glue and hand-rubbed to a handsome
finish. ~ Dale Road, just off Route 226, about two miles north
of the Blue Ridge Parkway, Spruce Pine; 828-765-9277.

The **Gallery at Penland School** showcases exquisite blown ◀ HIDDEN
glass, jewelry, pottery and other works by crafters at this nationally acclaimed school. Closed Monday; closed mid-December to
early March. ~ 3135 Conley Ridge Road, about three miles north
of Spruce Pine; 828-765-6211.

Of the many mountain nurseries in the valley, **Gardens of the** ◀ HIDDEN
Blue Ridge is most renowned. Tucked down a quiet road at the
4000-foot elevation, it flourishes with Appalachian ferns, shrubs,
trees and wildflowers, including many rare and exotic species. You
can wander among the snow trilliums, butterfly weeds, spider-

worts and other beauties that fill these eight acres. Owners Robyn, Paul and Katy Fletcher will tell you what grows best "back home," and will even ship your selections for you. ~ 9056 Wildflower Lane, off Route 181, near Blue Ridge Parkway Milepost 312.5, Pineola; 828-733-2417; www.gardensoftheblueridge.com.

NIGHTLIFE   You can't buy cocktails in the valley, which puts a damper on nightlife, to say the least. Best to have dinner and curl up with a good book.

PARKS   **LINVILLE GORGE WILDERNESS** 🏃 🛶 A deep, ragged crease in the mountains, Linville Gorge offers some of the most formidable terrain in the East. Stretching for 18 miles and bounded by Jonas Ridge and Linville Mountain, the gorge was carved by Linville River, which drops a fast 2000 feet into the valley. The protected wilderness spans nearly 11,000 acres, and appeals most to serious hikers, fishers and backcountry campers. Fishing for trout is excellent in the Linville River. Facilities include an information center, hiking trails and scenic overlooks. ~ The major access roads are Routes 181 and old 105 off of 183 in Linville Falls, and Route 221 north of Marin. The information center is along Kistler Memorial Highway, off Route 183, about three-fourths of a mile south of Linville Falls; 828-652-2144.

▲ Backcountry camping only; permit (no fee) required for weekends and holidays from May through October.

▼▼▼▼▼▼▼▼▼▼▼▼▼▼▼
Linville & Banner Elk

There is money in Linville. You can tell by the vast log homes set discreetly along the mountain, the country clubs with championship golf courses and private airstrips, by the expensive condominiums and villas dotting the valleys. Many are occupied only during summer months, revealing just how wealthy their owners are.

SIGHTS   Old Linville money is the reason **Grandfather Mountain** became such a splendid attraction. Hugh Morton, whose family has lived in the area for two centuries, created a private park on this famed mount whose summit looks like an old man in repose. An accomplished outdoor photographer and avid environmentalist, Morton's mountain was declared an International Biosphere Reserve by the United Nations and is protected by the Nature Conservancy. Grandfather is the highest mountain in the Blue Ridge and one of the most treacherous. A sign near the top warns that "you are on the most rugged mountain in Eastern America. Be careful!" It seems a valid statement as you wind up the mountain road whose sides drop down into rocky chasms. Admission. ~ Route 221, just north of Linville; 828-733-4337, 800-468-7325; www.grandfather.com.

Since it opened in the late 1940s, millions have come to enjoy this compelling place, and families especially like it. There are hiking trails, scenic overlooks, picnic areas and a **Nature Museum** (828-733-1059) with keen displays on Appalachian flora, fauna and minerals. There's also a **Wildlife Habitat** with deer, river otters, black bears, eagles and cougars. Near the summit is the **Visitors Center** and the famed **Mile-High Swinging Bridge**. Walk out onto the suspension bridge, look way down into a ravine, and feel the cold air pushing at your feet.

Except for the bridge and hiking trails, Grandfather Mountain attractions are wheelchair accessible. Unfortunately, you can't see the old man's profile unless you climb up **Linville Bluffs**. Anyway, by far the best view of his shaggy brows and pointed nose is down on Route 105 south of Boone.

A little north of Grandfather Mountain, Route 184 winds up through mountains to the Carolinas' two biggest ski resorts. The first is 5300-foot **Sugar Mountain**. The road into Sugar is lined with woods and chalets rented to skiers in the winter, home to many flatlanders in the summer. Right next to Sugar Mountain, the atrocity protruding from Little Sugar Mountain's summit is a condominium tower that caused local outrage (much inaccurately vented at the ski resort, which had nothing to do with the development) and prompted the Ridge Line Law, which prevents any more mountaintop graffiti.

Four miles north on Route 184, the attractive village of **Banner Elk** is enveloped in mountains. There's a bit of a college scene here, as well as exclusivity. Pricey boutiques and restaurants blend with casual cafés and a coffeehouse. This is where skiers from Sugar Mountain and **Beech Mountain**, a couple of miles up Route 184, like to hang out. At 5505 feet, Beech Mountain has the highest downhill action in the eastern United States. (For more on skiing, see "Outdoor Adventures" at the end of this chapter.) For information on local sights, visit the **Banner Elk Chamber of Commerce**. ~ Route 184, High Country Square, Banner Elk; 828-898-5605, 800-972-2183; www.avery-county. com. Another place to go for information is the **Beech Mountain**

AUTHOR FAVORITE

sights   The **Mile-High Swinging Bridge** made me feel like I was riding an arctic air wave. Problem was, once I made it to mid-bridge and looked down the bottomless, silver-blazed ravine, I froze in space. Thank goodness the kids behind me (fearless mountaineers that they were) coaxed me to the other side. See above for more information.

Chamber of Commerce. ~ 403-A Beech Mountain Parkway, Beech Mountain; 828-387-9283, 800-468-5506, fax 828-387-3572; www.beechmtn.com.

LODGING

The Eseeola Lodge is a venerable place whose longtime devotees return every summer to indulge in beautiful surroundings and sumptuous food and service. The entry of stone and bark-covered logs looks like something from the brothers Grimm; the 24 rooms and suites are light and airy, with pretty wallpapers and wool carpets, and colorful quilts for keeping warm on cool nights. In the evenings guests stroll across the green lawns decorated with firs and maples and arched footbridges, and there is much laughter in the expansive dining room. A swimming pool, golf course, tennis courts and croquet are among the possibilities offered. There's also a two-bedroom cottage. Breakfast and dinner (coat and tie required for men) are included in the price tag. Closed November through May. ~ Route 221, Linville; 828-733-4311, 800-742-6717, fax 828-733-3227; www.eseeola.com. ULTRA-DELUXE.

Hidden down a quiet lane, Linville Cottage welcomes guests with a white picket fence, English gardens, two antique-filled suites and an upscale suite called Grandfather's Nook, complete with jacuzzi, gas fireplace and its own secret garden. There are also two pet-friendly cottages on the property and a secluded cabin set in a rhododendron forest about a mile down the road. ~ 154 Ruffin Street, Linville; 828-733-6551, 877-797-1885, fax 828-733-9950; www.linvillecottage.com. DELUXE.

Villas, condominiums and homes can be rented through local lodging services. For information, call Sugar Mountain. ~ 828-898-4521, 800-784-2768; www.skisugar.com. Or try Ski Beech. ~ 828-387-2011, 800-438-2093; www.skibeech.com.

The 1912 Banner Elk Inn sits right in the engaging village of Banner Elk, with six guest rooms filled with style and solace. Among the decor: original Victorian wood and brass beds, floral tapestries, and a Peruvian bench. If you want to hide out, unpack in the honeymoon suite, complete with a "lounging room" with tub for two overlooking English gardens. ~ 407 Main Street East, Banner Elk; 828-898-6223, 800-295-7851, fax 828-898-6224; www.bannerelkinn.com. MODERATE TO DELUXE.

The focus at the Perry House is on scenic comfort: All five rooms come with handmade quilts, down comforters, and private bathrooms. The Jennifer Room, the only first-floor bedroom, is especially atmospheric with its canopy bed and hardwood floors. A full breakfast (don't miss the baked apple pancakes) and refreshments that are available throughout the day enhance this serene mountain experience. ~ 153 Klonteska Drive, Banner Elk; 828-898-3535, 877-806-4280; www.perryhouse.com, e-mail perryhouse@skybest.com. MODERATE TO DELUXE.

All five guest rooms at the **1902 Turnpike House Bed and Breakfast** flow with Euro-Southern nostalgia. In the Thomas Lower Room, for instance, you'll find wing-back chairs, a tilt-top table, and iron bathtub. Elegant breakfasts are served on heirloom crystal and china set among tables on the big front porch. Come evening, retreat to the "Gathering Room," where a wood-burning hearth warms you in winter. ~ 317 Old Turnpike Road West, Banner Elk; 828-898-5611, 888-802-4487, fax 828-898-5612; www.1902turnpikehouse.com, e-mail info@1902 turnpikehouse.com. MODERATE TO DELUXE.

About five minutes from the slopes of Ski Beech, **Archers Mountain Inn** is set along the mountainside overlooking the Elk River Valley. The inn has two buildings with fifteen rooms and suites, all with wood-burning fireplaces and most with smashing views of the valley. The presidential suite, which is warmed by a massive stone fireplace, features a king-sized four-poster bed, a jacuzzi tub and a private porch where you can gaze out on the mountains. Enormous country breakfasts are included. ~ Route 184, Banner Elk; 888-827-6155; www.archersinn.com, e-mail theinn@archersinn.com. DELUXE.

Right next to Ski Beech, **The Inns of Beech Mountain** are the only lodges within walking distance of downhill skiing. The **Beech Alpen Inn** is the main lodge; there's a fine restaurant here and spacious, simple rooms with carpeting, window boxes and views all the way to the Tennessee mountains. Four rooms have gas fireplaces. Next door and slightly more rustic, **Top of the Beech** has a living room with vaulted ceiling and a big fireplace. Continental breakfast is set out every morning. The rates fall into the budget range on summer and fall weekdays. Special two-night budget rates are available in the winter. ~ Route 184, Beech Mountain; 828-387-2252, fax 828-387-2229. MODERATE TO DELUXE.

◆◆◆

SCENIC REPASTS

Exquisite views meet sophisticated cuisine at **Jackalope's View**. Have a seat at a table covered in pressed linens, order the venison in puff pastry (a special that is frequently available), and gaze out across Sugar and Grandfather mountains. The venison, embellished with baby spinach and portobello mushrooms, is tucked inside hot pastry drizzled with garlic chili butter. Start with the gorgonzola-topped Vidalia onion stuffed with sauteed mushrooms, roasted garlic and shallot balsamic reduction, paired with a buttery borgogne blanc—Jackalope's has made the *Wine Spectator*'s "Best Restaurant Wine List" since 1999. ~ 2489 Beech Mountain Parkway, Banner Elk; 828-898-9004, 888-827-6155; www.archers inn.com. DELUXE TO ULTRA-DELUXE.

DINING

With reservations you can dine at **The Eseeola Lodge,** enjoying what some say is the High Country's finest cuisine. Offerings tend to change nightly, but you might find chilled Carolina peaches-and-cream soup or cornmeal crusted Carolina flounder with sesame-ginger slaw. Among the possible entrées are pan-seared venison with lingonberry pecan relish and black currant ginger sauce, and sauteed shrimp and jumbo lump crab in sherry cream with morels, sweet peppers, corn and leeks. Many diners are guests at the lodge—and have been here numerous times before. A coat is required for men. Closed late October to mid-May. ~ 175 Linville Avenue, off Route 221, Linville; 828-733-4311; www.eseeola.com. ULTRA-DELUXE.

The hottest High Country nightlife is in Banner Elk—but don't expect Bourbon Street; what you're more likely to find is a cozy place to listen to music.

The culinary experience at **Louisiana Purchase** is less formal but equally gratifying. Nawlins'-style through and through, the classy dining room is flooded with spicy smells and painted with murals of the Crescent City. Seafood leads the menu, but there's also rack of lamb, chicken and pork tenderloin. Try the pan-fried trout filet with baby shrimp and shiitake mushrooms. The hefty, cork-bound wine list has garnered awards from the *Wine Spectator*. If you'd rather just have wine, the *cuvinét* loft upstairs features more than 20 wines by the glass. Dinner only. ~ Route 184, Banner Elk; 828-898-5656. DELUXE TO ULTRA-DELUXE.

HIDDEN ►

Banner Elk's elegant bistro is **Morels.** It's a single room colored intensely green, with linen-topped tables threatening to crowd too close, but a menu that's vastly imaginative. Escargot with potato gnocchi and roasted garlic cream might start the meal. For the main course, there may be honey and tamari-seared Norwegian salmon, veal tournedo with jumbo lump crab meat, spring asparagus with a cilantro Bearnaise, or crispy sautéed sweetbreads with mustard caper sauce. It's dinner only, and reservations are usually necessary. Closed Monday in season, Monday through Wednesday in winter. ~ Off Route 194, down the side street beside B.J.'s Resortwear, Banner Elk; 828-898-6866. DELUXE.

Before and after skiing, everyone goes to **Fred's General Mercantile** for coffee and muffins, sandwiches and soups—but mostly just to hang out. Fred's is most definitely an institution, a modern, airy, New American–style general store frequented by people of some affluence. On summer Sunday mornings, Floridians and other flatlanders flock to Fred's patio to sip coffee and read their hometown newspapers. ~ 501 Beech Mountain Parkway, Beech Mountain; 828-387-4838. BUDGET.

SHOPPING

There's not much in Linville, but Banner Elk does have a few shops worth browsing.

J.W. Tweed's offers the oxford look for men (button-down shirts, leather and nubuck jackets, designer socks and belts) and a casual but elegant look for women (linen, khakis, dresses and jewelry). ~ Route 184, Banner Elk; 828-898-6166.

At the ever-popular **Fred's General Mercantile,** you can buy a paintbrush or ski jacket as easily as a ham sandwich. Cookbooks, fireplace tools, kitchenry, keys made—it's all here. ~ Beech Mountain Parkway, Beech Mountain; 828-387-4838.

Besides spectacular views and proximity to Ski Beech, **Archer's Mountain Inn** offers a cozy place for a drink in its upstairs bar. ~ Route 184, Banner Elk; 828-898-9004, 888-827-6155.

NIGHTLIFE

Destiny Inn serves up dishes from empanadas to gourmet pizzas, with live music on Saturday night. ~ 1001 Beech Mountain Parkway, Beech Mountain; 828-387-2266.

▼▼▼▼▼▼▼▼▼▼▼▼

Boone & Blowing Rock Area

To many people, Boone and Blowing Rock *are* the High Country, for here is the hub of vacationing: fine inns and eateries, golf greens and forays to the farmers' market, folksy attractions and outlet shopping. Only a few miles separate the two towns, though they could not be more different.

SIGHTS

Boone is the area's commercial pulse. Routes 105 and 221-321 around Boone are thronged with fast-food eateries and other suburban sprawl, so concentrate on historic **downtown**, centered around Depot and King streets. You'll see buildings of red brick housing mercantile stores and eateries, and the handsome **Appalachian State University**. Nearly 12,000 students create a vigorous campus atmosphere and fuel a pub and grub scene that's considerable for a town that allows only beer and wine to be sold. ~ Along Route 321 and Rivers Street, Boone; 828-262-2179.

Long before there was a campus here there was a log and stone cabin that belonged to Daniel Boone, who lived in the High Country during the 1760s and helped bring skilled, hard-working settlers to the area. For a look back at Boone (the man and the town), stop by the **Appalachian Cultural Museum.** The museum explores Boone history from its geologic development to the present. There are American Indian artifacts, exhibits of clothing, furnishings, farm tools, quilts and music from the 1700s, and more. Closed Monday. Admission. ~ University Hall, University Hall Drive off Route 321, at Appalachian State University; 828-262-3117.

The **Daniel Boone Native Gardens** are filled with Boone details: the iron entrance gates were forged by Daniel Boone VI, the logs in the reflecting pool cabin came from a grand nephew's home, and a big cherry tree arrived in the area with Boone's brother—making it more than two centuries old. Take a leisurely walk through the woods and the rockery. Fall is the best time to be here, when the trees rage orange and yellow and purple. Some areas are not wheelchair accessible. Open May through October, weather permitting. Admission. ~ 651 Horn in the West Drive off Route 321-421, Boone; 828-264-6390.

More on Boone, and the whole High Country area, is available south of the gardens at **High Country Host**. This visitors center can also provide information and referrals for buying a Boone summer home—a popular venture these days. ~ Route 221-321; 828-264-1299, 800-438-7500; e-mail info@highcountryhost.com.

No doubt Boone's popularity has caused interest in neighboring **Valle Crucis**, translated "Valley of the Cross." Situated a few minutes northwest of Boone along Routes 1112 and 194, the town sits where two mountain streams intersect into a cross. Only ten years ago Valle Crucis was a quiet mountain hamlet; now it's a mainly quiet mountain hamlet that's very "in." People hurrying to buy land here have driven prices way up. Secluded bed and breakfasts are booked months ahead. And the old-time general store is now a stop on the tourist track.

That would be **Mast General Store** where Charles Kuralt opined that you could "find the soul of the South." Built in 1883 and going stronger than ever, Mast seems to carry everything under the sun, lye soap and rosebud salve included. It's the potent nostalgia, though, that draws visitors far and wide. ~ Route 194, Valle Crucis; 828-963-6511.

Southeast of Boone, the **Tweetsie Railroad** train is nearly as old as Mast General Store, though it's hard to imagine Charles Kuralt waxing nostalgic over it. In fact, I can't imagine even taking this "trip back to the Old West" lest children were involved, pesky, relentless children begging for a ride. In that case, swallow hard and cough up the admission ($18 for children, $25 for adults), then ride the train around the mountain on its three-mile run, stopping for a cancan dance and a street shoot-out. There's also a petting zoo and kiddie rides. Closed November to late May. Admission. ~ Route 321; 828-264-9061, 800-526-5740; www.tweetsie.com.

Not as pricey but still frightfully hokey, **Mystery Hill** is a house where gravity is supposedly askew. Objects seem to fall upward, and so does your body. Magic mirrors, glowing rocks and other funhouse oddities thrill the kids. Admission. ~ Route 221-321 southeast of Boone; 828-264-2792; www.mysteryhill-nc.com.

A little farther south on Route 221-321 is **Blowing Rock**, both the town and the namesake rock. The town is an engaging mountain village whose fieldstone and wood buildings rest beneath high-reaching maple and poplar trees. Turn-of-the-twentieth-century manses are parked along steep crooked lanes, and mountains float in the distance. Flowers pour from window boxes along Main Street, galleries, boutiques and cafés are tucked beneath bright awnings, and park benches invite rest.

If something seems to be missing, it is. The commercial chaos of greater Boone is gone, but it did not stay away easily. Residents of this 1889 town have long fought the trappings of development—successfully. It didn't hurt that they had money.

Despite the town's apparent wealth, prices for lodging and dining are not prohibitive. Well-tended motels and lodges, neighborhood eateries and affordable shops are plentiful. And one of the most rewarding activities—walking around town—is free. Take a stroll down Laurel Lane to the **Annie Cannon Memorial Gardens** and **Broyhill Park,** small city parks with vigorous, immaculate plantings.

Right on Main Street, **Blowing Rock Chamber of Commerce** has information on lodging, dining and sights. Closed Sunday. ~ Beside the Town Park; 828-295-7851, 800-295-7851.

As for the biggest local sight, **The Blowing Rock,** this you will pay to see. The rock is 4000 feet high and pokes out from a mountain. It looks a bit like the head of a monster with its jaw cocked. Wind barrels up from the gorge below, and if you toss something off the rock it may get blown right back at you—hence the name. A pathway, with steps that make it impossible for wheelchairs, winds out to a platform. From here you can look over at the rock, and across mist-shrouded mountains. From January to mid-March you can only visit on weekends, weather permitting. Admission. ~ Route 321, two miles south of town; 828-295-7111; www.blow ingrock.com.

> Roadside pit stops along Route 321 into the Piedmont offer "hillbilly dolls," strange statuary and big jars of honey with the comb still in it.

South from the rock, Route 321 snakes down into the Piedmont, running alongside sheer cliffs with neck-craning views across the Blue Ridge.

LODGING

Near Hawksnest Golf & Ski Resort, **Smoketree Lodge** is a good buy. For a decent price, you get an oversized motel room with furnished kitchenette and cable TV, an indoor pool, whirlpool, dry sauna, weight room and complimentary morning coffee. Need a bottle of wine or groceries? The lodge will kindly dispatch someone for you. ~ Route 105, 11 miles south of Boone; 828-963-6505, 800-422-1880, fax 828-963-7815; www.smoketree-lodge.com. MODERATE.

Set up on an out-of-the-way hill with mountains all around, **Willow Valley Resort** is a timeshare that rents rooms by the night (with a two-night minimum required). Accommodations are in chalets, log cabins or condominiums, each with one, two or three bedrooms with carpeting, a kitchen and either a fireplace or a stove. None have air conditioning. Bring your racket and clubs; there are three tennis courts and a 9-hole, par-3 golf course, as well as an outdoor heated swimming pool. ~ Off Route 105, three miles south of Boone; 828-963-6551, fax 828-963-6812; www.willowvalley-resort.com, e-mail willowvalley@boone.net. MODERATE.

If you prefer the exclusive confines of a country club, there are **Hound Ears Club** and the **Inn at Yonahlossee Resort & Club**. Every imaginable pursuit—golf, tennis, swimming, hiking—is found at Hound Ears. It offers rooms and suites in a lodge, some with balconies, as well as chalet, villa and home rentals. ~ 328 Shulls Mill Road, off Route 105, south of Boone; 828-963-4321, fax 828-963-8030; www.houndears.com. ULTRA-DELUXE. Yonahlossee has no golf course but it devotes 130 of its 300 acres to horseback riding, and runs one of the premier equestrian centers in North Carolina. Manicured golf greens fill the valleys, and mountain scenes fill the skies. Chalets, villas and great big homes are parked on the hillsides. Yonahlossee has cottages and villas. Winter brings moderate room rates. ~ 226 Oakley Green, off Shulls Mill Road, near Route 105, south of Boone; 828-963-6400, 800-962-1986, fax 828-963-7902; www.yonahlossee.com. ULTRA-DELUXE.

High Country Inn is perfect for ski digs. Cozy, rustic and kitschy (water wheel out front, ducks and trout in the concrete pond), it has 120 spacious rooms with refrigerators and coffeemakers, some gas fireplaces and jacuzzis. If you're traveling with several people or just want space to spread out, consider the four three-bedroom, ultra-deluxe-priced cabins. They are equipped with a full kitchen, washer and dryer, gas grill and a jacuzzi out on the porch. The inn has an indoor/outdoor pool, hot tub and sauna, laundry facility, and a restaurant. ~ 1785 Route 105, Boone; 828-264-1000, 800-334-5605, fax 828-262-0073; www.highcountryinn.com, e-mail info@highcountryinn.com. MODERATE.

ROOMS WITH VIEWS

From its hideout along Sunset Mountain, **Window Views Bed and Breakfast** indeed offers vistas from every room. The best scenes are from the Gathering Room, which looks across wide-open Blue Ridge Mountains and the village of Valle Crucis. But you'll also see peaks and valleys from the two guest rooms, decorated in country comfort with rocking chairs and heirloom antiques. ~ 204 Stoneleigh Lane, Boone; 828-963-8081, 800-963-4484, fax 828-963-4484; www.windowviews.com, e-mail innkeeper@windowviewsb-b.com. MODERATE TO DELUXE.

The name **Broyhill Inn & Conference Center** suggests a grand place (Broyhill is the furniture conglomerate), but expect something like an upscale dorm house, which makes sense, as the inn is on the campus of Appalachian State University and caters to college functions. The two-story rambling brick buildings offer some mountain views. ~ 775 Bodenheimer Drive, Boone; 828-262-2204, 800-951-6048, fax 828-262-2946; www.broyhillinn. com. DELUXE.

If cocooning on a nineteenth-century Southern farmstead sounds appealing, stay at **Mast Farm Inn**. The front porch is   ◀ HIDDEN
lined with old rockers and a screen door that clunks. The sweeping grounds are sprinkled with a dozen rustic buildings, all on the National Register of Historic Places, including a smokehouse, springhouse, apple house, rustic cottages and an 1810 cabin where three generations of Masts lived. The main house was built in 1885 with 13 bedrooms and one bath, though today each of the eight guest rooms has a private bath. You can also spend the night in the old loom house, blacksmith shop, a granary or woodwork shop, all adorned in warm, unassuming fashion. Innkeepers Wanda Hinshaw and Kay Hinshaw Philipp make the whole experience enjoyable, from the cookies offered at check-in to the enormous but healthy breakfasts. ~ Route 1112, three miles from Route 105, Valle Crucis; 828-963-5857, 888-963-5857, fax 828-963-6404; www.mastfarminn.com, e-mail stay@mastfarminn.com. DELUXE TO ULTRA-DELUXE.

The imposing white 1911 farmhouse that's **Taylor House Inn**   ◀ HIDDEN
has been impeccably restored. The lobby has two gas-burning fireplaces, the guest rooms are plushly carpeted, their king-sized beds piled with down comforters and soft pillows. All have private baths. What more do you need? Closed mid-December through March. ~ Route 194, around the corner from Mast General Store, Valle Crucis; 828-963-5581, 800-963-5581, fax 828-963-5818; www.taylorhouseinn.com. DELUXE TO ULTRA-DELUXE.

Set on 16 wooded acres and overlooking the Watauga River, **Baird House Bed & Breakfast** is a grand hideaway. The main house was built in 1790 and still boasts some of its original hand-planed hard-wood paneling and glass windows. All seven rooms (four in the main house, three in the carriage house) are beautifully decorated in persimmon, teal and olive, and have private baths and sitting areas; some with gas log fireplaces, balconies and river views. Enjoy fresh-baked bread for breakfast, relax in a hammock, fish in the river or visit the cemetery that holds the Bairds. ~ 1451 Watauga River Road, Valle Crucis; 828-297-4055, 800-297-1342; www.bairdhouse.com, e-mail bairdhouse@charter.net. DELUXE.

A mansion in the mountains, **Westglow Spa** is the plushest place to stay in the High Country. It certainly does look beautifully haunting there on the hill, and the worn roadside is testament to the legions of people who've pulled over to stare. The 1916 former home of artist Elliott Daingerfield, it's a European-style fitness and pampering spa with every imaginable extravagance, from body wraps, aromatherapies and facials to the Victorian rooms filled with antiques and objets d'art. Inside, the white-columned antebellum manse is much as Daingerfield left it; his 2500-volume library (some books still have personal notes to his daughters) and his furnishings are here, as well as his famous painting of St. Mary's of the Hills. Rates include all meals, fitness classes and spa treatments. ~ Route 221, three miles south of Blowing Rock; 828-295-4463, 800-562-0807, fax 828-295-5115; www.westglow.com, e-mail info@westglow.com. ULTRA-DELUXE.

True to their name, **Boone's Country Cabins** are out in the woods, tucked among nine acres with Blue Ridge Mountains all around. Of the eight cabins offered by innkeepers Penny and Tony Boone (a descendant of Daniel), the largest and most luxurious is the Keystone Phoenix. Crowned with a blue tin roof, the Phoenix comes with a native stone fireplace and master bedroom with a dormer window, hand-carved cedar poster bed, and bubbling whirlpool. Despite all this seclusion, though, Blowing Rock awaits but five miles away. ~ 130 Cameron Drive, Blowing Rock; 828-295-4836, fax 828-295-4761; www.boonescountry cabins.com, e-mail info@boonescountrycabins.com. DELUXE TO ULTRA-DELUXE.

In 2002, all 11 rooms at the **Maple Lodge** were renovated with modern comforts—goose-down comforters on lacy canopy beds, private baths with fresh flowers—while still keeping their mountain mood. Hardwood floors gleam beneath your feet, and heirloom antique sofas offer spaces for rest. Don't miss breakfast, served in a glass-walled dining room overlooking a wildflower garden.~ 152 Sunset Drive, Blowing Rock; 828-295-3331; www.maplelodge.net, e-mail innkeeper@maplelodge.net. MODERATE TO ULTRA-DELUXE.

Right in Blowing Rock, **The Inn at Ragged Garden** is located in a one-acre setting of roses and rhododendrons, with massive trees and a walled garden. Among the twelve floral-themed rooms is Monet's Garden, painted a rich burgundy and appointed with a handcrafted king-sized bed, fireplace, jacuzzi, tub, and private balcony. In the attic, the Rock Garden Garret spreads across two rooms and is highlighted by a fountain and an interesting rock garden. Other features are skylights, a jacuzzi tub, window seats and English pine antiques. ~ 203 Sunset Drive, just off Main Street, Blowing Rock; 828-295-9703, fax 828-295-6534; www.ragged-gardens.com. MODERATE TO ULTRA-DELUXE.

Space and luxury are key at **Gideon Ridge Inn,** where ten rooms feel more like suites stocked with exclusive amenities such as Swiss soaps and hypoallergenic shampoos. You'll also find mahogany canopy beds, fireplaces, hand-embroidered pillows, and baths of marble or tile. For private outdoor space, ask for the Colonial Room, where French doors open onto your own terrace. ~ 202 Gideon Ridge Road, Blowing Rock; 828-295-3644; www.ridge-inn.com, e-mail innkeeper@ridge-inn.com. DELUXE TO ULTRA-DELUXE.

Mountainaire Inn & Log Cabins will put you up for reasonable rates. The motor court with cabins is a little noisy but as neat as can be. Front doors are adorned with country wreaths, room interiors are carpeted and have cable TV and air conditioning. The cabins, priced in the deluxe to ultra deluxe range, have fireplaces. ~ 827 North Main Street, Blowing Rock; 828-295-7991; www.mountainaire-inn.com. BUDGET TO MODERATE.

Across from The Blowing Rock, grand old **Green Park Inn** is located at the 4300-foot elevation along the Eastern Continental Divide. Built in 1882, its long guest list includes presidents and other history makers. The sprawling, green-shuttered white manse looks down into the valleys and across mountains, and is flanked by rolling golf greens. Most of the 85 simple rooms have terrific views; all are cooled by mountain breezes and ceiling fans. There's a lounge and fine restaurant here. ~ Route 321, two miles south of downtown Blowing Rock; phone/fax 828-295-3141, 800-852-2462; www.greenparkinn.com. DELUXE TO ULTRA-DELUXE.

DINING

"A Collaboration in Food & Art" awaits diners at **The Bistro.** The food is a fusion of French and Italian—blackened tuna with bechemal sauce; beef medallions in mushroom *veloute* over penne pasta—and the art is provided by North Carolina talent. Vegetarians will love it here, too, as the menu offers nearly a

AUTHOR FAVORITE

Any place with its own cookbook should be good, and the **Mast Farm Inn** definitely is, with garden-grown cooking and gracious service. Dinner is served in two cozy rooms (and on a terrace when the weather is nice) at this 1800s eatery, with oil lamps and quilts on the walls, and wood tables for two or more. Among the delectable dishes: roasted organic beet and local goat cheese timbales, tempura-fried soft-shell crab and yellowfin tuna, fennel and eggplant wellington. Wine and beer available. Reservations recommended. ~ Route 1112, Valle Crucis; 828-963-5857; www.mastfarminn.com. ULTRA-DELUXE.

dozen inventive, meatless entrées. ~ 115 New Market Boulevard, Boone; 828-265-0500; www.thebistrorestaurant.com. MODERATE TO DELUXE.

As its name suggests, **Red Onion Cafe** is no run-of-the-mill place. It's a colorful, animated, smoke-free eatery with healthful offerings. The black-bean pesto lasagna and grilled chicken and fontina pizza are exceptional, and so are the turkey reuben sandwiches. ~ 227 Hardin Street, Boone; 828-264-5470. MODERATE.

Angelica's Vegetarian Restaurant & Juice Bar is in downtown Boone—all three blocks of it. Students flock to this cozy restaurant for cheap and organic open-face sandwiches like the portobello melt (with grilled onions, baby spinach and feta). The sushi rolls feature unusual fillings like sweet potato, jalapeño cream cheese and roasted red peppers. Lots of windows in the front overlook a deck where you can eat when the weather's nice. ~ 506 West King Street, Boone; 828-265-0809. MODERATE.

HIDDEN ▶   The **lunch counter** in back of Mast General Store makes a great tofu sandwich, and the homemade soups are chunky and extra rich. Plenty of other deli sandwiches are offered, all generously adorned with meats and cheese and tasting extra fresh. You can eat inside or out on the porch. ~ Route 194, Valle Crucis; 828-963-7049. BUDGET.

Blowing Rock village has several prime lunch stops. **Cheeseburgers in Paradise** offers both regular-size patties and gorge-yourself, one-pound burgers. The jalapeño cheese is great on top. Quesadillas, nachos and BLTs are also on the menu—but then Jimmy Buffett never sang about those. Grab a table outside under the umbrellas. ~ North Main Street, Blowing Rock; 828-295-4858. BUDGET.

Blowing Rock Café is where folks call each other by their first names, and the owners ask, "Are you OK today?" Go for lunch and order the homemade soup, a salad and sandwich—you won't be able to finish them. Pasta, seafood and chicken dishes are offered at dinner, and there's good breakfasts, too. ~ 349 Sunset Drive, off Main Street, Blowing Rock; 828-295-9474. MODERATE.

The restaurant at **Crippen's Country Inn** offers a daring gourmet menu that constantly changes. Your dinner at the inn might include marinated and grilled leg of lamb with eggplant marmalade, lentils and mint aioli; grilled rack of lamb with truffle sauce, grilled zucchini and asparagus, truffled mash and crispy potatoes; or Coca Cola–marinated grilled kangaroo. ~ 239 Sunset Drive, Blowing Rock; 828-295-3487, 877-295-3487; www.crippens.com. DELUXE TO ULTRA-DELUXE.

In an old, atmospheric log cabin hidden in the most unlikely of places—behind a Food Lion grocery—the **Best Cellar** entreats with exquisite dishes such as rack of lamb, stuffed veal chops, marinated fresh tuna and roast duckling. The homebaked breads and array of nightly vegetables, including baked acorn squash and stuffed zucchini, are superb. Stone arches and stained glass parade around the inside, and three fireplaces offer warmth. Closed Monday and Tuesday. Dinner only. ~ Off Route 321, Blowing Rock; 828-295-3466; e-mail thebestcellar@boone.net. MODERATE TO DELUXE.

Since it broke onto Blowing Rock's restaurant scene in 2001, **Canyon's** has been the hot spot for locals and travelers alike. The fare pleases everyone: Choose from all-American cheeseburgers, Southwestern/Mexican specialties or the chicken, salmon or sirloin dishes. The ambience speaks more to the American desert, with Southwestern-style paintings and collages by local artists. ~ Route 321, Blowing Rock; 828-295-7661; www.canyonsbr.com. BUDGET TO MODERATE.

Woodlands Barbecue & Pickin' Parlor is the local favorite for barbecue. Upstairs and down are picnic tables, their pine tops worn to a perfect patina by years of elbows and beer mugs. Order pork or beef (sliced or chopped), chicken or turkey (smoked whole out back), or opt for "The Hog," a mountain-size platter of chicken, ribs, beef and pork. Sandwiches are served on pig-shaped wooden plates. Closed Monday in the winter. ~ Route 321 Bypass, Blowing Rock; 828-295-3651; www.woodlandsbbq. com. BUDGET TO MODERATE.

Creekside Galleries is two terrific galleries plus an artist's studio. **SHOPPING** The largest space, **Carlton Gallery** (828-963-4288), is a former weaving studio that now displays works from more than 300 local and regional artists. Glass work, jewelry, paintings, sculpture and pottery can be found here. ~ Route 105, ten miles south of Boone.

In downtown Boone, the **Candy Barrel** has every sweet imaginable. Make sure the kids have already eaten. ~ King Street; 828-262-0000.

AUTHOR FAVORITE

One of the most enjoyable ways to spend a Boone summer night is watching **Horn in the West**. The lively outdoor pageant tells the early High Country story—from the white man's point of view, of course. Daniel Boone figures prominently and so do American Indians; a Cherokee fire dance is always a favorite. Performances are staged Tuesday through Sunday from mid-June to late August. All seats reserved, but walk-ups welcome. Admission. ~ Off Route 421; 828-264-2120; www.horninthewest.com.

Next door, you'll find the **Mast General Store and Old Boone Mercantile**. This is a satellite of the famous, century-old store in nearby Valle Crucis on Route 194 (828-963-6511). The big question at both stores is: What *won't* you find here? Hiking boots, hammered silver jewelry, duck decoys, bark bird feeders, barrels of candy and blue jeans are just some of the things for sale. The folks working here are extra helpful, and prices are surprisingly decent for such a popular place. ~ King Street; 828-262-0000.

Blowing Rock is great for shopping. Stroll along Main Street and watch your afternoon disappear. Antiques, oriental rugs, Christmas decor, resort wear—it's all here.

Pandora's Mailbox is fairly packed with New Age and avant-garde selections. There are racks of jewelry made all over the world, stacks of CDs by offbeat but terrific musicians, and loads of greeting cards. ~ Main Street, Blowing Rock; 828-295-4238.

The selection at **Starwood Gallery** is vast and varied, from pottery, stained glass and jewelry to dolls, basketry and kaleidoscopes. ~ Main Street, Blowing Rock; 828-295-9229.

The Dulcimer does have dulcimers—hammered dulcimers and mountain dulcimers, books on dulcimers and kits for making dulcimers. Closed January through April. ~ Main Street, Blowing Rock; 828-295-3616.

The fashion at **Almost Rodeo Drive** is decidedly conservative. Sports wear, sweaters, and silk coordinates satisfy the classy dressers in the family. ~ Main Street, Blowing Rock; 828-295-3422.

The **Sky Land Books/Chickory Suite Coffee** has flavored coffees, fine teas and books to peruse. ~ Main Street, Blowing Rock; 828-295-4231.

NIGHTLIFE It's beer and wine only in Boone (hard liquor sales are taboo). Everything's legal (relating to alcohol, that is) in Blowing Rock, though you won't need the leather and lycra. Most places are low-key, not wild and crazy.

Okay, it does get a little wild and crazy at **Woodlands Barbecue & Pickin' Parlor** when the banjos start cooking. Bluegrass and folk musicians play most nights—but you still won't need the lycra. Full bar. ~ Route 321 Bypass, Blowing Rock; 828-295-3651.

The **Blowing Rock Stage Company** presents shows like *Grace and Glorie* and *The Legend of Sleepy Hollow* year-round. ~ Blowing Rock Community Arts Center, Route 321, Blowing Rock; 828-295-9627; www.blowingrockstage.com.

Green Park Inn's **Divide Tavern** has billiards and darts, and a decidedly classy atmosphere. Full bar. ~ Route 321, two miles south of downtown Blowing Rock; 828-295-3141.

PARKS The Blue Ridge Parkway skirts the area (it's only feet from Blowing Rock) and offers great picnicking, fishing, hiking and sightseeing. (For more information on the parkway, see Chapter Five.)

As far north and west as you can get in
North Carolina, the northern High **Northern High Country**
Country is what folks in Boone refer to
as "out there." You won't find much lodging, dining, shopping
or nightlife. What you will find is plenty of open space, hills and
pasture and sky running in all directions, cows grazing beside
red-roofed barns, signs for feed stores and Baptist revivals, valleys dipping and rising, and rivers running clear and clean through
the countryside.

The New River flows north from Blowing Rock, splintering
into a north and south fork and little creeks and streams. The
oldest river in the country, it is designated a State Scenic River.
Its waters are superior for canoeing and fishing.

Several back roads wind north from Blowing Rock, including the **SIGHTS**
Blue Ridge Parkway. From the parkway, Route 163 angles up
through folded hills and farmlands to **West Jefferson**, home to
North Carolina's only cheese factory. It's not a terribly impressive
place, but **Ashe County Cheese Company**
does make a whole lot of cheese, up to   The Ashe County Cheese
20,000 pounds on some days. Visitors can   Company will provide you with
sometimes watch more than 180,000 pounds   some cheesy trivia. For exam-
of milk become cheese from the viewing room. ple, it takes up to three
Walk by the factory windows and watch the   months for mild cheese to
curds being weighed (and squeezed of whey), then age, six for medium and up
pressed, dried and sealed in wax to age. Closed to two years for extra
Sunday. ~ 106 East Main Street; 336-246-2501. sharp.

Nearby, the **Ashe County Chamber of Commerce
and Visitors Center** provides maps and information on the
area. Closed Sunday. ~ 6 North Jefferson Avenue, West Jefferson;
336-246-9550; www.ashechamber.com.

The chamber can also tell you the way to the **frescoes of St.**   ◄ HIDDEN
Mary's Church. The 1902 church is small and white, very Rock-
wellish, bordered by white picket fence and four gravestones. The
three frescoes are inside on the walls, painted on plaster and ma-
sonry in the 1970s by Ben Long IV. A native of Statesville, North
Carolina, Long trained in Italy as a fresco artist. Upon returning
to his home state, he could find no church to paint, and was re-
jected again and again by ministers. In 1973, he approached Father
Faulton Hodge at a Blowing Rock party. Hodge agreed to let
Long paint his St. Mary's church, then asked: "What is a
fresco?" Soon after Hodge got his frescoes, the teeny church became famous, and now thousands stop by every year to see the
richly painted works of "Mary, Great With Child," "John the
Baptist" and "The Mystery of Faith." ~ 400 Beaver Creek School
Road, about one-half mile off Route 163, West Jefferson; 336-
982-3076.

HIDDEN ► Long suddenly became sought after, and was commissioned to paint four frescoes at **Holy Trinity Church** in nearby Glendale Springs. His portrait here of "The Last Supper" is vast and sumptuous to the eye. ~ Route 16, about two and a half miles north of Route 163; 336-982-3076.

Both churches welcome visitors any time.

LODGING Chain lodgings are available in West Jefferson and Jefferson. For something out of the way, you'll have to go to Laurel Springs.

HIDDEN ► There you'll find **Burgiss Farm Bed & Breakfast** on a 200-acre cattle farm ringed in deep green hills and Christmas tree farms, and crisscrossed by cold-water creeks. Few places provide such peacefulness. Nancy and Tom Burgiss have opened their 1896 farmhouse to visitors, offering a bi-level, two-bedroom suite with lots of privacy. The enormous wood-and-stone living room has a trough where water is piped in from a nearby spring. Besides the trough, you get a TV, a CD player, mountain bikes, a hot tub and elaborate breakfasts (guests select from seven different menus and a dozen varieties of coffee). ~ 102 Thistle Meadow, three miles north of Blue Ridge Parkway Milepost 246, Laurel Springs; 336-359-2995, 800-233-1505; www.breakfastinn.com, e-mail tom@breakfastinn.com. MODERATE.

DINING The towns of West Jefferson, Jefferson and Glendale Springs have fast-food places, pizzerias and coffee shops.

A few miles north of Jefferson in Crumpler, **Shatley Springs Inn** is the place of local renown. Breakfast, lunch and dinner are family-style, with sleep-inducing portions of Southern home cooking: fried chicken and country ham, mashed potatoes and creamed corn, biscuits and gravy, and tall, dewy glasses of sweet tea. Get there early, especially on weekends, or you'll wait for a seat. Closed late November through April. ~ Route 16, Crumpler; 336-982-2236. BUDGET TO MODERATE.

SHOPPING The locally made cheeses at **Ashe County Cheese Company** are good quality. If it's cool out, they'll keep a few days on the road. ~ 106 East Main Street, West Jefferson; 336-246-2501.

Shatley Springs Inn has a gift shop stocked with local crafts, jams, rugs and country decor. A good place for browsing while waiting for a table at the inn's ever-popular restaurant. Closed late November through April. ~ North of Glendale Springs along Route 16; 336-982-2236.

NIGHTLIFE It's awful quiet most nights. But on many Saturday nights from April through December, you can head for the big barn at **Burgiss Farm Bed & Breakfast**. Owners Tom and Nancy Burgiss throw a huge hoedown, complete with barbecue, mountain music and "wild and crazy dancing," says Tom. Wear your blue jeans and boots. ~ 102 Thistle Meadow, three miles north of Blue Ridge Parkway Milepost 246, Laurel Springs; 336-359-2995.

MOUNT JEFFERSON STATE NATURAL AREA 🏃 A tiny park with all-encompassing vistas, this 555-acre wilderness caps Mount Jefferson. The mountain is 4683 feet high, shooting straight up from surrounding valleys, a pinnacle amid low seas of greenery. A road winds up to the summit and parking lot, where there is a sensational Blue Ridge panorama, with views into Virginia and Tennessee. The park forests are dense oak and hickory. Sorry, no camping. Facilities include park office, picnic tables and hiking trails. ~ Off Route 221 between West Jefferson and Jefferson; 336-246-9653.

PARKS

NEW RIVER STATE PARK AND SCENIC RIVER 🏃 🚣 ⬛ A canoer's heaven, the 1400-acre park follows the river through remote mountain countryside. The New River is intensely beautiful and barely intruded upon by humans. Five canoe outfitters (see the "Outdoor Adventures" section at the end of this chapter) provide rentals and guided trips, including overnight treks, through the park. Canoe rentals are not available in the park. The New River is excellent for smallmouth bass and redeye bass (live bait required); try for trout in the tributaries. Facilities include a park office, hiking trails and picnic areas. ~ The park office is eight miles southeast of Jefferson. Take Route 88 from Jefferson to Route 1590, then follow the signs; 336-982-2587.

◄ HIDDEN

⚠ Backcountry, canoe-in camping along the New River; $9 per site per night for up to six people. Permit required, available at the park office.

STONE MOUNTAIN STATE PARK 🏃 🐎 ⬛ Cool woods, towering and green in summer and sparse in winter, fill this 13,450-acre park. The high point is Stone Mountain, though its glistening bald patch of granite is only about 600 feet high. Cliff climbers scramble up the stone summit, while hikers take a rugged trail up—less risky, but just as exhausting. Permit (no fee, available at the trailhead) required for rock climbing. More than 17 miles of streams offer good trout fishing; try for rainbow and brown trout on lower streams, brook trout on higher waters. Fishing fee is $15 per person. Facilities include park office, picnic areas, hiking and bridle trails. ~ The park's main entrance is along Route 1002, off Route 21 and the Blue Ridge Parkway, seven miles southwest of Roaring Gap. In summer, take the twisting, dirt-and-gravel John P. Frank Parkway up from Route 1002 into the park. Along this re-

◄ HIDDEN

A mid-nineteenth-century historic homestead at Stone Mountain State Park offers a glimpse into the everyday lives of early area settlers.

mote route are crude cabins, streams, sometimes turtles and snakes sunning in the road. There are hardly any other cars; 336-957-8185.

▲ A family campground has 37 sites for tents or RVs (no hookups); grills, restrooms, hot showers and laundry tubs provided; $15 per family per night. A group camping area has four primitive sites with fireplaces and pit toilets; $1 per person per night. There are also six primitive backpacker sites; $9 per night.

Outdoor Adventures

▼▼▼▼▼▼▼▼▼▼▼▼▼▼▼

SPORT-FISHING

High Country rivers, streams and lakes offer many prospects for trout, as well as small and largemouth bass, muskies and catfish. Among the top spots are: the **Toe River** and its tributaries; the **Linville River**, especially through Linville Gorge; the **Elk River** (Route 194 between Banner Elk and Elk Park); **Boone's Fork**, a tributary of the Watauga River (above Hound Ears Club); **Howard's Creek** (off Route 194 north of Boone); the **Globe portion of the Johns River Gorge** (Globe Road, off Route 321, eight miles south of Blowing Rock); and **Anthony Creek, Johns River** and **Big Horse Creek** (located upstream from the Lower Route 1361 bridge to the Virginia state line).

There's also terrific fishing along the Blue Ridge Parkway. For information, see Chapter Five.

Among the local fishing outfits, **Foscoe Fishing Company** goes out on the Watauga and fishes for rainbow and brown trout as well as smallmouth bass. ~ 4533 #5 Tynecastle Highway, Banner Elk; 828-898-7555.

Wahoos rents canoes for fishing on the New River. ~ Route 321; Boone; 828-262-5774, 800-444-7238.

Fishing licenses, available from most hardware and general stores, are required for anyone 16 and older. Various laws govern the use of lures as well as fish size. A list of regulations is available with your license.

No license is needed to fish stocked trout farms. At these farms you will pay a per-fish fee and a permit fee. Local farms include **Grandfather Trout Farm**. ~ Route 105, near Seven Devils; 828-963-5098. **Springmaid Mountain** has six ponds for trout or catfish. ~ 2171 Henredon Road, Spruce Pine; 888-297-0725.

RAFTING & CANOEING

There's superb rafting on the Nolichucky River, whose headwaters begin as the Toe River. The trip passes through the deep and deeply scenic Nolichucky River Gorge, which has Class III and IV rapids.

Nantahala Outdoor Center offers whitewater trips on the Nolichucky River. ~ 800-232-7238. **Cherokee Adventures Whitewater Rafting** offers these trips as well. ~ 800-445-7238; www.cherokeeadventures.com.

Among the repertoire of adventures offered by **High Mountain Expeditions** are whitewater rafting along the Watauga and Nolichucky rivers and "funyaking" (with one-person inflatable kayaks) through the Wilson Creek Gorge. Choose from mild to wild rapids, and half-day to overnight trips. The company also organizes caving trips. ~ 915 North Main Street, Blowing Rock; 828-295-4200, 800-262-9036. **Wahoos** offers canoeing on the Toe River and hosts a slew of outdoor expeditions. ~ Route 321, Boone; 828-262-5774, 800-444-7238; www.wahoosadventures.com.

The New River is *the* place for canoeing. **Zaloo's Canoes** rents   ◀ HIDDEN
canoes, kayaks and innertubes, and hosts overnight and week-long excursions with backcountry camping in New River State Park. ~ 3874 Route 16N, about a quarter mile from Route 16S-88, Jefferson; 336-246-3066, 800-535-4027; www.zaloos.com.

New River Outfitters also takes canoers on the New River. ~ Route 221, at the New River General Store between Jefferson and Sparta; 336-982-9192.

Four major ski resorts, with High Country mountains ranging   **SKIING**
from 4000 to 5500 feet, offer downhill action, including snowboarding. A lot of the snow is machine-made, but it's groomed daily to a crumbly consistency, and sometimes it's downright powdery. The resorts are so close together—anywhere from 15 to 50 minutes apart—that it's possible to ski a different mountain each day. Most people, though, become attached to one place and never leave.

The New River is the second oldest river in the world (behind the Nile) and one of the few that flow northward.

All of the High Country's ski areas are open for night skiing, and sell discounted "twilight" passes good from early afternoon through the evening. This works perfectly for those who like to spend the day sightseeing and the evenings on the slopes—easiest done in March, when the mercury is well above zero at night.

If you have children, **Sugar Mountain** is a good choice since 80 percent of the 19 trails and slopes are designed for beginner or intermediate skiers. The Sugar Bear Ski School takes 5- to 10-year-olds, and the Sugar Mountain Nursery looks after the ones too little to ski. There's also a snowboard park. ~ Route 184, two miles east of Banner Elk; 828-898-4521, 800-784-2768; www.skisugar.com.

About seven miles northeast of Sugar at the 5505-foot tip of Beech Mountain, **Ski Beech** calls itself "the highest ski area in Eastern North America." The vertical drop is only 830 feet, but it's a straight down, don't-look-now plunge. There's a snowboard program for children, as well as a ski and snowboard center and ski lessons for young skiers. You'll find a quad lift and plenty of intermediate slopes. ~ Route 184; 828-387-2011, 800-438-2093; www.skibeech.com.

Teenagers head to **Hawksnest** in the town of Seven Devils, not far from Boone. This growing resort has something for everyone, from short beginner slopes to expert runs, including the testy **Top Gun** that plunges right from summit to ski lodge. There's an entire area devoted to snowboarders and two areas for "glade skiing," a kind of kamikaze skiing through thinned forest. If you like trees on your trail, this is definitely your place. ~ Route 105; 828-963-6561, 800-822-4295, fax 828-963-6564; www.hawksnest-resort.com.

The skiing at **Appalachian Ski Mountain** is more conservative. Like Sugar Mountain, Appalachian is big with families and beginners, not in the least because of its French-Swiss Ski College. Classes are kept small (6 to 10 people) so the instructors can work one-on-one to help skiers hone their skills. The SKIwee children's school, designed by *SKI* magazine, incorporates skiing and play for kids 4 to 10 years old. ~ Route 221-321, about halfway between Boone and Blowing Rock; 828-295-7828, 800-322-2373; www.appalachianskimountain.com.

The mood at Appalachian is low-key and friendly and the setting gentle, with low-lying blue ridges painting the horizon and a peak height of 4000 feet. An ice-skating rink offers nonskiers a way to pass the day (other than on that slope-front barstool). The 6000-square-foot outdoor rink is parked on a knoll, with compelling views of the slopes.

Ski Rentals   You can rent equipment at all the ski resorts. Or, several private outfits rent equipment at (usually) slightly reduced rates. Check with **Ski Country Sports** for skis and snowboard rentals. ~ Route 184, across from the entrance to Sugar Mountain; 828-898-9786, 800-528-3874. **Edge of the World Outfitters** rents snowboards. ~ Route 184, about halfway between Sugar Mountain and Ski Beech; 828-898-9550. Try **Fred's General Mer-**

AUTHOR FAVORITE

I found heaven on skis in Oz—the Oz Run at **Ski Beech**, that is. Like a secret escape hatch, it bends down the back of the mountain and is clear of other skiers (they're back on Beech's excellent black diamond slopes). The only thing I saw on Oz, in fact, was a white-tailed deer. Ski Beech has a lot going on; there's a festive little village at the base where music is played all day long, and where an assortment of restaurants and boutiques crowd around an ice-skating rink that's nearly as popular as the slopes. See page 179 for more information.

cantile for skis, snowshoes or snowboards. ~ Route 184, Beech
Mountain; 828-387-4838. Near Hawksnest is **French Swiss Ski
Rentals.** ~ Route 105, near Hawksnest; 828-963-6410. **1st Tracks
Ski Team** has skis and snowboards. ~ Route 105, Boone; 828-
264-7368. **Farmer's Backside** will outfit you with skis or snow-
boards. ~ 140 South Depot Street, Boone; 828-264-4565. **Ski
Country Sports** will provide you with skis or a board. ~ Route
184, Banner Elk; 828-898-9786.

The mountains make for wonderful trail rides. Guided horseback
trips are offered through **Springmaid Mountain.** ~ Off Mckinney
Gap Road and the Blue Ridge Parkway, in the Toe River Valley;
828-765-2353. You can also try **Banner Elk Riding Stables.** ~
Shoemaker Road, off Route 194, Banner Elk; 828-898-5424.

**RIDING
STABLES**

   Blowing Rock Stables has rides along turn-of-the-twentieth-
century carriage trails at Moses H. Cone Memorial Park on the
Blue Ridge Parkway. ~ Located on Laurel Lane, off Route 221,
Blowing Rock; 828-295-7847.

   Northwest of Boone, in Vilas, there's **Chadi Farm Horseback
Carriage & Haywagon** for sleigh rides, carriage trips, hayrides
and horseback excursions. ~ 4365 Route 194 South; 828-963-
5399; www.chadifarm.com.

   Many stables operate from spring through fall and require
reservations, so call ahead.

High Country golf courses, like the **Grassy Creek Golf and Country Club** are famous for their mountain scenery. ~ Route 226,
Grassy Creek, about two miles south of Spruce Pine; 828-765-
7436. Among the courses open to the public is the semiprivate
Quaker Meadows Golf Club. ~ 826 North Green Street, Mor-
ganton; 828-437-2677. The 18-hole **Hanging Rock Golf Course**
is open to the public. ~ Hawksnest Golf & Ski Resort, Route 105,
Seven Devils; 828-963-6565. In Banner Elk, try **Sugar Mountain
Golf Club.** ~ off Route 184, Banner Elk; 828-898-6464. While
in Boone, head down to the **Boone Golf Club.** ~ 433 Fairway
Drive, Boone; 828-264-8760. Just south of Boone, you'll find
Willow Creek Golf Course. ~ Route 105, three miles south of
Boone; 828-963-6865. Or try the **Mountain Aire Golf Club.** ~
Off Route 221, West Jefferson; 336-877-4716.

GOLF

Most courts are outdoors, so plan on playing spring through fall.
You'll find courts at **Brad Ragan Memorial Park.** ~ School Road,
Spruce Pine. **Banner Elk Community Park** also has courts. ~ Route
194, Banner Elk. **Appalachian State University** has courts. ~
River Street, Boone. In Boone, try **Watauga Recreation Complex.**
~ Complex Drive, Boone; 828-264-9511. **West Jefferson Park** is
the place to go in West Jefferson. ~ Long Street, West Jefferson.

TENNIS

BIKING   Mountain bikers appreciate the High Country and its steep, muscle-building terrain that's also extremely picturesque. Try to plan your ride during the warmer months as the roads are usually too icy in winter and, anyway, who really wants to be out of doors unless it's to ski? For excellent bike-trail maps, contact the North Carolina Department of Transportation's Bicycle Program. ~ 1552 Mail Service Center, Raleigh, NC 27699-1552; 919-733-2804.

The **Blue Ridge Parkway** is the place of choice for many bikers. The **Brown Mountain Lights** segment of the trail starts on the Parkway just south of Little Switzerland and winds 52 miles to Jonas Ridge at Route 191. Along the way you can stop at the Museum of North Carolina Minerals and Linville Falls.

For more on biking the Blue Ridge Parkway, see Chapter Five.

Bike Rentals   Mountain bikes are available from **Beech Mountain Sports**. ~ 325 Beech Mountain Parkway, Banner Elk; 828-387-2795. **Boone Bike & Touring** is another place to go. ~ 899 Blowing Rock Road, Boone; 828-262-5750.

HIKING   A hiker's heaven, the High Country has hundreds of miles of trails through gardens and gorges, beside rivers and creeks, around lakes, and up steep rocky ledges. For an extensive list of trails, contact the **High Country Host**. ~ Route 321, Boone; 828-264-1299, 800-438-7500; www.mountainsofnc.com. All distances listed for hiking trails are one way unless otherwise noted.

TOE RIVER VALLEY   On Roan Mountain, the leisurely **Gardens Trail** (1 mile) wends through the world's largest natural rhododendron garden. The 600-acre mountaintop patch peaks in mid- to late June. The trailhead is off Route 261 just before the North Carolina–Tennessee line.

About a mile past the Gardens Trail, but still in North Carolina, **Cloudland Trail** (3 miles round-trip) is a little more challenging. It presses through fir and spruce forest to 6267-foot Roan High Bluff, where views are spectacular.

Hard-core hikers should consider the trails at Linville Gorge in Pisgah National Forest. Going down into the gorge is not too bad, but coming back out is another story: steep, ragged rocks make the hike more of a climb. Seven trails descend from the gorge's west rim, and are accessed along Route 1238 off Route 183 south of the town of Linville Falls. From the east rim, along National Forest Road 210, there are two trails. All are classified by the forest service as "more difficult" or "most difficult." Within the gorge, **Linville Gorge Trail** (12 miles) is a strenuous hike alongside Linville River.

Permits (there is no fee) are required for the Linville Gorge trails on weekends and holidays from May through October, and can be procured from the **Grandfather Ranger District Office**. ~

Located off Route 40, at the Nebow–Lake James exit, Nebow;
828-652-2144.

LINVILLE & BANNER ELK   The nine trails on Grandfather
Mountain are almost all rocky and strenuous, but they're unsur-
passed for rugged scenery. The arduous **Grandfather Trail** (2.3
miles) has ladders and cables to help you scale various cliffs.
Most of the trail is through high-elevation forest, with backcountry campsites to choose from. The **Nuwati Trail** (1.2 miles)
is much easier, though rocky, with a panorama of glacier-carved
Boone Fork Bowl.

A permit is required to hike and camp on Grandfather Mountain. The fee is $6 per day for adult hikers, $12 per day for adult
campers. The separate admission to get on the mountain (a private
attraction), means you don't need to pay the day fee for hiking. ~
828-733-4337.

BOONE & BLOWING ROCK AREA   The best trails around Boone
and Blowing Rock are off the Blue Ridge Parkway, which skirts
both towns. For a list of hikes, see Chapter Five.

NORTHERN HIGH COUNTRY   Within Mount Jefferson State Natural Area, the **Service Road Trail** (.6 mile) goes to the top of the
mountain. It's an easy gravel trail, but, unfortunately, the view
from the summit is partly blocked. Keep going from here on the
Rhododendron Trail (1.4 miles round-trip), which does reward
with numerous scenic overlooks. Vegetation and outlying mountains and valleys are marked on this easy trek.

Steep and strenuous, **Stone Mountain Loop Trail** (4 miles) in
Stone Mountain State Park curls up to the granite summit that gives
the mount its name. The scenery is spartan and rocky; the forests
are thin, the outcroppings windblown into futuristic shapes. The
superb view from the top is across Blue Ridge Mountains and
rolling Piedmont.

Also in Stone Mountain State Park, **Wolf Rock Cedar Rock
Trail** (3 miles) cuts a sloping path through hardwood forest and
patches of rhododendron. Parts of the trail are moderate, but
most are difficult.

▼▼▼▼▼▼▼▼▼▼▼
Transportation

CAR

There are no major highways leading into the High
Country, just scenic two- and four-lane roads that wind
up through the mountains. Route 321 is a fairly straight
shot northwest from Hickory to Blowing Rock and Boone.

From Asheville, **Route 19** wends north to the southern end
of the High Country. Or visitors can take **Route 40** east of
Asheville for 30 miles, then veer north on **Route 221** to Linville
and Boone. Route 221 also brings motorists down from Virginia
into the High Country.

If time is not of the essence, use the **Blue Ridge Parkway**. The picturesque byway, part of the National Park System, curls up from Asheville and runs right through the High Country.

AIR

About two hours away by car, **Asheville Regional Airport** near Asheville is serviced by Atlantic Southwest, ComAir, US Airways and US Airways Express.

CAR RENTALS

At Asheville Regional Airport (828-684-2226), there's **Avis Rent A Car** (800-331-1212), **Budget Rent A Car** (800-527-0700), **Enterprise Rent A Car** (800-261-7331) and **Hertz Rent A Car** (800-654-3131).

SEVEN

The Piedmont

Between the bluish peaks of North Carolina's western mountains and the flat white expanse of its coast is the Piedmont—a ruddy, rambling region sculpted with soft hills, sprinkled with loblolly pines and mahoganies, and colored with clay. This is the geographic heart of the state and a hub of the New South, where art, education, research and industry are all growing rapidly and creating a whole new way of doing things.

Technically, the Piedmont neither starts nor ends in North Carolina but reaches down from New York's Hudson River all the way to Birmingham, Alabama, a long, lazy plateau of rolling foothills framed by mountains and sea. It is the "crescent" of Carolinas hills, however, that gives the Piedmont its name, and it is North Carolina's big cities that shape its modern image.

Winston-Salem, Charlotte, Raleigh and Durham and their environs constitute the nation's fifth-largest urban area, home to over three million people. Here are the factories that churn out Piedmont textiles and tobacco, and the highrises of glass that house banking, insurance and computer giants. Here, too, are the brooding Gothic college campuses of red brick, white columns and ancient gardens, and the sprawling sports arenas (and their basketball games) that are treated with the same reverence as the stately churches that decorate the landscape.

In the beginning, though, before the textile mills, skyscrapers and churches, Piedmont life was all about clay. The earliest settlers, eighteenth-century Moravians, Quakers, Shakers and Scotch-Irish, were at the mercy of the acid-rich orange soil. It wasn't much good for growing corn or any other vegetable, so the settlers had to be enterprising, concentrating on trades instead of crops. They became masons and potters, coaxing the clay into bricks and bowls—and jugs to stash moonshine. They learned blacksmithing and tinsmithing, weaving and barrel-making (called coopering). They felled trees and turned them into furniture. They built wagons, filled them with wares, and sent men out to trade them. And they grew cotton.

Cotton is a scavenger crop, prolific in even the most barren of soils. By the mid-1800s, cotton fields had taken hold of the Piedmont clay. These weren't plantations like the ones across the Carolina coastal plain, but small- and medium-size plots worked by the yeoman farmer, the backbone of Southern cotton.

Tobacco is also a scavenger, thriving in the merciless clay. American Indians had been growing and smoking tobacco for centuries, but it wasn't until the 1850s, when Piedmonters concocted the lighter, brighter "brightleaf" tobacco, that the crop became a profitable industry. An exhausted Caswell County slave helped the tobacco cause when he fell asleep in a barn, allowing a fire to smolder the bright leaves he was curing. The leaves tasted so good that the rest of the Piedmont started charcoal-curing tobacco. Soon the Civil War created an instant demand: both Rebel and Yankee troops had to have their "weed," as tobacco was called back then. Women weren't supposed to smoke but they could dip snuff, which gave them a bigger buzz, anyway.

Washington Duke was one Civil War soldier who not only enjoyed smoking tobacco but also had a mind to market it. Most every Piedmonter knows the story of how, at war's end, a broke Washington Duke walked 225 miles from New Bern, North Carolina, back to his small Durham farm. There, in a teeny, one-room barn, he started the South's first tobacco "factory," sifting the cured tobacco and packing it into cloth bags. He labeled the bags *Pro Bono Publico* ("for the good of the public"), put them in his wagon, and peddled them across the Piedmont. Cigarettes being cigarettes, Duke became wildly successful and went on to build the largest tobacco empire in the world.

The Piedmont's other tobacco magnate, R. J. Reynolds, was assembling his own cigarette empire around the same time. In 1874 he settled not far from Durham in Winston, population 400. By the early 1900s, Reynolds had built his own factory, employing more than 10,000 people. Thanks to Reynolds, Winston got so big so fast it grew right into the Moravian town of Salem. In 1913, the two officially became known as Winston-Salem.

While the tobacco fields were spreading, cotton nearly disappeared. In the 1890s, the Mexican cotton boll weevil crossed the Rio Grande River and had most of the cotton belt for lunch. Today, you'll only find small patches of cotton around the Piedmont, though there is a vast patchwork of tobacco. Much of the tobacco crop makes its way to the monstrous R. J. Reynolds Plant near Winston-Salem, where one of every four cigarettes is made.

Tobacco kept the Piedmont in the national news for much of the 1990s, and not because it is *pro bono publico*. At best, tobacco is a troublesome crop; at worst, it's a deadly drug that has divided not only the South but the entire country. Cigarette sentiments run strong in these parts, and whether you're driving through brightleaf fields or eating in a restaurant (no-smoking sections have *not* caught on here), you feel tobacco's presence. Throughout the region, numerous sights and museums offer a fascinating look back at how the industry was born, right in the clay.

Clay is at least in part responsible for the region's second big industry: furniture. Ever since those early pioneers turned away from the harsh soil and to the trees for a trade, Piedmonters have been crafting furniture for folks around the country. Today, some 65 percent of all American furniture is made in the Pied-

The Piedmont

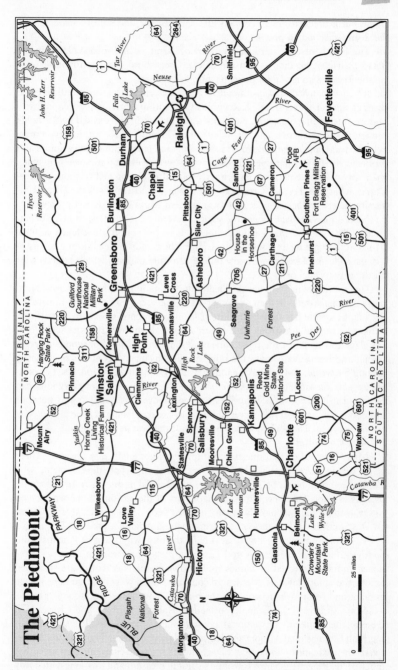

mont. Furniture factories and outlets fill the landscape, and visitors converge here for deeply discounted prices.

The Piedmont tour starts at the heart of furniture and tobacco land, in the Triad. A trio of big cities—Winston-Salem, Greensboro and High Point—make up the Triad, with slivers of green pasture in between.

It's easy to tell that Winston-Salem started as two cities, for it still has two distinct sides. There is the R. J. Reynolds side, with its thriving tobacco industry and its outstanding museums, parks, inns and art academies created by Reynolds money. And then there is Old Salem, one of the Piedmont's top attractions, a marvelous Moravian village of restored eighteenth- and nineteenth-century homes and workshops. The German-speaking Moravians were brilliant tradesmen who made their way to the Piedmont from Pennsylvania, after having fled religious oppression in what later became Czechoslovakia. Winston-Salem has Wake Forest University, where celebrated poet and local resident Maya Angelou is a professor.

Next door, Greensboro was the sight of several major battles, from a Revolutionary War conflict that included thousands to the nation's first lunch counter sit-ins in the fight against segregation. High Point and the neighboring towns of Thomasville and Lexington are the hub of furniture making, which extends west all the way to Hickory.

Due south of the Triad lies the Piedmont destination that has perhaps secured more national attention than any other—and not because of tobacco. In barely a decade, Charlotte has transformed itself from an obscure, unexciting textile and banking center to a lustrous New South star. Its downtown sparkles with vertical glass and metal of the most current design, and its neighborhoods of regal homes and immaculate lawns fan out for miles. Its airport connects major cities around the world, and its banking industry ranks third in the nation. The performing arts are thriving here, and so are the visual arts. Museums of every kind can be found in Charlotte, including historic neighborhoods qualifying as outdoor museums. Culinarily, it offers everything from exciting ethnic experiences to New South nouveau. The soul food here is some of the best in the South.

Why Charlotte?

Many have asked that question but few have gotten an easy answer. "There is no apparent reason, by the usual standards of urban development, why Charlotte should be doing so well," notes an editorial in the *Charlotte Observer*, the city's major daily newspaper. Perhaps part of the reason, the paper goes on to say, is that Charlotte has always invited new people and new ideas, and "is not an Old South town that moves at a crinoline and magnolia pace. . . ."

Two hundred miles east of Charlotte lie the tiny twin towns of Pinehurst and Southern Pines, where serious golf has been played for nearly a century. Three dozen courses, designed by names well known in the PGA world, are sprinkled among the sandy clay hills. Manicured country clubs, a New England–style village and a grand resort are just some of the reasons why visitors keep coming back.

North of here is the Triangle, formed by Raleigh, Durham and Chapel Hill. Despite their link in the national consciousness (mainly because of Raleigh-Durham International Airport and Research Triangle Park, a high-tech center between the two cities), Raleigh and Durham are separate cities, and not even that much alike. Raleigh is North Carolina's capital, pleasant and low-key, with a tidy downtown of classical-style state buildings and lovely historic neighborhoods. The busy North Carolina State University campus is on Raleigh's outskirts.

Durham has more bustle, taller buildings, faster-walking business people with serious looks on their faces. Like Winston-Salem, it grew up as a tobacco town; Washington Duke's homestead, now a state historic site, is minutes from downtown. Of course, his name is more often linked with Duke University, founded by his son James Buchanan "Buck" Duke. The Gothic campus is not only gorgeous to look at, it is a hub of Durham medical research.

The research continues at the 6800-acre, high-tech Research Triangle Park, whose tenants include IBM, Northern Telecom and Burroughs-Wellcome. The drug AZT was developed here, and Nobel Prizes have been awarded to park researchers. The park is a big reason *Fortune* magazine in 1993 named Raleigh/Durham the number-one U.S. city (really, cities) for business, saying "this chunk of piney-woods real estate in central North Carolina has smartened up over the past two decades and become a genuine intellectual capital."

> Yankee blood, it is said, gives the region's soil its color, though of course it comes from something much more prosaic—an overdose of iron oxides.

Many of the park's employees live (or want to live) in Chapel Hill, with neighborhoods filled with princely old homes, well-tended gardens and vast oaks and sycamores. The beautiful University of North Carolina is the centerpiece of the small town and, in fact, someone just passing through might think it the town, with the constant hubbub emanating from its groomed grounds.

Despite the rich academia and industry and New South growth, the old ways can still be found across the Piedmont. You don't need to look far to find weather-worn farmhouses set amongst shaggy fields of tobacco, centuries-old curing barns emitting sweet tobacco smells, the cattle grazing in plain view of a downtown highrise. Just outside Winston-Salem, there lies a Wild West–style town, Love Valley, where no cars—only horses—are allowed on Main Street. Unmarked side roads, whose names are known only to locals, lead up to time-forgotten general stores or perhaps a pharmacy museum whose pharmacist was born in the cabin next door.

Then, too, there is still all that clay. It sticks to your shoes and squishes between your toes. Dry, it's as tough as cement. Clay attaches itself to a person and won't let go, staining fingers for days and shoes forever. If you drive around the Piedmont for very long, both your car and mind will be indelibly rouged.

Winston-Salem Area

The R. J. Reynolds empire put Winston-Salem on the modern map in the 1950s when it named its cigarettes after the city (both Winstons and Salems). But two centuries earlier, a hard-working, health-minded band of Protestants put it on the geographic map.

When the Moravians came to the Piedmont from Bethlehem, Pennsylvania, in 1752, there was nothing here but trees, bears and rattlesnakes. The German-speaking people, religious dissidents from Bohemia and Moravia (later Czechoslovakia), instantly loved the land. They bought nearly 100,000 acres and called it *der Wachau*, after their leader's ancestral estate. The word soon became Wachovia, pronounced Wa-KO-vee-a, and today everything from banks to dry cleaners has taken the name Wachovia.

The idea for the original Wachovia, now known as Old Salem, was actually born six miles away at what is now **Historic Betha-bara Park**. More of an archaeological site than restored village, the serene, forested, 195-acre park is speckled with the wood and stone remains of one of the Piedmont's first frontier settlements. There's a film to tell you about the place, and a guided tour of the 1788 Gemeinhaus House, where religious services were held. You can also visit the 1782 Potter's House, the reconstructed French and Indian war fort and eight log buildings that replicate how the village looked in the eighteenth century. Here also is another God's Acre, with timeworn epithets scripted in German. Admission. Closed December 1 through April 1. ~ 2147 Bethabara Road, just north of Silas Creek Parkway, Winston-Salem; 336-924-8191; www.bethabarapark.org.

A century after the Moravians began building their Salem, Richard Joshua "R. J." Reynolds was creating the city of Winston. There the tobacco giant opened a factory, and by the early 1900s was mass-producing cigarettes, bringing in thousands of new residents. In 1917, Reynolds and his wife, Katherine, used some of their new fortune to buy an estate that's now the **Reynolda House Museum of American Art**. The manor and its 100 rooms and galleries are positively exquisite, and yet done with such warmth and familiarity as to seem like the Reynolds just stepped out for a carriage ride. In R. J. Reynolds' former den, for instance, wall lamps shimmer against fine Georgian oak paneling, a Gothic Revival oak desk and walnut armchairs. The art on the walls seems secondary, though it includes such intriguing pieces as a nineteenth-century oil by Edward Hicks, a sign painter and Quaker preacher. In the attic, a costume collection that includes the wedding "suit" Katherine Smith made and then wore when she married R. J. Reynolds in 1905, in nearby Mount Airy. The tour of Reynolda House is self-guided and accompanied by a booklet detailing every room. Docents roam the place hoping you'll ask questions, and they know *a lot*, including gossipy anecdotes about the Reynolds men and their womanizing, scandalous ways, so don't hesitate to ask! Closed Monday. Admission. ~ Reynolda Road, south of Silas Creek Parkway, Winston-Salem; 336-725-5325, fax 336-758-5704; www.reynoldahouse.org.

There's nothing more American than kitsch. Where else would you find a gas station built in the shape of a shell? You can't drive by this yellow concrete clamshell without taking a second look. Built by the Quality Oil Company in the late 1930s, **Preservation North Carolina** saved this bit of Americana from destruction and now uses the structure as a regional office. ~ 1111 Sprague Street, Winston-Salem; 336-788-0765.

Before heading out of town, bring the kids to learn and play at **Sciworks**. The 15-acre environmental park, nature trails, a state-of-the-art planetarium and several interactive exhibits are sure to keep you occupied. Closed Sunday. Admission. ~ 400 West Hanes Mill Road, Winston-Salem; 336-767-6730; www.sci works.org, e-mail info@sciworks.org.

For loads of information on tours and places to stay and eat and play, stop by the **Winston-Salem Convention and Visitors Bureau**. ~ 200 Brookstown Avenue, Winston-Salem; 336-728-4200, 800-331-7018.

Driving north from Winston-Salem, it's less than 30 minutes before the city scenes transform into bucolic ones. From the lonely two-lane stretches of **Routes 66** and **89**, you can look into forests with feet of clay and across open fields laced with white plank fence. Church steeples spire upward, wash flaps in the wind and

feed stores are attended by hound dogs and old farmers idly chewing pieces of straw. And then there will be mountains.

West of these byways, the four lanes of **Route 52** head northwest of Winston-Salem and eventually run smack into the Blue Ridge Mountains. On the way is a perfectly hidden stop, **Horne Creek Living Historical Farm**. The way to Horne Creek is down many country roads, past rippled fields of tobacco and their rugged curing sheds, and hillside cemeteries the size of postage stamps. The farm, a state historic site, is out in the woods, which is exactly where Thomas Hauser wanted to be back in the mid-1800s. His family's 1847 log barn and 1870s house are still here; the house has the original grain bin and has been restored to its original condition. Initially 400 acres but now 100, the farm is being fashioned as a turn-of-the-twentieth-century "living" outdoor museum, meaning the animals, crops and farm tools mimic those early ones (forget those gas-guzzling tractors!). There are plots of rare corn, some types of endangered farm animals, a kitchen garden with turnips, orchards of heirloom apples and peaches, a chicken coop, turkeys, a mule, feed barn and hog lot. Closed Sunday and Monday. ~ From Route 52, exit at the town of Pinnacle and go about six miles west; 336-325-2298, fax 336-325-3150.

HIDDEN ►

Back southeast of the foothills on Route 66 is a bucolic break called **Kernersville**. The town has several big old houses nestling under giant trees, but the one that gets everyone's attention is **Korner's Folly**, a state historic site. It's an outrageously elaborate, somewhat crumbling house built in the 1870s by local artist and eccentric Jule Korner, with a zany exterior, fanciful carved ceilings and walls, strange mismatched doors and tiny thresholds that seem made for dwarfs. Built on seven levels, the house con-

HIDDEN ►

sights

AUTHOR FAVORITE

For a gander at the opulence cigarette money could buy in the early twentieth century, stop by the **Reynolda House Museum of American Art**, originally the 100-room estate of tobacco king R. J. Reynolds. All three floors of the house are filled with architectural and artistic intrigue, with hundreds of paintings, prints and sculptures spanning 300 years, each piece marvelously varied and accompanied by a one-page background on the art and artist. In one stair corridor there's a 1922 abstract of Lake George, New York, by Georgia O'Keeffe along with a 1957 watercolor by Andrew Wyeth depicting a farm scene near his Pennsylvania home. In a second-floor gallery there's a wonderful painting of Mount Whitney by nineteenth-century landscape artist Albert Bierstadt. See page 190 for more information.

tains a total of 22 rooms and 15 fireplaces. If you plan on arriving during the week, call ahead to make an appointment. Closed Monday through Wednesday. Admission. ~ South Main Street, Kernersville; 336-996-7922; www.kornersfolly.org.

About 20 miles farther east, along Route 40, **Greensboro** is plain but pleasant enough and, though not a traveler's city, it does offer a few sites for those passing through. On the north side of town, **Guilford Courthouse National Military Park** covers 220 acres of forest and is the site of a key battle of the Revolutionary War. Monuments and markers nestled under sun-streaked elms guide you through the various stages of the battle that took place on March 15, 1781, between 4400 American troops and 2000 British soldiers. ~ 2332 New Garden Road, Greensboro; 336-288-1776.

In 1960, downtown Greensboro was the sight of a different kind of protest. It was here that four African-American college students sat down at the old F. W. Woolworth's lunch counter for the nation's first protest against segregation. A **marker** on Elm Street near Sycamore Street memorializes the history-altering event.

You can learn more about the sit-down nearby at the **Greensboro Historical Museum**. A striking Romanesque building sparkling with stained glass, it has had many past lives, including church and Confederate hospital. Numerous additions have been made over the years and now two floors are packed with engaging exhibits on Piedmont life. There's a terrific display of Piedmont furniture, and rooms filled with mementos of Dolley Madison and the writer O'Henry (real name William Sidney Porter), who spent his childhood in Greensboro. Closed Monday and the month of January. ~ 130 Summit Avenue, Greensboro; 336-373-2043, fax 336-373-2204; www.greensborohistory.org.

On the south side of town, **Blandwood Mansion** has the distinction of being the "earliest, still standing, Italianate Tuscan villa in the United States." It's really not a terribly impressive villa, but the docents are quite friendly and effusive about the history and architectural details. Closed Monday and the month of January. Admission. ~ 447 West Washington Street, Greensboro; 336-272-5003; www.blandwood.org.

Built in 1927, the historic **Carolina Theatre of Greensboro** is a community performing arts showplace. Tours through the magnificent building take you center stage and behind the scenes. Admission. ~ 310 South Greene Street, Greensboro; 336-333-2605, 336-333-2600, fax 336-333-2604; www.carolinatheatre.com.

South of Greensboro, the **Richard Petty Museum** is a shrine ◄ HIDDEN to the local boy who became history's winningest race car driver. Older kids should like this place because they can see several of his cars, dozens of his trophies and awards, photos of his various crashes, and his "cool suit." Closed Sunday. Admission. ~

A few blocks from the highrises of downtown Winston-Salem is the original Wachovia's main town, remarkably preserved as Old Salem. Nearly 90 buildings have been restored from the 1700s and 1800s; seven of the restored buildings feature guided tours (fee). You can stroll and drive through the village without paying admission, but to really feel Old Salem you should take the guided tours.

GUIDED TOURS   The seven guided tours—with Moravian history and culture passionately related by docents, and with cabinetmakers, blacksmiths, cobblers and others demonstrating their trades—is a must to fully experience the village. If you were to take all seven tours, wander leisurely through several more restored buildings and have lunch at the village's **Salem Tavern** (which you must), you would need two days. Not coincidentally, tickets are good for two days. Admission. ~ 600 South Main Street; 336-721-7300.

VISITORS CENTER   Pick up a map at the visitors center and start walking these tranquil streets, exploring the homes and trade shops of proper red brick and deep-toned clapboard, with their crisp white-picket borders, gushing gardens and steeply pitched roofs. ~ Old Salem Road at Academy Street. Walking around town, you'll see workers padding about in eighteenth-century garb and speaking in hushed, respectful tones as would have been done in the town's beginning. Like the Quakers and Mennonites, the Moravians lived a peaceful, productive existence, though unlike those other communities, theirs focused on trades instead of farming. Men and women lived separately until marriage, leaving home when they turned 14 to live in dormitories and learn a trade.

SINGLES AND SILVERSMITHS   Stop at the **Single Brothers House**, which housed up to 50 men and boys teaching and learning everything from tailoring to blacksmithing. Built in 1769, the brick-and-timber

142 West Academy Street, off Route 220, Randleman; 336-495-1143; www.pettyracing.com.

It only makes sense that the Carolinas' premier zoo is not near people but way out in the sticks of central Piedmont, where the elephants, giraffes and rhinoceros can really roam. Plan to spend **HIDDEN ►** at least half a day at the superb **North Carolina Zoological Park**, and wear some comfortable shoes (for wheelchair visitors, there are wide, paved, gently sloped paths). Admission. ~ Route 159, off Route 220, near Asheboro; 336-879-7000, 800-488-0444.

house has much that's original, including the great hearth. Around the corner, the Federal-style **John Vogler House** belonged to early Salem's most famous silversmith. Vogler's signature doorhandle, a hand gripping a bar and representing "the hand of hospitality," became the rage back then. Today, one still greets visitors to his 1819 house.

WINKLER BAKERY   From Vogler's place, you can smell the doughy, sugary aromas singular to Moravian baking. Walk a block and a half to the Winkler Bakery and watch robust women feeding dough into a brick oven. The domed oven, connected to the house by a trap door, is just like the one put here in 1800 by master builder Johann Gottlob Krause. Today women still rake the hot coals in early morning, laying out the dough on big trays of sheet iron, using long-handled paddles to pull the shapely loaves of bread dark as midnight, and the cakes and cookies dusted white with sugar. The baked stuff is for sale, by the way, though you'll have to wait in line behind everyone else lured here by their noses. Sunday is the only day they don't bake. ~ 525 South Main Street, Winston-Salem; 336-721-7302.

MUSEUM OF EARLY SOUTHERN DECORATIVE ARTS   Make sure you stop in the Museum of Early Southern Decorative Arts (separate admission), where two dozen rooms and galleries splendidly showcase the furniture and architecture of the Old South. Then have your letters postmarked "Salem" at the **post office**. At **God's Acre cemetery**, you can see how Moravians are buried, segregated by gender.

THE LARGE COFFEEPOT   Nothing, however, is as fitting an ending to Old Salem as the Large Coffeepot. Walk down to the line where Old Salem and Winston-Salem meet and you'll see it standing, tall and strange, like something the Mad Hatter might have concocted. It was, in fact, created by Moravian brothers Samuel and Julius Mickey. Built in 1858 of tin, the coffeepot stands seven feet and three inches high, an advertising ploy for their tinmaking business. No one seems to know if it ever worked. ~ Main Street at Brookstown Avenue.

Four miles of paths cut through the 1400 acres of habitats, for the most part big, open spaces designed more for animals than spectators. A tram circles the zoo; you can ride it all the way around, but in order to see the habitats you'll have to get off the tram.

On the **African-style plain** you'll find antelope and rhinoceros; in the forest edge, giraffes, zebras and ostriches; and in the forest glade, gorillas. Elsewhere you'll see baboons, chimpanzees, elephants and lions. And you'll also encounter some state-of-the-art exhibits opened in the last few years.

Most talked about are the three polar bears who live in the imitation Arctic Rocky Coast Habitat, part of the 200-acre **North American region**. The bears play in their pool, licking peanut butter, smeared by zoo employees, off a glass wall so visitors can get up-close looks.

The **Sonora Desert** is a domed hothouse with special heating and cooling and ventilation to keep relative humidity at 20 percent. That's how roadrunners, Chihuahuan spotted lizards, gila (pronounced HEE-la) monsters and the hundreds of other Sonora residents like it. The gilas, by the way, are warty-looking lizards, poisonous but shy.

Nearby, the gargantuan **R. J. Reynolds Aviary** is a jungle under mesh, a damp and musky space of flamboyant foliage and dazzling birds, from the turquoise tanager to the silver-eared mesia. Bromeliads burst from the elbows of great kapok trees and leggy African spoonbills—whose pinkish bills really are spoon-shaped —scoop fish from a pond. The resplendent, watermelon-colored scarlet ibis is almost too beautiful to believe.

HIDDEN ▶ About 15 miles from the zoo, at the junctions of Routes 220 and 705, the hamlet of **Seagrove** has a few thousand people and more than 90 potters. Seagrove pottery had its beginnings 200 years ago when Piedmonters turned to clay to make vessels for everyday use. During Prohibition, business picked up as people needed jugs to stash their hooch, and Seagrove thrived with some 250 potters. The law died, plastic was invented, and pottery making nearly disappeared from Seagrove. In the past ten years, tourism has brought it back, though longtime local potters warn of all the amateurs in town. "You can tell right away when you walk in (to a studio) if the quality's not there," said one potter who's been around 20-odd years. Unfortunately, to my untrained eyes, the pottery looked pretty much the same everywhere.

For a map to the potters, stop by the **North Carolina Pottery Center**. The center can also direct you to specific types of potters, such as those making elegant crystalline glazed pottery. Closed Sunday and Monday. ~ Route 705, near Route 220; 336-873-8430.

Other than all those potters, Seagrove has a couple of filling stations, a hardware store and three restaurants—the Dairy Breeze, the Seagrove Family Restaurant and the Jugtown Cafe. If you don't love pottery, you probably won't love Seagrove.

LODGING **Brookstown Inn** is on the outskirts of Old Salem but has much of the same Early Americana atmosphere. In a restored 1837 textile mill that's listed on the National Register of Historic Places, it's a handsome red-brick building whose rooms are all suites, full of space and light and character, with high-beamed ceilings and exposed brick walls, and furnishings reflecting early Mora-

The Real Mayberry, U.S.A.

Sheriff Andy Taylor used to say there's no place like home, and in real life that would be **Mount Airy**. The sheriff, you may remember, was played by Andy Griffith, a fresh-faced, down-home fella who was born and raised in this upper Piedmont town just south of the Virginia line off Route 52, 51 miles northwest of Winston-Salem. That's where he fished for trout in the wooded creeks and hung out at the Snappy Lunch counter on Main Street, just like he did in Mayberry on **The Andy Griffith Show**.

Mount Airy was the inspiration (though not the setting) for the fictional town of Mayberry and, amazingly, it still resembles its TV counterpart today. There are the same big gracious oaks lining the sidewalks and the same friendly folks sitting in swings on their front porches (remember how Andy used to sit with Helen Crumb?). On Main Street there's **Floyd's City Barber Shop** where Barney might have had a shave, and **Lamm's Drug**, once famous for cherry smashes.

To really get in the Mayberry swing of things, visit Mount Airy in September during "Mayberry Days," featuring a pie-eatin' contest, a pig-pickin' cookout and Opie's Backyard playground where kids can dig for worms and play hopscotch.

Two of Mount Airy's other famous residents were Eng and Chang Bunker. The twin Chinese boys, joined at the chest, had been touring in a freak show when they settled here in 1839. Desperate for a "normal" life, they bought 100 acres of farmland and married Sallie Ann and Adelaide Yates, two local sisters who were daughters of a wealthy farmer. They bought slaves, rallied for the Whig party, and fathered 21 children (which raises several questions I won't delve into at the moment). In 1874 Chang got bronchitis and died. Eng panicked and died several hours later, though an autopsy showed he was perfectly healthy and had likely died from fright. The twins are buried at the **White Plains Baptist Church** cemetery (Route 601, two miles west of Mount Airy) in a large grave.

Mount Airy has lots more history as well as some fine places to stay, shop and eat. To find out more, stop in the **Mount Airy Chamber of Commerce** and pick up brochures, a walking-tour map and a copy of The Mayberry Confidential newspaper. ~ 200 North Main Street; 336-786-6116, 800-948-0949.

vian styles. Guests do not go hungry: rates include continental breakfast, afternoon wine and cheese, and evening cookies and milk. ~ 200 Brookstown Avenue, Winston-Salem; 336-725-1120, 800-845-4262, fax 336-773-0147; www.brookstowninn.com. DELUXE.

Converted from a historic 1920s home with red brick facade and white fluted columns, the **Thomas-Welch House** continues the Victorian style inside with several large white-mantle fireplaces, dark wood floors, wingback chairs and period furnishings. The three guest rooms are clean and bright, featuring private baths, antique beds and floral quilts. The living room is so homey and personable you'll forget you're not relaxing on your *own* comfy couch. A full breakfast is served in the charming lime-green dining room. ~ 618 Summit Street, Winston-Salem; phone/fax 336-725-3303; e-mail dpoorbaugh@triad.rr.com. MODERATE TO DELUXE.

Right in historic Old Salem, the lobby of the 1700s **August T. Zevely Inn** welcomes guests with the warmth of corner fireplaces, flickering candles and antiques from the Old Salem Collection. There's even more warmth in the 13 rooms—some of which come with heated floors, fireplaces, steam baths, whirlpool tubs and Salem Arch beds. Have a continental breakfast in Mr. Zevely's former office. ~ 803 South Main Street, Winston-Salem; 336-748-9299, 800-928-9299, fax 336-721-2211; www.winston-salem-inn.com. MODERATE.

Once the 1100-acre estate of William Reynolds (R. J.'s brother) and his wife Kate, Tanglewood is now a big and beautiful county park offering many activities and several places to stay. Best is the **Tanglewood Manor House Bed and Breakfast**, Reynolds' former home that was built in 1859 and restored. There are only ten rooms, all with ample space and all impeccably furnished in the style of a country manor, with swag drapes, louvered wood blinds and rich hues of cranberry and hunter green. The windows look out on lawns of dogwood trees and towering pines. Moderate rates include breakfast. Several rustic **cabins** can be

AUTHOR FAVORITE

I never expected to find a lodge inside a city park, let alone the polished **Tanglewood Manor House Bed and Breakfast**, though the manor's pedigree—the Reynolds Family and its tobacco millions—instantly explains the composed, old-money cool of the place. When you have breakfast in the Dogwood Room, take a good look at the stone hearth: there are dogwood blooms hidden in the design. See above for more information.

rented by the week. ~ Off Route 158 in Clemmons, southwest of Winston-Salem; 336-778-6370, fax 336-778-6379. MODERATE.

About 30 minutes north of Winston-Salem, deep in the coolness of a forested mountain with not even a sign to announce its presence, is **Pilot Knob Bed and Breakfast Inn**. As soon as you see the log cabins with balconies looking into the woods, the whirlpool tubs and stone fireplaces, the swimming pool and sauna staring at the rocky knob of Pilot Mountain, you know it's a place where you could hole up for a long time. The innkeeper intended it that way, for though he built the cabins from an 1800s tobacco barn, he gave them luxurious touches and plenty of spaces for whiling away long afternoons. And though hidden, the place is not far from Mount Airy, several state parks and the Blue Ridge Parkway. ~ From Route 52, take the exit for Pilot Mountain State Park, then turn down New Pilot Knob Lane, the dirt gravel road immediately east of the overpass, Pilot Mountain; 336-325-2502; www.pilotknobinn.com, e-mail info@pilot knobhill.com. DELUXE.

DINING

Whether it's lunch or dinner, make time for a meal at **Old Salem Tavern**. In the midst of Old Salem, it's a handsome place, built in 1816 as the main tavern's annex. There are six dining rooms simply but warmly adorned with wood floors and tables where you can enjoy old-fashioned fare like chicken pot pie, sauerkraut stew and crab and lobster cakes. When it's warm you can eat out on the back porch, beneath a huge hood of wisteria. No dinner on Sunday. ~ 736 South Main Street, Winston-Salem; 336-748-8585. DELUXE.

◄ *HIDDEN*

Tell someone you went to the **Marshall Street Smokehouse** and they'll respond incredulously, "You found it?" It's in a warehouse district, down a side street next to the now-defunct Holsum Bakery, but it's a wonderful space, bright and open, with an outdoor patio for when the weather's warm. The menu focuses on comfort food, from beef brisket to mac and cheese. ~ 924 South Marshall Street, Winston-Salem; 336-723-0430. MODERATE TO DELUXE.

On seeing its blasé stucco exterior, the temptation is to drive by **South By Southwest** and keep going. Resist, go inside, and order some of their great Southwestern cuisine. Start with the Star Canyon shrimp, then progress to the pepita-crusted salmon or the Wrangler ribeye *asada*. ~ 241 South Marshall Street, Winston-Salem; 336-727-0800. DELUXE.

Where can you go for fabulously innovative food at a good price? **Mary's Of Course!** Lively walls with unique artwork invite you to enter this funky café. The menu changes daily, but might include inventions like sweet potato lentil soup, polenta bake with chili, vegetarian Reubens or a scrumptious blueberry peach pie. Breakfast and lunch only. Closed Monday. ~ 301 Brookstown Avenue, Winston-Salem; 336-725-5764; www. marysofcourse.com. BUDGET.

Head to **Christopher's New Global Cuisine** and dive into some of the chef's original creations: lavender honey–glazed wild salmon with peppercorn dijon sauce; roasted duck with tropical fruit salsa and maple sauce; and cornmeal-fried oyster salad with peaches, walnuts, pancetta and blue cheese. This house-converted restaurant features rich red and green walls, a large abstract mural and nightly live music—a great atmosphere for an exciting dining experience. ~ 712 Brookstown Avenue, Winston-Salem; 336-724-1395, fax 336-724-1392; www.christophersngc. com, e-mail info@christophersngc.com. MODERATE TO DELUXE.

Among the city's finer dining establishments, **Zevely House** was built around 1815 by Moravian cabinetmaker Van Neman Zevely as the centerpiece of his plantation. In 1974 the house was moved to its current downtown venue and beautifully furnished in period style. In winter, fires blaze in the hearths; in summer, the garden patio is the place for Sunday brunch. The fare is Continental and stimulating: salmon in potato crust with red wine beurre rouge, roast duck breast with bourbon-orange sauce, and scallops with apricots and jarlsberg cheese. All meals are accompanied by Moravian pumpkin muffins. No dinner on Sunday. Closed Monday. ~ 901 West Fourth Street, Winston-Salem; 336-725-6666. DELUXE TO ULTRA-DELUXE.

In Greensboro, **Southern Lights** is a bistro both bright and boisterous, a good-feeling place serving fresh, inventive fare for lunch and dinner. You can order sandwiches and salads from the regular menu, or check the blackboard for something like oatmeal-crusted grouper with ginger honey glaze, cheese polenta with roasted vegetables and green chile sauce, or grilled sirloin with barbecued onions. There is a full bar. Closed Sunday. ~ 105 North Smyres Place, Greensboro; 336-379-9414. MODERATE TO DELUXE.

In Mount Airy, **Snappy Lunch** has an entire wall devoted to its famous former resident's popular television series, "The Andy Griffith Show." Owner Charles Dowell, a meek and exceedingly friendly man, started working at Snappy Lunch in 1943 as a floor sweeper. He was 14. By 1961 he not only owned the place, he had created a famous pork chop sandwich. Today he sells over a thousand pork chop sandwiches every week in his tiny, time-worn lunch counter with old school desks for tables. His visitors have come from all 50 states. Dowell personally cooks each pork chop, dipping the boneless chop in a not-too-thin-or-thick batter, frying it until crisp and bronze, laying it between steamed buns lathered with mustard, and mounding on tomato, onion, chili and sweet coleslaw. Price: $3.75. His menu also offers cheeseburgers (breaded or all-meat), BLTs and bologna sandwiches, all under $3. Get there before 1 p.m. Closed Sunday. ~ 125 North Main Street, Mount Airy; 336-786-4931. BUDGET.

For pictorials, oil paintings, toys and other Moravian items, try the **Moravian Book and Gift Shop**. You'll find cookbooks, too, if you'd like to try making your own Moravian treats (though they probably won't be quite as good). Closed Sunday. ~ 614 South Main Street, Winston-Salem; 336-723-6262.

SHOPPING

The most enjoyable place to shop in Winston-Salem is **Reynolda Village**. Located next to Reynolda House and part of the old Reynolds' estate, the green-roofed white cottages were once barns, cattlesheds, corncribs, smokehouses and homes to various employees. Now they house upscale restaurants, shops and galleries. **Linda Weaver Studios** (336-725-5812) will restore and copy old photos, or paint or snap your portrait. Closed Sunday. ~ 106 Reynolda Road.

Also within Reynolda Village, **Reynolda Antique Gallery** will satisfy that yearning to redecorate your home you've been having ever since you left Reynolda House. Closed Sunday. ~ 336-724-2500. At **The Niche**, you'll find basketry, pottery, jewelry, kaleidoscopes and fabric dolls. Closed Sunday. ~ 336-724-3912.

If you hang around the Piedmont very long, you will hear talk of **Seagrove pottery**. If you are a pottery person, you'll find Seagrove's in little studios, many of them modest, kudzu-enveloped homes along Routes 220 and 705, and down dirt and gravel side roads. At last count, there were 78 "turners and burners" making Seagrove pottery, though the numbers change weekly. ~ Located in the hamlet of Seagrove, off Route 220, about 40 miles south of Greensboro.

Winston-Salem's burgeoning coffeehouse culture offers alternative nighttime prospects. At **Bistro 420**, you might hear live acoustic guitar. ~ 425 West Fourth Street; 336-721-1336; www.bistro420.com. **Morning Dew Herb and Coffee Co.** has acoustic entertainment some nights. Closed Sunday. ~ 1047 Burke Street; 336-723-5282.

NIGHTLIFE

◆◆◆

MOUTH-WATERING MORAVIAN MORSELS

You can buy your Moravian sugar cakes and cookies at the airport, but it's much more fun to go to **Winkler Bakery** in Old Salem. The women bake everything in a big brick oven, using the same methods and secret recipes as the original Moravians did 200 years ago. ~ 525 South Main Street, Winston-Salem; 336-721-7302.

Ziggy's has the best bands around, with concerts six nights a week. Bo Diddley, Dave Matthews Band, Hootie & The Blowfish and Insane Clown Posse are among the big names who've played here, but the local and regional talent is hot, too. Cover. ~ 433 Baity Street, Winston-Salem; 336-748-1064; www.ziggy rock.com.

THEATER, OPERA AND DANCE   With more than 50 cultural and entertainment groups, the performing arts thrive in Winston-Salem. The **North Carolina School for the Arts** hosts 400 performances alone, ranging from dance to music to drama. ~ 1533 South Main Street; 336-721-1945; www.ncarts.edu. The **Something for Everyone Series** showcases plays and musical performances. ~ 405 West 4th Street; 336-721-1945. The **Piedmont Opera Theatre** puts on two full-scale productions annually at the Stevens Center. ~ 405 West Fourth Street; 336-725-7101. The **North Carolina Black Repertory Company** produces four major shows a year, as well as the National Black Theatre Festival. ~ 610 Coliseum Drive; 336-723-7907.

GAY SCENE   Unlike most other areas of North Carolina, many of the Piedmont's fast-growing, New South cities offer a thriving young gay scene.

In Winston-Salem, the scene inside **Club Odyssey** is definitely hot. Popular with gay men and women, it features entertainment by male dancers and female impersonators. Cover. ~ 4019 Country Club Road, Winston-Salem; 336-774-1077.

The fashionable **Warehouse 29** is a hoppin' destination for gay men and women, with mainstream music for dancing and a patio bar for outdoor relaxing. All-male revues and female impersonators are also featured. Cover. ~ 1011 Arnold Street, Greensboro; 336-333-9333.

PARKS   **TANGLEWOOD PARK**   🚶 🐎 🚣 ⛴ 🎣   As county parks go, this one's a showplace, thanks to its beginnings as the luxuriant nineteenth-century estate of Will and Kate Reynolds, brother and sister-in-law of R. J. Reynolds. Rambling green lawns, ivy-clad pines and oaks, two lakes, rose gardens and "fragrance" gardens —filled with good-smelling greenery—grace these 1200 acres, and there are thick woods filled with deer. In spring when the roses bloom, the deer come out to nibble at the buds and you can watch them eat in the early morning. There are myriad places to stay, including the historic Reynolds' manor house and a cozy motel, and myriad ways to spend your time, from golfing at one of the two championship courses to taking a hayride. The Tanglewood Steeplechase is one of Winston-Salem's most celebrated events. Fishing is good in the park's two lakes; $1.50. Facilities include paddleboat, canoe, rowboat and johnboat rentals; a farm offering guided horseback rides, hayrides and riding lessons; nature trails and a sandwich grill. Day-use fee, $2. ~ Off Route 158 in Clemmons, about eight miles southwest of Winston-Salem; 336-778-6300.

HANGING ROCK STATE PARK 🏃 🚶 👫 🚣 ⛵ If you just ◄ HIDDEN want to be in the woods, screened from civilization by 6000 acres of tall trees and the sides of mountains, come to this place less than an hour's drive north of Winston-Salem. It's in the Saura-town Mountains, an intensely scenic range as evidenced by the nubby outcropping that gives the park its name. There are many more rocks, which is why rappelers and rock climbers especially love this place. Climbing and rappelling are allowed in designated areas. A permit is required, but there's no fee. Check with the park office. For picnicking and swimming, there's a 12-acre lake edged with forest and a mocha-colored beach. Swimming is good only at the protected, shallow, sandy area in the lake in summer. The fishing is excellent for bass and bream in the Dan River. Facilities include a visitors center, picnic tables with grills, hiking trails, restrooms (pit toilets only in the winter), a bathhouse and snack bar at the lake and canoe rentals in the summer. Many other facilities are closed in the winter. ~ Located about 32 miles north of Winston-Salem, 4 miles northwest of the hamlet of Danbury. You can reach the park from several paved roads (called "hard roads" by local folk) including Routes 89, 8 and 66. From Pilot Mountain State Park, take Moore's Lake Road; 336-593-8480.

> The Sauratown Mountains, at 1700 to 2500 feet, are short as far as mountains go.

🔺 Seventy-three sites accommodate tents and RVs (no hookups); $12 per site per night. Six rustic cabins can be rented by the week only in the summer, daily the rest of the year; closed in winter.

PILOT MOUNTAIN STATE PARK 🏃 🐎 🚣 ⛵ From a long way away, the rocky knob of Pilot Mountain looks like a bump on the head. From its summit, in turn, the landscape ripples in car-pets of forest, a tremendous vista stretching into Virginia. The bump is made of quartzite and was used by American Indians and early settlers as a guidepost. It's now a national landmark. The wild and clear waters of the Yadkin River cut through this 3703-acre wilderness park, and you can follow riverside trails through luscious foliage. There is no swimming. Fishing is good in the Yadkin River for largemouth bass, sunfish and catfish. Facilities include a park office, picnic areas with grills, pit toilets and canoe and hiking and bridle trails. ~ Located about 25 miles north of Winston-Salem off Route 52, near the town of Pinnacle; 336-325-2355.

🔺 Family camping area with 49 primitive sites for tents or RVs (no hookups); hot showers; $15 per site per night.

▼▼▼▼▼▼▼▼▼▼▼▼▼▼▼▼

High Point to Hickory

Spread between the metropolises of Winston-Salem and Charlotte is this peculiar part of the Piedmont, where a traveler's main endeavor would likely involve buying furniture.

SIGHTS

The furniture fun starts just south of Winston-Salem at **High Point**, which calls itself the "Furniture and Hosiery Capital of the World." Ninety-one miles west, **Hickory** is simply the "Furniture Capital of the World." Both claims would seem justified, considering more than 250 furniture manufacturers and more than 100 hosiery companies make their homes in the area. In fact, some 65 percent of all American furniture is manufactured within a 200-mile radius around High Point and Hickory.

Before doing any furniture shopping, you may want to bone up on furniture history and lingo at the **Furniture Discovery Center**. Located downtown in a restored fabric warehouse, it's where one discovers just how a Queen Anne Highboy begins life (with a lot of carving, cutting and staining), and how adept you must be at using an air-powered nail gun to make a love seat. At the tour's climax, "the mysteries of upholstery are unveiled." Closed Monday from November through March. Admission. ~ 101 West Green Drive, High Point; 336-887-3876, fax 336-887-2159; www.furniturediscovery.org.

Adjacent to the Discovery Center, the **Angela Peterson Doll and Miniature Museum** invites visitors to "See the World in Dolls!" It showcases one woman's collection of more than 2200 dolls (including 115 Shirley Temples) and miniatures from 54 countries. Even if you're not a doll lover, you may be intrigued by all those pensive eyes staring at you from their faces of china, wood and wax. There's even a Princess Di doll in a wedding dress, and a doll made of seaweed. Closed Monday from November through March. Admission. ~ 101 West Green Drive, High Point; 336-885-3655.

Even odder is the **World's Largest Bureau**. More than three stories high, 27 feet long and 14 feet wide, the wooden chest of drawers was built in 1926 to keep up with neighboring Thomasville, which had (and still has) the world's biggest chair. The High

◆◆

NON-BUYERS BEWARE

Two times when you don't want to be in the Hickory–High Point area are during the two, week-long International Home Furnishings Markets held every April and October in High Point. It's open to retailers only, who arrive by the tens of thousands and fill up hotels all the way to the Blue Ridge Mountains.

Point Jaycees used to keep their offices inside the bureau, and people would show up asking to look in their drawers. Now the bureau is locked tight, though you're welcome to take pictures. ~ 508 Hamilton Street, High Point; 336-889-8151.

Off Route 29-70, a long skinny bridge delivers you across the Yadkin River to tiny, historic **Spencer**. Like many small Southern towns, its neighborhoods are populated with pretty Victorian and antebellum homes. But Spencer's claim to the map is **The North Carolina Transportation Museum at Historic Spencer Shops**. It's   **◄ HIDDEN** housed in a brick building that rambles along the railroad tracks, and that used to be Southern Railway Company's steam locomotive headquarters (the town is named for Samuel Spencer, first president of the railway). Exhibits trace the history of local transportation, from a dugout canoe to the 1970s-era Coot-A Amphibian seaplane designed by North Carolinian Bill Motes. There's a 1913 Tin Lizzie and a 1935 gangster-style North Carolina Highway Patrol car with a bulletproof windshield. From March to mid-December, you can take a 50-minute ride around the 57-acre property in a restored steam or diesel locomotive. Admission to ride the train. ~ 411 Salisbury Avenue, Spencer; 704-636-2889, fax 704-639-1881; www.nctrans.org.

Next door, the bigger town of **Salisbury** is a marvelous place to spend an afternoon. George Washington, in fact, visited in 1791 and wrote that it was "a pleasant village." First stop at the **Rowan County Convention and Visitors Bureau** and pick up a walking-tour map and information guide. The map will direct you to more than 90 historic houses and points of interest. ~ 204 East Innes Street, Salisbury; 704-638-3100, 800-332-2343; www.visitsalisburync.com.

Salisbury has been around since 1747, when Scotch-Irish settlers first crossed the ruddy Piedmont. German immigrants soon followed and then others, making their way along the Great Pennsylvania Wagon Road from Lancaster County or on the Trading Path from Virginia. Daniel Boone spent his childhood here fishing the Yadkin River and hunting surrounding woods, and Andrew Jackson studied law in Salisbury in the 1780s.

Located in Rowan County, the village gets its name from an English cathedral town, not from the steak you're thinking of, though it did produce a locally famous beverage called Cheerwine. Created in 1917 by a man named L. D. Peeler, the wine-colored, sweet and syrupy soft drink tastes a little like Dr. Pepper and is "full of good cheer," according to the label. If you'd like to try a swig, do it in Salisbury. It's tough to find Cheerwine anywhere else.

It takes a couple of hours to explore the 30 square historic blocks of Salisbury. Make sure you walk down **South Fulton Street** for a look at the fabulous homes with their luscious gardens and long, lazy driveways. The architecture is wildly varied, from Victorian storybook with rampant filigree to Neoclassical Revival with great porticoes to Italianate and Colonial Revival.

One block over, the **Rowan Museum** gives a glimpse at life in the early 1800s inside one of these moneyed abodes. Built in 1819, the Federal-style townhouse is the handiwork of master builder Jacob Stirewalt, who designed an elaborate curved staircase and fanciful moldings. Period furnishings and many other fine Rowan County artifacts are displayed. Closed Monday through Wednesday. Admission. ~ 202 North Main Street, Salisbury; 704-633-5946.

HIDDEN ►

About 14 miles west of Salisbury, off roving rural Route 150, awaits one of North Carolina's most unexpected and rewarding hidden sights: camels, antelope, water buffalo and hundreds more exotic animals, all roaming the range at **Lazy 5 Ranch**. Owner Henry Hampton is a wildlife collector who invites people to turn into the pastures (but stay in the car) and take a 3.5-mile auto tour of the animals. Along the rutted paths you're apt to see rare albino elk from the Rocky Mountains, antelope from India, deer from the Far East, and Watusi cattle from Africa, whose horns get as wide as 12 feet. Horse-drawn wagon rides are available by appointment, and there's a petting zoo where children can spend hours. Among Hampton's list of rules for visitors: "Don't honk your horn or turn on your lights unless you need help because it gives our animals heartburn." Admission. ~ Route 150, Mooresville; 704-663-5100, fax 704-664-1549.

HIDDEN ►

From here, backtracking east on narrow, lonely **Route 152** is another real drive in the country, past vast Hereford ranches stenciled in rough-hewn fence, farmhouses and gazebos parked on wandering lawns, and intermittent tin shacks selling such diverse items as pottery and farm tools. You will pass a town called **China Grove**, named for chinaberry groves found here in the 1700s, and see soft, sculpted pastures ebbing and flowing along the horizon. You will definitely know you are outside the mainstream by all the cow manure on the road.

LODGING

In Salisbury, the magnificent **Rowan Oak House Bed and Breakfast** is a Victorian fantasy, complete with a cupola, rich wall tapestries and elaborate carved wood. Guests are invited to stay in one of four bedrooms, each with a private bath (one has a jacuzzi tub set in a bay window and two with a two-person marble shower), and all plushly adorned. A fountain and gazebo encourage quiet reflection. ~ 208 South Fulton Street, Salisbury; 704-633-2086, 800-786-0437, fax 704-633-2086; www.rowanoakbb.com. DELUXE.

Step through the beveled-glass and copper-wheel engraved front doors of **Turn of the Century Victorian Bed and Breakfast** into a parlor where a fire blazes beneath the 1905 marble man-

Barbecue Capital of the World

Furniture gave **Lexington** its name, but barbecue gave it fame. Just south of Winston-Salem, the plain town of weathered, whitewashed homes has 20,000 residents and 18 barbecue joints—which should easily make it the barbecue capital of the world. Lexington even hosts an annual Barbecue Festival with a parade of pigs.

Lexington barbecue was born in the 1920s when local fellas Sid Weaver and Varner Swicegood set up cinderblock cookers across from the Lexington County Courthouse and started cookin' on big court days. They cooked only pork shoulders and only over hickory wood fires, and it became *the* way to make Piedmont barbecue. (Elsewhere in the Carolinas, whole pigs are cooked and not always on wood fires but in gas and electric cookers and ovens—methods that horrify Lexington folks.) Typically, the pork is pulled by hand off the bone, hence the term "pulled pork," a food that you will see across the Carolinas.

Exactly who in Lexington serves the best barbecue is naturally a point of contention and great competition. Some folks like their pork shoulder sliced paper thin, some insist on fine-chopped till it's nearly shredded, and yet others prefer those coarse-chopped, stew-size chunks. Lexington sauce is vinegar-based, as opposed to tomato-based in the rest of the world, and it's slathered on the meat at the table, not back in the kitchen. Sauce is usually served in plastic squirt bottles—clear for mild; red for spicy. Coleslaw is doused in the same sauce, then heaped on the meat inside a sandwich. Sandwiches, by the way, are simply called "barbecues." The ultimate barbecue, in my experience, is one that's light on the slaw, heavy on the pork, nestled between soft but sturdy buns, with just enough spicy sauce to moisten the bread but not make it mushy.

Such a sandwich can be found at **Speedy's**, advertising "The Best Barbecue Anywhere." Locals start wandering in around 10:30 a.m. every morning, sliding into the tattered vinyl booths in anticipation of getting their daily barbecue fix. There are also pork plates that come with french fries and hushpuppies, and there are burgers, but don't order the latter unless you're prepared to endure the consternation of the waitress. Closed Sunday. ~ Winston Road, on the north end of town; 336-248-2410. BUDGET.

"You all right today?" is how the waitresses greet you at **Lexington Barbecue**, opened in the 1960s and famous for its owner, nicknamed "Honey Monk," and for having Tom Cruise and Ronald Reagan as former patrons. The sauce here is wonderfully tangy and rust-colored; the sandwiches are served on the teeniest of paper plates. Closed Sunday. ~ 10 Route 29-70 South; 336-249-9814. BUDGET.

tle. There are just three guest rooms and one suite, but all are lav-
ishly, intriguingly decorated with everything from fainting
couches to iron clawfoot tubs. Ask for the room with the "half-
tester" canopy bed—a brass beauty adorned with dragon and
lion heads—or the one with bath tiles of black and white basket-
weave patterns. ~ 529 South Fulton Street, Salisbury; 704-642-
1660, 800-250-5349; www.turnofthecenturybb.com. DELUXE.

Almost everything else is a chain motel or hotel; for a comprehensive list, contact the **High Point Convention & Visitors Bureau.**
~ 300 South Main Street, High Point; 336-884-5255, 800-720-
5255. In Hickory, go to the **Hickory Metro Convention and
Visitors Bureau.** ~ 1960-A Thirteenth Avenue Drive Southeast,
Hickory; 828-322-1335, 800-849-5093.

DINING

Like the local lodging, dining is almost strictly a chain restaurant
experience. Breaking the chain mold is **1859 Café**, where dressed-
up fare is served in dressed-up surroundings. Imaginative pasta
dishes, seafood, fowl and beef are featured. Try the cedar-planked
salmon with orange-marmalade horseradish sauce, or the roasted
duck with port-wine cherry sauce. ~ 443 Second Avenue
Southwest, Hickory; 828-322-1859. DELUXE.

Another eatery with equally inventive, though lighter, fare is
Jessica's Porch, a terrific place for lunch while you're furniture
shopping. Closed Sunday. ~ 2220 Route 70 Southeast, in the
Hickory Furniture Mart; 828-324-7204. BUDGET.

SHOPPING

Think furniture. You'll recognize the big names—Broyhill, Lexington, Thomasville, Drexel Heritage—whose factories sprawl around
High Point and Hickory. Most have showrooms attached where
you can browse the latest lines and styles. Furniture retail outlets
and warehouses also abound in the area. Prices are often so low
that even with the cost of shipping your purchases back home, you

---

SHOPPING SAVVY

A couple of tips for tackling the furniture mega-shopping that awaits you in
the High Point and Hickory areas: Some discounters do not accept credit
cards, only cash or sometimes personal checks with proper identification.
Most places require a deposit of 25 to 50 percent when you place an
order. Delivery charges are typically based on weight and distance, though
some discounters charge according to the price of your order. If you
order from several stores within one furniture mart, you can usually
consolidate the shipping charges. Make sure you inform each store of
your other purchases, and that the sales people write "Consolidation"
on your orders.

can save up to 50 percent. The amount of savings depends on how much you buy, how far you live and how committed you are to finding the best deal. Folks are known to make furniture forays from as far away as Canada, hoping to furnish their houses at deeply discounted prices.

If this, too, is your hope, then come prepared. With hundreds of stores and thousands of styles to choose from, it's best to know what you want *before* you arrive. Furniture consultants suggest shopping stores at home and making a list of the lines and styles you like. Then you can comparison shop in High Point and Hickory. Two of the best times to shop are in March and September, right before the International Home Furnishings Market. This is when manufacturers and discounters offer clearance prices to make room for the new lines they'll show at the market.

Comprehensive lists of furniture showrooms and outlets are available from the **High Point Convention & Visitors Bureau.** ~ 300 South Main Street; 336-884-5255. You can also get lists from the **Hickory Metro Convention and Visitors Bureau.** ~ 1960-A Thirteenth Avenue Drive Southeast, Hickory; 828-322-1335, 800-849-5093. Both places can also provide the names of furniture consultants who, for a fee, will assist with your hunt.

Among the megastores and furniture marts: **The Atrium,** spanning some 250,000 square feet—over five football fields— of furniture. Twenty galleries represent more than 900 manufacturers. ~ 430 South Main Street, High Point; 336-882-5599. **Rose Furniture Company** is about half the size of the Atrium but carries just as many lines. ~ 916 Finch Avenue, High Point; 336-886-6050. **Furnitureland South** boasts a million square feet of furniture displays and 500 different lines. There's also a third-floor library with catalogs and fabric and wood samples, and more than 50 telephones that put you instantly in touch with a salesperson. ~ 5635 Riverdale Drive, Jamestown; 336-841-4328.

The megalopolis you hear about most is **Hickory Furniture Mart,** covering 20 acres and four stories of windowed showrooms. One hundred galleries, outlets and discounters showcase more than 1000 lines, and there are places to buy reduced-price linens, lighting, wallpaper and bath fixtures. Furniture styles range from American Colonial, Art Deco and French provincial to Queen Anne, contemporary and Louis XV. Closed Sunday. ~ 2220 Route 70 Southeast, Hickory; 828-322-3510, 800-462-6278.

If you are one of those people who would rather get in the car and drive, stopping randomly at factory showrooms and warehouse outlets, then get on **Route 321** in Hickory and head north for 20 miles. Dozens of places offer bargains, and it's a pleasant drive in the country besides. **Route 70** between Statesville and Morganton also features scores of discount furniture stores.

NIGHTLIFE It's quiet around furnitureland. Most folks have a drink at their hotel or, in High Point, at **Restaurant J. Besul Noble**. The jazzy restaurant has a polished bar with live jazz Thursday through Saturday nights. ~ 101 South Main Street, High Point; 336-889-3354.

PARKS   **BOONE'S CAVE STATE PARK** 🏃 A 110-acre primitive park set along the Yadkin River, it's where Daniel Boone hunted and

HIDDEN ► fished as a child, and where he supposedly spent nights in a cave along the riverbank. Boone's Cave isn't very big or comfortable, though, only two to three feet high and eighty feet long, and you have to worm your way between dark, clammy walls. Small kids don't seem to mind, but they'll need a flashlight. Facilities include a picnic shelter, a restroom and a hiking trail. ~ Located on Boone's Cave Road, about four and a half miles east of Route 150, north of Salisbury and near the hamlet of Churchland; 336-242-2958.

▼▼▼▼▼▼▼▼▼▼▼▼▼ Anyone who knew Charlotte before the 1980s and
Charlotte Area
hasn't been back is in for a big surprise. In little more than a decade the city has gone from a low-key, low-slung urban hub to an upscale, uptown metropolis of the New South. Nearly half a million people now call Charlotte home, and every day many more are moving in. It's the biggest city between Atlanta and Washington, D.C., though not at all overwhelming, either physically or traffic-wise. How long it can stay that way will no doubt depend on the abilities of city politicians and planners, and how fast the city grows.

SIGHTS Charlotte's renaissance is most obvious downtown, where soaring, variously contoured buildings of metal and glass and granite create a modern symphony in the sky. Downtown is actually referred to as **Uptown Charlotte**, and this is where you should begin exploring, your first stop being the **Charlotte Convention & Visitors Bureau,** on the northwest side of Uptown. The bureau has more brochures than you would care to count, but you should definitely pick up the *Visitors Guide to Charlotte*, which has key-coded maps of virtually every area sight. Closed weekends. ~ 500 South College Street #300, Charlotte; 704-334-2282, 800-722-1994; www.visitcharlotte.com.

Most major Uptown sights are concentrated on the north end and are easy to see on foot. From the visitors bureau, walk east to the **intersection of Trade and Tryon streets,** and you will be where it all began. Several hundred years ago, two American Indian trading paths cut through the woods and ran right into each other at this very spot. After the Europeans arrived, mostly Scotch-Irish settlers, they took over the trading post and began building homes here. To get better trade deals from the British, they named the crossroads Charlotte, after the queen of England, then named the county Mecklenburg, after her German birthplace. Today, Charlotte calls itself "The Queen City," and calls this particular crossroads—now overshadowed by twentieth-century buildings of business and trade—**The Square**.

A couple of blocks away is Charlotte's loftiest building, **NationsBank Corporate Center and Founders Hall**. Opened in 1993 and rising 60 stories, the big banking center is the highest building in the Southeast, at least until a higher one comes along (and when one does, don't be surprised if it's in Charlotte). Head through the glass doors and you're met by an enormous glass atrium with a winter garden flooded with sunlight, and walls transformed by a trio of frescoes depicting the building's creation, as well as city scenes. The frescoes are the work of Ben Long, North Carolina's famed fresco artist whose rural church frescoes in the Blue Ridge Mountains have drawn thousands of spectators. Now just as many people are coming to experience his Founders Hall work. Founders Hall also has two floors of

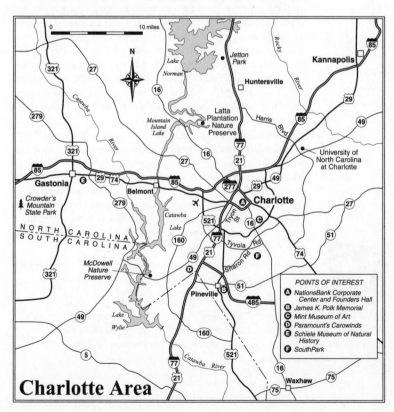

Charlotte Area

POINTS OF INTEREST
- Ⓐ NationsBank Corporate Center and Founders Hall
- Ⓑ James K. Polk Memorial
- Ⓒ Mint Museum of Art
- Ⓓ Paramount's Carowinds
- Ⓔ Schiele Museum of Natural History
- Ⓕ SouthPark

restaurants and shops, in case you care to browse. ~ 100 North Tryon Street, Charlotte; 704-386-0120.

If you have children, you must take them to **Discovery Place**. Charlotte's science showpiece, it is a science museum like no other in the South, perhaps even the nation, with engaging and engrossing exhibits lodged in big and bright rooms painted in bold, bright colors that seem never-ending, leading you on a journey through a re-created rainforest, solar galaxy, mission control and space station, science circus, undersea world, dinosaur habitat and many other worlds and places. Giant panels and whole walls beep and blink in a blaze of neon, contraptions swirl, grind and pop, and children swarm in an ecstatic frenzy, giving the distinct feel of a juvenile Las Vegas. Admission. ~ 301 North Tryon Street, Charlotte; 704-372-6261, 800-935-0553, fax 704-337-2670; www.discoveryplace.org.

The rainforest, however, is different. It is subtle and nearly quiet, a wedge of real plants and vines and trees, all very green and very damp, lodged behind a colossal wall of glass. Step inside and stroll through the forest on a catwalk, listening to the hoots and howls emanating from the tangle of luscious greenery. The noises are compliments of the rainforest residents: birds such as the Latin American aracari, deeply colored with a banded breast; the Victoria crowned pigeon, from New Guinea; and the wonderfully named "touraco-go away" from Africa. Some of the birds are involved in daily shows put on by the museum's animal trainers. Daily, five-minute thunderstorms also happen in the forest; check the front desk for times.

In an adjacent room, sea exhibits are just as absorbing. There's a simulated wave that rolls behind glass, giant tanks with everything from queen triggerfish and loggerhead turtles to camouflage fish (which become transparent when enemies come around) and nurse sharks who seem to be only inches away. Children especially love the shallow pool where they can touch snails and hermit crabs underwater. They also enjoy the **Butterfly Pavillion**, where thousands of chromatic insects wing their way around gardens within a glass dome.

sights

AUTHOR FAVORITE

Having spent weeks in the Central American jungles, you'd think I'd find the rainforest at **Discovery Place** a shabby substitute. Wrong! In fact, the luscious cove of damp green is startlingly similar, right down to the screaming aracari birds and regular "thunderstorms." See above for more information.

There are, of course, plenty of other exhibits in this two-level museum, enough to keep a visitor busy at least two days. You can duck into a kaleidoscope and see hundreds of images of yourself (frightening for some folks), build a simulated sandwich on a computer and learn its nutritional details (much healthier without the cheese), and search for cavities in a mouthful of teeth.

The Discovery Place is also home to the **Omnimax Theatre** and the **Space Voyager Planetarium**, both exceptional places with frequent, everchanging shows. The Omnimax, with its overwhelming, omnipresent dome of screen and six-track sound system, feels more like a ride than a theater. Sink down into a cushiony seat, recline all the way back, and look up and around at the screen. The shows are often cosmic in nature, taking you on mental trips through time and space, and causing many to pitch and scream at various points (and some even to get seasick; just close your eyes for a few minutes if you feel woozy).

You can buy separate tickets for the museum, theatre and planetarium, or pay a combined admission for two or all three—definitely the best deal.

From Discovery Place, you can walk two blocks north and one block east to Charlotte's most famous neighborhood: **Fourth Ward**. Victorian fantasy homes, painted in sherbet colors and amusingly adorned with turrets and gables, high-peaked roofs and woodshakes, and spectacular stained glass, parade up and down the lamp-lined brick streets. Parks the size of postage stamps offer benches for resting and fountains that bubble at your feet. Mint-colored liriope grass spills over the sidewalks, and rose gardens perfume the air. All in all, an enlightening place to stroll, and no doubt live, though quite expensively. Before you start exploring, pick up the guide *A Walk through Historic Fourth Ward* from the Charlotte Convention & Visitors Bureau. ~ Northeast corner of Uptown, bounded roughly by Seventh, Graham, Tenth and Church streets.

Fourth Ward began life as an upscale place in the mid-1800s, but did not stay that way. One of the city's four political wards, it was established by doctors and merchants and other well-to-do people. Time passed, the original owners eventually died, and the homes were not maintained. After World War II, many houses were divided into apartments or became boardinghouses or trade schools for veterans. By the early 1970s, some places were even selling liquor and sex. But the brothels and boardinghouses were soon bought up by citizens committed to saving the Fourth Ward, and during the 1980s, an extraordinary restoration took place.

On the south end of Uptown, a short drive from Fourth Ward, the **Afro-American Cultural Center** is a striking, early 1900s building of red brick with great Greek Revival columns and stained-glass windows shimmering all around, looking very much like the church it used to be. There's a small theater and larger amphitheater, and a gallery with changing exhibits of African and African-American art of stellar quality. Closed Monday. ~ 401 North Meyers Street, Charlotte; 704-374-1565, fax 704-374-9273; www.aacc-charlotte.org.

There are a lot of old houses around Charlotte, but none as old as the one stuck out in the sprawling suburbia just east of Uptown

HIDDEN ► at the **Charlotte Museum of History & Hezekiah Alexander Homesite**. The shuttered, unassuming, two-story rock house was built in 1774 by Hezekiah Alexander, who called himself a planter but was a whole lot more—including a justice of the peace and signer of the Mecklenburg Declaration of Independence, which created North Carolina's state government. He had a wife and ten kids; the latter shared three bedrooms upstairs and must have loved roving the woods around the house.

As you stroll through the forest of black walnut and rhododendron today, notice the "placer pits," little craters dug by prospectors searching for gold. Though none of the original belongings remain, the house has been furnished with Piedmont antiques, and most likely looks the same as it did two centuries ago. Similar antiques can be seen in the Museum of History adjacent to the home. Wheelchair visitors can easily tour the museum and grounds, but do not have access to the inside of the home. Wheelchairs are available at the front desk. Closed Monday. Admission. ~ 3500 Shamrock Drive, Charlotte; 704-568-1774; www.charlottemuseum.org.

South of Uptown Charlotte, hidden in a moneyed neighborhood of elegant, vast homes whose roofs reach up into the treetops, is the inspirational **Wing Haven Gardens and Bird Sanctu-**

HIDDEN ► **ary**. After decades of hard work, Elizabeth and Edwin Clarkson transformed a barren field of clay into a lush three-acre bird habitat. More than 100 varieties of birds have visited the brick-walled gardens since they opened in 1927. Hummingbirds, woodpeckers, mockingbirds, hawks and warblers come here, and so do brown-headed nuthatches, great horned owls and blue-gray gnatcatchers. An illustrated brochure guides you through the luxuriant flowers and trees, describing the history of the fountains and statuary and marking important places (such as where the Clarksons were sitting when they chose the name Wing Haven). Among the reflective inscriptions scattered throughout the greenery: "A garden is the mirror of a mind," by Henry Beston. Open Tuesday and Sunday afternoons and on Wednesday morning. ~ 248 Ridgewood Avenue, Charlotte; 704-331-0664; www.winghavengardens.com.

The first branch of the United States Mint opened in Charlotte—a fitting location considering the amount of gold discovered around the Piedmont in the 1800s. Built in 1836 in what's now Uptown Charlotte, the mint churned out $5 million in gold coins—a lot of dough in those days, but today not even enough to build the SouthPark Mall down the road. The Mint stopped being a mint around 1913, and 20 years later was nearly demolished before history lovers rescued it. They moved the low-lying building to the south end of town and made it the **Mint Museum of Art**, opening in 1936 as North Carolina's first art museum.

Today, the museum's permanent collection includes a fine sampling of American and European art, as well as outstanding pre-Columbian and Decorative art, spread across two floors. Among the diverse American selections are twentieth-century blown glass, papier-mâché, and metal collages; a Hudson River scene by Thomas Doughty, one of the founders of the Hudson River School of Art; and an 1836 portrait of a roseate spoonbill by Audubon. There are also some spectacularly ornate pieces of nineteenth- and twentieth-century furniture. Closed Monday. Admission. ~ 2730 Randolph Road, Charlotte; 704-337-2000, fax 704-337-2101; www.mintmuseum.org.

If you want to see a prime example of New South growth, take a drive around **SouthPark**. Just 20 years ago, promotional brochures tell us, this was a cow pasture. Thanks to the daring dreams of big businessmen, including Charlotte mover-and-shaker John Belk of Belk Department Stores, the area is now a "masterpiece community," with miles of glossy retail and corporate buildings and reproduction antebellum homes and condos, and a complex grid of asphalt that constantly hums with New South traffic. Today, if you want to see the cows, you'll have to travel another ten miles south. ~ Four miles south of Uptown Charlotte; major SouthPark routes are Park, Sharon, Tyvola, Fairview and Woodlawn roads.

Notice that the cabin at the James K. Polk Memorial has no nails; it was built in the half-dovetail design popular during the late 1700s.

Which is not a bad way to go, considering there are many terrific sights on the outskirts of metropolitan Charlotte and just beyond, side trips ranging up to 30 miles that can easily be undertaken in an afternoon. Here are just some of the possibilities:

About ten miles south of downtown Charlotte, the **James K. Polk Memorial** remembers the birthplace of the eleventh president of the United States. Nicknamed "Young Hickory," Polk lived here with his family until he was eleven. Polk's original homestead was destroyed, but a similar, authentic log cabin has been moved here. Guides offer tours of the cabin and the cookhouse, describing the furniture, farm tools and other items of Polk's day. Closed Sunday and Monday. ~ Route 521, Pineville; 704-889-7145.

Just west of here, **Paramount's Carowinds** straddles the line between North and South Carolina. The 100-acre theme park boasts ten rollercoasters, including the *Top Gun* water park, though in fact the place is more folksy than fantasy. Most of the rides work on the gravity principle as opposed to the high-tech Disney principle, and most of the entertainment is down-home country.

A family-pleaser since it opened in 1973, the park was purchased in 1992 by Paramount Parks, which has added some movie-themed touches, including the Star Trek–based Borg Assimilation ride. The *Drop Zone* lets riders experience the sensation of freefall as they drop 100 feet at 56 mph.

For an extra charge, and more of a hanggliding experience, the *Xtreme Skyflyer* rises over 150 feet in the air and then freefalls for 50 feet.

And at the *WaterWorks* water park, you can splash through a water jungle gym (watch out for the 1000-gallon "dumping bucket"), ride a raft down the four-story *Tidal Wave* or ride a surfboard in the *Big Wave Bay* pool.

Carowinds can easily eat up a long day, especially if you spend part at WaterWorks, and a long day is what you should spend after forking over the hefty admission ($41.99 for ages 7 through 54). Among the rides worth repeating during your visit: the *VORTEX*, a mind-scrambling rollercoaster you ride standing up; *Whitewater Falls*, a wet plunge down a 45-foot chute; and the *Carolina Cyclone*, a rollercoaster with four (count them) 360° loops and a 450° uphill helix for a finale. The *Skytower*, an air conditioned cabin that climbs 32 stories high, provides the best view around. For the little ones, *Nickelodeon Central* offers pint-sized rides and *Zoom Zone* has three-and-a-half acres where kids can fly elevated helicopters, ride a mini-rollercoaster of taxi cabs and police cars, or drive in a Cadillac or Corvette "road rally."

Carowinds is closed in winter, and open weekends-only during spring and fall. Dates and times vary, so call for hours of operation. Admission. ~ Off Route 77; 704-588-2606, 800-888-4386; www.carowinds.com.

HIDDEN ►

Leave theme-park land and head for the country, traveling east on Route 51, then south on Route 16 about 13 miles, until you reach the small and engaging town of **Waxhaw**. The population is only 2600, but the town is home to upwards of 50 antique shops. Main Street proper is only about three blocks long, though it is split by railroad tracks, and there's an arched wooden bridge to take you from one side of the road to the other. You will definitely want to cross the road, lest you miss some of the antique shops that parade up and down each side, waiting behind gaily painted storefronts in red-brick buildings.

Just east of downtown Waxhaw off Route 75, you'll find the headquarters for JAARS Bible translators and their interesting **Museum of the Alphabet**. A series of decorative panels details the   ◀ HIDDEN
history and logic of language, from Maya and Egyptian hieroglyphs to the Cherokee alphabet. Definitely not a place to take the kids, as the displays are erudite, though fascinating. Despite the Biblical connection, there's no religious hype, here. In fact, the friendly volunteer docents aren't even JAARS members. Closed Sunday. ~ Davis Road, Waxhaw; 704-843-6066; www.jaars.org/museum/alphabet.

> The Cherokee alphabet was developed by Sequoyah, the only illiterate person known to have created a written language.

To the west of Charlotte on Route 85, in the unexciting town of **Gastonia**, is an exciting place called the **Schiele Museum of Natural History**. Rooms and exhibits are given over to the natural world, including plants, animals, minerals and native peoples both near and far. The North American Wildlife Hall is filled with taxidermied beasts, from a moose and mountain goat to grizzly bear and antelope. The Hall of Earth and Man hones in on the geological and biological sides of things, and includes models of what some of the earliest, hairiest humans might have looked like. There's also a planetarium and a one-mile nature trail that's a good introduction to Piedmont plants. Extra admission to the planetarium. ~ 1500 East Garrison Boulevard, Gastonia; 704-866-6900, fax 704-866-6041; www.schielemuseum.org.

South of Gastonia, hidden along the banks of Catawba Creek, **Daniel Stowe Botanical Garden** is splendid for those with a fond-   ◀ HIDDEN
ness for flowers. In spring, the beds are bursting with azaleas, begonias, caladium and bleeding hearts. By fall, the chrysanthemums and asters have taken over. And even the depths of winter feature some decor: pansies and ornamental cabbages. In case you don't know a caladium from a chrysanthemum, all the flowers are labeled. Admission. ~ 6500 South New Hope Road, Belmont; 704-825-4490, fax 704-829-1240; www.dsbg.org.

For a look at how wealthy Piedmonters lived in the early 1800s, check out **Latta Place**, within Latta Plantation Nature Preserve, off of Beatties Ford Road, northwest of downtown Charlotte. The restored clapboard, two-story plantation manse, furnished with Federal period pieces, was home to James Latta, a prosperous lawyer, merchant and planter, and his wife, Jane Knox. A smokehouse, log cabin, dairy, well house and barn are part of this working farm. Historic breeds of cattle, sheep and chickens are among the current residents. Tours are available several times a day. Closed Monday. Admission. ~ 5225 Sample Road, Huntersville; 704-875-2312, 704-875-1391; www.lattaplantation.org.

Birds of prey also live at Latta Plantation Nature Preserve. Each year, the **Carolina Raptor Center** receives about 500 injured birds from across the Carolinas, most having been struck down by a car. About half are nursed back to health and set free. Eagles and owls, vultures and falcons all live in mesh enclosures, peering down from perches with their powerful raptor eyes. You will learn about raptor habits, including how they swallow whole mice and chicks and then regurgitate what their bodies can't digest. The regurgitated part is called a pellet. Admission. ~ 6000 Sample Road, Huntersville; 704-875-6521, fax 704-875-8814; www.carolinaraptorcenter.org.

HIDDEN ►

Nearby, the **University of North Carolina at Charlotte Botanical Gardens** combines indoor and outdoor gardens. Begin your visit at the **McMillan Greenhouse**, a research and education center with maps to the gardens. Within the greenhouse are rooms simulating five of the world's growing environments. In the moist "tropical" room, there's chocolate, coffee and papaya; in the dry and sunny "desert" room grow cactus and other succulents. Outside are plants native to the southeast United States, such as carnivorous pitcher plants, sundews and Venus flytraps. Next door, you'll find showy bromeliads and orchids from Guatemala, Venezuela and Mexico. Even more intriguing is the two-story "rainforest" with more than 400 plant species. The greenhouse is closed Sunday, but the gardens are open daily. ~ Mary Alexander Road, off Route 49 southeast of Huntersville; 704-687-2364; gardens.uncc.edu.

From here, take Route 49 east to Route 601, then head south to Route 200. By this time you will know you're way out in the sticks, beyond any likeness of Charlotte, but keep pressing deeper

HIDDEN ►

into the country by taking the turnoff at Route 200 for **Reed Gold Mine State Historic Site**. The gold mine is in the woods, between the eye-blink hamlets of Georgeville and Locust, precisely where young Conrad Reed found a seventeen-pound hunk of gold—America's first nugget. The year was 1799, and Conrad showed the big "yellow rock" to his pa, a poor farmer named John Reed, who promptly used it as a doorstop.

Three years later, a Fayetteville jeweler noticed the doorstop and asked John Reed to name his price. Reed got $3.50 for the nugget but later discovered it was worth $3600, so he feverishly took to panning his creek. By 1824, he and a small crew of slaves and unsavory miners had dug up more than $100,000 in gold.

A film at the historic site, located on the old Reed farm, tells you this story and its ending (not a great one, as the farm was eventually closed due to a Reed family squabble, though John did die a wealthy man). After the film, a guide will take you five stories down into the dim, clammy shafts and wormy tunnels where Reed and his crew dug for gold as well as other minerals and gems.

He'll show you the "veins" running along the quartz rock where gold and silver are born, and tell you how the Reeds used candles and oil lanterns to find their riches. From April through October, for a small fee, visitors can try their own luck at panning the Reed creek (something kids really enjoy), though you should know there have been no major finds reported lately. Closed Sunday and Monday. ~ 9621 Reed Mine Road; 704-721-4653.

LODGING

Most downtown Charlotte hotels are highrises of the chain variety, which makes the **Dunhill Hotel** especially inviting. Since its opening in 1929 as the Mayfair Manor, the hostelry has been providing intimate accommodations and stellar service. Today there's a piano, a bar and original art by North Carolinian Philip Moose on the walls. Every room is desirable, having been restored with reproduction period pieces, poster beds and pedestal sinks. The one-bedroom penthouse suite is complete with a king-sized bed, separate living room, fireplace and jacuzzi. ~ 237 North Tryon Street, Charlotte; 704-332-4141, 800-354-4141, fax 704-376-4117; www.dunhill hotel.com. MODERATE TO ULTRA-DELUXE.

In 1802, a 28-pound gold nugget was found in the Charlotte area by Peter, a slave who didn't even enjoy a last name, but whose find set off the nation's first gold rush.

Duke Mansion opened in the late 1990s, but its architecture—a grand Colonial Revival—recalls the early part of last century. In fact, the third-floor "treetop" rooms look down on 100-year-old oaks and pines. The remainder of the 20 rooms have sleeping porches—a nice touch—and all the spaces come with goose-down pillows, plush robes and bedside chocolates. ~ 400 Hermitage Road, Charlotte; 704-714-4400, 888-202-1009; www.dukemansion.org. DELUXE TO ULTRA-DELUXE.

Set on the spectacular acreage of an old strawberry farm three miles from the heart of uptown Charlotte is the **VanLandingham Estate Inn**. Quaint and sprawling, this residence was built in 1913 and offers nine rooms in two different buildings. The California-style bungalow features five of the rooms and a beautiful common space with rich red walls, hardwood floors and a fireplace. Browse the library and enjoy the light-bathed solarium in the main house. The guest rooms here are big, bright and elegant, each with a private antique bath. The equally historical grounds contain a world of delights: rose and butterfly gardens, petite waterfalls, a lily pond, a tree swing, a mosaic fountain and a European orangery and greenhouse. ~ 2010 The Plaza, Charlotte; 704-334-8909, 888-524-2020, fax 704-940-8830; www.vanlandinghamestate.com. DELUXE.

Amid posh SouthPark's highrise silhouettes and snazzy shops is the **Park Hotel**. Here things are polished and refined, from the lavish bouquets adorning the lobby to the hotel initials perfectly imprinted in the ashtray sands. Rooms are furnished with English reproductions, and turndown service includes a weather forecast card for the next day. There's a small gym, whirlpool, steam room, outdoor swimming pool and a restaurant. ~ 2200 Rexford Road, Charlotte; 704-364-8220, 800-334-0331, fax 704-365-4712; www.theparkhotel.com. DELUXE TO ULTRA-DELUXE.

The outside of **Ms. Elsie's Caribbean Bed and Breakfast** may be plain and cedar-ranch style, but the inside flows with Caribbean cool and color. Kiwi-washed walls, vibrant Spanish tiles, and palms from Elsie's own atrium garden fill the three guest rooms. Breakfast is just as lively, with island specialties like St. Maarten Creole shrimp. ~ 334 North Sharon Amity Road, Charlotte; 704-365-5189; www.mselsies.com. DELUXE.

For country quietude close to the city, check into **Victorian Villa Inn.** Just eight miles from downtown Charlotte, the 1929 inn rests on Lake Wylie among gardens and long, lazy green lawns. A dramatic curving staircase whisks you to five guest rooms with formal touches like floral, English-style wallpapers and stained-glass windows. The very best space, though, is the Lincoln Suite, with its stone fireplace and domed-ceiling bath overlooking the lake. ~ 10925 Windy Grove Road, Charlotte; 704-394-5545; www.victorianvillainn.com, e-mail manager@victorianvillainn.com. DELUXE TO ULTRA-DELUXE.

HIDDEN ►

In a few minutes' drive, you can abandon the city for something silent and deeply wooded and lakeside. That would be **Still Waters Bed and Breakfast** at the upper end of Lake Wylie, where red-bellied woodpeckers play in tall maple and dogwood trees and blue herons swoop low over the water. The 1920s-era log-veneer house has two bedrooms and a suite, all decorated in homey style. One has a queen four-poster bed and plank walls, another a waterbed with mirrored canopy. A separate wooden cottage features a free-standing fireplace and jacuzzi tub in the private bath. Breakfast is served in the glass sunporch with views of the lake. ~ 6221 Amos Smith Road, near Charlotte-Douglas International Airport; 704-399-6299; www.bbonline.com/nc/stillwaters, e-mail rdyer399@aol.com. MODERATE.

DINING

You would expect the Carolinas' largest city to have the most and best restaurants, and it does. You can have wholesome health food or wonderful deep-fried chicken with mashed potatoes and gravy, fiery Jamaican fare or something cucumbery from the Middle East or French country with a Southern twist—the list won't quit. Here are a few suggestions.

On the edge of historic Fourth Ward, in an exquisite century-old house painted in "jewel tones," is one of Charlotte's best places to dine. Jackets *and* reservations are required at the **McNinch House Restaurant,** the latter required several days in advance. Dining here is French and fabulous, and not to be

The Valley of Love

Love first came to the valley in 1954 when Charlotte developer Andy Barker chucked city life for some benevolent green Piedmont pastures. He and his wife, Ellenora, bought a chunk of land north of Statesville but nowhere near anything in particular, save some scattered farmhouses and tobacco fields. Then they threw up some wood shacks and began building a Wild West utopia. It was Andy's lifelong dream, and he and Ellenora called it **Love Valley**.

Throughout the 1960s, love kept coming to the valley as hippies dropped out of society and pitched wigwams and tents and planted gardens. Soon "downtown" Love Valley began to take shape. Log and bark buildings and split-rail fences lined the one-block Main Street, and there was even a general store. Townsfolk lived mostly in tents or trailers and hardly ever drove cars, preferring to ride horses. Andy became the mayor and hired a town marshal, head shop owner Joe Ponder.

Little has changed today. In fact, cars aren't allowed on the sawdust Main Street, though you're welcome to tie your horse to one of the many hitchin' posts—everyone else does. The **General Store**, decorated with an old wooden balcony, sells hot dogs, barbecue and Cheerwine; a toy horse out front runs on a quarter. Open Friday through Sunday. ~ 704-592-5425. Andy's still the mayor, except for those intermittent years when he's voted out by Love Valley's 100 or so residents.

On weekends from Easter through Halloween, there's usually a rodeo at the **Love Valley Arena** and there's always a big square dance. People come from surrounding states to dance and to join the weekend trailrides, arriving en masse on Friday nights with their horse trailers and RVs, setting up camp on the picturesque pastures around Love Valley. Ask Tony about campsites. ~ 704-592-2243. To rent a horse, call Buddy and Debbie Price. ~ 704-592-2024.

To get to Love Valley, you must drive down no-name country roads that squiggle through gentle hills speckled with whitewashed farm-houses sporting weathervanes. Fields of tobacco stretch to the horizon. *Directions:* From Route 40 just west of Statesville, take Route 115 North. Then follow the faded red heart-shaped signs to Love Valley.

undertaken with a skinny wallet. The six-course prix-fixe menu changes weekly and may include choices such as red bell-pepper bisque or shiitake mushroom and wild-rice soup, rack of lamb or Maine lobster tail in tomato vodka cream sauce over ravioli (some entrées have a Continental twist). Chocolate rules the desserts: go for the ganache cake with hazelnut mousse laced with Frangelica. Closed Sunday and Monday. ~ 511 North Church Street, Charlotte; 704-332-6159. ULTRA-DELUXE.

Over the years, young downtown professionals have worn a path to **Alexander Michael's**, a popular, publike Fourth Ward eating and meeting place. The long, polished walnut bar is trimmed in brass, the ceiling is low and wood-paneled, and a bay window overlooks the lovely Victorian neighborhood. There are cocktails and wine and light eats—dressed-up sandwiches and burgers, pasta and salads—though the food is really secondary to the friendly atmosphere. Closed Sunday. ~ 401 West Ninth Street, Charlotte; 704-332-6789. MODERATE.

Despite the name, there's nothing that will get you down at **Blue Restaurant & Bar**. From the intricate tile mosaics to the mood lighting to the blue-tinted martini, this hip hangout is true blue in every sense. The Mediterranean cuisine dazzles in taste and presentation with Sicilian, Spanish and Moroccan-style specialties. Indulge in the lamb tangine simmered with almonds, dates and carrots, or the seared tuna wrapped in prosciutto and sage. No need to head to an after-dinner nightspot—the innovative martini bar and live jazz acts make Blue a great place to linger. ~ 214 North Tryon Street, Charlotte; 704-927-2583, fax 704-927-0555; www.bluerestaurantandbar.com. DELUXE TO ULTRA-DELUXE.

HIDDEN ►   **Anthony's Caribbean Cafe** is in the most unlikely of places (the back corner of a strip shopping center) serving the most unlikely cuisine—island spice. Naturally, the place is wildly popular, especially with yuppies, who crowd in for Anthony's rotisserie chicken, basted with a secret sauce he concocted in Guaya and served with heaps of calypso rice and callaloo greens. The Guayanese man is there at the door, wearing his tropical flowered shirt, smiling at diners before they're seated beneath bright umbrellas next to walls painted colors reminiscent of the tropics. Anthony's sauce, by the way, is for sale—either by the bottle or by the case. No lunch on Saturday. Closed Sunday. ~ 2001 East Seventh Street, Charlotte; 704-342-0749. BUDGET.

Several healthful options await at the **Peaceful Dragon**, an Asian cultural center featuring an excellent restaurant. Perhaps after an introductory tai chi course or a Japanese facial massage, your appetite may be whetted for Asian fusion dishes such as shiitake mushroom and tofu-stuffed crêpes and vegetable dumplings with ginger sauce. Breakfast brings entrées like orange-scented french toast and apple buckwheat pancakes. Everything is fresh and vegetarian, a welcome change from hearty Southern food. ~ 12610 Steele Creek Road, Charlotte; 704-504-8866; www.the peacefuldragon.com, e-mail staff@thepeacefuldragon.com. BUDGET TO MODERATE.

The legendary **Lupie's Cafe** is cluttered and crazy, and not a   ◄ HIDDEN
little worn-out, residing in a soot-stained building with ductwork running along the ceiling and walls papered with fliers and posters and photos of known and unknown people. Lupie's is famous for big chili—order it vegetarian, Cincinnati- or Texas-style— and other gratifying fare like macaroni 'n' cheese, chicken 'n' dumplings, vegetable plates and banana pudding. Closed Sunday. ~ 2718 Monroe Road at Seventh Street, Charlotte; 704-374-1232; www.lupiescafe.com. BUDGET.

Looking for a good cup of java? Then visit **Dilworth Coffeehouse**. This quaint store roasts its own beans for the five fresh brews served daily. Bagels, pound cakes, danishes and muffins fill the glass cases at the counter of this local hangout. Enjoy your coffee inside or out on the patio. ~ 1235 East Boulevard, Charlotte; 704-358-8003. BUDGET.

Downtown Charlotte's best soul kitchen is the **Coffee Cup Grill**. Country-fried steak, chicken 'n' dumplings, pork chops, pigs' feet, corn bread and the like are fixed for lunch. There's no breakfast menu, but mention something Southern like fried eggs, grits and sausage patties, and you're sure to get it. Closed Sunday. ~ 914 South Clarkson Street, Charlotte; 704-375-8855. BUDGET.

If you go antique shopping in Waxhaw, have lunch at the **Bridge and Rail**. It's Carolinas country all the way. Dating back to 1904, the downtown diner offers two daily lunch and dinner entrées (chicken pie, spaghetti and meatloaf are possibilities) accompanied by green beans, fried okra, corn, squash—what-

AUTHOR FAVORITE

I could get fanatical and insist you haven't tasted the Piedmont if you don't eat at **McDonald's Cafeteria**. When the place opened in 1971, it was instantly the place for awesome cafeteria food. Over the years it has expanded and is still going strong, daily feeding more than 2000 customers such country wonders as teeny crispy-fried chicken pieces and volcanoes of mashed potatoes, slow-stewed black-eyed peas and lima beans, and the tenderest rib roast in the universe. The pies are also celestial. ~ Route 85 and Beatties Ford Road, Charlotte; 704-394-8848. BUDGET TO MODERATE.

ever's in season. No lunch or dinner on Sunday. Closed Monday. ~ 112 East South Main Street, Waxhaw; 704-843-5005. BUDGET.

SHOPPING   If you're looking for arty, New Age stuff, try **Seventh Street** between Hawthorne and Pecan streets, southeast of downtown Charlotte. Nestled under the magnolias are great galleries and shops selling crystals, tie-dye, African tribal prints, bangle and beaded jewelry and more.

It would be easy to spend hours at the **Paper Skyscraper** poring through the wonderfully peculiar housewares, books, cards and sundry gifts. Think Christmas shopping! ~ 330 East Boulevard, Charlotte; 704-333-7130.

For Charlotte's best assortment of gay books, magazines and newspapers, head to **White Rabbit Books and Things**. One in a chain of stores around the Piedmont, White Rabbit also stocks music, clever gifts and T-shirts with gay themes. ~ 1401 Central Avenue, Charlotte; 704-377-4067.

In a world of megamalls, it's nice to know that a shop like **Park Road Books** is thriving. This intimate store in Charlotte boasts a highly trained staff that provides quality service you won't find at a larger franchise. Patrons are welcome to browse or sit next to the fireplace to read at their leisure. If you can't find a book, just ask—they can special order a title or help find that author you can't remember. ~ 4139 Park Road, Charlotte; 704-525-9239; www.parkroadbooks.com.

For power shopping, head to the SouthPark area. The sprawling **SouthPark Mall** has four department stores and a slew of boutiques, galleries and music stores. ~ Sharon and Fairview roads, Charlotte; 704-364-4411; www.southpark.com. Just across the street, **Specialty Shops of SouthPark** offers even more exclusive places to drop your cash, in a setting of fountains, stone piazzas and bubble canopies.

HIDDEN ▶   If you're interested in antiques, there's no place like the town of **Waxhaw**, about 23 miles south of Charlotte on Route 16. More than two dozen antique stores line up along downtown Main Street, and there's more on the outskirts of town. Most places are open 10 a.m. to 5 p.m., Wednesday through Sunday, though some close for lunch, their owners wandering over to the Bridge and Rail Restaurant for chicken pot pie and fried okra.

Clock-o-holics will love **The Antique Clock Shop** and its bountiful selection of vintage clocks, watches, music boxes and other gadgets. ~ Route 16 and Price Street, Waxhaw; 704-843-4120.

Switch gears and head 30 miles northeast of Charlotte on Route 85 to the textile town of **Kannapolis**. Since the late 1800s, it's been the headquarters for Cannon Mills, the well-known maker of towels and linens, which operates **Cannon Village**. The village draws shoppers from miles around who come for discount prices not only on bed and bath items but on furniture, clothing, shoes, hosiery and toys. More than 35 factory outlet stores and boutiques are located here along pleasant streets with lushly landscaped medians and brick sidewalks. ~ 200 West Avenue, Kannapolis; 704-938-3200.

NIGHTLIFE

Charlotte has many ways to spend an evening, from the grittiest, get-down honky-tonks with great country and blues to cool-aired, after-work lounges where Southern yuppies linger over their imported beer. Some places import reggae from the sub-tropical south, others bring in big-name entertainers and acts.

Some of the city's most elaborate productions are at the **North Carolina Blumenthal Performing Arts Center**, opened in 1993. Three theaters, including a beautiful European-styled opera hall and a proscenium fashioned in a courtyard, host Broadway performances, national and international dance (including lavish cabaret) and symphony concerts. Locally, **Opera Carolina**, the **Charlotte Symphony**, **North Carolina Dance Theater**, **Oratorio Singers** and **Charlotte Repertory Theater**, among many others, perform at Blumenthal. ~ 130 North Tryon Street, Charlotte; 704-372-1000; www.blumenthalcenter.org.

For information on gay and lesbian events and resources in North Carolina, visit www.onevoicechorus.com and go to the community links page.

The **Graduate Food & Pub**, voted the "Best College Bar" by a local paper, has rock bands playing on Friday and Saturday nights. Cover for live music. ~ 123 West Trade Street, Charlotte; 704-358-3024.

For a night of dancing until you're ready to melt, hit up one of the two dancefloors at the **Liquid Lounge**, which has hosted international house legends like Charles Feelgood, Keoki and Angel Alanis. The red brick walls, bold neon lights and smoky ambiance evoke a club straight out of underground east Berlin—with trendy patrons replacing the punk crowd. The outdoor patio is a nice break from the drum 'n' bass and old-skool hip-hop—although sometimes it serves as a third dancefloor spinning a more subtle genre. ~ 127 West Trade Street, Charlotte; 704-374-0111; www.liquidlounge.net.

In the heart of downtown Charlotte, the **Carpe Diem Restaurant and Lounge** caters to a mostly professional crowd. The space is large but loveseats and coffeetables make it a cozy spot for an after-dinner drink. ~ 1535 Elizabeth Avenue, Charlotte; 704-377-7976.

Offering top-notch blues in no-nonsense surroundings, the **Double Door Inn** books bands from all over the country. Eric Clapton and Stevie Ray Vaughan are among those who have stopped in over the past twenty years. Cover. ~ 218 East Independence Boulevard, Charlotte; 704-376-1446; www.doubledoorinn.com.

Tremont Music Hall gets great bands spanning the universe of rock and alternative rock, punk, ska, hardcore and emo. Cover. ~ 400 West Tremont Avenue, Charlotte; 704-343-9494; www.tremontmusichall.com.

South End Brewery and Smokehouse gets its share of sports fans and also the after-work, Armani-and-martini crowd. Live bands playing everything from jazz to alternative rock are featured on Friday night. ~ 2100 South Boulevard, in the South End entertainment complex; 704-358-4677.

In Charlotte, the only spot offering live Dixieland jazz every night of the week is the **Cajun Queen**. This New Orleans–style restaurant and bar crowds both stories of a renovated house with happy patrons. The atmosphere is always fun and festive and there is never a cover. ~ 1800 East Seventh Street, Charlotte; 704-377-9017.

The **Palomino Club** is essentially two clubs under one roof, with live music four nights a week. One club showcases national country bands, while the other hosts pop and rock bands. Cover. ~ 8801 East W.T. Harris Boulevard, Charlotte; 704-568-6104.

GAY SCENE   Where better to find a happening gay scene than "the queen city"? Charlotte hosts a number of gay gathering spots, from leather bars to strip clubs.

An upscale gay crowd gathers at **Liaison's**. The old Victorian house features an upper-level veranda with a commanding view of the city skyline. ~ 316 Rensselaer Avenue, Charlotte; 704-376-1617.

The enormous **Scorpio** could be North Carolina's most popular gay and lesbian nightspot, consisting of several clubs within a club, including a vast dance bar and a down-home country bar called the Queen City Saloon. On weekends, its an endless sea of bodies. Cover. ~ 2301 Freedom Drive, Charlotte; 704-373-9124.

With an eclectic crowd sporting anything from dreadlocks to tube tops, **Club Myxx** is Charlotte's most diverse gay destination. This melting pot features myriad events such as spoken word open mics and freestyle rap performances. Expect to hear mostly reggae, hip-hop and R&B, and house and dance music on Saturday. ~ 3110 South Tryon Street, Charlotte; 704-525-5001.

Chasers bills itself as "Carolina's first and hottest cruise bar," and it is indeed a cruisey place, with an assortment of exotic dancers constantly performing. Men only. Cover. ~ 3217 The Plaza, Charlotte; 704-339-0500.

Eccentric and off-beat, **DAKS Tavern** puts on a number of get-to-know-each-other events: drag shows, talent searches, casino nights and themed parties (call ahead to find out what's going on). Couches, a pool table and pinball machines make this intimate bar fun and cozy. ~ 1704 Shamrock Drive, Charlotte; 704-347-6826; www.dakstavern.com.

MCDOWELL NATURE PRESERVE 🏃 🚣 🛥 🛶 Mecklenburg County's first nature preserve spans 1100 acres with more than 100 species of wildflowers and ferns. The centerpiece is pretty Lake Wylie, with its verdant, steep shoreline featuring a patch of white-sand beach. Seven miles of trails lead through the hardwood forest (one trail is designed for wheelchair hikers), and there's a nature center with hands-on exhibits that kids love. Swimming is not permitted. Fishing is good for bass, bream, carp, catfish and crappie. Facilities include picnic areas, restrooms, hiking trails, paddleboat and canoe rentals, and a boat launch. Day-use fee (March through October only). ~ Route 49, about 12 miles south of downtown Charlotte; 704-588-5224.

▲ There are 13 RV sites and 26 drive-to tent and pop-up camper sites, all at $18 per night; 10 primitive tent sites that require a short hike are $9 a night. In addition, the park has several tents already set up; they are $38 per night and must be reserved in advance; 704-583-1284.

CROWDER'S MOUNTAIN STATE PARK 🚣 🛶 This 2857-acre wilderness is ruled by the twin 800-foot peaks of Crowder's Mountain and Kings Pinnacle. The rocky monadnocks are an oddity in an otherwise flat land, having survived eons of erosion while the remaining Piedmont succumbed. Rock climbers seek out their jagged faces for a windblown experience (permit required but free). Clear, fast-flowing streams elbow through the park, and there's also a nine-acre lake that entices both boaters and anglers. Try fishing for bass, crappie and bream. Animal life in the park is abundant but subtle; though you may spot a gray squirrel or chipmunk, it is doubtful you will see one of the shrews, foxes or salamanders that make their homes here. Swimming is not permitted. Facilities include a visitors center, restrooms, picnic areas, hiking trails and canoe rentals. ~ Sparrow Springs Road 5 miles south of Route 29-74, about 25 miles west of Charlotte and 6 miles southwest of Gastonia; 704-853-5375; www.ncsparks.net/crmo.html.

More than 160 species of birds have been sighted in Crowder's Mountain State Park, making it a big draw for birders.

▲ There are 6 primitive, hike-in group tent sites; $1 per person per night, with a $9 minimum per site. There are 10 primitive, hike-in family tent sites; $9 per site per night.

LATTA PLANTATION NATURE PRESERVE 🏃 🏇 🚣 🛶 This is Mecklenburg County's biggest park and also its showpiece, with 2247 acres almost entirely devoted to nature. Waterfowl flock to

PARKS

◄ *HIDDEN*

◄ *HIDDEN*

the shores of manmade Mountain Island Lake, and so do canoers and those with johnboats. There's an equestrian center where you can rent horses; 12 miles of horseback trails wend through the woods. There's also Latta Place, a historic plantation home, and the Carolina Raptor Center that's home to injured birds of prey. There's bass and catfish in the lake; fishing permit is $2 per day. Swimming is not permitted in Mountain Island Lake. Facilities include a nature center, a volleyball court, ten miles of hiking trails, picnic areas, and canoe, johnboat and paddleboat rentals. ~ 6211 Sample Road in Huntersville, 12 miles northwest of downtown Charlotte; 704-875-1391.

HIDDEN ►   **JETTON PARK** 🚲 This outstanding park offers one of the few public accesses to colossal Lake Norman. On a map the 32,500-acre lake looks like a miniature sea ready to burst in on Charlotte. Much of Jetton's 105 scenic acres ramble along a peninsula, and there are fancy wood picnic decks parked right along the water. There's also a gazebo for picnicking, a small, white-sand beach for sunning, bike trails for sightseeing, and many fine spots for catching a lovely liquid sunset. Swimming is not permitted. Facilities include picnic tables, restrooms, seasonal bike rentals on the weekends, a playground, paved trails that are wheelchair-accessible, and lighted tennis courts. Day-use fee, $5 on weekends and holidays. ~ 1900 Jetton Road in Huntersville, off Route 77 north of Charlotte; 704-896-9808.

▼▼▼▼▼▼▼▼▼▼▼▼▼▼▼▼
Pinehurst & Southern Pines Area

A hundred miles of seamless back roads and rambling rivers separate Charlotte from Pinehurst and Southern Pines. Then there is golf. More than 35 championship-caliber courses pepper these sandhills, their soothing names—Whispering Woods, Legacy Links, Hyland Hills—suggesting long, languid days on well-tended turf. They hint at the money that's been coming to Pinehurst and Southern Pines ever since James Walker Tufts got it in his mind to build something great here.

It was the late 1800s when the Boston inventor and philanthropist bought 5500 acres near a speck of a village called Southern Pines. He began building a health retreat, hiring famed landscape architect Frederick Law Olmsted to design the grounds and a neighboring New England–style village. In 1901 Tufts opened the most opulent resort for miles around. He called it The Carolina.

Originally, wealthy folks came to relax, play croquet and take shooting lessons from Pinehurst Gun Club instructor Annie Oakley. But with the popularity of golf in the early 1900s, guests were soon bringing along their clubs and little white balls. Never a man to ignore a business opportunity, Tufts hired Donald Ross—the Frederick Law Olmsted of golf course designers—to create a couple of courses.

SIGHTS

Now there are eight courses, including the famously challenging Course Number Two. The Carolina, restored and just as spectacular, has been given the more contemporary moniker **Pinehurst Resort and Country Club**. Its grand white walls and copper cupola reign over charming Pinehurst, Olmsted's lovely little village, which attracts shoppers and strollers. ~ Carolina Vista Drive, Pinehurst; 910-295-6811; www.pinehurst.com.

The entrance to **Pinehurst Village** is through a throng of tall loblolly pines, magnolias and dogwoods, with handsome homes set within their shady recesses. The village is an orderly place, very proper, with traffic circles and lots of white picket and pine mulch, and more trees than concrete. There are cafés and confectionaries, antique emporiums and a bank with a "garden walk-up." Before looking around, stop by the **Pinehurst Area Convention & Visitors Bureau** for information. ~ 10677 Route 15-501, Southern Pines; 910-692-3330, 800-346-5362, fax 910-692-2493; www.homeofgolf.com.

> In the nineteenth century, the pretty little town of Cameron was the "Dewberry Capital of the World."

For strolling among beautifully sculpted greenery, make your way over to **Sandhills Horticultural Gardens**. The highlight is the Sir Walter Raleigh Gardens, a one-and-a-half-acre replica of a formal English garden. In the spring the Hackley Woodland Garden is bursting with colorful rhododendrons, camelias and azaleas. Southwestern plants adaptable to the Carolina climate make their home in the succulent garden. Take a look at the Ebersole Holly Collection, said to be the East Coast's largest array of hollies, and the Conifer Garden, with its assembly of firs and pines. Conifers, by the way, are cone-bearing trees. The boardwalk of the Desmond Wetland Trail takes you out over a wetland. ~ 3395 Airport Road at Sandhills Community College, Pinehurst; 910-692-6185.

A few miles east you'll encounter the town of **Southern Pines** (along Route 1). Not nearly as gentrified as Pinehurst, it embraces more of the simple Southernness found in most small Carolina towns. Golf may be the point of it all in Pinehurst, but in Southern Pines, folks experience real workdays, funneling into storefronts of red brick and painted plank. There are bakeries and a jeweler, a barber shop and banks, and trains that trundle through town regularly. The train tracks run right through downtown, slicing through a median planted with magnolias and awash with the orange-red of azaleas.

To the east and south of Southern Pines, **Fort Bragg Military Reservation** is a giant yawn in the landscape, covering over 200 square miles that finally end at the city of **Fayetteville**. As you'd expect, Fayetteville's economy is fueled by the military (there is also the nearby Pope Air Force Base), and the area is more oriented to those in the service than those out for a Sunday drive. But if you'd like a peek at this side of life, stop by the **Fort Bragg/**

Pope Air Force Base Welcome Center for driving-tour maps of the military reservation. ~ Randolf and Knox streets, Fayetteville; 910-907-2026. To find out if there are any scheduled parachute jumps, call 910-396-6366.

The **82nd Airborne War Memorial Museum** follows the missions of the 82nd Airborne from World War I through the Persian Gulf War and the Haitian Civil War. A section focusing on the Battle of Normandy will excite D-Day buffs. Closed Monday. ~ Within the Fort Bragg/Pope Air Force Base, corner of Ardennes and Gela streets, Fayetteville; 910-432-5307.

HIDDEN ▶

From battle history to dewberries—that's what happens if you drive north from Fort Bragg to **Cameron**, once the hub of dewberry growing, harvesting and shipping. Unfortunately, the dewberry's fate was sealed when strawberries and blackberries came along, as these were not only sweeter but easier to grow. These days, only a few backyard patches remain, but there are many antique shops in Cameron—the reason most travelers find it. Take a stroll around town and check out the terrific finds. ~ On Route 24-27, just east of Route 1.

HIDDEN ▶

From Cameron, wind west on Route 24-27 to Carthage and pick up Route 1006 for ten miles through lonesome sandhill country. Here you'll come to a place where the Whigs and Tories had a nasty encounter. The bullet holes in the **House in the Horseshoe** testify to the 1781 shootout between Whig Philip Alston and Tory David Fanning and their respective bands of troops. It was Alston's home, and Fanning was threatening to firebomb it. After ten men were killed, Alston's wife Temperance negotiated a deal with Fanning: her husband would stop his rebellions against the British crown if Fanning retreated. All this history and more is part of the tour of the gabled, double-shouldered, whitewashed plantation house, built in 1772 at the horseshoe bend in the Deep River. Closed Sunday and Monday. ~ 324 Alston House Road, 12 miles north of Carthage; 910-947-2051.

LODGING

Ever since its New Year's Day opening in 1901 as The Carolina, the **Pinehurst Resort and Country Club** has ruled as the area's supreme moneyed retreat. James Walker Tufts' palatial creation is crowned with a sparkling copper roof and cupola and cushioned in thick forest. Wide, whitewashed porches overlook gnarled limbs of magnolias. The resort offers every imaginable pursuit, from swimming in one of five outdoor pools to carriage rides, croquet and lawn bowling—very Southern and very clubby. And, as of 2002, spa lovers can find solace in a 31,000-square-foot spa with gleaming copper-domed towers, original yellow-pine-paneled dressing rooms, and a waterfall whirlpool. Of course, most guests come to chase the little white ball around one of the resort's eight golf courses. Within the hotel's ivory walls are more than 500 attractive rooms and suites; sprinkled in surrounding woods and around a lake are 140 condominiums and villas perfect for families. ~ Carolina Vista Drive, Pinehurst; 910-295-6811, 800-487-4653, fax 910-235-8503; www.pinehurst.com. ULTRA-DELUXE.

Magnolia Inn looks just like it sounds: a whitewashed, gabled turn-of-the-twentieth-century house with a rambling porch and three magnolia trees parked on the front lawn. Right in the village of Pinehurst, it is naturally a golfers' haven ("Golf attire is always acceptable dress," says the inn brochure). Rooms and public areas are Southern-comfortable, the walls prettily papered and the floors laid with wood plank. There's fine dining, a small pub and a pool. ~ Magnolia and Chinquapin roads, Pinehurst; 910-295-6900, 800-526-5562, fax 910-215-0858; www.themagnoliainn. com, e-mail magnolia@pinehurst.net. ULTRA-DELUXE.

Built in 1927 as a holiday home for a wealthy Philadelphia family, **The Knollwood House** was transformed last decade into an elegant retreat for travelers. Just six rooms keep things intimate in the two-story English Manor house, set on five acres filled with long leaf pines and magnolias. Turkish-woven robes and monogrammed towels await in the baths, distinct with their original, octagon-shaped tiles. Whether you take breakfast inside or out (in warm weather), you'll dine on English china with sterling flatware. ~ 1495 West Connecticut Avenue, Southern Pines; 910-692-9390, fax 910-692-0609; www.knollwoodhouse.com. DELUXE.

Inn at the Bryant House is hidden off the main highway between Aberdeen and Southern Pines, sequestered in a neighborhood of handsome antebellum homes. The bed and breakfast is well run—owners Lee and Sharon Steele make you feel at home but provide plenty of privacy—and the rooms are extra comfortable, decorated with sponge-painted nightstands and pretty linens, and

◄ HIDDEN

NO HORSIN' AROUND

Coming into Carthage, north of Pinehurst and Southern Pines, you can't miss the **Old Buggy Inn**: The imposing, 6000-square-foot Queen Anne manse stands right at the entrance to the historic district. You'll also spy W. T. Jones' original horse-drawn buggy on the wraparound, gingerbread porch (Jones, president of a buggy manufacturing company, built the 1897 home for his wife Florence). Inside, five guest rooms come with gas fireplaces and floor-to-ceiling windows offering views of the turn-of-the-twentieth-century town—and passersby gazing at the beautiful Buggy Inn. ~ 301 McReynolds Street, Carthage; 910-947-1901, 800-553-5247, fax 910-947-1345; www.oldbuggyinn.com, e-mail sesmith@pinehurst.net. MODERATE.

thick terrycloth robes hang in the closet. There's courtyard parking and a good breakfast included in the rate—all in all, great value for an expensive area. ~ 214 North Poplar Street, Aberdeen; 910-944-3300, 800-453-4019, fax 910-944-8898; www.innatbryant house.com, e-mail bryanthouse@pinehurst.net. MODERATE TO DELUXE.

Your best bet for lodging in Fayetteville is the **Radisson Prince Charles Hotel**, built in 1925 and renovated in 1992 to the tune of $7.5 million. Marble floors, Palladian windows, columns and pilasters adorn the eight-story hotel, and the 84 rooms and suites all have modern comforts. ~ 450 Hay Street, Fayetteville; 910-433-4444, 800-333-3333, fax 910-433-4472; www.radisson.com. DELUXE.

DINING

A little bit fancy and festive, **Theo's Taverna** is great for traditional Greek dishes like moussaka, *souvlaki* and *pastitsio*, plus nightly specials such as grilled veal chops or blackened striped bass with tomatoes. Take a linen-topped table in the main dining room, or opt for a chair at the long polished bar. Closed Sunday. ~ 140 Chinquapin Road, Pinehurst; 910-295-0780. MODERATE.

For lunch, the **Greenhouse Restaurant** offers a simple but hearty menu of homemade soups and sandwiches such as spicy meatball. Wash it all down with the variety of beers, wine and cocktails available. Don't miss the homemade signature mudpie. Bright, spacious and filled with luscious hanging plants, the Greenhouse delivers. ~ 905 Linden Road, Pinehurst; 910-295-1761. BUDGET.

195 American Fusion Cuisine is a comfortable dining room with hardwood floors, evening candles and tablecloths. The fare is fresh, imaginative and organic, different from anything else around. The menu changes daily, but for lunch you may find organic miso summer vegetable soup and pan-fried fresh salmon cake sandwich. At dinner, try the Yucatán marinated free-range chicken fajitas with black beans, or the grilled halibut with curried corn sauce and chive mashed potatoes. There's a full bar. No dinner on Tuesday. Closed Sunday and Monday. ~ 195 Bell Avenue, Southern Pines; 910-692-3811. MODERATE TO DELUXE.

In the tiny, farflung town of Cameron, the **Dewberry Deli** is an old-fashioned soda fountain and eatery, full of nostalgia and warmth with its checkered floor, wood-beamed ceiling and assorted curios. People crowd into cozy booths and out to sunny patio tables for salads and burgers, pita sandwiches and soups, lemonade and sweet dewberry cobbler (with dewberries from local backyards). A favorite lunch stop for Cameron antique hounds. Closed Sunday and Monday. ~ 129 Carthage Street, Cameron; 910-245-3697. BUDGET.

Start in **Pinehurst Village**, a perfectly pleasant place to shop and   **SHOPPING**
browse among galleries, boutiques and antique shops. You in-
stantly sense the shops' pedigree by their dressy scalloped awnings,
sobering price tags, and signs that announce branches in Palm
Beach and Greenwich, Connecticut. Most stores are closed Sunday
year-round.

Razook's has such a sign. Step inside to cultured couture for
women—extremely prim, chic styles, suits and dresses and accessories with that Jackie O. look. ~ 105 Chinquapin Road, Pinehurst; 910-295-6141.

If you're inclined to investigate the history of Pinehurst, **The
Country Book Shop** has several volumes for sale, along with other
local-interest books and bestsellers. ~ 140 Northwest Broad Street,
Pinehurst; 910-692-3211.

Just outside Pinehurst Village, **Midland Crafters** is a low-slung
building nearly obscured by pines, filled with thousands of fine
crafts: candles, pottery and glassware, chess sets, stone garden
accessories and sculpture. ~ 2220 Midland Road, one mile east of
the Pinehurst traffic circle; 910-295-6156.

Downtown Southern Pines does offer some shopping prospects,
mainly shoes, cookware and antiques. Most are along **Broad Street**,
on both sides of the railroad tracks (the tracks and a broad median
split the road in half). A store directory can be found at the corner of North Hampshire Avenue and Northwest Broad Street.

About ten miles northeast of Southern Pines, Cameron is an
attractive little town with nine or so antique stores. They're all on
Carthage Street, Cameron's main drag, so you can park and prowl   ◄ HIDDEN
the showrooms for old furniture, pottery and jewelry, glassware,
trains and artwork. Much has been beautifully restored—with price
tags that reflect it.

Definitely make a stop at **The Old Hardware**, in a 1920 building whose past lives include housing a Ford agency and mule auction center. Today it holds unusual, good-quality antiques: perhaps
a camel-back trunk, English cottage bed or a Scottish hunting
horn. Closed Sunday and Monday. ~ Carthage Street, Cameron;
910-245-7001.

BIRDIES AND BOGIES AT BURCHFIELD'S

Where but in Pinehurst would you find an entire store devoted to golf art?
At **Burchfield's Golf Gallery** you can buy a sketch of Jack Nicklaus or
a painting of Greg Norman. There's even a bronze sculpture of Bobby
Jones in the British Open. ~ 80 Magnolia Road, Pinehurst; 910-295-
6842; www.burchfields.com.

NIGHTLIFE   The word "nightlife" is a stretch for this area. You can, however, have a drink at **Dugan's Pub**, where there are usually live rock bands on weekends in the spring months. ~ Market Square, Pinehurst; 910-295-3400. Or try **Theo's Taverna**, where a long, polished wood bar and a friendly bartender make for pleasant before- or after-dinner relaxation. ~ 140 Chinquapin Road, Pinehurst; 910-295-0780.

In Southern Pines, **Brooks** is one option for a drink and the occasional live band. Cover for live music. ~ 155 Northwest Broad Street, Southern Pines; 910-692-3515.

The **Sunrise Theater**, originally a hardware store and a cinema, hosts a classical concert series, film festivals, theater, ballet and children's performances. ~ 250 Northwest Broad Street, Southern Pines; 910-692-3611; www.sunrisetheater.com.

PARKS   **WEYMOUTH WOODS NATURE PRESERVE** 🏃 These 905 acres of woods are dotted with wildflower fields and crisscrossed with streams. Four and a half miles of trails wind through the preserve. You'll find a park office, picnic tables, restrooms and hiking trails; a naturalist is available by appointment. ~ 1024 Fort Bragg Road, across from Highlands Trails, in Southern Pines; 910-692-2167.

▼▼▼▼▼▼▼▼▼▼

Raleigh

It would seem logical to begin exploring North Carolina's capital city from the downtown hub of state government, but it is entirely more pleasant to start in Historic Oakwood. This engaging Victorian neighborhood on the northeast corner of town is filled with lyrical architecture and dashing color, a meld of Neoclassical style and Second Empire and Steamboat Gothic.

SIGHTS   Bounded roughly by East Edenton Street, North Person Street, Franklin Street and the Oakwood Cemetery, **Historic Oakwood** is an oasis from downtown hubbub, with birds trilling from massive magnolias and oaks, children playing along sloping sidewalks, and passersby waving at everyone they see. In the neighborhood, more than 100 homes, most beautifully restored and many dating back to the 1800s, are spread over a span of about 22 blocks.

Each home is different, yet many share the same Southern features: wide porches for staying cool in summer, high-pitched roofs for attic insulation in winter, and porch ceilings painted blue to match the sky—and supposedly chase the flies away.

One of the many eye-catching residences is the **Wayne Allcott House** with its bright lavender paint. ~ 414 North East Street. Allcott also owned the house two doors down, at **500 Polk**

Street, now painted bubblegum pink and trimmed in forest green shutters and wavy shingles.

Down the way are a pair of **shotgun houses,** only one room wide, narrow enough for a bullet fired at the front to travel cleanly through the back. Built as spec homes for the working class, the tunnel-like designs saved developers money since less street frontage meant fewer taxes. ~ 407 and 409 North East Street.

Anything but narrow, the big and bold **Charles B. Hart House,** built around 1897, offers high drama with its great metal-wrapped tower, bold gables trimmed in bargeboard, delicate lancet windows and exterior of purple haze. ~ 412 Oakwood Avenue.

Don't be surprised if Raleigh is more cosmopolitan than you expected. Not only is it the state capital, it's also just 20 minutes from Research Triangle Park and its 30,000-plus scientists, computer programmers, and other high-tech minds.

Along the neighborhood's eastern border is the **Oakwood Cemetery,** wherein lie the remains of many of the people responsible for creating the neighborhood. Some of the people responsible today for preserving the neighborhood—The Society for the Preservation of Historic Oakwood—publish a handy walking-tour guide to the area. The guides are available at the **Capital Area Visitors Center.** ~ 5 East Edenton Street; 919-807-7950.

Kitty-corner to the visitors center is Raleigh's premier historic building, the **Executive Mansion.** Fashioned in Queen Anne cottage style and home to North Carolina's governor, it is a red-brick house of tremendous design and beauty, with whimsical eaves, great steps of granite and many gables. The immaculate grounds are shaded by giant trees. Inside awaits a showcase of North Carolina wood, elaborately carved and polished to a high sheen, and opulent chandeliers and works of art. Here, too, is much history. In 1891, then-governor Daniel Fowle moved into the Queen Anne manse after prisoners and craftsmen labored on the place for nine years (some of the bricks bear the initials of the prisoners who made them). Fowle's ghost is said to inhabit the building, for subsequent governors have been awakened by a knocking noise at precisely the same time each night. Extensive investigations have produced no explanation for the knocking. Free half-hour tours of the mansion's interior are offered only during the spring, the fall and part of December, though dates and times are sporadic. For tour schedules and reservations, call the Capital Area Visitors Center. ~ 200 North Blount Street; 919-807-7950.

A few blocks away is the heart of state government, an assemblage of low-slung, somber, sand-colored buildings. The classic-style **State Legislative Building,** carved of homegrown granite and laced with square columns, has free guided tours if you call ahead —not a bad idea, since the building's interior is a maze of look-alike rooms, corridors and courtyards famous for confounding even those with the keenest sense of direction. "Some visitors to the legislature become so hopelessly confused they become desperate," notes the book *Raleigh: A Guide to North Carolina's Capital.* "One legislative aide advises visitors to bring a bag of popcorn and leave a trail." ~ Jones and Salisbury streets; 919-807-7950.

When the Greek Revival **State Capitol** was built in the 1830s, someone called it "a Grecian temple on a hog pasture." The hogs have since been crowded out by sprawl, and the capitol's great stone walls and copper rotunda now enjoy a more somber setting. ~ Capitol Square, bounded by Edenton, Salisbury, Morgan and Wilmington streets; 919-733-4994.

Sunlight streams in on **North Carolina Museum of History**'s spacious high-ceiling galleries, spotlighting some 250,000 artifacts that tell a story of the Tarheel State. In the lobby you can view a replica of the Wright Brothers' plane and a hang glider built by hang glider inventor Francis Rogallo; in the Sports Hall of Fame are Richard Petty's race car and Arnold Palmer's Ryder Cup golf bag. The Health and Healing Experiences exhibit explores self-care, conventional medicine, faith and other healing systems. By now, you should realize you could spend all day here, and you didn't even have to pay to get in. Closed Monday. ~ 5 East Edenton Street; 919-807-7900; www.ncmuseumofhistory.org.

The **North Carolina Museum of Natural Sciences** is also free but not nearly as absorbing, though kids love it. They can stare at taxidermied northern hogsuckle fish and finger-size short-tailed shrews in the Piedmont Plateau exhibit, see salamanders and frogs in the wetlands exhibit and walk through an imitation mine where ultraviolet light is beamed at brilliant gems. In the Discovery Room, they can actually touch live animals and work on fossils. The Discovery Room, naturalist center and living conservatory are closed on Monday. ~ 11 West Jones Street; 919-733-7450, 877-462-8724; www.naturalsciences.org.

Even more fun for children, **Playspace** is an indoor and outdoor playground located in Raleigh's restored City Market. Parents pay by the hour and kids play by the hour, dressing in costumes and performing on stage, "working" in the imaginary hospital and grocery store, and climbing triple-tiered sand tables. *Note:* In case you're tempted to leave the little dears, you can't. All Playspace kids have to be supervised. Closed Monday. Admission. ~ 410 Glenwood Avenue; 919-832-1212; www.play spacemuseum.com.

To see what life was like in the old days, drive to the north end of town and tour **Mordecai Historic Park**. It occupies a single city block, the remnant of a huge plantation that before the Civil War sprawled for thousands of acres in every direction, taking in much of what is now downtown Raleigh. You can tour the

Raleigh-Durham-Chapel Hill

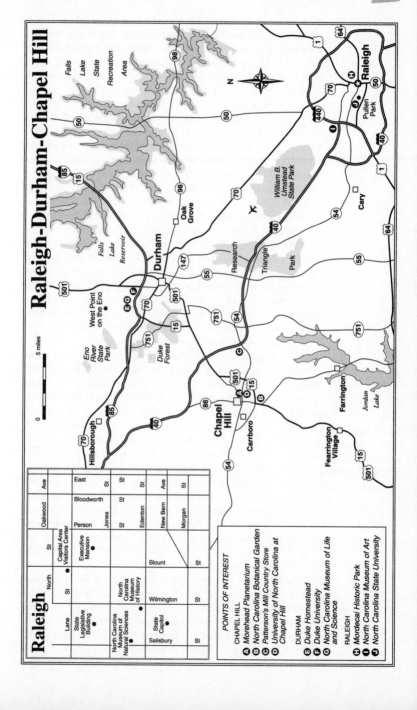

0 _____ 5 miles

Raleigh

North St	Oakwood Ave			
		East	St	St
Lane St	Capital Area Visitors Center	Bloodworth	St	St
State Legislative Building	Executive Mansion	Person	Jones	St
			Edenton	St
North Carolina Museum of Natural Sciences	North Carolina Museum of History		New Bern	Ave
		Blount	Morgan	St
	State Capitol	Wilmington		St
	Salisbury			St

POINTS OF INTEREST

CHAPEL HILL
- Ⓐ Morehead Planetarium
- Ⓑ North Carolina Botanical Garden
- Ⓒ Patterson's Mill Country Store
- Ⓓ University of North Carolina at Chapel Hill

DURHAM
- Ⓔ Duke Homestead
- Ⓕ Duke University
- Ⓖ North Carolina Museum of Life and Science

RALEIGH
- Ⓗ Mordecai Historic Park
- Ⓘ North Carolina Museum of Art
- Ⓙ North Carolina State University

Falls Lake State Recreation Area

Falls Lake Reservoir

Eno River State Park

Hillsborough

West Point on the Eno

Durham

Oak Grove

Duke Forest

Chapel Hill

Carrboro

Research Triangle Park

William B. Umstead State Park

Cary

Fearrington Village

Farrington

Jordan Lake

Raleigh

Pullen Park

N

time-beaten 1785 **Mordecai House** (with additions in 1826), named for its second occupant, Moses Mordecai, one of Raleigh's first Jews. Home to five continuous generations, the house showcases the Mordecai family's eighteenth- and nine-teenth-century furniture, portraits and books. Behind the house is a lane lined with six historic buildings, moved here from other parts of Wake County. Smallest and most significant is the hum-ble log kitchen apartment where Andrew Johnson, the 17th pres-ident of the United States, was born in 1808. Another plantation kitchen, built in 1842, is strung with dried herbs and outfitted with great antique cookware, from old butter churns and pie safes to tin candlemakers and spice grinders. Closed Sunday and Monday. Admission. ~ 1 Mimosa Street, off Wake Forest Road; 919-834-4844.

The enormous state-of-the-art **Exploris Museum** is an inter-active global learning experience. You can build your own web page, travel the world in a step and gaze at the million-marble mural to see what the earth looks like from space. Artifacts of note include a four-ton section of the Berlin Wall, handcarved doors from Zanzibar, an audio diary entry from Jimmy Carter and the only unpublished photo of Anne Frank. There is also an IMAX theater. Closed Monday from September through May. Admis-sion. ~ 201 East Hargett Street, Raleigh; 919-834-4040, fax 919-834-3516; www.exploris.org.

Raleigh is not exactly a place you associate with great art— which makes the **North Carolina Museum of Art** such a welcome surprise. Thanks to avid art collector and phil-anthropist Samuel Kress (of Kress & Co. five-and-dimes), the museum not only exists, it boasts more than 500 pieces by masters such as Botticelli, Titian, Giotto, Rubens, Cellini and Canaletto. You'll find them in the vast European art wing, where ten galleries spanning 600 years of works dazzle the eye. Most people spend all their time here, but save an hour to peruse the other galleries, featuring classical, Egyptian, African, Oceanic, New World and Judaic art as old as 450 B.C. The museum, which is free by the way (except for spe-cial exhibits), also has a great little café and gift shop. Closed Mon-day and Tuesday. ~ 2110 Blue Ridge Road, off Route 40; 919-839-6262; www.ncartmuseum.org.

Behind the Country Doctor Museum is a medicinal herb garden, a replica of the Botanic Garden at Padua, Italy, the oldest medicinal garden in the world.

For an entirely different look at the past, drive about 30 miles east of Raleigh to the far-flung country town of **Bailey**. Here the

HIDDEN ►

Country Doctor Museum is in a building made of two real rural doctors' offices, where rooms are filled with strange and incred-ible cures and their containers. There are antidotes for toothaches, fevers and freckles, and even one marked Manhood Cure, for an ailment one can only ponder. Among the fascinating and fearsome items in the surgical office are the implements of Dr. Matthew Moore Butler, the surgeon who amputated Stonewall Jackson's arm after the Battle of Chancellorsville in 1863. Alas, the Confederate general did not survive the ordeal. In a century-old house next to the doctor's offices, 1500 volumes of medical books span two centuries, from the 1700s to the early 1900s. The museum's Art of Nursing exhibit highlights North Carolina's pioneering role in the development of nursing. Closed Sunday and Monday. Admission. ~ Vance Street, just off Route 581 South; 252-235-4165.

Different, but equally engrossing, is the **Ava Gardner Museum**   ◀ HIDDEN
in **Smithfield**, about two dozen miles southeast of Raleigh. The museum is a modest place, but atmospheric. Docents will show you a 1941 family photo of Ava as a teenager, and dozens of other photos of Ava's Smithfield and Rock Ridge days. They'll walk you through original movie posters from some of Ava's 61 films, and show you some of Ava's wardrobe, including the black velvet and chiffon gown she wore in 1949's *The Great Sinner*, with Gregory Peck. Admission. ~ 325 East Market Street, Smithfield; 919-934-5830; www.avagardner.org.

Raleigh is mainly chain-hotel territory, sporting only three bed-   **LODGING**
and-breakfast inns. Only a few Raleigh lodges break out of the chain mode.

One place that's truly unusual is the **Oakwood Inn**, an 1871 Victorian house located in Historic Oakwood, Raleigh's finest neighborhood, and within walking distance from downtown. From the parlor of mahogany and leaded glass to the fancy Italian Revival eaves and big wraparound porch, it's a most appealing place inside and out. Six handsome bedrooms have private baths, thick throw rugs, clawfoot tubs, fireplaces and high, downy beds to climb into at night. Owners Gary and Doris Jurkiewicz see to your every need, offering cordials and "sweets" at night and hearty but healthy breakfasts (whole-wheat pancakes, stewed fruit hinting of nutmeg). ~ 411 North Bloodworth Street; 919-832-9712, 800-267-9712, fax 919-836-9263; www.oakwoodinnbb.com, e-mail innkeepers@oakwoodinnbb.com. MODERATE TO DELUXE.

Cameron Park Inn was built in 1916 but only opened to guests in 2000. All four rooms are filled with heirlooms (check out the poster bed and turn-of-the-eighteenth-century heart pine fireplace mantle from Al's grandmother), and modernized with decor such as chenille bedspreads and navy-striped drapes drawn across bay windows. ~ 211 Groveland Avenue; 919-835-2171, 888-257-2171, fax 919-754-1005; www.cameronparkinn.com. DELUXE.

The **William Thomas House**, an 1881 vintage, vanilla-washed house, harbors an elegant parlor and high-ceiling library, where guests enjoy afternoon wine and cheese. In the dining room a full Southern breakfast is served on a long clawfoot table. Four bedrooms with private baths are decorated with antiques such as poster and spindle-post beds and grand armoires. It's located a few blocks from downtown, though, unfortunately, on a busy street. ~ 530 North Blount Street; 919-755-9400, 800-653-3466, fax 919-755-3966; www.williamthomashouse.com. DELUXE.

The **Clarion Hotel State Capital** looks like a cylinder rising in the middle of downtown Raleigh. With a pleasant lobby, tidy rooms and a central location, it's not a bad choice. ~ 320 Hillsborough Street; 919-832-0501, fax 919-833-1631. MODERATE.

Near Saint Mary's College and North Carolina State University, the **Velvet Cloak Inn** is a lodging phenomenon, being both elegant and motelish. Mozart streams through the lobby hung with gilt-frame portraits and adorned with rhinestone lamps. But the 171 rooms are small and laid out like a motor court, with 1960s-era, low-slung buildings facing a parking lot. Among the unexpected pluses: a heated pool in a huge atrium, and the first-rate Baron's lounge. ~ 1505 Hillsborough Street; 919-828-0333, 800-334-4372, fax 919-828-2656; www.velvetcloakinn.com. MODERATE.

Many of the guests at **Brownestone Hotel** have children or business at the adjacent North Carolina State University. The building's 188 rooms are oversized and comfortable. (Ask for an upper floor, with views of the campus or city.) There's an outdoor swimming pool, and the YMCA is next door. ~ 1707 Hillsborough Street; 919-828-0811, 800-237-0772, fax 919-834-0904; www.brownstonehotel.com. DELUXE.

DINING

Many people come to Raleigh with low culinary expectations only to be amazed by the variety of eateries. If it weren't for the big red Coca-Cola mural on the side, you might drive right by the

HIDDEN ►

funky building called **Side Street** in Historic Oakwood. It's better to stop and take a seat inside the little neighborhood café,

TIME FOR A TIPPLE

The homegrown beers at **Greenshields Brewery and Pub** come from the giant steel fermentation tanks occupying the center of the restaurant. There are usually five or six brews on tap, and a terrific pub menu ranging from pork tenderloin and bangers and mash to Jamaican jerk chicken and seared ahi. Decor is equally publike, with lots of oak and brass and rich green carpets. ~ 214 East Martin Street, in downtown's City Market; 919-829-0214; www.greenshields.com. MODERATE.

crowded with regulars assaulting huge, elaborate sandwiches and dense desserts (the black-bottom pecan pie and fudge pie are definite winners). Closed Sunday. ~ 225 North Bloodworth Street; 919-828-4927. BUDGET.

With so many historic buildings around downtown, it seems only logical to dine at an old-time eatery. **Person Street Pharmacy**   ◄ *HIDDEN*
Soda Fountain is just the place (its motto: "Old Fashioned Goodness The Way You Remember!"). The rock-bottom budget prices definitely remind of bygone days: a burger is $2.25; a hot dog, $1.35. Meals, which also include tasty breakfasts, deli sandwiches, soups and ice cream, are prepared by a cheery girl behind the counter. Dining is on little tables facing the pharmacy aisles but, at these prices, who cares? Closed Sunday. ~ 702 North Person Street; 919-832-6432. BUDGET.

That infamous rule of dining—never order seafood unless water is in sight—can definitely be broken at **Cappers Restaurant and Tavern**. Fresh fish and shellfish arrive daily for dishes such as scallops florentine, seafood enchiladas, and Cajun beer-battered shrimp. Savor the seafood among warm, cherry-red walls enhanced with abstract art. And if you absolutely need a red meat fix, go for the New Zealand rack of lamb. ~ 4421 Six Forks Road; 919-787-8963, fax 919-787-8979; www.cappersrestaurant. com. DELUXE TO ULTRA-DELUXE.

Red candles flicker on each table at the **Red Room Tapas Lounge**, just one of the chic accents at this popular spot. Delicious bites include fried calamari with spicy tomato aioli, scallops with mango and ginger chutney, baby-back ribs in a spicy glaze and chorizo with sweet peppers. Traditional paella is also served family-style. ~ 510 Glenwood Avenue South, Raleigh; 919-835-1322; www.redroomraleigh.com. MODERATE TO DELUXE.

Upon entering **Neomonde Bakery & Deli**, you are assaulted   ◄ *HIDDEN*
by a sea of smells so good you desperately want to order one of everything in the glass case. Impossible, unfortunately, as there are dozens of choices, all Middle Eastern and all just made, from the meat and cheese pies, stuffed grape leaves and tabbouleh to spinach *fatayer* (spinach, onion and tomato baked inside pita dough) and *kibbeh* (ground beef, onions, hummus and pine nuts on a sub roll). There are also regular deli sandwiches, loaves upon loaves of fresh bread, and "sweets" such as *ballouria*, layered with egg noodles and pistachios and sprinkled with rose water. Go early or late for lunch or dinner; otherwise, expect to wait for a table. ~ 3817 Beryl Road, off Hillsborough Street near North Carolina State University; 919-828-1628. BUDGET TO MODERATE.

Downtown Raleigh's **City Market**, centered around a restored   **SHOPPING**
1914 markethouse, is where you'll find unusual and offbeat shops

and galleries. ~ Bounded by Martin, Person, Davie and Blount streets; 919-832-9300.

Foremost for gallery shopping is **Artspace**, home to nearly 40 artists and their studios. Within three floors are all sorts of paintings —silkscreen, acrylic, pastel, oil, portraiture—running the gamut from traditional to experimental. There's also jewelry, photography and sculpture. Artspace participates in a "gallery crawl," when neighboring galleries open their doors the first Friday of every month. ~ 201 East Davie Street; 919-821-2787.

Displaying the works of both Carolinian and national artists, the **Raleigh Contemporary Gallery** has a diverse selection of paintings, lithographs, sculpture and contemporary stained glass. Closed Sunday. ~ 323 Blake Street; 919-828-6500.

The **American Indian Company** carries goods made by tribes all across the county. Their pottery collection is one of the largest in the state. Also available are jewelry, original artwork, wooden flutes, and tapes and CDs of both traditional and contemporary American Indian music. ~ 311 Blake Street; 919-834-9655.

Nearby, Raleigh's gay literary crowd gathers at **White Rabbit Books**, a charming establishment with extensive gay readings, including periodicals from around the world, as well as specialty items and gifts. A bulletin board lists local gay happenings. ~ 309 West Martin Street; 919-856-1429.

A little west of downtown, **Cameron Village** is not a real village but six blocks of low-slung buildings lined with brick walkways and brimming with shopping possibilities. The 80-plus stores include a Talbots and several other chains, but you will also encounter the unusual. ~ 1900 Cameron Street; 919-821-1350.

Accipiter, for example, focuses on folk art and beaux arts— things like crazy clocks and wavy wine glasses. ~ 2046 Clark Avenue; 919-755-9309. **Flink's Fine Art** carries ceramics, photographs and paintings by local artists. ~ 427 Woodburn Road; 919-821-7172.

Upscale antiques, Mexican imports, jewelry and baseball cards are just a few collectibles sold at the **Fairgrounds Marketplace**. Bargains are so good here that you might bump into a professional decorator competing for that Chinese inlaid marble table. Closed October during the North Carolina State Fair. ~ Blue Ridge Road and Hillsborough Street; 919-829-3533.

NIGHTLIFE   With three major universities and a history steeped in blues, the Triangle is a nucleus of nightlife.

At the **Berkeley Cafe**, the bands play traditional stuff as well as newer R&B and folk rock; there's a patio bar for hanging out when it's warm. Occasional cover. ~ 217 West Martin Street; 919-821-0777.

Comedy or disco, take your pick at the mammoth **Charlie Goodnight's**. Jerry Seinfeld, Chris Rock, Drew Carey, Ray Romano, Robin Williams, Jay Leno and Rich Hall are among the greats to perform here and autograph the wall in the comedy club, though lesser knowns are usually featured. ~ 861 West Morgan Street; 919-828-5233; www.charliegoodnights.com. In the adjacent **NewBar**, the disco's loud, the hair big, and the attire heavy on black lycra. Cover.

Blue Martini serves the only two things a person really needs: a killer martini and some sweet jazz. Everyone must agree—patrons line up outside on weekends just to get in. Located in the heart of Raleigh's nightlife district, this classy bar hosts live jazz or blues bands—a great follow-up to a concert or a show at the theater. ~ 116 North West Street, Raleigh; 919-899-6464; www.bluemartiniraleigh.com.

It's a mellow but hip scene at the **Red Room Tapas Lounge**, where deejays spin chill tunes and dance grooves nightly. Take your adventurous mixed drink (red, of course!) and plunk down on one of the red and black couches for some conversation or people watching. ~ 510 Glenwood Avenue South, Raleigh; 919-835-1322; www.redroomraleigh.com.

Melissa Etheridge, Bruce Hornsby and Living Colour are among the acts who've graced **The Brewery**. It's mainly a rock-and-roll club, though, with local and regional bands jamming on a sound system that's just short of nuclear. Cover. ~ 3009 Hillsborough Street; 919-838-6788.

You'll find a bit of everything at the **BTI Center for the Performing Arts** where Broadway musicals, large-scale performances and regional theater are the mainstay. The complex includes the Meymandin Concert Hall, Fletcher Opera Theater and Kennedy Theater. The North Carolina Symphony, Carolina Ballet and National Opera Company stage shows here. ~ Raleigh Conven-

HOLLYWOOD IN SMITHFIELD

A farmer's daughter and youngest of five children, Ava Gardner was born right outside Smithfield in a place called Grabtown. She owed her Hollywood career at least in part to her sister, who married a New York photographer. He displayed Ava's picture in his studio; a scout for Metro-Goldwyn-Mayer saw the photo and liked it, and Ava waved goodbye to Smithfield for a big Hollywood career. Ava Gardner died of pneumonia in 1990 at the age of 67. She is buried at the Sunset Memorial Garden Cemetery in Smithfield.

tion and Conference Center Complex, Salisbury and Wilmington streets; 919-831-6060; www.raleighconvention.com.

The **Carolina Ballet** was founded in 1998 by Robert Weiss, a dancer who studied under George Balanchine. This classical ballet troupe has already gained national recognition in *Time* magazine as "America's most promising young company." ~ 3401-132 Atlantic Avenue; 919-719-0900; www.carolinaballet.com.

Burning Coal focuses on alternative theatrical productions. New works by living playwrights and fresh interpretations of traditional favorites are entertaining and provocative. ~ 512 Saint Mary's Street, Suite 104, Raleigh; 919-834-4001.

> Piedmont Blues, a soft, melodic blues, got its start in the tobacco houses of Raleigh's Triangle, but there are still many places to go to hear a harmonica wail.

GAY SCENE   Opened in 1976 and one of North Carolina's oldest gay clubs, **CC** is a friendly cruise bar with video screens, a big dancefloor and live entertainment every Wednesday and Friday. Cover. ~ 313 West Hargett Street; 919-755-9599; www.cc-raleigh.com.

Across the street from Capital Corral, the tastefully decorated **Legends** is the place to dance, dance, dance. Those dancing are generally gay men with astonishingly well-toned torsos; the music is typically progressive. Lesbians and straights also come to Legends. Cover. ~ 330 West Hargett Street; 919-831-8888; www.legends-club.com.

PARKS   **PULLEN PARK** 🚶 🚣   Local families and college students love this park, spread across 70 pretty green acres next to North Carolina State University. There are many good picnic spots as well as a pool and tennis courts, but the draws are definitely the 1912 Dentzel Menagerie Carousel and the miniature train that chugs around the park. Listed on the National Registry and kept sparkling by two artists, it's one of only 170 in existence. Kids love taking the beautiful tigers, horses and other animals for a spin. One ride will set you back $1. There is swimming in the swimming pool. Facilities include picnic shelters, tennis courts, pedal-boats and a kiddie boat. Day-use fee for the pool, $3. ~ 410 Ashe Avenue, next to North Carolina State University; 919-831-6468.

WILLIAM B. UMSTEAD STATE PARK 🚶 🚲 🐎 ⛴ 🚣 🎣
Physically, there is nothing particularly compelling about this park. Its mere existence, however, is enough, for it is a breath of green amid the gaseous traffic and concrete sprawl of Raleigh, Durham and Research Triangle Park. During segregation, Umstead was actually two parks, Reedy Creek and Crabtree. Today Ulmstead is one park but no roads connect the two sections, only hiking trails. Both have woodsy areas for hiking, biking and picnicking. Crabtree has horseback riding trails and Big Lake, where you can

rent boats and fish. Mostly, though, you can just relax before getting back on the interstate. You can get groceries about three miles from either park. Swimming is not permitted. Fishing is best at Big Lake. Try for bluegill, crappie and bass. At Crabtree, facilities include a visitors center, picnic tables and covered pavilions, hiking, biking and bridle trails, and boat rentals. At Reedy Creek there is a picnic area and hiking trails. ~ To reach the Crabtree Park section, take Route 70 six miles northwest of Raleigh; to reach Reedy Creek, take Route 40 west of Raleigh for 11 miles and exit at Harrison Avenue; 919-571-4170.

▲ Crabtree features 28 family tent sites; $15 per night. Camping allowed only Thursday through Sunday.

Durham

Durham is a working city, a hustling hub of research, technology and—foremost—medicine. Dubbed "The City of Medicine," it is home to numerous hospitals, clinics and laboratories and boasts five times more physicians per person than the national average. Keeping this in mind, then, unless you are inordinately interested in the medical field, you would do best to focus your explorations away from downtown and toward the more scenic parts of Durham.

SIGHTS

One site not to be missed would be **Duke University**. "Gothic wonderland" is the cliché applied to this renowned campus. Indeed, it is not an untrue moniker, as the quixotic buildings of stone, spires and arches, cloaked deeply in forest, look pulled from the pages of a medieval tale. Wending along the streets overhung with mammoth oaks, hickories and gum trees, there is the sense of the ancient and surreal, and the only things out of place are the students, with their cutoff jeans and neon backpacks.

The school goes back to 1838 when some Quakers and Methodists started Union Institute in nearby Randolph County. Over the years, it was reorganized and renamed (at one point called Normal College), and then in 1897 tobacco king Washington Duke offered $100,000 if the school would admit women and move to Durham. Having let a few females slip in before, and not minding the sound of a hundred grand, the institution accepted. But it was Washington's son, Buck Duke, who in 1924 transformed it from a smalltime college to a major university. All it took was $46 million—$6 million initially and $40 million in an endowment—and the Duke name was forever imprinted on the school and on Carolinians' minds. ~ Just west of downtown Durham, with main entrances off Main Street, Duke University Road, and Cameron Boulevard; 919-684-8111.

Duke is actually three separate campuses: west, central and east. The west is the main campus, the heart of Gothicism, presided over by **Duke Chapel**. When you turn onto Chapel

Drive and face the chapel squarely in the distance, you have no choice but to admit it is, quite simply, spectacular. Its jagged finials aim heavenward, its arched windows are bathed in glittering stained glass, its bell tower soars 21 stories. Modeled after the Canterbury Cathedral, the chapel is just as exquisite inside, with a 73-foot-high nave that overwhelms, a breathtaking sea of stained glass and an endless stream of pews. It is strangely silent and echoey in here, and when the front door opens it makes a thunderous sound. ~ 919-684-2572.

Washington Duke, the namesake of Duke University, began the first tobacco "factory" (a rickety, one-room barn) on his meager farm and parlayed his business into the world's biggest tobacco empire.

If by now you are feeling pensive, take a stroll through the **Sarah P. Duke Gardens** near the chapel. Its 55 acres are marbled with more than 1500 varieties of flora. Pond banks explode with lilies, dawn redwood trees spiral in the sky and azaleas form waves of raging color in spring. The terraced garden, designed in the 1930s by noted landscape architect Ellen Shipman, is decorated with Southern magnolias and impatiens. The Asiatic arboretum features trees and shrubs from the Far East. Paved paths and ramps allow wheelchair visitors access to most everything. ~ Anderson Street; 919-684-3698.

The **Nasher Museum of Art at Duke University** focuses on modern and contemporary art. Formerly the Duke University Museum of Art, the Nasher Museum is housed in a 65,000-square-foot facility, and offers three large gallery spaces, an auditorium, an education wing, a museum shop, sculpture gardens and a café. ~ On the central campus, at Duke University Road and Anderson Street; 919-684-5135, fax 919-681-8624; www.duke.edu/nasher.

To really get back to the beginning of Duke University and even Durham, head north several miles to **Duke Homestead**, a state historic site and keen place. Exhibits in the visitors center explore the history of tobacco and there's plenty of nostalgia here. Old TVs play old cigarette commercials. (Remember Marlboro Man and Marlboro Country? The man eventually died of lung cancer; the cigarettes still make millions.) A wall detailing the age-old tobacco debate quotes an 1884 *New York Times*, which decreed that "the decadence of Spain began when the Spaniards adopted cigarettes and if this pernicious practice obtains among adult Americans it will bring the ruin of the Republic."

After the exhibits, you'll follow a guide out back for a walk under the trees to the old Duke house, dating to 1852; to their third factory, built in 1869; and to their early-1900s packing house, where the women had to check each tobacco leaf for quality and grade it. There's also a late-1800s curing barn, moved here from another farm. Closed Sunday and Monday. ~ 2828 Duke Home-stead Road, off Guess Road north of Route 85; 919-477-5498.

A short drive east of the homestead, the **North Carolina Museum of Life and Science** brings you back to the present, with more than 50,000 square feet of fun for kids. Hundreds of gizmos, gadgets and giant apparatus teach and entertain; there's a cloud you can stick your hand into, a tiger skeleton to be touched and a space shuttle you can guide to catch a satellite. Outside, kids can romp in the playground, explore nature trails, pet farmyard animals and take a train ride. Admission. ~ 433 Murray Avenue; 919-220-5429, fax 919-220-5575; www.ncmls.org.

West Point on the Eno is a historic city park that highlights a nineteenth-century milling community. Adjacent to Eno River State Park, it features a reconstructed 1778 corn and wheat mill in full operation, a restored 1850 farmhouse and an original 1800s tobacco barn that is now a photography museum. Hiking trails, picnic areas and environmental education programs are offered here. The park is open year-round; the historic buildings are open only on weekend afternoons from March through December. ~ 5101 North Roxboro Road, six miles north of downtown Durham; 919-471-1623.

If you would like to explore further around Durham, stop by the **Durham Convention & Visitors Bureau**. Located downtown and run by the friendliest people, it's the best source for information and maps, including walking-tour maps of the downtown historic district. Closed Sunday. ~ 101 East Morgan Street; 919-687-0288, 800-446-8604; www.durham-nc.com.

LODGING

In Durham's historic Holloway neighborhood not far from downtown, the **Blooming Garden Inn** was built in the late 1800s and restored in the 1990s. The Victorian venue has the feel of a dollhouse, painted in bright pastels, trimmed in antique lace and stained glass and festooned with clever keepsakes. There are three attractive bedrooms as well as two suites with whirlpool tubs big enough for two. Guests are treated to an extraordinary gourmet breakfast, after which they usually find a comfortable spot on the big wraparound porch. ~ 513 Holloway Street; 919-687-0801, 888-687-0801, fax 919-688-1401; www.bloominggardeninn.com, e-mail bloominggardeninn@msn.com. DELUXE TO ULTRA-DELUXE.

Situated in one of Durham's most historic districts, the **Old North Durham Inn** is the city's oldest B&B. This 1900 Colonial Revival home offers four individually decorated guest rooms with queen-size beds, fireplaces, coffered ceilings and oak floors, as well as boldly patterned wallpaper and period furnishings. The parlor provides a charming common space for relaxing in front of the fireplace or playing a tune on the piano. A complimentary breakfast is served in the intimate dining room. ~ 922 North Magnum Street; 919-683-1885, fax 919-682-2645; e-mail ondi@nc.rr.com. MODERATE TO DELUXE.

"Inn" hardly seems an appropriate description for the **Washington Duke Inn**, Durham's grandest hotel. Presiding over the Duke University campus and its eighteen-hole golf course, the English cottage–style manse is named for the man who built the world's biggest tobacco empire and along the way built much of Durham. Duke family belongings decorate the lobby. The 146 guest rooms are contemporary, with fine linens, mahogany and cherry headboards and leather-back chairs. There is a restaurant, a jogging path and tennis courts. ~ 3001 Cameron Boulevard; 919-490-0999, 800-443-3853, fax 919-688-0105; www.washingtonduke inn.com. ULTRA-DELUXE.

HIDDEN ▶

An eighteenth-century manor house, the **Arrowhead Inn** offers relaxed, home-style accommodations on six acres several miles north of downtown Durham. The inn maintains nine guest rooms, all with working fireplaces, embellished with both period pieces and modern comforts such as telephones and private baths (most have double whirlpool tubs). There's also the spacious Carolina Log Cabin, with a sitting room, large fireplace and bedroom loft. After a full breakfast, guests can mingle in the "Keeping Room," which has a piano, a VCR, a video library and TV. ~ 106 Mason Road, off Route 501; 919-477-8430, 800-528-2207, fax 919-471-9538; www.arrowheadinn.com, e-mail info@arrowheadinn.com. DELUXE TO ULTRA-DELUXE.

DINING

Fishmonger's would look more at home parked at the end of a pier, but it's in downtown Durham, filled with the salty smells of the sea. The restaurant smokes its own bluefish, tuna and salmon, and sells fresh seafood from a glass case. The decor is picnic tables covered with plastic—all the better for delving into the lobsters, crabs (including Dungeness), mussels, clams and oysters that come out of the steamer. Grilled and fried fish are also for dinner; lunch features British-style fish-and-chips, oyster and crab cake sandwiches. No lunch on Monday. ~ 806 West Main Street; 919-682-0128. MODERATE.

The culinary signals at **Parizade**—Hebrew for "Message from Heaven"—are conveyed through zesty Mediterranean dishes such as linguine with spicy clam sauce and risotto with shrimp and artichokes. It all meshes with a gallery-like milieu of Renaissance-inspired murals and surreal acrylics. No lunch on the weekend. ~ 2200 West Main Street; 919-286-9712; www.parizade.com. MODERATE.

If you're craving salsa, cilantro and spices, head to **Blue Corn Café**, the only Latin American restaurant in town. Adventurous palates will want to try creative entrées such as chicken sautéed with lemon and orange juices and ginger or plantain-crusted mahimahi with saffron rice; you'll also find classics like burritos, fajitas and quesadillas, as well as vegetarian options. Enjoy a margarita, *mojito* or sangria at one of the streetside tables, or in the equally pleasant dining room. Salsa music from speakers gives this casual café an extra kick. ~ 716 Ninth Street; 919-286-9600, fax 919-416-0862; www.bluecorn-tosca.com, e-mail danielle@bluecorn-tosca.com. MODERATE.

Famed around Durham for its gourmet dinner menu, **Nana's** combines Italian, country French and American cuisine. Chef Scott Howe's entrées include his own potato pancakes with vodka-cured gravlax and caviar and a roast Long Island duck with lentils and field greens. Choose a wine from one of the many bottles on display in the dining room—a classy place with white linen, fresh-cut flowers and everchanging local artwork. Reservations recommended. Closed Sunday. ~ 2514 University Drive; 919-493-8545. DELUXE.

Since 1952, **Bullock's Bar-B-Q** has been churning out savory Southern edibles to anyone who wanders in, which would include celebrities Robert Duvall and Dolly Parton. Most everything on the menu is fattening, filling—and delicious. Barbecue platters come with brunswick stew; fried chicken and spareribs are served with a heap of fries, cole slaw and hushpuppies. You can also order salisbury steak or meatloaf. The vegetables, from stewed corn to black-eyed peas, have that incredible fresh flavor. Closed Sunday and Monday. ~ 3330 Quebec Street; 919-383-3211; www.bullocksbbq.com, e-mail whenpigsfly@bullocksbbq.com. BUDGET.

At the turn-of-the-twentieth-century, the buildings of **Brightleaf Square** were warehouses for the American Tobacco Company. (In case you've forgotten, the company was run by Washington   **SHOPPING**

SOUTHERN STAR

The place in Durham with the culinary reputation is **Magnolia Grill**, a simple brick building parked along a busy road, with an interior of peach walls and white tablecloths. The star is absolutely the menu, vast and varied every day depending on whatever chef-owners Ben and Karen Barker conjure up. Expect such Southern-inspired creations as black-eyed pea soup with cornmeal dumplings, country ham and greens, or grilled yellowfin tuna with smoked tomato barbecue vinaigrette on red-pepper grits and Southern greens "sandwich." Save room for the stellar desserts. Closed Sunday and Monday. ~ 1002 Ninth Street, Durham; 919-286-3609. DELUXE.

Duke and produced 90 percent of the world's tobacco at the time.) Now you can stroll along the lengthy red-brick corridors in the hopes of finding a book, an artpiece or even some clothing. Most shops are closed Sunday year-round. ~ Main and Gregson streets.

In the Square, **Wentworth & Leggett Rare Books** is packed floor-to-ceiling with wonderful old volumes, prints and world maps. ~ 919-688-5311.

Durham's hippest browsing and buying are along **Ninth Street** across from Duke University's east campus. Bookstores and bakeries, music stores and vintage boutiques appeal to shoppers of all stripes.

The Regulator Bookshop is a place of local renown where you can find reams on every subject, from the Civil War and Old South to New Age and gay studies. The children's section is outstanding. ~ 720 Ninth Street; 919-286-2700.

Vaguely Reminiscent has women's jewelry and clothing updated from the '60s for the modern day. ~ 728 Ninth Street; 919-286-3911.

One World Market is a not-for-profit store with a collection of worldly trinkets including hand-crafted jewelry, pottery and artwork. You'll find free-trade items from over 50 different countries. ~ 811 Ninth Street, Durham; 919-286-2457.

NIGHTLIFE   A gleaming, grand, beaux-arts beauty, the **Carolina Theater** began life in 1926 and enjoyed a thorough renovation in 1994. It hosts the North Carolina Symphony series every fall, plus everything from international choirs to chamber music. ~ 309 West Morgan Street; 919-560-3030.

Next door and just as palatial, the **Durham Arts Council** is headquarters to a vast performing arts network that includes the Durham Symphony, African-American Dance Ensemble, Young People's Performing Company and The Durham Chorale. ~ 120 Morris Street; 919-560-2787.

For the latest on the gay night scene, pick up *The Front Page* newspaper, available from stores along Ninth Street.

Within Brightleaf Square, **Satisfaction Restaurant & Bar** is a lively restaurant by day and a livelier bar by night, first with the after-work professional crowd and later with college students making the bar rounds. Food is served throughout the evening, of course. Closed Sunday. ~ 905 West Main Street; 919-682-7397.

Right next to the square, **Devine's Restaurant & Bar** entices sports fans with seventeen TVs airing games. ~ 904 West Main Street; 919-682-0228.

GAY SCENE   If conversation, good music and a game of pool are what you seek, you should head on over to **Boxers**. The congenial, publike atmosphere draws mostly gay men. Cover. ~ 5504 Chapel Hill Boulevard; 919-489-7678.

Visions is easily the most popular lesbian meetingspot in the Carolinas. With a patio bar, volleyball court and huge dancefloor, it's super-crowded on weekends. Cover. ~ 711 Rigsbee Avenue; 919-688-3002.

Durham's alternative theater scene is alive thanks to **Manbites Dog**. This company's success is in its ability to take on controversial topics and artistic risks. Most productions address alternative lifestyles, but the company does not limit its scope to gay themes. ~ 703 Foster Street; 919-682-3343; www.manbites dogtheater.org.

ENO RIVER STATE PARK Coming upon this park, you feel like you might have left the Piedmont for the mountains. Cool forest carpeted with ferns and wildflowers and studded with mountain laurel frame the rocky, rippling Eno River. Along the river are several mill sites dating back to the late 1700s. Fishers and naturalists love these 3900 acres, a nature break from Durham's urban sprawl and home to barred owls, box turtles, beavers and river otters. The fishing is excellent, with lots of good fishing holes along the Eno River banks. Try for largemouth bass, bluegill, crappie and chain pickerel. There is no swimming. Facilities include a park office, a picnic area, restrooms and 20 miles of hiking trails. A convenience store is located three miles away. ~ 6101 Cole Mill Road, off Route 85, about seven and a half miles northwest of downtown Durham; 919-383-1686.

▲ There are five primitive riverfront sites a one-mile hike from the parking lot; $9 per site per night. There is also a primitive group site with a maximum of 26 persons; $1 per person per night with a $9 minimum.

PARKS

FALLS LAKE STATE RECREATION AREA
This enormous park reaches into three counties and is largely underwater—some 12,000 of its 38,000 acres belong to Falls Lake. There are numerous places around the lake to have fun, including three beaches with clayish sand (one with a concrete ramp for wheelchair access), and there are many possibilities for landing a fish. A marina rents boats for getting out on the water. Away from the lake, the forest is typical of the Piedmont: loblolly pine, yellow poplars, hickories and oaks. Swimming is good from all three beaches, with shallow water sloping gently over hard-packed sand. Fishing is good year-round. Try for bluegills, crappie, sunfish and largemouth bass. Facilities include the park office, several picnic areas and boat ramps, marina with boat rentals and restrooms. Day-use fee, $5. ~ The main entrance is at 13304 Creedmoor Road, off Route 50, east of Durham and north of Raleigh.

Other entrances are off of Route 50 just north of Route 98, and off Route 98 west of Route 50; 919-676-1027.

▲ There are 350 sites for tents and RVs (most with hook-ups); $20 per night.

▼▼▼▼▼▼▼▼▼▼▼▼▼▼▼
Chapel Hill Area

Chapel Hill has been called "the southern part of heaven" and it's easy to see why, for it is an instantly pleasurable place, small and personable and well-established, with lofty trees sheltering the dignified brick and stone manses and filigreed clapboard homes that make up some of the Piedmont's most desirable neighborhoods. The lovely University of North Carolina (just call it UNC) sprawls across the center of town, and in fact is *the* town, for beyond the red-brick campus and the hubbub it generates, there are mainly homes and woods and then the neighboring town of Carrboro.

A lot of people who live in Chapel Hill and Carrboro aren't from the South (you'll be hard-pressed to find a southern drawl here) but have come from the Northeast and the West to work at UNC, nearby Research Triangle Park or one of the dozen or so publishing houses. People walk around Chapel Hill carrying books—and not just the students, but everyday people. Coffee-house conversation churns over the latest releases and book-stores brim with literary finds.

SIGHTS

Most Chapel Hill action happens on **Franklin Street**, lined on one side with columned brick houses, pizza joints, yuppie-ized head shops, coffeehouses, chain stores like The Gap, and women selling cut flowers on the sidewalk. On the other side is **University of North Carolina** and *the wall*, made of stone and decorated for blocks with students, studying and chatting and people-watching.

Parking around here is horrendous, and the least stressful thing to do is to find a spot in one of the UNC's visitor lots (the main lot is off Cameron Avenue) and pay by the hour. While you're here, take at look at the **Ackland Art Museum**, with its extensive collection of sculpture dating from the Renaissance to the present, along with European and American paintings and ancient Greek and Roman art. Closed Monday and Tuesday. ~ South Columbia and East Franklin streets, Chapel Hill; 919-966-5736; www.ackland.org.

There's more art inside the grand rotunda of UNC's **Morehead Planetarium**, including a 1632 portrait Rembrandt painted of his sister, Liesbeth Van Rijn. The planetarium also hosts regular astronomical shows (admission) on everything from wormholes to flying objects that show up on Earth. ~ East Franklin Street; 919-962-1236. In the building's west lobby, the UNC **Visitors**

Center dispenses maps and information and arranges walking tours of the campus. Closed weekends. ~ 919-962-1630.

For more information on the area, be sure to check with the **Chapel Hill/Carrboro Chamber of Commerce**, a little north of UNC. Closed weekends. ~ 104 South Estes Drive, Chapel Hill; 919-967-7075.

On the southeast edge of UNC, the **North Carolina Botanical Garden** is set in and around 80 acres of Piedmont woods. From the many walking trails, visitors can learn about vegetation native to the Southeast. In the main garden, plants grow geographically by coastal, Piedmont and mountain habitats. Bog and aquatic plants such as waterlilies, pondweed and spatterdocks decorate ponds and streams; endangered plants, including the bunched arrowhead, are also here, as are carnivores like the Venus flytrap. Good-smelling herbs, wildflowers, ferns and brick walkways surround the visitors center. Some of the gardens are wheelchair accessible; special assistance can be arranged by calling ahead. ~ Off Old Mason Farm Road, just south of Route 15-501 and 54 bypass; 919-962-0522.

> Did you know that BC Tablets and Headache Powder originated in Durham, Bromo Seltzer in Chapel Hill, and Vicks Vapor Rub in Greensboro? Find out more at the Pharmacy Museum in Patterson's Mill Country Store.

From here, jog over to Route 54 east and go three and a half miles to Farrington Road. Go north on Farrington Road (turning at the Hardees) and drive through rural countryside for one and a quarter miles until you see it, set up on a hill with its old Esso gas tank, looking like something out of an old photograph. **Patterson's Mill Country Store** is actually a 1973 replica of the ◀ *HIDDEN* original store that opened in 1870, but you could never tell it. Inside the wonderfully cluttered clapboard building is the real thing—moonshine jugs, bonnets, seed bins, cornshuckers, dolls, the occasional old Coca Cola poster, you-name-it, stacked and strung and hung everywhere.

The woman in charge, Gail Booker, is the daughter-in-law of Elsie Booker. Elsie was born in the green farmhouse next door, and the surrounding farmland has been in her family "better than 200 years." A feisty woman with a voice that booms, Elsie was one of the first female pharmacists in North Carolina, receiving her degree from UNC in Chapel Hill in the 1940s and practicing for 40 years. Her memento to those times is her Pharmacy Museum filled with ancient-looking medicinals: well-dusted potions and vials, mortars and pestles, pillboxes, tattered prescriptions.

Elsie's husband, John, has his own place of nostalgia upstairs, a Tobacco Museum packed with thousands of items he collected while working more than 30 years for Liggett & Myers. There's

Text continued on page 256.

Fearrington Village

Eight miles south of Chapel Hill off Route 15-501, Fearrington Village comes as a surprise. For it rises up from the North Carolina countryside, its meticulous shuttered buildings of white plank and flourishing arbors strangely juxtaposed against Piedmont scrubland and forgotten mill towns, and pine woods sheltering shacks and hound dogs and old pickup trucks.

Drive inside the village, park in the raked gravel, and step beneath the wash of crabapple trees. It does not take long to become accustomed to the place, where everything speaks to the art of living: the handsome inn and fountained courtyards, rambling dovecote and tiny white potting shed, the music room where Verdi reigns, the bookstore that invites all-day browsing, the sun-warmed bistro and market that carry the *New York Times*, delicate scents, and shelf after shelf of unusual wines.

Flowers engulf all the buildings—tall rugosa roses and fountains of lavender, ribbons of geraniums and pansies, tulips and iris—and in between the buildings are knot gardens, shrubs that are woven over and under each other in tight bond. Pecan trees with enormous arms serve as a cathedral for warm-weather weddings. There are hollyhocks that were seeded from Monet's garden in France. The herb garden is a daily source for the village restaurants, and if you order a summer salad, you may well find violas or passion flowers on your plate.

Much of Fearrington's style and mood are linked to Europe, where owner R. B. Fitch and his late wife, Jenny, made dozens of visits, researching architecture and horticulture, food and wine, and ways to run a place. They had purchased the 1786 Fearrington family farmstead in 1974 and started building homes on its 640 acres. But they were determined not to end up with a typical subdivision, the kind of development that infests suburbs across the country.

Now their singular village draws thousands of yearly visitors who come to shop and dine, play croquet and bocce, or bike along leafy streets hooded with elms and maples.

Some stay at **Fearrington House Inn**, in one of 33 handsome rooms, spacious and adorned with plank floors, canopied beds, antiques and original paintings. Styled like an English country manor, and somewhat lavish, it is a favorite of Europeans, who use their "Relais & Chateaux" guides (in which the inn is listed) to find their way to Fearrington. ~ 2000 Fearrington Village Center, Pittsboro; 919-542-2121, fax 919-542-4202; www.fearrington.com. ULTRA-DELUXE.

Next to the inn, **Fearrington House Restaurant** is a formal place to dine, with small, intimate rooms whose walls are prettily stenciled and whose windows look out onto lush gardens. The prix-fixe dinner menu changes monthly, but selections are supremely Southern. Among the possibilities: lobster bisque with swiss cheese and tarragon croûte, yellowfin tuna tartare with cucumbers, herb salad and vegetable ratatouille and filet mignon with seared foie gras, shaved black truffles, carrots and a red wine reduction. ULTRA-DELUXE.

Across the street, in the old farm granary, the bistro-style **Fearrington Market Cafe** has pale green walls, flowery Provençal tablecloths and sunlight streaming from windows up high. My favorites here are the portobello mushroom sandwich, the tricolored ravioli with pesto and goat cheese, and the Israeli couscous risotto. There's also a deli for takeout sandwiches and soups. Sunday brunch. ~ 2000 Fearrington Village Center, Pittsboro; 919-542-5505. BUDGET TO MODERATE.

Once a week, from March to November, people come from all around to browse the bins of fresh produce and locally made cheeses and artistry that line Fearrington's country lanes. Tuesday there is a farmer's market in the village, and it is a festive few hours, with people crowding the shops and market and gardens, stirring around the 1700s barn and silo, eating creamy, herb-crusted rounds of goat cheese and sipping pinot noir on the lawns.

a 1910 Piedmont cigarette sign and packs of bizarre brands like Vello, Total, Stage III and System III. If you've never seen generic cigarette packs, you'll see them here. Closed Monday. ~ 919-493-8149.

From Chapel Hill, you can instantly be in **Carrboro** in your car, and in fact not realize you had switched cities except for the small "Welcome to Carrboro" sign along West Franklin Street. Carrboro is as New Agey as its neighbor, though smaller. The little downtown is strung with arty storefronts advertising holistic foods and treatments, organic groceries and colorful galleries, and small publishing houses.

HIDDEN ▶   It takes longer to arrive in **Hillsborough,** about twenty minutes. From Carrboro, Old Route 86 dips and climbs and winds ten miles northwest through piney countryside, woods and hayfields. You see whitewashed homes, trailers parked along the highway, lawns planted with tulips in spring and pumpkins in fall.

The town of Hillsborough dates to 1754, and it feels like it. Handsome old clapboard homes with brick chimneys are set up along the slopes of town, just off cobbled stone sidewalks. Kudzu swarms over massive pecan and elm trees, and in the spring daylilies and hot pink azaleas ripple in the breeze. There are a handful of historic inns, fine spots for lunching and shopping.

Before exploring, stop in the **Orange County Historical Museum** and pick up a walking-tour map and brochures on antiquing and local sights. Closed Monday. ~ Located inside the Confederate Memorial Building, 201 North Churton Street, Hillsborough; 919-732-2201.

LODGING   With its coat of red brick and rows of gables and tall chimneys, the **Carolina Inn** fits right into its UNC setting. The lobby is decorated with white columns, antiques and overstuffed chairs; the guest rooms look very Southern with their easy chairs, armoires and desks. The 77 rooms in the historic section of the inn are most desirable; each one has a unique shape and features a pedestal sink in the bathroom. Owned by the university, the hotel boasts a great location. ~ 211 Pittsboro Street, Chapel Hill; 919-933-2001, 800-962-8519, fax 919-962-3400; www.carolina inn.com. ULTRA-DELUXE.

The **Siena Hotel** is as jazzy as lodging gets around Chapel Hill, and it is in fact a fine place, though a little odd (its brochure inviting guests to "Experience Italy right in the heart of North Carolina"). The owner, a native of Siena, Italy, has decorated the inn exclusively with Italian furnishings. The experience includes Italian gilt-frame paintings and fine sculpture, armoires and embroidered chairs decorating the large, lively lobby and 80 rooms. Guest rooms are spacious, with marble baths and cushy carpets. There's a shuttle service around town. ~ 1505 East Franklin

Street, Chapel Hill; 919-929-4000, 800-223-7379, fax 919-968-8527; www.sienahotel.com. ULTRA-DELUXE.

If you stay at **Windy Oaks Inn**, you'll be sleeping in the former   ◀ HIDDEN
home of Paul Green. The Pulitzer Prize–winning playwright no doubt found inspiration in these deep wood surroundings, which now cover 25 acres. The driveway is lined with magnolias, the backyard graced with gardens and picket fence. The five guest rooms, two with shared bath, are warmly decorated. Rates include a country breakfast (reservations required). ~ Take Route 15-501 three miles south of Route 54 to Old Lystra Road and go one mile; 919-942-1001; www.windyoaksinn.com. DELUXE.

Twelve miles west of Chapel Hill, **The Inn at Bingham School**   ◀ HIDDEN
is a tranquil place among rolling Piedmont hills. The Greek Revival and Federal bed and breakfast was home to Bingham's headmaster during the mid-1800s. Now it has been restored to a polished patina, with five bedrooms furnished in period antiques. All have private baths. There's also a restored milkhouse with a large bedroom, sitting room and whirlpool tub. Full breakfast and afternoon wine and cheese are included in the rates. ~ 6720 Mebane Oaks Road, off Route 54; 919-563-5583, 800-566-5583, fax 919-563-9826; www.chapel-hill-inn.com, e-mail fdeprez@aol.com. MODERATE TO DELUXE.

The best breakfast in town is at **Carolina Coffee Shop**. Small and   **DINING**
inviting with tall, straight-back booths, the eatery has been a Franklin Street favorite since 1922. There are gourmet coffees, eggs Benedict and other extravagant day starters. ●●●●●●●●●●●●●●●●●●●●●●●●●
There's also lunch (homemade soups, sandwiches) and dinner (uptown steak fillet, crab meat and artichoke crêpes), and even a full bar. ~ 138 East Franklin Street, Chapel Hill; 919-942-6875. MODERATE.

If it's lunchtime, go to **Jack Sprat Cafe** and have a salad or sandwich. The green and pasta salads, and portobello panini sandwiches are the best. The brick-walled eatery has a view to the sidewalk buzz. ~ 161 East Franklin Street, Chapel Hill; 919-933-3575. BUDGET.

> If you want to meet someone in Chapel Hill, don't go to a nightclub. Go sit on the UNC–Franklin Street wall.

Penang serves Thai and Malaysian cuisine in a light, open space. Stand-out dishes include the mango chicken, curried sting ray with tomatoes and okra, *pasembur* salad with cucumber jicama and pan-fried egg noodles. ~ 431 West Franklin Street; 919-933-2288. MODERATE.

The Weathervane is enormously popular. The atmosphere is quite calm—comfy booths brightened by oil lamps, jazz pouring from the speakers, diners a little dressed up—and there's a spacious patio for warm-weather dining. Menus focus on seasonal fare. Try the grilled chicken melt sandwich made with sun-dried tomato bread, or the smoked duck and spinach salad. The wine list is excellent. No breakfast on Sunday. ~ Located within A Southern Season, 201 South Estes Drive; 919-929-9466. MODERATE.

Four Eleven West has good pasta and burgers and wood-grilled pizza, but mostly it gives good atmosphere: waitresses with wisps for waists, students in tall black platforms, walls of exposed brick and ceilings high and lofty. Go even if you're not hungry and have a cocktail or espresso. Sunday brunch. No lunch on Monday. ~ 411 West Franklin Street, Chapel Hill; 919-967-2782. MODERATE.

Crook's Corner is everybody's favorite for contemporary Southern cooking: jalapeño cheddar hushpuppies, shrimp-and-grits, fried green tomatoes with sweet corn in a butter sauce, fluffy cornbread with a hood of black pepper. The atmosphere is bluesy, a little funky, with little bottles of Tabasco on silver-rimmed tables and a patio that's full as soon as the place opens. Sunday brunch. Closed Monday. ~ 610 West Franklin Street, Chapel Hill; 919-929-7643; www.crookscorner.com. MODERATE.

Cup A Joe is the unofficial college hangout for both gay and straight students. You'll see them huddled over homework at the schoolhouse desks, tossing back their third espresso, Janis Joplin wailing on the stereo, traffic buzzing outside big open windows. The pastries are homemade, the coffees available in a variety of concoctions. ~ 1129 A.D. Weaver Dairy Road, Chapel Hill; 919-967-2002. BUDGET.

The fill-you-up country cookin' at **Mama Dip's** is good stuff, not too greasy or heavy. Their slogan: "Put a taste of the South in your mouth." Slip into a vinyl booth and order chicken and dumplings, the best mashed potatoes you ever had or baked chicken breast with sour cream and wild mushrooms. Old ceiling fans circulate good kitchen smells, and grilled corn cobs fill ceramic pitchers. ~ 408 West Rosemary Street, Chapel Hill; 919-942-5837. BUDGET.

WU WEI TEA AND BUMBLEBEES

On a Chapel Hill afternoon, go to **Caffé Driade** and sit outside at one of the little round tables in the woods. Order a cup of wu wei tea, a hot and heady elixir plied with lavender and orange peel, and watch the bumblebees drink nectar from wildflowers. The music will be moody and so will the crowd at this former bookbindery, reincarnated as an Asian-aura coffee-and teahouse. Driade sits back off the highway, an infinitesimal sign announcing its existence, and can be maddening to find. Don't miss it. ~ 1215-A East Franklin Street, behind Traditions Bridal Salon; 919-942-2333; www.caffedriade.com.

In Carrboro, **Aurora** is an Italian bistro, modern and somewhat elegant, with five separate dining areas, including an outdoor piazza. The prevailing scent of garlic and olive oil is very pleasant. The fare is different each day, but expect seasonal, imaginative creations and lots of choices. Possibilities include mixed green salad with goat cheese, walnuts, olives, tomatoes and artichoke hearts; wood-fired tuna; and lamb with grilled new potatoes and wood-roasted vegetables. ~ 1350 Raleigh Road, Chapel Hill; 919-942-2400; www.aurorarestaurant.com. MODERATE.

Go casual at **Elmo's Diner** with "square meals" like Italian meatloaf, turkey and gravy with mashed potatoes, or chicken and dumplings. There are also burgers and salads and breakfast anytime. The diner is clamorous, a big, open room with brick walls and a ceiling floating somewhere high overhead, steam drifting up from soup bowls. Locals like it here. ~ Carr Mill Mall, 200 North Greensboro Street, Carrboro; 919-929-2909. BUDGET.

In downtown Hillsborough, **Saratoga Grill** occupies a second-floor perch, with big arched windows overlooking the street. Ambiance is country-casual, with cane-laden chairs, Southern prints on the walls and classical music filling the air. The fare is uncomplicated Continental—barbecue shrimp, grilled portobello mushroom salad, assorted fish and seafood, chicken, lamb and steaks for entrées. Best of all, you can order smaller size portions of many dishes. Closed Sunday and Monday. ~ 108 South Churton Street, Hillsborough; 919-732-2214. MODERATE.

On the third Sunday of the month you can drive to **Celebrity Farm** and have a goat cheese dinner. The farm is out in the piney Piedmont woods between Pittsboro and Siler City, about 30 miles west of Chapel Hill. The afternoon dinner is a prix-fixe family-style affair, with two dozen diners gathered at long tables inside Fleming and Britt Phann's inn. Every course the Phanns serve will have goat cheese, perhaps a butternut squash soup with goat cheese curd, a chicken breast stuffed with rice and herbed goat cheese, and finally a goat cheese cheesecake or flaming banana-cheese surprise! The cheese comes from the goats out in the Phanns' barn (actually it comes from their milk). You can have a look at the goats after dinner, but be prepared for some affection: "Goats like to be held," explains Britt, "and happy goats make good milk." Reservations required. ~ Located two miles north of Route 64 on Mount Vernon–Hickory Mountain Road; 919-742-5176. ULTRA-DELUXE.

◄ HIDDEN

In Chapel Hill, an easy stroll down **Franklin Street** will deliver you to everything from The Gap to head shops to bookstores and places selling nothing but Tar Heel (UNC's revered basketball team) accessories.

SHOPPING

Owner Lisa Heyward designs some of the hip female garb at **Modern Times**—soft, flowing skirts and sheer dresses, satiny pants and stunning jackets. Great jewelry and handbags, too. ~ 402 West Franklin Street, Chapel Hill; 919-929-8119.

HIDDEN ►　　**Internationalist Books & Community Center** has a small but interesting selection of gay and lesbian reading as well as other progressive and alternative books. The place is run by knowledgeable gay volunteers who are happy to tell visitors about local gay events. ~ 405 West Franklin Street, Chapel Hill; 919-942-1740.

Focusing on designer jeans and the latest styles, **Uniquities** does have unique stuff. Plus the salesgirls are gorgeous waifs who seem to drift among the merchandise. ~ 452 West Franklin Street, Chapel Hill; 919-933-4007.

Just outside downtown Chapel Hill, **A Southern Season** is a restaurant and gourmet food store; it's an enormous space filled with beautiful and unusual items, from kitchenry, candles and coffee mugs to cookbooks and greeting cards. There's even an espresso bar and a wine "corner" with a superb selection. ~ 201 South Estes Drive, Chapel Hill; 919-929-7133.

Women should start at **Shoes at the Square**, whose inventory of women's platforms, chunky-heel loafers and high-heeled tennis shoes are as cool as can be. Closed Sunday. ~ In University Mall, 201 South Estes Drive, Chapel Hill; 919-942-2044.

Next door to Chapel Hill in downtown Carrboro, **Carr Mill Mall** is an 1898 cotton mill that's been recycled into a shopping arcade. Beamed ceilings, wood floors and exposed brick walls lend atmosphere to the shopping experience. Stores inside the mall run the gamut from used books and local arts and crafts to designer duds. ~ Corner of Greensboro and Weaver streets, Carrboro; 919-942-8669.

HIDDEN ►　　If you've never experienced an old-time Southern store, go to **Patterson's Mill Country Store**. The crafts, kitchenwares and pieces of nostalgia fill every nook and cranny, and the owner is a character who was born in the house next door. ~ Farrington Road, one and a quarter miles north of Route 54, east of Chapel Hill; 919-493-8149.

Fearrington Village, designed like a European village in the countryside, is a most enjoyable place to shop. ~ Route 15-501, eight miles south of Chapel Hill, Pittsboro.

In the village, the warm and personal **McIntyre's Fine Books and Bookends** is designed for hours of browsing, with entire rooms devoted to travel, children's readings, and home and garden. There's a big selection by local authors, who give frequent readings here. ~ 919-542-3030.

Walking into the **Dovecote** is like stepping into the pages of a British *Home & Garden* magazine. Flowers, birdhouses, porcelain boxes, painted garden tables—everything here is artfully done. ~ 919-542-1145.

A Stone's Throw has gemstones set every imaginable way, even as the top of a wine cork. Closed Monday and Tuesday. ~ 919-542-1055.

The **Fearrington Grocery Co.** is perennially abuzz with customers gushing over all the unusual things to buy, from local beers and hard-to-find wines to green tomato relish and tangerine marmalade. ~ 919-542-5505.

NIGHTLIFE

Chapel Hill is wonderful at night (picture a small Berkeley, with a Southern twist). Clubs and cafés crowd along Franklin Street and just off it, and you can prowl for hours and not experience everything. Good bands play here, too—artists on the verge of making it (or who should be) and experimental musicians with new sounds. Expect the whole spectrum of music, from roots and reggae to Southern rock and alternative country. One music junkie in his 50s says he moved to Chapel Hill because "I can see the same groups I saw in New York and L.A. without all the crowd hassle. The people here are great." To find out who's playing where in Chapel Hill, pick up a copy of the *Independent*, a weekly tabloid at bookstores and cafés around town.

The place to be for students is **He's Not Here**. In warm weather, the outdoor courtyard with picnic tables and benches is packed to the hilt during happy hour. Classic rock is played real loud, and beer is dispensed in the ever-popular "Big Blue Cup." There's live music on Friday and Saturday nights during the spring and summer and they charge a cover then. ~ 112½ West Franklin Street, Chapel Hill; 919-942-7939.

The **Dead Mule** is where UNC grad students go to escape the undergrads; professors and professionals come here, too, for afternoon scotch-on-the-rocks and jazz. In the summer, local alternative and rock bands crank up at night. Members only—though if you fit the clientele a member will usually sign you in. ~ 303 West Franklin Street, Chapel Hill; 919-969-7659.

Choose from over one hundred different wines at **West End Wine Bar,** where vintage couches, terra-cotta walls, wood floors,

SOUND SCENE

Local musicians hang out at **Local 506**, listening to live everything, from surf and garage to roots and alternative country. Private club, but visitors won't have a problem getting a pass. Cover. ~ 506 West Franklin Street, Chapel Hill; 919-942-5506; www.local506.com.

low lighting, and live music create sultry vibes. The hand-tiled mosaic bar and artwork-spattered walls add a funky flair to the earthy interior. Shoot a round of pool in the downstairs "cellar" or take in the stars on the rooftop balcony. ~ 450 West Franklin Street, Chapel Hill; 919-967-7599; www.westendwinebar.com.

Enter **Hell** and discover it's not as tortuous as you might have thought. Decked with plastic skeletons, rubber rats and red walls, this smoky dive bar with a twist offers an evil list of drinks with names like the Devil's Elbow and Crime & Punishment. Pool tables, air hockey, video games and a jukebox will keep you entertained for hours. ~ 157½ East Rosemary Street, Chapel Hill; 919-929-9666.

One of the best concert venues around is a minute from Chapel Hill in Carrboro. **Cat's Cradle**, a beer-only SRO club that's a black-on-the-inside warehouse, brings in local, regional and national talent. Snake River Conspiracy, Jupiter Coyote, Dark Star Orchestra—they all play here. Cover. ~ 300 East Main Street, Carrboro; 919-967-9053; www.catscradle.com.

PARKS   The closest major park is Eno River State Park located near Durham. For information, see the "Durham Parks" section earlier in this chapter.

There are plenty of open green spaces around Chapel Hill perfect for picnicking, the premier place being the **University of North Carolina campus**. Try along Franklin Street. There's also the **North Carolina Botanical Garden**. ~ Off Old Mason Farm Road, south of Route 15-501 and 54 bypass. Or try the grounds of **Fearrington Village**. ~ Route 15-501, eight miles south of Chapel Hill.

▼ ▼ ▼ ▼ ▼ ▼ ▼ ▼ ▼ ▼ ▼ ▼ ▼ ▼
Outdoor Adventures
Piedmonters take their clubs seriously—more than 150 courses can be found in these clay and sand hills.

GOLF   **WINSTON-SALEM AREA**   In Winston-Salem, tee off at **Reynolds Park Golf Course**. ~ 2931 Reynolds Park Road; 336-650-7660. **Heather Hills Golf Course** is another choice. ~ 3801 Heathrow Drive; 336-788-5785. Also in the area is **Long Creek Club**. ~ Bethania–Tobaccoville Road; 336-924-5226. One of the two 18-hole courses at **Tanglewood Park** was designed by Robert Trent Jones. ~ Route 158, Clemmons; 336-778-6320.

The **Pleasant Ridge Golf Club** is near the Piedmont Triad International Airport. ~ 1518 Pleasant Ridge Road at Regional Road; 336-668-7107. In Pfafftown, go to **Grandview Golf Course**. ~ 3401 Grandview Road; 336-924-9146. Try the **Jamestown Park Golf Course**. ~ 7041 East Fork Road, Jamestown; 336-454-4912. While in Kernersville try the **Pine Tree Golf Club**. ~ 1680 Pine Tree Lane; 336-993-5598. In Brown Summit, go to **Bryan Park**. ~ 6275 Bryan Park Road; 336-375-2200.

HIGH POINT TO HICKORY   The **Oak Hollow Golf Course**'s 18 holes, designed by Pete Dye, have been ranked among the nation's best by *Golf Digest*. ~ 1400 Oakview Road, High Point; 336-883-3260.

CHARLOTTE AREA   The **Charlotte Golf Links** is designed in the Scottish style. ~ 11500 Providence Road, Charlotte; 704-846-7990. **Highland Creek Golf Club** has courses open to the public. ~ 7001 Highland Creek Parkway; 704-875-9000. The **Renaissance Park Golf Course** is also open to the public. ~ 1525 West Tyvola Road; 704-357-3373. Another option is the **Sunset Hills Golf Club.** ~ 800 Radio Road; 704-399-0980.

PINEHURST & SOUTHERN PINES AREA   Pinehurst and Southern Pines have been called the "World's Most Famous Birdie Sanctuary," and there is definitely no lack of great greens. Lovely links in the area include **The Club at Longleaf.** ~ Route 2, Pinehurst; 910-692-6100, 800-542-0450. Also in Pinehurst is **The Pit Golf Links.** ~ Route 5; 910-944-1600. There are many courses in Southern Pines, such as at the **Mid Pines Resort.** ~ 1010 Midland Road; 910-692-2114. **Talamore** is another. ~ 1448 Talamore Drive, Southern Pines; 910-692-5884. Along Route 2, you'll find **Pine Needles Lodge & Golf Club.** ~ Route 2, Southern Pines; 910-692-8611. And a final course in Southern Pines can be found at the **Hyland Hills Golf Club.** ~ 115 Fairway Avenue; 910-692-3752. In Aberdeen, there's **Legacy Golf Links.** ~ Route 15-501 South; 910-944-8825.

In addition to championship courts, the J. Spencer Love Tennis Center is home to the North Carolina Tennis Foundation's Hall of Fame.

RALEIGH   In the Raleigh area, you'll find **Cheviot Hills Golf Course.** ~ 7301 Capitol Boulevard, Raleigh; 919-876-9920. **River Ridge Golf Course** is also in the area. ~ 3224 Auburn-Knightdale Road, Raleigh; 919-661-8374.

DURHAM   The **Duke University Golf Club** course was originally designed by Robert Trent Jones. ~ Route 751 and Science Drive; 919-681-2288. George Cobb was the architect for the **Hillandale Golf Course.** ~ Hillandale and Sprunt roads; 919-286-4211.

CHAPEL HILL AREA   In Chapel Hill, try **Finely Golf Course.** ~ Finely Golf Course Road, off Route 15-501; 919-962-2349. In Hillsborough, you'll find **Cedar Grove.** ~ 619 McDade Store Road; 919-732-8397.

WINSTON-SALEM AREA   There are more than 100 courts in Winston-Salem, including 20 at **Joe White Tennis Center.** ~ 625 West End Boulevard; 336-727-2137. You might also enjoy playing at **Tanglewood Park**, which has lighted clay and hardtop courts. ~ Route 158, Clemmons; 336-778-6300. In Greensboro,

TENNIS

the **J. Spencer Love Tennis Center** has 12 championship courts. ~ Jaycee Park, on Forest Lawn Drive; 336-545-5320.

CHARLOTTE AREA A number of public courts exist in Charlotte, such as **Hornets Nest Park**. ~ 6301 Beatties Ford Road; 704-336-3854. **Kilborne Park** also has public courts. ~ 2600 Kilborne Road. Or try **Mason Wallace Park**. ~ 7301 Monroe Road. A final option for the Charlotte area is **Jetton Park**. ~ 19000 Jetton Road, Cornelius; 704-896-9808.

PINEHURST & SOUTHERN PINES AREA In Pinehurst, try **The Lawn and Tennis Club of North Carolina**. ~ 1 Merrywood, Pinehurst; 910-692-7270. The **Pinehurst Parks and Recreation Department** has courts at various locations. ~ 910-295-2817.

RALEIGH Raleigh has tennis courts at **Pullen Park**. ~ 520 Ashe Avenue; 919-872-4129. Also in Raleigh is **Millbrook Exchange**. ~ 1905 Spring Forest Road; 919-872-4129.

DURHAM You can play at **Oval Park**. ~ Knox and Roxboro streets. **East End Park** is another option. ~ 1204 Alston Avenue. Or try **Forest Hills Park**. ~ 1639 University Drive; 919-560-4355.

CHAPEL HILL In Chapel Hill, there's **Phillips Park**. ~ Estes Drive, Chapel Hill. ~ 919-929-2188.

RIDING STABLES

Several equestrian centers offer opportunities for a romp in the woods. The stables at **Tanglewood Park**, near Winston-Salem, not only rent horses, they'll take you on a carriage ride through gardens and forests. ~ Route 158, Clemmons; 336-778-6300.

The best place to saddle up in Charlotte is **Latta Plantation Nature Preserve**. The equestrian center offers guided tours along the park's 12 miles of trails. Horse shows are held on the weekend. ~ Sample Road, off Beatties Ford Road; 704-875-0808.

In Pinehurst, the **Carriage Tours of Pinehurst Village** features day- or night-time carriage tours with advance reservations. Closed Monday. ~ Spur and Everett roads; 910-235-8456.

In Durham, **Crane Creek Ranch** will outfit you with horses. ~ 3516 Bivins Road; 919-620-9313.

AUTHOR FAVORITE

Not to sound melodramatic, but something about saddling up a horse and striking out across clay-tipped pastures catapults you into the days of covered wagons and corn fields. My favorite place to hitch a ride is **Latta Plantation Nature Preserve**, where a network of bridle paths meander through an oak and hickory forest. See above for more information.

For excellent bike-trail maps, contact the North Carolina Depart-   **BIKING**
ment of Transportation's Bicycle Program. ~ 1552 Mail Service
Center, Raleigh, NC 27699-1552; 919-733-2804.

The Piedmont's hard-packed, gently sloped terrain makes for
ideal cycling. One of Winston-Salem's most scenic tours is through
Historic Bethabara Park. ~ 2147 Bethabara Road, off University
Parkway; 336-924-8191. The other is **Tanglewood Park**. ~
Route 158, Clemmons; 336-788-6300. Greensboro has nine designated bicycle routes, including the 13.4-mile **Battleground Loop**
through pretty neighborhoods and historic battle sites. For a map
of the various routes, call the City of Greensboro Department of
Transportation. ~ 336-373-2332.

Around Charlotte, **McAlpine Creek Park** features a two-mile
trail for bicycling. ~ 8711 Monroe Road, Charlotte; 704-568-4044.
Jetton Park has a one-mile trail along the shores of Lake Norman.
~ 1900 Jetton Road, Huntersville; 704-896-9808. If you care for
more challenging terrain, get on the mountain bike trails at **York
Road/Renaissance Park**, which trudges through mudholes, up steep
hills and over downed trees. ~ 1200 West Tyvola Road, Charlotte;
704-336-3854.

Pinehurst and Southern Pines are ideal for leisurely cycling;
their village settings offer lonely lanes and quiet neighborhoods.

Duke Forest, in Durham, covers 7700 acres crisscrossed with
bike trails. For information on trails, call 919-613-8013.

Bike Rentals   Despite the abundant bike trails, rentals are tough
to find, but there is **Durham Cycle Center**. ~ 639 Broad Street,
Durham; 919-286-2453. Near Raleigh, the **Spin Cycle** can get
you pedaling. ~ 1241 Kildaire Farm Road, Cary; 888-774-2925.

The Piedmont may be the most urban stretch of the Carolinas, but   **HIKING**
it does not lack in nature trails. Hundreds of miles of hikes exist
within the parks, offering everything from a lakeside stroll to a
steep mountain climb. All distances listed for hiking trails are one
way unless otherwise noted.

WINSTON-SALEM AREA   North of Winston-Salem in Hanging
Rock State Park, the **Hanging Rock Trail** (1.2 miles) is a moderate trek through sun-streaked forest, along drop-off ridges up to
the top of the dangling rock itself. The trailhead starts near the
end of the first parking lot.

Near here, take the trailhead for **Window Falls and Hidden
Falls Trail** (.5 mile) and you won't be disappointed. Two sets of falls
form myriad shapes, and you can even walk under one cascade.

In the northern part of the park, the **Lower Cascades Trail**
(.3 mile) is an easy, scenic walk down to the bottom of Cascade
Creek Falls, where water gushes, tier-like, for 120 feet. The trailhead is at the parking lot on Hall Road. ~ 336-593-8480.

Tougher but even more panoramic, **Ledge Springs Trail** (2 miles) in Pilot Mountain State Park skirts the edge of high cliffs with stunning vistas across rippled blue horizons. Mountain laurel and rhododendron are thick, and the steep, rugged terrain requires a bit of rock scrambling. The trailhead begins at the main parking lot.

If it's a clear day at the summit of Hanging Rock Trail you can see the Reynolds Building in Winston-Salem, 30 miles away.

The **Owl's Roost Trail** (10 miles) in Greensboro is truly unusual, first because few people know about it, and second because it is one of the few trails to circle an undeveloped North Carolina lake. The 785-acre lake provides water to Greensboro; the trail looks across the watery expanse but also wends into deep, old forests. The trailhead is in Bur-Mil Park, off Owl's Roost Road. ~ 336-373-3802.

CHARLOTTE AREA   McDowell Park in Charlotte has nine easy to moderate walks in the woods and along Lake Wylie, ranging from .25 mile to 1 mile. The **Four-Season Trail** (.33 mile), designed for wheelchair visitors, is a combination path that goes along the edge of the lake.

Crowder's Mountain State Park near Gastonia has a network of trails that start at the main parking lot. Pick up a brochure for **Fern Nature Trail** (.9 mile) to learn about the birds, animals, trees and plants that thrive in the woods and creek along the easy path. If you take **Crowder's Trail** to **Rocktop Trail** (5.3 miles together roundtrip), you'll scale the summit of Crowder's Mountain, along the way navigating rugged, rocky terrain with stomach-turning views down the sides of cliffs. The trek is moderate to strenuous. ~ 704-853-5375.

RALEIGH   Seventeen miles of trails follow rocky creeks and forest ridges through William B. Umstead State Park. In the Crabtree section there is the **Oak Rock Trail** (.6 mile) that is marked with signs describing the forest. Over in Reedy Creek, get on the **Company Mill Trail** (.5 mile), which goes by an old gristmill, to the **Sycamore Trail** (7.2 miles roundtrip), which meanders past granite outcroppings and an abandoned quarry.

DURHAM   Of the trails in Eno River State Park, **Cox's Mountain Trail** (3.8 miles) loop is the most contemplative, wending through wooded quietude to the Cox's summit, the highest place in the park. Portions of the trail are pretty steep, but the view is worth it.

Nearly 40 miles of trails delve into the 7900-acre **Duke Forest**, with entrances off Routes 571, 15-501 and 70. For a map, call 919-613-8013.

Transportation

CAR

Several interstate highways connect the Piedmont with the rest of the South. From Atlanta, **Route 85** cuts through South Carolina and into Charlotte, then makes its way up to Greensboro and over to Durham. **Route 77** comes up from

Columbia, South Carolina, and into Charlotte, continuing north through Statesville and Mount Airy.

Route 40 connects North Carolina's coast with its mountains, arching through the heart of the Piedmont on the way. Winston-Salem, Greensboro, Hickory, Raleigh and Chapel Hill are all linked by Route 40.

Three major airports serve the Piedmont: the Piedmont Triad International Airport, the Charlotte-Douglas International Airport and the Raleigh-Durham International Airport.

AIR

Piedmont Triad International Airport, centrally located to Winston-Salem, Greensboro and High Point, is serviced by American Airlines, Continental Airlines, Delta Air Lines, Independence Air, Northwest Airlines, United Airlines and US Airways. ~ www.flyfrompti.com.

Flying into **Charlotte-Douglas International Airport** are Air Canada, American Airlines, Continental Airlines, Delta Air Lines, Independence Air, Lufthansa, Northwest Airlines, United Airlines and US Airways. ~ www.charlotteairport.com.

Raleigh-Durham International Airport is served by Air Canada, American Airlines, Continental Airlines, Delta Airlines, Independence Air, Northwest Airlines, Southwest Airlines, United Airlines and US Airways. ~ www.rdu.com.

For shuttle service from Piedmont Triad International Airport to area cities, contact **PTI Airport Transportation.** ~ 877-796-5466.

Queens Transportation (704-752-9858) offers shuttle service around Charlotte.

To get to the Triangle area from Raleigh-Durham Airport, call **Carolina Trailways** (919-833-3601) or **Triangle Transit Authority** (919-549-9999).

Greyhound Bus Lines (800-231-2222; www.greyhound.com) has several locations around the Piedmont area. There are stops in Greensboro at 234-A East Washington Street, 336-272-8950; in Winston-Salem at 250 Greyhound Center, 336-724-1429; in Charlotte at 601 West Trade Street, 704-375-3332; in Raleigh at 314 West Jones Street, 919-834-8275; and in Durham at 820 Morgan Street, 919-687-4800.

BUS

Intrastate and interstate service is provided by **Amtrak** (800-872-7245; www.amtrak.com). Stops are in Greensboro at 2603 Oakland Avenue, 336-855-3382; in Charlotte at 1914 North Tryon Street, 704-376-4416; and in Raleigh at 320 West Cabarrus Street, 919-821-3615.

TRAIN

If you fly into Piedmont Triad International Airport, you can rent a car from **Alamo Rent A Car** (800-327-9633), **Budget Rent A Car**

CAR RENTALS

(800-527-0700), **Dollar Rent A Car** (800-800-4000), **Hertz Rent A Car** (800-654-3131) or **Triangle Rent A Car** (800-643-7368).

Rental agencies providing service to Charlotte-Douglas International Airport include **Alamo Rent A Car** (800-327-9633), **Avis Rent A Car** (800-331-1212), **Budget Rent A Car** (800-527-0700), **Dollar Rent A Car** (800-800-4000), **Enterprise Rent A Car** (800-325-8007), **Hertz Rent A Car** (800-654-3131), **National Car Rental** (800-227-7368) and **Thrifty Car Rental** (800-367-2277).

Raleigh-Durham International Airport has **Alamo Rent A Car** (800-327-9633), **Avis Rent A Car** (800-331-1212), **Dollar Rent A Car** (800-800-4000), **National Car Rental** (800-227-7368), **Budget Rent A Car** (800-527-0700), **Hertz Rent A Car** (800-654-3131), **Thrifty Car Rental** (800-367-2277) and **Triangle Rent A Car** (800-643-7368).

PUBLIC TRANSIT

The **Winston-Salem Transit Authority** will get visitors around Winston-Salem. ~ 336-727-2000. In Greensboro, there's SCAT. ~ 336-332-6445.

The Greater Charlotte area is served by **Charlotte Area Transit Systems**. ~ 704-336-7433.

Capital Area Transit operates public buses around Raleigh. ~ 919-828-7228. The **Durham Area Transit Authority** handles the routes around Durham. ~ 919-683-3282. If you need a bus ride across Duke University, call **Duke University Transit**. ~ 919-684-2218. Around Chapel Hill, catch one of the **Chapel Hill Transit** buses. ~ 919-968-2772.

TAXIS

Blue Bird Cab Company (336-722-7121) provides taxi service into Piedmont Triad International Airport. Around Greensboro, try **Bluebird-Diamond** (336-272-5112) or **United Yellow Taxi** (336-273-9421).

For taxi service to Charlotte-Douglas International Airport, call **Crown Cab Company** (704-334-6666) or **Yellow Cab Company of Charlotte** (704-332-6161).

At Raleigh-Durham International Airport, there's **American Cab Company** (919-821-0095), **Cardinal Cab Company** (919-828-3228) and **Triangle Yellow Cab Company** (919-832-5811). Around Durham, you'll find ABC **Cab Company** (919-682-0437).

EIGHT

The North Carolina Coast

Where North Carolina meets the Atlantic Ocean the state opens big and wide, taking a huge hunk of coast that stretches for nearly 300 miles between Virginia and South Carolina. A vast scrollwork of swamp and scrubland, sounds and rivers, it was once the bed of a sea. Now called the Coastal Plain, it is dotted with small towns and even a few big ones, and many fishing villages attended by shrimp boats whose nets fan out like wings.

Then there are the Outer Banks, a scant strand of sand and dunes lying offshore, a half-dozen islands elbowing out to sea. The Banks are forever being shaped and reshaped by whipping winds, simmering surf and tides that get out of bounds. On a cold full moon, the water may rear up and cross the road, smothering whole islands in its wavy froth. The seafood shack that's now on the sound used to sit at the dunes—before the wind and waves erased the dunes. The row of cottages atop the dunes was claimed one day by the sea, which does not care about a developer's beachfront schemes. The Outer Banks may help protect the mainland from wicked winds and oftentimes perilous waves and currents, but there is nothing to protect the Outer Banks.

The wind is most always blowing on the Outer Banks, sweeping the sand into giant castles—the tallest dune in eastern America is here—and casting the water into strange shapes. When the water gets angry, it demands victims; more than 600 ships have been flayed by the rough seas off the Outer Banks, called the "Graveyard of the Atlantic."

On land, the winds cool your hair and whisper in your ear. After a few days on the Banks, you grow accustomed to the whispering, and returning to the mainland brings a pang of silence. Kites and hang gliders, sailboards and surfboards are the toys of the Outer Banks. If someone wants to be airborne or surfborne, then the Outer Banks are the place to go.

Orville and Wilbur Wright desperately wanted to be airborne, so they came to this windswept waterfront in 1900. They brought with them a 17-foot glider and trusted it to the wind, but it only acted like a big kite. Not discouraged, they built a shack along the dunes in a place called Kill Devil Hills and moved in with their glider, sleeping in burlap hammocks strung from the rafters. Over the next couple of years they increased the glider's wingspan and arch, and installed a small engine. In 1903, after hundreds of failed tries, Orville aimed the airplane into a serious headwind and flew 120 feet—the first human flight.

Three centuries before the Wrights were catching air currents, two English ships made their way through wind and waves to land at what is now known as Ocracoke Inlet. It was 1584, and they had instructions from Sir Walter Raleigh to explore the New World. In a report to Raleigh, Captain Arthur Barlowe told of the "beating and surging of the sea" upon the sandy land. The shoal-studded waters, he said, "smelled so sweetly as if we had been in the midst of some delicate garden." On the mainland, the woods were rich with wildlife and "the highest and reddest cedars of the world."

Excited about the findings, Raleigh sent 107 men to establish a colony. They lasted less than a year before running out of supplies and catching a boat back to England. A second colony arrived in 1587, including 91 men, 17 women and 9 boys. Soon a child named Virginia Dare was born, the first English child born in North America. Now the Dare name appears on everything from inns and eateries to shopping centers—odd, since no one knows what happened to her, or to the rest of the colonists for that matter.

For when they, too, ran low on food, they dispatched a ship to England, but it got caught up in the war with Spain. When it finally returned three years later, the colonists' cabins were gone and in their place a fort had been built. On the fort was carved the word "croatoan," the name for an Indian village. The ship sailed for Croatoan but got sucked into a storm and damaged, and barely made it to Trinidad for repairs before returning to England.

The conundrum of the lost colony is played out every year on Roanoke Island, in an outdoor drama written by Pulitzer Prize–winning playwright Paul Green. The fort has been reconstructed and is now a State Historic Site, though its mystery is far more intriguing than its appearance—a low-lying, grassy berm in the woods.

North Carolina's first permanent settlement happened in a place more permanent than the Outer Banks: the northern Coastal Plain. Planters streamed down from Virginia in the 1650s, loaded with horses, pigs, cattle and sheep, and the idea of owning huge chunks of land. They found the land they wanted around the Albemarle Sound, where the soil was fertile and the meadows "interwoven with beautiful flowers, of most glorious colours, which the several seasons afford. . . ."

Over the next century more outposts were sewn into the fabric of North Carolina's coast. Most were fastened along the rivers and sounds, though for a long time there was no north–south route and so little sense of coastal cohesion. North Carolina's first town, Bath, cropped up on the Pamlico River in 1705, and by 1708 the town boasted 12 houses and a population of almost 50. Bath later lost a bid for state capital and stayed small. Today, it is a riverfront speck that looks lost in those early days—a great place for delving into coastal beginnings.

Five years after Bath was born, New Bern became North Carolina's second town. Located south of Bath where the Neuse and Trent rivers meet, it was founded by a group of Swiss and German immigrants (the town is named after Bern, Swit-

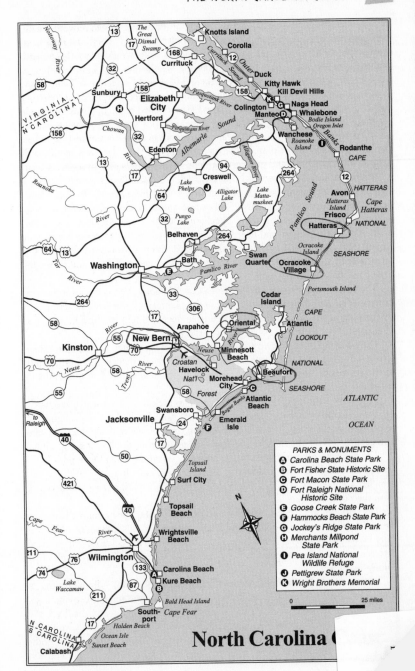

North Carolina

PARKS & MONUMENTS
- **A** Carolina Beach State Park
- **B** Fort Fisher State Historic Site
- **C** Fort Macon State Park
- **D** Fort Raleigh National Historic Site
- **E** Goose Creek State Park
- **F** Hammocks Beach State Park
- **G** Jockey's Ridge State Park
- **H** Merchants Millpond State Park
- **I** Pea Island National Wildlife Refuge
- **J** Pettigrew State Park
- **K** Wright Brothers Memorial

0   25 miles

zerland) determined to make it great. They built beautiful homes beneath the cypress and oak trees, reveling in Georgian and Federal designs. They built docks and warehouses to service the tar and turpentine that ships would carry to England, and the rum and sugar they brought from the West Indies.

New Bern thrived so much that in the 1760s Royal Governor William Tryon declared it capital of the North Carolina colony. He immediately ordered construction of a capitol building, and when Tryon Palace opened in 1770, it was the grandest place in the Carolinas. Tryon lived there only one year before being sent to New York to be governor, but other men governed in New Bern until 1798 when the palace burned. More than 150 years passed before the palace was rebuilt, and now its imposing halls and groomed gardens see thousands of visitors every year.

While the Coastal Plain was being civilized, the Outer Banks were being ruled by pirates. After having been chased out of the West Indies by the British, Blackbeard, Stede Bonnet and dozens of other buccaneers (including several women) found the Banks' secret coves and treacherous waters a perfect place to do business. Blackbeard met his end near Ocracoke Inlet when British Navy Lieutenant Robert Maynard raided his lair and slaughtered his crew. Maynard sliced off the pirate's head and mounted it in his ship's rigging, sailed into Bath and then continued all the way to England.

The Civil War came early to the North Carolina coast. Union troops took New Bern in 1862 and then wiped out most of the plantations along the eastern plain. By the turn of the century, locals turned to lumber and textiles for a living, shipping them from their port towns all over the world.

Only a small band of gritty, gutsy folk lived on the Outer Banks, many shipwreck survivors who had nowhere else to go. They built their homes in the safety of the soundside and drew their salaries from the sea, selling fish and crabs to mainlanders.

Even now, "Bankers," as year-round residents are called, are a scarce and hardy lot, only 32,000 people scattered along 175 miles of islands. They understand and respect the winter, when the wind comes calling, and cottage walls shudder and windows clatter. If you like the idea of nature banging at your door, visit in the winter.

The majority of visitors, of course, prefer the summer, when the wind is kindest and the toast-colored sand warms the feet. Most hole up in one of the woodshingled, long-legged cottages that huddle behind the dunes, a few seconds' stroll from the pounding surf.

The cottages are biggest, prettiest and priciest on the northernmost banks, in the towns of Corolla, Sanderling and Duck. All the action's just south of here in Kitty Hawk, Kill Devil Hills and Nags Head, and so is all the development. Wedged between here and the mainland is Roanoke Island, where Sir Walter Raleigh's first colony was lost.

Farther south, Hatteras Island has the Pea Island National Wildlife Refuge, a sliver of wide open dunes and beach and wispy seagrass, and snow geese who flock to safe shores. It also has a few small towns but scant development, thanks to the 50-mile-long Cape Hatteras National Seashore. Southwest from Hatteras, you must take a ferry to get to Ocracoke, a lovely, lost-in-time island with miles of nothing but beach and then a pretty fishing village laced around Silver Lake Harbor.

Two-day Getaway

Ocracoke Escape

DAY 1
- On Hatteras Island, pack a beach bag and picnic and get an early start so you can arrive at the Hatteras ferry docks by 8:30 a.m. Register your car for the 9 a.m. free ferry ride to Ocracoke Island. Then find a comfortable place on deck and enjoy the highly-scenic, 40-minute ferry ride.

- Don't hurry when you reach **Ocracoke Island** (page 281)—these 14 wilderness miles have a lonesome beauty you won't find anywhere else on the Outer Banks. Make sure you stop after five miles at the **Ocracoke Pony Pens** (page 281), take a stroll on the boardwalk and a look at the wild ponies. Then stop at one of the beach access areas for a few hours of sand and surf. (This is also when your picnic comes in handy.)

- Late afternoon, check into your Ocracoke lodging. You may want to shower the sand off and sneak a nap before heading over to **The Jolly Roger** (page 292) for a sunset cocktail. You won't need your car tonight, by the way; after sunset take a stroll over to the **Back Porch Restaurant** (page 290) for dinner.

DAY 2
- Sleep in and have a big breakfast at the **Island Inn Dining Room** (page 289). Then check out of your lodge and enjoy a few hours around **Ocracoke Village** (page 281), stopping first at the **National Park Service Visitors Center** (page 281) for island history and information. From there, walk among the picket-fenced neighborhoods to **Ocracoke Lighthouse** (page 281).

- Now you're ready for some spiffy island shopping. Definitely don't miss **Village Craftsmen** (page 291) and **Teach's Hole** (page 291). If you care to bring the beach (or the atmosphere, at least) back home, pick out a hammock from the **Ocracoke Island Hammock Company** (page 291).

- Have an early afternoon lunch at **Fig Tree Deli** (page 289). Then hop on the ferry for the ride home.

- Alternately, if you're not returning to Hatteras Island, you could spend another night on Ocracoke and take the morning ferry from the village to Cedar Island. It's a toll trip with two and a quarter hours of great, on-the-water scenery. From Cedar Island, Routes 12 and 70 curl along the coast for 50 miles to historic Beaufort—a perfect place to unpack your bags.

A series of sounds separate the Outer Banks from the Coastal Plain. Some, like the narrow, sheltered Currituck Sound, are calm and welcoming; others, like the vast Pamlico Sound, range from rough to treacherous. On a windy winter day, the two-and-a-half-hour ferry across the Pamlico feels like a wild ride on open seas.

Along the Coastal Plain are some of the Carolinas' most romantic names—Swan Quarter, Magnolia, Cape Fear, Emerald Isle—as well as some quirky hidden places: Frying Pan Landing, Gum Neck, Stumpy Point. The Coastal Plain tour starts north in the Albemarle Region, working southward from Virginia through the Great Dismal Swamp and then the port towns of Elizabeth City, Edenton and Bath.

The Neuse River Region takes in New Bern with its 150-plus historic homes, along with charming Beaufort, remote Cedar Island, and a string of developed beaches along Bogue Sound. At the southern foot of eastern North Carolina is the Cape Fear coast, whose centerpiece is graceful old Wilmington, where it's just as enjoyable to spend several hours or several days.

Despite its vast size, the North Carolina coast offers little glamour. There are no mind-numbing metropolises, no glitzy resorts, no possibilities for jackpot winnings. Instead, for the most part the land is given over to the intimacies of back-country fishing, searching the shallows for crabs, settling on a harborfront porch, listening to the wind, and watching the tide roll in.

The Outer Banks

The wisps of barrier islands known as the Outer Banks begin and end in wilderness. What's in between ranges from exclusive communities nicely spaced along the sand to crowded hodgepodges of funky cottages and motels to national seashores sprinkled with eye-blink towns. Always there is subtle beauty: the curve of the dunes, the lash of the wind, the great vault of ocean and sky opening to the east.

Sitting right below Virginia are the Banks' northernmost shores, though they can be reached only by four-wheel-drive vehicles, and preferably with someone familiar with the territory, as the trek requires much beachfront driving where patches of deep sand are famed for waylaying cars. The traveler lucky enough to drive way up here is rewarded with vistas of lush green farms and lonely, wind-lashed shores that seem to have no end.

SIGHTS

The paved road goes only as far north as **Corolla** (locals say "Car-ALL-a"), a beachy village at the dead end of Route 12 that's known for two things: wild mustang ponies and an 1800s-vintage lighthouse.

No one's exactly sure how the ponies got here, though a popular story is that they came aboard Spanish ships in the sixteenth century. Others say they are offspring of early colonists' herds. Either way, they roamed wild for several hundred years, feeding on sea oats and romping in the surf. But in the mid-1980s, Route 12 was extended up to Corolla, bringing instant tourism, planned developments, and thousands of visitors who came to feed the

Ocracoke - Cedar Island

7A	3P
930A	6P
12N	8:30P

On the Sea
for Free

252-225-3551
for reservations $15

On the North Carolina Coast, the best way to get from here to there is not always by car but by boat. State-run ferries cut across rivers and sounds, cutting travel time by hours and even days. The fleet of 23 boats range from 157-footers that can ferry 18 cars to 220-foot vessels with a capacity for 50 vehicles. They're clean and usually smooth riding, depending on weather, of course, and have air conditioned lounges to relax in. The salty fellows who run the boats are companionable and comfortingly well-informed on seafaring matters.

Best of all, some ferries are free.

If you choose the ferries between Knotts Island and Currituck, Hatteras Island and Ocracoke Island, Aurora and Bayview, or Minnesott Beach and Cherry Branch, you don't have to pay, not even if you take your bicycle or car aboard.

You should, however, be out on deck for most of the trip or you'll miss the scenes of tidal grass rippling in the breeze, the points of land capped with villages and their attendant fishing boats, the deep blues of the sound, the foggy bronze of the river. You can watch the shrimp trawlers drag their nets across the water's bottom, then unload their contents on deck. You can see the sun rise and set on the water, if you time your ferry rides right.

Trips are as short as twenty minutes and as long as two and a half hours. The three ferries that do charge fees—between Ocracoke and Cedar Island, Ocracoke and Swan Quarter, and Southport and Fort Fisher—are not expensive; pedestrians pay between 50 cents and $1. Reservations are usually required for these routes; call the **North Carolina Ferry System**. ~ 252-726-6446, 800-293-3779; www.ncferry.org. You can also check weather conditions. High winds can mean a rough ride, especially on the Ocracoke routes, though ferries don't operate when it's truly high seas.

beautiful animals and clamor for their photos. Traffic jams were a regular occurrence and the horses often got killed by cars. Now the 60 or so horses reside in more private surroundings on 1500 government- and private-owned acres north of Corolla, out of the tourists' camera range. You'll need a four-wheel drive to visit them now.

Corolla's other big attraction, **Currituck Beach Lighthouse**, is a red-brick beauty built in 1875 and restored in the late 1980s. The northernmost of the Outer Banks' "famous four" lighthouses, it's a prime place to catch a sky view. Take all 214 steps spiraling up to the top and look out across swirling sea oats and surf-laced sand. The beacon still flashes every 20 seconds. Closed late November until Easter. Admission. ~ Route 12, at Corolla Village Road; 252-453-4939.

Most places in the Outer Banks give their addresses in mileposts, since it's the easiest way to find them.

Route 12 is the only road out of here, indeed the only main road south for more than 20 miles. From late fall through early spring it can be a wonderfully moody drive, with few cars on the road, cottages all boarded up, the sky bundled in charcoal-colored clouds, and the sand and sea clutched by cold wind. Come summer, the road itself is clutched in traffic, cars creeping along two lanes, horns honking, tempers flaring. Weekends can be especially bad, so come prepared for crowds and allow extra travel time.

This goes for all the Outer Banks. Even remote Ocracoke, which can be reached only by ferry, is so thronged with cars on some summer days you feel certain there must be a secret bridge to the mainland. Ocracokers say there's no telling which days traffic may strike, though it usually clears up within a couple of hours—until the next ferry expels a new load of cars.

The 22 miles of Route 12 south of Corolla are designated a Wild Horse Sanctuary, so obey speed limits and be on the lookout. This stretch of northern beach is also a sanctuary for those with money, who have staked their spacious spots in well-tended dunes. Their sprawling, multilevel stilt homes are secured behind brambly foliage and at the foot of roads that stop just before the surf. Most lie within the towns of **Sanderling, Duck** and **Southern Shores**, where real estate offices with banners flapping in the wind foretell the future of this quiet, exclusive northern stretch of the Outer Banks.

South of here the future has already arrived. Starting with **Kitty Hawk** and running for 20 miles through **Kill Devil Hills** and **Nags Head**, virtually every inch of land, be it beachside or soundside, is cluttered with weathered wood-shingled cottages, cheesy motels, seafood shacks, putt-putt golf, shopping centers, surf shops, and just about every other manner of campy beach venue. This is where most Outer Banks' visitors come to play, to ride the wind on a hang glider, surfboard or windsurfer, to spread their towels cheek-to-jowl on the tawny sand, to shoot pool and eat oysters, to dangle in a hammock and be rocked to sleep by sea breezes.

This is also where four-lane Route 158, also called "The Bypass Road" and "Croatan Highway," parallels Route 12, providing faster driving, and where distances are measured in mileposts. You'll see the little green signposts with numbers on the roadside, which get bigger as you head south.

When you're in Kitty Hawk, stop at the **Aycock Brown Welcome Center**, the beach headquarters for the Outer Banks Visitors Bureau. It's fashioned as one of the Banks' old lifesaving stations. You can load up with maps, brochures and other information on the Outer Banks. ~ Milepost 1 on Route 158; 252-261-4644, fax 252-261-1053; www.outerbanks.org, e-mail visitorinfo@outerbanks.org. Extensive information and pamphlets can also be procured from the **Outer Banks Visitors Bureau**'s office on Roanoke Island, located at the foot of the bridge connecting the island to the mainland. ~ Route 64; 252-473-2138, 800-446-6262; www.outerbanks.org, e-mail visitorinfo@outer banks.org.

There weren't any mileposts around when Orville and Wilbur Wright arrived in 1900 and told gravity to take a hike. You can learn how the bicycle mechanics from Dayton, Ohio, pulled off the first powered human flight at the **Wright Brothers National Memorial**. Exhibits at the visitors center detail the ins and outs of aerodynamics, and how the Wrights first got their souped-up glider aloft in 1903. The famed event took place in a field near Big Kill Devil Hill, which looms near the visitors center and is punctuated by a 60-foot granite pylon aimed at the sky. You can drive the loop road around the hill, but most prefer to take the slow walk up the smoothly rounded knoll where, with the wind slapping at your back, you can understand precisely why the men chose this spot. Wheelchair visitors have full access to all the sights here. Though the memorial is closed at night, the pylon is all lit up and can be seen from Route 158, looking like a great dagger in the dark. Admission. ~ Route 158, Milepost 8, Kill Devil Hills; 252-441-7430, fax 252-441-7730; www.nps.gov/wrbr.

A couple of miles south of the memorial, take the western turnoff for **Colington**. The way to the crusty old fishing village is along three miles of narrow road that curls around inlets and harbors swirling with seagrasses, roadside shacks selling softshell crabs, a hilltop cemetery, and cottages crouched beneath big oak trees.   ◄ HIDDEN

Back on Route 158 and heading south, another side road delivers you to the little-known **Nags Head Woods Preserve**. With all the hubbub around Nags Head, it's hard to believe that these 1400 acres of forest exist, let alone harbor walnuts, hickories,   ◄ HIDDEN maples and other big hardwoods. Visitors can take part or all of the five miles of trails through woods and swamp and along Roanoke Sound. ~ Ocean Acres Drive, off Route 158, turn at Pigman's Bar-B-Q, Milepost 9½; 252-441-2525, fax 252-441-1271.

Farther south there's Route 64/264, where a bridge arches across Roanoke Sound to **Roanoke Island**, tucked between the Outer Banks and mainland North Carolina. The island has two contrasting sides: the south side largely smothered in marsh and punctuated by the busy little fishing village of **Wanchese**; and the

HIDDEN ►

north side, where the main town of **Manteo** (locals say "MAN-te-o") is haphazardly dotted with fast-food chains, car lots, and double-decker buses filled with sightseers. The most appealing part of Manteo is **The Waterfront**, where a handful of shops, eateries and inns gather along the sound. Some buildings date back to the late 1800s when Manteo was found, but most are twentieth-century replicas. ~ Route 400 East, just off Route 64/264.

Docked at The Waterfront in Shallowbag Bay, the **Elizabeth II** gives you a good idea of how North America's first colonists got to Roanoke Island in the 1500s. A visit to this State Historic Site starts with a short film about the hardships they endured on those early voyages. The regal, triple-masted ship, a replica of those early vessels, is great to explore, especially for kids, who can roam all 69 feet of polished wood deck. Closed January. Admission. ~ The Waterfront in Shallowbag Bay; 252-473-1144, fax 252-475-1507; www.roanokeisland.com, e-mail risp.information@ncmail.net.

The colonists actually landed down the road at a place that's now **Fort Raleigh National Historic Site**. There were 117 English settlers in all, and they were among the first Europeans to try fulltime life in the New World. After several months they ran short of food and supplies and sent a ship back to England, but the vessel, due to the war against Spain, could not return for three years. By then, the colony had vanished, and all that remained was a

AUTHOR FAVORITE

sights

Funny how a pile of sand can make your soul soar. When I kicked off my sandals and climbed the big dune at **Jockey's Ridge State Park**, it was like tackling a piece of the Sahara Desert. The sand dune moves three to six feet southwest every year, thanks to prevailing northeast winds. At the top, you can watch hang gliders leaping and swooping, and sandboarders (the dune equivalent of snowboarders) cruising down the dune's rippled southwest face. Sunsets from up here are incredible. And though you can look across rippling Roanoke Sound to what is most definitely Roanoke Island, you still feel like you're in the desert. See page 293 for more information.

small earthen fort. ~ Route 64/264; 252-473-5772, fax 252-473-2595; www.nps.gov/fora.

Earlier in the 20th century the fort was reconstructed and is now the centerpiece of the historic site. It's not much to see, for the fort is not big and formidable but low-lying and grassy, although the 150-acre wooded setting is certainly enjoyable. Loblolly pines form cool canopies for the trails that meander around the fort all the way to Roanoke Sound. There is wheelchair access to the fort.

Within the site is also the orderly **Elizabethan Gardens**, which explode with color year-round. Springtime is best, though depending on the season you can witness azaleas, rhododendrons, gardenias, magnolias or hydrangeas at their height. Crepe myrtles grow geometrically, and a fountain pool and whimsical stone statuary dominate the pristine Sunken Garden in the park's center. Above the garden is a handmade brick terrace dating from the late 1800s. A small gazebo reminiscent of the sixteenth century overlooks Roanoke Sound, where the colonizers first landed. Admission. ~ 252-473-3234; www.outerbanks.com/elizabethangardens.

At the **North Carolina Aquarium on Roanoke Island**, there's an ample representation of aquatic animals native to North Carolina. Fish, alligators, otters and turtles are on display in the freshwater aquarium. Saltwater species include lobster, stingrays and triggerfish. Kids gravitate toward the touch tank, where they can reach down and hold horse shoe and hermit crabs, sea stars and other small creatures. Even more popular is the shark gallery, where the sinister-looking creatures prowl along the windows of their 285,000-gallon tank. Admission. ~ Airport Road, off Route 64/264, Manteo; 252-473-3493, fax 252-473-1980; www.ncaquariums.com.

To keep exploring the Outer Banks, head back east on Route 64/264 to Route 12, then drive south along **Bodie Island**. Bodie (say "Body") actually was an island but isn't anymore, since the tides and winds sealed up the inlet in the 1800s. Now it's a low-key strand of pale white sand, called Coquina Beach, that's part of Cape Hatteras National Seashore. Bodie's southernmost tip is pinpointed with the **Bodie Island Lighthouse**. With black-and-white stripes racing around its 150-foot cylinder, it's a favorite of photographers. Unfortunately, you can't enter the lighthouse.

The lighthouse stands sentinel over the **Oregon Inlet**, perpetually congested with fishers hopeful of snagging a bluefish, sea bass, flounder, or dozens of other varieties that funnel through this small opening between the Atlantic Ocean and Pamlico Sound. The Herbert C. Bonner Bridge spans the inlet and delivers you to **Hatteras Island** and the solitude of **Pea Island National Wildlife Refuge**. Thousands of waterfowl such as snow geese, tundra swans, and green-winged teal have found safety on these 6000 acres running along the sides of Route 12. ~ Headquarters located on Route 12; 252-473-1131.

Seven towns are sprinkled along the skinny 58-mile length of Hatteras Island. All are little more than gathering spots for bait-and-tackle shops, campgrounds, and a handful of motels and cottages. The island owes its laid-back ambiance and abundance of silent shores to the Cape Hatteras National Seashore, which protects not only Hatteras but also Ocracoke Island to the south.

You can drive right on these shores in certain areas, provided you have a four-wheel-drive vehicle and stay well between the dunes and the surf. Access ramps are marked along Route 12 on Hatteras and Ocracoke, though before setting out you should check with the National Park Service for current weather and tide conditions. Lest you're tempted to take your two-wheel-drive car on the beach, the park's brochure says, "we think you will be sorry." ~ 252-995-4474, 252-473-2111.

Rodanthe (pronounced "Ro-DAN-thee") is Hatteras' northernmost town and also where you'll find the **Chicamacomico Life-saving Station**. One of seven stations along the Outer Banks (and the only one open to the public as a museum), it operated from 1874 until after World War II. The men who guarded the shores from this demure-looking shingled cottage were truly fearless—or crazy, depending on how you look at it. When a ship wrecked, they would launch a line out to the sinking vessel in the hopes of reeling it in. Then they would launch rowboats into the ocean's tumult and row out to collect survivors. Naturally, wrecks occurred on the nastiest of days, and even if dark thoughts of dying never crossed a lifesaver's mind, one would imagine he at least got a stomachful of saltwater. Those heroic and hair-raising feats are remembered through exhibits at the station, open Monday through Friday, Memorial Day through Thanksgiving weekend. ~ Route 12; 252-987-1552; www.chicamacomico.net, e-mail chicamacomico@earthlink.net.

Also helping steer ships to shore was the **Cape Hatteras Lighthouse** in the town of Buxton. The most famous Outer Banks lighthouse, it's the one you see in all the vacation ads looking a lot like a black-and-white striped barber's pole perched on a point of land, with whitecaps boiling at its feet. At over 200 feet (depending on where you start your measurement), it's the tallest brick lighthouse in the United States. From Easter until Columbus Day you can climb up inside the slender silhouette for the Banks' best vista (unless you go parasailing). The adjacent lighthouse keeper's quarters offer some displays on lighthouse lore. There is a limit on how many people can enter at once, so it's recommended to get there by 10 a.m. Children must be 38 inches or taller. Admission. ~ Off Route 12, Buxton; 252-995-4474, fax 252-995-4633.

The next town south, Hatteras, is where you can catch the free 30-minute ferry over to **Ocracoke Island**, the only way to Ocracoke from the north.

Mentally, the trip seems much longer, for when you arrive on Ocracoke, it's as if you were transported to an entirely different region. Gone are the spaceships hawking hot dogs, the legions of fishing boats, the clutter of cottages. What you find here is a lonely, desolate, wind-lashed island ribboned with wide, whitish sand and bristly scrublands not burdened by a single manmade structure for nearly 13 miles. The only interlude in the scenery is the **Ocracoke Pony Pens**, where from a boardwalk you can look across pastures and watch the wild horses that once had the whole island to themselves. ~ Route 12, five miles south of the Hatteras Ferry.

Route 12 is the only road on the island until **Ocracoke Village**, near the southern end. There is nothing contrived about this tiny place of whitewashed and weathered cottages sprinkled among the gnarled boughs of live oaks. Narrow lanes curl through the neighborhoods where vegetable gardens are edged in white-plank fence. Here, too, is the **Ocracoke Lighthouse**, thickest and squattest of the Outer Banks' lighthouses. Built in 1823, its mortar walls are five feet thick, its nonrotating light still shining, making it the second-oldest operating beacon in the nation. ~ Point Road.

Ocracoke is wonderful at sunset. The great orange orb dives down across a wide-open horizon unhindered by development, leaving in its wake scarlet clouds bunched across the sky. A better day's end cannot be imagined.

Ocracoke activity culminates at **Silver Lake Harbor**, a sort of "downtown" area of little shops, eateries and bait stores so pleasantly arranged you instantly reach for your camera. The vanilla-washed, clapboard **National Park Service Visitors Center at Ocracoke Island** provides insight on the island and tourism information. Ships' horns blow frequently as ferries head out for Swan Quarter or Cedar Island for voyages across the breadth of Pamlico Sound. ~ Across from the Cedar Island/Swan Quenta ferry landing; phone/fax 252-928-4531.

◆◆

FAR-OUT FRISCO

South of Buxton, the town of Frisco has perhaps the Outer Banks' quirkiest, tackiest site: a former hot-dog shop called **Out of This World** that's shaped like a spaceship. (Remember the old TV series "Lost in Space"? This could be that spaceship.) ~ Route 12, Frisco.

LODGING   Most Outer Banks visitors rent cottages. The choices are many, from the ubiquitous two-room, cedar-shingled shacks huddling behind the dunes to the multilevel homes confronting the ocean. They are usually rented by the week or weekend, and priced according to the size of the place, the time of year and the location. Generally, cottages in the northernmost Banks are most expensive, while those in Kill Devil Hills and Nags Head cost less. Families often opt for a place on the soundside of the banks, as the water is safer for swimming.

As you might guess, the list of rental agencies is rather long. Try **Resort Quest** for northern Banks rentals. ~ 252-261-3566, 800-334-6315; www.resortquestouterbanks.com. **Atlantic Realty** also provides rentals. ~ 252-261-2154, 800-334-8401. Or call **Seaside Vacations**. ~ 252-261-5500, 800-395-2525.

On Hatteras Island, contact **Dolphin Realty**. ~ 252-986-2562, 800-338-4775; www.dolphin-realty.com. For rentals on Ocracoke Island, call **Ocracoke Island Realty**. ~ 252-928-6261. The alternative on Ocracoke Island is **Sandy Shores Realty**. ~ 252-928-5711.

When it comes to full-service lodging, it's tough to match the **Sanderling Inn**. Located in Duck, it bills itself as one of the most exclusive resorts in the area, and it is. Resembling the old shingled cottages dotting the island, it sits squarely on the oceanfront, with sound views from the upper floors. The lobby is a warm wooden entry with duck decoys and Audubon prints scattered across high walls. All of the 88 rooms have private porches that lend an open-air feel, as if they were secluded beach cabanas. All the rooms have kitchenettes; others offer wet bars. Tennis courts, spa facilities and an indoor swimming pool are available for those not content with mere sea oats and sand; there are also two restaurants on the property. ~ 1461 Duck Road, Duck; 252-261-4111, 800-701-4111, fax 252-261-1638; www.thesanderling.com, e-mail info@ thesanderling.com. ULTRA-DELUXE.

Ferries bring thousands of visitors to Ocracoke in summer, though permanent residents number about 900. Says one resident: "Ten folks died last year but a bunch more were born, so it usually evens out."

The **Sea Ranch Hotel** is known for catering to a tourist's every whim; there's an indoor pool, beauty salon and health spa. Even as newer resorts have cropped up across the beach, the Sea Ranch is still considered one of the best. All the rooms are clean and moderately sized with microwaves and refrigerators, many have an ocean view. ~ Beach Road, Milepost 7, Kill Devil Hills; 252-441-7126, 800-334-4737, fax 252-441-0408; www.searanch hotel.com. DELUXE.

Some of the rooms in the eccentric little **Ocean House Motel** are decorated with a particular theme. For example, a patch-quilt comforter, kerosene lantern and wagon wheel can be found in the

"Tobacco Belt Room." Some of the rooms have oceanfront access and refrigerators, while others are decorated a little more conservatively. If you're looking for elegance, though, stay away: for the most part, Ocean House looks like an overnight costume party that got a little out of hand. Closed mid-October through March. ~ Beach Road, Milepost 9½, Kill Devil Hills; 252-441-2900, 800-699-1963; www.oceanhousemotel.com, e-mail info@ocean housemotel.com. MODERATE TO DELUXE.

The **Nags Head Inn** is located at the southern end of Nags Head Beach, a bit out of the congestion of mid-beach. Still, don't let the name fool you; this is no cozy B&B, but one of the largest and newest hotels on the island. Reminiscent of a big chain hotel, the inn offers such amenities as an oceanfront indoor pool and a spa and sun deck. The guest rooms are carbon-copy simple but comfortable. Ask for one with a private oceanfront balcony. ~ Beach Road, Milepost 14, Nags Head; phone/fax 252-441-0454, 800-327-8881; www.nagsheadinn.com, e-mail info@nagsheadinn. com. DELUXE TO ULTRA-DELUXE.

The red cedar **First Colony Inn**, listed on the National Register of Historic Places, is beachy and intimate, just 27 rooms with encircling verandas and dormers set near the dunes. There's a heated pool, croquet court, and boardwalk angling down to an oceanside gazebo. The rooms are some of the Banks' plushest, furnished with English antiques, poster and canopy beds, and soft, pale carpets. Take your complimentary breakfast on the sunporch or on a silver tray in your room. ~ 6720 South Virginia Dare Trail, off Beach Road, Milepost 16, Kitty Hawk; 252-441-2343, 800-368-9390, fax 252-441-9234; www.firstcolony inn.com, e-mail innkeeper@firstcolonyinn.com. ULTRA-DELUXE.

You get a lot for your dollar at **Scarborough Inn**, where hosts Rebecca and Fields Scarborough treat guests like old family friends. Each room is decorated in antiques, collected by family members when traveling. (Microwaves, refrigerators and coffeepots are available in each room.) Though it may be quite tempting to simply lie around your room, it's far better to borrow one of the bicycles lining the wooden porch and pedal along the waterfront. Continental breakfast included. ~ 524 Route 64/264, Roanoke Island; 252-473-3979; www.scarborough-inn.com, e-mail scarinn@aol.com. MODERATE.

Overlooking Shallowbag Bay on the Manteo waterfront, the **Tranquil House Inn** is designed like a nineteenth-century beach resort. The cypress woodworking and stained-glass windows give it a tasteful appearance, and all 25 rooms are individually decorated with accoutrements like four-poster beds. The most appealing rooms are on the soundside, offering a view of the docked *Elizabeth II* and shrimp boats. In the morning, there's a continental breakfast buffet; in the early evening, there are wine receptions. ~ 405 Queen Elizabeth Street, The Waterfront, Roanoke Island; 252-473-1404, 800-458-7069, fax 252-473-1526; www.tranquilinn.com. DELUXE TO ULTRA-DELUXE.

Even Sparky will appreciate the hospitality at the pet-friendly **Island Guesthouse & Cottages**. The fourteen rooms in the guesthouse are comfy and affordable, while the three cottages offer more luxurious amenities: a full kitchen, private bath and a two-person jacuzzi tub. The two-bedroom cottage with a living room and fireplace is perfect for a family or two couples. Just a five-minute walk from the heart of Manteo, this hostelry is a great base for exploring Roanoke Island. ~ 706 Route 64, Manteo; 252-473-2434; www.theislandmotel.com, e-mail admin@theisland motel.com. MODERATE TO ULTRA-DELUXE.

Tranquil and petite, the **Inn on Pamlico Sound** is a cozy retreat on the shores of Hatteras Island. Guests choose between five individually decorated rooms, each of which offers a bright and elegant theme. The queen-size beds are plush and inviting; the furnishings are cheerful; and each room has a view of the sound or the inn's surrounding gardens. Soak up the rays out on the sun deck, take a dip in the seaside pool or watch your favorite film in the small in-house theater. Despite its spectacular location, the complimentary breakfast just might be the highlight—each morning the three-course gourmet meal includes seven different types of fresh juices and entrées such as brown sugar–baked French toast. ~ 49684 Route 12, Buxton; 252-995-7030; www.innonpamlicosound.com, e-mail innkeeper@innon pamlicosound.com. DELUXE.

The **Cape Hatteras Motel** spans from soundside to beachside. The lodging itself is nothing spectacular, just basic and comfortable. The hotel offers many different types of accommodations;

JOIN THE INN-CROWD

An Outer Banks treasure, the **Island Inn** began life in 1901 as the Oddfellows Lodge of Ocracoke and part-time schoolhouse. Since the 1950s, the gabled, whitewashed building has been welcoming overnight guests who enjoy its charm and character and slow pace (but not slow service). The inn has one of the best dining rooms on Ocracoke and the only heated swimming pool. All of the rooms are decorated differently, and though none are fancy, they are spacious, warm and welcoming—just what you'd hope from a far-flung island inn. Four villas built in 1998 feature two bedrooms, a living room, dining room, kitchen, modern decor and views of Silver Lake Harbor. ~ 100 Lighthouse Road, Ocracoke Island; 252-928-4351, 877-456-3466, fax 252-928-4352; www.ocracokeislandinn.com, e-mail info@ocracokeislandinn.com. MODERATE.

standard rooms on the ocean are plainly adorned with king-sized beds and a few kitchen appliances. There are efficiencies on the oceanside and apartments on both sides of the water. There's also a pool and a hot tub. ~ Route 12, Buxton; 252-995-5611, 800-995-0711, fax 252-995-4303; www.capehatterasmotel.com, e-mail info@capehatterasmotel.com. ULTRA-DELUXE.

At the southernmost tip of Hatteras Island, the **Sea Gull Motel** is reminiscent of the 1950s, with a few concessions to more current tastes. Other than the welcome addition of air conditioners, little has changed over the years at this bi-level brick motel, which includes 15 oceanside units (each with a microwave and refrigerator). Several apartments come with fully equipped kitchens. There's a pool here but not much else in the way of amenities. Closed late November through February. ~ Route 12, Hatteras Island; 252-986-2550; www.seagullhatteras.com, e-mail seagullmotel@earthlink.net. DELUXE.

The **Castle on Silver Lake Bed and Breakfast** is a historical inn with eleven individually decorated rooms and eight courtyard villas. Built in the 1950s, the hotel retains its grandeur today with vintage furnishings such as brass chandeliers and dark oak tables. Because of the castle-like architecture, each room is unique in shape and size, offering a private bath (some with whirlpool tubs), a queen-size bed and hardwood floors. The newer two- or three-bedroom courtyard villas are bright and modern and have separate entrances. Relax and take advantage of the heated pool, sauna, steam rooms and bike rentals on the property, all of which are free for guests. ~ 155 Silver Lake Road, Ocracoke; 252-928-3505, 800-471-8848, fax 252-928-3501; www.thecastlebb.com, e-mail innkeeper@thecastlebb.com. DELUXE TO ULTRA-DELUXE.

Built in 1936, **Blackbeard's Lodge** conveys the feeling of a cozy summer camp. Barefoot children run freely through the pine-paneled lobby while older guests read the paper in wide, welcoming chairs. Most of the rooms are rustic but comfortable and air-conditioned. But penthouse rooms on the upper floor have modern amenities: wet bars and whirlpools. The harbor and beaches are but a bicycle ride away, and if you don't like the salt and sand you can splash around in Blackbeard's heated pool. ~ Ocracoke Village; phone/fax 252-928-3421, 800-892-5314; www.blackbeardslodge.com. MODERATE TO ULTRA-DELUXE.

DINING

Small, intimate and immensely popular, **Nicoletta's Italian Café** serves some of the best Italian fare on the Outer Banks. One reason: all vegetables and seafood are fresh and local; nothing frozen is ever served on the seasonal menu. Try the seafood risotto, lasagna or the chicken florentine. Dinner only. Hours vary according to the season, so be sure to call ahead (reservations are wise, too). ~ Route 12, in the Corolla Light Town Center; 252-453-4004. MODERATE TO ULTRA-DELUXE.

Blue Point Bar & Grill looks like a 1950s diner, with chrome tables and red-vinyl barstools lining the black-and-white checkerboard floor. The menu, which runs the gamut from simple Southern to complex, includes crab cakes, grilled Atlantic salmon, pan roast of jumbo shrimp, smoked bay scallops and fresh fish. Try the bourbon pecan pie for dessert. No lunch on Monday; call ahead for off-season hours. Reservations are recommended. ~ Route 12, Duck; 252-261-8090, fax 252-261-7284; www.goodfoodgoodwine.com. DELUXE TO ULTRA-DELUXE.

The spectacular sunset is just the icing on the cake at the seaside **Fishbones Sunset Grille & Raw Bar**. A gazebo extending into the sound and a nightly sushi bar makes this hotspot hard to resist, but it's the creative menu that keeps the crowds coming back for more. You'll find unique appetizers such as warm brie in a pastry shell topped with raspberry sauce or Caribbean-inspired entrées like cashew mango mahimahi and coconut curry lobster. Palm trees and tiki torches adorn the patio, and if you're lucky, you might find yourself sipping a mai tai in a coconut shell while you groove to the tropical tunes of a live reggae band. ~ 1264 Duck Road, Duck; 252-261-3901; www.fishbonessunsetgrille. com, e-mail sunsetinfo@earthlink.net. MODERATE TO DELUXE.

Rundown Cafe is fast becoming the best place on the beach for "fun food." The two-floor eatery has an encroaching bar and small wooden tables, ceiling fans, and bright art work on the walls. Don't expect the average fried-fish platter at this joint. The menu leans toward eastern flavors—Thai noodles with ginger and garlic and Indian garlic flatbread are staples. There are also plenty of seafood dishes. Weekends in season bring big, festive crowds, so be prepared to wait at the bar for a table. Closed Sunday, and November through January. ~ Beach Road, Milepost 1, Kitty Hawk; 252-255-0026, fax 252-255-0029. BUDGET TO MODERATE.

City meets beach at **Ocean Boulevard American Bistro & Martini Bar**. The view outside is of the dunes but inside it's more tropical gotham, with mustard-yellow walls, red brick alcoves, and floors of pebble and poured concrete in the bar. The cuisine that emanates from the open kitchen is complex and vigorous, perhaps the most stunning on the Outer Banks. Start with a composed salad of baby greens, seasonal fruit, melted brie and toasted almonds, then go for one of the "big plates," like the mango barbecue–glazed lamb steak with truffle-scented sauté of greens and goat-cheese whipped potatoes. Great wine list. Dinner only. ~ 4700 Virginia Dare Trail, off Beach Road, Milepost 2½, Kitty Hawk; 252-261-2546, fax 252-261-2083; www.ocean-boulevard.com. DELUXE.

Dark and cozy, with small candles glimmering at the tables and Tiffany lamps hanging from the ceiling, **Port O' Call** is one of the Banks' fancier eateries. The dinner menu ranges from veal to prime rib to pasta. Naturally, there is seafood, though it's more elegantly prepared than the garden-variety fried type. Dinner only. Closed January to mid-March. ~ Beach Road, Milepost 8½, Kill Devil Hills; 252-441-8001; www.outerbanksportocall.com, e-mail portocall@aginet.com. MODERATE TO ULTRA-DELUXE.

After a morning on the waves, surfers rejuvenate at **Pigman's Bar-B-Q** over plates piled high with pork and beef, hushpuppies and sweet-potato fries. An Outer Banks institution, "The Pigman" slow-smokes its meat in the Carolinas tradition, dousing the pork in a tangy vinegar-based sauce and the beef in a spicy tomato sauce. They get inventive with the turkey, tuna and catfish "q," in an effort to provide a few low-fat options. Smoked chicken and buffalo wings are also hot items at this no-frills wood eatery. Closed for three weeks in winter. ~ Route 158, Milepost 9½, Kill Devil Hills; 252-441-6803; www.pigman.com, e-mail pigman@pigman.com. BUDGET TO MODERATE.

Along the winding side road to Colington, look for **Colington   ◄ HIDDEN Café** tucked up on a hill. This pretty cottage that's loved by locals delivers French-international cuisine, some of the classiest food around. The shrimp and scallops are served with a delicious sherry cream sauce. The filet mignon, chicken filet and pork loin are equally mouth-watering. Closed Thanksgiving to Easter, except for the week of Christmas and Valentine's Day. Reservations recommended. Dinner only. ~ 1029 Colington Road at Milepost 8½; 252-480-1123. MODERATE.

The Dunes Restaurant is the best choice for family fare. This unimposing place packs tourists into three large dining areas. Don't be scared off if the waiting line extends out the door; turnover is usually quick. Breakfast is bountiful and served up on

SEASIDE SEAFOOD STATION

If you care to dine in a lovely 1899 lifesaving station, go to the **Lifesaving Station Restaurant** at the Sanderling Inn. From the main dining room, barnyard doors open to the sand dunes. The seaside ambiance continues indoors where a brass ringing bell, wooden oars and old photos of the station adorn the walls. The fare is inventive and nearly gourmet. Brown sugar and cinnamon french toast is on the breakfast menu. At dinner, waiters in dress shirts offer seasonal specials of fresh local seafood. ~ Route 12, Duck; 252-261-4111, 800-701-4111; www.thesanderling. com, e-mail restaurant@thesanderling.com. DELUXE TO ULTRA-DELUXE.

square, lunchroom-style platters; crab omelettes and steak and eggs are among the many choices. For lunch and dinner, there is everything from seafood to pasta, steak, pork chops and chicken. This is no-frills dining, but the food is good and your dollar goes a long way. Closed for dinner in January, but breakfast and lunch are served year-round. ~ Route 158, Milepost 16½, Nags Head; 252-441-1600; www.thedunesrestaurant.com, e-mail info@the dunesrestaurant.com. MODERATE.

Locals frequent **Sam & Omie's** year-round, and anything goes in this joint. Looking more like a weather-beaten shack than a restaurant, Sam & Omie's serves up breakfast, lunch and dinner, and some folks stay for all three. A rarely empty bar area extends into the dining room—little more than some wooden tables and booths. Among the more popular menu items: fried-oyster sandwiches and design-your-own omelettes. Closed December through February. ~ Beach Road, Milepost 16½, Nags Head; 252-441-7366, fax 252-473-6624. BUDGET TO MODERATE.

At Sam & Omie's, a casual restaurant, a shirt is required when dining but shoes are not!

Even if you're not staying at the Tranquil House, their restaurant **1587** should top your dining itinerary. If the thought of chargrilled beef tenderloin with herb asiago risotto, carmelized leek porcini cream, grilled onions and glazed carrots whets your appetite, you'll be coming to the right place. (They also offer a full vegetarian menu.) The chefs use only the freshest of ingredients, including herbs grown in the inn's own garden. Located right on the waterfront, the dining room is gorgeous, with softly lit gleaming wood giving way to views of bobbing sailboats. The prices are a little steep, but worth every penny. Dinner only. ~ 405 Queen Elizabeth Street, The Waterfront, Roanoke Island; 252-473-1587; www.tranquilinn.com, e-mail djust1587@aol.com. DELUXE TO ULTRA-DELUXE.

A rare find in this coastal community is the **Weeping Radish Brewery and Restaurant**. Tucked behind pine trees, it's German through and through, with Bavarian meals that include veal sausage, sauerbraten, and a liverwurst and onion sandwich. The microbrewery is on display behind glass, and patrons can enjoy homemade lager with their meal. A courtyard beer garden is a fine place to just have a brew. Closed January and February. ~ Route 64/264, Manteo, Roanoke Island; 252-473-1157, 800-896-5403; www.weepingradish.com, e-mail email@weeping radish.com. BUDGET TO MODERATE.

The **Froggy Dog** on Hatteras Island is one of the most popular places around. This morning-and-night joint has pine walls and low ceilings that make the dining areas somewhat dark, but the back room overlooks the reed-lined sound. The floor is tiled in slate; driftwood adorns the walls. The food is eclectic: seafood egg rolls, fried oysters with artichoke and spinach dip, sand-wiches and pasta, seafood and beef entrées. Considering there's not much else in the way of Avon restaurants, this place is usually hopping. Call for winter hours. ~ Route 12, Avon; 252-995-4106; www.froggydog.com, e-mail info@froggydog.com. MODERATE TO DELUXE.

At **Bubba's** the service is minimal. Just go up to the counter and order from the huge menu posted on the wall. The list leans toward barbecue; pork and chicken platters come with cornbread and two veggies. The drink of choice here is icy draft beer. Closed November through March. ~ Route 12, Frisco, Hatteras Island; 252-995-5421; e-mail bubbasbbq@coastalnet.com. BUDGET.

The **Island Inn Dining Room** has some of the best food on Ocracoke Island. The hushpuppies are sweet and light, not at all greasy, and the side dishes are many and varied, from spinach lasagna to marinated cucumbers to potatoes au gratin. Dinner entrées are long on fresh seafood, and breakfasts are bountiful and slightly Southern (try Gladys' homemade fishcakes). Both the main dining room and the sun-washed porch have the flavor of an intimate country inn. Breakfast and dinner only. ~ 25 Lighthouse Road, Ocracoke Island; 252-928-4351, 877-456-3466; www.ocra cokeislandinn.com/dining, e-mail info@ocracokeislandinn.com. MODERATE TO DELUXE.

Step off the boat and onto the patio of s**MacNally's Raw Bar and Grill**, where you can dine along the waterfront or down a cold beer among old salts. Specializing in local seafood, your dockside table will soon be overflowing with buckets of oysters, clams or crab legs. Thick Angus burgers and "sammiches" are delivered hot off the grill. Casual and friendly, this hip gathering spot serves "food so good, it'll make ya wanna smack yo mama!" The early bird catches the best view at this joint—if you show up at noon or 4 p.m., you'll witness the charter boats bringing in the fresh catch of the day. ~ Route 12, Ocracoke Island; 252-928-9999; www.smacnallys.com. BUDGET TO MODERATE.

Just a hop, skip and a jump from where the Ocracoke ferry departs, the **Fig Tree Deli** is a great place to grab a bite to eat before your trip back to the mainland. Specializing in breakfast (which you can order any time of the day), you'll find hot dishes such as country ham and eggs with fresh buttermilk biscuits or baked goods like nut breads and cinnamon rolls. Not in a hurry? Relax in the butterfly garden as you savor the homemade shrimp salad or a hot pastrami sandwich. Breakfast and lunch only. ~ 1015 Irvin Garrish Highway, Ocracoke Island; 252-928-4554; e-mail caroldav@beachlink.com. BUDGET.

Blue linen napkins adorn the small wooden tables at **Café Atlantic**. This tiny restaurant with vaulted ceilings and cypress walls is full of light and space. From the second floor, diners get a big view of the sound through picture windows. The popular Sunday brunch features sandwiches, soups and salads and a variety of egg dishes at a good value. The dinner menu features the usual seafood and pasta fare. Dinner only, and Sunday brunch. Closed November through February depending on weather. ~ Route 12, Ocracoke Island; 252-928-4861, fax 252-928-3771. MODERATE.

A favorite among locals and visitors, the **Back Porch Restaurant** sounds just like its name. A large porch has been screened and shaded with venetian blinds and green-striped awnings, and set with little tables. Serving dinner only, the Back Porch offers seafood that departs from the mainstream, including crab beignets, sautéed crabmeat and yellowfin tuna. The homemade bread and dessert tortes and tarts are extra good. Closed December to mid-April. ~ Off Route 12, Ocracoke Island; 252-928-6401. MODERATE TO DELUXE.

SHOPPING   In the Corolla Light Village Shops, in between the gaggle of T-shirt and flip-flop shops, are a few interesting boutiques and, surprisingly, several excellent art galleries. **Mustang Sally's** carries primitive-chic men's and women's clothing, handcrafted gifts, and accessories. Closed September to mid-March. ~ Route 12, Corolla; 252-453-4749.

Nearly two dozen stores and boutiques at **Scarborough Faire** handle exclusive gifts, clothing, jewelry, kitchen items and artwork. ~ Duck Road, Duck; 252-261-6224.

At **Greenleaf Gallery**, paintings, prints, ceramics, glass, one-of-a-kind jewelry and sculpture are just a few of the mediums on display in a bright, contemporary showroom. Closed January through March. ~ 1169 Duck Road, Duck; 252-261-2009.

Glenn Eure's Ghost Fleet Gallery showcases the innovative and expansive work of owner Glenn Eure, including acrylic and watercolor paintings, etchings, collagraphs and woodblocks. The gallery also presents special exhibits by guest artists. Closed in the winter. ~ Milepost 10 on Gallery Row, Nags Head; 252-441-6584.

CATCHING AIR

Wanna go fly a kite? **Kitty Hawk Kites** can set you up with a simple, inexpensive flier or something so elaborate you'll think you've bought an airborne BMW. This beach-goods megastore has smaller locations in Corolla, Duck and Manteo, and also in Avon on Hatteras Island and Ocracoke. ~ Route 158, Milepost 13, Nags Head; 252-441-4124, 877-359-8447; www.kittyhawk.com.

The most extensive and diverse collection of artwork on the Outer Banks is at **Seaside Art Gallery**. Among the everchanging offerings are works by Pablo Picasso, Winslow Homer and Mary Cassatt. Local artists are featured too, of course, and there's a large collection of animation cells from Disney and Warner Brothers. Closed Sunday in winter. ~ 2716 South Virginia Dare Trail, Nags Head; 252-441-5418; www.seasideart.com.

The Island Art Gallery and Christmas Shop has many small rooms loaded with floor-to-ceiling art. Paintings and prints, wood sculpture and duck decoys, woven baskets and pottery are among the finds. A special section is devoted to the paintings of P. Buckley Moss, who first displayed her works here. And, of course, as the name implies, there's a year-round selection of Christmas paraphernalia. ~ Route 64, Manteo, Roanoke Island; 252-473-2838; www.outerbankschristmas.com.

The best place for books, **Manteo Booksellers** has a selection on seafaring subjects, as well as tough-to-find volumes on Outer Banks myths and history. ~ 105 Sir Walter Raleigh Street, Roanoke Island; 252-473-1221, 866-473-1222; www.manteo booksellers.com.

If you like those <u>Adirondack chairs lining</u> local porches, stop by **All Decked Out**. Hammocks, rockers and picnic tables are also for sale. All can be shipped to your home. ~ Route 12, Frisco, Hatteras Island; 252-995-4319.

The whimsical creations at **Village Craftsmen** range from fish-shaped pewter spoons to teleidoscopes and bowed psalteries (triangular stringed instruments). A stellar array of North Carolina pottery is also displayed. Closed January to mid-February. ~ 170 Howard Street, off Route 12, Ocracoke Island; 252-928-5541; www.villagecraftsmen.com.

Parlaying local lore into a store, **Teach's Hole** sells books, videos, flags, jewelry and other items relating to Edward Teach, a.k.a. Blackbeard the Pirate, who lived and died on Ocracoke. Closed Sunday, and January and February. ~ Ocracoke Back Road, off Route 12, Ocracoke Island; 252-928-1718; www. teachshole.com.

At **Over the Moon** the offerings include hammock chairs, woodworks, pottery and contemporary crafts. Closed the occasional Sunday and December through March. ~ 64 British Cemetery Road, Ocracoke Island; 252-928-3555.

Books To Be Red has plenty of great beach reads, from modern thrillers and humor to the old classics you've been meaning to catch up on. Closed January and February. ~ 34 School Road, off Route 12, Ocracoke Island; 252-928-3936.

The locally woven hammocks at **Ocracoke Island Hammock** **Company** come in several styles, such as porch swing, hanging chair and deck chair. Call ahead for hours; closed January through March. ~ Across from the Historic British Cemetery; 252-928-4387; www.ocracokehammocks.com.

Arts, crafts and other fare sold around Ocracoke Village celebrate island life. **The Island Ragpicker**, for instance, has pirate tales and books on nature, rag rugs and woodworks by local sculptors. Closed January and February. ~ Route 12, Ocracoke Village; 252-928-7571.

NIGHTLIFE Alternative music and velvet Victorian decor? That's the scene at **Gaslight Saloon**. Upstairs on the catwalk, you can lounge in sinking sofas overlooking the dancefloor. The crowd here is just as diverse as the atmosphere—anyone and everyone seems to find a spot. Closed January to early March. ~ In the Port O' Call Restaurant, Beach Road, Milepost 8, Kill Devil Hills; 252-441-7484.

If you'd like to relax and have a drink, the upstairs, horseshoe-shaped bar at **Kelly's Restaurant** is a fine spot. The party here is low-key; the live music, anything from classic rock and Motown to beach tunes. ~ Route 158, Milepost 10, Kill Devil Hills; 252-441-4116.

Before testing the waters, check for riptides and strong currents (for weather conditions, call 252-473-2138, 800-446-6262; www.outer banks.org).

The much-acclaimed outdoor pageant, *The Lost Colony*, plays most summer nights on Roanoke Island at the **Waterside Theater**. Written by North Carolinian and Pulitzer Prize winner Paul Green, it recounts the arrival and mysterious disappearance of America's first permanent colonists. The production, complete with symphony and elaborate Elizabethan costumes, began in 1937 and has been playing to full houses every summer since. ~ Route 64/264, Fort Raleigh National Historic Site, Roanoke Island; 252-473-3414; www.thelostcolony.org.

It's beer and wine only on Hatteras Island, and only where there's food served. However, you can show up at **Mad Crabber** for a game of pool, or to watch a game on the big-screen TV. Closed in the off-season. ~ Route 12, Avon; 252-995-5959.

Nightlife on Ocracoke Island generally means finding a worn wood barstool, ordering a brew, and scanning for local color. Your best hope of finding the latter is at **Howard's Pub**, a year-round pizza, steak and burger joint and raw bar that even has cable TV (translation: televised sports). ~ Route 12, Ocracoke Island; 252-928-4441.

Otherwise, Ocracoke has **The Jolly Roger**, a weathered wood cottage on the harbor where bands play while the sun sinks beneath the water. Closed in the off-season. ~ Ocracoke Village; 252-928-3703.

BEACHES & PARKS As desperately as people try to define and permanently fix the shape of a beach, they cannot on the Outer Banks. What is today a wide, loosely packed swath of sand will tomorrow be narrow and hard packed—thanks to perpetual, ever-shifting winds and currents and intense tides.

Those same forces make swimming here a bit risky at times—and cold (in summer, the water temperature averages in the mid- to high-70s), though with proper precautions you can enjoy the surf of your life. Dangerous seas are marked with a red flag, so if you see one don't go swimming. To be completely safe, especially if you have small children, swim only at beaches where there are lifeguards (in-season only), located all along the northern Banks.

NORTHERN BANKS BEACHES The shores at Corolla are wide and windy. If you have a four-wheel-drive vehicle, you can head north toward Virginia until you find a truly deserted spot. South of Corolla, there's not much public parking until **Kitty Hawk**, where all the action starts and continues south nearly 20 miles through **Kill Devil Hills** and **Nags Head**. Cedar-shingled cottages crowd against the dunes, and so do eateries and little shops. In the height of summer, sun worshipers lay towel-to-towel, and from the air the dunes look bearded with oiled bodies. The sand is as tan as the bodies, and usually deep and finely grained, so you sink in up to your ankles. It's narrowest on the north end of Kill Devil Hills, where the water threatens the feet of the cottages. Facilities include plenty of eateries and convenience stores in the area and lifeguards stationed throughout the beaches from Corolla down to Nags Head. Swimming is good on calmer days. King mackerel has been caught off the Outer Banks Pier in Nags Head, also a prime place for snagging flounder and red drums. From the beach you might get a bluefish or even spotted sea trout. ~ Corolla beaches are just north of the village, which has a public parking lot on Corolla Village Road. The beaches at Kitty Hawk, Kill Devil Hills and Nags Head are off the aptly named Beach Road, which parallels Route 12. Regional beach access signs point the way to small parking lots near the dunes.

JOCKEY'S RIDGE STATE PARK When you first see this place along Roanoke Sound, you think a chunk of the Mojave Desert landed at Nags Head. Actually it's just a sand dune, albeit the highest in the eastern United States, 30 million tons of sugar-fine grains rearing up 80 to 100 feet, depending on wind speed and direction. Your first urge is to climb it. Go ahead—everyone else does. Go barefoot or wear sturdy shoes (and plan to get lots of sand in them). Ski goggles aren't a bad idea, though sunglasses will do fine. Back near the bottom, a little museum provides sand dune trivia. From the museum, a boardwalk wends through small dunes marbled with bayberry and southern wax myrtle and live oaks. Wheelchair travelers can take the boardwalk to the end for a big view of the big dune and the rest of the 426-acre park. Look down at the sand here and you might see tracks of park animals such as the gray fox or six-lined race runner lizard. Facilities here include a park office, a museum, an auditorium, restrooms, picnic tables, two hiking trails and restaurants nearby. You can swim on the sound side but there are no lifeguards. This is an excellent place for hang gliding and sandboarding. These activities are allowed in designated areas and only with a permit, available from park office. (Sandboarding is only allowed October 1 through March 31.) ~ Off Route 158 at Milepost 12 in Nags Head; 252-441-7132; www.jockeysridgestatepark.com.

Love to snowboard but hate the cold? Try the warm-weather equivalent: sand-boarding, which is allowed at Jockey's Ridge State Park from October 1 through March 31 (permit required).

COQUINA BEACH A broad shell-strewn corridor of whitish brown sand at the south end of Bodie Island, Coquina is the northernmost beach within Cape Hatteras National Seashore. Families like it here; you'll see lots of tots toting buckets. They sit hopefully at the surf, hoping to pluck a coquina before the teeny mollusk digs back into the wet sand. Things get crowded in summer, so stake your towel spot early. Facilities include restrooms, a bathhouse and picnic tables. Stores, restaurants and a marina are close by. Swimming is usually good. There is good surf fishing for whiting, pompano, small bluefish and flounder. ~ Off Route 12, about five miles south of Whalebone Junction; 252-473-2111, fax 252-473-2595.

▲ There are 120 tent and RV sites (no hookups) just south of Coquina at Oregon Inlet, open only in summer; facilities include cold-water showers, restrooms, picnic tables and grills and are on a first-come, first-served basis; $20 per night.

HATTERAS ISLAND BEACHES To some beachgoers, Hatteras is the Outer Banks beach—58 miles of little but sand and sea oats and dunes. Only seven villages (including one named Waves) interrupt the wilderness look created here by the **Pea Island National Wildlife Refuge** and **Cape Hatteras National Seashore**, which blanket most of the island. Hatteras is so skinny that the beach tends to be narrow and the sand damp and hard-packed in most spots. You can drive on the beach in designated places, but only with four-wheel drive. **Haulover Day-use Area**, three miles south of Avon on the sound-side, has major windsurfing action. Go at sunset and watch the orange globe light up the surfers' sails. Farther south, **Cape Hatteras** is also big with windsurfers and surfers, and anyone who likes to bask beneath the famous Cape Hatteras Lighthouse. Facilities include the Pea Island National Wildlife Refuge Headquarters, located on Route 12 north of Rodanthe; Cape Hatteras National Seashore Visitors Center in Buxton. Swimming is good on calm days. Three fishing piers offer good opportunities for bluefish, flounder, pompano, trout and croakers. ~ All facilities are accessed by Route 12, which runs the length of Hatteras Island and offers numerous beachfront parking areas; 252-473-2111, fax 252-473-2595.

▲ More than 329 tent and RV sites are available Memorial Day through Labor Day at campgrounds in Frisco and Cape Point. Cold-water showers, restrooms, picnic tables and grills are at each site and are on a first-come, first-served basis; $20 per night.

OCRACOKE ISLAND BEACHES 🏃 🏖 🚣 Who couldn't love a beach so remote you can only get there by boat? Even in the full heat of summer when ferries discharge hundreds of cars, there is always a silent stretch of sand to be had. **Cape Hatteras National Seashore** covers all 14 miles of Ocracoke, offering several parking areas within steps of the sand. The beaches are some of the Outer Banks' widest, thanks to the way the island angles inland, enjoying some protection from wind and waves and therefore erosion. Shelling is good, and so is staring at miles of unencumbered coast. Facilities include Cape Hatteras National Seashore Visitors Center in Ocracoke Village at the island's south end and nature trails. Swimming is good most everywhere, but especially near Ocracoke Village. Fishing is best close to the inlets on either end of the island; try for sea mullet, bluefish, pompano, red drum and croakers. ~ Route 12 runs the length of Ocracoke beaches; 252-473-2111, fax 252-473-2595.

▲ Reservations required for the 136 tent and RV sites, complete with restrooms, cold-water showers and grills; open Memorial Day through Labor Day; $20 per night; 252-473-2111.

▼▼▼▼▼▼▼▼▼▼▼▼

Albemarle Region

Only water—specifically the Currituck and Albemarle Sounds—separates the Outer Banks from the Albemarle Region. Yet the two places couldn't be more different, the beach with its pounding surf and raw bar scene, the Albemarle with its quiet country towns and folks resting on front porch rockers. Hound dogs rule the back roads, and sausage and grits rule the breakfast menu.

The peninsulas that edge out into the sounds are blanketed with pine woods where deer and bear roam. In some places, the distance between country stores is more than an hour. The only radio station plays John Denver. When you stop for gas, the attendant admonishes you to watch out for the deer and bear crossing the road. The next sign you see says "Red Wolf Crossing," and you wonder why he didn't mention the wolves.

SIGHTS

The northeast corner of North Carolina's Coastal Plain, the Albemarle Region begins at Virginia and heads south to the Pamlico River, taking in more than a dozen counties but only a handful

A Coastal Forest Cruise

East and south of Creswell, coastal forest goes on for hours. Occasionally there are signs of human life, outposts with names like Stumpy Point, Frying Pan Landing and Leechville. A trio of counties—Tyrrell, Dare and Hyde—cover this vast peninsula poking into the Albemarle and Pamlico sounds.

AROUND THE BIG PENINSULA   Take the long way around the peninsula, east from Creswell on **Route 64** and then south on **Route 264**. You'll be on lonely, two-lane roads that pass through sawgrass seas and pancake-flat farmlands studded with Colonial and antebellum farmhouses.

BATH   Stay on Route 264 and eventually you'll be heading west toward the place called Bath. It's off Route 92 and the Pamlico River, but more importantly it's the oldest town in North Carolina. When you arrive, you're not quite sure you're there, as there's nothing to denote so important a place save for some historical markers tucked among the trees and tidy clapboard homes. One of the markers on **Main Street** commemorates the James Adams Floating Theatre, which brought show biz to these coastal towns between 1913 and 1941. Bath was founded in 1705 with 12 homes and nearly 50 people. Over the centuries it saw wars with Indians, pirates and Union soldiers, yellow fever outbreaks

of cities. The biggest, **Elizabeth City**, is home to about 17,230 people. It curves around the Pasquotank River, which feeds into Albemarle Sound and then the ocean, a perfect locale for the country's largest Coast Guard station. ~ Junction of Routes 17 and 158.

Yachters, sailboaters and other recreational boaters also love Elizabeth City because it's at the end of the Dismal Swamp Canal, a scenic shortcut for anyone traveling the Intracoastal Waterway. None would dream of cruising past the city, lest they miss the **Rose Buddies**. Since the 1980s, a group of local seniors have been giving boats a big greeting down at **Mariners Docks**. ~ Water Street. When the boats arrive, the Buddies tool up on their golf carts, present each boater with a red rosebud, and lay out a spread of wine and cheese. The most famous Rose Buddy, Fred Fearing, got his golf cart from "Today Show" weatherman Willard Scott. The self-appointed regional historian was profiled by Scott, who then gave him the cart.

Downtown Elizabeth City is pleasant enough. Old, red-brick buildings line the streets, and shipbuilding yards pepper the water-

and even drought—odd, considering there's water at nearly every turn. The shore of Bath Creek squiggles along Main Street. The **Historic Bath Visitors Center** can provide maps for walking around town. To see everything, you'll need a couple of hours. Closed Sunday from November through March. ~ 207 Carteret Street; 252-923-3971, fax 252-293-0174; www.bath.nchistoricalsites.org, e-mail bath@ncmail.net. Make sure you look inside **St. Thomas Episcopal Church**—built in 1734, it's the oldest church in the state. The prim building nestled beneath big cedar trees is made of brick shipped from England. The walls are two feet thick, the floors are battered clay. The Bible encased in glass near the entrance is a 1704 edition, donated in 1740 by King George II. ~ Craven Street.

BELHAVEN   Five miles west of Leechville, taken the Route 99 turnoff toward Belhaven. Two miles later you'll arrive in Belhaven, a piece of locked-in-time South on the Pungo River. It's quiet and quirky (folks swattin' flies and watching soap operas in the diner) around town. Don't miss it!

GOOSE CREEK STATE PARK   From Bath, head west on Route 92 about eight miles to Goose Creek State Park (page 302). Before you turn off, though, pick up lunch from one of the local grocers. The pine-shaded tables are perfect for a picnic, and afterward you can hike through the forest, take a swim, or explore the environmental education center.

front. For a look back at the city's seafaring history, stop by the small but engaging **Museum of the Albemarle.** You can meander through wide corridors and see artifacts from early Colonial days, including a crude dugout canoe, farm tools and household items. There are also blueprints and photos of the first "moth" boat, designed in Elizabeth City by Captain Joel Van Sant in 1929. Closed Monday. ~ 1116 Route 17 South, just south of downtown, Elizabeth City; 252-335-1453; www.museumofthe albemarle.com/moa, e-mail moa@ncmail.net.

Delve even farther back in time south of Elizabeth City. North Carolina's oldest brick house, the **Newbold-White House,** was built in 1730 by Abraham Sanders. It's on the Perquimans River, two stories made of brick—unusual, since most homes back then were all wood. Inside, the walls are bathed in original pine, and leaded casement windows let in sunlight and crosswinds. Closed Monday and Thanksgiving through February. Admission. ~ 151 Newbold-White Road, off Route 17, Hertford; 252-426-7567, fax 252-426-3538; www.newboldwhitehouse.com, e-mail nbwh@ inteliport.com.

South of Hertford on Route 17, **Edenton** is the quintessential small port town, with several blocks of Colonial-style clapboard crisply painted and lawns and gardens well-tended, and streets shaded by the long arms of magnolias and pecan trees. On the cusp of the Chowan River, Edenton has been around since 1722, though barely 5400 people call it home. Many of the town's residents live in and take great care of homes built before the Civil War and now on the National Register of Historic Places.

Before a walk around town, stop by the **Historic Edenton Visitors Center** for information and brochures on local sights. If you'd care to take a guided tour of the historic homes and buildings, the center can arrange it. ~ 108 North Broad Street, Edenton; 252-482-2637, fax 252-482-3499; www.edenton.nchistoric sites.org, e-mail edentonshs@inteliport.com.

HIDDEN ▶

One of the area's most striking old homes lies southwest of Edenton near the village of Windsor. **Hope Plantation** was built in 1803 by David Stone, who served as North Carolina governor and also United States Senator. Fashioned with both Georgian and Federal accoutrements, the big, two-story manor is meticulously furnished to look as it did when Stone and his family lived here. In the beautiful library, Stone kept more than 1400 books, then one of the state's largest private collections. The plantation tour starts in the Roanoke-Chowan Heritage Center, which houses a gallery, library and gift shop. Closed late December to January 2. Admission. ~ Route 308, three miles west of Route 13; 252-794-3140; www.hopeplantation.org, e-mail hopeplanta tion@coastalnet.com.

HIDDEN ▶

Heading back east toward the eye-blink town of **Creswell**, you'll encounter another plantation, less lavish but historically intriguing and quite hidden. **Somerset Place** was one of the biggest, most productive plantations of the antebellum South. Prosperous planter Josiah Collins III built the mansion in the 1830s, owned over 300 slaves and put them to work harvesting rice, wheat and corn. The main house is elegant and well-maintained,

---

WHAT'S IN A NAME?

Hushpuppies—a.k.a. corn dodgers—are a staple of Southern cooking and are usually served with fried fish. The delicious (though artery-clogging) puppies consist of deep-fried nuggets of cornbread. The legend of their unusual moniker dates back to the Civil War. The story goes that Southerners, preparing their dinner around the campfire, found a way to calm their barking dogs and prevent discovery by Yankee soldiers: they would toss the animals bits of the cornbread cakes and warn, "Hush, puppies."

but the outbuildings, including a reconstructed slave cabin, kitchen, hospital, icehouse, smokehouse and salthouse, paint the most poignant picture of life in the 1800s. Closed Monday from November through March. ~ Off Route 64, seven miles south of Creswell; 252-797-4560; e-mail somerset@ncmail.net.

Elizabeth City Bed and Breakfast sits on a quiet, tree-lined corner one block from Main Street. Both buildings here date to 1847 and have been meticulously restored. A brick courtyard with a fish pond and gazebo is a peaceful spot for reading or sipping iced tea. There are only five guest rooms, and they get booked fast, so call way ahead for reservations. ~ 108 East Fearing Street, Elizabeth City; 252-338-2177; e-mail ecitybb@adelphia.net. MODERATE.

LODGING

Otherwise, the options for lodging in Elizabeth City are slim. If you're just passing through, you might try the **Hampton Inn**, whose 101 rooms are furnished in standard motel-chain blandness, but they're clean and comfortable, and there's an outdoor pool. ~ 402 Halstead Boulevard, Elizabeth City; 252-333-1800, fax 252-333-1801. MODERATE.

A lovely place to spend the night is **Lords Proprietors' Inn**. Three large houses, including a handsome Victorian with a charming wraparound porch, are sprinkled among these shady one and a half acres. Each building possesses an antique-filled parlor, and the 16 guest rooms and two suites are commodious and pleasingly furnished with an eye for detail. Telephones, TVs and VCRs are among the amenities. Breakfast is served every day; dinner is served Tuesday through Saturday. ~ 300 North Broad Street, Edenton; 252-482-3641, 800-348-8933, fax 252-482-2432; www.eden toninn.com, e-mail stay@edentoninn.com. ULTRA-DELUXE.

Surrounded by lush green spruce trees and adorned with white wood trim, the **Edenton Rose** brims with quintessential Southern charm. Housed in a 1912 Victorian, this delightful inn offers four rooms, each with queen-size beds, hardwood floors and white lace curtains. Snag Olivia's Garden Room if you can—three large windows, wicker chairs and an appealing yellow flowered quilt make it the brightest and most comfortable in the house. Two fireplaces in the living room and parlor create cozy niches where you can enjoy your morning cappuccino and home-baked bread and muffins. Take a stroll by night to the waterfront—a mere three blocks away. ~ 204 West Queen Street, Edenton; 252-482-1411; www.edentonrose.com, e-mail edenton rose@simflex.com. MODERATE.

A favorite among birders, the **Trestle House Inn**, the town's only waterfront inn, is adjacent to Chris Lake Wildlife Refuge, a rest stop for migratory birds. A wooden deck serves as a lookout over the lake. The five rooms are named for the birds commonly seen here: heron, mallard, osprey, cormorant and egret. Each room is tastefully decorated with quilts, oriental rugs and watercolors. By canoe (available for rent) you can paddle from the inn to Albemarle Sound. A full gourmet breakfast is served. ~ 632 Soundside Road, off Route 32, south of downtown Edenton; 252-482-2282, 800-645-8466; www.trestlehouseinn.com, e-mail peter@trestlehouseinn.com. MODERATE TO DELUXE.

DINING　At the tip of the Pasquotank River, **Groupers Waterfront Restaurant** is a town favorite. The place is spacious, with high ceilings, wood floors, and large windows facing the river. An expansive deck out back provides a view of the boat docks. Each dish is prepared by the chef/owner, who specializes in pasta and seafood. ~ 400 South Water Street, Elizabeth City; 252-331-2431. MODERATE TO DELUXE.

Open for breakfast, lunch and dinner, **The Colonial** is an Elizabeth City landmark that is always filled with locals who know each other. What they most enjoy are the breakfasts—eggs, hash browns, grits, bacon and most particularly the biscuits, which are split down the middle and toasted on the grill. And breakfast is a bargain at less than $3.50. For lunch and dinner, you can eat things like flounder, fresh oysters and meatloaf. Closed Sunday. ~ 418 East Colonial Avenue, Elizabeth City; 252-335-0212. BUDGET.

Fresh seafood, usually fried or baked, are the mainstays of the **Marina Restaurant,** but deep South dishes like ham and liver and onions are why locals have been coming here for years. The diningroom windows offer wide views of the Pasquotank River sprinkled with sailboats. During warm weather you can eat out on the deck. No lunch on Saturday. Closed Monday. ~ Camden Causeway, Route 158 East, Elizabeth City; 252-335-7307. MODERATE.

SHOPPING　The Albemarle Region is not a shopper's haven, though there are always ways to spend your money.

Local artisans display their works at the **Pasquotank Arts Council Gallery.** Watercolor and oil paintings reflect the region's rich seafaring past, and the gallery also has an array of pottery, jewelry and wood sculpture. Closed Sunday. ~ 609 East Main Street, Elizabeth City; 252-338-6455.

For reads ranging from pirate lore to airplane page-turners, **Page After Page** will have it, or do their best to get it for you. Closed Sunday. ~ 111 South Water Street, Elizabeth City; 252-335-7243.

In a recycled, turn-of-the-twentieth-century mill, **Waterworks** has a cache of boutiques selling everything from designer clothing and antiques to objets d'art and gourmet coffee. ~ 400 South Water Street, Elizabeth City.

In Edenton, you can browse antique shops and boutiques along **Broad Street** and the blocks surrounding it.

All the action's in Elizabeth City, but don't expect much.   **NIGHTLIFE**

Levels usually has a good party crowd at night. There's a large bar and two wide-screen TVs, karaoke, deejays and sometimes live music. When the bands aren't playing, the dancefloor is used for dart games. ~ 400 East Colonial Avenue, Elizabeth City; 252-338-5288.

Down at the docks, **Groupers Waterfront Restaurant** is a fine spot for a drink. Rock and blues bands occasionally play out back on the deck along the river on Friday and Saturday nights. ~ 400 South Water Street, Elizabeth City; 252-331-2431.

MERCHANTS MILLPOND STATE PARK 🚶 🛶 🚤 🎣 Perched   **PARKS**
at the northeastern head of North Carolina is this enormous vault
of forest, marsh and creeks—just over 3000 acres. For wildlife   ◄ *HIDDEN*
and waterfowl, it is a safe haven. For the human visitor, the thick
swamp seems an eerie, endless maze. Cypress trees, laden with
Spanish moss, grow out of the quagmire, and lilies waft upon the
murky water. Tree frogs, snapping turtles and snakes are abundant, as are as many as 200 species of birds. Whether you intend
to fish, hike, canoe or picnic, bring mosquito and tick repellent.
Facilities include a park office, a boat ramp, picnic tables, canoe
rentals, hiking trails and restrooms. Fishing is great for largemouth bass and bluegill. ~ The park's main entrance is along
Route 158 about five miles west of Sunbury; 252-357-1191, fax
252-357-0149.

▲ Twenty sites are available at the family campground; $15
per night in season. There are also five primitive, hike-in sites; $9
per night, and seven primitive canoe-in sites; $9 per night.

THE GREAT DISMAL SWAMP 🛶 🚤 🎣 This National
Wildlife Refuge spreads across more than 100,000 acres of wetlands extending from northeastern North Carolina to southeastern Virginia. A virtual animal kingdom, it harbors white-tailed deer and mink, foxes and black bears, and hundreds of bird species. Officially designated as a federal refuge in 1974, the swamp has been recognized as a valuable resource since 1763. In 1784, then-governor of Virginia, Patrick Henry, commissioned a 22-mile-long canal to be dug through the area, creating a trade route between Virginia and North Carolina. The canal is now popular with boaters, who enjoy its wilderness scenery. Facilities include boat docks, picnic areas and restrooms. Fishing is good in Lake Drummond in Virginia. Call for hours. ~ The visitors center is on Route 17, 18 miles north of Elizabeth City; 252-771-8333.

> George Washington invested in a portion of the Great Dismal Swamp to begin a logging business.

PETTIGREW STATE PARK 🚶 🚴 🏕 🛶 🚤 🎣 Most of   ◄ *HIDDEN*
this 19,000-acre park is underwater. All 25 square miles of Lake

Phelps lie within Pettigrew, offering exceptional fishing, sailing and even waterskiing. The shoreline is shrouded in bald cypress and sweet gum forest, and bogs and swamps heading out to Pungo and Alligator lakes. Next door is Somerset Place, a restored antebellum plantation run by the North Carolina State Department of History that draws visitors to these swampy netherlands. Facilities include boat ramps, piers, hiking trails, a biking trail, a picnic area, a playing field and restrooms. Fishing is excellent for largemouth bass (particularly during spring and fall), yellow perch (also called raccoon perch) and sunfish. ~ Located off Route 64, about seven miles south of Creswell; 252-797-4475, fax 252-797-7405.

▲ There are 13 sites for tent and RVs, with a central bathhouse that has hot water (except in winter); fees range from $8 to $15 per night, depending on the season. A group campground is available for a minimum of $9 per night.

HIDDEN ▶ **GOOSE CREEK STATE PARK** 🏃 ⛵ 🚤 🛥️ Running along the edges of Pamlico River and Goose Creek, the park is a subtle skein of brackish marshes, pine forest and sawgrass, and bald cypress and live oaks hung with moss. Boardwalks and boat ramps are the avenues for observing this watery cosmos. Bring mosquito repellent, even in the winter. A slice of beach along the river is good for sunning and swimming. Facilities include a park office, an environmental education center with interactive exhibits, picnic tables, restrooms, boat ramps and hiking trails. Groceries are nearby. Swimming is good in designated areas. Fishing's good in the creek and river for largemouth and striped bass, croaker and bluegill. ~ Off Routes 264 and 92, between Washington and Bath; 252-923-2191, fax 252-923-0052.

▲ Twelve primitive sites accommodate tents; $9 per night and a group campground available for a minimum of $9 per night.

▼▼▼▼▼▼▼▼▼▼▼▼▼

Neuse River Region

The south end of the Albemarle Sound meets up with the Pamlico Sound, which takes a great big gulp of water between the Coastal Plain and the southern Outer Banks. The Pamlico is like a small sea, flourishing with shrimp and fish and crabs and other good things for one's dinner table, and fed by rivers that flow in from the Piedmont. The Neuse is one of the those rivers.

SIGHTS   Several hundred years ago, American Indians built a settlement right where the Neuse and Trent rivers join before heading down to Pamlico Sound. They called it Chattawka, meaning "where the fish are." In 1710, German and Swiss colonists came poking around the area, found the settlement, and liked the idea of all those fish. They set up their own village and named it **New Bern**, after Bern, Switzerland.

New Berners were determined to have a sparkling, successful town. They built handsome homes along the shoreline, and began culling local lumber, tar and turpentine to load onto ships headed for England.

The town-altering event came in 1770, when Royal Governor William Tryon opened a 19-room "palace" and moved in, making New Bern the colony's capital. Various governors lived in Tryon Palace until 1794, when Raleigh was made the capital. Four years later, the palace burned. For 161 years, New Bern had no palace, not until 1959, when it reopened as a public attraction.

These days, **Tryon Palace** attracts thousands of visitors to New Bern each year. It is furnished with rare 18th-century American and English decorative arts, reflective of colonial America just before the Revolutionary War. Admission. ~ 600 block of Pollock Street, New Bern; 252-514-4900, 800-767-1560, fax 252-514-4876; www.tryonpalace.org, e-mail info@ tryonpalace.org.

This is how Maude Moore Latham hoped it would be. In 1944, the New Bern native gave much of her fortune to bring back Tryon Palace. Before it could be rebuilt, though, the state had to get back the land, which by then had more than 50 buildings. It took eight years before all the landowners could be persuaded (some more easily than others) and the land razed, and another seven for the palace to be built and opened as a state historic site.

In 1749, the New Bern colony's first printing press cranked up and two years later published their first newspaper.

When you first see the palace's proper brick facade, it seems as if it's been there for centuries. Secured at the end of a tunnel of big Darlington oaks, behind a pair of 1741 English castle gates, it does indeed sit upon its original foundation and retains most of its west wing. It is filled with early English art and costly antiques and ringed with formal English parterre gardens and their fountains.

But one thing Tryon Palace is not is palatial. Rather, it is orderly and symmetrical, precisely according to its Georgian architectural style. Each half of the chimneyed brick facade is identical to the other half. Every plaster molding has a match, every doorway a counterpart.

The tour of the palace, conducted by broad, buxom women in big Colonial dresses, takes about an hour. Afterward, you can wander through the luscious gardens of precisely pruned holly and bold plantings of flowers. The most famous and photographed is the Maude Moore Latham Memorial Garden, a scrollwork of dazzling flora decorated with statuary.

New Bern has several other historic sites and plenty of historic Georgian and Federal homes, some dating to the late 1700s, that are lovely to look at. The 1790 **Attmore-Oliver House** showcases exquisite eighteenth- and nineteenth-century furniture, as well as (could it be possible?) Civil War artifacts. Closed Sunday and Monday, and mid-December through March. ~ 510 Pollock Street, New Bern; 252-638-8558; e-mail nbhistoricalsoc@coastalnet.com.

Nearby is the **Dixon-Stevenson House**, which dates from the early 1800s and is furnished with antiques from the period. ~ 619 Pollock Street, New Bern. The **John Wright Stanly House** was built even earlier, around 1783, and is furnished accordingly; its garden is also straight out of the eighteenth century. ~ 307 George Street, New Bern.

It's easy to walk all of New Bern's sights, enjoying eateries and shops along the way. One place to pause is at the corner of **Pollock and Middle streets**, where a historical marker recalls the beverage, known as Brad's Drink, created in the building's basement back in 1898. Today the drink is known as Pepsi-Cola. There are still pockets in this region where you won't find Coca-Cola; these are loyal folks.

The folks at **New Bern/Craven County Convention and Visitors Bureau** have excellent walking tours and are eager to provide tips and information. ~ 203 South Front Street, New Bern; 252-637-9400, 800-437-5767, fax 252-637-0250; www.visit newbern.com, e-mail info@visitnewbern.com.

If you head east from New Bern you can travel solitary back roads and see a slice of coastal life that hasn't changed much this century. Start east on Route 55, then head south on Route 1005 toward Arapahoe, delving through roadsides thronged with slash pines and low bush, weathered old farmhouses selling collard greens, and brambly fields of cotton. In the fall picking season, the white puffs come loose from their bushes and the roads are sprinkled with cotton balls. The road holds such emptiness that there seems no possibility of anything at its end. Yet Route

HIDDEN ▶

1005 eventually rejoins Route 55, which dead ends at **Oriental**.

A mite-size village whose shores are decorated with shrimp boats and sailboats, Oriental sits where the Neuse River flows into Pamlico Sound. There's not much action around town, just loads of seafood pouring in nearly every day down at the docks. Restaurants here serve some of the freshest-tasting sea fare on the North Carolina coast, and even the local convenience store offers fresh fish and shrimp. It's no surprise, then, that Oriental is a favorite lunch and dinner stopover for boaters cruising the Intracoastal Waterway.

From Oriental, head west to Route 306, then south to Minnesott Beach. Here, a free twenty-minute ferry will take you across the Neuse River to Cherry Branch. Keep going south on

Route 306 until Route 101, then head southeast to the lovely port town of **Beaufort**.

Founded in 1709, Beaufort has a rich seafaring past and a successful modern story. In recent years it has been "found" by tourists, which is no surprise, considering the town has much to offer. The Beaufort scene, which centers around Front Street, is awash with the salty smell of the harbor. Its orderly little harborfront is lined on one side with sailboats and on the other with pretty brick and painted clapboard storefronts and colorful awnings. Cafés, seafood houses and shops displaying clever gifts and smart attire draw strollers from early morning till evening year-round. A few roads angle off the waterfront, where neighborhoods are filled with big rambling homes and even bigger trees.

> Lest you be ridiculed, be sure to say BO-fort when referring to the North Carolina town; BEW-fort is in South Carolina.

Before you start walking, stop by the **Beaufort Historical Association** for maps and information. The association also offers regular guided bus tours of town from April through October. Closed Sunday. ~ 130 Turner Street, Beaufort; 252-728-5225, 800-575-7483; www.historicbeaufort.com.

The association will first direct you to the **North Carolina Maritime Museum** for a look at the state's seafaring side. This roomy space has well-done exhibits on whaling and oystering, and naturally all kinds of boating, taking you from the time of oars to outboards. A 1910 "deadrise sail" skiff, also called a spritsail skiff and popular around the turn of the twentieth century, is here, and there's a 1958 Silver Clipper. Don't miss the terrific maritime reference library. ~ 315 Front Street, Beaufort; 252-728-7317; e-mail maritime@ncmail.net.

Many of Beaufort's earliest residents now reside at the **Old Burying Ground** in graves facing east, supposedly so they faced the morning sun when they rose for judgment. The headstones date to 1756, though there are thought to be older graves. A marked 1850 grave holds what remains of Captain Otway Burns, a naval hero in the War of 1812. Maps of the Old Burying Ground are available at the Beaufort Historical Association. ~ On Ann Street between Turner and Craven streets, Beaufort.

From Beaufort, it's 38 miles north along Routes 70 and 12 to **Cedar Island**. If it weren't for the ferry from Cedar Island to Ocracoke Island, few folks would find their way up here—and not too many actually do. For as Route 70 squiggles through the eye-blink villages of Otway and Williston and Stacy, the landscape courses with water and silky-looking seagrasses. There are patches of coastal woods, loblolly pines and live oaks dripping with Spanish moss, and there are tin-roofed homes tucked here and there.

West of Beaufort the scenery couldn't be any more different. Across the Beaufort Inlet is **Morehead City**, whose main drag,

Route 70, rumbles with the noise of gaseous traffic. Side streets do hold some pleasant old neighborhoods, and folks in Beaufort often drive "across the bridge" to dine in Morehead City.

Morehead City is also the gateway to the **Bogue Banks,** a 30-mile-long barrier island that calls itself "The Crystal Coast" and also the "southern Outer Banks" but in no way resembles either, having been for the most part heavily developed—and not in an attractive way. Route 58 runs the length of the banks. The easternmost town, **Atlantic Beach,** is chock-a-block with cheesy motels, nondescript condos, putt-putt golf courses, and multilevel glass T-shirt shops. The beach is thin and grayish. Farther west, things improve a little in **Emerald Isle,** where folks with money have bought big attractive homes in manicured developments.

HIDDEN ►

West of Emerald Isle, Route 58 veers across Bogue Sound to the mainland. Take a south turn onto Route 24 and stop in **Swansboro.** A teeny version of Beaufort, Swansboro curves along Bogue Sound, its streets angling up from the water and bordered by juniper and magnolia trees. Antique shops and art galleries look out from weathered clapboard buildings, and the adjacent neighborhood is sprinkled with shingled wood cottages.

LODGING

On a tree-lined street near Tryon Palace, **The Aerie Inn Bed & Breakfast** is distinguished by a bay window and red shutters. This handsome bed and breakfast has a formal parlor feel throughout. Seven rooms are furnished in contemporary style with reproduction and original antiques. Country breakfasts are included. ~ 509 Pollock Street, New Bern; 252-636-5553, 800-849-5553, fax 252-514-2157; www.aerieinn.com, e-mail aerieinn@aol.com. MODERATE TO DELUXE.

Harmony House Inn invites with a wide front porch lined with rocking chairs and a warm, prettily lit parlor. All seven guest rooms are big, offering separate sitting areas, and are tastefully appointed with antiques and reproductions made by local craftspeople. Private baths, ceiling fans, air conditioning and cable TV are standard. There are also three luxuriant suites named to honor the original owners. The Eliza Ellis room boasts a heart-shaped jacuzzi for two and the Benjamin Ellis features twin fireplaces and a queen canopy bed. Breakfast might feature stuffed french toast with homemade blueberry syrup, corn frittata or peach upside down french toast and egg and cheese casseroles. Wine is served in the evenings. ~ 215 Pollock Street, New Bern; phone/fax 252-636-3810, 800-636-3113; www.harmonyhouseinn.com, e-mail stay@harmonyhouseinn.com. MODERATE TO DELUXE.

A pair of handsome brick buildings right on the waterfront, the **Sheraton Grand New Bern** enjoys the city's premier location and accommodations. Choose from traditional hotel rooms in the main building or suites with whirlpool tubs in the newer, Georgian-style inn. All the rooms are plush, decorated in hunter green and cranberry tones, and look straight across the Neuse River. A brick promenade rambles along the river, and there's also a swimming pool and restaurant here. Tryon Palace is but a short and scenic walk. ~ 100 Middle Street, New Bern; 252-638-3585, 800-326-3745, fax 252-638-8112; www.sheratonnewbern.com. MODERATE TO ULTRA-DELUXE.

One of the prettiest buildings along Beaufort's waterfront belongs to **The Cedars**. Built in 1768, the stately, crisp white manse once belonged to Rhode Islander William Borden, who hosted visiting sea captains. Now the home, together with a newer building next door, welcomes travelers with plush, immaculate rooms, all different and ornamented with such pleasantries as lace draperies, eyelet bedspreads and clawfoot tubs. Popular with honeymooners are the four suites and attached cottage, complete with a sitting room, king-size canopy bed and whirlpool tub. All guests are treated to a full breakfast that often features banana walnut pancakes, lemon french toast, country ham, freshly baked biscuits and fresh fruit. ~ 305 Front Street, Beaufort; 252-728-7036, fax 252-728-1685; www.cedarsinn.com. DELUXE TO ULTRA-DELUXE.

An unmarked grave along Craven Street in Beaufort is said to contain a girl in a rum keg.

For simpler accommodations, check out the **Langdon House**, located in a neighborhood across from a church. Friendly owner Jimm Prest has restored his two-story 1730s house and offers four guest rooms with basic furnishings. All are downstairs and have private baths, and are done in masculine maritime style. Full breakfast and taxes are included in the upper-level prices. ~ 135 Craven Street, Beaufort; 252-728-5499; www.langdonhouse.com, e-mail inn keeper@coastalnet.com. MODERATE TO DELUXE.

The **Inlet Inn**, on the east end of the waterfront, has 35 spacious rooms done in heavy woods and pale walls and six have fireplaces. French doors open onto balconies overlooking the water or onto a courtyard area. The Inlet Inn is ideal for those who prefer lodge-style hostelries over more intimate bed-and-breakfast accommodations, though a continental breakfast is included here. ~ 601 Front Street, Beaufort; 252-728-3600, fax 252-728-5833; www.inlet-inn.com. DELUXE.

The **Henderson House Restaurant** in a lovely, restored New Bern residence, features four dining rooms, three with fireplaces, that serve a traditionally elegant menu with dishes such as roast duck with plum sauce, shrimp amandine and chicken cabernet. Dinner only. Closed Sunday and Monday. ~ 216 Pollock Street, New Bern; 252-637-4784, fax 252-637-6754. DELUXE TO ULTRA-DELUXE.

DINING

Housed in a lovely restored 1880s home in the historic district is the **Pollock Street Delicatessen**, whose turn-of-the-twentieth-century aura is perfect for sampling its homemade delights, including breakfast dishes, pasta and seafood, with a good old-fashioned brownie for dessert. Breakfast and lunch only. ~ 208 Pollock Street, New Bern; 252-637-2480. MODERATE.

Fred & Claire's is where locals gather for lunch, dinner and —more importantly—town gossip. For lunch this tiny kitchen located downtown serves grilled-cheese sandwiches, chicken salad, quiches, soups and salads and other homey eats. For dinner expect more elegant dishes emphasizing seafood. The handful of tables and booths are painted bright yellow. Closed Sunday. Call for winter hours. ~ 247 Craven Street, New Bern; 252-638-5426. MODERATE.

Publike and polished-looking, **The Chelsea** is New Bern's uptown eatery, complete with brass chairs, straight-back wood booths and a long wood bar against a brick wall. You can have a full meal such as Maryland crab cakes or opt for fun fare like fried green tomatoes or shrimp and grits. Closed Sunday. ~ 335 Middle Street, New Bern; 252-637-5469. MODERATE.

Beaufort Grocery Co. is a colorful, high-ceilinged venue full of light and space and wonderful smells. Everything on the menu sounds good, from the Grecian salad with crab cakes and *gougeres* (herb pastries) for lunch to the free-range chicken and grilled yellowfin tuna served at dinner. Start dinner with the *sagnaki*, a wedge of *kesseri* cheese flambéed at your table. Closed Tuesday from Labor Day to Memorial Day. ~ 117 Queen Street, Beaufort; 252-728-3899; www.beaufortgrocery.com. MODERATE TO ULTRA-DELUXE.

The **Sanitary Fish Market and Restaurant** started in 1938 as a shack that sold ice, shrimp and "shore dinners," and grew to a big rambly waterfront building selling seafood dinners daily by the hundreds. The atmosphere is crowded and noisy, the decor

AUTHOR FAVORITE

A longtime Beaufort favorite, **The Net House** is the perennial seafood place, nautically adorned with nets and lacquered wood tables framed in ships' lines. The fare is, of course, seafood, but it's not the heavy fried stuff. Flounder, grouper and other fresh catches come simply prepared, broiled or sautéed and ladled with light sauces. You can also order crab cakes and clams. Dinner only. Closed Sunday from Labor Day through Memorial Day. ~ Turner Street, a half block off Front Street, Beaufort; 252-728-2002. MODERATE TO DELUXE.

minimal, and the entrées listed by number. Number Eight, for instance, is a platter of broiled bluefish, jumping mullet or spots-in-the-round—whichever local fish is in season. A page explains the local fish (spots-in-the-round are sweet and flaky but require a bit of bone picking). Closed in December and January. ~ 501 Evans Street, Morehead City; 252-247-3111; www.sanitaryfish market.com. MODERATE.

The recipes at **Trateotu** hail not from the Carolinas but the Mediterranean, with influences from France (bouillabaisse) to Tuscany (pasta dishes) to Greece (spanakopita). The menu changes daily and the scenery is casual and vibrant, with murals of island scenes on the walls and palms gushing from big pots. Dinner only. Closed Sunday. ~ 506 Arendell Street, Morehead City; 252-240-3380. MODERATE.

The **Anchor Inn Restaurant** is where locals head for clam chowder. The nautical-themed decor verges on cheesy, but the fresh seafood, steak and pasta entries are hearty, no-nonsense and filling. Breakfast, lunch and dinner are served; no lunch on weekends; closed Sunday during the off-season. ~ 2806 Arendell Street, Morehead City; 252-726-2156. MODERATE TO DELUXE.

SHOPPING

In New Bern, concentrate your shopping efforts near the waterfront along Craven, Pollock and Middle streets. **Mitchell Hardware** is a great old place, dating to 1898, whose new and not-so-new inventory ranges from quaint antique farm tools and modern cookware to Venus flytrap insecticide and seeds for growing collards, black-eyed peas and squash. Closed Sunday. ~ 215 Craven Street, New Bern; 252-638-4261.

The locally made creations at **Carolina Creations** include pottery, jewelry, ink drawings, watercolors and stained glass. ~ 317-A Pollock Street, New Bern; 252-633-4369.

Few places have such a comprehensive selection of books and material on the Carolinas, especially the coast, as **Tryon Palace Museum Shop**. ~ Eden Street near Pollock Street, New Bern; 252-514-4900.

Beaufort's boutiques and antique shops parade along the harbor and just off it. Most are on Front and Turner streets.

Looking for a bag? Stop in at **The Bag Lady** and you'll find a whole world of hip totes to explore, from designer purses to brightly colored beach towels that fold into backpacks. In the midst of this bag madness, don't miss the other unique accessories such as earrings made from bottle caps and giraffe-patterned furniture. ~ 413 Front Street, Beaufort; 252-726-4388; www.bagladyofbeaufort.com.

Scuttlebutt purveys "land and seaworthy gifts," things like cruising guides and charts, model ships and lighthouses, and home and galley wares. ~ 433 Front Street, Beaufort; 252-728-7765.

Among the vintage stores in Beaufort, you'll find antiques and collectibles, as the name implies, at **Taylor's Creek Antiques**. The store specializes in items of the nautical and wicker persuasion. ~ 513 Front Street, Beaufort; 252-728-2275.

Over in Morehead City, **Seaport Antique Market** has 35 dealers under one roof—the perfect antidote for the antique bug. ~ 509 Arendell Street, Morehead City; 252-726-6606.

NIGHTLIFE The long polished bar at **The Chelsea** restaurant is always a good place for a drink. ~ 335 Middle Street, New Bern; 252-637-5469.

Grab a cocktail at the classy **Pro Sail Pub** and stroll out along the waterfront. The stars seem extra big here on summer and fall nights. On Friday and Saturday nights there is mellow live music. ~ Sheraton Grand New Bern, 100 Middle Street, New Bern; 252-638-3585.

The **New Bern Civic Theatre**'s amateur performers and stagehands do a good job of putting on a show. Drama, musicals and some original works are performed. ~ 414 Pollock Street, New Bern; 252-634-9057, 252-633-0567; www.newberncivic theatre.org.

In Beaufort, lots of people head to the deck at **Front Street Grill** for a drink on the harbor and the occasional evening of live jazz. Closed Monday. ~ 300 Front Street, Beaufort; 252-728-3118.

HIDDEN ► In a little courtyard off the waterfront, **Back Street Pub** is the town headquarters for live entertainment. Rock-and-roll, R&B, Cajun—you never know what will be playing. ~ 124 Middle Lane, just behind Clawson's Restaurant, Beaufort; 252-728-7108.

On the Atlantic Beach Causeway east of Beaufort in Morehead City, **Channel Marker** is a restaurant where waterfront decks are popular at cocktail hour. ~ 252-247-2344.

BEACHES & PARKS   **CROATAN NATIONAL FOREST** 🏃 ⛵ 🚤 🛥️ 🎣 Four rivers trace the edges of Croatan National Forest, and five spring-fed lakes speckle its interior. All that water seeps into swamps and bogs and marsh, utopias for wading birds, ducks, hawks and alligators. Hardwood and pine forest also marble some of these 160,000 acres. Some of the swamp cypress trees are enormous. Hiking trails and boardwalks provide access to the natural wonders. Facilities include boat ramps, a fishing pier, picnic areas, restrooms and hiking trails in various locations throughout the park. Seasonal swimming is permitted at Neuse River campground, Route 70 south of Fishers Landing. Freshwater fishing is good in the rivers. ~ Croatan National Forest runs south of New Bern to Bogue Sound. Main access roads are Routes 70, 17 and 58. The Croatan District Forest Service Office is along Route 141, off Route 70, south of New Bern; 252-638-5628.

▲ Free open tent camping is available year-round at Fishers Landing, off Route 70 on the Neuse River. South of Fishers Landing, 50 seasonal tent and RV sites are at the Neuse River campground off Route 70; $12 to $17 per night (closed December through February). At Cedar Point, on Route 24 east of Swansboro, you'll find 50 seasonal tent and RV sites; $12 to $17 per night.

MINNESOTT BEACH 🏊 Forget the roaring surf and dramatic dunes of the Outer Banks. This "beach" is a public patch of pale sand along the Neuse River near where the ferries discharge passengers coming from Cherry Point. Popular with families, it's a neighborly spot near the neighborhood of Minnesott Beach. Facilities include a picnic table; restaurant, grocery, golf course and marina are nearby. Swimming is fine in the Neuse River campground on Route 70 south of Fishers Landing (closed December through February). ~ On Route 306 on the north side of the Neuse River, south of Oriental.

CAPE LOOKOUT NATIONAL SEASHORE 🏖 Arguably the most ◄ *HIDDEN* remote of all Carolinas beaches, these three thin islands last for 56 miles from Ocracoke Inlet, near the southernmost tip of Ocracoke Island, all the way to Beaufort Inlet. Accessible only by personal boat or private ferry and offering only minimal facilities, the seashore is more suited to wildlife than human life.

The southernmost tip of the seashore, called Cape Lookout, is punctuated by a lighthouse painted in a black-and-white diamond pattern. You can't go inside the lighthouse, but the Keepers Quarters next door has a small museum with seashell exhibits and history on the islands. Beaches go on for miles, offering secluded sunbathing and surf casting. Unfortunately, strong currents and undertow make swimming dangerous, and there are no lifeguards. On the seashore's north end, closest to Ocracoke Island, is **Portsmouth Island** and uninhabited **Portsmouth Village**, where nineteenth-century buildings have been restored and are

♦♦♦

FEASTING ON FLIES

Few places in the world have more than one species of insect-eating plant. Croatan National Forest has five. One type, the rosette-shaped butterwort, catches bugs with its sticky leaves, then washes them in natural anesthesia. When a bug falls inside the tall, tube-shaped pitcher plant, the plant tilts its "hairs" downward so the bug can't crawl back out. Then it splashes the bug with fluid to drown and digest him. Of course, the most common insect eater, the Venus flytrap, is also found here. The plants are protected by law—so don't cut any.

listed on the National Register of Historic Places. Facilities include restrooms at Keepers Quarters, and picnic areas scattered throughout the seashore. Swimming is not recommended; strong currents and undertow create constant hazardous conditions. There is good surf fishing in the fall for flounder, drum, black sea bass and sea trout. ~ Private ferries provide passenger service from various locations, including Ocracoke Island, Harkers Island, Beaufort, Morehead City and the towns of Davis and Atlantic. (For a complete list of ferries, see the "Transportation" section of this chapter.) Round-trip fare ranges from $10 to $30, and most operate seasonally. Only four-wheel-drive vehicles are allowed on the island; 252-728-2250, fax 252-728-2160.

> Endangered loggerhead turtles and piping plovers (a teeny seabird) nest at Cape Lookout National Seashore, which is one reason the area has been designated a Biosphere Reserve.

▲ Open primitive camping, free of charge, for tents and pop-up campers; no RVs allowed. Bring your own water.

BOGUE BANKS BEACHES 🚲 🏊 〰 Not a particularly compelling example of sand and sea, the Bogue Banks have nonetheless been keenly developed and are keenly crowded in summer. A 30-mile-long barrier island along Bogue Sound, it starts east with Atlantic Beach, North Carolina's tiny version of Ocean City. Cheesy motels and T-shirt shops crowd every corner, and neon signs vie for visual space. Westward, Emerald Isle does not live up to its name, though the western point does have some exclusive homes. The beaches everywhere tend to be thin, the sand gray to pale brown, the waves big and good for surfing. Facilities include restrooms, a parking area and a boardwalk to beach in Salter Path; groceries, restaurants and bike rentals are widely available. For swimming check the surf conditions; strong currents and riptides are common. Fishing is best from one of the four piers. Possibilities include cobia, amberjack, king mackerel and tarpon. ~ A causeway from Morehead City will guide you over to Atlantic Beach on the eastern end. Emerald Isle on the west end is accessed by Route 58 from Cape Carteret. Route 58 runs the length of Bogue Banks; 252-726-8148; www.sunnync.com, e-mail vacation@sunnync.com.

FORT MACON STATE PARK 🚶 🏊 〰 On the barren, windworn eastern tip of Bogue Banks sits this 1834 fort, surrounded by nearly 400 acres of marsh and desert-like dunes and beach. In summer, the landscape swells with vacationers, particularly families, who explore the five-sided, brick-and-stone fort and then hit the beach. The fort has some history: During the Civil War, it was overtaken by Union soldiers after eleven hours of bombardment. Facilities include the Fort Macon museum, restrooms, picnic areas, a seasonal bathhouse and a snack bar. Swimming is good in a protected area, which is patrolled by lifeguards in season.

The fishing is good for drum, flounder, trout and bluefish. ~ Off Route 58 in Atlantic Beach, on the east end of Bogue Banks; 252-726-3775, fax 252-726-2497.

HAMMOCKS BEACH STATE PARK 🏊 Secluded and scenic,   ◄ HIDDEN with near-empty beaches and salt marsh that last for 892 acres, the park covers all of Bear Island. Unless you have a boat, the only way there is by ferry from Swansboro, which explains its peacefulness. Even during summer, when every ferry is filled, the island does not seem crowded. Estuaries and salt marsh run along the Intracoastal Waterway and Bogue Sound–side of the island, drawing many types of birds, including willets and American oystercatchers, that nest here. The Atlantic side of the island is rimmed with beaches and high sandy ridges and dunes. Facilities include a park office, a ferry dock, restrooms, picnic areas, and a snack bar, open in season. Shallow sandy shores along the Atlantic side offer great swimming; lifeguards are on duty in summer. There is surf casting for puppy drum, flounder and sea trout. ~ From April through October, pontoon ferries provide transportation to the park from the dock on Route 1572 in Swansboro. The ride takes about 25 minutes. Depending on the time of year, ferries leave every half-hour or every hour. On summer weekends, the ferries fill up fast, so get there early; 910-326-4881.

▲ There are 14 primitive tent sites, as well as group camping; $9 per night for individual sites.

The south end of the North Carolina Coast jags ▼▼▼▼▼▼▼▼▼▼▼▼▼ out into the sea as if making one last stand before **Cape Fear Coast** succumbing to South Carolina. Where the jag is most prominent is Cape Fear, at the point of far-flung Bald Head Island, home to a private resort community. From here, you can follow the Cape Fear River north to Wilmington.

The Cape Fear Coast's center of gravity, **Wilmington** is the larg-   SIGHTS est city in eastern North Carolina and the one everybody's talking about. *Rolling Stone* magazine deemed Wilmington's southern port one of the hottest spots on the eastern seaboard, and the town will come as a surprise to anyone accustomed to the quietude and rural scenes of the rest of the coast.

Downtown Wilmington has a happening feeling. Cafés, fine restaurants, ornate inns and trendy boutiques, many appealing to a gay clientele, crowd along the Cape Fear River. Streets of rippling red brick run rampant through the historic area, and so do exquisite old homes of Italianate, Romanesque and antebellum design. Many buildings date to the 1800s, but have recently been painted in crimson or cranberry or hunter green, and wrapped with contrasting porches of crisp white. Mammoth sycamore, oak and pecan trees blanket the neighborhoods, giving the sense they've been here a lot longer than anyone else has.

Most sights are concentrated along the river on Water Street and in the few blocks north of the water. The **Cape Fear Coast Convention & Visitors Bureau** has excellent maps of the area with details on dozens of sights. ~ 24 North Third Street, Wilmington; 910-341-4030, 800-222-4757; www.cape-fear.nc.us.

Two blocks east and nearly a century later, the **Zebulon Latimer House** was built before the Civil War, when Wilmington was a bustling railway hub and port. Zebulon Latimer, a wealthy merchant, prospered in this elaborate Italianate house, and his descendants lived there until 1963. Now the home is furnished with gorgeous period pieces and artwork, and the surrounding grounds are lush in the Victorian style. Closed Sunday. Admission. ~ 126 South Third Street, Wilmington; 910-762-0492, fax 910-763-5869; www.latimerhouse.org, e-mail latimer@latimer house.org.

Artists have also prospered in Wilmington, as evidenced by the works at the **Louise Wells Cameron Art Museum**. The museum, dedicated to the prolific artists of North Carolina, features paintings, prints, pottery and sculpture spanning the last two centuries. Closed Monday. Admission. ~ 3201 South 17th Street, Wilmington; 910-395-5999, fax 910-395-5030; www.cameron artmuseum.com.

For the big picture of Cape Fear life, past and present, visit the **Cape Fear Museum**. Hundreds of exhibits trace the history of this southeastern region, many designed especially for children. A model of Wilmington's waterfront depicts the city in 1863. The Michael Jordan Discovery Gallery displays exhibits on the ecosystem of the Lower Cape Fear Region and includes

◆◆◆

BETTER HOMES & GARDENS

The **Burgwin Wright Museum House and Gardens** is among Wilmington's finest old homes, distinguished by its Palladian doorway and double porches. John Burgwin, treasurer of the Carolina Colony, built the white Georgian beauty in 1770 on the thick stone foundations of the abandoned town jail. They proved to be solid foundations, for the house has stayed true to its design, having been restored in 1937 and opened for tours in 1950. The rooms are furnished in the styles of Burgwin's day; a kitchen building and parterre garden are also on the grounds. You can also peek into the dungeon, a relic from the house's stint as a jail. Closed Sunday and Monday and the month of January. Admission. ~ 224 Market Street, Wilmington; 910-762-0570, fax 910-762-8650; e-mail burgwinw@bellsouth.net.

Jordan memorabilia. Closed Monday in winter. Admission. ~ 814 Market Street, Wilmington; 910-341-7413; www.capefear museum.com.

A big, brooding presence in Wilmington's harbor, **Battleship North Carolina** was stationed in Pearl Harbor after the attack. Commissioned in 1941 and called "The Showboat" of World War II, it was the fastest, most powerful battleship of the time. Today, the mammoth gray ship welcomes sightseers, including plenty of children, who explore the maze of decks and rooms, from the galley and engine rooms to sick bay and crew's quarters. Admission. ~ Route 17, Wilmington; 910-251-5797; www. battleshipnc.com, e-mail ncbb55@battleshipnc.com.

Away from Wilmington's historic downtown are, regrettably, all the trappings of suburban America. Fast-food joints, gas stations and strip shopping centers seem to swallow the perimeter of town, and then go on for miles in every direction.

And then there are beaches. East of Wilmington across the Intracoastal Waterway on Route 74, **Wrightsville Beach** spans less than one square mile but harbors some of the area's best sand and surf. Sprinkled with modern resorts, seafood houses, sun-blistered cottages and sparkling new stilt homes (on the north end), it's foremost a family destination.

The beaches that lie south of Wilmington are campy, funky and crowded. From Carolina Beach to Kure Beach, it's mostly wall-to-wall cottages along the dunes and streets crammed with cheesy mom-and-pop motels, arcades and hot-dog stands—like an amusement park that's been going on too long. The whole island, not surprisingly, has been dubbed Pleasure Island.

Kure's historic moment would be lost in all the beach regalia were it not for the **Fort Fisher State Historic Site**. Here stood the largest Confederate earthworks fort, and the last to fall in the Civil War. The moment was in January 1865, when the fort fell victim to a three-day naval assault and was bombarded by 10,000 troops who destroyed it and then headed up the Cape Fear River to take Wilmington. Little remains of the fort, but the historic site re-enacts the event through slides and museum displays. Closed Sunday and Monday in winter. ~ Route 421, 20 miles south of Wilmington; 910-458-5538, fax 910-458-0477.

A mile farther south, the **North Carolina Aquarium at Fort Fisher** is a favorite of kids, who love looking at alligators, sea turtles and sharks, and handling the hermit crabs and other critters in the "touch tank." Admission. ~ Route 421; 910-458-8257, fax 910-458-6812; www.ncaquariums.com.

Kids also enjoy a ferry ride, available a little farther south at the Fort Fisher Ferry Terminal. For a minimal fee, you get a 30-minute cruise across the Cape Fear River over to **Southport**, a most agreeable sight after the clutter of Atlantic and Kure beaches.

In fact, from the graceful old mansions and pine trees of Southport all the way to the South Carolina line, the scenery is gentle
and agreeable, the beaches isolated and sedate.

HIDDEN ▶   The southernmost necklace of North Carolina isles, the **South
Brunswick Islands** are teeny, a little tough to reach, and esteemed
by Carolinians who make summer pilgrimages to their cottages
by the sea. **Holden Beach,** north in the chain, has 672 year-round
residents, most of whom fish or shrimp and live along the Intracoastal Waterway. On the oceanside of the island, vacationers
flock to beachfront cottages.

Ocean Isle is eight miles long and the most "developed," with
a handful of shops and eateries, motels and condominiums. Most
remote and probably most loved by locals and naturalists, **Sunset
Beach** is the southernmost barrier island in North Carolina. A
one-lane swing bridge connects Sunset to civilization—which is
just fine by most folks, as it tends to scare off anyone in a hurry.
At low tide, you can wade across Mad Inlet on Sunset's west end
HIDDEN ▶   to **Bird Island,** a speck of ground where osprey, herons, egrets
and other beautiful birds come to nest and feed. Endangered sea
turtles also lay their eggs on the beach here, sensing the safety of
such an isolated place.

LODGING   The choices of lodging in Wilmington are the finest on the North
Carolina coast. Within the lovely historic neighborhoods more
than 15 inns, bed and breakfasts and guesthouses entreat visitors
with elaborate architecture, luxuriant rooms and stellar Southern
service.

Six rooms with varied decor ranging from a wildflower motif
to an Asian theme constitute the **Rosehill Inn Bed & Breakfast.**
Breakfast is served at a long table in the elegant dining room, and
might feature orange-almond french toast or ginger pancakes
with mango butter. There's onsite massage available, and a selection of free videos, or you can easily walk to the historic district
for nighttime entertainment. ~ 114 South Third Street, Wilmington; 910-815-0250, 800-815-0250, fax 910-815-0350; www.rose
hill.com, e-mail rosehill@rosehill.com. DELUXE TO ULTRA-DELUXE.

Decorated with fanciful shingles and turrets, the **Worth House**
is a Queen Anne confection offering seven guest rooms. The atmosphere here is easygoing; you can relax on the porch under
the pecan and magnolia trees, or walk a few blocks to the waterfront. Every room is a little different, from the Rose Suite with
king bed to the Azalea Suite and Hibiscus Room, complete with
whirlpool, located in turrets and ensconced in windows. ~ 412
South Third Street, Wilmington; 910-762-8562, 800-340-8559,
fax 910-763-2173; www.worthhouse.com, e-mail relax@worth
house.com. DELUXE.

Business travelers like **The Wilmingtonian**. Every room is a suite, bright and airy and contemporarily decorated. Some have French doors that open onto a pretty courtyard; bigger suites offer full kitchens, washers and dryers and wet bars. A continental breakfast is served every morning. Downtown Wilmington is right outside the door. ~ 101 South Second Street, Wilmington; 910-343-1800, 800-525-0909, fax 910-251-1149; www.thewilming tonian.com, e-mail mail@thewilmingtonian.com. DELUXE.

At the **Camellia Cottage**, it feels like you're stepping into an artist's colony. You are, sort of—this beautiful 1889 home is the former residence of local artist Henry J. MacMillan. His Neo-Renaissance paintings cover the walls, as do other intriguing fixtures such as seashells, vintage radios and an accordion. The four guest rooms are spacious and comfortably elegant, with a queen-size beds, private baths and fireplaces. The Crane Suite is particularly enticing, featuring red-orange walls, a large bay window and a dressing room with tropical plants. The jasmine- scented garden, courtyard with running fountains and delectable three-course breakfast will make you want to never leave. ~ 118 South Fourth Street, Wilmington; 910-763-9171, 866-728-5272; www. camelliacottage.net, e-mail info@camelliacottage.net. DELUXE.

If you prefer less luxurious accommodations on the beach, consider staying on Wrightsville Beach.

The best place here is **Blockade Runner Beach Resort**, where 163 airy, casual guest rooms and suites are geared toward families. Located in twin rectangular buildings by the sea, the rooms look out at the ocean, the Intracoastal Waterway or Wrightsville Sound. The atrium lobby is done in ethereal tropical motif; the restaurant offers good food and views of the sand dunes and gardens. ~ 275 Waynick Boulevard, Wrightsville Beach; phone/fax 910-256-2251, 800-541-1161; www.blockade-runner.com. ULTRA-DELUXE.

◆◆◆

AUTHOR FAVORITE

Sure, the beach is a few miles away, but who needs an ocean view when you have the Renaissance splendor of **Graystone Inn**? I love the 1906 stone mansion's gorgeous mass of carved wood and chic antiques, and the tall chimneys beckoning on wintry nights. Inside there's a grand staircase of hand-carved red oak, ornate music and drawing rooms, formal dining room, a library, and seven bedrooms and two suites adorned in old-world grandeur. ~ 100 South Third Street, Wilmington; 910-763-2000, fax 910-763-5555; www.graystoneinn.com, e-mail reserva tions@graystoneinn.com. ULTRA-DELUXE.

By far the best way to stay on the South Brunswick Islands is in a cottage. For a cottage rental on Holden Beach, call **Alan Holden Realty.** ~ 910-842-6061, 800-720-2200. Or try **Brunswickland Realty.** ~ 910-842-6949. On Ocean Isle, there's **Cooke Realtors.** ~ 910-579-3535. Also on Ocean Isle is **R. H. McClure Realty.** ~ 910-579-3586.

Sunset Properties handles cottages and homes on Sunset Beach. ~ 910-579-9900, 800-525-0182; www.sunsetbeachnc.com. **Sunset Vacations** deals with this area as well. ~ 910-579-9000, 800-331-6428; www.sunsetvacations.com.

DINING

At **Caffé Phoenix**, the tables are faux marble, the walls decorated with original art, and the ceilings high enough to accommodate a loft for dining. You can have lunch, dinner or cocktails and light eats. Pizzettes, salads, pasta (try the bow tie pasta with pesto), seafood, chicken and vegetarian dishes are offered. The crowd leans toward a gay, avant-garde clientele. ~ 9 South Front Street, Wilmington; 910-343-1395. MODERATE.

Buffets rarely offer high-quality food and ambiance, but **Taste of Country Buffet** is an exception. Lunchtime crowds pour in from downtown to eat turkey and dressing, roast pork, sweet potatoes and mashed potatoes, squash, corn, cobblers—like Thanksgiving every day. The Victorian surroundings are pleasant, but don't quite go with the food. Open for lunch every day; open for dinner on Friday and Saturday. ~ 226 South Front Street, Wilmington; 910-343-9888. BUDGET.

Anyone who savors Charleston's Lowcountry cuisine should go to **The Pilot House**. Shrimp and grits, crab cakes with beurre blanc and crunchy catfish with grits are a few of the Southern flights of fancy here. Right on the Cape Fear River in the restored historic Craig House, it has a jazzy ambiance: multi-colored walls and oil lamps on the tables. Reservations recommended. ~ In Chandler's Wharf, corner of Ann and Water streets, Wilmington; 910-343-0200. DELUXE.

Elijah's is the casual compatriot of Pilot House, an all-wood former ship's store with leftover relics like ship's models and compasses. Order from the raw bar or the regular menu of uncomplicated sea fare—hot crab dip, stuffed shrimp, grouper teriyaki, and the like. You can choose to dine on the deck overlooking the river. ~ In Chandler's Wharf, corner of Ann and Water streets; 910-343-1448; www.elijahs.com. MODERATE TO DELUXE.

Solid German food served in an uproarious pub atmosphere is what you'll find at **German Café**. Brick walls and stained glass decorate the multilevel eatery, while kielbasas, wursts and schnitzels decorate the plates. No dinner on Monday. Closed Sunday.

~ 316 Nutt Street, in the Cotton Exchange, Wilmington; 910-763-5523. MODERATE.

Trails End is so hidden, I won't even attempt to give directions. You'll have to call the restaurant, brave the maze of neighborhood roads, and hope for the best (hint: stay on the gravel road *after* the sign says "Road Ends"). A most unusual place but one that's absolutely worth finding, it's a steak house on the water. The beef is broiled over hardwood charcoal and remarkably good, the salad bar arrayed with light bites, and the service exceptional (one waiter has been here for over 35 years; the waitstaff racks up over 150 years in combined service). The front door handles are actually shoes from the Budweiser Clydesdale horses; the cannonball pulley dates from the Civil War. Dinner only. Closed Sunday. ~ Located off Masonboro Loop Road near Whiskey Creek, Wilmington; 910-791-2034, fax 910-799-9617; www.trailsend-steaks.com. DELUXE TO ULTRA-DELUXE.

◄ **HIDDEN**

Get your grits and gravy at **The Middle of the Island,** better known as "The M.O.I." to locals who take their morning wake-up call here. The country breakfast house has fast waitresses and fast, fill-you-up fare, from butter-studded biscuits and fat pancakes to fish roe and eggs. ~ 216 Causeway, Wrightsville Beach; 910-256-4277. BUDGET.

With its many levels, peaked and gabled roof and pier angling out to sea, The **Oceanic Restaurant** is one of the prettiest places—with the best view—on the beach. Grouper pan-seared in cashew nuts and crab-stuffed shrimp are among the specialties. Another good bet is the freshest local catch of the day. Comfy booths, polished wood tables and lots of long windows create a perfect milieu for gazing at the sea. Sunday brunch. ~ 703

THE REAL CALABASH

The only thing between Sunset Beach and South Carolina is **Calabash**, a town whose image is much bigger than its size (they tout themselves as the "Seafood Capital of the World"). For out of this nowheresville village on a river came "Calabash" seafood: seasoned, crisp-fried niblets of fish, shrimp and clams heaped on plates and embellished with hushpuppies, fries and slaw. Hundreds of restaurants along the Carolinas' coast hawk Calabash seafood, many of them in Myrtle Beach, where it's served at all-you-can-eat buffets—a strange concept for fried food. For real Calabash seafood, you'll have to go to Calabash, of course. At last count, about 20 restaurants were serving here. Most cater to tourists who unload from big air-conditioned buses and funnel inside.

South Lumina Avenue at the Crystal Pier, Wrightsville Beach; 910-256-5551, fax 910-256-4527. MODERATE TO DELUXE.

SHOPPING The best shopping is along Wilmington's waterfront in places like **Chandler's Wharf.** ~ Corner of Ann and Water streets. The **Cotton Exchange** is another good choice. ~ 300 block of North Front Street; 910-343-9896; www.shopcottonexchange.com. Also try the dozens of shops lining the streets in between these two. Both complexes offer shopping in restored buildings whose many levels are filled with eateries, pubs and interesting stores and boutiques.

Filmmaking accounts for 11 percent of Wilmington's economy. The area has been host to 300 movies and six TV series, including the teeny-bopper hit "Dawson's Creek."

In Chandler's Wharf, **A Proper Garden** will fill all your formal and informal garden needs. ~ 2 Ann Street, Wilmington; 910-763-7177. In Lumina Station, **The Quarter** has smart resort wear for women. ~ 1900 Eastwood Road, Wilmington; 910-256-6011.

At the Cotton Exchange, look for the **Candy Barrel**, an expert purveyor of candy, fudge and taffy. This is not, however, the place to buy gifts for loved ones back home—the purchase probably won't make it past your hotel. Closed Sunday. ~ 910-762-3727.

Island Passage offers women's apparel that's both dressy and casual. ~ 4 Market Street, Wilmington; 910-762-0484.

The bins at **Wilmington City Market** overflow with colorful, fresh-cut flowers, plants and herbs, jewelry and arts and crafts. ~ 119 South Front Street, Wilmington; 910-763-9748.

NIGHTLIFE The night definitely moves in Wilmington. Come ten o'clock, lines start forming along the downtown sidewalks.

Attracting a loyal following of the hipper-than-thou, **Marrz** is the state's largest venue for live music. National and local acts headline here, including well-known names like Melissa Ferrick and Mushroom Head. You can take a break from the musical action in the game room (foosball, arcade games, pool tables), from which you can still view the band, or grab a breath of fresh air on the patio. ~ 15 South Front Street, Wilmington; 910-772-9045; www.marrz.net.

The Reel Cafe features live rock bands and deejays on weekends. The rooftop bar makes this one a favorite. Cover on Friday and Saturday. ~ 100 South Front Street, Wilmington; 910-251-1832.

The music often starts early evening at the waterfront **Water Street**, where you can hear jazz and blues bands. Occasional cover. ~ 5 South Water Street, Wilmington; 910-343-0042.

Stately **Thalian Hall**, built in the 1850s and designed by famed theater architect John Mantague Trimble, hosts a vast array of performing arts throughout the year. Zulu dance, big-name country and jazz artists, musicals, chamber music and ballet could be on the playbill. ~ 310 Chestnut Street, Wilmington; 910-343-3664; www.thalianhall.com.

Charley Brownz Downtown Lounge has live reggae on Sunday and karaoke on Monday. The popular dance spot brings in a mixed crowd. Occasional cover. ~ 21 South Front Street, Wilmington; 910-254-9499; www.charleybrownz.com.

Kinky cabaret meets mellow lounge at **Mixer's**, one of Wilmington's few gay bars. Men gather here nightly to converse over a cocktail or, on weekends, to catch the drag and strip shows. There's a small outdoor patio that's pleasant in warm weather. ~ 2325 Burnett Boulevard, Wilmington; 910-362-0200; www.mixerswilmington.com.

TOPSAIL ISLAND This 26-mile-long barrier island north of Wilmington isn't as appealing as Wrightsville Beach, but it's still a hotspot for beaching it. Fairly saturated with motels, seafood shacks and other development, it is trimmed in tan sand and dunes and sprinkled with fishing piers. Most are concentrated around Surf City near the middle and Topsail Beach on the south end. This happens to be where all the beach action is, too. Swimming is good in most spots. From the piers you can fish for everything from king mackerel and cobia to tarpon and jack crevalles. ~ From Wilmington, take Route 17 north 26 miles to Route 50, then go east 6 miles; 800-626-2780.

BEACHES & PARKS

WRIGHTSVILLE BEACH The sea and sands have been very generous to Wrightsville, the prettiest, broadest beach on the Cape Fear Coast. Lasting for a mile along the Atlantic Ocean, the tawny sands are edged with dunes and sea oats, and then weathered clapboard cottages. The south end of the beach is rugged and wind-whipped, with water too rough for swimming but sands ideal for secluded sunbathing. Sailboats cruise by frequently on their way to and from Masonboro Inlet. Windsurfers like the west side of the island, where they can go fast in Banks Channel. Swimming is good between Crystal Pier and Johnny Mercer Pier; lifeguards patrol in the summer. There is good fishing from both piers and good surf casting on the south end. ~ Wrightsville Beach is just east of Wilmington off Route 74. Regional beach access, with designated parking lots, are sprinkled along the island off Lumina Avenue; 800-222-4757.

CAROLINA BEACH STATE PARK An expansive park—761 acres—at the northern tip of Pleasure Island, it's not really on the beach, but is flanked on one side by the Cape Fear River and on the other by the Intracoastal Waterway. Grassy ponds, swamp forest and pine savannah dominate the terrain, and you will find Venus flytraps growing here. The Venus Flytrap Trail (see "Hiking" in this chapter) promises close-up looks, but don't touch—the insect-eating plants are protected. Facilities include a park office, restrooms, a marina with boat ramps, a picnic area and hiking trails. Swimming is not permitted. ~ Off Route 421 in Carolina Beach, ten miles south of Wilmington; 910-458-8206; e-mail carolina.beach@ncmail.net.

▲ A family campground features 83 tent and RV sites with two hot-water bathhouses; no hookups; $15 per night per family. ~ 910-458-8206.

SOUTH BRUNSWICK ISLAND BEACHES The Cape Fear Coast's most secluded beaches, they skirt a trio of islands: **Holden Beach**, **Ocean Isle** and **Sunset Beach**. Sunset is farthest south and barely developed, accessed by a single-lane bridge that swings open for passing boats. Ocean Isle has the most going on—though only about 425 people call it home. Holden has a busy fishing village and a summer resort community. All have a wilderness look: fine-sand beaches washed with foamy surf, soft dunes fringed with sea oats, and water in every direction. All three islands have eateries and grocery stores. Swimming is usually excellent, just check for strong currents or undertow before going in. Fishing is good off Ocean Isle Pier and Sunset Beach Pier. ~ Located at the southern end of coastal North Carolina, the Brunswick Island Beaches are accessed from Route 17.

Outdoor Adventures

SPORT-FISHING

There is no lack of boat captains ready to take you fishing. Below are a few of the charter companies that offer everything from deep-sea to light-tackle to fly-fishing. For details on pier, jetty and surf fishing, see the section titled "Where the Fish Are" in this chapter.

OUTER BANKS Along the Outer Banks, Oregon Inlet on Bodie Island is the hub for charter fishing. The fleet at **Oregon Inlet Fishing Center** includes 42 charter boats and one headboat (holding up to 50 people) ready to take you anywhere from the sounds all the way out to the Gulf Stream. The center is a concession of the Cape Hatteras National Seashore. Call for winter hours. ~ North side of Oregon Inlet; 252-441-6301, 800-272-5199; www.oregon-inlet.com.

On Roanoke Island, check with **Pirate's Cove Yacht Club** for charters and headboats. ~ Manteo Causeway; 252-473-3906. Down along Hatteras Island, head to **Teach's Lair Marina**. ~ Route 12, Hatteras; 252-986-2460. Teach's Lair and **Hatteras Harbor Marina** are lined with boats offering full- and half-day charters. ~ Route 12, Hatteras; 252-986-2166. In Ocracoke, get in touch with the captain of the **Drum Stick**. ~ Anchorage Marina; 252-928-5351, 800-825-5351. Also in Ocracoke is the **Miss Kathleen**. ~ 252-928-4841. Or try the **Rascal**. ~ 252-928-6111.

NEUSE RIVER REGION There are dozens of charter boats along at the marina on Evans Street in Morehead City. The Causeway to Atlantic Beach is also lined with charter companies. In the Causeway, try **Captain Stacy IV, VI and VII**. ~ 252-726-4675. You can join a headboat charter on the **Carolina Princess**. ~ Morehead City; 252-726-5479. Another choice is **Continental Shelf**. ~ Morehead City; 252-726-7454, 800-775-7450.

In 1996, off the coast of Beaufort, divers discovered underwater remains believed to be the *Queen Anne's Revenge*, Blackbeard's ill-fated ship that sunk in 1718.

CAPE FEAR COAST Charter companies along the Cape Fear Coast include **Carolina Beach Fishing Charters**. ~ Carolina Beach Docks; 910-458-1122, 800-288-3474. **Fish Witch II Charter Fishing** is another company in Carolina Beach. ~ Municipal Boat Dock, Carolina Beach; 910-458-5855. In Kure Beach is **Class Action Fishing Charters**. ~ Carolina Beach Municipal Docks, Kure Beach; 910-458-3348.

HANG GLIDING Persistent wind and summits of sand draw thousands of hang gliders to the Outer Banks every year. The largest hang-gliding schools in the world, **Kitty Hawk Kites** promises to get you off the ground within three hours. The beginner's lesson includes at least five flights, though don't expect to be doing any aerial stunts. Being airborne a few feet, with an instructor right beside you, is more like it. Jockey's Ridge State Park in Nags Head, with the highest sand dunes on the East Coast, is great for launching and landing. ~ Route 158, Milepost 13, Nags Head; 252-441-4124, 877-359-8447.

SURFING & WIND-SURFING If you're into riding waves, the Outer Banks has some big ones. To rent the right surf stuff, call **Ocean Atlantic Rentals**, which rents surfboards from outlets in Corolla, Duck, Nags Head and Avon. ~ 800-635-9559. **North Duck Watersports** rents windsurfers and offers lessons on how to use them. ~ 1446 Duck Road, Duck; 252-261-4200. On Ocracoke Island, you can rent a surfboard from **Ride the Wind Surf Shop**. ~ Located on the harbor in Ocracoke Village; 252-928-6311.

KAYAKING **Coastal Kayak Touring Company** will take you to Kitty Hawk Maritime Forest and Marsh, the Audubon Society's Pine Island Sanctuary, the Pea Island National Wildlife Refuge or the Alligator River National Wildlife Refuge. Their trained instructors are well-versed in the region's coastal ecology. Closed December through February. ~ 1240 Duck Road, Duck; 252-441-3393.

Text continued on page 326.

Where the Fish Are

Even on the wickedest windy days, you will see fishers along the North Carolina Coast, cocooned in down jackets, huddled against a horizon of frothy water, eyes trained on a multitude of monofilament angling out to sea. You ponder the obvious: They are either out of their minds, or they are catching a lot of fish.

It turns out to be the fish (though some would argue the former, too). Something's nearly always running off the coast of North Carolina: channel bass in spring; Spanish mackerel, whiting and flounder in summer; small bluefish in fall. Pompano, the perennial surf fish, shows up in spring and isn't chased off until wintertime, though it's often most plentiful in September. Spiny dogfish, a beach shark, prefers the winter. Sea trout can appear any time of year.

Big bluefish, one of the most exciting catches, are hunted relentlessly nearly year-round. Writes Robert J. Goldstein in his *Coastal Fishing in the Carolinas*: "Bluefish are voracious. They will hit anything that moves and most things that won't, will chop schools of baitfish to pieces, leaving gore and flesh in the water, stuff themselves like angler fish with elastic bellies, chase food up onto the beach and even strand themselves in the process, engaging in feeding frenzies like packs of sharks."

But perhaps the most exciting part of fishing off the North Carolina coast is you don't need a boat. Along the 300 miles of coast, numerous beaches, jetties and piers put you in touch with the fish. More than a quarter of all Atlantic piers are located here.

Certain piers and beaches are renowned for certain fish. On the Outer Banks, the **Nags Head Fishing Pier** draws bluefish and channel bass in spring and fall; mullet, striped bass and speckled trout in early winter; and flounder all summer. ~ Milepost 12, Nags Head; 252-441-5141. The **Outer Banks Pier** is a haven for king and Spanish mackerel and also for flounder, spots, croakers, kingfish and cobia. Closed January through March. ~ Milepost 18½, Nags Head; 252-441-5740.

Cast your line in the surf at **Coquina Beach** on Bodie Island and you could land a whiting, flounder or pompano. Sand fleas, those white, beetle-like bugs that burrow in the surf sand, are the bait of choice.

Oregon Inlet, between Bodie Island and Hatteras Island, is the Grand Central Station of coastal fishing. Fast currents carry a stream of fish between the ocean and Pamlico Sound. From the catwalks along the Bonner Bridge, which spans the inlet, you can hook anything from a gray sea trout, big bluefish, or puffer to a croaker, flounder or young tautog. The local way to fish the inlet is from West Point, on the southern tip of Bodie Island, but you can only get there in a beach buggy or with four-wheel drive.

On Hatteras Island, **Avon Pier** and the beaches on either side are famed for red drum. ~ Route 12, Avon. The remote beaches of **Ocra-coke Island** offer good fishing for pompano, bluefish and sea mullet, with privacy to match. If you find they're not biting, try again close to the ends of Ocracoke, near the inlets.

The piers along the **Bogue Banks** in the Neuse River Region are known for big amberjack and tarpon. In the surf at **Wrightsville Beach** on the Cape Fear Coast, there's usually flounder and pompano, particularly near Carolina Beach Inlet. The southernmost beach in North Carolina, **Sunset Beach Pier** offers a secluded locale for pulling in spots, floun-der, speckled trout, bluefish, whiting, Spanish mackerel and even king mackerel. ~ 910-579-6630.

To find out what's biting and where, call the **Outer Banks Visitors Bureau**. ~ 252-473-2138, 877-629-4386. Of course, you won't need a tourist bureau to tell you when fish are biting. You'll know it by the roadways crowded with trucks whose front grills are fastened with fishing rod racks. The rods stick straight up in the racks in front of the truck and the windshield, and makes you wonder how all those fishers can see where they're going.

Carolina Outdoors has numerous kayak tours, one of the most popular being a trip around Roanoke Island, that wends through narrow creeks, marsh canals and maritime forest, with a stop at the softshell crab docks. Other kayak destinations: Pea Island National Wildlife Refuge (including a wonderful sunset foray), Alligator River National Wildlife Refuge (where you might glimpse the scaly creatures) and the Pine Island Sanctuary, which is a haven for migrating birds. ~ Route 158, Milepost 13, Nags Head; 252-441-4124, 877-359-8447.

When the weather's right, the kayaking's great along the sound side of Ocracoke. **Ride the Wind Surf Shop** combines kayaking with wildlife watching and local history. Afternoon tours, if the wind allows, include a trip up Teach's Hole, where Blackbeard supposedly met his demise. There are sunset and sunrise tours as well, and nighttime excursions when the moon is full. ~ Located on the harbor in Ocracoke Village; 252-928-6311; www.surfocracoke.com.

Ocracoke Kayaking

GOLF

Serious sand dunes and prevailing winds make for some challenging golf along the North Carolina Coast.

On the Outer Banks you can tee up at **Duck Woods Golf Course.** ~ Dogwood Trail, off Route 158; Southern Shores; 252-261-2609. In Kitty Hawk, go to **Sea Scape Golf Course.** ~ Milepost 2½, off Route 158, Kitty Hawk; 252-261-2158. In Nags Head, there's **Nags Head Golf Links.** ~ 5615 South Seachase Drive, Nags Head; 252-441-8074. There are also nine scenic holes on Hatteras Island at the **Ocean Edge Golf Course.** ~ Route 12, Frisco; 252-995-4100.

In the Albemarle Region, there's an 18-hole course at **Goose Creek Golf & Country Club.** ~ Route 158, Grandy; 252-453-4008. There's also an 18-hole course at **The Sound Golf Links.** ~ Albemarle Plantation, Holiday Island Road, Hertford; 252-426-5555.

Courses along the Neuse River Region include **Carolina Pines Golf & Country Club.** ~ 390 Carolina Pines Boulevard, between New Bern and Havelock; 252-444-1000. Also in the area is the 18-hole **Brandywine Bay Golf Course.** ~ Route 70 West, Morehead City; 252-247-2541. **Bogue Banks Country Club** is also in the region. ~ Pine Knoll Shores; 252-726-1034. Another golf club is **Star Hill Golf Club.** ~ 202 Clubhouse Drive, Cape Carteret; 252-393-8111. A final choice for the Neuse River Region is **Silver Creek Golf Club.** ~ Route 58, just north of Cape Carteret; 252-393-8058.

On the Cape Fear Coast, there's **Belvedere Country Club.** ~ 2368 Country Club Drive, Hampstead; 910-270-2703. **Beau Rivage Resort** is also on this coast. ~ 649 Rivage Promenade, Wilmington; 910-392-9022, 800-628-7080. Another option is the

Porters Neck Plantation and Country Club. ~ 8403 Vintage Club Circle, off Route 17 north of Wilmington; 910-686-1177. Also on the Cape Fear Coast is the Founders Club. ~ Route 211 East, Southport; 910-253-3008, 800-247-4806. From Southport it's a 25-minute ferry ride to Bald Head Island Club, a George Cobb masterpiece with ocean views and windy links. ~ Bald Head Island; 910-457-7310, 866-657-7311. A bit farther south on Ocean Isle, try Brick Landing Plantation. ~ Route 179; 910-754-4373.

If the wind's too wild on the Outer Banks, you can play indoors at Pine Island Racquet Club. ~ Route 12, two and a half miles north of Sanderling; 252-453-8525. Manteo Middle School also has outdoor courts. ~ Route 64, Manteo.

TENNIS

The Albemarle Region has Elizabeth Street Tennis Courts in Elizabeth City. ~ Elizabeth, Harney and Cedar streets.

In the Neuse River Region, grab a racquet and head for the West New Bern Recreation Center. ~ Pine Tree Drive, New Bern. Try Swinson Park if you're in Morehead City. ~ Country Club Road, Morehead City. Also in the region is Mariner's Park. ~ Sea Level; 252-808-3301.

There are seven courts at the city of Wilmington's Empie Park on the Cape Fear Coast. Courts here must be reserved in advance. ~ 3300 block of Park Avenue; 910-341-7855.

Flat terrain and hundreds of miles of back roads make the North Carolina coast ideal for bicycling. For excellent bike-trail maps, you should contact the North Carolina Department of Transportation's Division of Bicycle Transportation. ~ Raleigh; 919-733-2804; www.ncdot.org/transit/bicycle.

BIKING

If you like biking by the beach, head for the Outer Banks. Starting in Corolla, separate bike and golf cart paths parallel Route 12 for several miles south. The roads around Kitty Hawk and Kill Devil Hills aren't much fun in season (way too much traffic), but you can cruise the beach at low tide.

South of Kill Devil Hills, get on Route 12 in Whalebone and head south on Hatteras Island for 58 miles. Then you can board

RIDING BAREBACK ON THE BEACH

What could be more satisfying than exploring the beach on horseback? At **Cedar Island Stables**, you can choose a Thoroughbred, Morgan, Appaloosa, Quarter Horse or Tennessee Walker for the guided beach tours. ~ Cedar Island Ferry, Cedar Island; 252- 225-1185.

the ferry for Ocracoke and continue another 14 miles. Remote, scenic and punctuated with a picturesque fishing village, Ocracoke is a marvelous place for a bike ride. From the village you can catch a ferry south to Cedar Island and continue biking along Route 12, or west to Swan Quarter and ride along lonesome **Route 264**.

In the Albemarle Region, you might start in Currituck on **Route 168** and head west to Elizabeth City via **Route 34**. From Elizabeth City, **Routes 37 and 137** are pleasant western rides. For a cruise through coastal forest and serene fishing towns, pick up **Route 32** near Goose Creek State Park, follow it through Bath, North Carolina's oldest town. From Bath, **Route 99** to Belhaven is also a scenic road less traveled.

Both Beaufort and Swansboro in the Neuse River Region are wonderful places to ride. Beaufort has a six-mile designated bike route that takes in historic **Front Street** along the harbor. Swansboro is only a few blocks of skinny streets along the White Oak River.

Along the Cape Fear Coast, try the 38-mile **Venus Flytrap Route**. It starts on **Route 210** just south of Route 172 and runs along Topsail Island, then cuts inland to the woods north of Wilmington. Be on the lookout for Venus flytraps, native to the southern coast of North Carolina.

A five-and-a-half-mile route winds through scenic Southport along the Cape Fear River, taking in tranquil neighborhoods, an 1804 burial ground and a maritime museum.

The 36-mile **South Brunswick Islands Route** follows **Route 17** north from the South Carolina border, with opportunities for side trips to remote Sunset Beach, Ocean Isle and Holden Beach. **Bike Rentals**   On the Outer Banks, **Ocean Atlantic Rentals** has beach cruisers at locations in Corolla, Duck, Nags Head and Avon. ~ 800-635-9559. In Nags Head, try **Lifesaver Rent-Alls**. ~ Route 12, Milepost 9, Nags Head; 800-635-2764. On Hatteras Island, **Island Cycles** rents beach cruisers as well as six-speed cruisers and mountain bikes. ~ Route 12, Avon; 252-995-4336. **Lee Robinson General Store** has beach cruisers as well. Closed January and February. ~ Hatteras Village; 252-986-2381. **The Slushy Stand** is the place for beach cruisers on Ocracoke Island. ~ Route 12, Ocracoke Village; 252-928-1878.

Up in the Albemarle Region, bikes are for rent from **Party and Equipment Rentals**. ~ 408 West Queen Street, Edenton; 252-482-7368.

In the Neuse River Region, **Bikes-R-In** rents road, mountain, tandem and children's bikes. ~ Route 24, Cape Carteret; 252-393-7161; www.ronniesbicycleshop.com.

You can rent bikes on the Cape Fear Coast at **Wrightsville Beach Supply Company**. ~ 1 North Lumina Avenue, Wilmington; 910-256-8821.

All distances listed for hiking trails are one way unless otherwise noted.

THE OUTER BANKS The ultimate stroll by the sea, **Cape Hatteras Beach Trail** starts at Whalebone Junction (Route 12) south for 75.8 miles. The trail temporarily ends at land's end—the southern tip of Hatteras Island—then picks up again on the north tip of Ocracoke Island. Hikers need only take the scenic 2¼-hour free ferry ride between islands.

The **Nags Head Woods Preserve Trails** (5 miles) wind through coastal forest filled with hickories, maples and other hardwoods. Located on Ocean Acres Drive, off Route 158 (turn at Milepost 9½, across from Pigman's Bar-B-Q).

ALBEMARLE REGION An 1800s plantation **Carriage Trail** (8.2 miles round-trip) at Pettigrew State Park is now a nature trail that wends past Somerset Place (the plantation) and along picturesque Phelps Lake to the west end of Cypress Point.

The **Live Oak Trail** (1.2 miles) at Goose Creek State Park tunnels through caverns of live oak trees, following the sandy shoreline of the Pamlico River.

NEUSE RIVER REGION The **Island Creek Forest Walk** (.5 mile) within Croatan National Forest is a leisurely loop through colossal trees, some 12 stories high. Bald cypress, American beech, black walnut, and white and red oaks are some of the species labeled on the trail, which begins along Route 1004, off Route 17.

Boardwalks take you part of the way on the **Cedar Point Tideland Trail** (1.4 miles), a walk through an estuary in Croatan National Forest. Pine and hardwood forest and seagrasses are the landscape here. There are platforms for close-up looks at wildlife.

For a longer walk within the national forest, take the moderately difficult **Neusiok Trail** (20.4 miles) and journey through ford palmetto swamps, sandy ridges and beaches, loblolly pine woods and the swampy bogs called pocosins. The trailhead is at the Pinecliff Recreation Area, off Cherry Branch Road near Havelock.

CAPE FEAR COAST If you've never seen a Venus flytrap, take the **Flytrap Trail** (.5 mile) at Carolina Beach State Park. For a longer jaunt the trail joins up with the **Sugarloaf Trail** (2.8 miles), **Campground Trail** (1 mile) and **Swamp Trail** (.8 mile).

Transportation

CAR

The Outer Banks' main drag (and only road in some spots) is two-lane **Route 12**, which commences in Corolla and runs all the way through Ocracoke Island. The four-lane **Route 158**, known as "The Bypass," parallels Route 12 through Whalebone, Nags Head and Kill Devil Hills, providing faster but less scenic travel.

Route 17 is the common thread along the Coastal Plain. It comes in from Virginia and veers southwest through Elizabeth

City, New Bern and Wilmington to the South Carolina line. **Route 40** is the interstate highway that connects the coast with the rest of North Carolina, heading northwest from Wilmington to Raleigh and Durham, then on to Winston-Salem and, finally, to Asheville in the mountains.

AIR

Two small and pleasant commercial airports are located along the North Carolina Coast: **Craven County Regional Airport** (252-638-8591) near New Bern, served by US Airways, and **New Hanover International Airport** (910-341-4125) in Wilmington, served by Delta and US Airways.

Taxis are your best bet for transportation from the airports to towns in the surrounding area.

Many people headed for the north part of the coast fly into **Norfolk International Airport** in Virginia, 90 minutes by car from the northern Outer Banks. Norfolk is served by most major domestic airlines, including American Airlines, Continental Airlines, Delta Airlines, Independence Air, Northwest Airlines, Southwest Airlines and US Airways. ~ www.norfolkairport.com.

BUS

Carolina Trailways, a subsidiary of Greyhound Bus Lines, has locations in several cities. They are in Elizabeth City at 118 South Hughes Boulevard, 252-335-5183; in New Bern at 504 Guion Street, 252-633-3100; and in Morehead City at 105 North 13th Street, 252-726-3029.

Greyhound Bus Lines (800-231-2222; www.greyhound.com) has a station in Wilmington. ~ 201 Harnett Street; 910-762-6073.

FERRY

The **North Carolina Ferry System** operates seven year-round ferry routes along the coast: between Currituck and Knotts Island; Hatteras and Ocracoke; Ocracoke and Cedar Island; Ocracoke and Swan Quarter; Aurora and Bayview; Minnesott Beach and Cherry Branch; and Southport and Fort Fisher. ~ 252-726-6446, 800-293-3779; www.ncferry.org.

Automobiles, motorcycles and bicycles are welcome on all the boats, though reservations are recommended on some routes. In the summer, call two weeks ahead. For departures from Ocracoke, call 252-928-3841, 800-345-1665. For departures from Cedar Island, call 252-225-3551, 800-856-0343.

Several private ferries offer service to Cape Lookout National Seashore, mainly in the summer and fall. From Ocracoke Island, **The Austins** will take you to Portsmouth Island, the seashore's southernmost island. ~ 252-928-4361. **Morris Marina Ferry Service** leaves from the little town of Atlantic, near Cedar Island. ~ 252-225-4261. **Alger Willis Fishing Camps** departs from the village of Davis. ~ 252-729-2791. From Harkers Island, you can board a ferry at **Cape Lookout Ferry Service.** ~ 252-728-3575.

In Beaufort, **Outer Banks Ferry Service** has boats going over to Cape Lookout. ~ 252-728-4129.

For more on North Carolina ferries, see the section titled "On the Sea for Free" in this chapter.

In Elizabeth City, try **City Auto Rentals**. ~ 1500 West Church Street; 252-335-1224.

CAR RENTALS

At the Craven County Regional Airport just outside New Bern, there's **Avis Rent A Car** (800-331-1212), **Hertz Rent A Car** (800-654-3131) and **National Car Rental** (800-227-7368).

At New Hanover International Airport in Wilmington there is **Budget Rent A Car** (800-527-0700), **Hertz Rent A Car** (800-654-3131) and **National Car Rental** (800-227-7368). A few minutes from the airport you'll find **Enterprise Rent A Car** (800-325-8007) and **Triangle Rent A Car** (910-251-9812).

At Norfolk International Airport, you can rent a car from **Avis Rent A Car** (800-331-1212), **Budget Rent A Car** (800-527-0700), **Dollar Rent A Car** (800-800-4000) and **National Car Rental** (800-227-7368).

As you might imagine, most coastal towns are too small to support public bus service. However, **Inter-County Public Transportation** can get you around Elizabeth City and Currituck County. ~ 252-338-4480. Down south, **Wade Transit** operates routes in the city of Wilmington. ~ 910-343-0106.

PUBLIC TRANSIT

In the Outer Banks, catch a ride from **Beach Cab** (252-441-2500) or **Winslow Taxi Co.** (252-335-7180).

TAXIS

Cherry Cab Company (252-447-3101) serves Craven County Regional Airport. Around New Bern, there's also **New Safeway Cab Co.** (252-633-2828). **Yellow Cab** (910-762-3322) serves Hanover International Airport.

At the Norfolk International Airport in Virginia you'll find **Black and White** (757-489-7777) and **Norfolk Checker** (757-855-3333).

NINE

The South Carolina Coast

South Carolina's coast is not long, only about 200 miles, but its northern and southern stretches are nothing alike. In the north, Myrtle Beach and the Grand Strand resemble a big amusement park by the sea, all neon and newness, souvenir shops and chain eateries and golf courses appearing over and over, like a movie reel that keeps rewinding. The beaches are sugary silver, the water radiant and slurpy, the dunes silky swells of sand tracing the shore.

The south is the Lowcountry, dark, watery and mysterious, a mosaic of marshland and blackwater swamps, rivers and creeks flushed by tides. In the salty haze of a Lowcountry morning, you can see the silhouette of those wading out onto the flats to catch crabs and gather oysters. Shrimp boats, their nets spread wide much like angels' wings, slip into shore burdened with the night's bounty. Gullah women, African Americans descended from plantation slaves, wade into the marshes to cut sweetgrass for their baskets. It is said that at night, some of them steal into the moss-sheltered depths of cypress swamps to practice voodoo.

The Lowcountry seems ancient. Gnarly cypress trees ramble low and long over rivers, and mammoth live oaks festooned with Spanish moss arch above country lanes. Bridges snake along seas of tidal grass glinting green in the sun and rippling in the wind. At low tide, the brown caps of oyster beds poke up and spread their primal scent into the air.

These are the tides of Pat Conroy's book *The Prince of Tides*, which was made into a movie. "Breathe deeply, and you would . . . remember that smell for the rest of your life," Conroy wrote, "the bold, fecund aroma of the tidal marsh, exquisite and sensual, the smell of the South in heat, a smell like new milk, semen and spilled wine, all perfumed with seawater."

The scent of Charleston is equally as sensuous, though different. Musky sprays of Confederate jasmine perfume the sidewalks, and honeysuckle and yellow jessamine overtake the cemeteries. To walk among the tombstones is a heady experience. Magnolia trees thrust their fragrant blossoms above cobbled streets. There is the smell of loquat and wintersweet and sweet bay, of gardens growing for centuries and barely contained by walls of wrought iron and brick.

Charleston is old, the oldest city in South Carolina. The English founded the settlement in 1670 and named it Charles Town after King Charles II. He was a hedonistic king who loved women and wine, horses and the theater. Four of his many mistresses were actresses. And so his Colonial trading port grew as a place of societal pleasures, with music and art and galas lavished with food and drink. English, French and Irish immigrants poured into Charleston and got rich trading deerskins, sugar and rum. They built the grandest homes in Colonial America and planted exquisite formal gardens. Then everyone planted rice.

The Lowcountry's labyrinth of rivers and tidal creeks made it perfect for growing rice. The Europeans didn't know how to grow it but the Africans did, having cultivated it for centuries in the Congo–Angola region. Rice growing is labor-intensive, and the slave trade grew vigorously. Indigo soon joined rice as a major crop. White traders couldn't import enough slaves to work the rice and indigo plantations springing up across the Lowcountry. Crowds could be counted on at the Charleston slave market, where gaunt, shackled Africans were auctioned like livestock. The city became the Hades of Africans and slave port of America.

The Civil War brought Charleston to its knees. After a siege in February 1865, the "Cradle of Secession" was nearly in ruins, the gardens a tangle of weeds, slave markets and rice warehouses deserted, slaves finally freed. Plantations became the ghosts of the Lowcountry. Reconstruction was slow and disasters many. A hurricane struck Charleston in 1885 and a great earthquake in 1886.

Charleston's story is of a city that should not have been. It is impossibly built on a tongue of marshland with rivers on either side, threatened by tides at every turn, and by the ravages of weather and war. Fires have five times rearranged the town. But despite the tornadoes, earthquakes and hurricanes, invasions by Indians, Revolutionary forces and Sherman's Army, Charleston barely budged. By the 1920s, the city was again firmly the aristocrat of the South. Now its historic area, saturated with more than 4000 buildings, is a monument to the city's tenacity.

For centuries, writers have tried to typify Charleston, to explain its existence, but this is not an easy task. The city is complex, with attitudes and ways that can either enchant or dismay, seduce or frustrate. The place William Allen White called "the most civilized town in the world" is indeed vastly charming, slavish to manners, though proud, stubborn and eccentric.

Charlestonians have always been selective with their tolerance. In the late 1600s, Quakers and Huguenots, Jews and Baptists, and other religious rebels were warmly welcomed into town. A hundred years later, Charleston embraced slavery like no place else in the South. Today, it is the only city in South Carolina with a considerable gay scene, and the only one where, six generations removed from the Civil War, people still haven't forgiven Abraham Lincoln for interrupting their garden parties. The Civil War started in Charleston, and here it is simply called "The War" or "The Late Unpleasantness."

Today's Charleston is a walking town, its brick and cobblestone blocks filled with architectural exquisitry: glorious Gothic Revival churches, Classical Revival synagogues, Art Deco theaters, and seemingly endless manses of Georgian, Colonial, Federal, Italianate and Neoclassical design. The Charleston Museum, founded in 1773 and the oldest museum in the nation, looks back at the city's florid history.

The past may be worshiped in Charleston, but the present is in full force. Bohemian coffeehouses, gay cafés, extravagant inns and guesthouses, and the savviest shops in the Carolinas are here. Excellent restaurants are abundant, with many eateries focusing on distinctive Lowcountry cuisine—those sweet, sultry flavors of farm and sea.

Just outside the city and reposing across the countryside are proud old plantations, their walls reduced to cinder by the Civil War and remarkably revived this past century. The enormity and elaborateness of their antebellum manors stand in harsh contrast to the cold brick cavities that were their slave quarters. Four plantations are open for touring, though it would take several days to see them all fully—and that's not counting Charleston.

As for the rest of the South Carolina coast, it can easily be canvassed in a week or two. Some people, however, prefer to park their blankets in the sand at Myrtle Beach and stay all summer. Nearly ten million visitors crowd into this beachy town every year, primarily from March through September, when the ocean is clear and clement and the boardwalk alive with amusement rides and the smell of popcorn and cotton candy.

Promoters call the Myrtle Beach area the Grand Strand, a ribbon of beach towns beginning below the North Carolina border at North Myrtle Beach and running south 60 miles to Litchfield. Besides being some of the Carolinas' best sands (some would say *the* best), the Strand has a lengthy parade of strip shopping centers, miniature golf courses, fast-food joints, buffet seafood houses and campgrounds—Disney World by the sea, only without the theme parks. Families naturally love it here, and so do golfers; more than 80 courses are set along the Strand.

The Lowcountry starts nearly a hundred miles south of Myrtle Beach in Charleston, situated almost halfway down the South Carolina coast. South of Charleston, the pine and palmetto forests are immense and dense, the tourist scene slow-paced. Kiawah and Seabrook are resort islands with groomed grounds and an affluent clientele. Edisto Island, with its weathered stilt cottages, is more casual and kind of cluttered.

Then there's Beaufort (say BEW-furt; BO-fort is in North Carolina), antebellum all the way, a sparkling port town with beautiful old houses and a fast-growing tourist business. From Beaufort, a bridge leads to a series of secluded sea islands, including St. Helena Island, Hunting Island and Fripp Island, swirled with marshlands and trimmed in lonesome beaches.

South across the Broad River, the scenery couldn't be more different. Hilton Head Island, civilization's last fling before Savannah, Georgia, is an exclusive, expensive enclave for golfers, shoppers and beachgoers. Sprawling resorts and country club communities have been meticulously placed among the pine woods, their entrances and lawns given a Disneyesque manicure. The beaches here are long, lovely and—like the roadways—jammed in summer, though if you care to walk a bit you can always find a hidden stretch of sand.

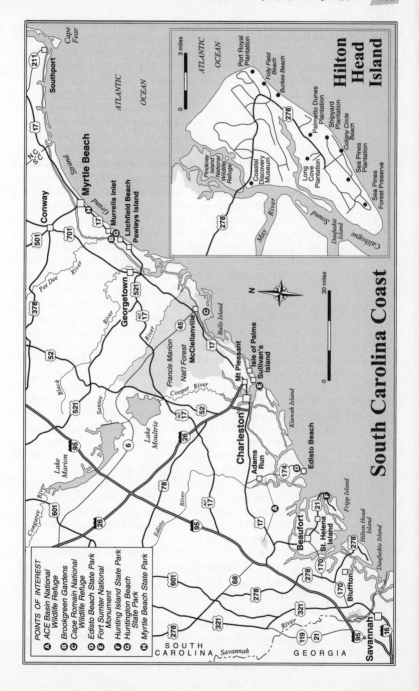

Hilton Head Island

Port Royal Plantation
Folly Field Beach
Burkes Beach
Palmetto Dunes Plantation
Shipyard Plantation
Coligny Circle Beach
Sea Pines Plantation
Pinckney Island National Wildlife Refuge
Coastal Discovery Museum
Long Cove Plantation
Sea Pines Forest Preserve
Daufuskie Island
Calibogue Sound
May River
ATLANTIC OCEAN

3 miles
0

278

South Carolina Coast

POINTS OF INTEREST
Ⓐ ACE Basin National Wildlife Refuge
Ⓑ Brookgreen Gardens
Ⓒ Cape Romain National Wildlife Refuge
Ⓓ Edisto Beach State Park
Ⓔ Fort Sumter National Monument
Ⓕ Hunting Island State Park
Ⓖ Huntington Beach State Park
Ⓗ Myrtle Beach State Park

Cape Fear
Southport
211
ATLANTIC OCEAN
N.C.
S.C.
17
Myrtle Beach
Grand Strand
Conway
501
701
521
17
Murrells Inlet
Litchfield Beach
Pawleys Island
378
Pee Dee River
Georgetown
521
45
McClellanville
Francis Marion Nat'l Forest
Bulls Island
Isle of Palms
Sullivan's Island
Mt Pleasant
Santee River
Black River
Lake Marion
Lake Moultrie
6
Cooper River
Charleston
Kiawah Island
95
26
78
Edisto River
Congaree River
601
26
95
17
Adams Run
174
Edisto Beach
68
278
601
321
Beaufort
St. Helena Island
170
21
Fripp Island
Hilton Head Island
278
170
Bluffton
Daufuskie Island
278
321
119
21
Savannah River
95
16
Savannah
SOUTH CAROLINA
GEORGIA

N
30 miles
0

▼▼▼▼▼▼▼▼▼▼▼▼▼▼▼
Myrtle Beach Area

Plenty of people who live in Myrtle Beach are older than the city. Incorporated in 1938 with about 1200 residents, it was mostly a thick forest of pine and myrtle trees by the Atlantic Ocean. There was a hotel as early as 1901, though guests of the Seaside Inn had to contend with razorback hogs rooting beneath their cottages.

As late as the early 1970s, Myrtle Beach was a laid-back community that slowly swelled in summer with the arrival of a few thousand families, college students and older folks who liked to shag. The shaggers, who started coming in the late 1940s, hung out around North Myrtle Beach and danced their jitterbug-like dance to beach music. The families rented quiet cottages among the dunes, while the college students flocked to the Myrtle Beach Pavilion and its carnival atmosphere. Winters were frightfully quiet.

Today, an estimated 13.7 million people pack into the Myrtle Beach area every year. They are drawn by sun, sand and surf, and by the pop-top fun of a place swarming with pancake houses, waterslides, all-you-can-eat seafood houses, batting cages, outlet stores, T-shirt shops and big-name country music show houses. The selection of golf is mind-jolting: 115 regular courses and 46 miniature courses, including one of the former with a gondola ride over water and one of the latter with an imitation erupting volcano. In the bar at one course, waiters stand on your table and throw napkins at you. A few patches of coastal forest and marsh remain, but they are fast being eaten by development. The last empty oceanfront lots were for sale in 1995.

SIGHTS

Route 17, called Kings Highway through Myrtle Beach, is the main north–south Grand Strand thoroughfare, but it won't let you see the beach. For the most part, it is a monument to neon and visual chaos, with more businesses and signs crowding along than it is possible for a motorist going a reasonable speed to glimpse. There are also many signs for "plantations," though they hold no resemblance to their historic counterparts, but are sprawling modern developments and country club communities. There are numerous restored and rebuilt plantations along South Carolina's coast, but only a few, mainly those around Charleston, open their doors to the masses.

From Route 17, various side roads make it easy enough to cut over to the ocean and small communities like **Cherry Grove Beach**, near the northern end of the Strand. It's quieter, campier and less expensive up here than in Myrtle Beach. Mom-and-pop motels gather near the sea, and vendors sell hot dogs and pretzels.

Just south of Cherry Grove, **Ocean Drive Beach** is the heart of shagging and beach music, pop culture of the late 1940s and 1950s. Carolinas beach music was born of Southern black rhythm-and-blues; shagging was born of the jitterbug, the former being a softer, sultrier dance ritual. In 1985, South Carolina made shag the official state dance. Each spring and fall, thousands of shaggers pour into Ocean Drive for the S.O.S. (Society of Stranders) weekend.

From Ocean Drive Beach, Route 65 follows the shore through the breezy, laidback communities of Crescent Beach, Atlantic Beach and Windy Hill Beach, where families settle into the many cottages lining the dunes during summer. The sands are usually quieter up here than in Myrtle Beach, about ten miles south.

The central nerve of **Myrtle Beach** is the **Myrtle Beach Pavilion Amusement Park**, an old-time, horseshoe-shaped complex with over 35 carnival rides and roller coasters, go carts, a carousel and loud rock-and-roll parked right next to the sand. Admission. ~ Ocean Boulevard and 9th Avenue North, Myrtle Beach; 843-913-5200, fax 843-913-5215; www.mbpavilion.com.

A blur of neon and fluorescent light emanates around The Pavilion, with souvenir shops, video arcades and places selling pizza, corn dogs and fried onion rings. There is the constant prowl of traffic, which reaches deadlock during spring break and holidays and some summer weekends. Here, too, is **Ripley's Believe It or Not! Museum** with such unbelievable exhibits as a four-eyed man and an eight-foot model of Cleopatra's barge made with pastry sugar. Best are the hair balls, especially the 5¾-pounder extracted from the stomach of a cow and donated by Lancaster Frozen Foods of Lancaster, South Carolina. Admission. ~ 901 North Ocean Boulevard, Myrtle Beach; 843-448-2331; www.ripleys.com, e-mail myrtleb@ripleys.com.

The Strand is lately being called "Nashville by the Sea" for the country music theaters mushrooming along the coast.

A few blocks away, the **Myrtle Beach Area Chamber of Commerce** has loads of information on area sights and pursuits, including golf. ~ 1200 North Oak Street, Myrtle Beach; 843-626-7444, 800-356-3016, fax 843-626-0009; www.myrtlebeachinfo.com.

Only twelve miles south of Myrtle Beach, the sandy shores melt into salt marsh and the tourist trappings transform into caverns of live oaks laced with moss. Here, along Business Route 17, **Murrells Inlet** has several thousand residents and over two dozen seafood shacks tucked beneath the trees. The fishing village of weathered clapboard homes and sloops is much older than Myrtle Beach, having been founded in the early 1700s. Blackbeard and other pirates supposedly sailed up into the inlet.

◄ HIDDEN

An outdoor gallery, **Brookgreen Gardens** holds more than 500 sculptures of bronze, marble, metal, limestone and granite. You'll need several hours to stroll these several hundred acres of cloistered quiet, punctuated by birdsong and tablets of poetry (tickets are good for seven consecutive days, so feel free to return

to finish your wandering). There are reed-filled ponds and gushing fountains, fields of Irish ivy and flowering quinces. There are
extraordinary live oaks with crazily twisted trunks trailing high
into the sky, and white-barked crepe myrtles whose lithe, mar-
ble-smooth trunks are natural sculptures.

Walk down the Magnolia Allée and be overwhelmed by
glossy green leaves and redolent white blossoms. Go to the
Palmetto Gardens and have a look at the state tree. Walk within
the Cypress Bird Sanctuary, an aviary under mesh, and watch the
ibis sweep the black muck for insects. Then stroll through the
other wildlife areas, where forested enclosures contain birds of
prey, fox, deer, otters and alligators. You can bring a lunch to
picnic at one of the tables, or eat at the Pavilion Restaurant,
which has good, budget-priced soups, salads and sandwiches.
The cypress swamps and hammocks surrounding Brookgreen
were thriving rice plantations until the Civil War. Today, Brookgreen offers a 50-minute tour aboard a pontoon boat. As you
cruise the Waccamaw River you will be introduced to the flora,
fauna and history of this part of the Lowcountry. Admission. ~
Route 17 South; 843-235-6000, 800-849-1931; www.brook
green.org, e-mail info@brookgreen.org.

South of Brookgreen on Route 17, you know you're in **Litchfield** and **Pawleys Island** when the medians take shape, lushly
planted and looking like they have their own personal gardener.
On the roadsides, exclusive shopping enclaves and country club
communities are sheltered in the recesses of ambling, moss-draped
oaks. Two hundred years ago, the area was equally as prosperous—but because of rice. **Litchfield Plantation** was the center of
the universe back then, and today it holds its own in country club

AUTHOR FAVORITE

If you need a reprieve from Myrtle Beach's pop-top delirium,
here's my prescription: **Brookgreen Gardens**. The atmosphere is so serene
it's almost sacred, with amazing sculpture and poetry tablets ruling over the
ivy fields like a benediction. Once home to the rice and indigo plantations
of prominent Old South families, it is now the oldest and largest public
sculpture garden in the country. In 1930, New York millionaires Archer and
Anna Hyatt Huntington bought the land as a winter retreat. Anna was a
sculptress who needed a place to showcase her work. She designed a
garden in the shape of a butterfly and set within it her bold, hauntingly
detailed pieces of bronze. Soon she collected other works, and began
devising a museum of American sculpture, as well as a wildlife sanctuary. See page 337 for more information.

society. The plantation's manor house, built in 1750, offers sumptuous accommodations, though you cannot enter the grounds without an appointment (or preferably, a reservation). ~ Kings River Road, off Route 17, Pawleys Island; 843-237-9121, 800-869-1410, fax 843-237-1688; www.litchfieldplantation.com, e-mail vacation@litchfieldplantation.com.

Pawleys Island has long been a summer retreat. Take one of the causeways (North or South) over from Route 17 to the thin ribbon of land, the marsh on one side and the ocean on the other, with stilt homes on wood shakes tucked among the foliage. Islanders like to say Pawleys is "four miles long and one house wide." Most of the cottages are along Myrtle Avenue. Several are made of cypress wood culled from local swamps.

Keep on Route 17 south of Pawleys and after about ten miles you'll come to **Georgetown**, parked at the confluence of six rivers. Your first impression is of a sooty port town; smokestacks spew blackness and paper mills pour an acrid scent into the air. But past the port scene lies historic Georgetown, where neighborhoods are layered with live oaks and magnolias, prim brick churches and proud old antebellum homes wrapped in big porches. Park along the harbor at Front Street, where several blocks of storefronts are washed in pink, green and blue and edged with brick walkways.

Two small museums on either end of Front Street recall the earliest days of South Carolina's third-oldest city, founded in 1729. The **Rice Museum** has modest but informative displays on the pervasive rice culture that began in the 1730s and lasted nearly 200 years. On the third floor is a 50-foot ship from the 1700s. In the 1850s, Georgetown exported more rice than any other port in the world. Closed Sunday. ~ Front and Screven streets, Georgetown; 843-546-7423, fax 843-545-9093; www.ricemuseum.com.

The **Kaminski House Museum** sits on a bluff overlooking the Sampit River. Built in the late 1700s and home to the town's first intendant, or mayor, the whitewashed house is warmly decorated with antiques, including an nineteenth-century Spanish wedding chest. Admission. ~ 1003 Front Street, Georgetown; 843-546-7706, 888-233-0383, fax 843-527-4871.

Several local people offer walking tours, the most animated being "Miss Nell" Morris Cribb, a native Georgetonian whose tales are peppered with ghost trivia. Contact **Miss Nell's Tours**. Admission. ~ 843-546-3975. If you'd rather see the city by water, **Captain Sandy's Plantation Tours** cruise the rice plantation mansions along the Sampit River and promises "history, mystery, romance and yes gators." ~ 843-527-4106. For more information on Georgetown, visit the **Georgetown County Chamber of Commerce**. ~ 1001 Front Street, Georgetown; 843-546-8437.

Text continued on page 342.

Taking the Country to the Sea

Myrtle Beach has gone country. In little more than a decade, nine country music theaters have sprung up within stomping distance of the sand—elaborate imitations of colonial showhalls that resound with twangy tunes. The shows range from big-name country concerts and patriotic pageants to orchestral extravaganzas with a little gospel and Elvis thrown in. The entertainment is clean, feel-good fun—no booze or smoking inside. Families love the shows, and so do church and school groups. Charter buses pour in daily for matinees and nighttime shows.

Missourian Calvin Gilmore got the country show ball rolling in Myrtle Beach. A good guitar player but a much better businessman, Gilmore opened The Carolina Opry in 1986 and was instantly successful. Others were quick to open theaters, including country superstars Alabama, Dolly Parton and Ronnie Milsap. Then came developers, who fashioned elaborate entertainment complexes with showhalls that offered more than country—big-band and jazz, variety and comedy acts, Vegas-style magic shows and impersonators, and an improbable genre called rock-and-roll gospel.

Now, Gilmore's own **Carolina Opry**, located in uptown Myrtle Beach, mixes shimmery costumes and big-band with Western swing, comedy, bluegrass and gospel. It all happens in a sparkling sandstone show house surrounded by palm trees and crowned with a cupola. Closed Sunday. ~ 8901-A Business Route 17, Myrtle Beach; 843-913-4000, 800-843-6779, fax 843-913-1442; www.carolinaopry.com.

Country supergroup Alabama (which played its first gig in Myrtle Beach at a hole-in-the-wall called The Bowery) has **The Alabama Theatre**. They perform about fifteen times a year and host weekly celebrity concerts by artists such as Emmylou Harris, Merle Haggard,

Charley Pride and Crystal Gayle. Most nights, there's the "One," a vigorous song-and-dance fest by an ensemble of young, fresh-faced performers. ~ Route 17 South, in Barefoot Landing, North Myrtle Beach; 843-272-5758, 800-342-2262, fax 843-272-7748; www. alabama-theatre.com, e-mail info@alabama-theatre.com.

Dolly Parton's $7.8-million **Dixie Stampede** dinner theater promises "belles, beaus, bridles, buckles and big-time fun." The cast of 250 includes 32 horses and even some ostriches. It's a rodeo-style Civil War saga that's dreadfully hokey, but folks seem to enjoy it while they're loading up on hickory-smoked pork loin, chicken, corn on the cob and "homemade stampede bread." There's even a non-alcoholic saloon where you can have a frozen drink in a souvenir boot mug. Closed January through the third week of February. ~ 8901-B Business Route 17, Myrtle Beach; 843-497-9700, 800-433-4401, fax 843-497-6767; www.dixiestampede.com.

The biggest, priciest showplace around is **The Palace**, a $13-million theater with 2600 seats in Broadway at the Beach, yet another Myrtle Beach entertainment complex. Big-name performers like Englebert Humperdink, Jerry Seinfeld and Debbie Reynolds appear here. Order your tickets at least one month in advance. Closed January. ~ Route 17 bypass between 21st and 29th avenues north, Myrtle Beach; 843-448-0588, 800-905-4228; www.palacetheatre myrtlebeach.com.

You can see unknown performers imitating superstars at **Legends in Concert**. Some of the superstars are no longer of this world— Marilyn Monroe and Elvis Presley being two that come to mind. No shows on Sunday. Closed January to early February. ~ Business Route 17, Surfside Beach; 843-238-7827, 800-960-7469; www.legendsin concertsc.com, e-mail boxoffice@legendsinconcertsc.com.

Twelve miles south of Georgetown, rambling along the North Santee River, **Hopsewee Plantation** is the Lowcountry's northernmost plantation open to the masses. For five dollars you can roam the live oak– and magnolia-shaded grounds, picnic by the river and prowl through cypress outbuildings littered with old farm tools. For five bucks more you get a guided house tour—worth it, because it's occasionally given by the owner, Mr. Beattie, a man with a passion for the particulars of his 1740s rice plantation. He'll show you the eave flounces that keep the rain out, chair rails that double as window sills, carved cypress mouldings patterned with lighted candles and antiques collected over the decades at Hopsewee. And he'll tell you that Thomas Lynch, Jr., was born in one of the bedrooms in 1749 and, in case you don't know, he signed the Declaration of Independence. Regular tours run Tuesday through Friday. ~ 494 Hopsewee Road, off Route 17; 843-546-7891, 800-648-0478, fax 803-648-0479; www.hopsewee.com, e-mail mail@hopsewee.com.

LODGING   Mom-and-pop motels proliferate the northern Strand, while nondescript highrises crowd along Myrtle Beach central. Sprinkled in between are a few places with character, some offering rock-bottom budget rates in winter.

At the north end of Myrtle Beach but across the street from the beach, **The Mariner** is a tiny, two-story place with a tile roof, wood shakes, a cupola and a weather vane. The motel rooms, efficiencies and one- and two-bedroom apartments are variously decorated with crude wood beams and walls, terrazzo floors and driftwood decor—pretty funky, all in all, but completely clean. Amenities include air conditioning and television. ~ 7003 North Ocean Boulevard, Myrtle Beach; 843-449-5281; www.myrtlebeachmariner.com, e-mail marinerhotel@hotmail.com. BUDGET TO MODERATE.

Also across the street from the sand, **St. John's Inn** is a pleasant compound of three-story buildings around a courtyard with a swimming pool and very green grass. The rooms are beachy and a little outdated, but extra roomy and clean as can be. Some have kitchenettes. ~ 6803 North Ocean Boulevard, Myrtle Beach; 843-449-5251, 800-845-0624, fax 843-449-3306; www.stjohnsinn.com. MODERATE TO DELUXE.

HIDDEN ►   **Serendipity** is entirely unexpected, a Spanish Mission–style house in a sleepy neighborhood a few minutes' walk from the beach. Small and full of charm, the sand-colored stucco building with arches is enveloped by big trees (the window of one room looks into the blossoms of a magnolia). There's a heated swimming pool, a hot tub and a garden room where continental breakfast is served every morning. Rooms, studios and suites are tastefully decorated in different periods, some with four-poster canopy beds and carpets. ~ 407 71st Avenue North, Myrtle Beach; 843-449-5268, 800-762-3229, fax 843-449-3998; www.serendipity inn.com, e-mail serendipity-inn@worldnet.att.net. DELUXE.

The Strand's best beach resort is the **Kingston Plantation**, a meticulously planned community where waterways snake around condominiums and peaked-roof townhouses with fine trimmed lawns. The hotel is an all-suite affair, with kitchens and separate bedrooms and views of the ocean. The lobby is classy and subdued, the pool area sprawls along a sweet stretch of sand. There's a top-notch spa and health club and several restaurants. If you'd rather go home-style, you can reserve a condo or townhouse, too. ~ 9800 Queens Way Boulevard, off Route 17 North, Myrtle Beach; 843-449-0006, 800-876-0010, fax 843-497-1017; www.king stonplantation.com. ULTRA-DELUXE.

The area's other big chain hotel, **Wyndham Myrtle Beach Resort** also commands ultra-deluxe summer rates but is not nearly as plush. Indeed, the whole place feels quite campy. The atrium lobby is minimally decorated, the room doors open onto breezeways. Rooms are smallish, with wall-to-wall carpets, but every one has a look at the ocean. Unfortunately, erosion has eaten away most of the beach here, and waves threaten the edge of the swimming pool. For a minimal charge kids can participate in daily activity programs during the summer. ~ 10000 Beach Club Drive, Arcadian Shores, off Route 17 North, Myrtle Beach; 843-449-5000, fax 843-497-0168; www.wyndham.com. ULTRA-DELUXE.

Litchfield Beach & Golf Resort is a massive place, 4500 acres of low-rolling hills and ponds, villas and cottages, and beachfront tower condominiums. You can rent any of these or opt to stay in the allsuite hotel, where rooms are spacious and decorated with embroidered sofas and wallpapers of rich navy and

---

SEA-WORN CHIC

It doesn't take long to figure out what most guests do at **Sea View Inn**: nothing. The clapboard Pawleys Island house is that kind of place, slightly shabby and plenty weathered, miles of cypress deck and porch set with rocking chairs and chaise longues, everything open to the grumbling waves, wind and sea. The rooms have bleached floors and sailcloth curtains that blow in the breeze—very simple. The cottage has air conditioning; all have a half bath. There are showers down the hall, but most guests prefer the private hot water showers a few steps off the beach. Rates include all meals. No TVs and just one phone, for those who must keep a link with reality. Closed Thanksgiving to mid-April. ~ 414 Myrtle Avenue, Pawleys Island; 843-237-4253; www.seaviewinn.net, e-mail seaview inn@sc.rr.com. ULTRA-DELUXE.

burgundy. All have balconies overlooking a pond. Everything's geared toward families. There are swimming pools, a health club and spa, restaurants and three golf courses. Only the condos are right on the beach; everywhere else, you'll have to walk or drive to the sand. Some units rent by the week in summer. ~ Route 17, Pawleys Island; 843-237-3000, 888-766-4633, fax 843-237-3282; www.litchfieldbeach.com, e-mail info@litchfieldbeach.com. MODERATE.

HIDDEN ►

The drive into **Litchfield Plantation** is precisely what you'd hope for from an Old South plantation: a tunnel of live oaks lasting a quarter-mile and framing the crisp white facade of a manor house. The house, built in 1750, for a century ruled the rice fields for miles around. Today it is a country inn, regally furnished, with four lavish suites, including one in the former ballroom that has a living room, fireplace, kitchen and veranda overlooking the lawns. It's all within a country club community, with swimming pool and cabana, tennis courts and gourmet dining in the Carriage House. A reservation or an appointment is required to enter the property. Full breakfast is included. ~ Kings River Road, off Route 17, Pawleys Island; 843-237-9121, 800-869-1410, fax 843-237-1688; www.litchfieldplantation.com. ULTRA-DELUXE.

DINING

HIDDEN ►

Just off busy Route 17, **Hamburger Joe's** huddles beneath oaks and pines in a tin-roofed building with a wraparound gingerbread porch. You can eat on the porch or inside in full view of the guys searing burgers on a grill. Joe's patties aren't big and heavy, just juicy and tasty. If the kids don't like burgers, there's fried bologna, hot dogs and grilled cheese. ~ 809 Conway Street, North Myrtle Beach; 843-272-6834. BUDGET.

Behind the faux stable facade of **Thoroughbreds** you'll find warm, inviting spaces, walls of wood and brick and banquettes of leather, all prettily lit with flickering sconces and fireplaces. The menu lists some of the Strand's finest cuisine: roast duckling and chicken dijon, filet mignon with brandy sauce and green pep-

AUTHOR FAVORITE

Murrells Inlet offers around two dozen seafood shacks. **Oliver's Lodge** is the oldest such shack, and, some will say, among the best. The 1860 clapboard house down by the marsh serves fantail shrimp, crab cakes, softshell crab, grouper Francaise and plenty of other seafood for dinner. The dining room is comfy and rustic, with Shaker-style chairs parked on the walls, simple wood tables and a view of the pelicans out back. Dinner only. Closed Sunday through Tuesday. ~ 4204 Business Route 17, Murrells Inlet; 843-651-2963. MODERATE.

percorns, and always a fabulous daily "fresh catch" special. Reserve ahead on weekends. ~ 9706 Route 17 North, Myrtle Beach; 843-497-2636; www.thoroughbredsrestaurant.com, e-mail scott@thoroughbredsrestaurant.com. DELUXE TO ULTRA-DELUXE.

Collectors Cafe is easy to miss, wedged in a blur of strip shopping centers bordered by chaotic traffic. But the mood inside is entirely civilized: gleaming clay tile floors, tables topped with white linen and radiant bouquets, original art on the walls. A good place before or after a show, the coffeehouse and gallery serves Mediterranean cuisine (grilled fish, pasta, veal, lamb and chicken dishes) as well as elaborate coffees and desserts. Closed Sunday. ~ 7726 North Kings Highway, Myrtle Beach; 843-449-9370. DELUXE TO ULTRA-DELUXE.

One of the few restaurants right on the beach, **Sea Captain's House** resides in a wonderful gray house built in the 1930s, with wood shakes on the sides, twin white chimneys on top and big windows and a covered patio looking at the ocean. The interior is homey and hospitable, the fare focused on seafood. There's shrimp and asparagus baked in phyllo, Cajun jambalaya, broiled scallops and Lowcountry favorites like she-crab soup and fried oysters. Breakfast, lunch and dinner. ~ 3002 North Ocean Boulevard, Myrtle Beach; 843-448-8082, fax 843-626-6960; www.seacaptains.com. MODERATE TO DELUXE.

In downtown Myrtle Beach, **The Library** is about as chichi as the Strand gets. Walls are shelved with old and new volumes, the tables crowned in starched red linen. The cuisine is French continental. The rack of lamb and caesar salad served tableside are highlights. There are nightly fresh seafood specials. Dinner only. Closed Sunday. ~ 1212 North Kings Highway, Myrtle Beach; 843-448-4527. ULTRA-DELUXE.

Go to **Bovine's** for great wood-fired food like mesquite-grilled salmon finished with red pepper hollandaise, or the popular jambalaya. Some of the booths are patterned with cowboy boots, the walls are decorated with saddles and cow heads, and big windows look across salt marsh. A fun place, one of the best of the Inlet's eateries. Dinner only. ~ 3979 Business Route 17, Murrells Inlet; 843-651-2888, fax 843-651-0211. MODERATE TO ULTRA-DELUXE.

Located on an old tobacco farm circa 1886, **Tyler's Cove** is a splendid spot for Lowcountry sampling. Seafood strudel, flounder stuffed with crabmeat and fried oysters and she-crab soup are well prepared. Brick floors, copper lanterns and beamed ceilings provide warm, atmospheric dining for lunch and dinner. ~ 727 Wachesaw Road, Murrells Inlet; 843-651-5135, fax 843-651-5408; www.tylerscove.com. MODERATE.

If you are not able to stay at Litchfield Plantation, at least have dinner (or breakfast) at its **Carriage House Club**. The 1750s ◄HIDDEN

English carriage house of red brick and slate has a tabby out-building once used for drying indigo. At its back is a sweeping marsh (a former rice field) that at sunset becomes a theater of bird and frog and alligator sounds, and reeds tinted rosy red. Inside the tables are dressed in white linen and the hearth has a fire. The menu features both Lowcountry and Classical delicacies, with olive fried tomato soup or Caesar salad prepared at the table to start, Lowcountry crab cakes and herb-roasted lamb chops for entrées. Reservations required. ~ Kings River Road, off Route 17, Pawleys Island; 843-237-9322, fax 843-237-1688. DELUXE TO ULTRA-DELUXE.

Pawley's Island Tavern is a casual, backyard kind of place at the end of an alley, with wood decks wandering everywhere, tin roofs and oak trees providing shelter. Home cooking is the name of the game, Old and New South–style. Fried flounder, crab cakes, fried chicken, shrimp and yellow grits—you can't go wrong. Closed Monday. ~ 10635 Ocean Highway, just north of Waverly Boulevard, on the west side of the highway, Pawleys Island; 843-237-8465. MODERATE.

The fare at **Frank's** is some of the best on the Strand. You never know what the chef's up to, maybe grilled yellowfin tuna on a bed of fried spinach with Moroccan barbecue sauce, or sautéed red snapper with poached oyster cream sauce on grits. The rack of lamb with garlic mashed potatoes is heady stuff. The setting—painted tin ceilings, carved mahogany bar back, and wood floors worn to a perfect patina—is funky and relaxed. If you want even more relaxed, eat out back in the courtyard. Here, coral-washed **Frank's Outback** serves lighter dishes. Dinner only. Frank's is closed on Sunday; Frank's Outback is closed on Sunday and Monday. ~ Route 17, Pawleys Island; 843-237-3030, fax 843-237-1778; www.franksandoutback.com. MODERATE TO DELUXE.

There are several fine places to eat in Georgetown. The small, friendly **Kudzu Bakery** is located in a former horse stable with wooden floors. Open for breakfast and lunch, with a lineup of pastries, muffins, sandwiches, cookies, coffees and fresh-squeezed lemonade. Closed Sunday. ~ 120 King Street, Georgetown; 843-546-1847. BUDGET.

For fancier Georgetown dining, the **River Room** resides behind glass along the Winyah Bay. There's lots of brick and brass inside, and plenty of chargrilled fish on the menu. The daily specials are very good; try the herb-encrusted grouper. Closed Sunday. ~ 801 Front Street, Georgetown; 843-527-4110. MODERATE TO DELUXE.

Otherwise in Georgetown, there's **Rice Paddy**, low lit and lying in an old stone building, once a bank. There are linen-covered tables and the two-story area is surrounded by huge windows. The business crowd streams in during lunch for hot crab sandwiches. At dinner, there's plenty of fish—sautéed grouper with capers, olives and sun-dried tomatoes or baked snapper stuffed with spinach and shrimp. Closed Sunday. ~ 732 Front Street, Georgetown; 843-546-2021, fax 843-546-0211. DELUXE TO ULTRA-DELUXE.

SHOPPING

Formerly marshland and now an ersatz Cape Cod by a lake, **Barefoot Landing** is where everyone who comes to Myrtle Beach simply must shop, or so it seems. It is admittedly an appealing milieu: tin-roofed buildings with cupolas and green awnings and boardwalks wending along fountain-filled ponds. There are factory outlet stores, T-shirt shops, beachwear boutiques, children's stores, book nooks and eclectic emporiums, as well as more than a dozen eateries, some with music venues. ~ 4898 Route 17 South, North Myrtle Beach; 843-272-8349; www.bflanding.com.

Know your terminology: South Carolinian factory outlet stores are called factory "direct."

For "mystical merchandise," head for **Instant Karma**, which also has a fine collection of jewelry and sculpture. ~ 843-272-4035.

The merchandise at **Barefoot Landing General Store** ranges from candles to pickles to Coca-Cola collectibles. ~ 843-272-1230.

The imitation architecture at **Broadway at the Beach** includes not only New England but Caribbean styles, and you can shop among brick and cobbled avenues and painted tin roofs. Over a hundred shops offer typical and atypical stuff, from kites, books and hammocks to sandals, trains and candles. ~ Route 17 bypass between 21st and 29th avenues north; 843-444-3200; www. broadwayatthebeach.com.

Within Broadway at the Beach, **Marvelous Magnets** carries mainly magnets—animal magnets, cartoon character magnets, celebrity magnets and magnet games. You'll also find the typical selection of souvenirs here, such as posters, keychains and the like. ~ 843-444-3240.

Build-a-Bear Workshop is a family attraction where kids— and adults—construct their own stuffed animals and outfit them from a choice of over 200 ensembles. You'll also get a personalized birth certificate for your fluffy new friend. People line up in the rain to get into this immensely popular store. ~ 843-445-7675, 888-560-2327; www.buildabear.com.

Elsewhere around Myrtle Beach, there are souvenir and T-shirt shops. Hundreds of them line Route 17 and Ocean Boulevard, and every year they keep increasing, little neon and fluorescent cubicles mutating across the land. One T-shirt shop called Wings has 24 stores along the Grand Strand, though it is not the king of souvenirs.

That designation is reserved for the **Gay Dolphin**, opened in the 1940s in a place the size of a cubbyhole and mutated many times until reaching its current multilevel extravaganza near the

Myrtle Beach Pavilion. Within this sea of silly stuff are all kinds of seashells, plastic toys galore, shirts monogrammed with every imaginable slogan, sharks in a jar, baseball caps . . . you get the picture. ~ 916 Ocean Boulevard, Myrtle Beach; 843-448-6550.

The shopping in Pawleys Island is considerably more cultured. There are some lovely clapboard venues at **The Hammock Shops**. ~ 10880 Route 17; 843-237-8448. These shops include **The Original Hammock Shop**, where it is said the first Pawleys Island cotton hammock was woven in the late 1800s by a riverboat captain. Today, you can choose a cotton weave or one soft-spun in polyester, a rope swing or a cottonduck pillow. Terrific handmade jewelry and books on the Lowcountry are also for sale at The Original Hammock Shop, which does mail order in case you can't visit. ~ 843-237-9122, 800-332-3490; www. hammockshop.com.

Also here is **The Hammock Shop General Store**, stocked with Lowcountry gifts, wind chimes, resort wear, candles and sauces. Other Hammock Shops stores sell everything you could possibly need, from sporting goods and Christmas decor to ice cream and toys. ~ 843-237-9021.

Across the street, **The Island Shops** have a dozen more places to spend money. ~ Route 17, Pawleys Island.

NIGHTLIFE   Dick's Last Resort promises "fun, surly help and crummy atmosphere," so don't be surprised when the waiters stand on your picnic table and throw napkins at you. There's stuff to eat, but most people come to guzzle beer and watch everyone act stupid. It's a huge hit with tourists. Live bands perform most days after 5 p.m. ~ Barefoot Landing, 4700 Route 17 South, North Myrtle Beach; 843-272-7794; www.dickslastresort.com.

Three nightclubs reside under the roof of **2001**. **Razzie's** is flooded with beach music and oldies, and an older crowd. **Touch** pulsates with Top-40 dance music and spinning strobe lights, and is the place to wear your painted-on lycra. The lounge area is a good place to relax and have a drink to the sounds of retro tunes. Cover. ~ 920 Lake Arrowhead Road, off Route 17 North, Myrtle Beach; 843-449-9434; www.2001nightclub.com.

The latest in one-stop nightclubbing action is **Celebrity Square**, located within the $250-million mega-entertainment park called Broadway at the Beach. The square is imitation French Quarter, with cobblestone and brick streets, gaslamps and wrought-iron balconies overhead. Ten themed places offer drinks and possibly entertainment, from the piano and comedy club **Crocodile Rocks** and **Froggy Bottomz Jazz & Blues** to **Malibu Surf Bar**, **Club Boca**, **Margaritaville** and **Blarney Stones**. **Hard Rock Cafe** is here and so is **Fat Tuesday**, its assembly line of spinning drink machines dispensing high-octane frozen cocktails. ~ Route 17 bypass between 21st and 29th avenues north, Myrtle Beach; 843-444-3200; www.broadwayatthebeach.com.

At the Myrtle Beach Pavilions, **The Attic** is a teenage night-club with loud music and no alcohol. Hours are quite limited so call ahead. Cover. ~ 812 North Ocean Boulevard, Myrtle Beach; 848-448-6456.

Mother Fletchers has bikini and wet T-shirt contests, a dee-jay that spins pop tunes, live bands, and a three-level deck right on the beach. Most summer nights, the clientele that packs this place is barely old enough to (legally) drink. Cover, with discounted tickets avail-able in advance. ~ Ocean Boulevard and Eighth Avenue, Myrtle Beach; 843-448-2545. The other way to spend an evening in Myrtle Beach is at one of the country music theaters in town. To know where to go, see the section in this chapter titled "Taking the Country to the Sea."

Wheelchair-accessible ramps cross the dunes at 15 locations at Myrtle Beach, and some life-guard stands have free beach-going wheelchairs.

To find a nightspot with true Lowcountry character, you'll have to look in Pawleys Island, off Route 17, at the end of an alley lined with wood-shack art galleries and studios. There, under the big trees at **Pawleys Island Tavern**, you can hear blues bands with talent crank it out several nights a week. The own-ers are friendly and the food's good, too. Closed Monday. ~ 10635 Ocean Highway, just north of Waverly Boulevard, on the west side of the highway, Pawleys Island; 843-237-8465.

NORTH MYRTLE BEACH 🏊 🎣 🚤 🛥️ ⛵ This northern stretch of Grand Strand takes in several small seaside communities, including Cherry Grove Beach, Ocean Drive Beach, Crescent Beach and Windy Hill Beach. Most of the action's at Ocean Drive Beach, birthplace of shagging, where the spring and summer sands are jammed with sun worshipers and "The Horseshoe," a road just off the sand, is packed with cruisers. There are public beach access walkways at various spots along North Myrtle Beach and lim-ited parking, especially around Ocean Drive Beach. The swim-ming is excellent. Facilities include public restrooms and showers along First Avenue South at Ocean Drive Beach, and lifeguards stationed all along North Myrtle Beach. ~ Located on Cherry Grove Beach, Ocean Drive Beach and Crescent Beach are along Route 65, off Route 17. To get to Windy Hill Beach, take 48th Avenue south from Route 17; 843-281-2662.

BEACHES & PARKS

MYRTLE BEACH 🏊 🎣 🚤 🛥️ ⛵ Ten miles of hard-packed to fine brown-sugar sand make up Myrtle Beach, but it's the few yards in front of The Myrtle Beach Pavilion and Amusement Park that sticks in everyone's consciousness. From spring through fall the towels are wall-to-wall, the umbrellas vying for space beyond the blinking neon of arcades, carnival rides and cotton-candy stands. Families and beachgoers wanting mental peace head several miles north of The Pavilion, where lovely neighborhoods with luxuriant myrtle trees line the wide beaches and there are patches of public parking. Lifeguards and eateries are located at various spots along Myrtle Beach, though they're most abundant around the Myrtle Beach Pavilion and Amusement Park. Swimming is good everywhere, but especially nice on the north end of Myrtle Beach, where the water is less crowded and shallow for quite a ways. ~ Along Ocean Boulevard, starting around 79th Avenue North and ending around 29th Avenue South. The Myrtle Beach Pavilion and Amusement Park is at Ocean Boulevard and 9th Avenue North; 843-626-7444.

MYRTLE BEACH STATE PARK At the southern tip of Myrtle Beach, these 312 acres include generous stands of pine woods and a pretty swath of oyster-colored beach. The shore is skirted with dunes decorated with sea oats and wildflowers. It's almost always windy. The fishing pier and campground were both firsts on the Grand Strand. Swimming is good here. Fishing is great from the pier for mackerel, flounder, whiting, pompano, bluefish and trout. Facilities include a park office, restrooms, picnic tables and pavilions, a snack bar, fishing pier, playground, nature center and trails. Day-use fee, $1.50 to $4. ~ Located along Route 17 at the south end of Myrtle Beach; 843-238-5325.

There are 350 sites for tents and RVs (100 of which are reservable), most with hookups for water and electricity; $25 to $27 per night. Families love the five cabins and two apartments, all budget-priced and requiring a two-day to seven-day minimum, though you'll have to book a year ahead to get one in season.

HUNTINGTON BEACH STATE PARK The way into this 2500-acre park is through dense woods and across

INSPIRING ART

Huntington Beach State Park's coastal wilderness was once owned by sculptress Anna Hyatt Huntington and her husband, Archer, the late creators of Brookgreen Gardens, across Route 17 from the park. For their winter home they built **Atalaya**, an enormous, Moorish-style stone-and-brick fortress by the sea that's now a National Historic Landmark. In 1930, Anna wrote in her diary that "Archer has also decided to build something and what he has in mind would probably be a hair-raiser to an architect." Indeed, there was no construction plan. The windows were randomly spaced, a watchtower perched on top, and the walls so crude that fig vines were planted to hide their harshness. Still, Anna, said to be deeply in love with Archer, sculpted one of her most significant works at Atalaya— "Don Quixote."

freshwater lagoons and saltwater marsh where oyster beds are exposed at low tide. An observation deck runs out over the marsh, and you can walk down and watch the egrets wading, waiting for fish. There are lots of sea oats and dunes, then wide, firm, lonely beach, the sand tinted orange by crushed seashells.

Swimming is good in designated areas. There's good fishing in the surf and from the jetty at the northern end of the beach; try for whiting, pompano, puppy drum and flounder. The boardwalk along the salt marsh is a prime place for snagging blue crabs. You'll need a dip net, a lead weight and string, available from the trading post, and some chicken necks and backs, available from local groceries. In case you've never crabbed before, here's how it works: You tie the chicken and weight to the string and drop it in the water. When the crabs come crawling for dinner, dip them out with the net. Facilities include a trading post, picnic areas, historic house, restrooms and nature trails. Day-use fee, $5. ~ The beach is located along Route 17, three miles south of Murrells Inlet; 843-237-4440.

▲ There are 133 tent and RV sites with hookups, and a hot-water bathhouse. Four wheelchair-accessible sites are available and can be reserved in advance. Remaining sites are $25 first-come, $26 reserved from March through October; $22 first-come, $23 reserved from November through February.

PAWLEYS ISLAND BEACH 🏊 🚶 Waves thunder and the   ◀ HIDDEN
wind never rests, yet Pawleys is very much an intimate beach, accessed along sandy lanes between private cottages and little boardwalks over the dunes and frequented by summering families. The sand is more gray than white but it's soft as silk and stretches nearly four miles along the barrier island. Swimming is best at high tide; at low tide, watch out for sand holes. If the surf's not too rough, try fishing for whiting and flounder. ~ Access is by either a north or south causeway from Route 17. Beach parking is located in small sandy lots, at intervals along Atlantic Avenue.

For the 56 miles between Georgetown and Charleston, Route 17 offers leisurely, uneventful driving. **Charleston Area**
Low palmetto forest and dense stands of pine, road-
sides swallowed by kudzu, and scattered farmhouses whose lawns bloom with gardenias and magnolias make up much of the scenery. There is also the broad sweep of Francis Marion National Forest, stretching westward more than 40 miles from Route 17 to Lake Moultrie.

East of Route 17 and 60 miles south of Georgetown, Pinckney   **SIGHTS**
Street will take you on a short detour through the scenic, strange, very small town of **McClellanville**. Small wood homes trimmed   ◀ HIDDEN
in spindle rail sit back under moss-draped oaks, their porches

occupied by blank-faced people. The Intracoastal Waterway winds through, and alongside it are shrimp boats with high-flying masts strung with nets.

A few yards from the noisy gaseous blur of Route 17 exists a place of forested calm, the 260,000-acre Francis Marion National Forest, where yellow-billed cuckoos play among the cypress trees and bald eagles loom overhead. The **Sewee Visitor & Environmental Education Center** center has an air-conditioned building with wildlife films, classrooms, laboratories and exhibits on the ecosystems of the adjacent forest and the Cape Romain National Wildlife Refuge. Take a walk on the boardwalk into the forest and swamp, watching for warblers, hawks, butterflies and other wild things, until you reach the mesh enclosure containing four red wolves. The wolves are one of the world's most endangered animals and are extremely shy. If you want to see them, don't make any noise. Closed Monday. ~ 5821 Route 17 North, Awendaw; 843-928-3368, fax 843-928-3828; seweecenter.fws.gov.

Back on Route 17 South, ramshackle carts offer "Hot Boiled P-Nuts" and "Sweet P-Cans, Shelled." Just north of Mount Pleasant, the road is lined on both sides with lean-tos and stands selling sweetgrass baskets.

In Mount Pleasant, take the turnoff at Route 703 for **Patriots Point Naval and Maritime Museum**. Here, the aircraft carrier *Yorktown* looms in the Cooper River, a gray giant rimmed with guns and mounted with helicopters and planes. Kids really enjoy exploring this World War II carrier, parked here since 1975, with its hull encased in 28 feet of river silt and encrusted with weird barnacles. The depths of the ship harbor military and seafaring fascination: fire rooms and engineering flats, a torpedo workshop, combat information center, scullery (which held cookware and dishes) and Korean War Room. The Sick Bay is small and stuffy enough to make one sick. Admission. ~ 40 Patriots Point Road, Mount Pleasant; 843-884-2727, fax 843-881-5923; www.state.sc.us/patpt.

Also here is the destroyer *Laffey*, which fought at Normandy; the Coast Guard cutter *Ingham*; and the World War II submarine *Clamagore*. The inside of the sub is cramped and hot; the sleeping quarters a Lilliputian maze of metal and tiny bunks.

From Patriots Point you can catch a tour boat over to **Fort Sumter** on a tiny manmade island at the head of Charleston Harbor. It's an enjoyable ride across the harbor, whose waters have seen battles with the French, Spanish, British and, finally, Union soldiers. Fort Sumter is, of course, where the Civil War officially began, though it was not a terribly exciting start. Admission for the boat. ~ 843-881-7337, fax 843-881-2960.

Fort Sumter was occupied by a Federal garrison in 1860 when South Carolina became the first state to secede. In April 1861, renegade Confederates demanded the fort back. Union Major Robert Anderson, in charge of Fort Sumter, refused. On April 12 at 4:30 in the morning, Confederate Brigadier General Pierre Beauregard fired the first shots on the fort—and of the war. For 36 hours he shelled the fort, and then Anderson surrendered. No one was killed.

Today, the fort is a National Monument run by the National Park Service. Rangers give ten-minute talks on various details of the fort, such as how it took eleven years and 70,000 tons of rock and granite just to build the island it sits on. The fort had five-foot-thick brick walls and was originally 50 feet high, though today it is considerably less. From atop its batteries you can look across the harbor to surrounding islands and watch the pelicans diving for fish. Everything here is wheelchair-accessible; special elevators even deliver wheelchair visitors to the batteries.

Back in Mount Pleasant heading south, Route 17 dramatically climbs the twin steel spans of the Cooper River Bridge, whose top gird rails trace the sky like rollercoasters. You'll soon find yourself at the north end of downtown Charleston. Get on King Street

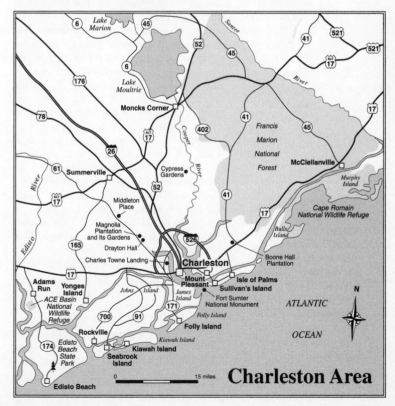

Charleston Area

going south, and you will drive through the most exquisite old city in the Carolinas.

Nothing can prepare you for **Charleston**: The processions of beautiful buildings, Italianate and Victorian, Art Deco and Gothic Revival, Federal and Colonial, most centuries old, all splendidly preserved. The Old World cathedrals with their medieval gates, stained-glass towers and spires flung against bright blue sky. The curve of magnolias wearing white, the heady walks through waist-high lilies in teeny cemeteries. The luscious gardens with marble fountains that have been flowing for more than 100 years, the outdoor markets filled with Lowcountry fruit and art and sweets. The smell of green gardens and salty ocean air, and of shrimp and sausage simmering in Lowcountry kitchens. The sun dispensing light in theatrical doses, shaping and reshaping the historical stage called Charleston.

The quietest times in Charleston are just after dawn and before dusk, when business is done and workers retreat to the suburbs. During the day there is the typical bustle of a modern city, with crowded cafés and streets, and traffic slowed by horse-drawn carriages carrying tourists (Charlestonians have their own unmentionable names for the traffic-congesting surreys). Parking is not a problem, as long as you seek out one of the many garages noted on local maps. The downtown historic area is extremely walkable, and even at its busiest feels scaled-down, even intimate.

Charleston is also very hip. Bistros, coffee and tea houses, tony shops and pretty inns crowd along the streets, and are concealed down skinny brick alleys and in flourishing courtyards. This is a great place to go people-watching. Retro garb with a bit of modern embellishment is in. Being young is also in. Lots of people in their 20s and 30s have lately made an exodus from Atlanta, preferring the happening scene of a small historic town to the faceless, frenzied sprawl of a Southern metropolis.

Home to just 97,000 people and host to 4.6 million annual visitors, Charleston is a low-lying city—church spires define its ceiling—that sits on a tongue of filled marsh. The Cooper River runs along its east side, the Ashley River is on the west. They meet at the southern end and proceed out into the Atlantic Ocean. Tour guides like to say that the Cooper and the Ashley form the ocean, and they also point out that plenty of people born in Charleston die there, never having ventured off the peninsula. One soon grows accustomed to such sentiments from the place Edgar Allen Poe called "the kingdom by the sea."

It is at the tip of the tongue, **The Battery**, where Charleston is most opulent. Storybook mansions washed in sherbet colors and embellished with iron fretwork and red brick march along the harbor. Many are occupied by Charleston's oldest families with some of its oldest money. The wonderful Queen Anne manse at **Two Meeting Street Inn** offers public lodging, though you can't go in without a reservation. White as a wedding cake and nearly as decorative, its gates are constantly thronged with people looking through the wrought iron and boughs of ancient oaks. ~ 2 Meeting Street, Charleston; 843-723-7322; www.twomeetingstreet.com.

Formerly called White Point, The Battery was created in the 1850s, when a high stone seawall and wide promenade were built. Twenty years earlier, **White Point Gardens** had been planted next to the sea, and ever since has been a wonderful place for walking. Colossal oaks shade vast green lawns sprinkled with monuments and rimmed in cannons that remember wars and other momentous times in the city's illustrious history. That would include the hanging of Stede Bonnet, British Navy major-turned-pirate who was captured with Blackbeard in 1718

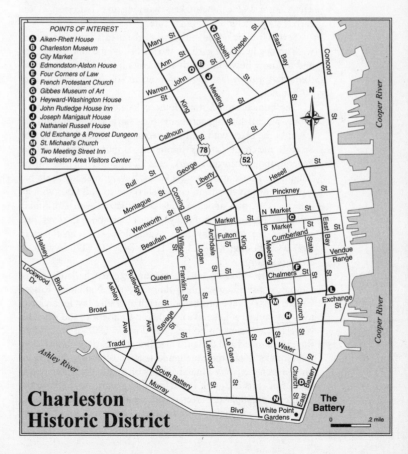

POINTS OF INTEREST
- Ⓐ Aiken-Rhett House
- Ⓑ Charleston Museum
- Ⓒ City Market
- Ⓓ Edmondston-Alston House
- Ⓔ Four Corners of Law
- Ⓕ French Protestant Church
- Ⓖ Gibbes Museum of Art
- Ⓗ Heyward-Washington House
- Ⓘ John Rutledge House Inn
- Ⓙ Joseph Manigault House
- Ⓚ Nathaniel Russell House
- Ⓛ Old Exchange & Provost Dungeon
- Ⓜ St. Michael's Church
- Ⓝ Two Meeting Street Inn
- Ⓞ Charleston Area Visitors Center

Charleston Historic District

The Battery

0 ———— .2 mile

at Cape Fear, North Carolina. The gentlemanly Bonnet pleaded for his life, even offering to cut off "all my limbs from my body, only reserving the use of my tongue to call continually on, and to pray to the Lord," but he was hanged anyway at White Point.

Pirate Stede Bonnet was hung at White Point Gardens, despite his claim that he became a pirate due to "domestic problems."

North of The Battery, lovely neighborhoods fan out, their homes residing within enormous vaults of trees. Gardens pour perfume into the air. There is the sound of fountains unseen.

Most of the homes are not of this era but of a prosperous, pre–Civil War world where European men grew absurdly wealthy trading rice, cotton and indigo through Charleston's port, and African men and women were their slaves. The merchants money was poured into extravagant architecture that gave jobs to hundreds of builders, carpenters and designers. There were 142 cabinetmakers working in Charleston in the early 1800s, including Thomas Elfe.

Several public house museums in the area allow outsiders to walk among luxuriant gardens and see behind the fanciful facades, and to know how Old South aristocrats lived. There are guided tours that usually last about an hour or so, offered every 15 to 30 minutes.

The **Edmondston-Alston House** is located on The Battery, its roomy piazzas looking across the busy harbor. Not opulent, but a handsome place with odd architecture, it was built in 1825 by Scottish merchant Charles Edmondston. His design was late Federal, though thirteen years later, rice planter Charles Alston bought the house and gave it a Greek Revival makeover. He put a parapet across the front, embellished the second floor with an iron balcony, and added a third-floor piazza with Corinthian columns. Many Alston family furnishings, books, silver and paintings are on display here. Admission. ~ 21 East Battery Street, Charleston; 843-722-7171, fax 843-722-4176; www.mid dletonplace.org.

Walk a few blocks north on Meeting Street to Charleston's most famous, most photographed domicile, the **Nathaniel Russell House**. Russell was a prosperous merchant with a lust for architecture. He wanted a home like no other in Charleston, and when his Neoclassical "mansion house" was done in 1808, it was indeed singular in mood and design. Three floors high, three rooms deep, three bricks thick, the tour guide tells you, though there is no known architect, only a massive book on architecture memorized by Russell. His hallmark is the free-flying staircase, built on the cantilever principle and erected with wooden pegs, that swirls up three floors as though it were floating. Admission. ~ 51 Meeting Street; 843-724-8481; www.historiccharleston.org.

Like many early Charlestonians, Russell and his wife Sarah were big on society and status, and they ran their house in a most formal way. English tea was served in French porcelain on Italian marble tables in the fancy front parlor. The day's main meal was promptly at 3:00, and it was a lavish affair lasting several hours and requiring many slaves to prepare, serve and clean up (the Russells had 18 slaves in all). Afterward, the men had their brandy and cigars in the drawing room or library, for it was disrespectful to smoke in front of a woman.

Before or after the house tour, have a walk around the rambling, fragrant gardens, with perfect circles of hedges, ivy climbing the walls, petite rosebuds and fat camellias, and statuary tucked here and there.

George Washington overnighted at the **Heyward-Washington House**, whose three simple stories of red brick are wedged among the row houses of Church Street. Built in 1772 by rich rice planter Daniel Heyward, it was home to his son, Thomas Heyward, Jr., one of the many signers of the Declaration of Independence. The inside is bathed in cypress and furnished with marvelous Charleston antiques, including a priceless secretary-bookcase in both Chippendale and Hepplewhite styles. The kitchen is original, having amazingly survived centuries of fires, earthquakes, hurricanes and wars. Admission. ~ 87 Church Street, Charleston; 843-722-0354.

Next door, you can look at the outside of **Cabbage Row**, where DuBose Heyward set his 1920s novel *Porgy*, though in the book the black tenement was called Catfish Row and located two blocks over on East Bay Street. A white Charleston writer hailing from New Hampshire, Heyward was one of the first American novelists to depict black life. His *Porgy* was modeled after crippled beggar "Goat Sammy" Smalls, who used to roam King Street with his goat and cart. Sammy's "woman" was Bess and his world was that of many Southern blacks: poor and segregated, cut off from the opportunities of the white elite. The novel was turned into an opera and then the musical *Porgy and Bess*, immediately a smash hit all across the country, with the now-famous first line: "Summertime and the livin' is easy." ~ 89–91 Church Street, Charleston.

But living wasn't easy for Charleston blacks. From the 1930s through the 1960s there were repeated attempts to cast the musical here, but white Charlestonians insisted on segregated theaters and the blacks refused to attend. Finally, more than three decades after its initial production, *Porgy and Bess* played in Charleston.

Across the street from Cabbage Row are several privately owned **single houses** typical of 1700s Charleston. One room wide, two rooms deep and set lengthwise to the street, they were aimed into the prevailing breezes. Historian Samuel Gaillard Stoney once likened them to a sailing fleet, "trimmed to the sacred Charleston wind that every hot afternoon blows up from the southwest across the Ashley River," according to Charleston Houses and Gardens. People with a little more money and land would build "double houses," two rooms wide and often Georgian in style. ~ 90–94 Church Street, Charleston.

Walk over to East Bay Street and you will see an entirely different set of row houses. **Rainbow Row** looks just like it sounds: a parade of radiant facades washed in purple, salmon and yellow, then cinnamon, aqua and olive. There are black ironwork balconies decorated with potted roses and sculpted boxwood. Built in the mid- to late 1700s as merchants' homes and stores, they were restored in the 1900s to become the private homes they are now. ~ 82–107 East Bay Street, Charleston.

North from here, **East Bay Street** is a pleasant piece of road with patches of brick and cobblestone edging the Cooper River and culminating with pretty cafés, nightspots and shops. Called simply "The Bay" during the early days, the street was the pulse of eighteenth-century Charleston, when rice, indigo, tobacco, fine porcelain and silk passed through these docks.

On East Bay Street you'll find the **Old Exchange and Provost Dungeon**, a strange, massive place with subterranean caverns where prisoners were kept. Completed in 1771, the stately, Palladian-style Exchange acted as town hall and hub of social, economic and political life. You can wander through the grand Colonial halls, then slip downstairs for a guided tour of the darkened dungeon honeycombed with brick arches. Admission. ~ 122 East Bay Street, Charleston; 843-727-2165, 888-763-0448; www.oldexchange.com, e-mail oldexchange@infoave.net.

From East Bay Street you can walk west on Broad Street to **St. Michael's Episcopal Church**, whose soaring white steeple and bell tower dominate the city. It's the oldest of Charleston's churches, built between 1751 and 1761, and it is very English,

DELVING BENEATH THE SEA

The brand-new **South Carolina Aquarium** swarms with tourists and critters. There's a series of walk-through exhibits like the Mountain Forest gallery (birds and native plants roam freely through a mountain ravine). The Great Ocean exhibit is particularly popular: over 300,000 gallons of water support hundreds of sea animals and plants; the sharks always get a big gasp from first-timers. Although the aquarium is one of the most touristy sites in town, its popularity is warranted. Admission. ~ 100 Aquarium Wharf, Charleston; 843-720-1990; www.scaquarium.org.

designed in the same manner as Trafalgar Square's St. Martin-in-the-Fields. St. Michael's has an illustrious history involving several wars and an earthquake. It survived the 1886 quake, but its steeple sank eight inches. It was painted black and used as a lookout during the Civil War. Its eight bells have crossed the Atlantic five times (once in the American Revolution when they were stolen by the British). Robert E. Lee and George Washington have graced these pews. John Rutledge is buried beneath crepe myrtles in the cemetery here. ~ Meeting Street at Broad Street, Charleston; 843-723-0603; www.stmichaelschurch.net, e-mail office@stmichaelschurch.net.

St. Michael's makes up one of the **Four Corners of Law** at the intersection of Broad and Meeting streets. (The church supposedly represents God's law.) The other "corners" are **City Hall**, built in 1801, **Charleston County Courthouse**, dating to 1792, and the federal **Courthouse and Post Office**, built in 1898 in the Renaissance style, after the first structure fell in the great earthquake of 1886.

More interesting than the buildings here are the **flower ladies** who gather every morning along the sidewalks to weave and sell sweetgrass baskets. They sing rich Gullah hymns, songs passed on through generations of women who've attended these sidewalks. Gullah is one of the purest forms of Creole, originating on the earliest plantations of coastal South Carolina.

Several blocks northeast of Four Corners, the **French Protestant (Huguenot) Church** was built back in 1845, though it was the third church on this plot to serve Charleston Huguenots (the first was as early as 1681). It's a stellar sample of Gothic Revival, with pointed arches and eyebrows, finials and stone tracery parading all over the sand-colored building. Open for tours mid-March to mid-June and mid-September to mid-November. Closed Saturday. ~ 136 Church Street, Charleston; 843-722-4385, fax 843-722-4388.

Just south of the church, **Chalmers Street** is one of Charleston's most charming thoroughfares, ancient curving cobblestone edged with fanciful and timeworn facades.

At one time, three out of every four enslaved Africans passed through Charleston's public slave markets. An 1808 ban on U.S. participation in the international slave trade prompted an equally prosperous domestic commerce. Charleston became a major hub for reselling, the bulk of which took place at the Old Exchange Building. When public sale of slaves was prohibited in 1856, the practice moved to a series of rooms, yards and markets along Chalmers, State and Queen streets. The **Old Slave Mart Museum** once belonged to a complex of structures, including a four-story slave jail (where the "merchandise" was housed before sale), a kitchen and a morgue. The museum, the last surviving slave auc-

Text continued on page 362.

Charleston Plantations

To find Charleston's four public plantations you'll have to follow the rivers out from the city, away from the commotion of downtown to cool, calming countryside ruled by mighty oaks. The rivers are the reason for the plantations. They fed the fields of rice, cotton and indigo that dominated the landscape nearly 200 years ago. African slaves were the reason the fields thrived.

From downtown Charleston, take Route 61, also called Ashley River Road, nine miles northwest to the first of three plantations lining the Ashley River. The drive into **Drayton Hall** is typically long, lovely and oak-lined, with sun pouring through massive, mossy boughs. The house is a red-brick Georgian-Palladian, built between 1738 and 1742 by young planter John Drayton and occupied by seven generations of Draytons (Draytons still live in Charleston). Though neighbors called it "Mr. Drayton's palace," it was not his primary plantation but was used as headquarters for managing his many other plantations. Extremely wealthy when he died, his possessions included some 500 slaves. He was not well-liked, and history recounts that he "lived in riches—but without public esteem."

The inside of the house is as bare as can be—which is good, as one can admire the handsome bald cypress paneling in the great hall, the intricate thistle and lotus blossom carvings around the ceilings, the mahogany garlands over the drawing room windows, and many other intricacies without being distracted by fancy furnishings. Drayton is the only Ashley River plantation the Civil War did not destroy. Admission. ~ 3380 Ashley River Road; 843-766-0188; www.draytonhall.org, e-mail dhmail@draytonhall.org.

A mile northwest of Drayton on Route 61, **Magnolia Plantation and Its Gardens** is sprawling, multi-faceted, quite modern and touristy. The focus here is the gardens. The original house, built in the 1680s by the Draytons of Drayton Hall, burned and was replaced by another house, which was leveled by Union troops. The current manor dates to 1873 but it looks nothing like a Southern plantation house, more like a gingerbread confection with gables and chimneys and curving eaves.

The gardens have been growing since about 1680, though their real architect didn't come along until much later. In the 1840s, Reverend Grimke-Drayton inherited the plantation. He eschewed formal gardens, preferring the random, romantic plantings of azaleas, camellias and magnolias. His sisters were staunch abolitionists, and so Grimke-Drayton called his slaves "black roses" and taught them to read and write. They cultivated his garden, and today his wending paths are bordered by walls of flowers and greenery. Many of the blooms are higher than your head. The camellias come in 900 varieties, and there's usually one in bloom. Fanciful flower-lined bridges cross the blackish-green Ashley River, which wanders through the 50-acre gardens, and there are several lakes.

Also here is the **Audubon Swamp Garden**, a 60-acre blackwater cypress and tupelo swamp inhabited by alligators, and the small Barbados Tropical Gardens whose greenhouse burgeons with bromeliads, pandanus and other warm-weather beauties. Paved nature and bike trails accommodate wheelchair visitors, and there's a 45-minute tram tour several times daily. Admission. ~ 843-571-1266, 800-367-3517, fax 843-571-5346; www.magnoliaplantation.com.

Four miles farther northwest lies **Middleton Place**. The gardens are vast, French and formal, laid out in geometric patterns and embellished with long terraced lawns and twin lakes in the shape of butterfly wings. Entire embankments explode with azaleas in spring. Oaks twist toward the sky like gnarled giants. Swans repose on the glassy waters of a rice mill pond. Crabapple and myrtle trees parade around, and hidden hollows with a single bench provide cool retreats. The backdrop of all this is the dark, brooding Ashley River.

Middleton was begun in the early 1700s. Most of its buildings were burned by Union troops and then finished off by the 1886 earthquake; the fault line actually runs through the gardens. Portions of a 1755 bachelor guest wing remained and were restored after the devastating earthquake. Today there are guided tours of the red-brick house decorated in the manner of early Charleston.

There is much more to see at Middleton, including numerous outbuildings, a slave chapel, a sugarcane mill, and a working stableyard with a smithy, horses, goats, sheep and pigs. Have lunch or dinner inside the cypress-paneled restaurant; their *prix-fixe* lunch menu offers such dishes as cold melon soup, tomato pie, fried chicken and ceviche. Dinner only on Monday. Admission. ~ Ashley River Road; 843-556-6020, 800-782-3608, fax 843-766-4460; www.middletonplace.org.

Boone Hall Plantation lies six miles north of Charleston along the Wando River. Its high point is a half-mile alley of oaks, their spidery limbs locked high over the entrance road. The house is faux plantation, built in 1935 where once stood an eighteenth-century house. Tours of the first floor are given by women in hoop skirts; the upper floors are used by the home's current owners, no relation to the Boones. Most historic here is the slave street built some time between 1790 and 1810, lined with one-room, red-brick cubicles with dirt floors. Walk along the street and look inside the dark, dank cavities. Admission. ~ Route 17; 843-884-4371, fax 843-884-0475; www.boonehall plantation.com.

tion in South Carolina, is currently closed for renovations. But in the meantime, you can walk by the chilling site and wonder how such inhumanity was possible. ~ 6 Chalmers Street, Charleston; 843-724-7395.

A couple of blocks northwest on Meeting Street, **Gibbes Museum of Art** resides in a handsome Colonial building with one room of permanent exhibits, mainly American art dating to the 1700s. There's a collection of miniature portraits numbering more than 400, and notable works by South Carolinians Benjamin West, Thomas Sully and Rembrandt Peale. Closed Monday. Admission. ~ 135 Meeting Street, Charleston; 843-722-2706; www.gibbes.com.

The **Joseph Manigault House** is considerably north of Charleston's historic heart, so it's best to catch a public shuttle bus or drive. In 1803, wealthy French Huguenot Gabriel Manigault fashioned the house for his brother, Joseph. It was one of Gabriel's first residential creations, but it foretold his bright future as a renowned Charleston architect. The mansion is in the Adams style and designed as a parallelogram, with bows on two sides and a curving piazza on another. The interior is striking, with a flowing staircase, handsome period pieces and portraits more than 200 years old. Admission. ~ 350 Meeting Street, Charleston; 843-723-2926.

The **Charleston Museum** was founded in 1773, making it the nation's first museum. Its current quarters, however, were built in 1979 and are, unfortunately, some of the city's dullest: a big block of brick. The inside is much more enlightening, with exhibits on the Lowcountry's florid history. A whole room of hands-on fun for kids was under construction at press-time. The museum operates two of Charleston's house museums and sells discounted combination tickets. Admission. ~ 360 Meeting Street, Charleston; 843-722-2996; www.charlestonmuseum.org, e-mail info@charlestonmuseum.org.

Across the street, the **Charleston Area Visitors Center** is the place for information. The friendly, well-informed people here will help plan tours, suggest dining itineraries, provide walking-tour maps (including one of King Street architecture) and even direct you to great hidden spots. ~ 375 Meeting Street, Charleston; 843-853-8000, 800-868-8118; www.charlestoncvb.com.

Parallel to Meeting Street, **King Street** is a bustling commercial haven edged with some of Charleston's best inns and eateries and shops, especially those selling stellar antiques. The architecture is vast and varied: a German Gothic church, Art Deco theater, Georgian and Neoclassical hotel, plenty of Federal and antebellum designs, and even some Victoriana.

Before visiting Charleston, contact the excellent **Charleston Area Convention & Visitors Bureau** for information. ~ 423 King

Street, Charleston; 843-853-8000, 800-868-8118; www. charlestoncvb.com.

One block east of the Visitors Center, the 1817 **Aiken-Rhett House** was home to South Carolina governor William Aiken, Jr., and then war room for Confederate General P.G.T. Beauregard. It began as a Federal manse and was later given Greek Revival flairs. All of the furnishings are original; the slave quarters and stable look barely changed. Admission. ~ 48 Elizabeth Street, Charleston; 843-723-1159.

Your best bet for parking is at the Charleston Area Visitors Center. ~ 375 Meeting Street.

There are many guided walking tours of Charleston, with seemingly endless themes. If you are interested in the Civil War go on the **Civil War Walking Tour of Charleston**. ~ 843-722-7033. Another interesting tour is the **Charleston Tea Party Walking Tour**. ~ 843-577-5896. Those interested in architecture should try the **Architectural Walking Tours of Charleston**. ~ 843-893-2327, 800-931-7761.

Or you may want to consider the **Revolutionary Colonial Buildings Tour**, the **Slavery and Freedom Tour**, the **Civil War Tour** or the **History and Ghost Tour**, all offered by Charleston Walks. ~ 58½ Broad Street, Charleston; 843-577-3800.

Chai Y'all Tours explores the city's Jewish heritage (either on foot or by car). ~ 843-556-0664. **Gullah Tours by Alphonso Brown** recounts the rich Gullah history from a van. ~ 843-763-7551.

Horse-drawn carriage rides are available from numerous companies, most stationed along Market Street near Church Street. One of these companies is **Classic Carriage Tours**. ~ 843-853-3747. Another is **Old South Carriage Company**. ~ 843-577-0042.

Outside Charleston is plantation country. Four historic plantations, including two with extraordinary gardens, are open to the public and are within a 30-minute drive of downtown Charleston. For more on these, see the section titled "Charleston Plantations" in this chapter.

Across the Ashley River from the city is the site of the original Charleston. **Charles Towne Landing** is where English settlers first set up camp and lived for several years. Today it's a pretty park and nature preserve set among wooded clearings. There's a small seventeenth-century-style crop garden and a 53-foot replica of a 300-year-old trading ship. Gravel paths wend through woods where black bears, otters, pumas and other animals live in roomy, grassy enclosures. You can have a picnic, rent a bike or stroller, or take a walk along the forested footpaths. Admission. ~ 1500 Old Town Road, Charleston; 843-852-4200, fax 843-852-4205.

North of Charleston, deep in old rice plantation country, you can explore the blackwater swamp at **Cypress Gardens**. Birders

◀ HIDDEN

and naturalists enjoy this 173-acre retreat along the Cooper River, where you can get in a little rowboat and wander along the inky, silent water studded with giant cypress trees. The gardens are a tiny remaining piece of Dean Hall, a 3000-acre antebellum plantation that flourished until the Civil War. During the spring, the shore is masked with azaleas, wisteria, dogwoods and daffodils that burst with color. This is the best time to visit, though fall is also quite pleasant. If you go in summer, take your mosquito repellent. It's muggy and very buggy. Admission. ~ 3030 Cypress Gardens Road, off Route 52 North, Moncks Corner; 843-553-0515; www.cypressgardens.org.

South of Charleston, the Lowcountry spreads out like a watery apron, with rivers seeping through farm fields, stilt homes perched against seas of marsh, and bridges connecting a series of sea islands. None of the islands are easy to get to. Most are cul-de-sac destinations, and you will travel the same way out as you did on the way in. The drives are atmospheric: long, silent journeys across interminable stretches of salt marsh and tidal creeks and seagrass rippling softly in the wind.

Several 1700s plantation homes and churches are still standing on Edisto Island.

Even **Kiawah Island**, the most developed and most visited, requires a lengthy, twisting drive through the countryside, first along Route 700 south from Charleston, then southeast down Bohicket Road. Kiawah is a private, gated resort community, impeccably planned and planted with perfect shrubs and tall oaks. Five championship golf courses, several restaurants, a 150-room inn, rental cottages and villas, and tawny beaches are among the offerings. For information, call **Kiawah Island Resort**. ~ 843-768-2121, 800-654-2924, fax 843-768-9339; www.kiawahresort.com.

HIDDEN ►

As the crow flies, **Edisto Island** is but a few miles across the Edisto River from Kiawah. In your car, it is many miles, about 55, as you backtrack north along Bohicket Road to Route 17, then south to Route 174, which burrows eastward into Edisto. Along Route 174 is tall pine forest and modest country homes set under magnolias, and the village of **Adams Run** with a country store selling hunting and fishing supplies and a post office the size of a postage stamp.

HIDDEN ►

Cathedrals of moss-draped oaks, ivy and kudzu snaking around their trunks, deliver you to the town of Edisto Island. There are no traffic lights here (the closest is 26 miles away) but there is the **Edisto Island Museum**, whose brief but well-done displays provide a portrait of sea island life. There is pottery from the island's earliest occupants, the Edistow Indians, and coil baskets made by the first Africans who were plantation slaves. The famed Sea Island Cotton, so fine it skipped local markets and was shipped straight to France to make lace, was grown here, as was rice and indigo. The museum is open afternoons on Tuesday, Thursday, Friday and Saturday. Admission. ~ 8123 Chisolm Plantation Road; 843-869-1954.

Mostly, though, Edisto is great for beachgoers. The scene here couldn't be any more different than at Kiawah. Edisto is casual, funky, a little rundown. Rows of rental cottages line the beach and pickup trucks line their driveways. Local cafés are staffed by sweet-talking waitresses and have been owned by the same family for half a century.

The **Edisto Chamber of Commerce** can supply information on the island. Closed Saturday and Sunday. ~ 430 Route 174; 843-869-3867, 888-333-2781; www.edistochamber.com, e-mail eichamber@aol.com. Jann Poston, a descendant of a local plantation family and owner of **Island Tours n T'ings**, takes groups on tours of the island's historic churches and plantations. ~ 843-869-1110, fax 843-869-0510. The second week of October, the Edisto Island Museum hosts the annual **Edisto and Beyond Tour**, which features several of the island's surviving plantation homes, graveyards, churches and other historic sites. ~ 843-869-1954.

If you visit Charleston in high season—spring and fall—you'll need a fat wallet. Rates at most inns are deluxe and ultra-deluxe then. In summer and winter, many of those same places offer moderate rates.

LODGING

The **Lodge at Lofton's Landing** is actually a house, a big and beautiful Japanese-style pole home sitting at the cusp of marsh wilderness, with a grand veranda encircling it and a 550-foot dock running down to Doe Hall Creek. The veranda is fashioned of redwood, the roof of spruce. The floors are heart of pine salvaged from a country school. Three bedrooms, a loft and 3000 square feet of space provide room for a big family or two small ones, or eight good friends. The kitchen is furnished for extensive cooking, or opt for catered meals (biscuits and shrimp for breakfast, frogmore stew for dinner). And lest you fear boredom out here in the Cape Romain wildlife refuge, kayaking, birding, chartered sailing and fishing provide plenty of options. And there is always Charleston, a half-hour away. Two-night minimum stay. ~ Route 17, five miles south of McClellanville; 843-720-7332, fax 843-887-4358; www.loftonslanding.com, e-mail makaira1@aol.com. MODERATE.

◄ *HIDDEN*

"Charleston goes to the beach" is how the designer of **The Boardwalk Inn** describes its five coral-washed stories crowned with cupola. The $12-million inn is within the country club confines of Wild Dunes Resort, 20 miles north of Charleston. Lobby floors gleam with Brazilian cherry and chairs have sunburst motifs copied from those in a St. Croix museum. Paintings by a George-town artist hang in many of the 93 rooms and suites that are out-fitted with plush waffle-weave robes and down pillows. The beach is a short stroll down the boardwalk and all the Wild Dunes activities—golf, tennis, boating, fishing—are a golf cart ride away. ~ 5757 Palm Boulevard, Isle of Palms; 843-886-6000, 800-845-8880; www.wilddunes.com, e-mail concierge@wilddunes.com. ULTRA-DELUXE.

Charleston easily has the finest lodging in South Carolina. Many inns here are old, saturated with history and judiciously restored, lavished with creature comforts and Southern pleasant-ries. To stay here is to enter another time, a slower mode.

Two Meeting Street Inn is a wonderful white house right on The Battery, with views across oak-dotted White Point Gardens and Charleston Harbor. The Queen Anne manse, as fanciful as a wedding cake, was indeed a wedding gift in 1890. Carved oak paneling graces much of the interior and Tiffany stained glass fills the windows. There are lovely arched piazzas. Antiques and canopy poster beds decorate three floors of rooms, all have pri-vate baths. Continental breakfast and afternoon tea are included. ~ 2 Meeting Street, Charleston; 843-723-7322; www.twomeet ingstreet.com. ULTRA-DELUXE.

The Mills House is a twentieth-century reconstruction of the 1850s antebellum hostelry once called "the finest hotel south of New York." Today's Mills House is still quite fine, its lobby bathed in floors of white marble, its 214 rooms and suites done in soothing tones of ice blue and peach and furnished with hand-some reproductions. The patio rooms have French doors open-ing onto a private alcove above the second-floor swimming pool.

AUTHOR FAVORITE

The first clue that **Jasmine House** had ultra-Charleston cool was the sign—it was so tiny I could barely see it from the street. It's located along quiet Hasell (pronounced "Hazel") Street in Charleston's eighteenth-century Ansonborough neighborhood, though Jasmine was built in the 1840s. The vanilla-washed Greek Revival mansion has ten luxurious rooms, with four inside a carriage house, all outfitted in grand style with antiques and finds from the Far East to England. There's barely a hint of a hostelry here—visitors check in across the street at Indigo Inn (One Maiden Lane), which shares the same owner—and after a few hours you feel like the place belongs to you. ~ 64 Hasell Street, Charleston; 843-577-5900, 800-845-7639, fax 843-577-0378; www.jasminehouseinn.com, e-mail info@jasminehouseinn.com. ULTRA-DELUXE.

~ 115 Meeting Street, at Queen Street, Charleston; 843-577-2400, 800-842-8022, fax 843-722-0623; www.millshouse.com. ULTRA-DELUXE.

Families like **The Meeting Street Inn**. Four stories tall and coral-washed, it's a casual place with a spacious courtyard and the faint feel of a motor court. All 56 rooms come with poster beds and simple baths with tubs, though some are showing wear. Buffet breakfasts of ham biscuits, pecan bread and honeydew melons are served in the lobby, and there are wine and hors d'oeuvres every afternoon. The staff is extra friendly. ~ 173 Meeting Street, Charleston; 843-723-1882, 800-842-8022, fax 843-577-0851; www.meetingstreetinn.com. ULTRA-DELUXE.

Charleston's most prominent lodging entrepreneur, Rick Widman, is known for his stellar yet varied taste in decorating and his affinity for impeccable service. His properties include Wentworth Mansion, King's Courtyard Inn, Fulton Lane Inn, Victoria House Inn, all described below, and the **John Rutledge House Inn**, which Rutledge built in 1763 for his bride, Elizabeth Grimke. Ornate ironwork and eyebrows decorate the outside of the three-story townhouse, while the inside is grandiose, endlessly detailed. All the doors and floors are original; the first-floor parquet floors are copies of European castle floors. There are eight bedrooms and three suites, the latter entirely overwhelming with its fourteen-foot ceilings, Italian marble fireplaces, grand canopy beds and whirlpool tubs. Eight additional rooms are spread between two carriage houses in back, though these are not as large or opulent. Pastries and coffee are delivered to your room each morning; wine and sherry are served in the grand ballroom afternoons and evenings. ~ 116 Broad Street, Charleston; 843-723-7999, 800-476-9741, fax 843-720-2615; www.johnrutledgehouseinn.com, e-mail jriddle@charminginns. com. ULTRA-DELUXE.

A throwback to America's Gilded Age, **Wentworth Mansion** was built in the 1880s by a wealthy cotton merchant with a weakness for opulence: Tiffany stained-glass windows, hand-carved marble fireplaces, elaborate fretwork and crystal chandeliers, and a grand staircase floating up to a cupola. In 1998 Rick Widman resurrected all the finery, opening 21 guest rooms, a formal library and parlor, and an enclosed sunporch where glasses of sweet tea and cool golden wine help pass summer afternoons. Rates are some of Charleston's priciest—and worth every penny. ~ 149 Wentworth Street, Charleston; 843-853-1886, 888-466-1886, fax 843-720-5290; www.wentworthmansion.com, e-mail bseidler@charminginns.com. ULTRA-DELUXE.

The Elliott House Inn is not as stylish as many other Charleston inns, but it is comfy enough and, most importantly, has rates starting in the moderate range in the fall and winter. Twenty-four rooms gather around a brick courtyard thick with palmettos, ficus and fountains, and a big spa beneath a trellis of purple wisteria. Plush throw rugs, exposed plumbing, vases of fresh flowers, and small baths round out the simple rooms. Pastries, fruit, juice and coffee are served in the morning, wine and cheese in the evening. The only drawback: occasional noise from the restaurant next door, so ask for a room across the courtyard. ~ 78 Queen Street, Charleston; 843-723-1855, 800-729-1855, fax 843-722-1567; www.elliotthouseinn.com. MODERATE TO ULTRA-DELUXE.

The 1853 Greek-Revival **King's Courtyard Inn** does indeed have a courtyard—actually, three of them, one of which is a sunlit brick hideaway with fountains flowing and ivy climbing the walls. Rooms aren't fancy but elegant, high-ceilinged expanses with long windows and the original hardwood floors. Some rooms have lace canopy beds and fireplaces. Continental breakfast, afternoon drinks, and bedside chocolates are included in the rates. ~ 198 King Street, Charleston; 843-723-7000, 800-845-6119, fax 843-720-2608; www.kingscourtyardinn.com. ULTRA-DELUXE.

HIDDEN ► Never mind there's no sign for **Twenty-Seven State Street Bed & Breakfast**. Word has leaked out, and you'll likely have to call weeks or months in advance if you hope to secure one of the two handsome rooms. Both the main house and adjoining carriage house date to 1800. The living room and one of the bedrooms have original exposed brick. The other room has a flower-trimmed balcony for sunset watching; both have kitchenettes. ~ 27 State Street, at Queen Street, Charleston; 843-722-4243, fax 843-722-6030; www.charleston-bb.com. ULTRA-DELUXE.

HIDDEN ► Tucked neatly down a brick alley along King Street's antique row, **Fulton Lane Inn** is a most desirable address, with two floors of sumptuous, smart-looking rooms, all totally nonsmoking. Another of Rick Widman's choice properties, Fulton Lane offers guest rooms and suites with poster canopy beds and big whirlpool tubs, some with fireplaces, cathedral ceilings and kitchenettes. Your continental breakfast arrives on a silver tray every morning. ~ 202 King Street, Charleston; 843-720-2600, 800-720-2688, fax 843-720-2940; www.fultonlaneinn.com. ULTRA-DELUXE.

Victoria House Inn resides in a Romanesque brick building whose past lives include YMCA and boardinghouse. Impeccably restored and opened in 1992, it is an intimate, private place with a lovely parlor for a lobby and two floors of plushly carpeted rooms painted deep plum and green. Big windows are fitted with wood blinds and lace shades, and cabinets and headboards are fashioned of rich wood. In the morning, a chambermaid brings you a champagne breakfast. ~ 208 King Street, Charleston; 843-

720-2944, 800-933-5464, fax 843-720-2930; www.thevictoria houseinn.com. ULTRA-DELUXE.

A landmark Charleston caravanserai since 1924, the **Historical Francis Marion Hotel** reopened in 1996 after being closed since Hurricane Hugo's unwelcome visit in 1989. Extensive refurbishing has not obscured the hotel's stunning historic features. The lobby is just as grand as ever, with soaring ceilings, and its original chandeliers and marble countertops at the front desk. The 227 guest rooms are accented with antique furnishings and white linen down bedspreads. Amenities here are many: weight room, day spa, lobby bar, coffee shop and restaurant. ~ 387 King Street, Charleston; 843-722-0600, 877-756-2121, fax 843-723-4633; www.thefrancismarion.com, e-mail info@thefrancismarion.com. ULTRA-DELUXE.

Charleston Place sprawls in the midst of historic downtown, its 440 luxuriant rooms sequestered within a complex of savvy shops. It has everything a visitor could want, from the grand lobby of marble and glittering chandeliers to the spacious rooms with beautiful reproduction furnishings, plush draperies and views of the city or courtyard. Service is superb. A fitness center with an indoor-outdoor pool and the excellent Charleston Grill are here, too. It's owned by the exclusive Orient-Express, which is continually adding exclusive touches—European-style spa, fountain entry with bronze sculpture, a club level sweep of floors with silver service breakfasts and teas, and nighttime cordial hours. ~ 205 Meeting Street, Charleston; 843-722-4900, 800-611-5545, fax 843-939-8541; www.charlestonplacehotel.com. ULTRA-DELUXE.

In the downtown area, **Planters Inn** manages to beautifully walk the line between luxury and lack of pretension. The 62-room hostelry surrounds a courtyard with a fountain and tables, flanked on one side by palm trees. The rooms are lovely: mine had a working fireplace and a four-poster bed with a lace canopy. Evening turndown service includes thoughtful touches like clas-

WELCOME HOMES

Many Charlestonians open their homes to visitors, offering simple to formal accommodations and prices ranging from budget to ultra-deluxe. **Historic Charleston Bed & Breakfast** can help you find a place. Most of their listings are within the historic district and so are walking distance to everything. Some accommodations are in separate carriage houses with living rooms and kitchens. Closed Saturday and Sunday. ~ 57 Broad Street, Charleston; 843-722-6606, 800-743-3583, fax 843-722-9589; www.historiccharlestonbedandbreakfast.com.

sical music and a sound machine. The lobby sitting room provides a constant flow of ice water and tea, and a bowl of apples for snacks on the run. Some bathrooms have whirlpool tubs; if bathroom luxury is important to you, make sure you request it. The inn is a member of Relais & Chateaux, an exclusive international group of hotels and restaurants, with standards that show in every touch. ~ 112 North Market Street, Charleston; 843-722-2345, 800-845-7082, fax 843-577-2125; www.planters inn.com. DELUXE TO ULTRA-DELUXE.

HIDDEN ▶   Northwest of downtown Charleston and next door to Middleton Place plantation is the highly unusual **Inn at Middleton Place**. Its stark granite exterior has a Gotham look, but inside, the 52 rooms are commodious spaces full of light and warmth, with lustrous wood cabinets, wood-burning fireplaces, thick glass blocks curving around sunken tubs, and floor-to-ceiling windows looking out on the woods and Ashley River. Frank Lloyd Wright fans will love it here. Free admission to Middleton Place gardens and house is included in the rate. ~ Ashley River Road, fourteen miles from Charleston; 843-556-0500, 800-543-4774, fax 843-556-5673; www.middletonplace.org. DELUXE TO ULTRA-DELUXE.

Only 35 minutes inland from Charleston lies an English-style refuge of profuse luxury and pampering. How else to explain the Alfred Gratien chilling in your room at **Woodlands Resort & Inn**, or the Swedish massage awaiting your tired body at the spa? Guests at the 19-room Relais & Chateaux resort are also treated to nightly handmade chocolates, plush robes, and romantic suites (ask for one with a fireplace and whirlpool tub) fashioned by New York designer David Eskell-Briggs. Relax on the sun patio by the heated pool, borrow a bike for a countryside ride or stroll along trails through the 42 acres of nonstop woods. ~ 125 Parsons Road, Summerville; 843-875-2600, 800-774-9999, fax 843-875-2603; www.woodlandsinn.com, e-mail reservations@ woodlandsinn.com. ULTRA-DELUXE.

South of Charleston, the lodging choices at **Kiawah Island Resort** include a 150-room inn and myriads of cottages, villas and homes for rent. Families especially enjoy these private, landscaped environs with ten miles of beaches, several restaurants, oceanfront pool, five golf courses and sixteen miles of bike trails. Reservations required to enter the property. ~ Kiawah Island; 843-768-2121, 800-654-2924; www.kiawahresort.com. DELUXE TO ULTRA-DELUXE.

Cottage and home rentals on Edisto are available by calling the **Atwood Agency**. ~ 843-869-2151, 800-476-0126. You may also want to try **Edisto Sales and Rentals Realty**. ~ 843-869-2527, 800-868-5398. Another option is **Lachicotte & Harper Realty**. ~ 843-869-1930, 800-962-1930.

Up north of Charleston, **The Crab Pot** is a simple side-of-the-road stop with red cinderblock walls and white butcher paper on the tables, not a lot of atmosphere on the surface. But back in the kitchen wonderful things are being done with just-plucked crab, and you should not leave without trying the she-crab soup or the crab balls (bundles of sweet lump crab seasoned and deep-fried), the hot crab open-face sandwich or the deviled crab cake plate (order it with red rice and cole slaw). Try them all—you won't be sorry. Closed Sunday. ~ Route 17, McClellanville; 843-887-3156. MODERATE.

Lowcountry cuisine reaches its zenith in Charleston, and you'll find wonderful French and Italian food as well.

Gaulart & Maliclet, known around the city as "Fast and French," or simply "F&F," is deep and skinny and lined with lots of little bars and counters. Grab a newspaper from a wall rack, have a seat at a bar, and choose from homemade soups and pâtés, smoked salmon and stuffed baguettes, and fruit, sandwich and cheese plates. There's petit and grand *dejeuner* every morning, and hearty dinners of escargot, fondue, chicken and fish. Go for the daily budget-priced specials with five items, including soup and a glass of wine. No dinner on Monday. Closed Sunday. ~ 98 Broad Street, Charleston; 843-577-9797, fax 843-723-1018; www.fastandfrench.org. MODERATE.

With a name like **High Cotton**, you expect some uppityness, if not from the cuisine then certainly from the clientele. Here you get both, though it's all very playful and chic, from the spry young cocktail crowd slipped into ostrich-skin banquettes, to the live jazz seven nights a week, to classic fare like filet mignon with mushroom gravy. Not that Chef Jason Scholz doesn't detour on occasion. Order his buttermilk fried oysters with green goddess

---

AUTHOR FAVORITE

French meets Lowcountry at **The Sea Island Grill**, where Swiss-born chef Enzo Steffenelli offers pecan-encrusted scallops; chicken stuffed with lobster; flounder stuffed with crab meat and served with a shrimp and corn succotash; and wasabi-encrusted grouper pan-fried with ginger hollandaise. His dishes are richly textured, flawlessly seasoned, and lovely to look at. The white linen restaurant has French doors, a mahogany bar, and wrought-iron chandeliers patterned after Charleston garden gates—though it is not in Charleston but at the Boardwalk Inn on Isle of Palms. Breakfast, lunch and dinner are served. ~ 5757 Palm Boulevard, Isle of Palms; 843-886-2200. DELUXE TO ULTRA-DELUXE.

dressing and enjoy them beneath the slow-drawl of palm frond fans. No lunch on weekdays. ~ 199 East Bay Street, Charleston; 843-724-3815, fax 843-724-3816; www.high-cotton.net. DELUXE.

It's no coincidence that the initials of **Slightly North of Broad** spell SNOB; the restaurant is a pecan toss from Charleston's lofty old houses just off the Battery. But there's nothing stuffy about this place, so big and open and high-ceilinged and situated in a restored warehouse, with friendly waiters and arty accoutrements. The elegant Southern and regional fare includes grilled barbecued tuna topped with fried oysters and country ham, and maverick grits, a thick stew with shrimp, scallops, ham and sausage. There are grilled salads and sandwiches for lunch. No lunch on weekends. ~ 192 East Bay Street, Charleston; 843-723-3424, fax 843-724-3811. MODERATE TO ULTRA-DELUXE.

Magnolia's is Charleston's premier Lowcountry haunt. The crisp linens are starched and as white as a magnolia, the light as soft and low as a Southern full-moon night. The patrons are trendy, very trendy. Chef Donald Barickman turns out such creations as spicy shrimp and sausage over creamy white grits. His signature "Down South" egg roll is stuffed with collard greens, chicken and ham and served with a trio of sauces: red pepper purée, spicy mustard sauce and peach chutney. If you can't go for dinner, go for lunch. ~ 185 East Bay Street, Charleston; 843-577-7771, fax 843-937-4027; www.magnolias-blossom-cypress.com. MODERATE TO ULTRA-DELUXE.

Adjacent to Magnolia's and sharing the same owners, **Blossom** is a stylish indoor/outdoor bistro for "seafood with a Southern accent." The open kitchen allows you to observe the creation of barbecue jumbo shrimp, Carolina crab ravioli, cornmeal fried oysters and—from the wood-burning oven—the po' boy pizza. The service is stellar, the wait staff comprised of vibrant people. Workday crowds pack in just before noon and just after 5 p.m. ~ 171 East Bay Street, Charleston; 843-722-9200,

---

WHERE THE HIP EAT HAMBURGERS

In a little, blue-painted shack near the U.S. Customs House, you'll find **Your Place**. Citadel cadets and other college students have made it their place, crowding into the beat-up wood booths and ordering Charleston's juiciest, beefiest burgers. Order them plain or lavished with bacon, cheese or jalapeños, and wash them down with long, tall glasses of sweet tea. The waitresses sport tattoos, the walls are festooned with useless nautical items, the concrete floors flood when it rains a lot. Closed Sunday. ~ 6 Market Street, Charleston; 843-722-8360. BUDGET.

fax 843-937-4027; www.magnolias-blossom-cypress.com. MOD-
ERATE TO ULTRA-DELUXE.

Venerable yet still chic, Charleston's **Carolinas** retains many
loyal patrons. The specialty is nouveau Lowcountry fare, and
there will undoubtedly be something on the menu to please you.
Among the favorites are the almond-crusted grouper and the
flounder in sweet potatoes. There are also plenty of poultry, pasta
and beef dishes. Expect a memorable dining experience. Reservations are recommended on the weekend. Dinner only. ~ 10
Exchange Street, Charleston; 843-724-3800, fax 843-722-9493;
www.carolinasrestaurant.com. MODERATE TO DELUXE.

You can dine inside tony **82 Queen**, but ask for a seat out in
the rambling brick courtyard with tables tucked beneath a gazebo and hoods of wisteria and rose trees. People gush about 82
Queen and its Lowcountry nouveau cooking, and this is under-
standable. One could eat bowls of the barbecued shrimp and
grits crowned with cheddar cheese and scallions, and the pudding-
thick she-crab soup laced with sherry. There's also roast duckling
with bing cherry–Grand Marnier glaze and grilled Georgia lamb
chops with mozzarella risotto. For both lunch and dinner, the
mood is momentous: waiters hurrying from the dining room, the
front door mobbed with hopeful diners, the clientele Southern
and smartly dressed. Don't go without a reservation. ~ 82 Queen
Street, Charleston; 843-722-4428; www.82queen.com, e-mail
info@82queen.com. DELUXE.

Dark, small and savvy, **Fulton Five** is Italian all the way, from
the platters of carpaccio, prosciutto and buffalo mozzarella that
greet you at the door to the ruby wine poured in small, glittering glasses. The music is like something from a Mickey Rourke
flick—fast, anxious, angst-filled. The people are polished and
pretty. The pasta, chicken, veal and seafood dishes are good to
great. Dinner only. Closed Sunday. ~ 5 Fulton Street, Charleston;
843-853-5555. DELUXE TO ULTRA-DELUXE.

Long, narrow and lively all day, **Baker's Cafe** has an inventive lineup of eggs (they're known for their poached dishes) and
turnovers, quiches and pasta, seafood and soups (you should try
the chicken chili with cheddar). There's art parked on the walls
and tables squeezed in tight. A back dining room offers more
space—if there are any empty seats. A good place for breakfast.
~ 214 King Street, Charleston; 843-577-2694; www.bakerscafe.
com. BUDGET TO MODERATE.

For long, leisurely, Lowcountry dining go to **Charleston Grill**.
You can listen to live jazz and eat Russian malosal caviar on buckwheat blinis, something tart and heady like baby lola rosa leaves
with Clemson blue cheese, or marinated shiitakes and roasted
hazelnuts in a sweet port and rosemary sauce. The floors are her-
ringbone and the carver chairs curved and comfortable. The

wine list numbers 1000 labels, and there are momentous wine tasting dinners throughout the year, including first-growth bordeaux paired with sweetbreads and foie gras. On Sunday the Grill hosts a "plantation supper" accompanied by classical guitar and violin. ~ 224 King Street, in Charleston Place; 843-577-4522, fax 843-724-8405. ULTRA-DELUXE.

Peninsula Grill has the look and feel of a supper club, its darkened candlelit recesses set with white-linen tables and a bar with booths of gold crushed-velvet brocade. Anyone inclined toward champagne will be happy at the Peninsula, for the champagne bar menu there presents both affordable and exquisite bubblies by the glass. For starters there's an iceberg salad with smoked bacon jerky and buttermilk dressing. For entrées try the grilled pork or veal chop with choice of sauces, from horseradish crème fraiche to toasted pecan Roquefort butter. Heady stuff. Dinner only. ~ 112 North Market Street, Charleston; 843-723-0700, fax 843-577-2125; www.peninsulagrill.com. ULTRA-DELUXE.

HIDDEN ► To get to **Circa 1886**, slip inside a pair of wrought-iron gates through a secret garden and back to the carriage house of a Victorian mansion. The clandestine Charleston spot is the domain of chef Marc Collins, who parlays the freshest, seasonal Lowcountry ingredients into fabulous-tasting dishes such as peppercorn-crusted antelope medallions with Carolina pecan butter, and poached wreck bass with rice noodle frittata and chanterelle mushroom *duxelle*. Dine inside on champagne-colored linens in suede-covered high-back chairs, or outside in the little garden. Dinner only. Closed Sunday. ~ 149 Wentworth Street, Charleston; 843-853-7828; www.circa1886.com, e-mail circa1886@charming inns.com. DELUXE TO ULTRA-DELUXE.

The atmosphere at **Anson** is enjoyable enough: little café tables and gold-back chairs, velvet booths and a balcony where one can dine with a view to St. Phillip's steeple. But mainly Anson is about food, seamlessly crafted cuisine of the Lowcountry designed to liven the eye and tongue. Fried cornbread oysters with green tomato relish, cashew-crusted grouper with champagne sauce, and double-cut, deep-fried pork chops with collards and mushroom cream sauce. And to end it all there is the chocolate oblivion torte. Dinner only. ~ 12 Anson Street, Charleston; 843-577-0551, fax 843-722-1955; www.ansonrestaurant.com. DELUXE.

Vickery's Bar & Grill is a popular hangout serving Lowcountry cuisine with a Cuban flair. Opt for the classic Cuban sandwich or the black beans and rice and you will be transported to Havana. Or stay closer to home with the roast half-chicken or the turkey pita with mixed greens, brie and raspberry mayonnaise. The bar is lively and the outdoor patio is, regulars say, the best in town. ~ 15 Beaufain Street, Charleston; 843-577-5300, fax 843-577-5020; www.vickerys.com. BUDGET TO MODERATE.

39 Rue de Jean may well be in the emerging design district called ChoHo, but its ambience is straight from Paris. Smoky mirrors, hammered tin ceilings and a zinc bar set the scene for brasserie staples such as duck confit, *coq au vin* and scallops St. Jacques. ~ 39 John Street, Charleston; 843-722-8881. DELUXE.

Amid the sea of seafood eateries in Charleston, none is as fresh and fashionable as **Fish**. In this 1837 Charleston "single-style" house, diners are served pepper-seared diver scallops amid rooms with black wingback chairs and lamps draped in scarves. In summer, ask for a seat (all are curvy and metallic) in the courtyard, next to the mermaid fountain. ~ 442 King Street, Charleston; 843-722-3474, fax 843-937-0406; www.fishrestaurant.net. MODERATE.

In the South, collard greens and black-eyed peas are served on New Year's day; this tradition is said to bring good luck in the coming year.

If you stay on Edisto Island, have dinner at the **Old Post Office**. The cream plank-board building with big blue mailboxes out front is topped with tin and backed by an enormous live oak. Within the high-ceiling dining rooms you can enjoy such unusual offerings as grilled onion sausage, homemade deviled crab cakes, pecan chicken with blueberry sauce, and shrimp and scallop grits. Ribeye steak and a ten-ounce filet topped with goat cheese and hollandaise sauce are among the more familiar entrées, and there is salmon, smoked out back over apple wood. Dinner only; reservations recommended. Closed Sunday. ~ Route 174 along Store Creek, Edisto Island; 843-869-2339, fax 843-869-2372. DELUXE.

SHOPPING

People from all over the Carolinas make shopping forays into Charleston. This isn't bargain shopping (though there are many deals to be had); we're talking antiquing and boutiquing at its very best. Whether you seek eighteenth-century English silver or Gothic garden statuary, the sassiest clothes or headiest chocolate truffles, things both bazaar and bizarre, you will find them among these brick and cobbled streets.

Utopia has the ultimate in cool clothes and shoes for women. Not a big selection, but smart-looking stuff. There are also paintings by Beki Crowell, the highly talented artist who owns the boutique. ~ 27 Broad Street, Charleston; 843-853-9510.

Candle bunches, "floaters," outdoor candles, even Hanukkah candles are in full aromatic display at **Candle Lover's Delight**. They also have bins of "crumble melts": pellets for placement in wax burners. Exotic scents like lemongrass, toasted coconut and caramel pecan pie may leave you hungry. ~ 58 Broad Street, Charleston; 843-723-6115; www.candleloversdelight.com.

With a sister store in Atlanta, **Metropolitan Deluxe** is a purveyor of stylish furniture, fine linens, cards and fresh flowers. ~ 164 Market Street, Charleston; 843-722-0436; www.metropolitandeluxe.com.

SHOPPING TOUR
Charleston's King Street

King Street is the king of shopping rows in Charleston. On the south end, between Broad and Wentworth streets, you'll find Tiffany, Chippendale and other
traditional highbrow names as well as familiar chains (Talbot's, Victoria's Secret
and, alas, even The Gap). But north of Wentworth, savvy shoppers will discover
the city's first design district—nicknamed ChoHo—where more than two dozen
boutiques have opened in Civil War–era buildings.

CHARLESTON TO CANTERBURY SQUARE   If after a day of sightseeing
you are completely charmed by Charleston, go to the **Preservation
Society of Charleston Bookstore.** Anything you could possibly want
to know about the place, from floor coverings to private gardens to
restoring old homes, is offered within the pages of a book. Besides that,
the employees here are anxious to help you get to know the city. Closed
Sunday. ~ 147 King Street, Charleston; 843-722-4630. Need a tie or a
blazer button? **Ben Silver** has thousands of both, with price tags reaching into the thousands. The London-based store will also sell you attire
for your cricket or croquet match. ~ 149 King Street, Charleston; 800-
221-4671. **George C. Birlant & Co.**, around since 1929, sells all manner of eighteenth- and nineteenth-century furniture, silver, china and
crystal, as well as Charleston Battery benches. Closed Sunday. ~ 191
King Street, Charleston; 843-722-3842.

BATH AND HOME COUTURE   If you're looking for a cool kitchen gadget
or something to spruce up the bath, check out **fred.** The 2000-square-

The Shops at Charleston Place is downtown Charleston's chic
mini-mall. In a rambling red-brick complex that includes the
Charleston Place Hotel, the stores are for the most part familiar
chains (Benetton, Godiva, Gucci, Laura Ashley), though you will
find a few singular boutiques. There's a parking garage here. ~
Market Street, between Meeting and King streets.

Even if you aren't shopping for paintings, stop by The Pink
House Gallery. It's a wonderful old building, Charleston's oldest,
built in the 1690s of Bermuda stone. There's just one room on
each of three floors. The walls are filled with watercolors and
prints by local artists. Closed Sunday. ~ 17 Chalmers Street,
Charleston; 843-723-3608.

For flea market items and those a notch above, go to The
City Market. Even if you're not buying, the market's weary old-

foot shop looks upscale, but don't let that scare you away. There's plenty in here that is affordable for budget-conscious travelers. The store's wide selection of adorable basics and accessories makes it hard to leave empty-handed. ~ 237 King Street, Charleston; 843-723-5699.

THINGS TO WEAR   The great-smelling **Stella Nova** stocks luxuriant body lotions, aromatherapy oils and playful gadgets for your hair. ~ 292 King Street, Charleston; 843-722-9797. The eighteenth-century home that houses **Croghan's Jewel Box** is the perfect backdrop for this shop specializing in antique gems and novelties. Over 80 years old, the store's unusual array of silver will dazzle anyone with an affinity for this precious metal. There is also a fine selection of designer pieces to satisfy those with modern taste. Closed Sunday. ~ 308 King Street, Charleston; 843-723-3594; www.croghansjewelbox.com. The zany **Granny's Goodies** carries both new and used oddities, from Jerry Garcia ties to costumes and old movie posters. ~ 301 King Street, Charleston; 843-577-6200.

FOR DESIGN DIVAS   In ChoHo, snap up a wide, hip-hugging belt or low-cut denim halter from **Rosita Jones**, which has a lounge-like interior. ~ 440 King Street; 843-958-0120. Top things off with a hand-blocked, felt cheetah cocktail chapeau from **Magar Hatworks**. ~ 557½ King Street; 843-577-7740. Slip down a side street to **Filigree**, where Charleston designer Heather Key Tiller fashions such singular pieces as gemstone lariats. ~ 47 John Street; 843-722-6189. In the district's home department, **Dwelling** displays mohair throws and curvaceous lidded vases. ~ 474 King Street; 843-723-9699. Neighborhood pioneer Robert Hines has been producing stained-glass windows and mosaic panels at **Hines Studios** for over a decade. ~ 579 King Street, Charleston; 843-722-0207.

brick walls and wood-beam ceilings are atmospheric, and you can't help but get swept along in the flush of shoppers. ~ Market Street between Meeting and East Bay streets.

NIGHTLIFE

Clichés about the lazy pace in the South don't hold true for Charleston's bar-hopping nightlife. Charleston cooks at night. Bar-hopping is *de rigueur*, and plenty of places are geared toward early or late-night crowds.

The twice-a-night shows at **Cumberland's** headline hot rock and Delta blues bands. The beer's extra cold, too. ~ 301 King Street, Charleston; 843-577-9469.

Looking for laughs? Check out **The Have Nots**, an improvisational comedy troupe that makes its home at Theatre 99. After touring the country for several years, the group decided to put down some roots. The 8 p.m. shows on weekends are a huge draw. Audience participation is a big part of the fun, so don't be shy. ~ 446 King Street, Charleston; 843-853-6687; www.thehavenots.com.

Wild Wing Cafe, one in a chain around the Carolinas, can get crazy most anytime, but later is better. Come for beer by the bucket, chicken wings and insanity. Live bands play every night. ~ 36 North Market Street, Charleston; 843-722-9464; www.wildwingcafe.com.

Save **Kaminsky's** for after dinner. The "Most Excellent Café" has brick walls and a glass case filled with tempting chocolate trappings. There's good wine and music, a gay and straight crowd, and a lineup of sassy coffee drinks. ~ 78 North Market Street, Charleston; 843-853-8270.

Classy **Charleston Chops** has hardwood and brass decor and a prettily lit piano bar. Wear your long black cocktail dress and order a martini. ~ 188 East Bay Street, Charleston; 843-937-9300.

The polished, postmodern bar at **Blossom** is tended by young men in ponytails. Young professionals settle in at the bar for happy hour, and an older crowd appears in the after-dinner hours. ~ 171 East Bay Street, Charleston; 843-722-9200.

In a big recycled warehouse and looking like a mini concert hall, the **Music Farm** hosts regional and big-name rock-and-roll, reggae, new wave and jazz bands several days a week. Advance tickets available. The scene is young and happening. ~ 32 Ann Street, Charleston; 843-722-8904.

The place to go in Edisto is **Coot's Lounge**, a funky joint situated right on the beach that hosts good blues and beach bands most summer evenings. The rest of the year, there are live acts featured on weekends. ~ The Pavilion, 102 Palmetto Boulevard, Edisto Island; 843-869-3063.

THEATER, BALLET AND SYMPHONY For three weeks each spring, the **Spoleto Festival**, a Charleston-based performing-arts festival, presents internationally acclaimed opera, dance, jazz, theater and symphonic programs at venues throughout the city. ~ 14 George Street, Charleston; 843-722-2764; www.spoletousa.org.

SKY-HIGH SUNSETS

Just before sunset, go to the **Rooftop Bar** at the Vendue Inn. The rooftop roost, peopled with pretty faces, is prime for watching the golden globe sink down along the Cooper River, with views across Waterfront Park and Charleston Harbor. Live music Sunday through Friday. ~ 23 Vendue Range, Charleston; 843-723-0485; www.vendueinn.com.

Charleston's best plays come from the **Charleston Stage Company**, which produces classical and cutting-edge musicals, drama and comedy, as well as children's theater. ~ 135 Church Street, Charleston; 843-577-5967.

Dancers with the **Charleston Ballet Theater** come from as far as Austria, San Francisco and New York. South Carolina's only full-time professional dance company, the ballet presents traditional and contemporary dance throughout the year. ~ 477 King Street, Charleston; 843-723-7334; www.charlestonballet.org.

Classical, chamber and pop music concerts are presented September through May by the **Charleston Symphony Orchestra**. ~ P.O. Box 20397, Charleston, SC 29413; 843-723-7528; www.charlestonsymphony.com.

GAY SCENE   Gay and straight night owls mingle at most Charleston nightspots. For a strictly gay scene, try **Dudley's**, the "men's Cheers of Charleston." ~ 42 Ann Street, Charleston; 843-577-6779.

Bar hop over to **Pantheon**, located near the visitors center, where the action gets started around 11:30 p.m. This 5000-square-foot dance club has a cabaret and dancers, lots of shirtless men, and a well-deserved cover charge. Closed Monday through Wednesday. ~ 28 Ann Street, Charleston; 843-577-2582; www.clubpantheon.com.

Beaches are not the Lowcountry's high point, for obvious reasons: dozens of creeks and rivers delivering mud and silt out to shore and ocean. The surf gets cloudy and the sand ruddy. Near the mudflats, the beaches are littered with pesky oyster fragments. Among the few exceptions are the far-flung islands north of Charleston called Cape Romain.

BEACHES & PARKS

CAPE ROMAIN NATIONAL WILDLIFE REFUGE 🏃 🦌 🛶 This 22-mile crescent of barrier islands between the Intracoastal Waterway and the Atlantic Ocean is wild, windswept—and extremely remote. Unless you have your own boat, you must take a ferry to the island, and it only operates four days a week, from March thorough November. The rest of the year, it runs on Saturday only. **Bulls Island**, the southern end of the refuge, is the only place you can go ashore. Here are some of the South Carolina coast's best sands, a lonesome strand of fine, deep white. Shelling is excellent. The twenty-minute boat ride over is through dense salt marsh populated by pelicans, egrets, herons and other shorebirds. Take along comfortable walking shoes, binoculars, insect repellent, a picnic and plenty to drink, including fresh water. This place is primitive. Swim here at your own risk; the water can be rough and the currents strong. As far as fishing goes, there is good surf casting, though it's a pain to lug the rods and

◄ HIDDEN

tackle. Facilities include restrooms, picnic tables, and sixteen miles of nature trails. The Sewee Visitor and Environmental Education Center on Route 17 has informative displays and information on ferry schedules and prices. ~ Ferries (there is a ferry fee of $30 per person) leave from Garris Landing, off Route 17 about twenty miles north of Charleston, just before Awendaw. From Route 17, turn east on Seewee Road; 843-928-3368, fax 843-928-3828; www.seweecenter.fws.gov.

ISLE OF PALMS AND SULLIVAN'S ISLAND ⚊ These twin islands just north of Charleston are where the city folk go for sun and sand. Big stilt homes line the dunes, and then there is silvery, hard-packed sand that often runs thin on high tide. Both islands are packed in summer, with traffic crawling along Route 703. Isle of Palms is favored by families and older people; there's wheelchair access across the dunes. Swimming is good along beaches at both islands and lifeguards are occasionally on watch. Facilities include restrooms, public parking lots and showers at Isle of Palms. ~ The islands are located along a twelve-mile stretch of Route 703, about nine miles north of Charleston; 843-886-3863, fax 843-886-8943.

FOLLY BEACH COUNTY PARK ⚊ On one side of this park is Folly River and a spacious sweep of seagrass, on the other is a string of beach, silvery, silty and whipped by waves. The winds lash constantly at this land's-end point of Folly Island, just south of Charleston. Everyone loves the 1045-foot pier with 170 benches designed for fishing or just wave watching. Wooden ramps provide wheelchair access to the beach. The gay and lesbian crowd gravitates to the southernmost end of the beach. Strong tides and currents and hidden deep areas make swimming here more challenging. Swim only in designated areas, where lifeguards patrol in summer. Facilities include picnic tables and shelter, outdoor showers and restrooms year-round; a snack bar, beach rentals and gift shop operate during the summer. Day-use fee, $5. ~ Located on the west end of Folly Island, off Route 171, about 12 miles southeast of Charleston; 843-588-2426.

HIDDEN ▶   **BEACHWALKER PARK** ⚊ This is the only public beach on Kiawah Island, and it is a fine one. Tremendous vistas of windblown seagrass end in forests of oak and palms, and there is the dark, snaking Kiawah River. The Atlantic Ocean borders one side of Beachwalker, complete with wide, windy beach—up to 200 feet wide at low tide. The condos and townhouses of private Kiawah Island Resort are visible in the distance. There are strong winds and currents; swim in the designated area, staffed by lifeguards in summer. Facilities include restrooms, outdoor showers, picnic area, and a seasonal snack bar. The park is closed November

Sweetgrass Baskets

Along the country roadsides of Route 17 near Mount Pleasant, you will see ebony-skinned women sitting beneath roofs of tin and plywood and selling sweetgrass baskets. They are intricate baskets, tightly woven and as resilient as the women who have spent years learning their art. Properly cared for, a sweetgrass basket will last generations. No two baskets are alike.

It is an old Lowcountry art, the making of sweetgrass baskets, originating about 300 years ago when the first Africans were shipped to the South to be slaves. The women waded into the marsh and cut the wispy, plume-like grass and took it home to dry. Its scent was good, like fresh-cut hay. They bound it with palmetto fronds, stitching the grass with slivers of frond in interlocking patterns (a maddeningly meticulous task) until it became rows of coil.

The baskets were used on the plantations; commodious ones carried produce to market, while wide, flat, winnowing trays called "fanners" separated chaff from rice. Deep baskets, which African men often made from bulrush, stored grain, cotton and fish. Ornamental baskets were filled with fruit and placed on sideboards and dining tables of plantation manors. Today, they are exhibited in museums and sold at art shows.

Mount Pleasant, across the Cooper River from Charleston, is the heart of sweetgrass country. From the humble shacks and lean-tos alongside Route 17, the Mount Pleasant Sweetgrass Basketmakers' Association sells beautiful vessels that cost up to several hundred dollars. The smallest basket (the size of a tea cup) sells for about $20. Fruit baskets with thin, graceful handles start at $75, and urn-shaped containers are over $100. Some baskets are woven with bulrush and longleaf pine needles.

Many of the women speak Gullah, a pure, rich Creole language developed by their plantation ancestors. As they sell their baskets they sing the soft, strong Gullah hymns. Besides the stalls on Route 17, you'll find Gullah basket weavers in Charleston at **The Old Charleston Market**. ~ Market Street between Meeting and East Bay streets. You can also find them at **The Four Corners of Law**. ~ Meeting and Broad streets. Down in the Sea Islands, **The Red Piano Too** has a small selection of baskets. ~ 870 Sea Island Parkway, St. Helena Island; 843-838-2241.

through February. ~ Located on the west end of Kiawah Island, off Bohicket Road, about 30 miles southeast of Charleston; 843-762-2172, fax 843-762-2683.

HIDDEN ▶ **EDISTO BEACH STATE PARK** 🏃 ⌂ ⌟ Spread across 1255 acres of dunes, marsh and tidal creeks, maritime forest and shelly sand, the park extends from the Atlantic Ocean well into Edisto Island. The park was built in the 1930s by the Civilian Conservation Corps and today is a nesting ground for endangered logger-head turtles. The beach is a combination of brownish, dirtlike sand and crushed oyster shells, so bring a chair. Five air-conditioned cabins with screened porches, picnic tables and barbecue grills overlook Scott Creek. The budget-priced cabins have a three-night minimum stay; reservations required. Swimming is okay in the ocean, though the water is often cloudy. Fishing is superb. Come in late fall and fish for trout, bass, flounder, whiting, spot and even shark. Crabbing and shrimping are also excellent. Facilities include a park office, an interpretive center and gift shop, restrooms and nature trails. Day-use fee, $4. ~ Off Route 174 on Edisto Island, about 50 miles southeast of Charleston; 843-869-2756, fax 843-869-3023.

▲ There are 89 RV and tent campsites, including 31 with partial hookups; $17.50 to $23 per night. Reservations: 866-345-7275.

▼▼▼▼▼▼▼▼▼▼▼
Beaufort & the Sea Islands

On a map, the 69 inland miles between Charleston and Beaufort look empty. Route 17, which is two lanes most of the way, ambles through scrub pine and oak forest sprinkled with scant towns like Parkers Ferry, Jacksonboro and Ashepoo, then enters the hushed, hazy domain of ACE Basin National Wildlife Refuge.

SIGHTS The ACE Basin, where the Ashepoo, Combahee and Edisto rivers meet, encompasses some 350,000 acres of marsh and rivers and swamps, creating one of the last coastal wildernesses in the Carolinas. Nearly 12,000 acres of this vast area has been preserved as the **ACE Basin National Wildlife Refuge**, home to alligators, wading birds, wintering waterfowl and migratory birds. There are 27 known pairs of bald eagles that can be spotted year round.

HIDDEN ▶

A few miles south of the basin, take the eastern turnoff for Route 21 and after 15 miles you'll arrive in **Beaufort**. It's a superb small Southern port town with rich Colonial and antebellum flourishes and only 12,000 residents. Grand old mansions number more than 150. They march along a waterfront of salt marsh and frilly palmetto trees. The streets have ceilings of ancient oaks and magnolias. The air is perfumed by the sea.

Beaufort's first homes weren't grand but very simple, sturdy structures built by Barbadian planters, religious refugees, English indentured servants and others who came seeking a new life in the early 1700s. The settlers burned oyster shells with lime to make tabby, strong as cement, and used it to secure their clapboard homes. They faced the homes southward at the river, to catch prevailing breezes, and gave them Georgian, Greek Revival and tropical Spanish touches.

A hundred years later, sea island cotton came to Beaufort and neighboring islands and made a lot of people very rich. It was an unusual cotton, soft and silken and extremely prized in Europe. From 1820 to 1860, wealthy planters built furiously across Beaufort, fashioning plantation-style homes with formal gardens on big lots all over town. Today, they fill the downtown, creating a kind of outdoor, privately owned museum. Filmmakers like Beaufort. Its fanciful homes and boundaries of river and vast salt marsh and sky, so surreal and Hollywood-like, have been the backdrop for many films.

> Films such as *The Big Chill*, *The Great Santini*, *The Prince of Tides* and *Forrest Gump* were filmed in Beaufort.

Walk into the **Greater Beaufort Chamber of Commerce and Visitors Center** and the first thing you'll hear is: "Have you seen *The Prince of Tides*? Well, right out here on this dock is where Nick Nolte was at the end of the movie," and so on about many scenes that really did or didn't take place around town. The chamber folks will explain how to best explore Beaufort and the nearby sea islands, including tips on carriage, walking and boat tours. ~ 1106 Carteret Street, Beaufort; 843-524-3163, 800-638-3525, fax 843-986-5405; www.beaufortsc.org, e-mail chamber@beaufortsc.org.

About a half-mile north of the chamber is the pretty **Henry C. Chambers Waterfront Park**, dotted with oak trees and paved with brick piazzas and those made of crushed oyster shells. There are lots of benches and even swings and a playground along the seawall. Bay Street runs along the park and the water, and this is where you should start your walk around Beaufort. Shops, eateries and inns are sprinkled along Bay Street and the few blocks just off it.

The west end of Bay Street is laced with fabulous homes and manses and immense trees strung with Spanish moss. At low tide the bay reveals brown caps of oyster beds and waves of seagrass.

Near the center of Bay Street you'll find the **John Mark Verdier House Museum**. Built by a prominent merchant in 1800, it is not a prominent place but one filled with fascinating details on early Beaufort life. The Federal-style house faces south to catch river breezes and is built up high to avoid flooding (like so many early Beaufort homes, the first of its three floors is called the "garden floor"). The woodworking is outstanding, from the ocean waves carved along the staircase to cable and rope detailing along the fireplace mantles. There's a fireplace in each of the eight rooms. Closed Sunday. Admission. ~ 801 Bay Street, Beaufort; 843-379-6335, fax 843-379-3371.

You'll also find plenty of history at **The Beaufort Museum**. It's two blocks north of Bay Street in the 1798 Beaufort Arsenal, sunny yellow and Gothic in style with its pointed arches and heavy, castlelike gates. One large gallery holds artifacts and information about the history of Beaufort County, from prehistory to the twentieth century. Closed Sunday. Admission. ~ 713 Craven Street, Beaufort; 843-379-3331.

Near the east end of Bay Street, Route 21 crosses the Beaufort River and for 18 miles threads across a series of secluded **sea islands**. Also called the Sea Island Parkway, the road is the only way in and out of these Lowcountry lairs. It passes first along **Ladys Island** and then **St. Helena Island**, with bucolic scenes of small pastures dotted with grain silos, signs for pick-your-own tomatoes, matchbook-size seafood markets, and stands of tall cabbage palm trees. No-name dirt roads trail off from the Sea Island Parkway.

On St. Helena Island, you'll find the town of **St. Helena Island**, home to a few shops, gas stations, eateries and residences. Out of town, bridges bring endless horizons of salt marsh, their grassy shallows and mudflats attended by hopeful shorebirds. Snapping turtles cross the road. Shrimp boats send out their wide nets, like birds opening their wings, and drag the bottom for the pearly pink shellfish. There is a restaurant here called the Shrimp Shack where you can eat a shrimp burger.

After St. Helena comes tiny **Harbor Island**, a gated resort. Then densely wooded **Hunting Island**, where all 5000 acres are protected as a state park. The last of the sea islands, the end of the cul-de-sac, is **Fripp Island**, a private resort that you can enter only with a reservation. ~ 843-838-3535, 800-845-4100.

LODGING

Plan your accommodations carefully: In summer many inns and resorts in this area rent by the week only.

On the west side of Beaufort's Bay Street, **TwoSuns Inn** is a homey and inviting bed and breakfast housed in a 1917 Neoclassic Revival manse. There are six guest rooms painted deep colors and given ruffly, floral flourishes. One has a country quilt theme, another is pure Victorian. In the skylight room, you sleep beneath the stars. All have views of the salt marsh and bay. There is a croquet lawn in front, and a ramp that accommodates wheelchair visitors. Full breakfast is included in the rates. ~ 1705 Bay Street, Beaufort; 843-522-1122, 800-532-4244; www.twosunsinn.com, e-mail info@twosunsinn.com. DELUXE TO ULTRA-DELUXE.

Riding with the Rev

For the very best "insider" look at the Sea Islands, join **The Rev's Step-On Gullah Tours** ($20 per person for a three-hour tour; 843-838-3185). Beaufort native Joseph P. Bryant (just call him "Rev," like the parishioners at his Baptist church and everyone else in town) will take you around in his van, explaining the rich, obscure Gullah culture of the Sea Islands. Descendants of African slaves, the Gullah were abandoned after the Civil War because these isles was considered worthless. "There were no bridges, and the mosquitoes were so thick they'd carry you off," says the Rev. That abandonment, and more than a century of isolation, have preserved the Gullah language, culture and daily way of life. Families live for generations on the same farm, grow much of their own food, pick sweetgrass to make baskets, and attend the one-room praise houses of their slave ancestors, where hymns are harmonized in Gullah.

After stops at a praise house and a Gullah plantation (you can chat with the owners but can't take a tour, since the farms are private), the Rev heads to **Gullah Grub Café**. This is the venue for terrific, traditional Gullah cooking—barbecued chicken, collard greens and sweet potato pie. ~ 877 Sea Island Parkway, St. Helena Island; 843-838-3841. MODERATE.

From the front window of the studio and gallery at **Ibile Indigo House**, white doves coo inside a cage as artistic director Arianne King Comer tells how indigo patterns are created with everything from broomsticks to chicken feathers. In recent years, King Comer and Sea Island farmers have worked to bring back the lost African art. *Ibile*, pronounced "ee-beh-lay," is a Yoruba term for "those who are messengers of our ancestors." The messages here resound from intricate images of African village life—seasons and harvests, births and deaths—depicted on brilliant fabrics, lampshades, and rugs that are for sale. ~ 27 Penn Center Circle East, St. Helena Island; 843-838-3884, fax 843-838-8023; www.ibileindigo.com.

Near tour's end, if you find yourself dreaming of moving to the Sea Islands, you're not alone. "Tourists are so infatuated by the simplicity of this place," the Rev says, "that they sometimes change their address."

The Cuthbert family built a Federal-style house in 1790 and lived there until their capture by Union forces in 1861. Today, the home is a charming bed and breakfast with seven guest rooms. **The Cuthbert House Inn** features pine floors, oriental rugs and gleaming mahogany and cherry furniture. Each room has a private bath, phone and cable TV. A full Southern breakfast is served each morning in the dining room. In the evening, guests head to the veranda for refreshments and sunset. ~ 1203 Bay Street, Beaufort; 843-521-1315, 800-327-9275; www.cuthbert houseinn.com, e-mail info@cuthberthouseinn.com. DELUXE TO ULTRA-DELUXE.

As charming as a dollhouse, the award-winning **Beaufort Inn** sits in the heart of the Historic Landmark District. The common area, with mahogany trim and marble-and-slate fireplaces, is impeccably decorated with period furniture. The inn's centerpiece is a stairway that curves around a 50-foot-high atrium and connects rooms on the second and third floors. Each of the 25 guest rooms, which vary in size and decor, is named after a Lowcountry plantation and features photographs of the room's namesake. There are modern amenities as well: wet bars and televisions. In addition is a self-contained cottage with two bedrooms, living room, dining room and kitchen. Despite this modernity, the proprietors retain Southern hospitality and rocking chairs on the front porch beckon to guests. ~ 809 Port Republic Street, Beaufort; 843-521-9000, fax 843-521-9500; www.beaufortinn.com, email information@beaufortinn.com. DELUXE TO ULTRA-DELUXE.

HIDDEN ▶   Stashed down a Sea Island lane, **Beaulieu House** is an airy, welcoming B&B with a postcard-perfect location on Chowan Creek. The three-story Victorian-style house has nine rooms decorated in simple, seaside style—pastel coverlets, antiques and

AUTHOR FAVORITE

One of Beaufort's most desirable guesthouses resides but a block from Bay Street and the harbor. **Rhett House Inn** is lovely, quite Southern and civilized in every way. Classical music is played at breakfast, and sugar-dusted french toast is served on English china. Guest rooms are high-ceilinged and plushly adorned with down comforters, handsome antiques and thick pile towels. There is a lush courtyard and two floors of wide piazzas wonderful for relaxing and listening to birdsong. Owners Stephen and Marianne Harrison are former Manhattaners (her father started Anne Klein) who are completely cordial, seeing to your every need. ~ 1009 Craven Street, Beaufort; 843-524-9030, 888-480-9530, fax 843-524-1310; www.rhetthouseinn.com, e-mail info@rhetthouseinn.com. DELUXE TO ULTRA-DELUXE.

dolls. Ask for a room with a water-view veranda, and you can gaze across honey-colored marsh. In nearby historic Port Royal, Beaulieu also offers three roomy suites in a nicely renovated 1899 Island house. ~ 3 Sheffield Court, Cat Island; 843-575-0303, 866-814-7833, fax 843-770-0303; www.beaulieuhouse.com, e-mail beaulieubb@aol.com. DELUXE TO ULTRA-DELUXE.

You can rent a cottage, villa or efficiency within the private, quiet confines of **Fripp Island Resort**. The southeasternmost sea island, Fripp has more than three miles of beach, much of it secluded, and a golf course along the ocean. If you don't like golf, you can gather clams and oysters along the flats. There are tennis courts, restaurants, swimming pools, shops, a marina and a church. Nature trails and golf cart paths meander around the island, and golf carts are the vehicle of choice. Great for families, the resort even has a camp for kids. ~ Route 21, Fripp Island; 843-838-3535, 800-845-4100, fax 843-838-9079; www.frippislandresort.com, e-mail info@frippislandresort.com. MODERATE TO ULTRA-DELUXE.

◄ HIDDEN

Plums, at Beaufort's Waterfront Park, is a casual café with a porch overlooking the river and multicolored tile floors. Go for the shrimp roll, homemade soup or any of the very good sandwiches. The lengthier dinner menu includes pasta, chicken and steak. ~ 904½ Bay Street, Beaufort; 843-525-1946, fax 843-986-5092. MODERATE TO DELUXE.

DINING

Emily's is Beaufort's bistro and *tapas* bar, a colorful, cozy nook with painted wood beams. Salads and soups (try the she-crab or French onion) are mainstays, and there's a *tapas* lineup that includes herring in wine or Cajun sausage. For dinner, there is steak *au poivre*, blackened lamb chops and duck à l'orange. Dinner only. Closed Sunday. ~ 906 Port Republic Street, Beaufort; 843-522-1866. BUDGET TO DELUXE.

For leisurely, civilized dining, try the restaurant at the **Beaufort Inn**. The atmosphere is elegant and formal, but you're not required to dress the part. The dinner menu changes four times a year, but longstanding favorites will appear again: roast rack of lamb with Creole mustard glaze, crispy whole flounder with a watermelon-strawberry chutney, and sliced roast duck breast with a raspberry puree sauce. Sunday brunch. ~ 809 Port Republic Street, Beaufort; 843-521-9000; www.beaufortinn.com, e-mail beaufortinn@hargray.com. DELUXE TO ULTRA-DELUXE.

Go to the sea islands and have lunch at the **Shrimp Shack**. In a humble gray house with fishnets strung out front, you can sit in a screened porch, look across the salt marsh and enjoy a shrimp burger. The shrimp are pressed into a patty, lightly battered and crisp-fried, then laid in a soft, buttery bun—very nice. Hushpuppies, fried sweet-potato fingers, and red rice piled with andouille sausage are possible sides. The iced tea is as sweet as honey. You could also have a shrimp hamburger, fried flounder, crab or scallops, but hardly anyone does. In summer, the shack serves a hundred pounds of shrimp a day. Dinner also served May through September. Closed Sunday year-round. ~ Route 21, east end of St. Helena Island; 843-838-2962, fax 843-838-5945. BUDGET.

SHOPPING   Boutiques, galleries and antique stores are plentiful in Beaufort, especially along Bay Street and the blocks immediately north. The best antiquing is on Carteret Street.

The fine **Rhett Gallery** displays paintings and prints of the Lowcountry, as well as Civil War art and memorabilia, first-edition Audubons, wood carvings and antique nautical charts. ~ 901 Bay Street, Beaufort; 843-524-3339; www.rhettgallery.com.

At **Beaufort Butterfly Company & John Cody Gallery**, enthusiastic owner Steve Mix will show you his extensive collection of butterflies and moths from Beaufort and the sea islands. For sale are butterfly soaps, T-shirts, kites and many other things with winged themes. Closed Sunday. ~ 928 Bay Street, Beaufort; 843-986-0555.

Sunlight streams in the wood and glass cupola of **Firehouse Books & Espresso Bar**, which is indeed in a restored brick fire station. Browse the ample selection of hard and paperbacks and periodicals, then have a cappuccino and a pastry. ~ 706 Craven Street, Beaufort; 843-522-2665.

If you're fond of folk art, go to the **Red Piano Too Art Gallery**. The co-op building in "downtown" St. Helena Island is a gallery of brightly painted birdhouses, chairs and tables, mobiles made of watermelon sculptures, jewelry, Lowcountry paintings and other fine pieces. ~ 870 Sea Island Parkway, St. Helena Island; 843-838-2241; www.redpianotoo.com.

BEACHES & PARKS   **HUNTING ISLAND STATE PARK** 🏃 🏊 🎣 At the eastern end of the sea islands, this far-flung, 5000-acre island park is filled with slash pine and palmetto forest and edged in beach that lasts more than four miles. The sand is hard-packed and silver from intruding bits of oyster shells; the beach is thin at high tide and wide at low. There is a brick-lined lighthouse, completed in 1875 and moved to its current spot in 1889 because of beach erosion. A previous lighthouse was destroyed by Confederate troops. Displays in the visitors center tell about the lighthouses, maritime and fishing history, and the island's abundant wildlife, which includes white-tailed deer. Lodging is offered in fourteen furnished, budget-priced cabins near the ocean, all with air conditioning, heating and one, two or three bedrooms. Try to book at least a year in advance. Swimming is good within designated, protected areas, in season only. **Hunting Island Fishing Pier**, one of the longest freestanding piers on the East Coast, is at the park's southern point. It is extremely popular. Try for trout, spot, drum and tarpon. Monster tarpon have been caught in previous decades. You can also fish in the lagoon near the southern end of the park. The facilities here include a visitors center, picnic areas, a beach store, nature trails, a fishing pier and a marsh boardwalk. Day-use fee, $4. ~ Route 21, 16 miles east of Beaufort; 843-838-2011, fax 843-838-4263.

▲ The campground has 180 sites for tents or RVs, most with electrical and water hookups. Two sites accommodate wheelchair visitors and can be booked in advance, as can 59 of the other sites. Remaining sites are first-come; $19 to $23 per night. A park store and hot-water showers are located in the campground.

Hilton Head is often called "the original island green." In this community of only 40,000, there are 30 golf courses and room for no more.

Hilton Head Island Area

From Beaufort, Route 170 runs southwest across the Broad River for 13 miles to Route 278. Get on Route 278 heading south and then east toward Hilton Head Island, and you will see signs for Vidalia onions and Georgia peaches. Magnolia blossoms, big, fat and white, hang from 30 feet above in towering trees along the road. The city of Savannah, Georgia, is only ten miles south.

SIGHTS

◄ HIDDEN

Along Route 278 take the western turnoff on Route 46 and drive two miles through pine forest to **Bluffton**. Things haven't changed much the past few decades in this Lowcountry village, which was settled around 1825 as a summer resort for rice and cotton planters and nearly leveled by Union troops in the Civil War. Folks take their noon meals at the Squat & Gobble, a roadside dive with newspaper racks parked out front.

The heart of town runs along Calhoun Street, where little clapboard homes are buried beneath the spidery branches of live oaks. Funky emporiums offer terrific art and second-hand finds. Where Calhoun ends at the river, you'll find a peaceful setting occupied by the stunning **Church of the Cross**. The Gothic wood church, built in 1854, looks like something from medieval England with its pointed arches and heavy, castle-like doors. ~ Calhoun Street, Bluffton; 843-757-2661.

◄ HIDDEN

Back on Route 278 east a few miles, the bucolic scenes evaporate when you reach **Hilton Head Island**. Twelve miles long, five miles wide and shaped like a shoe, it is foremost a resort island, heavily developed, with seemingly every chain restaurant, motel and hotel represented and many shops and real estate offices, though all in a tasteful, intensely planned and regulated setting. A band of beaches goes on for twelve miles.

Like so much of the Lowcountry, Hilton Head was once covered in plantations. Sea Island cotton was first grown here in 1790, and rice, indigo and sugarcane soon thrived. When the Civil War barreled through, there were 24 plantations on Hilton Head. More than 12,000 Union and Federal troops with fifteen warships landed here in 1861 and took the island in five hours. For 90 years Hilton Head was nearly deserted. Within its dense pine woods, hot and mosquito-infested in summer, lived several hundred Gullahs, former slaves who lived simply by farming and fishing.

All that changed in 1956 when Charles Fraser, whose family owned Hilton Head land, decided to pair fairways with fancy housing. He built a bridge connecting the island with civilization, and within two decades, country club communities mushroomed across the island.

Golf courses spill over the bridge to the mainland and stretch for several miles. The eleven "plantations" of Hilton Head are of recent invention, modern planned communities with homes and villas and condos, seaside resorts, restaurants and shops, tennis and golf. They all look much the same with their well-shaped pine woods, pretty plantings and homes in muted tones of gray, green and brown.

On tradition-steeped Daufuskie Island, some of the private homes don't have indoor plumbing.

About 34,000 people live on Hilton Head, although more than a million and a half more visit each year. The season lasts from about early March to early November, and in summer the roads are thick with cars, the beaches thronged with sun worshipers. Families find all they need here, including kids camps, all manner of sports and an excellent network of bike paths.

Begin your exploring with a stop at **The Coastal Discovery Museum**. The brief exhibits here include taxidermied birds that are extinct or endangered. ~ 100 William Hilton Parkway, one mile east of the Route 278 bridge; 843-689-6767; www.coastal discovery.org, e-mail info@coastaldiscovery.org.

Sharing the same building with the museum is the **Hilton Head Island/Bluffton Chamber of Commerce**, where you can pick up information on the island, including a map, which you will need to find your way around. More extensive information is available from the chamber's main office. ~ 1 Chamber Drive, off William Hilton Parkway, just east of Long Cove Plantation; 843-785-3673, 800-523-3373, fax 843-785-7110; www.hilton headisland.org.

Four-lane William Hilton Parkway, also Route 278, is the main drag through Hilton Head. Hundreds of roads splinter off, nary a one of them straight. From the parkway you can access the various "plantation" communities, some with a security gate and an officer who will take your license plate number but allow you to pass through. The parkway ends at **Sea Pines Plantation**, the toe of the Hilton Head shoe, the only community charging

an entrance fee. Sea Pines is Charles Fraser's original development, the genesis of Hilton Head. Many consider it the island's
most desirable setting; it is extremely wooded, dotted with beautiful homes and deer crossing signs. There are riding stables and
pretty gardens. The 605-acre **Sea Pines Forest Preserve** is thick
with loblolly pines (called sea pines) and live oaks and bordered
by marsh. Nature trails wind through. ~ Along Greenwood Drive
and Lawton Road.

Here also is the **Heritage Farm**, where gardens of sunflowers,   ◄ HIDDEN
roses and vegetables have been planted by local folks. Open the
wood-slat gate and take a stroll through the community farm,
and you may see gardeners tending their rented plots. ~ Greenwood Drive, across from Lawton Stables.

From the northern edge of Sea Pines you can see a mile across
the Intracoastal Waterway to **Daufuskie Island**. Five miles long   ◄ HIDDEN
and three miles wide, it is accessible only by boat. Plantations
prospered here in the 1800s, and timbering, oystering and a rich
Gullah culture thrived during the first half of the twentieth century. In the 1950s, Savannah factories dumped pollution into the
Savannah River, the oysters died and Daufuskie's oyster plants
closed.

Today, the humble, picturesque village on Daufuskie's south
end is occupied by a few dozen islanders, many who still cling to
Gullah traditions, living in painted wood cottages. The streets are
made of sand. There's only one speed-limit sign, near the two-
room clapboard elementary school. Life is slow and seabreezy
most all year.

You can walk around the village, have a look at the one-room
1912 **Daufuskie Island Elementary School** (near the public dock,
on the island's southwest side) and the **First Union Baptist Church**
(mid-island on the south end), built in 1880 with, count 'em, *two*
front doors—one for men and one for women. At the island's
southern tip, buried within trees at the end of a dirt road, the
teeny **Mary Dunn Cemetery** bears the 1790 gravestone of Mary
Martinangele. Most of the old epitaphs are too worn to read.

Hilton Head is famed for pricey, amenity-packed lodging. Beau-   **LODGING**
tiful resorts owned by big luxury chains are draped along the
beaches, tucked within the lush confines of plantation communities. For these you will pay ultra-deluxe rates in season (about
mid-March to mid-November) and deluxe the rest of the time.
Several motels, mostly chains, offer less expensive rates, and
home and villa rentals are also an option.

For a complete list of all island lodging, contact the **Hilton
Head Island/Bluffton Chamber of Commerce**. ~ 1 Chamber Drive,
off William Hilton Parkway, just east of Long Cove Plantation;
843-785-3673.

Hilton Head Central Reservations handles bookings for villas and homes on Hilton Head Island. ~ 843-785-9050, 800-845-7018, fax 843-686-3255.

Leading the list of luxury haunts, **Westin Resort Hilton Head Island** enjoys a loyal following who wouldn't think of parking their beach towels anywhere else. The tropical green tin-topped building curves against the beach among 24 acres of fantasy gardens, swimming pools and a whirlpool nestling under a waterfall. A wooden boardwalk delivers you across the dunes to a beach that disappears in the distance. The 412 rooms are plush, handsomely decorated, and all have private balconies overlooking the ocean or island. Three golf courses, four restaurants, tennis, health club, daily family activities—it's all here. ~ 2 Grasslawn Avenue, Port Royal Plantation; 843-681-4000, fax 843-681-1096; www.westinhiltonhead.com. ULTRA-DELUXE.

Marriott Beach and Golf Resort occupies a vast piece of oceanfront, with more than 500 rooms, two outdoor pools and palmy gardens spread next to a wide beach and an indoor pool tucked beneath a glass solarium. The elegant lobby has glass windows that look out to sea. Rooms are typical of the chain: thick carpets, modern furnishings, attractive drapes and fine bedspreads. Half of the rooms face the ocean, the other half look at the island. Three golf courses, 25 tennis courts, several restaurants and lounges complete the offerings. ~ Queens Folly Road, Palmetto Dunes Plantation; 843-686-8400, 800-228-9290, fax 843-686-8450; www.hiltonheadmarriott.com. ULTRA-DELUXE.

The glittering lobby of **Crowne Plaza Resort** soars five floors, with glossy wood floors and balconies trimmed in theater lights. The resort has a roving courtyard with swimming pools, ponds, waterfalls and streams winding through, then long green lawn running down to the dunes and beach. The 340 rooms are nicely appointed with blonde oak furniture, chintz love seats, marble vanities, and balconies overlooking the courtyard treetops or ocean. There's golf, tennis, fine dining, kids' camp and anything else you care to do. ~ 130 Shipyard Drive, Shipyard Plantation, Hilton Head Island; 843-842-2400, 800-334-1881, fax 843-842-9975; www.crowneplazaresort.com, e-mail info@cphilton head.com. ULTRA-DELUXE.

Several of Hilton Head's plantation communities offer villa lodging. For details, contact **Palmetto Dunes Resort**. ~ 843-785-1161, 800-845-6130, fax 843-842-4482. For villas at Sea Pines call **Sea Pines Villa Resorts**. ~ 843-785-3333, 800-925-4653, fax 843-842-1475.

Among the general home and villa rental agencies, you might try **Coastline Rentals, Inc.** ~ 843-842-5866, 800-752-3506, fax 843-785-9119. ESP **Resort Rentals** is another choice. ~ 843-671-

4700, 800-368-5975, fax 843-671-5899. Or try **Hilton Head Vacation Rentals.** ~ 843-689-3010, 800-346-0426, fax 843-689-3011.

The family-friendly **Carolina Cafe** serves up fantastic she-crab soup, one of the regional specialties, as well as combinations like grilled beef filet with mushroom ragout. Breakfast, lunch and dinner are served. ~ At the Westin Resort, 2 Grasslawn Avenue, Port Royal Plantation; 843-681-4000, fax 843-681-1096. MODERATE TO DELUXE.

DINING

The three dining rooms at **Charlie's L'Etoile Verte** are homey yet elegant, and the open bar provides overstuffed chairs perfect for relaxing. The dinner menus are handwritten on white paper every day, and possibilities might include omelettes, fish cakes, and lamb shank with bordelaise sauce. Tilapia sautéed in a parmesan crust, or perhaps filet mignon with jalapeño butter for dinner. You don't want to miss this place. Closed Sunday. ~ 8 New Orleans Road, Hilton Head Island; 843-785-9277; www.charliesof hiltonhead.com. DELUXE TO ULTRA-DELUXE.

Locals wear a lunch path to **Remy's Sports Bar and Grill** for simple Southern and Lowcountry fare like fried chicken, oyster po'boys, okra and tomatoes, mashed potatoes and sweet corn. The floors and high ceiling are unfinished wood, the TVs are on in the bar, the dining room is quite small. If you can't make it for lunch, this late-night spot occasionally serves until 4 a.m. Closed Sunday. ~ 28 Arrow Road, off William Hilton Parkway, near Sea Pines Circle; 843-842-3800, fax 843-842-3292. MODERATE TO DELUXE.

◄ HIDDEN

"A bit of Scotland on the road to Hilton Head"—an odder motto cannot be imagined, but when you see **Scottish Mill Shop** you must agree it is steeped in all things Scottish, and it is indeed on the way to Hilton Head. Here are kilts, golf caps, Celtic jewelry,

SHOPPING

AUTHOR FAVORITE

Captain John's Gallery is a Lowcountry seafood house, perhaps Hilton Head's best, with dining on a glass porch overlooking a marina and salt marsh, and the smell of the sea inside and out. Flounder sautéed and seasoned with white wine, lemon and butter, seafood pot pie and Braddock's Steamer pot, a kettle full of crab legs, shrimp, scallops, oysters, sausage and corn on the cob are among the savory offerings. ~ 232 South Sea Pines Drive, Sea Pines Plantation; 843-671-5199. MODERATE TO ULTRA-DELUXE.

lap robes and tartans galore. Closed Sunday. ~ 1200 Fording Island Road, Bluffton; 843-837-4696.

HIDDEN ▶ Don't be put off by the "Elvis Lives" sign above the door of **The Store**, for inside this quirky century-old shop is some fine local and international art, painted sideboards, cookbooks, beeswax candles and great second-hand stuff. Closed Sunday. ~ 56 Calhoun Street, Bluffton; 843-757-3855.

HIDDEN ▶ An old Bluffton gas station was reincarnated as **eggs 'n tricities**, an art boutique with singular, eccentric pieces and clothing. Closed Sunday. ~ 71 Calhoun Street, Bluffton; 843-757-3446.

You could technically shop for days on Hilton Head, though it would take a lot of driving, diving in and out of traffic between the mind-numbing array of strip shopping centers and plazas and mini-malls. The official store count is over 300. Selections are typically islandy and upscale, colorful resort wear, tropical-themed art, crafts and collectibles, kitchenry and books on boating and golf.

If you must have a mall, there's the **Mall at Shelter Cove**. Victoria's Secret, Talbots, Williams-Sonoma, Saks Fifth Avenue and other familiar names are located here. ~ William Hilton Parkway, a half-mile north of Palmetto Dunes Plantation entrance, Hilton Head Island; 843-686-3090.

The **Red Piano Gallery** has nineteenth- and twentieth-century paintings and sculptures by regional, national and international artists. Closed Sunday. ~ 220 Cordillo Parkway, Hilton Head Island; 843-785-2318; www.redpianoartgallery.com.

Coligny Plaza, across from the island's most popular beach, has more than 80 stores assembled around courtyards and duck ponds. ~ Located at the corner of Pope Avenue and North Forest Beach Avenue, Hilton Head Island; 843-842-6050; www.coligny plaza.com. Among them, **The Magic Puppet and Toys Too** supplies neat magic tricks and books on magic, entertaining beach games and pretty puppets. ~ 843-785-3280; www.worldsbesttoys.com.

Beneath Hilton Head's red-and-white-striped lighthouse are the colorful galleries, boutiques and plazas of **Harbour Town Shops**. ~ North end of Lighthouse Road, Sea Pines Plantation.

ALL THAT JAZZ

Dinner at **The Jazz Corner** is a musical and gastronomic experience. The chef has designed the menu to complement the high-quality tunes that fill the house. Dine on delectable entrées such as crispy duck with raspberry and blackberry glaze, and pork tenderloin rolled in cashews and served with sweet honey-mustard brown sauce. Dinner only. ~ The Village at Wexford, Hilton Head; 843-842-8620; www.thejazzcorner.com, e-mail lesliejazzgm1@aol.com. DELUXE.

Here, the **John Stobart Gallery** is the place to browse for nautically themed paintings, including nineteenth-century port and harbor scenes. Closed Sunday in winter. ~ 843-671-2739.

Wild Wing Café gets crazy at night. Beer, chicken wings and a prevailing college crowd. Live bands stay mellow on weeknights, and crank it up on weekends. ~ 72 Pope Avenue, Circle Center, Hilton Head Island; 843-785-9464.

NIGHTLIFE

The Jazz Corner is a sophisticated and intimate jazz, blues and swing club where well-known performers such as Rebecca Parris, Freddy Cole (brother of Nat) and the Paul Brown Quartet pack 'em in. Cover. ~ The Village at Wexford, Hilton Head; 843-842-8620.

The community drama, musicals and comedy at the **Arts Center** tend to be high quality, and shows often sell out. ~ Self Family Art Center, 14 Shelter Cove Lane; 843-842-2787.

The worn-wood environs of **Remy's Sports Bar and Grill** are a late-night local haunt. Live entertainment happens weekend evenings, and you can have munchies until the wee hours. ~ 150 Arrow Road, off William Hilton Parkway near Sea Pines Circle; 843-842-3800.

◄ HIDDEN

There's always a crowd at **Salty Dog Cafe**. The shingled, peak-roofed bar and attendant picnic tables sit outside next to a marina, where you can hear live island music (Jimmy Buffett tunes, etc.) Thursday through Sunday in summer. ~ 232 South Seas Pines Drive, Sea Pines Plantation; 843-671-5199.

Visitors staying at a seaside villa or on Hilton Head will have access to quiet sands. If you seek a livelier scene, the following are Hilton Head's three public beaches:

BEACHES & PARKS

FOLLY FIELD BEACH ≈ Here's a generous stretch of tawny sand and a small, quiet cove where you can sometimes find shells, especially sea olives. There's a lot with metered parking. Swimming is good. Concessions closed in winter. ~ Located at the end of Bradley Road, off William Hilton Parkway, just south of Port Royal Plantation.

BURKES BEACH ≈ Immediately south of Folly Field Beach and less crowded, this pretty swath of sand is reached by a short dirt path across the dunes. The sand is hard-packed, moist and gray, laced with dried seagrass and reeds that wash ashore. The surf is gentle. Arrive early for parking. Stores and restrooms are only a short walk away. Swimming is excellent. ~ At the end of Burkes Beach Road, off William Hilton Parkway.

◄ HIDDEN

COLIGNY CIRCLE BEACH ≈ Next to and spilling over into the Holiday Inn, this is Hilton Head's most popular beach, with sunbathers crowding in towel-to-towel spring through fall. The sands are tan and hard-packed, the water warm in summer. There are teenagers galore when school's out. The metered parking here is expensive (25¢ for fifteen minutes), so use the all-day lot. Get here early in season or you won't get a parking spot. Swimming is good. Restrooms and refreshments are nearby. ~ At Coligny Circle, at the intersection of Pope Avenue and Forest Beach Drive.

Outdoor Adventures

GOLF

There is great golf on South Carolina's coast. More than 100 courses dot the Grand Strand and Lowcountry, many created by big-name designers like Jack Nicklaus, Donald Ross, George Cobb, Tom Fazio, Robert Trent Jones and Pete Dye, who have replaced coastal woods and wetlands and wild shores with meticulously tended greens and holes of championship caliber.

Most of these courses are in the Myrtle Beach area, which hosts a slew of annual tournaments. Some courses run alongside pine and palmetto woods or ancient, cypress-draped rivers, others follow the windy ocean or the stillness of marshlands. Some appeal to scratch golfers, others are kind to duffers. You can play on a traditional design created in the '60s or on a cutting-edge course carved in the '90s.

> The Myrtle Beach Area Chamber of Commerce estimates golfers spend nearly $700 million a year on their games.

Several places offer mega-golf, several courses within one club. For a detailed list of courses, pick up a copy of the *Myrtle Beach Golf Holiday* from the Myrtle Beach Area Chamber of Commerce. ~ 1200 North Oak Street, Myrtle Beach; 843-626-7444, 800-356-3016, fax 843-626-0009; www.myrtle beachinfo.com.

You can pick from three courses at **The Legends Golf Complex,** including the Moorland Course and its 16th hole, nicknamed "Hell's Half Acre." The enormous Scottish-style clubhouse here is surrounded by 40 acres of practice and putting greens. ~ 1500 Legends Drive, off Route 501 South, Myrtle Beach; 843-236-9318, 800-552-2660.

Pine Lakes is called the "Granddaddy" of Myrtle Beach. Built in 1927 by Robert White, the first PGA president, the Scottish-influenced course features subtle curves, contours and pitches and woodsy scenery to match. ~ 5603 Woodside Drive, off Route 17, Myrtle Beach; 843-449-6459, 800-446-6817.

Several holes at **River Hills** have a Scottish feel, as well as unexpected hills, sharp doglegs and non-parallel fairways. ~ Route 17 North, Little River; 843-399-2100, 800-264-3810.

Classic Golf Group represents seven courses. ~ 843-626-1658, 800-833-6337. Among these is **Quail Creek Golf Club,** designed by Gene Hamm in 1968 with soft curving greens and fairways and riotous beds of azaleas. ~ University Drive, West Myrtle Beach; 843-347-0549. The **Burning Ridge** is another—a double course with several lakes, big bunkers and sand traps. ~ Route 501 West, Conway; 843-347-0538.

The front nine holes of **The Witch** wend through wetlands, the back nine climb along gentle hills. Designed by Dan Maples, it's not too witchy, but playable by high handicappers. ~ 1900 Route 544, Conway; 843-347-2706.

In Georgetown, **Wedgefield** course is especially scenic. The fairways snake alongside big old magnolias and oaks, and camellias punctuate the setting with color. ~ 129 Clubhouse Lane, Georgetown; 843-546-8587.

The Charleston area has plenty of fine courses, including **Wild Dune Links** and **The Harbor Course** at Wild Dunes Resort. ~ 5757 Palm Boulevard, Isle of Palms; 843-886-2164. There is also **Dunes West**. ~ 3535 Wando Plantation Way, off Route 41, Mount Pleasant; 843-856-9000. Try **Shadowmoss Plantation Golf Club** in Charleston. ~ 20 Dunvegan Drive, Charleston; 843-556-8251. At John's Island head over to **Oak Point**. ~ 4255 Bohicket Road, Hope Plantation, John's Island; 843-768-2121. On Kiawah Island try **Turtle Point** and **Osprey Point**. ~ Kiawah Island Resort, Kiawah Island; 843-768-2121. And finally there is **Edisto Beach Golf Club**. ~ 24 Fairway Drive, Edisto Island; 843-869-1111.

Around Beaufort and the Sea Islands are a couple of courses. In Beaufort is the **Country Club of Beaufort**. ~ 8 Barnwell Drive, Beaufort; 843-522-1605. On Ladys Island is **Ladys Island Country Club**. Closed Monday. ~ 139 Francis Marion Circle, Ladys Island; 843-522-9700.

Golf needs no introduction on Hilton Head Island. The 18 courses include some of golf's most famous and famously expensive. Green fees at **Harbour Town Golf Links** are $250, though tee times are scarce in season at this famed course. Designed by Pete Dye and the site of the annual PGA tournament, its trademark is the red-and-white-striped lighthouse across a canal from the 18th green. The last two holes look across Calibogue Sound. ~ 11 Lighthouse Lane, off Lighthouse Road, Sea Pines Plantation; 843-363-4485.

Sea Pines Plantation also has the **Sea March** course and **Ocean Course**. The Ocean Course was Hilton Head's first fairway, built in 1962, and the country club catalyst for developers across the nation. Despite its name, the Ocean Course has only one seaside hole. ~ Both at 100 North Sea Pines Drive; 843-363-4475.

Among the other prime public island greens on Hilton Head is **Country Club of Hilton Head**. ~ 70 Skull Creek Drive, Hilton Head Plantation; 843-681-4653. At Port Royal Plantation, you'll find **Planters Row**. ~ 10-A Grasslawn Avenue, Port Royal Plantation; 843-681-1750. In Palmetto Dunes Plantation try the **Rob-**

ert Trent Jones Course. ~ 7 Trent Jones Lane, Palmetto Dunes Plantation; 843-785-1136. In the Shipyard Plantation is **Shipyard**. ~ 45 Shipyard Drive, Shipyard Plantation; 843-686-8802.

**SPORT-
FISHING**

Numerous outfits will take you deep-sea fishing along the coast.

In Calabash, **Hurricane Fleet** has four boats that go out on fishing charters. ~ Captain Jim's Marina, Calabash; 843-249-3571. **Capt. Dick's Marina** has half-day and all-day trips to the Gulf Stream, as well as deep-sea overnighters. ~ Murrells Inlet; 843-651-3676.

In Charleston, **Blue Boy** leaves out of the Ripley Light Marina on Ashley Point Drive. ~ 843-814-0067.

Edisto Water Sports and Tackle offers inshore and offshore trips around Edisto Island. ~ 3071 Dockside Road; 843-869-0663. Coast Guard–certified **Captain Ron Elliott** will take you fishing on the river. ~ 843-869-1937.

SeaWolf departs from Port Royal Landing Marina near Beaufort, but will pick up customers on Hilton Head Island. ~ Beaufort; 843-525-1174. The **Boomerang** in Hilton Head will take you out for fish from mackerel to grouper. ~ South Beach Marina, Hilton Head; 843-363-2900.

TENNIS

You won't have trouble finding a court on South Carolina's coast. In the Myrtle Beach area, try **Sports and Health Club at Kingston Plantation**. ~ 9760 Kings Road, Myrtle Beach; 843-497-2444. Also in the area is **Grand Dunes Tennis Club**. ~ On Route 17 Bypass North, across from Dixie Stampede; 843-449-4486.

The City of Charleston maintains a number of courts. For suggestions on where to play, call the **Charleston Tennis Center**. ~ 19 Farmfield Avenue, Charleston; 843-724-7402.

In Beaufort, you can play at **Beaufort Tennis Courts**. ~ Boundary and Bladen streets; 843-525-4009.

There's mega-tennis on Hilton Head Island. The courts at **Palmetto Dunes Tennis Center** include 23 clay and 2 hard. ~ 6 Trent Jones Lane, Palmetto Dunes Plantation; 843-785-1152. **Van der Meer Tennis University** comes in second with 17 hard courts (4 are covered and lighted). ~ 19 DeAllyon Road; 843-785-8388, 800-845-6138. Other public courts include **Port Royal Racquet Club**. ~ 15 Wimbledon Court, Port Royal Plantation; 843-686-8803. Another is **South Beach Racquet Club**. ~ 230 South Sea Pines Drive, Sea Pines Plantation; 843-671-2215.

**RIDING
STABLES**

Lawton Stables will take you on a guide ride through a nature preserve and wildlife habitat, with history on the island's old working plantations. ~ 190 Greenwood Drive, Sea Pines Plantation; 843-671-2586.

BIKING

With flat terrain barely above sea level, South Carolina's coast is easy on the legs. The 227.2-mile **Coastal Route** runs from North Carolina to Georgia, curling along lonesome wooded back roads and passing through minuscule towns.

From Rhems (about ten miles north of Georgetown), it's a 121.6-mile trek south to Givhans Ferry State Park, along the Edisto River about 31 miles west of Charleston. Routes 41, 51 and 17 are the main routes.

Charleston can be done on a bicycle, though downtown traffic can make riding tedious. The most enjoyable cycling is along **The Battery** and through the historic neighborhoods just north.

Hilton Head Island was designed with bikers in mind. Paved bike paths wend along William Hilton Parkway from Folly Field Road to Palmetto Bay Road. On Palmetto Bay Road, the path curves south to Forest Beach Drive, then runs both north and south along the public beach.

> The best place to go to the beach is behind your hotel—it will always be less crowded and chaotic than a public beach.

Bike Rentals   To get rolling around Cherry Grove, visit the **Bike Doctor**. ~ 315 Sea Mountain Highway, Cherry Grove; 843-249-8152.

In Charleston, **The Bicycle Shoppe** rents bicycles. ~ 280 Meeting Street; 843-722-8168. So does the **Charles Towne Landing Nature Preserve and Historic Site**. ~ 1500 Old Town Road, off Route 171; 843-852-4200.

Beaufort has the **Lowcountry Bicycle Shop**. ~ 102 Sea Island Parkway; 843-524-9585.

On Hilton Head Island, bikes are available from **Fish Creek Landing**. ~ 77 Queens Folly Road, Palmetto Dunes Plantation; 843-785-2021. Or try **Hilton Head Bicycle Company**. They'll deliver your wheels right to your door. ~ 112 Arrow Road; 843-686-6888. **Pedals** is another choice. ~ 71 Pope Avenue; 843-842-5522. In Sea Pines Plantation, go to **Bikes Plus**. ~ 79 Lighthouse Road, Sea Pines Plantation; 843-785-5470.

HIKING

It's easygoing along the pancake-flat coast. Every trail listed here falls in the "leisurely" category. Mosquitoes can be tenacious, however, even hellish in summer, so don't hike without repellent. All distances for hiking trails are one way unless otherwise noted.

MYRTLE BEACH AREA   Beachwalking is the best way to work your legs here. The sand is wide and hard-packed in most spots.

If you'd prefer to walk through woods, the **Sculptured Oak Nature Trail** (1 mile) at Myrtle Beach State Park cuts through live oak and loblolly pine, poplar, hickory and magnolia trees. There is even a stream running through.

CHARLESTON AREA   Much of the coastal forest and marsh life is marked along the **National Recreation Trail** (2 miles) on Bulls

◄ HIDDEN

Island, within Cape Romain National Wildlife Refuge. You're apt to see alligators and in spring, flocks of egrets, coots, warblers and painted buntings. Besides this interpretive trail, the island has 16 miles of roads that can be hiked. Bulls Island is accessed only by ferry; for information, see the "Charleston Area Beaches & Parks" section of this chapter.

Downtown Charleston is best seen on foot and though it may not technically be hiking, you will be tired after a couple of days. Numerous companies offer guided walks around town. For a list, see the "Charleston Area Sights" section of this chapter.

A few minutes from downtown, **Charles Towne Landing** offers an enjoyable stroll. Follow gravel and dirt trails through lush plantings of azaleas, camellias and myriad other bloomers, then wander the woods where enclosures harbor black bears, otters, pumas and other animals.

The **Spanish Mount Trail** (2.5 miles round-trip) at Edisto Beach State Park heads through coastal forest of palmetto and oak, red cedar and wax myrtle to a heap of shells that may have been left by American Indians.

BEAUFORT AND THE SEA ISLANDS At Hunting Island State Park, the **Salt Marsh Boardwalk and Nature Trail** (1.1 miles) starts out along a wooden walkway across the salt marsh, then follows the shore lined with dunes and sea oats.

HILTON HEAD ISLAND AREA The **Pinckney Island National Wildlife Refuge main trail** (7 miles) is a dirt road, accessed on bicycle or foot, that starts at the refuge parking lot. On its trek across the island, it meanders through maritime forest with pine plantations and ponds with wading birds and rookeries. An additional ten and a half miles of trails split off from this main trail.

HIDDEN ▶   The **Audubon-Newhall Nature Preserve Trail** (1.5 miles round-trip) traverses dense, sunlit woods filled with the music of birds and crickets. You'll circle a pond, passing popcorn trees (also called Chinese tallowtrees), pitcher plants and a pocosin (a boggy trough of land), all described in the brochure available at the trailhead on Palmetto Bay Road, one half-mile north of Greenwood Drive, in Sea Pines Plantation.

American Indian shell rings are among the things you'll see if you walk the seven miles of trails that wend through **Sea Pines Forest Preserve**, a 605-acre woodland by the ocean on the west end of Hilton Head Island (entrance fee).

▼▼▼▼▼▼▼▼▼▼▼▼
Transportation

CAR

Route 17, sometimes two lanes and at other times four, runs the length of South Carolina's coast and connects most major towns and metropolitan areas. Interstate highway **Route 95** comes up from Georgia, near Savannah, and runs along the eastern side of South Carolina. From Route 95, you can wind over to Hilton Head Island along **Routes 46** and **278**. Interstate highway **Route 26** connects Charleston with Columbia, South Carolina.

Several commercial airports provide service to South Carolina's coast. **Myrtle Beach Jetport,** located within Myrtle Beach Air Force Base, has regular flights via major airlines including Atlantic Southeast Airlines, Delta Air Lines, Northwest Airlines and US Airways.

AIR

Charleston International Airport is served by several domestic and foreign airlines, including Continental Airlines, Delta Air Lines, Independence Air, Northwest Airlines, United Express and US Airways. ~ www.chs-airport.com.

The small **Hilton Head Island Airport** handles commuter flights from Charlotte, Raleigh and Atlanta via US Airways Express. ~ www.hiltonheadairport.com. Some visitors to Hilton Head Island fly into **Savannah International Airport,** about 45 minutes away and serviced by Continental Express, Delta Air Lines, Independence Air, Northwest Airlines, United Express and US Airways. ~ www.savannahairport.com.

Shuttle service from Myrtle Beach Jetport to points around the Grand Strand is provided by **Coastal Cab** (843-448-4444).

North Area Taxi (843-554-7575) provides area shuttle service to Charleston International Airport.

Lowcountry Taxi will give you a ride from Hilton Head Island Airport or from Savannah International Airport. ~ 843-681-8294.

Greyhound Bus Lines (800-231-2222; www.greyhound.com) are located in Myrtle Beach at 511 Seventh Avenue North, 843-448-2472; in Georgetown at 2014 High Market Street, 843-546-4535; in Charleston at 3610 Dorchester Road, 843-744-4247; and in Beaufort at 3659 Trask Parkway, 843-524-4646.

BUS

Try **Amtrak's** "Silver Meteor" (800-872-7245; www.amtrak.com). It brings visitors from surrounding regions to Charleston. ~ 4565 Gainor Avenue, Charleston; 843-744-8264.

TRAIN

Myrtle Beach Jetport is serviced by several rental companies, such as **Alamo Rent A Car** (800-327-9633), **Avis Rent A Car** (800-331-1212), **Budget Rent A Car** (800-527-0700), **Enterprise Rent A Car** (800-325-8007), **Hertz** (800-654-3131) and **National Car Rental** (800-227-7368).

CAR RENTALS

Rental agencies at or near Charleston International Airport include **Alamo Rent A Car** (800-327-9633), **Avis Rent A Car** (800-331-1212), **Budget Rent A Car** (800-527-0700), **Hertz Rent A**

Car (800-654-3131), **National Car Rental** (800-227-7368), and **Thrifty Car Rental** (800-367-2277).

On Hilton Head Island, try **Alamo Rent A Car** (800-327-9633), **Avis Rent A Car** (800-331-1212), **Budget Rent A Car** (800-527-0700) and **Enterprise Rent-A-Car** (800-325-8007).

At Savannah International Airport, you'll find **Avis Rent A Car** (800-331-1212) and **Thrifty Car Rental** (800-367-2277).

PUBLIC TRANSIT

Catch a **Coastal Rapid Public Transit Authority** bus along the Grand Strand. ~ 843-626-9138.

Charleston Area Regional Transportation Authority runs public buses in Charleston, including **D.A.S.H.** (Downtown Area Shuttle), which makes regular city rounds, stopping often at the Visitors Center. ~ 36 John Street; 843-724-7420; www.ridecarta.com.

For bus service around Beaufort, call **Lowcountry Regional Transit Authority**. ~ 843-757-5782.

TAXIS

The Myrtle Beach area has lots of taxis. Among them are **Coastal Cab** (843-448-4444) and **Beachside Taxi** (843-448-8888).

In Charleston, try **Yellow Cab** (843-577-6565).

Around Beaufort and the Sea Islands, call **Yellow Cab** (843-522-1121). On Hilton Head, **Lowcountry Taxi** (843-681-8294) will take you around the island or up to Savannah.

TEN

Inland South Carolina

Once you get away from the coast, South Carolina slows down. Pounding surf and golf greens transform into fuzzy fields of cotton and long-lasting forests of scrub pine. Sun-blistered farmhouses dot the horizon. Cinderblock shanties sell fresh catfish. Folks wave from their tractors and pickup trucks.

The land angles northwest 250 miles in gentle crescendo, rising to soft hills across the middle of the state and then above 3000 feet just before North Carolina. Sassafras Mountain, which peaks at 3560 feet, is South Carolina's highest place, though it is not lofty or breathtaking. Like most of inland South Carolina, it is subtle, simple, peaceful.

Inland South Carolina is also wet—very wet. A vast river system sprawls toward the ocean like a spiderweb, sending out creeks and streams and opening onto vast lakes. The most furious river, the Chattooga, runs along the Cherokee Foothills in northwestern South Carolina and is famed for whitewater rafting. The dark, disturbing movie *Deliverance* was shot on the Chattooga. Dark, secretive swamps once covered much of the state, but they were erased by loggers or drowned behind dams. Only one virgin watery wilderness, 22,000-acre Congaree Swamp, remains near the middle of the state and is protected as a National Monument.

Hundreds of small towns are sprinkled across inland South Carolina, but there are only a handful of cities. The biggest, Columbia, has just under 100,000 residents and is the state capital. Nestled at the confluence of three rivers, it's also a haven of history.

In February 1865, General William Tecumseh Sherman crushed Columbia on his death march through the South, nearly burning the city to the ground. He slashed telegraph wires, mangled railroad ties and ignited the bridges that linked Columbia with the rest of the world. A few homes were salvaged and restored, and today their stately Federalist, Italianate and antebellum facades are reminiscent of pre–Civil War days. The State House, half-built when Sherman arrived, now bears the shell scars of his destruction.

Just as the Civil War looms large across South Carolina, so does the American Revolution. All but one of the streets in downtown Columbia are named for Revolutionary War generals and officers. Some of those men successfully led forces in 1776 against Loyalists and Cherokees who had joined the British. Four years later, however, General Charles Cornwallis had nearly overrun the state.

Two South Carolina battles helped turn things around. In September 1780, a rugged band of "over-mountain" men trounced the Tories at Kings Mountain in northern South Carolina. Four months later, a similar defeat at nearby Cowpens helped decide the fate of the British in the war. Today, you can tour the misty green pastures and cool woods at both Kings Mountain and Cowpens National Battlefields.

You can also immerse yourself in Civil War days, and the times before and after. Immaculately tended plantation homes, some 200 years old, invite exploration across the state. Entire towns are listed on the National Register of Historic Places, their red-brick streets and marketplaces, soda fountains and steepled churches virtually unchanged for over a century. Old railroad and mill towns populate the countryside, with nothing but pastures and cornfields in between. State parks abound, but there is no blatant tourism: no enormous theme parks, no kitschy boardwalks, no towns contrived for visitors. Indeed, it seems sometimes that it's easier to find the Old South in South Carolina than the new.

Columbia is a good place to start the inland South Carolina tour. It's precisely in the center of the state, a hundred miles from either coast or mountains, and its airport is easy to get in and out of. Explore downtown and the artsy Five Points area, then head to nearby Lake Murray for golfing, boating, fishing or camping in the woods.

Southwest of Columbia, Aiken is a refined old town with big graceful homes, groomed lawns and gardens, and lots of horse racing action. Hundreds of horses train during winter in preparation for the Aiken Triple Crown competition every spring. Between Aiken and northern Abbeville, there's Sumter National Forest and four state parks, and the lonesome Savannah River Scenic Highway that wends through pine forest.

South Carolina's most dramatic landscape is in the Upstate, the northwestern crescent of the state. Here the land swells to 2000 and 3000 feet, and water gushes down rock walls. Greenville, Spartanburg, Clemson (home to the university) and Anderson are the main towns of the Upstate. Greenville and Spartanburg, 30 miles apart, are a growing hub of industry in the emerging New South, with companies such as Michelin and Adidas located there. In 1994, after a worldwide search of cities, BMW selected nearby Greer as the site of its United States auto manufacturing plant.

Beyond the borders of the towns, there is little but beautiful scenery and little-traveled roads. Lodges, restaurants and shops are scarce, and six state parks stay packed during warm months.

The Upstate also has the far-flung Chattooga River, a National Wild and Scenic River and one of the best whitewater trips in the South. Take a wild and fast rafting trip, then plan to relax. The Upstate, like the rest of inland South Carolina, is all about downshifting into slow gear.

Text continued on page 408.

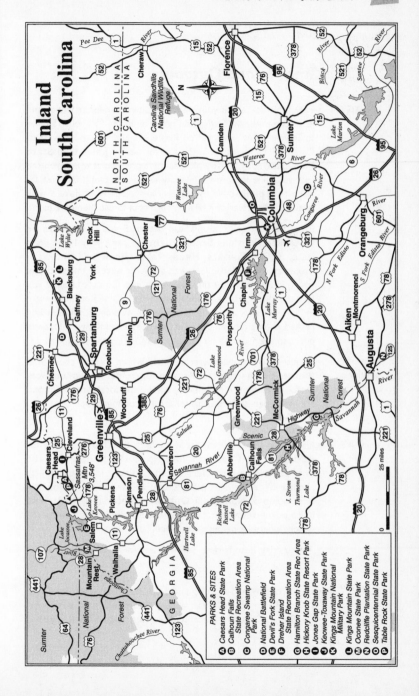

Inland South Carolina

PARKS & SITES
- Ⓐ Caesars Head State Park
- Ⓑ Calhoun Falls
   State Recreation Area
- Ⓒ Congaree Swamp National
   Park
- Ⓓ Devil's Fork State Park
- Ⓔ Dreher Island
   State Recreation Area
- Ⓕ Hamilton Branch State Rec Area
- Ⓖ Hickory Knob State Resort Park
- Ⓗ Jones Gap State Park
- Ⓘ Keowee-Toxaway State Park
- Ⓙ Kings Mountain National
   Military Park
- Ⓚ Kings Mountain State Park
- Ⓛ Oconee State Park
- Ⓜ Redcliffe Plantation State Park
- Ⓝ Sesquicentennial State Park
- Ⓞ Table Rock State Park

The Great Inland Outdoors

DAY 1 • Pack a picnic—and if you're a trout fisher, your fishing gear—and leave Greenville by 9 a.m. Head north on Route 25 about 15 miles to Travelers Rest, then get on Route 276 and wind northwest to Cleveland. Here you'll see the sign for nearby **Jones Gap State Park** (page 437), a lovely mountainside playground where you can cast your line for brown, rainbow and brook trout. But first, lay claim to a picnic table by the swirling Saluda River. Take a walk (wade?) in the river or a hike through cool forest, then have lunch.

• Early afternoon, pack up and head west on Route 11, known as the **Cherokee Foothills Scenic Highway** (page 428). Three great state parks—**Caesars Head**, **Table Rock** and **Keowee-Toxaway** (pages 438–39)—await along the next 35 miles, so take your pick. If you're big on views, duck into Caesar's Head. If you love the idea of a brisk mountain dip, stop at Table Rock for a swim in Pinnacle Lake, though if it's a summer weekend it's liable to be packed. There's rarely a crowd at heavily forested Keowee-Toxaway, but then again, there's no place to swim. So instead opt for a hike.

• It's just six more miles west to Salem, where you can check in at **Sunrise Farm** (page 432). Arrive before sunset to enjoy the wonderful, wide-open setting. There are several local dinner options; ask innkeeper Barbara Laughter for a recommendation.

DAY 2 • Have a big country breakfast at the farm, then head out early for **rafting on the Chattooga River** (page 442). (Guests of Sunrise Farm get a 10 percent rafting discount, so don't forget to ask!) It's about a 40-minute drive along Routes 130 and 28 up to Mountain Rest, home of **Nantahala Outdoor Center** (page 442). Have lunch at the restaurant, then join the half-day rafting trip on the waters where *Deliverance* was filmed.

• After rafting, head back to Sunrise Farm for the evening.

DAY 3 • Check out by mid-morning and work your way south on Route 130 to Route 76, then head west to **Clemson** (page 429). Stroll the **South Carolina Botanical Garden** (page 429) at Clemson

University and stop at the school's **Hendrix Student Center** (page 435) for some blue cheese. Then head three miles east on Route 28 to **Pendleton** (page 429). Have lunch at the venerable **Liberty Hall Inn** (page 433), following it up with a shopping stroll around town. Consider high tea on the village green before heading back to Greenville. Allow one and a half hours for the return trip.

Wade across a mountain creek. Have a picnic on an abandoned bridge overhung with hickories. Witness a summer rain, when thunderclouds darken the white cotton fields and lightning licks at the tips of oak trees. Get to know the local people—they're some of the friendliest folks you'll ever meet.

▼▼▼▼▼▼▼▼▼▼▼
Columbia Area

Columbia is one of the few planned cities in the nation. Its meticulous design began back in 1786, when the legislature decreed that a capital would be built dead center in the state where the Broad, Congaree and Saluda rivers meet. A surveyor laid out 400 blocks, with 10 blocks equaling one square mile. He made the streets 100 feet wide, with the belief that mosquitoes could fly only 60 feet before starving to death. This being absolutely false, mosquitoes buzzed right across the new city streets. Today, however, Columbia enjoys wide, roomy streets draped in oaks and magnolias.

SIGHTS

Downtown Columbia, a gridwork of streets covering precisely two square miles, is presided over by the **State House**. The grand Classical building has a copper dome, walls of Italian white marble, and elaborate columns parading along the front. Rich green lawns are ruled by vast oaks, and imposing monuments are scattered about. Some recall the three days in 1865 when General Sherman nearly leveled the city with guns and fire. Bronze stars on the building's west wall mark the wounds from Sherman's shell fire. Guided tours are available. Closed Sunday (except the first Sunday of every month). ~ Located at the corner of Main and Gervais streets, Columbia; 803-734-2430, fax 803-734-2439; www.myscgov.com.

Near the State House, the **Columbia Visitors Center** has maps and information on local sights. ~ 1101 Lincoln Street, Columbia; 803-545-0002, 800-264-4884; www.columbiacvb.com, e-mail visit@columbiasc.net.

Two blocks west of the State House, back on Gervais Street, is the heart of **Congaree Vista**, where antiques and art galleries, artists' studios, cafés and office suites occupy restored nineteenth-century buildings. Shop and dine among the weathered red bricks and pine floors and walls worn to a warm patina. Then walk down the street and tour downtown's four public historic homes. Start at the **Historic Columbia Foundation**, which sells individual or discounted combination tickets to the houses. Closed Monday. ~ 1616 Blanding Street, Columbia; 803-252-1770, fax 803-929-7695; www.historiccolumbia.org.

The Foundation is located behind **Robert Mills House and Park**, one of the historic home stops. An elegant place graced with magnolia trees, its three stories were commissioned in 1823 by prominent Columbia merchant Ainsley Hall. More prominent is the home's designer, Robert Mills, who was Federal Architect of the United States, State Architect of South Carolina and creator of the Washington Monument. Mills' trademark symmetry is everywhere; each room and door is offset by another (including some false doors added for congruity). His exquisite detailing is evident in the elaborate ceilings and curving walls, and in the columned Neoclassical porch out front. All of the doorknobs and key latches are sterling, and most of the Regency and Neoclassic furnishings are early 1800s. Unfortunately, Ainsley died before he could enjoy all this, and his widow sold the home to the Presbyterian Theological Seminary. Admission. ~ 1616 Blanding Street, Columbia.

Ainsley did live across the street at the **Hampton-Preston Mansion**. Built in 1818, the antebellum address is less grandiose than its neighbor, though still stately. A curving staircase glides to two upper floors, and a grand dining room is gilded and set with finery—including china that was rolled in bedsheets and stashed in the woods during Sherman's raid on Columbia. The house itself was spared when General John Logan decided it would serve as

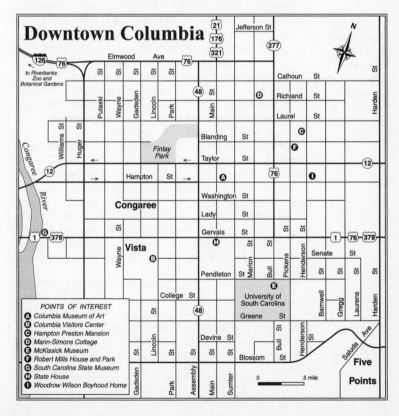

Downtown Columbia

POINTS OF INTEREST
- Ⓐ Columbia Museum of Art
- Ⓑ Columbia Visitors Center
- Ⓒ Hampton Preston Mansion
- Ⓓ Mann-Simons Cottage
- Ⓔ McKissick Museum
- Ⓕ Robert Mills House and Park
- Ⓖ South Carolina State Museum
- Ⓗ State House
- Ⓘ Woodrow Wilson Boyhood Home

his Union headquarters. There is much more history, most involving the Hampton family, who were sort of the Kennedys of the Old South. Wade Hampton I, a cotton plantation tycoon and general in the War of 1812, bought the manse in 1823. Wade II and Wade III, as famous as their father, were raised here and enjoyed vigorous lives of wealth and politics. Wade III became governor of South Carolina in 1876. Admission. ~ 1615 Blanding Street, Columbia.

A few years earlier, Woodrow Wilson was living a few blocks away in a pretty Tuscan villa. Today, the **Woodrow Wilson Boyhood Home** nestles beneath magnolias and is decorated with ivy. The inside is plush; the parlor is bathed in green, crushed-velvet draperies, the music room in red velvet. Many of the furnishings belonged to Wilson's family, who built the home in 1872. The 28th president lived there until 1875, when he was fourteen years old, and the family moved out of South Carolina. Admission. ~ 1705 Hampton Street, Columbia.

The last stop on the historic home tour does not speak of wealth or prominence, but the triumph of a black woman born in the plantation South. Celia Mann was a Charleston slave who also worked on the side as a midwife, saving enough money over several years to buy her freedom. She promptly left Charleston, which didn't care much for freed slaves, and walked 112 miles to Columbia. There, in the early 1850s, she purchased a small house that's now the **Mann-Simons Cottage**. She raised four daughters amid an often hostile environment. Admission. ~ 1403 Richland Street, Columbia.

Celia Mann, once a Charleston slave, started the Calvary Baptist Church for Blacks in her basement in 1865.

Art lovers must not miss the **Columbia Museum of Art**, South Carolina's international fine art museum featuring European and American art from the 1300s to the present. Most impressive are the Kress Collection of Baroque and Renaissance art and a display of Tiffany glass. Other permanent pieces include sculpture, stained glass, art glass, metal work, furniture and textiles. The museum also regularly hosts outstanding traveling exhibits. Closed Monday and Tuesday. Admission. ~ Main and Hampton streets, Columbia; 803-799-2810, fax 803-343-2150; www.colum biamuseum.org.

Just south of here, the **University of South Carolina** is wonderful for walks. Along Greene and Sumter streets, red-brick buildings, worn to a historic patina, are enveloped in tidy gardens and lawns. Flowers spill over brick walls and planters, and sun steams through pink-blossomed myrtle trees. Streets dip way down, trailing off into neighborhoods of early 1900s cottages masked in ivy. ~ Bounded by Greene, Sumter, Pendelton and Pickens streets, Columbia.

Stop inside USC's **McKissick Museum** for a look at its current   ◄ *HIDDEN*
art exhibit. That could be weavings, fiber art, glass works, pottery,
folk art—it's always different. In permanent residence is a collection of Baruch silver, gems and minerals. Closed Sunday. ~ 816
Bull Street, Columbia; 803-777-7251, fax 803-777-2829.

Across town to the west in an 1890s textile mill, the **South
Carolina State Museum** looks at the funky and serious side of state
styles and history. Natural history, science, transportation, culture and art displays are spread across four floors, with plenty of
hands-on fun for the kids, who also have their own discovery
center. There are whisper dishes and strange fossils, a 1904 Olds-
mobile horseless carriage, an authentic one-room schoolhouse (and
out house) and nineteenth-century decorative pottery, some made
by slaves. Closed Monday from Labor Day through Memorial
Day. Admission. ~ 301 Gervais Street, Columbia; 803-898-4921,
fax 803-898-4969; www.museum.state.sc.us, e-mail publicrela-
tions@museum.state.sc.us.

Civil War aficionados will want to drop by the **South Carolina
Confederate Relic Room and Museum**. Not a terribly big place,
but more than a Civil War cache, it showcases clothing, money,
stamps and keepsakes from Colonial to modern times. Open
Tuesday through Saturday, and the first Sunday of every month.
Admission. ~ 301 Gervais Street, Columbia; 803-737-8095, fax
803-737-8099.

If you have kids, take them to **Riverbanks Zoo and Botanical
Gardens**. Just west of downtown and the Congaree River, it's a
small but top-notch city zoo with wide paved paths (ideal for
wheelchair visitors), luscious plantings (the tulips rage in spring),
pony rides and roomy habitats for animals. Giraffes, ostriches,
warthogs and bongos (a kind of antelope) saunter around the
African Plains area and sea lions dive in a pool. The coolest place
may be the Coral Reef exhibit, where butterflyfish glide and sharks
prowl around a giant pool behind glass. Children love to ride the
endangered species carousel, whose 22 different animals are
hand carved and colorfully painted—not to mention educational.
Admission. ~ 500 Wildlife Parkway, off Route 26, Columbia;
803-779-8717, fax 803-253-6381; www.riverbanks.org.

When Columbians want a weekend on the water, they head for
Lake Murray about 15 miles to the west. These 78 square miles
of fresh water were corralled in 1930 when a mile-and-a-half-long
dam was built across the Saluda River. Electricity was made.
Homes, marinas, golf courses and campgrounds cropped up on
the new lakefront. Golfers, fishers and boaters were made happy,
not to mention realtors.

A day trip northeast of Columbia brings you first to **Camden**,   ◄ *HIDDEN*
about 32 miles away. Camden enjoys the designation of "the old-

est existing inland town in South Carolina," its township decreed by King George II in 1730. Fifty years later, it was a staunch Whig town captured by General Cornwallis. The British held Camden for nearly a year before retreating after nearby battle losses. Some of the British fortifications and redoubts have been unearthed today. Visitors can walk around the sites, as well as tour historic homes around town. ~ Off Routes 1 and 521, Camden. Pick up a walking tour map at **Historic Camden Revolutionary War Site**, a 98-acre Revolutionary War park. ~ Route 521 South; 803-432-9841; www.historic-camden.org, e-mail hiscamden@camden.net.

Fifty-four miles farther northeast on Route 1, **Cheraw** snoozes along the Great Pee Dee River. It started as a trading post in 1740 and became a real town in 1768. Now it's home to 6000 people and more than 50 beautiful old antebellum homes and buildings. Streets are broad and shady. Before a walk around town, stop by the **Greater Cheraw Chamber of Commerce**. Closed Saturday and Sunday. ~ 221 Market Street, Cheraw; 843-537-7681, 888-537-0014; www.cheraw.com, e-mail cherawchamber@bellsouth.com.

Straight north from Columbia, an easy 71-mile glide along Route 77, lies the city of **Rock Hill**. Some people call it the "southern side of Charlotte," as the North Carolina metropolis has edged farther and farther southward, though Rock Hill retains its own flavor. **Winthrop University**, founded in 1886, occupies much of downtown, its imposing Georgian buildings residing behind spidery arms of oaks. ~ Oakland Avenue, Rock Hill; 803-323-2211.

HIDDEN ▶   The quirky **Museum of York County** is so hidden it publishes instructions on getting there. (From downtown Rock Hill, you should take Route 274 northwest to Mount Gallant Road, then go east to Museum Road. There are signs along the way.) These rural South farmlands are about the last place you'd expect to find a fringe-eared oryx, lesser kudu or Lichenstein's hartebeest —taxidermied African animals. Together with giraffes, bushpigs, teeny Kirk's dik-dik and numerous other creatures, they look out from behind museum glass, set in imitation deserts, mountains and wetlands. Even if you can't fathom why humans desire to stuff and mount animals, you'll find the display intriguing. There are four galleries with rotating exhibits and one gallery devoted to the artwork of illustrator Vernon Grant; there's also a planetarium. Admission. ~ 4621 Mount Gallant Road, Rock Hill; 803-329-2121, fax 803-329-5249; www.yorkcounty.org.

About 41 miles southeast of Columbia, not quite halfway to Charleston, the city of **Orangeburg** harbors the universally appealing **Edisto Memorial Gardens**. They're spread across 150 acres, with fragrant seas of azaleas, camellias and roses, arching canopies of cypress and oak, and the shadowy Edisto River cutting

HIDDEN ▶

through. A wheelchair-accessible boardwalk extends across the river, where the cypress "knees," or knobby exposed roots, poke out of the water. ~ Route 301, Orangeburg; 803-533-5870, fax 803-533-6027.

LODGING

Built in 1928, **Claussen's Inn** was once a bakery but is now a handsome hostelry just off the University of South Carolina campus. Fashioned of red brick, it has a lobby full of light and space, and high-ceilinged rooms warmly decorated with reproduction Colonial furnishings. The private patios and jacuzzis are an added touch. Afternoon wine is served and a continental breakfast is delivered to your door, which is included in the room rate. ~ 2003 Greene Street, Columbia; 803-765-0440, 800-622-3382, fax 803-799-7924; www.claussensinn.com. DELUXE.

Columbia Northeast AmeriSuites provides modern suites equipped with TV and microwaves. A deluxe continental breakfast is included. ~ 7525 Two Notch Road, Columbia; 803-736-6666, fax 803-788-6011; www.amerisuites.com. MODERATE.

DINING

Near the University of South Carolina, **Garibaldi's** is a friendly place with class. Jazz pours from speakers above the long glossy bar. The dining room is decorated with Art Deco statuettes and lights, booths with embroidered backs and salmon-colored walls. Fresh seafood and gourmet pizza lead the menu. Veal, chicken and pasta dishes are also offered. Try the crispy flounder served with a spicy apricot glaze or the pasta Garibaldi—fettuccini alfredo with bacon, onions and mushrooms or shrimp marinara over angel hair pasta. Dinner only. ~ 2013 Greene Street, Columbia; 803-771-8888. MODERATE TO DELUXE.

Mr. Friendly's New Southern Cafe serves some of the best and most innovative cooking around. Charleston chicken salad

---

FUEL FOR THE FAMISHED

From auto parts to roasted Cornish hens with raspberry glaze and wild rice cakes—the merchandise has definitely changed at 920 Gervais Street. The downtown Columbia address was once an automotive store in the 1960s; now it's **Motor Supply Company Bistro**. In the hub of historic Congaree Vista, it's trendy, tastefully decorated and filled with imaginative fare that's different every day. A few lunch and dinner possibilities: potato-encrusted grouper, pink peppercorn–seared tuna with champagne and shallot beurre blanc, filet mignon with crabmeat and bearnaise, and woodland mushroom ravioli. The patio is a lovely spot for summer dining. Closed Monday. ~ 920 Gervais Street, Columbia; 803-256-6687. MODERATE TO DELUXE.

is a curry-spiced chicken breast topped over organic mixed greens and topped with peach chutney, toasted almonds, shaved red onions and diced tomatoes—order it at lunchtime. For dinner there's catfish, shrimp and grits, garlic mashed potatoes, filet mignon with French Quarter pimento cheese and wonderful pecan crab cakes (sans the breading) served with sherry-cayenne mayonnaise. Full bar. No lunch on Saturday. Closed Sunday. ~ 2001 Greene Street, Columbia; phone/fax 803-254-7828; www.mrfriendlys.com. MODERATE TO DELUXE.

If you're shopping in Five Points, stop at the **Gourmet Shop Café** for wine, cheese or fresh-tasting deli sandwiches. The bright and airy eatery is kin to the gourmet cooking shop next door. ~ 724 Saluda Avenue, Columbia; 803-799-3705, fax 803-256-2337; e-mail gourmetshop@msn.com. BUDGET.

If you tire of the chips and beer mentality of Five Points, spend a more mature evening at **Gracie's**. The 1920s building was renovated almost exclusively by the owners themselves and restored to match its original Art Deco splendor, complete with a 54-foot oak bar and an ornate working fireplace. Try the crab cakes, served with chili aioli and peach chutney, or the pesto portobello sandwich with goat cheese. Dinner only. Closed Sunday. ~ 711 Harden Street, Columbia; phone/fax 803-312-0012. BUDGET TO DELUXE.

On your way out of town for a day trip, don't miss the **Mulberry Market Bake Shop**. It's the perfect place to stock up on sugary breakfast treats: croissants, coffee cake, pastries and the like. One of their chocolate brownies alone should keep you fueled for a good couple of hours. Closed Sunday. ~ 536 East DeKalb Street, Camden; 803-424-8401. BUDGET.

SHOPPING In downtown Columbia, there's good shopping at **Congaree Vista**, a historic district bounded by Senate, Assembly and Lady streets and the Congaree River. Concentrate on Gervais Street, which runs down the vista's middle and where antique and art galleries gather beneath painted awnings.

Cucina is a smart-looking cook shop for the home chef. Closed Sunday. ~ 1219 Wayne Street; 803-779-9288. Situated across Park

SCORE FIVE POINTS

USC students spend a lot of time in **Five Points**, the artsy neighborhood next door to campus. It's named for the five-pronged intersection where Santee Avenue and Harden and Devine streets run together. Painted brick facades are emblazoned with bright shutters and awnings. Columbia's funkiest shopping is here, and there are some watering holes with real character.

Street, **Paul D. Sloan** is a chichi gallery of interior design, with reproduction and original period furnishings and objets d'art. Closed Sunday. ~ 929 Gervais Street; 803-733-1704.

The arts-and-crafts booths at **City Market Mall** purvey everything from silver, crystal and linens to glassware, original paintings and out-of-print books. ~ 705–709 Gervais Street, Columbia; 803-252-1589.

It's getting harder and harder to find independent bookstores, but **Happy Bookseller** is one of the best holdouts. They have just about everything, including a good selection of regional writers. There's a full lunch cafe in the back. You can even sip coffee while you browse. No wonder they're Happy. ~ 4525 Forest Drive, Columbia; 803-782-2665, 800-787-1503; www.happybookseller.com.

Southeast of downtown Columbia, the **Five Points** neighborhood has the hippest goods. Start on Saluda Avenue, the heart of funky stuff.

Joyful Alternative has far-out T-shirts, swirling candles, unique jewelry and clever cards. Closed Sunday. ~ 747 Saluda Avenue, Columbia; 803-771-9138.

Gibson's stocks eclectic birdhouses, nutcrackers and other unusual gifts. Closed Sunday. ~ 743 Saluda Avenue, Columbia; 803-771-4520.

Creative Kids has nothing but toys—stilts, stuffed animals, teeny push brooms and lots more fun. Closed Sunday. ~ 725 Saluda Avenue, Columbia; 803-779-8697.

Looking for comfort? **Loose Lucy's** has comfortable embroidered clothing as well as posters, candles and incense. ~ 709 Saluda Avenue, Columbia; 803-252-1390.

There is a thriving night scene in Columbia. Tammy Wynette may still croon from many a pickup truck radio, but Hootie & The Blowfish—that cool rock-and-roll foursome—are the most happening sounds around town.

NIGHTLIFE

Documentaries and foreign films are on the bill at the **Nickelodeon Theatre**, which showcases bright new talent and indie flicks you won't see at the mini-malls. Located across from the State House. ~ 937 Main Street, Columbia; 803-254-3433; www.nickelodeon.org.

Classic musicals, youth theater, cutting-edge cabaret, lesbian drama, gay falsettos—what better variety from a theater company called **Trustus**. The season culminates each year with the terrific Trustus Playwrights' Festival in August, then starts back up in September. Some Friday nights there are "Late Night" shows, with possibilities ranging from solo guitarists and cello choirs to one-act plays. Cover on Friday. Advance tickets available for all other events. ~ 520 Lady Street, Columbia; 803-254-9732; www.trustus.org.

Funky and cranking past midnight, **Art Bar** plays alternative dance music. Each night features a different genre, so call ahead. You wouldn't want to show up on Goth Night when you were expecting '80s Nostalgia. ~ 1211 Park Street, Columbia; 803-929-0198; www.artbarsc.com.

Sit down and enjoy excellent Southern wings, watch the game on one of the big screen TVs or hunker down to a pool table at **Wings and Ale.** ~ 125 C Outlet Pointe Boulevard, Columbia; 803-750-1700.

Calmer and classier, **Mr. Friendly's New Southern Cafe** draws an early-evening dinner and drink crowd. Full bar. Closed Sunday. ~ 2001 Greene Street, Columbia; 803-254-7828.

Columbia's coolest coffeehouse, **Goat Feathers** is a swanky Five Points haunt serving cocktails, foreign beers and ravishing desserts. The coffees are killer, too. ~ 2017 Devine Street, Columbia; 803-256-3325.

PARKS

FINLAY PARK 🏃 One of the prettiest city parks anywhere, Finlay is swirled with waterfalls, including a high one you can walk behind. People like to take off their shoes and stick their feet in one of the clear, cold streams running through these seventeen-plus acres. It's all manmade, of course, including the one-and-a-half-acre lake with an island stage. Rocky terraces cascade down a hill, and crepe myrtles and weeping willows decorate lengthy lawns. A row of bench swings overlooks Columbia's skyline, and an amphitheater hosts Shakespeare performances in the spring and fall. Facilities here include a picnic area, a playground, restrooms and walking paths. ~ 930 Laurel Street at Gadsden Street, Columbia; 803-733-8331, fax 803-343-8744.

SESQUICENTENNIAL STATE PARK 🏃 🚲 ⛵ Nicknamed "Sesqui," these 1419 acres northeast of Columbia were formerly occupied by cotton fields. Now they're oak and pine forest that sit along a strip of South Carolina sandhills running from North Augusta to Cheraw. The terrain is dry, scrubby, muggy in summer. Swimming at a 30-acre lake helps cool visitors down, while the four-mile jogging and exercise trail keeps them in shape. The lake has fine bream and bass fishing, though there are daily limits on each, so check with the park office, where you can also rent a canoe, kayak or paddleboat. There are picnic tables (including shelters by the lake), a playground and nature trails. Day-use fee, $2. ~ Off Route 1, 13 miles northeast of Columbia; 803-788-2706, fax 803-788-4414; e-mail sesqui@scprt.com.

Sesquicentennial State Park is mosquito territory. The little pests are vicious nearly year-round, so cover up and remember to bring repellent.

▲ A campground offers 87 tent and RV sites with water and electrical hookups. Two sites designed for wheelchair campers can be reserved in advance; $17 per night. A primitive camping area is available for groups (call for information).

DREHER ISLAND STATE RECREATION AREA 🧍 🏊 🚤 🛥️ ⛵ ◀ HIDDEN

Columbians love getting away to this park on weekends. It's hidden in the woods on a peninsula poking into enormous Lake Murray, with twelve miles of shoreline and lots of ways to be on the water. You can fish, waterski or just tool around in a boat. Fourteen picnic areas are next to the water and there's a lakefront campground. By far the best digs are five villas, modern, roomy and right on the water, with amenities (remote-control TVs, microwaves, coffeemakers, fireplaces and porches) a hotel would offer. One villa is designed for wheelchair guests. Weekly stays required in the summer; there's a two-night minimum the rest of the year. Rates are deluxe. Book several months in advance, and be flexible with your dates. Swimming is fine in the shallow areas along most of the shoreline, but there are no lifeguards. Fish from the shoreline; you might snag a bream or crappie. From a boat, the possibilities extend to largemouth bass and striped bass, called "stripers." State fishing license required. You'll find a park office, a grocery and tackle shop, a marina, boat ramps, a playground, picnic pavilions and a nature trail. Day-use fee, $2. ~ Route 571, off Routes 231 and 48, nine miles west of the town of Chapin. From Columbia, take Route 26 northwest about 25 miles to Chapin; 803-364-4152, fax 803-364-0756.

▲ A lakefront campground has 112 campsites (97 for RVs and tents and 15 for tents only). All have hookups for water and electricity. Three sites accommodate wheelchair visitors and can be reserved ahead of time. All other sites are $18 to $20 per night.

CONGAREE SWAMP NATIONAL PARK 🧍 🚣 ⛵ Twenty miles ◀ HIDDEN

south of Columbia, this 22,200-acre park is one of the last stands of virgin Southern swamp. Some of the loblolly pines are more than 300 years old; one of them is sixteen stories high and fifteen feet wide. The forests of sweet gum and sycamores are beautifully sunlit, the red maples and mulberries filled with bird whistles. The Congaree River squiggles along the southern side of this water-soaked wilderness, and creeks and lakes run all through it. Cypress trees drip with moss around the water's edge. A wooden boardwalk loop lets you walk across the water (wheelchair-accessible), and several trails wind along the water. Try fishing for largemouth bass, sunfish, garfish, catfish and bream; you will need a state fishing license. Certain park areas are closed to fishing, so check with visitors center. Night fishing is allowed within state regulations. There's also canoeing, and a free three- to four-hour canoe tour is offered once a month, canoe included. If you're not doing the tour you must bring your own canoe. Rentals are available in Columbia. Facilities include a visitors center, restrooms, a picnic pavilion with grills and hiking trails. ~ Route 48, about 20 miles southeast of Columbia. From Route 48, follow the park signs; 803-776-4396, fax 803-783-4241.

▲ Primitive and backcountry camping in various areas, but there are no facilities. Permit (no fee) required, available from the visitors center.

Aiken to Abbeville

Sixty miles southwest of Columbia on Route 20, Aiken emerges from the cotton fields like a grand Old South dame. Antebellum mansions and palatial pine and oak trees line the labyrinthine streets. Muscled, glossy-coated thoroughbreds graze behind serpentine walls of red brick. Clay and sand trails, deeply worn by equestrians and their horses, wend through town and disappear into the woods.

Charlestonians rode the train over to Aiken and liked its cool forest environs "secure from tides and ocean mists, and free from sleet and snow," as exulted by the late Thomas H. Williamson, one of Aiken County's first treasurers. Northerners discovered Aiken after the Civil War and brought their money and horses here for the winter. Society pages told of polo matches, fox hunting forays and lively steeplechases. Men were dashing, and women were their husbands' wives (even now, you'll rarely hear a woman's first name in polite conversation). The Yankee aristocrats built magnificent manses and called them "cottages," and called themselves "The Winter Colony."

SIGHTS

Winter colonist Thomas Hitchcock was an internationally known polo player who wanted a wooded park right in the city. Together with other Aiken elite, he established **Hitchcock Woods**, today one of the largest urban forests in the nation. Its 2000 acres are thick with birch and pine trees and flanked by sand and clay trails designed for horseback riding and walking. ~ Laurens Street and South Boundary Avenue, Aiken.

Running along the woods are some of the elegant Colonial "cottages" of **Aiken Winter Colony Historic District**, some with nearly a hundred rooms. Take a leisurely walk through Hitchcock Woods, then drive along South Boundary Avenue beneath its famous tunnel of live oaks. ~ Along South Boundary Avenue and Laurens and Newberry streets, Aiken.

Hopeland Gardens, set on a turn-of-the-twentieth-century estate, is also a beautiful spot to walk. Fountains and shimmering ponds, weeping willows and brick walls, gigantic deodora cedars and red-berried yopon holly, and other lush flora create a pleasurable, fragrant setting. A "Touch and Scent Trail" for blind visitors has bronze markers etched in Braille. ~ Whiskey Road and Dupree Place, Aiken.

Also at the gardens is the **Thoroughbred Racing Hall of Fame**, occupying the former carriage house of the Iselin family (Mrs. Iselin, an avid gardener who lived to be 102, used to park her Rolls Royce here). This is the place to absorb Aiken's horse history; rooms and galleries are given over to exhibits on polo, steeple-chasing and harness, or "sulky," racing. You'll learn how hundreds of horses are trained here every winter so they can compete in the Aiken Triple Crown. The three races—Aiken Steeplechase, Aiken Trials and harness racing—are held over three weekends in mid-to late March, when the town swells with thousands of equestrians and horse lovers. Open late afternoon Tuesday through Sunday from mid-October to mid-May. ~ 803-642-7758.

Of course, plenty of Aiken area folks have nothing to do with horses or big money. At the **Aiken County Historical Museum**, you discover that textiles and farming were the backbone of the region for over a hundred years. Here were lots of Southern "firsts," including the South's first cotton mill and first successful bathtub. Most intriguing, though, is the museum building, an elaborate Colonial Revival home built in 1931 by a Northern industrialist. It originally had 32 rooms and 15 bathrooms, though they've been altered over time; the ballroom, now used for special exhibits, has remained untouched. The property spans an entire city block. Closed Monday. ~ 433 Newberry Street Southwest, Aiken; 803-642-2015, fax 803-642-2016.

Aiken has many other millionaire homes, though most can be viewed only from the tree-covered sidewalks. Pick up a walking tour map from the **Aiken Chamber of Commerce**, which covers the Aiken Winter Colony Historic District. Closed Sunday. ~ 121 Richland Avenue East, Aiken; 803-641-1111, 800-542-4536; www.aikenchamber.net, e-mail chamber@aikenchamber.net.

The nearby town of **Montmorenci**, five miles east of Aiken ◄ HIDDEN
on Route 78, is a scattering of farmhouses enveloped by cotton, corn and peanut fields, and pecan groves. On summer afternoons,

IN HONOR OF WILLIAM AIKEN

Aiken's main avenues and parkways are broad, thanks to town engineers who, in 1835, designed Aiken with extra-wide streets. Two years earlier, a railroad was completed between Charleston and Hamburg, South Carolina—at the time the world's longest tracks. William Aiken, wealthy equestrian, cotton grower and president of South Carolina Canal and Railroad Company, was thrown from his horse and killed before the tracks were finished. Railroad workers, laying line near a woodsy outpost, named it Aiken.

storm clouds stack up big and black over the fields, and pecans click in the pre-rain wind.

HIDDEN ▶   Amidst a thousand acres of peanut, cotton and wheat, **Mont-morenci Vineyards** now emphasizes grape vines. Robert Scott, Sr., and son, Robert Scott, Jr., grow 60 varietals and bottle a dozen different wines. A charming, chimneyed cottage acts as tasting room, open Wednesday through Saturday. Closed the first two weeks of January. ~ 2989 Charleston Highway; 803-649-4870, fax 803-642-1834.

Northwest of Aiken, pick up Route 28 at the southern edge of Sumter National Forest. Here the road becomes the **Savannah River Scenic Highway**, trailing along the river north more than a hundred miles to South Carolina's Upstate region. The scenery is near-flat, scrub-pine forest pocketed with tiny towns, their one-room post offices and gas stations with attendant loungers. Semi-trailer trucks hauling fresh-felled trees explain occasional gaps in the forest.

For the first 40 miles, the river opens wide and becomes J. Strom Thurmond Lake, though the water eludes the road and the views are mostly of trees. Four state parks provide access to the lake and forest. In the town of Calhoun Falls, you can take a thir-teen-mile jog east on Route 72 to **Abbeville**. This timeworn town with brick streets and buildings was a frontier settlement founded in the 1730s by Patrick Calhoun. His son, John C. Calhoun, was a wealthy planter and politician who fought to keep slavery, even-tually becoming vice president of the United States.

The South's Ordinance of Succession was drafted in Abbeville right before the Civil War. Near war's end, the last meeting of the Confederate War Council took place here. This is why Abbeville residents like to say the town is the "birthplace and deathbed of the Confederacy."

Despite Southern history, there's really not much to do in Abbeville. Walk around **Court Square** (bounded by Trinity, Washington, Main and Pickens streets), the heart of historic downtown, where there's the **Abbeville Opera House**, built in 1908. The opera house was a stop on the vaudeville circuit, host-ing performers such as Jimmy Durante and Fanny Bryce. Next door to this ornate brick beauty, the stately **Abbeville County Courthouse** was built the same year. Also here is the **Greater Abbeville Chamber of Commerce**, which can provide walking-tour maps of historic homes. Closed Sunday. ~ 107 Court Square, Abbeville; 864-459-4600; www.abbevillechamber.org, e-mail abvchamber@wctel.net.

The best-known historic home, **Burt-Stark Mansion**, is the official deathbed of the Confederacy. Here, in May of 1865, Jeffer-son Davis met with the Confederate War Council for the last time

before losing to the Yanks. Tours are given on Friday and Saturday afternoons; group tours available by appointment. Admission.
~ 400 North Main Street, Abbeville; 864-366-0166; www.burt-
stark.com, e-mail info@burt-stark.com.

The place to stay in Aiken is **The Willcox Inn**, right in the heart
of the old-money Winter Colony neighborhood. Built in 1898
and beautifully restored, the imposing, crisp white house offers
15 spacious rooms with poster beds, gas fireplaces, huge baths
and equestrian prints on the walls. One suite opens onto a porch.
Cocktails are available in the lobby, where you can curl up in
front of the fire. A continental breakfast is included. ~ 100
Colleton Avenue, Aiken; 803-648-1898, 877-648-2200, fax 803-
648-6664; www.thewillcox.com. ULTRA-DELUXE.

LODGING

Annie's Inn is a pecan throw from cornfields and pecan groves,
a big, white, two-story antebellum house with twin columns and
wraparound porch. Built in the 1830s, it was once the centerpiece of a 2000-acre cotton plantation. All the bedrooms have
private baths, and are variously decorated in homey style. Six
spacious cottages, popular with corporate travelers as well as visiting polo players, are rented by the week. Rooms include a full
breakfast. ~ Route 78, about five miles east of Aiken, 3083
Charleston Highway, Montmorenci; 803-649-6836; e-mail an-
nizin@aol.com. MODERATE.

◀ HIDDEN

Next door to the Abbeville Opera House, the **Belmont Inn** was
heralded by the local paper as a "new and modern hotel" when
it opened in 1903. Over time, it deteriorated and eventually closed,
but now has been reincarnated as a no-frills, comfortable place.
Twenty-five individually decorated guest rooms have original
hardwood floors that creak with age, and period antiques. The
marble veranda overlooks Abbeville Square for refined people-
watching. ~ 104 East Pickens Street, Abbeville; phone/fax 864-
459-9625, 877-459-8118; www.belmontinn.net. MODERATE.

Close to the town square, in a two-story Princess Anne B&B
with a wraparound porch, you'll find the sweet little **Vintage Inn**.

AUTHOR FAVORITE

Annie's Inn stole my heart the second I learned a Civil War cannonball
lopped off the third floor. Naturally, repairs have been made since the
1860s, but you can still sense the sanguine Old South from the porch
rockers, looking across cornfields and listening to pecans click in the
twisted old trees. See above for more information.

Coincidentally, after renovating the home, the owner discovered that her great-grandparents once lived there. Perhaps hospitality is genetic: you'll find quilts and lace curtains, books and fireplaces, wood floors, clawfoot tubs, and even a collection of antique hats to play dress-up in. The inn consists of a main house (three eclectically decorated rooms) and a carriage house (two suites, a kitchen and a sitting room). ~ 1205 North Main Street, Abbeville; 864-459-4784, 800-890-7312; www.thevintageinn.com, e-mail info@thevintageinn.com. MODERATE TO DELUXE.

DINING

Go to **Malia's** for lunch and have soup. Different every day but always good, you might find black bean chili or—what locals crave—crab meat bisque. The menu also lists sandwiches, salads and full-course fare. The dining room of the downtown eatery runs deep, the facade is washed with sunny yellow. No dinner on Monday and Tuesday. Closed Sunday and from mid- to late May. ~ 120 Laurens Street Southwest, Aiken; 803-643-3086. MODERATE TO DELUXE.

In a restored 1837 house that's simple and elegant, **No. 10 Downing Street** serves savory Continental creations such as nutted pork tenderloin with ginger mayonnaise, sea bass with lemon beurre blanc, and rack of lamb. Save room for the chocolate-raspberry flan, then stroll around the lovely gardens. There's a full bar. Dinner only. Closed Sunday and Monday. ~ 241 Laurens Street Southwest, Aiken; phone/fax 803-642-9062; www.no10aiken.com. MODERATE TO DELUXE.

For a comprehensive list of antique shops, stop by the Greater Aiken Chamber of Commerce. ~ 121 Richland Avenue East; 803-641-1111.

The best eatery in Abbeville, **The Village Grill** is a comfy place with wood booths and walls painted watermelon and hunter green. Steaks, fish, shrimp and pasta selections come with side dishes like fried corn on the cob and baked beans. Among the heart-healthy items: rotisserie chicken and grilled salmon. Full bar. Closed Sunday and Monday. ~ 110 Trinity Street, Abbeville; 864-366-2500; www.thevillagegrill.com. MODERATE TO DELUXE.

SHOPPING

Look for antiques and country collectibles along Laurens and Newberry streets in downtown Aiken.

You'll find a wide range of artifacts at **Market Place Antiques**. Closed Sunday. ~ 343 Park Avenue Southwest, Aiken; 803-648-9696.

Take a meander through **Birds and Butterflies**, a repository of nature and garden items, statues, fountains and one-of-a-kind pieces made by local artists. They've also added a line of dog and cat specialty items. Closed Sunday. ~ 117 Laurens Street Northwest, Aiken; 803-649-7999.

Area farmers bring their crops to **Aiken County Farmers Market**. Depending on what's in season, you'll find watermelon, silver queen corn, pecans, peanuts and cantaloupe. Call before you go; they're open only during certain times of year. ~ Richland Avenue and Williamsburg Street, Aiken; 803-642-7630.

Westside Bowery, a restaurant on one end and pub on the other, pulls in huge happy-hour crowds, mostly thirty- and fortysome-things. It's SRO on Friday and Saturday nights, too. ~ 151 B Lane, Aiken; 803-648-2900.

The Opera House Players, a stock theater company, perform year-round at **Abbeville Opera House**. The former vaudeville and "talkie" movie house is a striking turn-of-the-twentieth-century showplace. ~ On Court Square, downtown Abbeville; 864-459-2157.

REDCLIFFE PLANTATION STATE PARK 🏃 Many people are surprised to discover this 1859 antebellum mansion, tucked fifteen miles southwest of Aiken near the Georgia state line. South Carolina Governor James H. Hammond chose this secluded spot along the Savannah River for his two-story plantation house, calling it "Redcliffe" for the high clay bluffs running along the water. Four generations of Hammonds lived here until descendant John Shaw Billings, former managing editor for *Time* and *Life* magazines, donated it to the state. You can tour the house (admission), which has many original furnishings and art pieces, then picnic and walk along the nature trail at this 369-acre park. Facilities include the park office, the plantation home with slave quarters, a picnic area and a nature trail. There is a $4 fee to tour the home. Closed Tuesday and Wednesday. ~ Off Route 278, three miles southwest of Beech Island and 15 miles southeast of Aiken; phone/fax 803-827-1473.

HAMILTON BRANCH STATE RECREATION AREA 🏃 🛥 🚤 ⚓
With more than 1200 miles of shoreline and a sea of fresh water teeming with bass, bream and catfish, this is a fisher's haven. The park is a 731-acre peninsula elbowing into J. Strom Thurmond Lake, pale blue water rimmed with slash pine forest rising up from the clay. Picnic tables and campsites are sprinkled along the shore of pine needles. Rarely crowded, even in the height of spring and fall seasons. There are no designated swimming areas, but plenty of shallow lakeshore with hard-packed clay bottom. Lake fishing is excellent for bass, bream and catfish; a state license is required. Facilities include the park office, picnic tables and shelters, a playground, a bike trail, a bath house, restrooms and boat ramps. ~ Located along Route 221 (Savannah River

Highway) just north of Route 23, 12 miles south of McCormick; phone/fax 864-333-2223.

▲ There are 200 tent and RV sites with electric and water hookups (most are right on the lake); $16 per site. Hot showers and restrooms available ~ 866-345-7275.

HICKORY KNOB STATE RESORT PARK 🏃 🏊 🛶 Just past the entrance of this vast wooded retreat, a velvety green golf course swirls against the blueness of Thurmond Lake. It's but one clue why this is called a "resort" park—and why it's wildly popular nearly year-round. Like a summer camp for adults and kids, it offers myriad activities and accommodations, including a motel-style lodge; basic but modern one-bedroom cabins with kitchenettes, TVs and telephones; and a historic, two-bedroom house with a full kitchen and fireplace. Budget rates for the lodge and cabins; moderate for the house. Book several months ahead, especially for the spring and fall. Swimming is best in the swimming pool; lake swimming is permitted, but there's no beach or lifeguards. You can catch bass, bream, yellow perch, saugers and catfish in Thurmond Lake. There are many facilities: an 18-hole golf course with putting green, a driving range, a pro shop and a clubhouse lounge; a swimming pool; two tennis courts; a skeet shooting range; an archery course; a playground; a restaurant and coffee shop; nature trails; and johnboat and kayak rentals. ~ Off Route 378, seven miles west of McCormick; 864-391-2450, 800-491-1764, fax 864-391-5390; e-mail hickory_knob_sp@scprt.com.

▲ There are 42 campsites for tents or RVs, all with hookups. A hot-water bathhouse is at the campground. Fee is $15 per site, available on a first-come basis.

HIDDEN ► **CALHOUN FALLS STATE RECREATION AREA** 🏃 🏊 🛶 🚤 🛶 There aren't any waterfalls here, just miles of pine woods and pale blue Lake Russell. (The falls disappeared when the lake was created.) Everything in this park is geared toward the water—Lake Russell covers 26,650 acres—with fishing and boating heading the list of park pursuits. Swimming is good off the lakefront beach, open during summer. There are excellent fishing opportunities for bass, bluegill, crappie, striped bass and catfish. Facilities include the park office, a marina with 36 boat slips, boat ramps, a fishing pier, a park store and tackle shop, a modern community building, a playground, basketball, volleyball and tennis courts, picnic areas and a bathhouse. ~ Off Route 81, two miles north of Route 72 and the town of Calhoun Falls; 864-447-8267, fax 864-447-8638.

▲ Eighty-six RV/tent sites, all with electric and water hookups; $19 per site per night; fourteen primitive sites; $15.50 per site per night; reservations accepted.

The flat pine woods and fields of central South Carolina slowly give way to soft sculpted hills in the northwest. Lakeshores angle against spires of trees, whitewashed farmhouses are propped on knolls, rivers run long and
lucid, and seamless roads twist above hazy valleys. The Upstate, as
this northwestern corner of South Carolina is called, is indeed the
highest part of the state, rising more than 3000 feet, a prelude to
North Carolina's Southern Mountains just across the state line.

Upstate

Greenville and Spartanburg are the commercial gateways to
the Upstate. Their downtowns are separated by 30 miles but
with ever-expanding commerce and industry, their metropolitan
areas are fast merging. The nearby town of Greer was chosen
over dozens of cities worldwide as the site of BMW's auto-manu-
facturing plant, a $5 million facility that opened in 1995. The
modern and attractive Greenville-Spartanburg Airport, almost
halfway between the cities, welcomes visitors to the area.

On the west side of Greenville stands **"Shoeless Joe" Jackson
Memorial Park,** homage to a native son who was one of the
greatest baseball players of the early twentieth century. It's located opposite the old Brandon Mill for whose Textile League team
Jackson played as a teenager. Jackson compiled the third-highest
career batting average in history before he was banished from
ball after being implicated in the 1918 Chicago Black Sox scandal.
~ West Avenue, north off Easley Bridge Road; 864-288-6470.

SIGHTS

Downtown **Greenville** is an enjoyable few blocks of tree-lined
streets and wide walkways. Browse the shops and have lunch,

AUTHOR FAVORITE

sights

I was seriously skeptical about the **Bob Jones University
Museum of Sacred Art,** fearing more evangelical fervor than museum (remember Jones' fiery Sunday TV sermons?). Four hours, 27 galleries, and 400
masterpieces later, I had miraculously found art heaven. There are icons that
are 4000 years old, including vases from ancient Egypt and Syria and a Hebrew Torah scroll written on gazelle skin. As for the impressive sampling of
Baroque and Renaissance paintings, you'll find works by no less than van
Dyck, Tintoretto and Rubens. Note that this is *not* the place to wear
your short-shorts, the university being of the fundamentalist Protestant
persuasion. Open Tuesday through Sunday afternoons. Children must
be at least six years of age. Admission. ~ 1700 Wade Hampton Boulevard, Greenville; 864-770-1331, fax 864-770-1306; www.bjumg.org, e-
mail contact@bjumg.org.

then stop at the **Greater Greenville Convention & Visitors Bureau** for information on the area. Closed Saturday and Sunday. ~ In the City Hall lobby, 206 South Main Street; 864-421-0000; www.greatergreenville.com, e-mail visit@greatergreen ville.com. You also can request maps and brochures by mail from the **Discover Upcountry Carolina Association**. ~ P.O. Box 3116, Greenville, SC 29602; 864-233-2690, 800-849-4766; www.the upcountry.com, e-mail visit@theupcountry.com.

The permanent pieces at **Greenville County Museum of Art** focus on Southern talent, from the colonial period to the present, including works by Henrietta Johnston and Jasper Johns. The museum's growing collection of twentieth-century American art features works by such masters as Josef Albers, Georgia O'Keeffe, Hans Hofmann, Andy Warhol and Andrew Wyeth. Traveling exhibitions span ancient to modern times and are usually excellent. Closed Monday. ~ 420 College Street, Greenville; 864-271-7570, fax 864-271-7579; www.greenvillemuseum.org, e-mail info@greenvillemuseum.org.

In addition to the collections at the county museum and Bob Jones University Museum, local and regional art is also displayed at Greenville's leading institution of higher learning, in the **Furman University Thompson Gallery**. Founded in 1826, the 750-acre campus also boasts rose and Japanese gardens as well as an Italian bell tower that rises from an island in a 30-acre lake. The gallery is open only on weekdays when an exhibit is on display, so call ahead. ~ 3300 Poinsett Highway, Greenville; 864-294-2074.

Civil War history buffs may also want to sneak a peek at the **Museum of Confederate History**, which—though small—has an interesting collection of military and personal relics from the 1860s. Operated by the 16th South Carolina Volunteers, it also has a research library. Open Wednesday, Friday night and on the weekend. ~ 15 Boyce Avenue, Greenville; 864-421-9039.

Greenville has a couple of lures for children, as well. The **Roper Mountain Science Center** combines a hands-on science museum and education center, an observatory, planetarium, and living-history demonstration farm with a series of nature trails. Operated by the county school district, it is open to the public on the second Saturday of each month except December; planetarium shows are offered every Friday night. Admission. ~ 402 Roper Mountain Road, Greenville; 864-281-1188, fax 864-458-7034; www.roper mountain.org.

The small but charming **Greenville Zoo**, at the edge of lovely Cleveland Park, features an international cast of animals in open-air exhibits, as well as a reptile house and waterfowl lagoon. Admission. ~ 150 Cleveland Park Drive, Greenville; 864-467-4300; www.greenvillezoo.com, e-mail info@greenvillezoo.com.

For those who prefer wildlife of a less common sort, a visit to the **Hollywild Animal Park** may be in order. Located east of   ◄ HIDDEN
Greer in Spartanburg County, this 100-acre spread offers safari-style rides through one of the largest private collections of rare and exotic animals in the southeastern United States. A miniature train (fee) tours areas of the park inaccessible by foot. Many of the animals have appeared in movies or commercials. Open March to October and Thanksgiving to January 1. Admission. ~ 2325 Hampton Road, Wellford; 864-472-2038, fax 864-472-6336; www.hollywild.com, e-mail info@hollywild.com.

The BMW **Manufacturing** plant is just off the interstate between Spartanburg and the regional airport. It's been the biggest thing in these environs since 1994, when the ◆◆◆◆◆◆◆◆◆◆◆◆◆◆◆◆◆◆◆◆◆
German auto manufacturer announced its intention to locate here, hire several thousand workers and open a visitors center to draw tourists. One-hour walking tours of the factory start at the Zentrum, as the center is called, and include a lengthy look at actual car assembly. No one under twelve years of age allowed on the tour. Admission. ~ 1400 Route 101 South, Greer; 864-989-5297, 888-868-7269, fax 864-989-5298; www.bmwzentrum.com.

> At Greer's BMW Manu-facturing plant, you'll get a glimpse of the Z3 roadster actor Roger Moore (as agent James Bond) drove in the movie *Golden Eye*.

Spartanburg lacks the contemporary edge of Greenville, but its downtown is pleasant enough. The best sightseeing is actually in the bucolic pastureland south of Spartanburg. Take Route 221 through sun-sprinkled forest and country fields until you see the signs for **Walnut Grove Plantation**. Park and follow the path be-   ◄ HIDDEN
neath arches of gorgeous crepe myrtles to the unassuming plantation house. It has changed little since 1765, when Charles Moore received the land by grant from King George III and built the house of local pine. He and his wife raised ten children, including daughter Kate, who was a scout for the Patriots during the American Revolution.

Incredibly, some of the Moore's original furnishings and books are well preserved here, and what didn't actually belong to them are still specific to the period. A closet door has its original paint—buttermilk dyed with indigo. The ruddy stains on a bedroom floor are from the blood of a Patriot captain slain by Tories. After a tour of the home and the adjacent schoolhouse (one of the first in the South), stroll the nature trail and the cemetery where Kate Moore and other family members are buried. Open weekends only from November through March; closed Monday from April through October. Admission. ~ 1200 Otts Shoals Road, Roebuck; 864-576-6546; www.spartanarts.org/history, e-mail walnutgrove@mindspring.com.

Text continued on page 430.

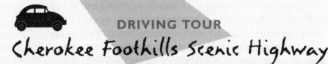

Cherokee Foothills Scenic Highway

If you head west from Chesnee along Route 11, you can experience the most scenic drive in inland South Carolina. For 135 miles, the road curves against the northwestern corner of the state, from Gaffney in the east to Route 85 in the west near Georgia. Called the **Cherokee Foothills Scenic Highway**, it runs alongside velvety green hills and forest-covered mountains, leafy peach orchards and bushy pea patches. Signs direct you to hidden hamlets like Pumpkintown, Pickens, Fair Play and Mountain Rest. The few rambling farmhouses, country stores and log homes are but pinpoints of civilization in this far-reaching wilderness. Six state parks are sprinkled along the highway's hilly length, some dating back to the 1930s, when their solid facilities were erected by the Civilian Conservation Corps. The parks provide most of the access to the vast blue lakes, the clear-as-gin streams, the rocky mountain trails.

TWO GREAT BRIDGES   A short, scenic side trip will take you to **Campbell's Bridge**, built in 1909 and now the last covered bridge left in South Carolina. To find it, go south at Gowensville on Route 14 for four miles, then head west on Route 414 for one half-mile. A little farther west on Route 11, detour north on Route 25 for a great drive in the country. The skinny road launches through forest and farmland where a few postage stamp–size homes have corn patches. After a couple of miles, you'll see the turnoff for **Poinsett Bridge**, a shaded stone beauty built in 1820 and thought to be the oldest bridge in South Carolina. Its Gothic arch presides over the fast-flowing Middle Saluda River, where you can wade through the clear, brisk water embedded with black granite. Spread out a picnic atop the bridge, look into the coves crowded with kudzu, and listen to the water rush by. You will most likely have the place to yourself.

TOWER POWER   A little farther west on Route 11, Route 178 North winds up through the woods. The trees get higher and higher, sunlight barely breaks through the tops and you'll realize you're climbing up the mountains. You can stop and wade in creeks that ramble by, or take a look at 3560-foot **Sassafras Mountain**, South Carolina's highest peak. The best view of the mountain is from the **Forest Service Lookout Tower** on Route 39-199, east of Route 178. If park personnel are on duty, they'll usually let you climb the tower.

A TOWN AND A TUNNEL   Toward the western end of Cherokee Foothills Scenic Highway, Route 28 jogs north to **Walhalla**, where a sign declares "This is a Great Town." It's not really much of a town, just some whitewashed houses and antique shops, patches of corn and an annual Hillbilly Festival. About eight miles north of Walhalla, through mountain gaps with panoramas of hazy valleys, **Stumphouse Mountain Tunnel Park** lies below the road in cool forest crisscrossed with streams. The tunnel is part of a brief, strange attempt in 1856 to connect South Carolina with the Midwest by railroad. The Blue Ridge Railroad decided to bore through granite mountains using Irish immigrants with sledgehammers and hand drills working twelve hours a day. It took them one month to chip away 200 feet. Money ran out, the Civil War struck, and all that's left are empty tunnels. In the 1950s, Clemson University used Stumphouse Mountain Tunnel for curing its locally renowned blue cheese, hanging the blue-veined curds in little pouches from the wet tunnel walls. The blue cheese is gone and the tunnel is sometimes closed due to precarious rock conditions. But you can peer through the barricades into its black, abysmal depths or, if it's open and you've dressed warmly, you can explore inside. . Afterward, hike along nearby Issaqueena Falls and through surrounding forest, wade in the streams or picnic at the tables. Call the Walhalla Chamber of Commerce for more information. ~ 864-638-2727.

AROUND CLEMSON   Route 11 curls south past Walhalla and crosses Route 123, which heads east to **Clemson**. The pretty, nineteenth-century town is joined in the Southern consciousness with **Clemson University** and its Tigers, and indeed the school (and mascot) is the focus of everything (there's even a Tiger Paw Car Wash). The campus is beautiful, brimming with ancient oak trees and nineteenth-century architecture. Drive along College Avenue and Perimeter Road, south of Route 123, and you'll get a good picture of the place. ~ 864-656-4789. On the campus's east side, **South Carolina Botanical Garden** offers a fine walk in the woods. Miles of paths cushioned with pine needles wind through forest, wooden footbridges arch over streams, and shady coves offer relief from summer heat. A thousand species of trees are here (unfortunately, few are labeled) as are gardens of camellia and daffodils. ~ Perimeter Road and Route 28.

HIGH TEA TIME   From Clemson, take Route 28 just three miles to **Pendleton**. If you arrive in the morning, you'll see folks out tending their gardens. This time-locked town with lovely old homes and enormous trees has a village green embraced by colorfully painted shops and restaurants, most dating to the 1800s. You can easily spend a day browsing, having lunch and exploring historic homes. Stop by **The Pendleton District Historical and Recreational Commission** for a walking-tour map. Closed weekends from November through March. ~ 125 East Queen Street, Pendleton; 864-646-3782, 800-862-1795.

A few miles south of Walnut Grove, Thomas Price built a beautiful brick home with chimneys and a steep gambrel roof—unheard
HIDDEN ▶ of for a 1795 plantation home. **The Price House** doesn't seem so unusual today, except that it is meticulously restored. The original plantation covered 2000 acres, with 28 slaves doing most of the farm work. Price ran the local post office and general store and entertained folks passing through by stagecoach, a good way to make extra cash and show off his place. Closed Monday through Friday. Admission. ~ 1200 Oak View Farms Road, off Route 26, Woodruff; 864-576-6546.

Northeast of Spartanburg along rural Route 29, you will know you are in peach country when you see the **Peachoid water tower** in **Gaffney**. Painted like a peach, its ruddy, sun-faded facade is a tribute to area peach growing.

Keep heading north on two-lane Route 29 and it will dip and climb through rolling green pastures with dirt roads that have names like Possom Trot. Turn off at Route 216 and follow the signs for **Kings Mountain National Military Park**, next door to Kings Mountain State Park. Kings is not really a mountain but a low spur of the Blue Ridge, covered in Southern hardwood forest and straddling the South and North Carolina border. The long, flat summit, rising only 60 feet, seemed an ideal place for the Tories to set up camp in October 1780. From here, they thought they could defend themselves against the Patriot "over-mountain men," a backwoods band of farmers who were marching down from Tennessee with knives and guns. But the surrounding oaks and hickories proved good cover for the mountaineers. They surrounded the Tories and "fought from tree to tree to the summit," according to one Loyalist account. In less than an hour, the over-mountain men had killed Tory commander Major Patrick Ferguson, and helped decide the end of the American Revolution.

Today, you can stroll through the forest along the ridge where the centuries-old skirmish occurred. Much of the trail is wheelchair-accessible. Historical markers help bring the battle into perspective. (Basically, these guys were shooting with muskets from behind trees. Imagine their stress level every time they had to stop to reload.) There's also an eighteen-minute film, shown in the visitors center, that traces local battles during the war. ~ 2625 Park Road, Blacksburg; 864-936-7921; www.nps.gov/kimo, e-mail kimo_administration@nps.gov.

HIDDEN ▶ The next big skirmish was in January 1781 at nearby **National Battlefield**. Once again, the British were defeated in an hour even though they enjoyed bigger and better forces. It helped that the Colonials were led by one Daniel Morgan, a brilliant field tactician of the Revolution. The frenzied fighting went on right next to the cows and horses who grazed at Hannah's Cowpens, a frontier pasture. The battlefield originally covered only about an acre, though the park stretches for 845 acres, providing areas for picnicking and walking. A one-and-a-quarter-mile interpretive trail and three-and-a-half-mile loop road, sprinkled here and there with historical markers, take you to the heart of the battle. A 24-minute film at the visitors center provides more background. ~ Route 11, about 11 miles west of Route 85, Chesnee; 864-461-2828, fax 864-461-7795; www.nps.gov/cowp.

LODGING

Most accommodations around Greenville and Spartanburg are chain hotels and motels. One exception in Greenville is the award-winning **Pettigru Place**, a gorgeous B&B in a historic neighborhood near downtown. The front lawn of the Georgian Federalist house is riotously planted with flowers. Inside, the rooms are striking, just like something out of a home decorating magazine. The Brass Giraffe has a primitive African theme, the Carolinian has a king sleigh bed, Charleston detailing and a jacuzzi for two, and the Greene Room has a fireplace and rich tones of cranberry and hunter green. Rates include a full gourmet breakfast. ~ 302 Pettigru Street, Greenville; 864-242-4529, 877-362-4644, fax 864-242-1231; www.pettigruplace.com, e-mail info@pettigruplace.com. MODERATE TO ULTRA-DELUXE.

◄ HIDDEN

If you prefer something of the motor hotel variety, we recommend **The Phoenix: Greenville's Inn**. Centrally located on a low hill near the Palmetto International Exposition Center, The Phoenix combines colonial ambience (construction is reminiscent of a spacious carriage house) with Southern hospitality, an elegant restaurant, a piano lounge and a sports pub. The nicely landscaped grounds include a central swimming pool surrounded by a large deck. A full breakfast buffet is available. ~ 246 North

AUTHOR FAVORITE

When you're watching the sunset over the Blue Ridge Mountains from your flagstone terrace at the **Red Horse Inn**, remember that we told you so. The six bedroom suites, each with a private bath and fireplace, are sumptuously decorated in draped fabrics and high windows. There are gardens to wander, a koi pond, and breathtaking views of mountains, grazing horses and the surrounding 190 acres. Five spacious cottages are also available, each individually decorated with murals, wing chairs and reproduction antiques. The units are each provided with a small fridge, which has been thoughtfully stocked with breakfast items. ~ About 22 miles northwest of Spartanburg, 310 North Campbell Road, Landrum; 864-895-4968; www.theredhorseinn.com, e-mail theredhorseinn@aol.com. DELUXE TO ULTRA-DELUXE.

Pleasantburg Drive, Greenville; 864-233-4651, 800-257-3529; www.phoenixgreenvillesinn.com, e-mail phoenixgreenvillesinn@ aol.com. MODERATE.

At the foot of the Blue Ridge Mountains, surrounded by 40 acres of vineyards, hides **La Bastide**, a hostelry imbued with the grace of southern France. A local craftsman provided the wrought-iron detailing that winds around the hotel, and the exquisite restaurant ensures you won't leave the grounds. Some of the 14 rooms and suites overlook the vineyards; others have views of the mountains. French antiques and reproductions, original artwork, and lovely balconies complete the effect: apparently, there's a touch of France alive and well in South Carolina (but without the cigarette smoke). Full breakfast is included. ~ 10 Road of Vines, Travelers Rest; 864-836-8463, 877-836-8463, fax 864-836-4820; www.labastide.com. ULTRA-DELUXE.

Lodging is scarce along the Cherokee Foothills. Several state parks have cabins and one rents contemporary villas, but they are tough to secure (for more information, see "Beaches & Parks" later in this chapter).

HIDDEN ► It's easier to reserve a room at **The Schell Haus**. Sharon and Jim Mahanes have opened their Victorian home in the woods to visitors, offering six bedrooms with homespun decor and a swimming pool out back. One room has a sumptuous view of Table Rock Mountain. There's also a lavish suite with living room, wet bar, whirlpool tub and more panoramic scenes. Full breakfast is included. ~ Off Route 11, across from Table Rock State Park; 864-878-0078, 877-283-0661, fax 864-878-0066; www.schell haus.com, e-mail schellhs@bellsouth.net. MODERATE.

The adjacent **Laurel Mountain Inn** is a five-room motel in a private, wooded setting. Each room has antique reproductions and a picture window with views of Table Rock Mountain. All come with coffeemakers, refrigerators, microwaves and one extra-large room is wheelchair-accessible. ~ Off Route 11, across from Table Rock State Park; 864-878-8500; e-mail shergeo@aol.com. MODERATE.

HIDDEN ► Off the western stretch of Cherokee Foothills Scenic Highway, **Sunrise Farm** was once a cotton plantation but is now a ten-acre property with picturesque pastures and mountains all around. The early 1890s farmhouse is big and beautiful, its lawns decorated with myrtle trees, magnolias and a split-rail fence. Owners Barbara and Ron Laughter offer two rooms and a suite that are spacious, colorful and extra comfortable. There are also two cottages, including a corncrib with a fireplace and private patio. ~ On Sunrise Drive, one mile from Route 130, Salem; 864-944-0121, 888-991-0121, fax 864-944-6195; e-mail sfbb@bellsouth. net. MODERATE TO DELUXE.

The four-acre grounds at **Liberty Hall Inn** are rich with lawns and gardens, while the seven bedrooms are informal, spacious and tasteful. All have telephones, televisions and air conditioning, but these are recent additions. When a wealthy Charlestonian built the handsome, two-story home in 1840 as a summer home, there was little but wood floors and walls, and cotton fields all around. A full breakfast is included. ~ 621 South Mechanic Street, Pendleton; phone/fax 864-646-7500, 800-643-7944; e-mail liberty hallinn@aol.com. MODERATE TO DELUXE.

DINING

Thanks in large part to the revitalization of Main Street, Greenville has become blessed with a spate of fine restaurants. Among the best is **Soby's**, whose changing menu of gourmet New South cuisine might feature seared yellowfin tuna with mustard greens or a grilled pork chop on hominy grits. Housed in a former brick warehouse almost opposite the peace center, Soby's also has one of the city's most popular wine bars for the 30-plus set. Dinner only. Closed Sunday. ~ 207 South Main Street, Greenville; 864-232-7007, fax 864-232-5282; www.sobys.com. DELUXE.

Only one block away is **Trattoria Giorgio**, whose young owner-chef indeed came to the Upstate directly from Italy. You won't find better homemade pasta dishes than in this intimate café with huge streetside windows that make it appear larger than it is. The Italian preparations of fresh seafood and veal piccata are (*mama mia!*) divine. Dinner only. Closed Sunday and Monday. ~ 121 South Main Street, Greenville; 864-271-9166. DELUXE TO ULTRA-DELUXE.

The **Augusta Grill**, which dominates a mini-mall about a mile south of downtown, has a strong following. The fare combines traditional and innovative American with Continental favorites. Closed Sunday. ~ 1818 Augusta Street, Greenville; 864-242-0316. MODERATE TO DELUXE.

◆◆

BARBECUE UNTIL YOU BURST

You really can't leave the Carolinas without indulging in a big barbecue buffet. **Just More Barbecue**, a place that epitomizes the Southern specialty, should fit the bill. All the meat is cooked onsite with natural wood and a fourteen-hour cooking and smoking process: chopped pork, smoked chicken quarters, baby back ribs. Sides include hushpuppies, two different types of coleslaw, corn on the cob, hash, and green beans (maybe the only vegetable you'll find here). Live music accompanies your meal, bands with names like "Wooden Nickel," "Saluda River Catfish" and "Buffalo Barfield." Open on Friday and Saturday nights only. ~ 1410 Cherry Street, Pendleton; 864-646-3674; www.justbbq.com, e-mail sauce@justbbq.com. MODERATE.

Long established in the Furman University area north of town is **The Peddler Steak House**, in a turn-of-the-20th-century stone building designed to look like a rustic log cabin with five big fireplace lounges. It feels more like a ski lodge than a restaurant. There's no menu; the server displays a choice of raw beef cuts and asks how you'd like yours cooked. Not recommended for vegetarians. Dinner only. Closed Sunday. ~ 2000 Poinsett Highway, Greenville; 864-235-7192, fax 864-235-4843. MODERATE TO DELUXE.

With its influx of international business people, Upstate South Carolina is getting more and more Asian restaurants. In Greenville, you'll find an array of Chinese, Thai, Korean, Vietnamese and Indian options.

One of the best Japanese restaurants in the area, **Irashiai Sushi Pub**, in a strip mall behind Kmart near Bob Jones University, has an extensive Japanese menu but specializes in raw-fish delicacies rolled as diners watch. Closed Sunday. ~ 23 Rushmore Drive off Wade Hampton Boulevard, Greenville; 864-244-2008, fax 864-268-0950; www.irashiai.com. MODERATE.

Classy and casual **Abby's Grill** offers a changing menu that might include crabcakes, lamb or Southwestern fare. The grill features live music Wednesday and Friday nights. No lunch on Saturday. Closed Sunday. ~ 149 West Main Street, Spartanburg; 864-583-4660; www.abbysgrill.com. MODERATE TO DELUXE.

The **Beacon Drive-In** is a scream. The cafeteria line moves fast and furious, with servers hollering orders and commotion radiating from the kitchen. There are more than 80 sandwiches guaranteed to blow your cholesterol for the day. Double chili cheeseburgers with bacon, fried perch, sausage and egg—order them regular or "a-plenty" with fried potatoes and Vidalia onions. Dozens of booths and tables fill this funky, timeworn eatery. You can dine in your car, but you'll miss all the crazy goings-on. Closed Sunday. ~ 255 John White Boulevard, Spartanburg; 864-585-9387. BUDGET.

There's not much cookin' along the 135-mile Cherokee Foothills Scenic Highway. For lunch, there's **Aunt Sue's Country Corner**, where organ music streams out front and waitresses are called "cousins." Deli sandwiches, BLTs, ice cream, fudge and sweet tea are the mainstays. Closed Monday. ~ Route 11, two miles east of Table Rock State Park; 864-878-4366. BUDGET.

There's no problem finding fine food in Pendleton. To dine in cultured country style, go to **Liberty Hall Inn**. With white linens, fresh-cut flowers and candlelight, the restaurant serves dinner Thursday through Saturday nights. Choose between the fresh grilled salmon with caper butter or pork tenderloin medallions with a reisling and rum raisin sauce and you won't be disappointed. Closed Monday. ~ Route 28 business, Pendleton; 864-646-7500. MODERATE TO DELUXE.

Across from the village green, **The Country Kettle** is a small cafeteria whose fresh fill-you-up farm fare features mashed potatoes, lima beans, stewed apples, stewed tomatoes, country steak, fried chicken and the best macaroni and cheese you've ever tasted. It's breakfast and lunch only, so leave time for an afternoon nap. Closed Saturday. ~ 129 North Mechanic Street, Pendleton; 864-646-3301. BUDGET.

SHOPPING

Concentrate your shopping efforts in Greenville, where the area around Main Street has splendid shopping. Look for traditional and primitive furniture, funky watches, hip garb, health food items, artwork and even maps.

Pick any place in the world and **The Map Shop** will surely have a map of it. There's even a world pocket atlas for sale at this fascinating place. Closed Sunday. ~ 5 East Coffee Street, Greenville; 864-271-6277; www.themapshop.com.

The gallery of **Llyn Strong Fine Jewelry** is a prettily lit space exhibiting pricey and unusual jewelry and hand-blown glass. Closed Sunday. ~ 119 North Main Street, Greenville; 864-233-0216; www.llynstrong.com.

Northwest of downtown Greenville, **Tempo Gallery, Art & Frame** showcases works by Upstate South Carolina artists—everything from oils, acrylics and serigraphs to pottery and works off and on paper. Closed Sunday and Monday, and sometimes on Saturday. ~ 125 West Stone Avenue, Greenville; 864-233-1070; www.tempogallery.com.

Clemson University has been making blue cheese for nearly half a century, and is good at it. You can buy the blue-veined delicacy at the school's **Hendrix Student Center**. ~ Palmetto Boulevard, Clemson; 864-656-3663.

Galleries and gift shops edge the Pendleton village green. The folks at **The Mercantile** will offer you coffee while you browse the porcelain, collectibles, candles and potpourri. Closed Sunday. ~ 149 East Queen Street, Pendleton; 864-646-9431.

NIGHTLIFE

Greenville is rightly proud of its $42 million **Peace Center for the Performing Arts,** the venue for touring Broadway musicals, symphony and dance, children's theater, and appearances by such top performers as Bill Cosby, Gordon Lightfoot and Mary Chapin Carpenter. It's home to the Greenville Symphony Orchestra and the Carolina Ballet Theatre. Facilities include a 400-seat theater, a 2100-seat concert hall, and an outdoor amphitheater. ~ 300 South Main Street; 864-467-3000, 800-888-7768; www.peacecenter.org.

The 16,000-seat BI-LO Center is Greenville's premier events facility. In addition to presenting big-name acts such as Billy Joel and Aerosmith, it plays host to the Greenville Grrrowl minor-league hockey team. ~ 650 North Academy Street; 864-467-0008; www.bilocenter.com.

A leading local theater company is the **Greenville Little Theatre**, which has stuck together since 1926. It performs a September-to-June season in the 600-seat Charles E. Daniel Theatre. ~ 444 College Street; 864-233-6238; www.greenvillelittletheatre.com. Less serious shows are mounted at **Café and Then Some**, a comedy dinner theater whose sketches tend to parody the Southern redneck culture. No shows Sunday through Tuesday. ~ 101 College Street, Greenville; 864-232-2287; www.cafeats.com.

Cinema complexes are rife throughout the Upstate, but opportunities to see foreign or independent "art" films are rare. That's where the **Coffee Underground** comes in. Besides being a coffee shop, it often shows hard-to-find movies. ~ 1 East Coffee Street, Greenville; 864-298-0494.

The **Blind Horse Saloon** is a rare country-and-western spot in this neck o' the woods. On any given night you'll find the floor packed with Stetson-hatted two-steppers and live music. Cover. ~ 1035 Lowndes Hill Road, Greenville; 864-233-1381.

> Because South Carolina bars must close by midnight on Saturdays, and do not open on Sundays, private clubs have become very popular. A one-time membership fee of $5 provides a convenient way to circumvent the conservative drinking laws.

The Dutch-owned **Addy's** is an oasis for jazz lovers, especially on live performance night on Tuesday and the occasional Friday. This popular watering hole also serves meals and offers a full cocktail menu. Closed Monday. ~ 17 East Coffee Street; 864-232-2339; www.addys.net.

The largest and liveliest of Greenville's private clubs is **Gametime/Rip Tide**. It has dance music most nights, 18 pool tables, and plenty of big-screen TVs and video-arcade games. There's a 24-hour waiting period for "membership" to the club, so plan your visit ahead of time; you can apply at the door or online. ~ 5 Webb Road (off Congaree Road); 864-297-6500; www.gametime-riptide.com.

Taprooms have become increasingly popular in the Upstate. Downtown Greenville has a couple, both of them excellent. There's **Barley's Taproom**. ~ 25 West Washington Street; 864-232-3706. Another option is the **Blue Ridge Brewing Company**, where you can savor craft brews at the custom wood bar while listening to the live entertainment. ~ 217 North Main Street, Greenville; 864-232-4677.

Outside of Greenville, evening action is less of a sure thing, although Spartanburg has a few clubs. **Ground Zero** may be the Upstate's best place to hear touring alternative bands. Closed Sunday. Occasional cover. ~ 3059 Howard Street, Spartanburg; 864-948-1661; www.groundzerorocks.com.

The **Music Foundation of Spartanburg** sponsors a concert season that includes classical and ethnic music, as well as performances by the local symphony orchestra. Shows are usually held in the Twichell Auditorium. ~ Spartanburg; 864-948-9020. Internationally known dance companies are presented by **Ballet Spartanburg**. ~ Spartanburg; 864-583-0339, 864-583-3776; www.sparklenet.com/balletspartanburg.

You can "talk sports with the local Clemson boys" at **Goober's Sports Pub**, a down-home bar with cheap beer and snacks. Closed Sunday. ~ 520-1 Old Greenville Highway; 864-654-7345.

Darts, snacks and pints of ale are served at the **Pendleton House Pub**, a handsome 1880 restaurant with a pub and drawing room near Clemson. ~ 203 East Main Street, Pendleton; 864-646-7795.

KINGS MOUNTAIN STATE PARK 🕺 🏊 🚣 🚤 🚣 Within the cool, shady confines of this oak and hickory forest is a nineteenth-century working farm. It's a poignant, peaceful setting, with split-rail fence running along grassy pastures and corn patches, and wildflower meadows attended by bumblebees and big grasshoppers. On weekends during the summer, a guide will take you through the 1860s log house built by a Civil War veteran and the blacksmith and carpenter shops dating to the 1820s, the cotton gin, corncrib and sorghum mill. On weekdays, you can stroll the farm by yourself. There's also a pretty lake in the park, named for a low-lying spur of the Blue Ridge—not a real mountain. Right next door, Kings Mountain National Military Park is a Revolutionary War battlefield. Try fishing for bass, bream and crappie in the lake. Facilities include the park office, picnic shelters, trading post, and johnboat, canoe and pedal boat rentals. Day-use fee, $2. ~ Off Route 161 north of York. From Blacksburg, take Route 29 north to Route 216 and enter through Kings Mountain National Military Park; 803-222-3209.

▲ There are 116 tent and RV sites with water and electrical hookups; $16 per night. There are ten primitive tent camping sites that have no facilities; $12 per night.

JONES GAP STATE PARK 🕺 🚣 The Middle Saluda River, cold and clear as air, hurries through Jones Gap mountain gorge and thus right through the park. The forest setting is immensely scenic and tranquil, filled with the rush of the river. Families love these 3346 acres; children wade in the river and play along the grassy banks sprinkled with picnic areas, including several for wheelchair visitors. A rock pond swirling with enormous trout was once the Cleveland Fish Hatchery but is now a park exhibit. The river offers excellent brown, rainbow and brook trout fish-

PARKS

◄ *HIDDEN*

ing; only artificial flies and lures permitted. No trash cans are located in the park, so be prepared to carry out your own refuse. Facilities include the park office, picnic areas, hiking trails and an environmental education center. ~ River Falls Road, north of Route 276, about one mile west of the town of Cleveland; 864-836-3647, fax 864-836-3647.

▲ There are 18 primitive tent sites along Jones Gap Trail, a strenuous, five-mile hike between Jones Gap State Park and Caesars Head State Park; $6 to $10 per site per night.

CAESARS HEAD STATE PARK 🏃 This place is all about views. Stand on a platform of rock and a torrent of Blue Ridge mountains sweeps before you, cool winds slapping at your face. Walk down into Devil's Kitchen, a sliver of space between rocks, and look across to the granite outcropping that someone once said looks like Julius Caesar. The sad, squatty face poking from the mountain could be anyone. Facilities include the park office, gift shop, small picnic area and hiking trails. ~ Located along Route 276, just north of Route 11 near the tiny hamlet of Caesars Head; phone/fax 864-836-6115.

▲ Primitive, trailside camping permitted along Jones Gap Trail, a strenuous five-mile hike between Caesars Head and Jones Gap State Park; $6 to $10 per site per night.

TABLE ROCK STATE PARK 🏃 ⛵ 🚤 🛶 The flat stony summit of Table Rock Mountain looms in the distance. Lofty, fragrant forest covers the mountainsides and most of the 3083-acre park. Perennially packed from spring through fall, it's a mecca for hiking, swimming, boating and fishing. Thirty-six-acre Pinnacle Lake, framed in bluish mountains, is the focus of activity in summer. A popular restaurant (currently under renovation) serves Southern cooking. A small chapel hosts woodsy weddings. Families like the fourteen budget-priced cabins with furnished kitchens, heat and air conditioning, though it's tough to get a reservation. There's a one-week minimum stay in the summer. There is swimming in the summer; Pinnacle Lake is clear but brisk. Both Pinnacle Lake and Lake Oolenoy are stocked with bass, bream and catfish. Facilities include the park office, a trading post, a restaurant, canoes, pedal boat and fishing boat rentals, picnic areas, nature and hiking trails. Day-use fee, $2. ~ Located along Route 11, about 16 miles north of Pickens; 864-878-9813.

▲ One hundred sites spread across two campgrounds are open to tents and RVs; hookups for water and electricity provided, and there are hot-water bathhouses, trading post and coin laundry. Two sites for wheelchair visitors can be reserved in advance; $16 per night (plus $1 for reserved sites).

KEOWEE-TOXAWAY STATE NATURAL AREA 🚶 ⚓ The park is a sliver of woods along 18,500-acre Lake Keowee. The Cherokees hunted and fished around the lake for centuries, naming it "place of the mulberries." Today, the waters are an impoundment for Duke Power, which makes nuclear and electrical energy. Facilities are limited to small picnic and camping areas—unfortunately, not on the lake. It's about a one-mile hike from the campground to the lake. A three-bedroom lakeside cabin can be rented; one-week minimum in the summer. Rate is moderate. Lake Keowee has good bream, crappie, bass and trout fishing. Facilities include picnic tables and two hiking trails. ~ Off Route 11, just west of Route 133, near the town of Salem; 864-868-2605.

> Several Upstate parks offer accommodations at reasonable prices. You should pick a park you'd really like to get to know however—the minimum stay in summer is usually one week.

▲ There are 14 tent sites and 10 RV sites with hookups; $12 per night.

DEVIL'S FORK STATE PARK 🚶 🚤 🛥 ⚓ The vast, pale blue of Lake Jocassee set against cloud-sprinkled sky and deep blue peaks—this is the scenery at Devil's Fork. Throughout these 622 acres are deep, dark woods and bright fields of wildflowers, where trout lilies, jack-in-the-pulpits and rare Oconee bells flourish. The park is one of South Carolina's most popular, not only for the stunning setting but for the twenty luxury villas set in the woods along the lake. For moderate to deluxe rates, you get two or three bedrooms, carpeting, fireplaces, screened porches, blenders, microwaves, and televisions. Two villas accommodate wheelchair visitors. In the summer, minimum stay is one week. The small clay beach along Lake Jocassee angles into clear, shallow waters. Jocassee is the only lake in South Carolina where you can fish for both smallmouth bass and trophy trout (translation: angling is exceptional). You'll also find largemouth bass, black crappie, white bass and bluegill. Facilities include the park office, a picnic area with shelters, a general store, boat ramps and hiking trails. ~ Route 25, about two and a half miles north of Route 11, near Salem; 864-944-2639, fax 864-944-8777.

▲ There are 59 RV sites (two wheelchair accessible) with hookups and 25 tent sites. Hot showers and coin laundry are provided; $18 for RVs, $13.50 for tents. Reservations are mandatory.

OCONEE STATE PARK 🚶 ⚓ ⚓ The Civilian Conservation Corps built Oconee in the early 1930s, making it one of the state's first parks. A favorite among seclusionists, it's flung deep in pine woods on a high plateau in the northwestern crook of South Car-

◀ HIDDEN

olina. There are two mountain lakes here and an old water wheel built by the Conservation Corps. Nineteen budget-priced cabins, most of them situated along a lake, are outfitted with fireplaces, heat and air conditioning, and kitchens. A one-week minimum stay is required during the summer months; there are two- or three-day minimums the rest of the year. There's good summertime swimming in the main lake, with lifeguards provided. In the main lake, try fishing for bass, bream and catfish. Facilities include the park office and museum, picnic tables and shelters, carpet golf, groceries and hiking trails. Day-use fee, $2. ~ Route 107, 12 miles northwest of Walhalla; 864-638-5353, fax 864-638-8776; e-mail oconee_sp@scprt.com.

▲ Next to the main lake are 140 wooded sites for tents or RVs; hookups provided. All sites are first-come, first-served except for 30 sites that can be reserved; $16 per night (plus $1 for reserved sites).

Outdoor Adventures

FISHING

Headed for Lake Murray near Columbia? **Just Add Water** rents out pontoons, johnboats, waverunners and other water craft. ~ Dreher Island State Park; 803-345-9682.

North of Aiken, you can rent johnboats at **Hickory Knob State Resort Park** for a trip on Strom Thurmond Lake. ~ Off Route 378, seven miles west of McCormick; 864-391-2450, 800-491-1764.

Vast clear lakes and swift streams in the Upstate make for superior boating and canoeing.

Mountain Lakes Vacation Center rents canoes, kayaks and johnboats for area waters. ~ Route 11, Fair Play; 864-972-0463, 800-610-0020.

SPORT-FISHING

Just Add Water, with two locations on Lake Murray, supplies guides for striped bass fishing on the lake. ~ 803-345-9682. **The Blue Heron** guide will pick you up near Dreher Island State Park for striped bass fishing in Lake Murray. ~ Prosperity; 803-364-2971; www.blueheronguide.com.

Hoyett's Grocery and Tackle, next to Devil's Fork State Park, offers guided trips on Lake Jocassee for smallmouth bass and tro-

AUTHOR FAVORITE

Maybe I'm a water wimp, but I'd just as soon poke around a dead-calm lake on a pontoon than roar down a boiling river in a raft. Best place to poke: **Jocassee Lake** in Devil's Fork State Park. Hoyett's Grocery and Tackle will supply the pontoons. ~ 516 Jocassee Lake Road, Salem; 864-944-9016.

phy trout. Reservations are mandatory. ~ 516 Jocassee Lake
Road, Salem; 864-944-9016.

Black Mountain Trout Farm is the only commercial trout   ◀ *HIDDEN*
farm in South Carolina. No license required, and there's no limit.
Call for directions: It's way out in the boonies. Closed Sunday
through Wednesday and November through February. ~ Northeast of Clemson on 198 Trout Farm Road, Westminster; 864-
647-9700.

Public courses abound across South Carolina. In Columbia,   **GOLF**
there's the P.B. Dye–designed **Northwood Golf Club**. ~ Farrow
and Parkland roads, in the Carolina Research Park; 803-786-
9242. There's nine-hole **Hickory Ridge Golf Club**. ~ 1300 Bitternut
Drive, off Trotter Road; 803-776-9900. Also in Columbia is
county-owned **LinRick Golf Course**. ~ 356 Camp Ground Road,
off Route 215 North; 803-754-6331. And finally there's 6900-
yard **Oak Hills Golf Club**. ~ 7629 Fairfield Road, off Route 321;
803-735-9830.

Not far from the city, you'll find **Indian River Golf Club**. ~
200 Indian River Drive, West Cola; 803-955-0080. You'll also
find **Coldstream Golf Club**. ~ 2121 Lake Murray Boulevard,
Irmo; 803-781-0114. In Chapin, go to **Timberlake Country Club**.
~ Amicks Ferry Road, off Route 26, Chapin; 803-345-9909.
Charwood Golf Club has 27 holes. ~ 222 Club House Drive,
West Columbia; 803-755-2000.

Aiken has several courses, including **Cedar Creek**. ~ 2475 Club
Drive; 803-648-4206. Another course is at **Aiken Golf Club**. ~ 555
Highland Park Avenue; 803-649-6029.

Between Aiken and Abbeville, there's superb golfing at **Hickory Knob State Resort Park**, which has an 18-hole championship
course, driving range and putting green. ~ Off Route 378, seven
miles west of McCormick; 864-391-2450, 800-491-1764.

Across the Upstate, you'll find public and semi-private
courses at numerous locations. In Greenville, there's one at
Bonnie Brae Golf Club. ~ 1116 Ashmore Ridge Road, Greenville; 864-277-9838. Southeast of Greenville, you'll find **Caro-
lina Springs Golf & Country Club**. ~ 1680 Scuffleton Road,
Fountain Inn, southeast of Greenville; 864-862-3551. In Spartan-
burg, tee off at **Cotton Creek Golf Club**. ~ 640 Keltner Avenue,
Spartanburg; 864-583-7084. **Falcon's Lair** is another alternative.
~ 1308 Southums Drive, north of Walhalla; 864-638-0000. Try
Cherokee Valley Golf Club in Tigerville. ~ 253 Chinquapin
Road, Tigerville; 864-895-6758. Or in Pickens head to the **The
Rock**. ~ 171 Sliding Rock Road, Pickens; 864-878-2030. In
Pendleton, you'll find **Boscobel Golf Club**. ~ Off Route 76,
Pendleton; 864-646-3991.

Text continued on page 444.

The Wild Waters
of Oconee

Where the Chattooga River starts in North Carolina, the water flows slow and steady, coursing south down a mountain gorge and gaining speed. Once it hits South Carolina, the Chattooga is on a rampage. The water foams and fizzes and hurls itself at boulders and trees, like a torrent in a pinball machine. It thunders down inclines in tremendous freefall, landing in silent baths.

The Cherokees called this land Oconee, or "water eyes from the hills." The Chattooga does appear to ooze from the Cherokee Foothills, the prelude to the Blue Ridge Mountains. The river races along the north-western edge of Oconee County, separating it from Georgia. Oconee is the northwesternmost corner of South Carolina, far-flung and wild, barely inhabited by people but home to many wild animals. The forests are dim, deep and Edenic, ablaze with color in spring and fall.

It was in this watery wilderness that the 1972 movie *Deliverance* was shot. And though today you may not see any banjo-pickin' hayseeds on the porch (or you may), you will find some of the best whitewater rafting in the country. The Chattooga has Section III and IV whitewater, and is ranked as a National Wild and Scenic River. Section III, a leisurely run culminating with serious rapids, allows rafters time to enjoy the cool forest and bizarre boulder formations.

Section IV is tricky business. The water is fast and furious, the drops frequent and steep. But they deposit you into dead-calm pools where you can relax and ponder your surroundings: straight-up sides of gorges decorated with wildflowers and enormous trees. The climax of Section IV is a series of rapids called Corkscrew, Sock 'em Dog and Jawbone.

The U.S. Forest Service permits only three whitewater outfitters to offer trips on the Chattooga River. All conduct guided trips as well as overnight excursions. **Nantahala Outdoor Center** is located in South Carolina. ~ Chattooga Ridge Road, Mountain Rest; 800-232-7238; www.noc.com. **Wildwater Ltd.** is a second outfitter in South Carolina. Closed December through February. ~ 1251 Academy Road, off Route 76, Long Creek; 864-647-9587, 800-451-9972. **Southeastern Expe-**

ditions is in Clayton, Georgia, just over the state line. ~ Route 76 East, Clayton, Georgia; 706-782-4331, 800-868-7238.

The Forest Service also limits the number of rafters, so the river rarely is crowded. It's easier to reserve a weekday; weekends are usually booked months ahead. Advance reservations are required for all trips, which are offered March through October.

If you'd prefer to enjoy Oconee's wild waters from the comfort of land, go waterfall watching. Dozens of falls can be reached by car, and then a short to long hike through the woods.

Spoonauger Falls, also called Rock Cliff Falls, are shaped like a giant spoon. You'll find them at Spoonauger Creek, a vein of the Chattooga River, near the town of Tamassee. From Route 28, take Route 107 north ten and a half miles to Burrells Fork Road. Turn left and go three miles to the Chattooga River bridge. From here it's an easy 20-minute walk to the falls.

Downriver, **Big Bend Falls** are the biggest on the Chattooga. The falls angle first in a watery sheet, then drop straight down in an angry torrent. It's a three-hour hike here, but worth it. The trailhead is at Cherry Hill Campground on Route 107 near Tamassee.

Blue Hole Falls are exquisite. Foamy white liquid freefalls 40 feet into a jewel-like pool of blue. Mist rises up and fills surrounding forest in the spring and fall. A sublime picnic spot. Getting there is a challenge, but here are the directions: From the town of Walhalla, take Route 28 north about seven miles, past the Stumphouse Ranger Station, to Route 193. Turn left and go .8 mile to Route 290 (also called Cassidy Bridge Road). Turn left and go 1.8 miles to Rich Mountain Road, a gravel road. Turn left and go .2 mile to Cedar Creek Road. Turn right and go three miles to Route 2658, a Forest Service road. From here, hike one mile to Route 2659 (also a Forest Service road) and turn right until you run into Cedar Creek. From here, you can hike down about 100 yards to the falls. If this fails, ask for directions at the Stumphouse Ranger Station!

Directions to many more hidden falls are available from the **Discover Upcountry Carolina Association**. ~ P.O. Box 3116, Greenville, SC 29602; 864-233-2690, 800-849-4766.

TENNIS   Need a workout with a racquet? Head for **Columbia Tennis Center**. ~ 1635 Whaley Street, Columbia; 803-733-8440. Also in Columbia is **Greenview Park**. ~ 6700 David Street; 803-754-5223. You can also opt for **Hampton Park**. ~ 1117 Brandon Avenue; 803-776-9082. A fourth option is **Woodland Park**. ~ 6500 Olde Knight Parkway, 803-776-1096.

In Aiken, you can play at the **Weeks Tennis Center**. ~ Whiskey Road, just north of Hitchcock Parkway; 803-642-7739. North of Aiken off the Savannah River Scenic Highway, **Hickory Knob State Resort Park** has two tennis courts for their guests. ~ Off Route 378, seven miles west of McCormick; 864-391-2450, 800-491-1764.

The city of Greenville has courts at **Cleveland Park**. ~ East Washington Street and Cleveland Park Drive, Greenville. There are also courts at **McPherson Park**. ~ North Main Street and East Park Avenue, Greenville.

BIKING   Inland South Carolina rises from flat farmland to gentle hills to steep mountains. Most everywhere, you can ride for hours without the hassle of traffic, enjoying long, lonesome stretches of road and eye-blink towns. As many of the roads have no shoulders, however, you'll have to keep constantly vigilant for a few inconsiderate drivers who think it's funny to use their pickup trucks to run bikes off roads.

The South Carolina State Park system offers several environmental and cultural programs, including an Annual Hawk Watch. ~ 803-734-0156.

The 221-mile **Carolina Connector** crosses the eastern side of the state. Starting at Route 381 north of McColl, it heads southwest along country roads through Sumter, then spans several rivers before commencing at the Savannah River on Route 119.

The **Central Route** is a 165-mile run starting on the coast at McClellanville. From here, it angles northwest along Route 45, picking up Route 6 on the west side of Lake Moultrie. Near Swansea it switches to Route 178 into Saluda, then takes Route 702 to Route 246 around Greenwood. It heads into the Upcountry on Route 20, ending along Route 133 at the Cherokee Foothills Scenic Highway.

All 135 miles of the **Cherokee Foothills Scenic Highway** are ideal for bicycling. The highway arcs along northwestern South Carolina, following Route 11 from Gaffney to Lake Hartwell.

HIKING   For a comprehensive list of trails, you should try to pick up a copy of *Hiking South Carolina Trails* by Allen de Hart (Globe Pequot Press). All distances listed for hiking trails are one way unless otherwise noted.

COLUMBIA AREA At Sesquicentennial State Park, the **Sandhills Nature Trail** (2 miles) begins its easy-going loop around a lake.

If you prefer a workout, the park's **jogging trail** (4 miles) features an obstacle course and places to stop and exercise.

Among the six scenic swamp trails in Congaree Swamp National Monument, **Weston Lake Loop Trail** (4.6 miles) is most scenic. It wends through damp, musky, centuries-old forest, passing one of the state's largest loblolly pines—16 stories high and 15 feet wide. Don't forget your mosquito repellent.

AIKEN TO ABBEVILLE   Aiken's Hitchcock Woods, a premier urban forest, has 20 miles of trails coiling through lofty forests of sweet gum, oak, pine and mulberry trees and alongside wildflower meadows. Equestrians frequent these trails, so watch where you step.

Within Hickory Knob State Resort Park, the **Turkey Ridge Trail** (.3 mile round-trip) and **Beaver Run Nature Trail** (1 mile) combine for a pleasant walk through loblolly woods. Part of the trail rims a lake.

UPSTATE   The Foothills Trail, South Carolina's longest trek, runs for 85 miles, with portions reaching into North Carolina. It began as a network of trails in Sumter National Forest, along South Carolina's northwest corner, and spread across the Cherokee Foothills. Today, it passes through Caesars Head State Park, Table Rock State Park and Oconee State Park.

Many of the steps along **Table Rock Trail** (3.4 miles) were laid in the 1930s by the Civilian Conservation Corps. The strenuous trek up Table Rock Mountain crosses several creeks and granite outcroppings (some badly eroded), rewarding with numerous Blue Ridge and lake views. It connects with **Pinnacle Mountain Trail** (3.3 miles), equally as arduous. This climb up Pinnacle Mountain edges cliffs and granite overhangs and pretty waterfalls. Both trailheads are at Table Rock State Park, and provide access to the Foothills Trail.

Jones Gap Trail (5 miles) links Jones Gap State Park with Caesars Head State Park. It's a moderate to tough trek through a rugged, rocky mountain gap, with the cold, clear Middle Saluda River coursing through. Trailside camping is available (fee charged); check with either state park.

Pick up the **Whitewater Falls Trail** (3.4 miles) at the Bad Creek Hydroelectric Station (Route 130, eight miles north of Salem). You'll hike through old-growth forest with massive fraser magnolias and tulip poplar trees, down to a platform where you can see Whitewater's Lower Falls. The Upper Falls are in North Carolina.

All highways lead to Columbia—or so it would seem on a map. **Route 26** angles up from Charleston to Columbia, continuing northwest to Spartanburg and into North Carolina. **Route 77** comes down from Charlotte, North Carolina,

Transportation

CAR

and into Columbia. And **Route 20** brings motorists from Atlanta to Columbia.

Also heading up from Atlanta is **Route 85**, which passes through Greenville and Spartanburg in the Upstate.

AIR   **Columbia Metropolitan Airport** (803-822-5000, 888-562-5002) in Columbia is serviced by Continental, Delta Air Lines, Independence Air, Northwest Airlines, United Express and US Airways.

The larger, modern **Greenville-Spartanburg Airport**, halfway between Greenville and Spartanburg in the Upcountry, is served by American Eagle, ComAir, Continental Airlines, Delta Air Lines, Independence Air, Northwest Airlines, United Express and US Airways. ~ 864-877-7426; www.gspairport.com.

BUS   **Greyhound Bus Lines** (800-231-2222; www.greyhound.com) has several locations around inland South Carolina. There is a location in Columbia at 2015 Gervais Street, 803-256-6465; in Greenville at 100 West MacBee Avenue, 864-235-4741; and in Spartanburg at 100 North Liberty Street, 864-582-5814.

TRAIN   **Amtrak** (800-872-7245; www.amtrak.com) makes several stops around inland South Carolina. There are stations in Columbia at 850 Pulaski Street, 803-252-8246; in Denmark at 200 West Baruch Street, 40 miles southeast of Aiken; in Greenville at 1120 West Washington Street, 864-255-4221; and in Spartanburg at 290 Magnolia Street.

CAR RENTALS   At the Columbia Metropolitan Airport, you'll find **Avis Rent A Car** (800-331-1212), **Budget Rent A Car** (800-527-0700), **Hertz Rent A Car** (800-654-3131), **National Car Rental** (800-328-4567) and **Thrifty Car Rental** (800-367-2277).

If you're flying into Greenville-Spartanburg Airport, try **Avis Rent A Car** (800-331-1212), **Budget Rent A Car** (800-527-0700), **Hertz Rent A Car** (800-654-3131), **National Car Rental** (800-328-4567) or **Thrifty Car Rental** (800-367-2277).

PUBLIC TRANSIT   **Central Midlands Regional Transit Authority** operates bus routes in Greater Columbia. ~ 803-255-7100.

Greenville Transit Authority provides extensive service around Greenville. ~ 864-467-5011. In Spartanburg, hop on a SPARTA bus. ~ 864-562-4287.

TAXIS   **Checker Yellow Cab** (803-799-3311) services Columbia Metropolitan Airport.

In Greenville, there's **Yellow Cab** (864-232-5322). **Checker Cab Co.** (864-583-2724) services the Spartanburg area.

Index

Lodging Index

Dining Index

HIDDEN GUIDES

Adventure travel or a relaxing vacation?—"Hidden" guidebooks are the only travel books in the business to provide detailed information on both. Aimed at environmentally aware travelers, our motto is "Where Vacations Meet Adventures." These books combine details on unique hotels, restaurants and sightseeing with information on camping, sports and hiking for the outdoor enthusiast.

PARADISE FAMILY GUIDES

Ideal for families traveling with kids of any age—toddlers to teenagers—Paradise Family Guides offer a blend of travel information unlike any other guides to the Hawaiian islands. With vacation ideas and tropical adventures that are sure to satisfy both action-hungry youngsters and relaxation-seeking parents, these guides meet the specific needs of each and every family member.

Ulysses Press books are available at bookstores everywhere. If any of the following titles are unavailable at your local bookstore, ask the bookseller to order them.

You can also order books directly from Ulysses Press
P.O. Box 3440, Berkeley, CA 94703
800-377-2542 or 510-601-8301
fax: 510-601-8307
www.ulyssespress.com
e-mail: ulysses@ulyssespress.com